STATISTICAL HANDBOOK ON AGING AMERICANS

1994 EDITION

STATISTICAL HANDBOOK ON AGING AMERICANS

1994 EDITION

Frank L. Schick and Renee Schick, Editors
Compiled by Renee Schick

Oryx Press
1994

The rare Arabian Oryx is believed to have inspired the myth of the unicorn. This desert antelope became virtually extinct in the early 1960s. At that time several groups of international conservationists arranged to have 9 animals sent to the Phoenix Zoo to be the nucleus of a captive breeding herd. Today the Oryx population is over 800 and nearly 400 have been returned to reserves in the Middle East.

© 1994 by The Oryx Press
4041 North Central at Indian School Road
Phoenix, Arizona 85012-3397

Published simultaneously in Canada
Printed and Bound in the United States of America

∞ The paper used in this publication meets the minimum requirements of
American National Standard for Information Science—Permanence of Paper
for Printed Library Materials, ANSI Z39.48, 1984.

Library of Congress Cataloging-in-Publication Data
Statistical handbook on aging Americans / Frank L. Schick and Renee Schick, editors.—
1994 ed. / compiled by Renee Schick.
  p.   cm.
  Includes bibliographical references and index.
  ISBN 0-89774-721-6
  1. Aged—United States—Statistics. 2. Aging—United States—Handbooks, manuals,
etc. I. Schick, Frank Leopold, 1918–1992. II. Schick, Renee.
HQ1064.U5S695   1994   93–36711
305.26'0973'021—dc20   CIP

The oldest hath born most; we that are young
shall never see so much nor live so long.

Shakespeare, *King Lear,* Act V, Scene 3, line 325

In loving memory of Frank who started this book but, alas, did not live to see it finished.

Contents

List of Tables and Charts   ix

Preface   xxi

A. Demographics   1

   A1. Age and Sex Distribution   3

   A2. Life Expectancy   12

   A3. Race and Ethnicity   18

   A4. Geographic Distribution and Mobility   29

   A5. Aging Around the World   41

B. Social Characteristics   47

   B1. Living Arrangements and Marital Status   48

   B2. Households, Housing, and Informal Supports   60

   B3. Education   64

   B4. Social Attitudes and Activities   80

   B5. Victimization and Abuse of the Elderly   92

   B6. Other Social Problems   103

C. Health Status   109

   C1. Health Assessment   110

   C2. Diseases and Disabilities   116

   C3. Death Rates and Causes of Death   132

   C4. Health Care Access and Utilization   145

   C5. Hospitals and Nursing Homes   151

   C6. Health Insurance Coverage   165

D. Employment   172

   D1. Labor Force Participation   173

   D2. Unemployment   189

   D3. Retirement Trends and Pensions   198

E. Economic Conditions   202

   E1. Sources of Income   203

   E2. Income and Assets   215

   E3. Living Costs   231

   E4. Poverty   246

F. Expenditures for the Elderly   260

   F1. Overview of Expenditures   261

   F2. Social Security   266

   F3. Health Care Expenditures   274

   F4. Public and Private Pensions   282

   F5. Veterans   288

Guide to Relevant Information Resources   303

Glossary   310

List of Sources   313

Index   331

List of Tables and Charts

A. DEMOGRAPHICS

A1. Age and Sex Distribution

A1-1   Total Population Aged 65 Years and Over: 1990

A1-2   Percent of Total State Population Aged 65 Years and Over: 1990

A1-3   Population 65 Years and Over, by State: 1990

A1-4   Total Population Aged 85 Years and Over: 1990

A1-5   Percent of Total State Population Aged 85 Years and Over: 1990

A1-6   Population 85 Years and Over, by State: 1990

A1-7   Resident Population, by Age and Sex: 1970 to 1991

A1-8   Population 80 Years and Over: 1900 to 1990

A1-9   Growth of the Older Population, Actual and Projected: 1900 to 2050

A1-10   Population 85 Years and Over: 1900 to 2050

A1-11   Number of Men Per 100 Women, by Age Group: 1989

A1-12   Population, by Sex and Age: 1990

A1-13   Population, by Sex and Age: 2010

A1-14   Population, by Sex and Age: 2030

A1-15   Population, by Sex and Age: 2050

A2. Life Expectancy

A2-1   Expectation of Life and Expected Deaths, by Race, Sex, and Age: 1989

A2-2   Expectation of Life at Birth, 1970 to 1990, and Projections, 1995 to 2010

A2-3   Life Expectancy by Sex: United States, 1970 to 1990

A2-4   Life Expectancy at Birth and at 65 Years of Age, by Race and Sex: Selected Years 1900 to 1989

A2-5   Life Expectancy at 65 Years of Age, According to Race and Sex: 1986 to 1990

A2-6   Expectation of Life at Selected Ages, by Race and Sex: United States, 1900–02 to 1990

A2-7   Percent Surviving from Birth to Age 65 and 85, by Sex and Race: 1900–02 and 1987

A2-8   Life Expectancy for Black Persons at Individual Ages 65 to 85 Years, by Sex: United States, 1986

A2-9   Projected Life Expectancy at Birth and Age 65, by Sex: 1990 to 2050

A3. Race and Ethnicity

A3-1   Persons 65 Years and Over, by Age, Sex, Race, and Hispanic Origin: 1990

A3-2   Persons 65 Years and Over for Regions, by Age, Race, and Hispanic Origin: 1990

A3-3   Persons 65 Years and Over, by Specific Race and Hispanic Origin: 1980 and 1990

A3-4   Percent of Elderly Persons, by Race, Hispanic Origin, and Place of Residence: 1990

A3-5   Black Population 65 and 85 Years and Over, Ranked by State: 1990

A3-6   Hispanic Origin Population 65 and 85 Years and Over, Ranked by State: 1990

A3-7   Asian and Pacific Islander Population 65 and 85 Years and Over, Ranked by State: 1990

A3-8   American Indian, Eskimo, or Aleut Population 65 and 85 Years and Over, Ranked by State: 1990

A3-9   Growth of the Minority Elderly Population: 1990 to 2050

A3-10   Persons 65 Years and Over, by Age, Race, and Hispanic Origin: 2050

A3-11   Percent of the Population 65 Years and Over, by Race and Hispanic Origin: 1990 and 2050

A3-12   Black Population Aged 65 Years and Over: 1980 to 2050

A3-13   Black Population Aged 85 Years and Over: 1980 to 2050

A3-14   Hispanic Origin Population 65 Years and Over: 1980 to 2050

A3-15   Hispanic Origin Population 85 Years and Over: 1980 to 2050

A4. Geographic Distribution and Mobility

A4-1   Persons 65 Years and Over for Regions, by Age, Race, and Hispanic Origin: 1990

A4-2   Percent Change of U.S. Population 65 Years and Over, by Region, Division, and State: 1980 and 1990

A4-3   Percent Change of U.S. Population 85 Years and Over, by Region, Division, and State: 1980 and 1990

A4-4   Population of the United States for Metropolitan/Nonmetropolitan Areas, by Age, Sex, Race, and Hispanic Origin: 1990

A4-5   Age Distribution of the Elderly, by Area of Residence: 1990

A4-6   Age Composition for the Elderly and Children, by Area of Residence: 1980 and 1990

A4-7   Percent Who Moved, by Type of Move and Age: March 1990 to March 1991

A4-8   Selected Characteristics of Persons, by Mobility Status and Type of Move: 1990 to 1991

A4-9   General Mobility, by Race and Hispanic Origin, Sex, and Age: 1990 to 1991

A5. Aging Around the World

A5-1   World's Population, by Age and Sex: 1991 and 2000

A5-2   Average Annual Percent Growth of Elderly Population in Developed and Developing Countries

A5-3   Countries with More Than Five Million Elderly (65+) and One Million Oldest Old (80+): 1990

A5-4   Elderly Population, by Age: 1985

A5-5   Speed of Population Aging in Selected Countries

A5-6   Countries with More Than Two Million Elderly Persons: 1991

A5-7   Countries with More Than Two Million Elderly Persons: 2020

A5-8   Countries with More Than One Million Octogenarians: 1991 (Projection)

A5-9   Countries with More Than One Million Octogenarians: 2020 (Projection)

A5-10   Population, by Age and Sex for Japan: 1991, 2000, and 2020

A5-11   Projections of Elderly Population, by Age: 1985 to 2025

B. SOCIAL CHARACTERISTICS

B1. Living Arrangements and Marital Status

B1-1   Living Arrangements of Adults, by Age: 1991

B1-2   Living Arrangements of the Elderly, by Sex, Race, and Hispanic Origin: 1992

B1-3   Living Arrangements of the Elderly: 1991

B1-4   Living Arrangements of the Elderly: 1980 and 1990

B1-5   Living Arrangements of Elderly Persons, by Residence: 1990

B1-6   Percent Distribution of Black Persons 65 Years of Age and Over, by Living Arrangement, According to Sex and Age: United States, 1986

B1-7   Percent of Persons 65 Years and Over Living Alone, by State: 1990

B1-8   Persons Living Alone, by Age and Sex: 1990, 1980, 1970, and 1960

B1-9   Marital Status of Persons 15 Years Old and Over, by Age, Sex, Region, and Race: March 1991

B1-10   Marital Status of Older People, by Age, Sex, Race, and Hispanic Origin: March 1989

B1-11   Marital Status of Persons 65 Years and Over, by Age and Sex: 1960 to 2040

B1-12   Percent of Older Men and Women Widowed, by Age, Race, and Hispanic Origin: 1989

B1-13   Percent Never Married, by Age, Sex, Race, and Hispanic Origin: 1992, 1980, and 1970

B1-14   Ratio of Unmarried Men Per 100 Unmarried Women, by Age: 1992, 1980, and 1970

B2. Households, Housing, and Informal Supports

B2-1　Adults in Unmarried-Couple Households, by Age, Sex, and Marital Status: 1990

B2-2　Size of Households for Householders 65 Years and Over, by Age, Race, and Hispanic Origin: March 1990

B2-3　Grandparents Maintaining Families with Grandchildren Present: 1991

B2-4　Support Ratios of Elderly Persons, by Age, Race, and Hispanic Origin: 1990 and 2050

B2-5　Percent Distributions of Caregivers, by Relationship to 65+ Individual with Activity Limitations: 1985

B2-6　Homeownership Rate for the Elderly, by Residence: 1989

B2-7　Percent of Owned Houses Owned Free and Clear (Nonmortgaged) for the Elderly, by Residence: 1989

B2-8　Housing Tenure of Aged Families and Unrelated Individuals, by Poverty Status: 1988

B3. Education

B3-1　Years of School Completed, by Selected Characteristic: 1991

B3-2　Selected Measures of Educational Attainment for People Age 25+ and 65+: 1950 to 1989

B3-3　Median Years of School for People 25+ and 65+: 1950 to 1989

B3-4　Educational Attainment of People Age 65+ in the United States, by Regions: 1987

B3-5　Educational Attainment of Elderly Persons, by Residence: 1989

B3-6　Measures of Educational Attainment, by Age Group, Sex, Race, and Hispanic Origin: March 1989

B3-7　Years of School Completed, by Age, Race, and Hispanic Origin: March 1989

B3-8　Highest Degree Earned, by Selected Characteristic: 1987

B3-9　Percent Literate for Persons 65 Years and Over and 14 Years and Over, by Race, Nativity, and Parentage: 1979

B3-10　Undergraduate Enrollment in Institutions of Higher Education, by Type of Institution, Sex, Attendance Status, and Age: 50 States and D.C., Fall 1989

B3-11　Enrollment in All Institutions of Higher Education, by Level of Study, Sex, Attendance Status, and Age: 50 States and D.C., Fall 1989

B3-12　Educational Attainment–Persons 18 Years Old and Over, by Total Money Earnings in 1991, Age, Work Experience in 1991, and Sex

B3-13　Years of School Completed by Persons 25 Years and Over, by Age, Race, Household Relationship, and Poverty Status in 1991

B4. Social Attitudes and Activities

B4-1　How Older Americans Feel About Themselves and Their Lives

B4-2　Percent of Persons 65 and Older Reporting Specific Leisure-Time Activities: 1980

B4-3　Percent of Adults Who Are Church or Synagogue Members, by Age Group: 1979

B4-4　Social Activities and Religious Attendance of the Elderly, by Residence: 1987

B4-5　Number of Friends/Relatives the Elderly Talked with in the Past Month, by Residence: 1987

B4-6　Number of Relatives the Elderly Can Call for Help, by Residence: 1987

B4-7　Number of Friends the Elderly Can Call for Help, by Residence: 1987

B4-8　Percent of Adult Population Doing Volunteer Work: 1989

B4-9　Characteristics of Unpaid Volunteer Workers, by Age Group: May 1989

B4-10　Type of Organization for Which Volunteer Work Was Performed, by Age Group: May 1989

B4-11　Persons Who Performed Unpaid Volunteer Work at Some Time During the Year Ended May 1989, by Sex and Selected Characteristics

B4-12　Volunteers Helping Younger Generations

B4-13　Productive Engagement: Contributions by Those 75+

B4-14　Volunteers Providing Direct Care

B4-15　Voting-Age Population, Percent Reporting Registered, and Voted: 1976 to 1990

B4-16 Percent Reported Voting in Congressional Election Years, by Region, Race, Hispanic Origin, Sex, and Age: November 1966 to 1990

B4-17 Percent of Persons 65 Years and Over Reported Voting in Congressional Elections, by Race and Hispanic Origin: November 1966 to 1990

B4-18 Percent Reported Voting in Presidential Election Years, by Region, Race, Hispanic Origin, Sex, and Age: November 1964 to 1992

B4-19 Percent Reported Registered in Congressional Election Years, by Region, Race, Hispanic Origin, Sex, and Age: November 1966 to 1990

B4-20 Reported Registration, by Region, Race, Hispanic Origin, Sex, and Age: November 1968 to 1992

B4-21 Average Annual Miles Per Licensed Driver, by Driver Age and Sex: 1969, 1977, 1983, and 1990 NPTS

B4-22 Distribution of Estimated Annual Miles, by Driver Age and Sex: 1969, 1977, 1983, and 1990 NPTS

B4-23 Travel by Individuals 65 Years and Older Compared to All Age Groups: 1983 and 1990 NPTS

B5. Victimization and Abuse of the Elderly

B5-1   Victimization Rates for Personal Crimes of Violence and Theft, Persons Age 65 or Older: 1973 to 1990

B5-2   Victimization Rates for Household Crimes, Head of Households Age 65 or Older: 1973 to 1990

B5-3   Average Annual Victimization Rates, by Age of Victim and Type of Crime: 1987 to 1990

B5-4   Relationship of Offenders to Victims of Violent Crime, by Age of Victim and Type of Crime: 1987 to 1990

B5-5   Place of Occurrence of Crimes of Violence, by Age of Victim and Type of Crime: 1987 to 1990

B5-6   Average Annual Victimization Rates of Persons Age 65 or Older, by Sex, Race, Marital Status, and Type of Crime: 1987 to 1990

B5-7   Average Annual Victimization Rates of Persons Age 65 or Over, by Location of Residence, Home Ownership, and Type of Crime: 1987 to 1990

B5-8   Average Annual Victimization Rates of Persons Age 65 or Older, by Family Income and Type of Crime: 1987 to 1990

B5-9   Average Annual Victimization Rates, by Age of Victim and Type of Crime: 1987 to 1990

B5-10 Average Annual Victimization Rates of Persons Age 65 to 74 and 75 or Older for Crimes of Violence, Crimes of Theft, and Household Crimes

B5-11 Injuries, Medical Treatment, and Hospital Care Received by Violent Crime Victims, by Age of Victim: 1987 to 1990

B5-12 Self-Protective Measures Taken in Violent Crimes, by Age of Victim: 1987 to 1990

B5-13 Percent of Victimizations Reported to the Police, by Type of Crime and Age of Victims

B5-14 Percent of Victimizations Reported to the Police, by Age of Victims and Victim- Offender Relationship

B5-15 Average Annual Homicide Rates, by Age of Victim and Victim-Offender Relationship: 1980 to 1987

B5-16 Average Annual Homicide Rates, by Age of Victim and Precipitating Circumstances: 1980 to 1987

B5-17 Types of Elder Abuse: 1990 and 1991 (Reports from 29 and 30 States)

B5-18 Effectiveness of Nine Factors in Identifying Elder Abuse

B5-19 Effectiveness of Eight Factors in Preventing a First Occurrence of Elder Abuse

B5-20 Sex of Elder Abuse Victims: 1990 and 1991 (Reports from 28 and 29 States)

B5-21 Age of Elder Abuse Victims: 1990 and 1991 (Reports from 22 and 25 States)

B5-22 Abusers of the Elderly: 1990 and 1991 (Reports from 21 States)

B5-23 Effectiveness of Eight Factors in Treating Elder Abuse

B6. Other Social Problems

B6-1 Alcohol Abuse or Dependence in the Past Year, by Age, Sex, and Ethnicity: Data from ECA (DSM-III) and 1988 NHIS (DSM-III-R), in Percentages

B6-2 Elderly Drinkers Who Are Heavy Current Drinkers, by Sex: 1990

B6-3 Blood Alcohol Content for Drivers Involved in Fatal Crashes, by Age

B6-4 Elderly Smokers Who Smoke Heavily, by Sex: 1990

B6-5 Percent of Persons 65 Years and Over Who Smoked Cigarettes at Time of Survey, by Sex and Race: 1965 to 1987

B6-6 Crash Involvements Per Million V.M. of Travel, by Age

B6-7 Self-Reported Driving Difficulties of Older and Younger Drivers

B6-8 Driver Fatality Rate, 1986

B6-9 Fatalities as a Percent of Serious Injuries, 1986

B6-10 Nonmotorist Fatality Rate Per 100,000 Population, by Age: 1975 to 1990

B6-11 State Prison Inmates—Selected Characteristics: 1979 and 1986

C. HEALTH STATUS

C1. Health Assessment

C1-1 Number of Persons and Percent Distribution, by Respondent-Assessed Health Status, According to Sociodemographic Characteristics: United States, 1990

C1-2 Self-Assessment of Health, According to Selected Characteristics: United States, 1985 and 1990

C1-3 Average Annual Percent Distribution of Persons 55 Years of Age and Over, by Respondent-Assessed Health Status, According to Sex, Race, and Age: United States, 1985 to 1987

C1-4 Percent Distribution of Persons 65 Years of Age and Over, by Number of Activities of Daily Living for Which Difficulty Was Reported, According to Sex, Age, and Respondent-Assessed Health Status: United States, 1986

C1-5 Percent of Elderly in Fair or Poor Health, by Race and Residence: 1985 to 1987

C2. Diseases and Disabilities

C2-1 Number of Acute Conditions, by Age and Type of Condition: United States, 1990

C2-2 Number of Acute Conditions Per 100 Persons Per Year, by Age and Type of Condition: United States, 1990

C2-3 Average Annual Number of Selected Reported Chronic Conditions Per 1,000 Persons 55 Years of Age and Over, by Type of Chronic Condition, Sex, and Age: United States, 1979 to 1981, 1982 to 1984, and 1985 to 1987

C2-4 Number of Selected Reported Chronic Conditions Per 1,000 Persons, by Age: United States, 1990

C2-5 Number of Selected Reported Chronic Conditions Per 1,000 Persons, by Sex and Age: United States, 1990

C2-6 Percent of Persons 55 Years of Age and Over Who Reported Joint Pain or Physician-Diagnosed Arthritis, by Sex, Race, and Age: United States, Selected Time Periods

C2-7 Average Annual Number of Selected Reported Chronic Conditions Per 1,000 Black Persons 55 Years of Age and Over, by Type of Chronic Condition, Sex, and Age: United States, 1985 to 1987

C2-8 Selected Chronic Conditions Among Adult Males and Females: Percent in the SAIAN and General U.S. Population with at Least One Condition, by Age and Sex: United States, 1987

C2-9 Number of Restricted-Activity Days Associated with Acute Conditions, by Age and Type of Condition: United States, 1990

C2-10 Number of Restricted-Activity Days Associated with Acute Conditions Per 100 Persons Per Year, by Age and Type of Condition: United States, 1990

C2-11 Number of Days Per Person Per Year and Number of Days of Activity Restriction Due to Acute and Chronic Conditions, by Type of Restriction and Sociodemographic Characteristics: United States, 1990

C2-12 Percent Distribution of Persons with Difficulty in Activities of Daily Living and Instrumental Activities of Daily Living, by Sex and Age

C2-13 Difficulties of the Elderly with ADLs and IADLs, by Residence: 1986

C2-14 Percent of Persons 65 Years of Age and Over Who Reported Receiving the Help of Another Person with Performing Activities of Daily Living, by Race, Sex, and Age: United States, 1986

C3. Death Rates and Causes of Death

C3-1   Provisional Death Rates for All Causes, According to Race, Sex, and Age: 1988 to 1990

C3-2   Crude and Age-Adjusted Death Rates: United States, 1940 to 1990

C3-3   Deaths and Death Rates, by Age, Race, and Sex: United States, 1990

C3-4   Percent Change in Death Rates Between 1989 and 1990, by Age, Race, and Sex: United States

C3-5   Deaths, by Selected Cause and Selected Characteristics: 1989

C3-6   Deaths and Death Rates for the 10 Leading Causes of Death in Specified Age Groups: United States, 1990

C3-7   Provisional Death Rates for the Three Leading Causes of Death, According to Age: United States, 1988 to 1990

C3-8   Death Rates for All Causes Among Black Persons 55 Years of Age and Over, by Sex and Age: United States, Selected Years 1960 to 1986

C3-9   Death Rates for Diseases of the Heart for Persons 65 Years and Over, by Age, Sex, and Race: 1988

C3-10 Death Rates for Malignant Neoplasms for Persons 65 Years and Over, by Age, Sex, and Race: 1988

C3-11 Death Rates for Cerebrovascular Diseases for Persons 65 Years and Over, by Age, Sex, and Race: 1988

C3-12 Death Rates for Diseases of Heart, According to Sex, Race, and Age: United States, Selected Years 1950 to 1989

C3-13 Death Rates for Malignant Neoplasms, According to Sex, Race, and Age: United States, Selected Years 1950 to 1989

C3-14 Death Rates for Cerebrovascular Diseases, According to Sex, Race, and Age: United States, Selected Years 1950 to 1989

C3-15 Percent Change in Death Rates for Persons 55 Years of Age and Over, According to Age, Sex, and Race: 1960 to 1986

C3-16 Percent Change in Death Rates for Diseases of the Heart for Persons 55 Years of Age and Over, According to Age, Sex, and Race: 1980 to 1986

C3-17 Percent Change in Death Rates for Malignant Neoplasms for Persons 55 Years of Age and Over, According to Age, Sex, and Race: 1980 to 1986

C3-18 Percent Change in Death Rates for Cerebrovascular Disease for Persons 55 Years of Age and Over, According to Age, Sex, and Race: 1980 to 1986

C4. Health Care Access and Utilization

C4-1   Annual Movement of Persons 65–74 Through the Health Care System

C4-2   Annual Movement of Persons 75 and Over Through the Health Care System

C4-3   Professionally Active Physicians Per 100,000 Residents, by Type of County and Population Size: 1987 to 1988

C4-4   Number of Dentists Per 100,000 Residents, by Type of County: 1987

C4-5   Dental Care/Visits and Toothlessness of the Elderly: 1989

C4-6   Average Annual Number of Physician Visits Per Person, by Race, Sex, Respondent-Assessed Health Status, and Age: United States, 1985 to 1987

C4-7   Number of Mentions of Most Common Patient Reasons for a Physician Visit for Ambulatory Patients 55 Years of Age and Over and Rank of Males and Females, by Age: United States, 1985

C4-8   Office Visits to Physicians, According to Selected Patient and Visit Characteristics and Physician Specialty: United States, 1985 and 1989

C4-9   Number and Percent of Persons 55 Years of Age and Over Currently Using Vitamin or Mineral Supplements, by Selected Characteristics: United States, 1986

C4-10 Number and Percent of Black Persons 55 Years of Age and Over Currently Using Vitamin or Mineral Supplements, by Selected Characteristics: United States, 1986

C5. Hospitals and Nursing Homes

C5-1   Average Length of Stay by Race, Sex, and Selected First-Listed Diagnoses for Persons 65 Years of Age and Over: United States, 1981 and 1987

C5-2   Percent of Elderly Hospitalized Persons Discharged Home and Percent Discharged to a Nursing Home, by Age: 1986

C5-3   Discharge Destination of Persons Discharged from Nursing Homes Expressed as a Percent of Persons Admitted, by Age: 1986

C5-4   Discharges and Average Length of Stay in Non-federal Short-Stay Hospitals, According to Sex, Age, and Selected First-Listed Diagnosis: United States, 1980, 1988, 1989, and 1990

C5-5   Patients Discharged from Short-Stay Hospitals, Days of Care, and Average Lengths of Stay, by Sex, Age, Race, and Income: 1989

C5-6   Patients Discharged from Short-Stay Hospitals, by Category of First-Listed Diagnosis, Sex, and Age: 1988

C5-7   Procedures Provided to Patients Discharged from Short-Stay Hospitals, by Sex and Age: 1988

C5-8   Nursing Home Residents 65 Years of Age and Over Per 1,000 Population, According to Age, Sex, and Race: United States, 1963, 1973 to 1974, 1977, and 1985

C5-9   Nursing Home and Personal Care Home Residents 65 Years of Age and Over and Rate Per 1,000 Population, According to Age, Sex, and Race: United States, 1963, 1973 to 1974, 1977, and 1985

C5-10 Nursing Home Population, by Region, Division, and State: 1980 and 1990

C5-11 Percent Change in Nursing Home Population: 1980 to 1990

C5-12 Nursing Home Residents Who Required Assistance, by Age and Activity: 1985

C5-13 Selected Characteristics of Nursing Home and Community Residents Age 65+: 1985 and 1984

C5-14 Nursing Home Length of Stay Probabilities, by Age of Entry and Marital Status

C5-15 Inpatient and Residential Treatment Episodes in Mental Health Organizations, Rate Per 100,000 Civilian Population, and Inpatient Days, According to Type of Organization: United States, Selected Years 1969 to 1988

C5-16 Admissions to Selected Inpatient Psychiatric Organizations and Rate Per 100,000 Civilian Population, According to Sex, Age, and Race: United States, 1975, 1980, and 1986

C5-17 Admissions to Selected Inpatient Psychiatric Organizations, According to Selected Primary Diagnoses and Age: United States, 1975, 1980, and 1986

C6. Health Insurance Coverage

C6-1   Percent without Health Insurance for at Least One Month: February 1987 to May 1989

C6-2   Health Insurance Coverage Status—Persons, by Age: 1990 and 1991

C6-3   Health Insurance Premiums Per Elderly Family: 1961 and 1991

C6-4   Health Care Coverage for Persons 65 Years and Over, by Type of Coverage: 1980 and 1989

C6-5   Health Insurance Coverage, by Age and Race: 1986 to 1989

C6-6   Firms That Offer Health Benefits and Firms That Do Not Offer Health Benefits, by Size: 1990

C6-7   Percent Distribution of Persons 70 Years of Age and Over, by Type of Private Health Insurance Coverage, According to Age and Sex: United States, 1984

C6-8   Percent Distribution of Persons 70 Years of Age and Over, by Health Care Coverage, According to Age and Sex: United States, 1984

C6-9   Percent Distribution of Persons 70 Years of Age and Over, by Type of Medicare and/or Private Health Insurance Coverage, According to Age and Sex: United States, 1984

C6-10   Health Insurance Coverage for the Elderly, by Residence: 1987

C6-11   Selected Characteristics of Persons, by Health Insurance Coverage Status and Poverty Status: 1991

D. EMPLOYMENT

D1. Labor Force Participation

D1-1   Labor Force Participation for Older People, by Age and Sex: 1989

D1-2   Labor Force Participation Rates for Older People, by Age, Sex, and Race: 1989

D1-3   Percent of Civilian Noninstitutional Population in the Labor Force, by Age and Sex: 1950 and 1990

D1-4   Labor Force Participation Rates for Persons Aged 45 to 49 Through 75 Years or Older, by Sex: Selected Years, 1950 to 2005

D1-5   Civilian Labor Force and Participation Rates, by Race, Hispanic Origin, Sex, and Age: 1970 to 1991, and Projections, 2000 and 2005

D1-6   Civilian Labor Force—Employment Status, by Sex, Race, and Age: 1991

D1-7   Employed Civilians and Weekly Hours, by Selected Characteristics: 1970 to 1991

D1-8   Percent Change in Labor Force Participation of Men 55 Years and Over, by Age: 1970 to 2005

D1-9   Occupation of Employed Older Workers, by Age: 1989

D1-10   Industry of Employed Older Workers, by Age: 1989

D1-11   Occupation of Employed Older Workers, by Age: 1989

D1-12   Civilian Labor Force Participation Rate, by Age and Sex: 1950 to 1988, and Projected for 2000

D1-13   Employment Status of the Civilian Noninstitutional Population, by Age, Sex, and Race: 1992

D1-14   Employed Civilians, by Age, Sex, and Class of Worker: 1992

D1-15   Employed Civilians in Agriculture and Nonagricultural Industries, by Age and Sex: 1991 and 1992

D1-16   Persons at Work in Nonagricultural Industries, by Sex, Age, Race, Marital Status, and Full- or Part-Time Status: 1992

D1-17   Labor Force Participation Rates for Men Age 60 to 64 and 65+ in Selected Countries: 1988

D1-18   Labor Force Participation Rates for Women Age 60 to 64 and 65+ in Selected Countries: 1988

D1-19   Work Experience During Year, by Selected Characteristics and Poverty Status in 1991 of Civilians 16 Years Old and Over

D2. Unemployment

D2-1   Unemployed Workers—Summary: 1980 to 1991

D2-2   Unemployed Persons, by Sex, Age, Race, Marital Status, and Duration of Unemployment: 1991 and 1992

D2-3   Persons Not in the Labor Force, by Reason, Race, Hispanic Origin, Age, and Sex: 1992

D2-4   Persons Not in the Labor Force, by Reason, Sex, and Age: 1992

D2-5   Persons Not in the Labor Force Who Desire Work But Think They Cannot Get Jobs, by Reason, Sex, Age, Race, and Hispanic Origin: 1992

D2-6   Unemployed Jobseekers, by Sex, Age, Race, and Jobsearch Methods Used: 1992

D2-7   Reason for Not Working or Reason for Spending Time Out of Labor Force, by Poverty Status in 1991 of Persons Who Did Not Work or Who Spent Time Out of Labor Force

D3. Retirement Trends and Pensions

D3-1   Pension Plan Coverage of Workers, by Selected Characteristics: 1990

D3-2   Beneficiaries Receiving a Retirement Pension from a Private Pension Plan as a Percent of All Persons Age 65 and Over: 1970 to 1989

D3-3   Demographic Characteristics of Wage-and-Salary Workers Offered an Employer or Union Pension Plan, by Employment Size of Firm, Small Firm Detail: 1988

D3-4   Percent of Employers Offering Health Care Coverage to Retirees, by Size of Employer

D3-5   Survival Status of New Retired-Worker Beneficiaries to 1989, by Selected Characteristics for Men and Women

E. ECONOMIC CONDITIONS

E1. Sources of Income

E1-1 Sources of Income of Persons 65 or Older: 1990

E1-2 Income Sources, by Age, Sex, and Marital Status: Percent of Aged Units 55 or Older with Money Income from Specified Sources: 1990

E1-3 Income Sources, by Age, Sex, Marital Status, and Social Security Beneficiary Status: Percent of Aged Units 55 or Older with Money Income from Specified Sources: 1990

E1-4 Income Sources, by Age, Sex, Marital Status, Race, and Hispanic Origin: Percent of Aged Units 55 or Older with Money Income from Specified Sources: 1990

E1-5 Income Sources, by Age, Race, Hispanic Origin, and Social Security Beneficiary Status: Percent of Aged Units 55 or Older with Money Income from Specified Sources: 1990

E1-6 Percent Composition of Total Income of Family Units, by Type of Income and Age of Unit Head: 1984 and 1989

E1-7 Relative Importance of Income Sources, by Age, Sex, and Marital Status: Percent Distribution of Aged Units 55 or Older Receiving Particular Sources of Income: 1990

E1-8 Receipt of Income of Aged Units from Various Sources, by Race and Hispanic Origin: 1990

E1-9 Source of Income—Number with Income and Mean Income of Specified Type—of Persons 65 Years and Over: 1991

E1-10 Composition of Gross Income of Families with Heads Age 65 to 74 in Selected Countries: 1979 to 1981

E1-11 Composition of Gross Income of Elderly Families, by Age of Head and Income Type in Selected Countries: 1979 to 1981

E2. Income and Assets

E2-1 Money Income of Households—Aggregate and Mean Income, by Race and Hispanic Origin of Householder: 1990

E2-2 Median Family Unit Income, by Age of Head: 1990

E2-3 Family Net Worth—Mean and Median of Net Worth, by Selected Characteristics: 1983 and 1989

E2-4 Median Net Worth of Households, by Age of Householder: 1988

E2-5 Distribution of Net Worth, by Age and Asset Type: 1988

E2-6 Total Income of Aged Units: 1990

E2-7 Median Family Income, by Age, Race, and Hispanic Origin: 1990

E2-8 Median Income and Percent of Aged Units, by Age, Sex, and Marital Status

E2-9 Median Income of Elderly Units, by Marital Status, Race, and Hispanic Origin: 1990

E2-10 Income Level for the Elderly, by Residence: 1987

E2-11 Median Income of Households, by Selected Characteristics, Race, and Hispanic Origin of Householder: 1991, 1990, and 1989

E2-12 Presence of Elderly—Households, by Total Money Income in 1991, Race, and Hispanic Origin of Householder

E2-13 Income from Earnings, by Race, Hispanic Origin, and Marital Status: Percent Distribution of Aged Units 65 or Older: 1990

E2-14 Income from Private Pensions or Annuities, by Age and Marital Status: Percent Distribution of Aged Units 55 or Older: 1990

E2-15 Income from Employer Pensions, by Sex, Marital Status, and Social Security Beneficiary Status: Percent Distribution of Persons Aged 65 or Older: 1990

E2-16 Income from Government Employee Pension, by Sex and Marital Status: Percent Distribution of Persons Aged 65 or Older: 1990

E2-17 Age of Householder—Households, by Median Money Income: 1967 to 1991

E2-18 Median Value and Ratio of Owned House Value to Current Income for the Elderly, by Residence: 1989

E3. Living Costs

E3-1 CPI-U: All Items and Food and Beverages: 1981 to 1992

E3-2 CPI-U: Housing and Apparel and Upkeep: 1981 to 1992

E3-3   CPI-U: Transportation and Medical Care: 1981 to 1992

E3-4   CPI-U: Entertainment and Other Goods and Services: 1981 to 1992

E3-5   Selected Characteristics, Annual Expenditures, Sources of Income, and Shares of Expenditures and Income, for Older Consumer Units, by Income Class, Consumer Expenditure Survey: 1988 to 1989

E3-6   Annual Expenditures, Expenditure Shares, and Characteristics of Single Consumer Units Classified by Sex and Selected Age Groups, Consumer Expenditure Survey: 1988 to 1989

E3-7   Consumer Units with Reference Person Age 65 and Over, by Income before Taxes: Average Annual Expenditures and Characteristics, Consumer Expenditure Survey: 1988 to 1989

E3-8   Monthly Housing Costs as a Percent of Income, by Tenure and Age of Householder: 1987

E3-9   Monthly Housing Costs as Percent of Income, by Age and Tenure of Householder: 1987

E3-10   Personal Health-Care Expenditures, by Age: 1977 and 1987

E3-11   Total Out-of-Pocket Health Expenditures by the Elderly

E3-12   Per Family Out-of-Pocket Health Expenditures by the Elderly

E3-13   Percent Distribution of Per Family Out-of-Pocket Health Expenditures by Elderly Families

E3-14   Elderly Family Out-of-Pocket Health Expenditures as a Percent of After-Tax Income

E3-15   Elderly Out-of-Pocket Health Costs Per Elderly Family

E3-16   Distribution of Out-of-Pocket Health Care Costs Per Elderly Family

E3-17   Elderly Out-of-Pocket Health Care Expenses as a Portion of After-Tax Income

E4. Poverty

E4-1   Number of Poor and Poverty Rate: 1959 to 1991

E4-2   Distribution of the Population Above and Below the Poverty Level, by Age: 1991

E4-3   Persons Below Poverty Level, by Race, Hispanic Origin, Age, and Region: 1990

E4-4   Persons 65 Years Old and Over Below Poverty Level, by Selected Characteristics: 1970 to 1990

E4-5   Number and Percent Poor in 1989 of Persons Aged 65 Years and Over, Ranked by State

E4-6   Percent Poor in 1990 for Persons 65 Years and Over, by Race and Hispanic Origin: March 1991

E4-7   Percent Poor Elderly in 1990, by Age, Sex, Race, and Hispanic Origin: March 1991

E4-8   Poverty Rates of Persons 85 Years and Over: 1981 to 1990

E4-9   Poverty Status of Persons, by Age, Race, and Hispanic Origin: 1959 to 1990

E4-10   Poverty Rates for Persons Aged 65 to 74: 1990

E4-11   Poverty Rates for Persons Aged 75 and Over: 1990

E4-12   Poverty Rates for White Persons Aged 65 to 74: 1990

E4-13   Poverty Rates for White Persons Aged 75 and Over: 1990

E4-14   Poverty Rates for Black Persons Aged 65 to 74: 1990

E4-15   Poverty Rates for Black Persons Aged 75 and Over: 1990

E4-16   Poverty Rates for Persons of Hispanic Origin Aged 65 to 74: 1990

E4-17   Poverty Rates for Persons of Hispanic Origin Aged 75 and Over: 1990

E4-18   Families Below Poverty Level—Selected Characteristics, by Race and Hispanic Origin: 1990

E4-19   Percent of Elderly Persons Below the Poverty Level, by Race, Sex, and Residence: 1990

E4-20   Poverty Status of Persons, by Age, Race, and Hispanic Origin: 1959 to 1991

E4-21   Family Income Below the Poverty Line and 125 Percent of the Poverty Line, by Age, Sex, Marital Status, Social Security Beneficiary Status, Living Arrangements, Race, and Hispanic Origin: Percent of Aged Units 55 or Older: 1990

E4-22   Percent of Elderly Persons in Poverty, by Definition of Income: 1979 to 1991

F. EXPENDITURES FOR THE ELDERLY

F1. Overview of Expenditures

F1-1   Federal Outlays Benefiting the Elderly: 1991

F1-2   Federal Outlays Benefiting the Elderly: 1990 and 1991

F1-3   Federal Pension and Health Programs as a Percent of GNP and the Budget: 1965 to 2040

F1-4   Gross National Product (GNP), National Health Care (NHC) Expenditures, National Physician Expenditures, Medicare Expenditures, and Medicare Physician Expenditures: Selected Calendar Years 1970 to 1988

F1-5   Estimates of Monthly Rent Subsidies, by Number of Bedrooms, Region, and Income Level: 1991

F1-6   Cost of Thrifty Food Plan: 1991

F1-7   Private Pension Plans—Summary, by Type of Plan: 1975 to 1988

F2. Social Security

F2-1   Social Security at a Glance: 1992

F2-2   Social Security Trust Funds: 1980 to 1990

F2-3   Social Security—Covered Employment, Earnings, and Contribution Rates: 1970 to 1990

F2-4   OASDI Benefits: Number and Average Monthly Benefit in Current-Payment Status for Adult Beneficiaries, by Type of Benefit, Sex, and Age: March 1992

F2-5   Amount of OASDI Benefits in Current-Payment Status, by Type of Benefit, Sex of Beneficiaries Aged 65 or Older, and State: December 1990

F2-6   OASDI Benefits in Current-Payment Status: Number and Percent of OASDI Beneficiaries Also Receiving Federally Administered SSI Payments, by Reason for SSI Eligibility and Type of OASDI Benefit: March 1992

F2-7   OASDI Benefits: Number of Monthly Benefits Awarded to Retired Workers and Their Spouses and Children and to Survivors: 1940 to 1992

F2-8   Proportion of Elderly Social Security Beneficiaries, by Sex and Residence: December 1990

F2-9   Average Social Security Benefit for Elderly Beneficiaries, by Sex and Residence: December 1990

F2-10   SSI: Number of Persons Awarded Federally Administered Payments, by Category: 1974 to 1992

F2-11   SSI: Number and Percent Distribution of Children and Adults Receiving Federally Administered Payments, by Age and Category: June 1992

F3. Health Care Expenditures

F3-1   Federal Health Outlays, by Several Measures: 1960 to 1995

F3-2   Real Per Capita National Health Expenditures: 1929 to 1989

F3-3   Federal Health Spending: 1965 to 1995

F3-4   Health Care and General Inflation Rates in the 1980s

F3-5   Relative Growth in Total National Health Care Expenditures, Physician Expenditures, Total Medicare Expenditures, and Medicare Physician Expenditures: Selected Calendar Years 1970 to 1988

F3-6   Per Capita Personal Health Care Expenditures for Persons 65 Years and More, by Age, Type of Service, and Source of Payment: 1987

F3-7   Mean Medicare Outlays Per Enrollee, by State and Risk Class: 1991

F3-8   Medicare Supplementary Medical Insurance Expenditures, Relative Index, and Percent Distribution, by Type of Provider: Selected Calendar Years 1970 to 1988

F3-9   Medicare Enrollment, Persons Served, and Payments for Medicare Enrollees 65 Years of Age and Over, by Selected Characteristics: 1967, 1977, and 1986

F3-10   Where the Medicare Dollar for the Elderly Goes: 1989

F3-11   Where the Private Health Care Dollar for the Elderly Goes: 1987

F3-12   Projected Nursing Home Expenditures for People Age 65+, by Source of Payment in 1990, 2005, and 2020

F3-13   Sources of Payment of Health Care Expenditures for the Elderly, by Functional Status of User: 1987

F3-14 Total Health Care Expenditures for the Elderly, by Functional Status of User and Residence: 1987

F4. Public and Private Pensions

F4-1   Assets of Private and Public Pension Funds, by Type of Fund: 1980 to 1991

F4-2   Accrual Costs and Funding for Major Federal Retirement Systems: 1991 Estimates

F4-3   Private and State and Local Government Pension Assets: 1950 to 1989

F4-4   Benefits and Beneficiaries Under Public Employee Retirement Systems, by Reason for Benefit Receipt: Fiscal Year 1988

F4-5   Percent Distribution of Benefits and Beneficiaries Under Public Employee Retirement Systems, by Reason for Benefit Receipt and Level of Administering Government: 1978 and 1986 to 1988

F4-6   Average Annual Benefit Amounts, by Reason for Benefit Receipt and Level of Government: 1978 and 1986 to 1988, in Current and Constant (1988) Dollars

F4-7   Benefits and Beneficiaries Under Public Employee Retirement Systems, by Reason for Benefit Receipt: 1954 to 1988

F4-8   Average Annual Retirement Pension from Private Pension Plans in Selected Countries: 1970 to 1989

F5. Veterans

F5-1   Number of Veterans Over 65 Years: 1965 to 2000

F5-2   Percent of Elderly Males Who Are Veterans, by Age: 1987

F5-3   Veterans Over 65 Years as Percent of All U.S. Males Over 65 Years: 1970 to 2000

F5-4   Estimates and Projections of the Elderly Veteran Population, by Age: 1980 to 2040

F5-5   Department of Veterans Affairs Medical Budget Obligations: 1993

F5-6   Department of Veterans Affairs Budget Obligations for Patient Care: 1993

F5-7   Percent of Elderly Veterans Receiving Selected Benefits, by Residence: 1987

F5-8   Source of Assistance for Elderly Veterans Receiving ADL/IADL Aid, by Residence: 1987

F5-9   Expenditures/Outlays for Disability Compensation: 1967 to 1991

F5-10   Expenditures/Outlays for Disability Pension: 1967 to 1991

F5-11   Expenditures/Outlays for Dependency and Indemnity Compensation or Death Compensation: 1967 to 1991

F5-12   Expenditures/Outlays for Death Pension: 1967 to 1991

F5-13   Monthly Disability Compensation Age of Veteran, by Combined Degree of Impairment: September 1992

F5-14   VA Nursing Home Census: FY 1988 to 2010

Preface

America is graying at ever increasing speed. In 1776, the total population of the American colonies was approximately 2.5 million; only one out of 50 persons was 65 years or older, and half the population was under age 16. In 1990, fewer than one-fourth of the people living in the United States were younger than 16, and 1 of 7 was over 65. Early in the next century, as the Baby Boom becomes the Grandparent Boom, the aging trend will accelerate. With steadily increasing longevity the proportion of the oldest old, those 85 years or older, will also be greater. The 1990 census counted nearly 1 million persons who reported their age as 90 years or older; 36,000 of those were centenarians, more than double the number reported in the 1980 census.

Social and economic issues concerning older Americans are important aspects in American life. As more people reach old age in good health, are able to maintain an excellent quality of life, and are comparatively affluent, they are changing the marketing strategies of industry. They are a powerful political influence on the federal, state and local scene. On the other hand, the soundness of the Social Security system is threatened as fewer and fewer young people are paying to support more and more older people. The middle-aged and the young elderly are often called upon to care for their children as well as their parents and grandparents. The poor elderly pose especially difficult social problems and are often victimized and abused. The aged are also a major factor in the economic and ethical problems of containing the costs of health care and providing quality care to all Americans.

Statistical data are helpful decision-making tools for government agencies, industry, educators and caregivers who are faced with these problems. The British economist Sir Josiah Stamp (1880–1941) once said that "the government is very keen on amassing statistics. They collect them, raise them to the nth power, take the cube root and prepare wonderful diagrams. But you must never forget that every one of these figures comes in the first instance from the village watchman who just puts down what he damn pleases" (Stamp, Sir Josiah, *British Income and Property: The Application of Official Statistics to Economic Problems*. London: P.S. King & Son, 1916, introduction). The village watchman in the United States has been replaced by the highly skilled staff of the U.S. Bureau of the Census, which collects, processes, and analyzes data on sophisticated computer systems. However, Sir Josiah's caveat should still be kept in mind and statistics used with caution and perspective. In 1790, the United States became the first nation in the world to establish a population census for the purpose of apportionment in Congress. In 1791, Thomas Jefferson expressed his concerns about the completeness and accuracy of the census; in a letter to David Humphrey, U.S. Minister to Portugal, he said: "Nearly the whole of the states have now returned their census . . . Making a very small allowance for omissions, we are upwards of four millions; and we know in fact that the omissions have been very great" (*The Works of Thomas Jefferson*, collected and edited by Paul Leicester Ford, 12 vols. New York: G. Putnam, 1901-1910, vi, 304).

In 1902 the Census Bureau was organized as a permanent agency of the federal government. Since then, the bureau has been on the forefront of developing data collection methodologies, sampling procedures and the use of statistical projections and analyses. Over the years, other government agencies entered the field of statistics in the areas of agriculture, commerce, education, health, labor, law, social security, and others. During the twentieth century, statistical data have been widely used as a base for the distribution of federal funds in various assistance and entitlement programs, for planning health and educational needs, and for estimating consumer demands. The 1990 census, as its predecessors, is estimated to have undercounted the population by several million, in spite of special efforts made to reach migrant workers, illegal immigrants, minority groups, and the homeless.

The first edition of the *Statistical Handbook on Aging Americans* appeared in 1986. This 1994 edition contains a totally new compilation of 378 tables and charts illustrating the changes in America's aging population, based on 1990 census data and on several new surveys. In 1991, Frank Schick and I contracted with Oryx Press to produce this volume. Sadly, he died suddenly in 1992. He had a keen lifelong interest in history and politics and in the numerical representation of findings and trends; I know he would have wanted me to complete the task.

To produce this book, we contacted various divisions of the U.S. Bureau of the Census, statistical units in other government agencies, the Administration on Aging, the American Association of Retired People (AARP), and other organizations for significant publications and works in progress. We waded through reports, books and serial publications in government document depositories, performed extensive online and manual literature searches, and massaged unpublished data on the computer. We fought the battle of ever changing telephone numbers and rarely returned voice mail messages; however, once an actual human being was reached, he or she was usually most knowledgeable and cooperative.

I hope that this volume will make it easier for researchers to put their fingers on relevant statistics concerning the elderly. The data presented here were the most recent available as of June 1993. Generally, information based entirely on pre-1985 data was not included. Comparatively little of the information presented comes from nongovernment sources. The tables and charts are given as they appeared in their original sources, without editorial changes, unless otherwise indicated. "The List of Sources" and the "Guide to Relevant Information Resources" will help users to obtain additional and more detailed statistics. A glossary of statistical terms and abbreviations and a subject index are also included.

The Bureau of the Census, Bureau of Labor Statistics, National Center for Health Statistics, and the AARP Information Center staff were most helpful in providing me with materials and leads to other information sources. I especially want to thank Cynthia Taeuber and Arnold Goldstein from the Bureau of the Census, Philip Rones from the Bureau of Labor Statistics, Paula Lovas and Diane Welsh from AARP, and Peggy Pruden from the Montgomery County (Maryland) Public Library for their support in this endeavor. To my son, Thomas Schick, thanks for lending me his ear and logical mind for many brainstorming sessions.

Renee Schick
Bethesda, MD

A. Demographics

The aging population is defined as persons 65 years and older. Since the first edition of the *Statistical Handbook on Aging Americans*, an increasing number of statistical tabulations have tried to distinguish among the component age groups of "the elderly" to illustrate the diversity within this population. The following terms are frequently used for the component age groups: the young old (65 to 74 years); the aged (75 to 84 years); and the oldest old (85 years and over).[1]

A1. AGE AND SEX DISTRIBUTION

The elderly comprise an ever increasing proportion of our population; they are living significantly longer and in better health than previously. Between 1980 and 1990, the elderly population grew by 22%, from 25.5 to 31.2 million, while the total population increased by 9.3%. Growth of the elderly population will increase dramatically in the second decade of the twenty-first century when the Baby Boom generation begins to reach age 65. In 1990, 1 in 8 Americans was over 65 years old; by 2050, 1 in 5 will be elderly. The oldest old group will have grown from 3 million in 1990 to over 17 million in 2050.

Elderly women outnumber elderly men by 3 to 2. The disparity is especially marked in the oldest age group of persons over 85: only 39 men per 100 women.

A2. LIFE EXPECTANCY

During this century, life expectancy in the United States has changed dramatically. In 1900, the average person could expect to live 47.3 years; by 1950, this figure had increased to 68.2, and in 1990, the average life expectancy for women had risen to 78.6 and for men to 72 years. More persons will survive to the oldest ages in the future.

A3. RACE AND ETHNICITY

The elderly population will be more diverse in terms of racial composition and Hispanic origin in the coming decades. The proportion of the nonwhite and Hispanic older population is expected to increase more rapidly than that of whites. During the first half of the century, life expectancy for the white population was considerably longer than for blacks; these differences have narrowed and today life expectancy is longest for white women, followed by black women, white men, and black men. In 1990, minorities made up 14% of the elderly population; this proportion is projected to increase to 32% by 2050.

A4. GEOGRAPHIC DISTRIBUTION AND MOBILITY

In 1990, nine states had more than 1 million elderly: California, Florida, New York, Pennsylvania, Texas, Illinois, Ohio, Michigan, and New Jersey. In Florida 18.3% of the population is over 65. The mobility rate of the older population is considerably less than that of the younger. Many who changed their residence moved to the Sunbelt; moves by older people to that region nearly doubled since 1950. During the last 10 to 15 years, a pattern of "countermigration" has developed, indicating that a substantial number of retirees, as they reach the oldest old cohort, return after a few years to their home states, families, and friends.

A5. AGING AROUND THE WORLD

The world's elderly population is also growing faster than the total population. In 1991, there were about 332 million people over the age of 65 in the world; by the year 2000, that number is expected to grow to 426 million. Sweden is the world's "oldest" country, with 17% of its population over age 65. Japan is the most rapidly aging country. The over-80 age group is expected to be the fastest growing portion of the elderly population throughout the world, especially in developed countries.

REFERENCE

1. Cynthia M. Taeuber, *Sixty-Five Plus in America*, U.S. Department of Commerce, Bureau of the Census, Current Population Reports, P23–178, August 1992, pp. 1-2.

A1. Age and Sex Distribution

A1-1. Total Population Aged 65 Years and Over: 1990

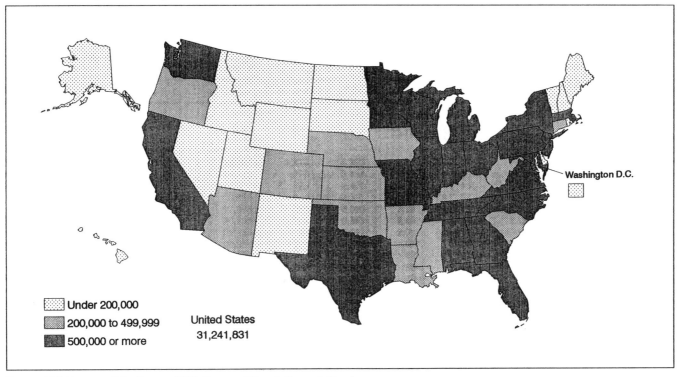

Washington D.C.

Under 200,000
200,000 to 499,999
500,000 or more

United States
31,241,831

Source: U.S. Bureau of the Census, 1990 Census of Population and Housing.

A1-2. Percent of Total State Population Aged 65 Years and Over: 1990

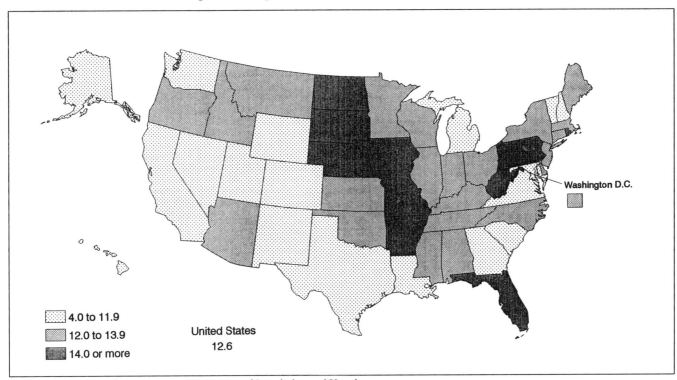

Washington D.C.

4.0 to 11.9
12.0 to 13.9
14.0 or more

United States
12.6

Source: U.S. Bureau of the Census, 1990 Census of Population and Housing.

A1-3. Population 65 Years and Over, by State: 1990

Population 65 Years and Over, by State: 1990

Rank, State	Population 65 years and over	Percent 65 years and over
UNITED STATES	**31,241,831**	**12.6**
1 Florida	2,369,431	18.3
2 Pennsylvania	1,829,106	15.4
3 Iowa	426,106	15.3
4 Rhode Island	150,547	15.0
4 West Virginia	268,897	15.0
6 Arkansas	350,058	14.9
7 South Dakota	102,331	14.7
8 North Dakota	91,055	14.3
9 Nebraska	223,068	14.1
10 Missouri	717,681	14.0
11 Kansas	342,571	13.8
11 Oregon	391,324	13.8
13 Massachusetts	819,284	13.6
13 Connecticut	445,907	13.6
15 Oklahoma	424,213	13.5
16 New Jersey	1,032,025	13.4
17 Montana	106,497	13.3
17 Wisconsin	651,221	13.3
17 Maine	163,373	13.3
20 New York	2,363,722	13.1
20 Arizona	478,774	13.1
22 Ohio	1,406,961	13.0
23 Alabama	522,989	12.9
24 District of Columbia	77,847	12.8
25 Tennessee	618,818	12.7
25 Kentucky	466,845	12.7
27 Illinois	1,436,545	12.6
27 Indiana	696,196	12.6
29 Minnesota	546,934	12.5
29 Mississippi	321,284	12.5
31 North Carolina	804,341	12.1
31 Delaware	80,735	12.1
33 Idaho	121,265	12.0
34 Michigan	1,108,461	11.9
35 Washington	575,288	11.8
35 Vermont	66,163	11.8
37 South Carolina	396,935	11.4
38 Hawaii	125,005	11.3
38 New Hampshire	125,029	11.3
40 Louisiana	468,991	11.1
41 Maryland	517,482	10.8
41 New Mexico	163,062	10.8
43 Virginia	664,470	10.7
44 Nevada	127,631	10.6
45 California	3,135,552	10.5
46 Wyoming	47,195	10.4
47 Texas	1,716,576	10.1
47 Georgia	654,270	10.1
49 Colorado	329,443	10.0
50 Utah	149,958	8.7
51 Alaska	22,369	4.1

Source: U.S. Bureau of the Census, 1990 Census of Population and Housing.

A1-4. Total Population Aged 85 Years and Over: 1990

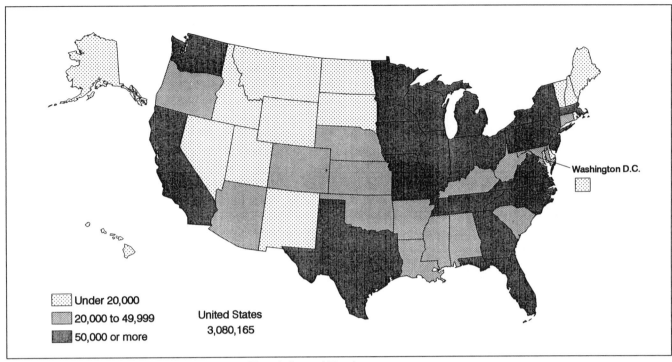

Legend:
- Under 20,000
- 20,000 to 49,999
- 50,000 or more

United States
3,080,165

Source: U.S. Bureau of the Census, 1990 Census of Population and Housing.

A1-5. Percent of Total State Population Aged 85 Years and Over: 1990

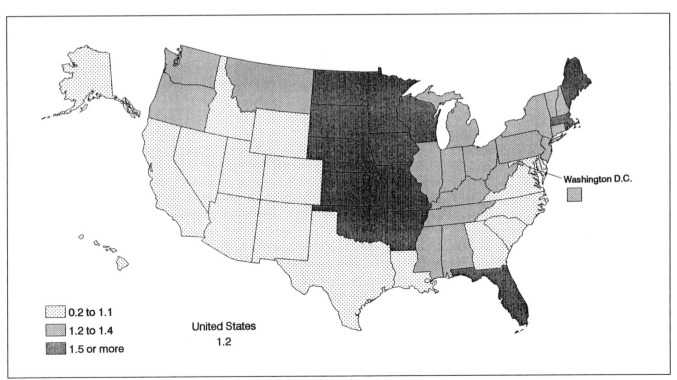

Legend:
- 0.2 to 1.1
- 1.2 to 1.4
- 1.5 or more

United States
1.2

Source: U.S. Bureau of the Census, 1990 Census of Population and Housing.

A1-6. Population 85 Years and Over, by State: 1990

Rank, State	Population 85 years and over	Percent 85 years and over
UNITED STATES	3,080,165	1.2
1 Iowa	55,255	2.0
2 South Dakota	13,343	1.9
2 Nebraska	29,202	1.9
4 North Dakota	11,240	1.8
5 Kansas	42,241	1.7
6 Florida	210,110	1.6
6 Rhode Island	16,016	1.6
6 Missouri	81,217	1.6
6 Minnesota	68,835	1.6
10 Massachusetts	92,209	1.5
10 Wisconsin	74,293	1.5
10 Arkansas	35,216	1.5
10 Maine	18,226	1.5
10 Oklahoma	45,848	1.5
15 Pennsylvania	171,836	1.4
15 Connecticut	46,993	1.4
15 West Virginia	25,451	1.4
15 New York	248,173	1.4
15 Oregon	38,815	1.4
20 Vermont	7,523	1.3
20 Montana	10,676	1.3
20 Indiana	71,751	1.3
20 District of Columbia	7,847	1.3
20 Illinois	147,549	1.3
20 Ohio	138,030	1.3
20 Kentucky	46,367	1.3
20 Mississippi	32,335	1.3
28 New Jersey	95,547	1.2
28 Tennessee	58,794	1.2
28 Alabama	48,507	1.2
28 New Hampshire	13,286	1.2
28 Washington	56,301	1.2
28 Michigan	106,907	1.2
34 Idaho	11,398	1.1
34 Delaware	7,142	1.1
34 North Carolina	69,969	1.1
37 Louisiana	43,633	1.0
37 Arizona	37,717	1.0
37 California	299,107	1.0
37 Wyoming	4,550	1.0
37 Colorado	32,953	1.0
37 Texas	166,605	1.0
37 Maryland	46,496	1.0
37 Virginia	59,709	1.0
45 New Mexico	14,232	0.9
45 Hawaii	10,397	0.9
45 Georgia	57,244	0.9
45 South Carolina	30,749	0.9
49 Utah	13,611	0.8
50 Nevada	7,463	0.6
51 Alaska	1,251	0.2

Source: U.S. Bureau of the Census, 1990 Census of Population and Housing.

A1-7. Resident Population, by Age and Sex: 1970 to 1991

[In thousands, except as indicated. Based on enumerated population as of **April 1**; 1991 based on estimated population as of **July 1**. Excludes Armed Forces overseas.]

YEAR AND SEX	Total, all years	Under 5 years	5-9 years	10-14 years	15-19 years	20-24 years	25-29 years	30-34 years	35-39 years	40-44 years	45-49 years	50-54 years	55-59 years	60-64 years	65-74 years	75 years and over	5-13 years	14-17 years	18-24 years	18 years and over	65 years and over	Median age (yr.)
1970, total[1]	**203,235**	**17,163**	**19,969**	**20,804**	**19,084**	**16,383**	**13,486**	**11,437**	**11,113**	**11,988**	**12,124**	**11,111**	**9,979**	**8,623**	**12,443**	**7,530**	**36,675**	**15,851**	**22,714**	**141,263**	**19,972**	**28.0**
Male	98,928	8,750	10,175	10,598	9,641	7,925	6,626	5,599	5,416	5,823	5,855	5,351	4,769	4,030	5,440	2,927	18,687	8,069	11,583	67,347	8,367	26.8
Female	104,309	8,413	9,784	10,208	9,443	8,458	6,859	5,838	5,697	6,166	6,269	5,759	5,210	4,593	7,002	4,603	17,987	7,782	12,131	73,920	11,605	29.3
1980, total	**226,546**	**16,348**	**16,700**	**18,242**	**21,168**	**21,319**	**19,521**	**17,561**	**13,965**	**11,669**	**11,090**	**11,710**	**11,615**	**10,088**	**15,581**	**9,969**	**31,159**	**16,247**	**30,022**	**171,196**	**25,549**	**30.0**
Male	110,053	8,362	8,539	9,316	10,755	10,663	9,705	8,677	6,862	5,708	5,388	5,621	5,482	4,670	6,757	3,548	15,923	8,298	15,054	81,766	10,305	28.8
Female	116,493	7,986	8,161	8,926	10,413	10,655	9,816	8,884	7,104	5,961	5,702	6,089	6,133	5,418	8,824	6,420	15,237	7,950	14,968	89,429	15,245	31.3
1990, total[2]	**248,710**	**18,758**	**18,035**	**17,060**	**17,742**	**19,132**	**21,328**	**21,833**	**19,946**	**17,689**	**13,744**	**11,313**	**10,487**	**10,625**	**18,045**	**13,033**	**31,226**	**13,340**	**26,942**	**191,536**	**31,079**	**32.8**
Male	121,239	9,599	9,232	8,739	9,173	9,743	10,702	10,862	9,833	8,676	6,739	5,493	5,008	4,947	7,907	4,586	16,295	6,857	13,734	91,964	12,493	31.6
Female	127,470	9,159	8,803	8,322	8,709	9,389	10,625	10,971	10,013	8,913	7,004	5,820	5,479	5,679	10,139	8,447	15,532	6,483	13,208	99,572	18,586	34.0
1991, total	**252,177**	**19,222**	**18,237**	**17,671**	**17,265**	**19,194**	**20,718**	**22,159**	**20,518**	**18,754**	**14,094**	**11,645**	**10,423**	**10,582**	**18,280**	**13,474**	**32,500**	**13,423**	**26,385**	**193,754**	**31,754**	**33.1**
Male	122,979	9,836	9,337	9,051	8,834	9,775	10,393	11,034	10,174	9,258	6,907	5,656	4,987	4,945	8,022	4,769	16,641	6,901	13,456	93,065	12,791	31.9
Female	129,198	9,386	8,900	8,620	8,371	9,419	10,325	11,125	10,344	9,496	7,188	5,989	5,436	5,637	10,258	8,705	15,859	6,522	12,929	100,689	18,962	34.3
Percent:																						
1970	100.0	8.4	9.8	10.2	9.4	8.1	6.6	5.6	5.5	5.9	6.0	5.5	4.9	4.2	6.1	3.7	18.0	7.8	11.7	69.5	9.8	(X)
1980[2]	100.0	7.2	7.4	8.1	9.3	9.4	8.8	7.8	6.2	5.2	4.9	5.2	5.1	4.5	6.9	4.4	13.8	7.2	13.3	75.6	11.3	(X)
1990[2]	100.0	7.5	7.3	6.9	7.2	7.7	8.6	8.8	8.0	7.1	5.5	4.5	4.2	4.3	7.3	5.2	12.8	5.4	10.8	77.0	12.5	(X)
1991	**100.0**	**7.6**	**7.2**	**7.0**	**6.8**	**7.6**	**8.2**	**8.8**	**8.1**	**7.4**	**5.6**	**4.6**	**4.1**	**4.2**	**7.2**	**5.3**	**12.9**	**5.3**	**10.5**	**76.8**	**12.6**	**(X)**
Male	100.0	8.0	7.6	7.4	7.2	7.9	8.5	9.0	8.3	7.5	5.6	4.6	4.1	4.0	6.5	3.9	13.5	5.6	10.9	75.7	10.4	(X)
Female	100.0	7.3	6.9	6.7	6.5	7.3	8.0	8.6	8.0	7.4	5.6	4.6	4.2	4.4	7.9	6.7	12.3	5.0	10.0	77.9	14.7	(X)

X Not applicable.

[1] Official count. The revised 1970 resident population count is 203,302,031; the difference of 66,733 is due to errors found after release of the official series.

[2] The data shown have been modified from the official 1990 census counts.

Source: U.S. Bureau of the Census, *Current Population Reports*, series P-25, Nos. 917 and 1045; *1990 Census of Population and Housing Data Paper Listing* (CPH-L-74); and unpublished data.

A1-8. Population 80 Years and Over: 1900 to 1990

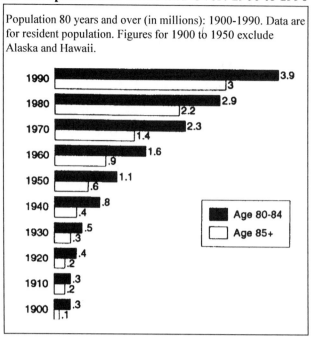

Population 80 years and over (in millions): 1900-1990. Data are for resident population. Figures for 1900 to 1950 exclude Alaska and Hawaii.

Source: 1990 CPH-L-74 tabulation and previous decennial census data.

A1-9. Growth of the Older Population, Actual and Projected: 1900 to 2050

(Numbers in thousands. Data for 1900 to 1990 are April 1 census figures. Data for 2000 to 2050 are July 1 projections.)

YEAR	Total (all ages) Number	Age in Years											
		65–74		75–79		80–84		80 and over		85 and over		65 and over	
		Number	Percent	Number	Percent	Number	Percent	Number	Percent	Number	Percent	Number	Percent
1900	75,995	2,187	2.9	520	0.7	252	0.3	374	0.5	122	0.2	3,080	4.1
1910	91,972	2,793	3.0	667	0.7	322	0.4	489	0.5	167	0.2	3,949	4.3
1920	105,711	3,464	3.3	856	0.8	403	0.4	613	0.6	210	0.2	4,933	4.7
1930	122,775	4,721	3.8	1,106	0.9	535	0.4	807	0.7	272	0.2	6,634	5.4
1940	131,669	6,376	4.8	1,504	1.1	774	0.6	1,139	0.9	365	0.3	9,019	6.8
1950	150,697	8,415	5.6	2,128	1.4	1,149	0.8	1,726	1.1	577	0.4	12,269	8.1
1960	179,323	10,997	6.1	3,054	1.7	1,580	0.9	2,509	1.4	929	0.5	16,560	9.2
1970	203,302	12,447	6.1	3,838	1.9	2,286	1.1	3,695	1.8	1,409	0.7	19,980	9.8
1980	226,546	15,581	6.9	4,794	2.1	2,935	1.3	5,175	2.3	2,240	1.0	25,550	11.3
1990	248,710	18,045	7.3	6,103	2.5	3,909	1.6	6,930	2.8	3,021	1.2	31,079	12.5
MIDDLE SERIES (Middle fertility, mortality, and immigration assumptions) /1													
2000	274,815	18,258	6.6	7,447	2.7	4,892	1.8	9,181	3.3	4,289	1.6	34,886	12.7
2010	298,109	21,235	7.1	7,217	2.4	5,550	1.9	11,252	3.8	5,702	1.9	39,705	13.3
2020	322,602	31,680	9.8	9,554	3.0	5,913	1.8	12,393	3.8	6,480	2.0	53,627	16.6
2030	344,951	37,865	11.0	14,154	4.1	9,438	2.7	17,819	5.2	8,381	2.4	69,839	20.2
2040	364,349	33,678	9.2	16,236	4.5	12,453	3.4	25,674	7.0	13,221	3.6	75,588	20.7
2050	382,674	35,217	9.2	14,264	3.7	11,744	3.1	29,396	7.7	17,652	4.6	78,876	20.6

[1]For the base year (1992): Lifetime births per 1,000 women, 2,052; Life expectancy at birth, 75.8; Yearly net immigration, 880,000. Assumptions for the year 2050 are respectively: [2]119; 82.1; and 880,000. Figures for 1900 to 1950 exclude Alaska and Hawaii. Figures for 1900 to 1990 are for the resident population; Projections for 2000 to 2050 include armed forces overseas.

Source: U.S. Bureau of the Census. Data for 1900 to 1940, 1960, and 1980 shown in 1980 Census of Population, PC80-B1, General Population Characteristics, Tables 42 and 45; Data for 1990 from 1990 Census of Population and Housing, Series CPH-L-74, "Modified and Actual Age, Sex, Race, and Hispanic Origin Data." Data for 1950 shown in "Estimates of the Population of the United States and Components of Change, by Age, Color, and Sex: 1950 to 1960," *Current Population Reports*, Series P-25, No. 1045, U.S. Government Printing Office, Washington, DC, 1990. Data for 2000 to 2050 shown in *Current Population Reports*, P25-1092, "Projections of the United States, by Age, Sex, Race, and Hispanic Origin: 1992 to 2050," U.S. Government Printing Office, Washington, DC, 1992.

A1-10. Population 85 Years and Over: 1900 to 2050

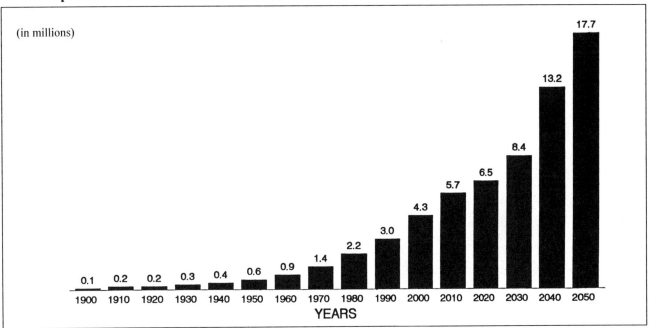

Source: U.S. Bureau of the Census, 1900 to 1980 Censuses of Population; 1990 from 1990 Census of Population and Housing, Series CPH-L-74, "Modified and Actual Age, Sex, Race, and Hispanic Origin Data"; 2000 to 2050 from Jennifer C. Day, "Projections of the United States, by Age, Sex, Race, and Hispanic Origin: 1992 to 2050," *Current Population Reports,* P25-1092, U.S. Government Printing Office, Washington, DC, 1992 (middle series projections).

A1-11. Number of Men Per 100 Women, by Age Group: 1989

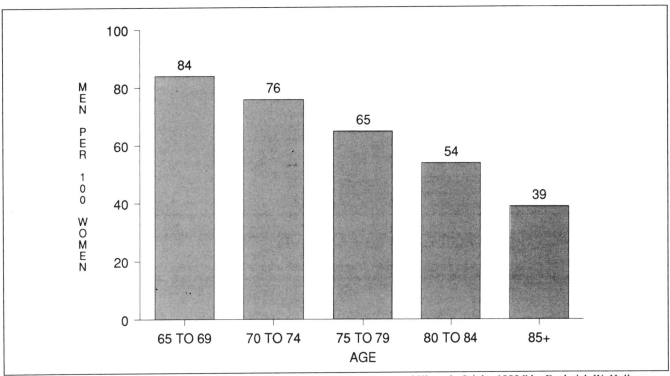

Source: U.S. Bureau of the Census, "U.S. Population Estimates, by Age, Sex, Race, and Hispanic Origin: 1989," by Frederick W. Hollman, *Current Population Reports* Series P-25, No. 1057 (March 1990).

A1-12. Population, by Sex and Age: 1990

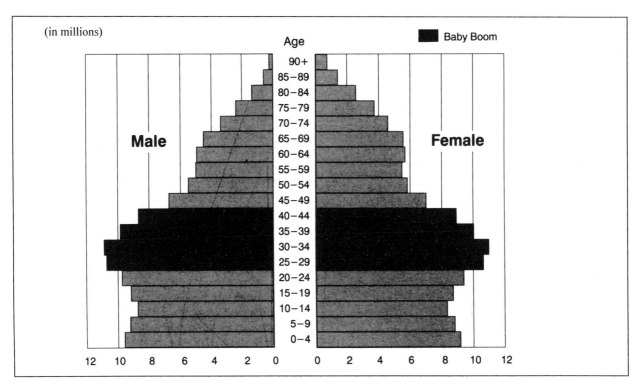

Source: U.S. Bureau of the Census, 1990 Census of Population and Housing, Series CPH-L-74, "Modified and Actual Age, Sex, Race, and Hispanic Origin Data."

A1-13. Population, by Sex and Age: 2010

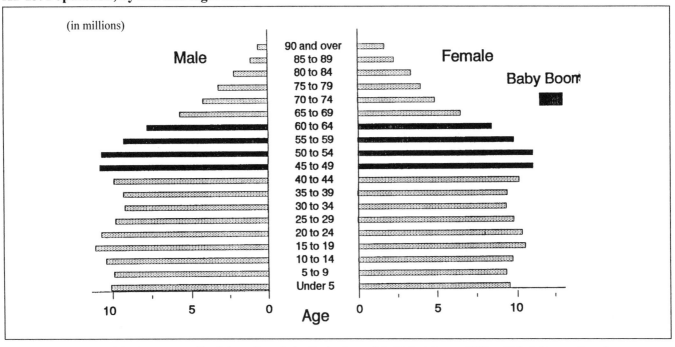

Source: U.S. Bureau of the Census, Jennifer C. Day, "Population Projections of the United States: 1992 to 2050," *Current Population Reports*, P25-1092, U.S. Government Printing Office, Washington, DC, 1992 (middle series projections).

A1-14. Population, by Sex and Age: 2030

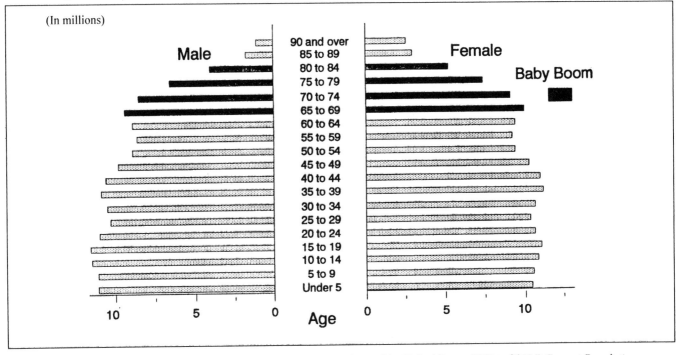

Source: U.S. Bureau of the Census, Jennifer C. Day, "Population Projections of the United States: 1992 to 2050," *Current Population Reports,* P25-1092, U.S. Government Printing Office, Washington, DC, 1992 (middle series projections).

A1-15. Population, by Sex and Age: 2050

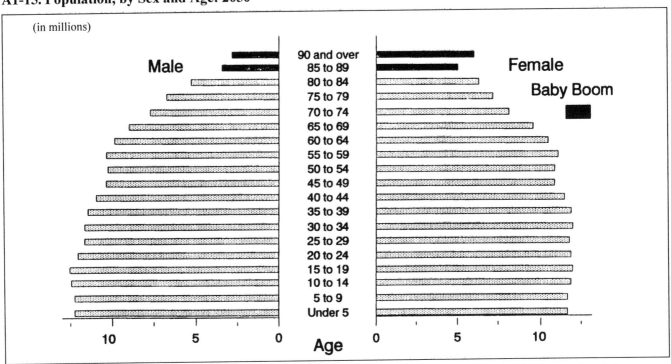

Source: U.S. Bureau of the Census, Jennifer C. Day, "Population Projections of the United States: 1992 to 2050," *Current Population Reports*, P25-1092, U.S. Government Printing Office, Washington, DC, 1992 (middle series projections).

A2. Life Expectancy

A2-1. Expectation of Life and Expected Deaths, by Race, Sex, and Age: 1989

AGE IN 1989 (years)	EXPECTATION OF LIFE IN YEARS					EXPECTED DEATHS PER 1,000 ALIVE AT SPECIFIED AGE [1]				
	Total	White		Black		Total	White		Black	
		Male	Female	Male	Female		Male	Female	Male	Female
At birth	75.3	72.7	79.2	64.8	73.5	9.86	9.08	7.15	20.04	17.17
1	75.0	72.3	78.8	65.2	73.8	0.69	0.69	0.53	1.18	0.91
2	74.1	71.4	77.8	64.2	72.9	0.52	0.50	0.41	0.91	0.75
3	73.1	70.4	76.9	63.3	71.9	0.40	0.38	0.32	0.72	0.61
4	72.1	69.5	75.9	62.3	71.0	0.33	0.32	0.27	0.59	0.49
5	71.1	68.5	74.9	61.4	70.0	0.29	0.29	0.23	0.51	0.40
6	70.2	67.5	73.9	60.4	69.0	0.26	0.27	0.21	0.45	0.32
7	69.2	66.5	73.0	59.4	68.0	0.24	0.26	0.19	0.40	0.27
8	68.2	65.5	72.0	58.5	67.1	0.21	0.23	0.17	0.34	0.23
9	67.2	64.5	71.0	57.5	66.1	0.18	0.20	0.15	0.28	0.22
10	66.2	63.6	70.0	56.5	65.1	0.16	0.17	0.13	0.24	0.23
11	65.2	62.6	69.0	55.5	64.1	0.17	0.17	0.13	0.24	0.25
12	64.3	61.6	68.0	54.5	63.1	0.22	0.24	0.16	0.34	0.27
13	63.3	60.6	67.0	53.5	62.1	0.32	0.39	0.22	0.55	0.30
14	62.3	59.6	66.0	52.6	61.2	0.47	0.59	0.30	0.83	0.33
15	61.3	58.6	65.1	51.6	60.2	0.63	0.82	0.39	1.16	0.37
16	60.4	57.7	64.1	50.7	59.2	0.79	1.03	0.48	1.47	0.42
17	59.4	56.8	63.1	49.8	58.2	0.91	1.21	0.53	1.78	0.48
18	58.5	55.8	62.1	48.8	57.3	0.99	1.31	0.55	2.07	0.54
19	57.5	54.9	61.2	47.9	56.3	1.03	1.37	0.53	2.33	0.62
20	56.6	54.0	60.2	47.1	55.3	1.06	1.42	0.50	2.61	0.70
21	55.6	53.0	59.2	46.2	54.4	1.10	1.47	0.48	2.89	0.79
22	54.7	52.1	58.3	45.3	53.4	1.13	1.51	0.47	3.10	0.88
23	53.8	51.2	57.3	44.4	52.4	1.15	1.53	0.47	3.23	0.95
24	52.8	50.3	56.3	43.6	51.5	1.17	1.55	0.49	3.28	1 03
25	51.9	49.4	55.3	42.7	50.6	1.18	1.55	0.50	3.32	1.10
26	50.9	48.4	54.4	41.9	49.6	1.20	1.56	0.52	3.38	1.18
27	50.0	47.5	53.4	41.0	48.7	1.23	1.58	0.54	3.50	1.28
28	49.1	46.6	52.4	40.2	47.7	1.27	1.62	0.56	3.69	1.39
29	48.1	45.7	51.5	39.3	46.8	1.32	1.67	0.59	3.94	1.51
30	47.2	44.7	50.5	38.5	45.9	1.38	1.73	0.62	4.20	1.65
31	46.2	43.8	49.5	37.6	44.9	1.45	1.79	0.66	4.47	1.78
32	45.3	42.9	48.6	36.8	44.0	1.51	1.86	0.70	4.78	1.91
33	44.4	42.0	47.6	36.0	43.1	1.59	1.93	0.73	5.14	2.02
34	43.5	41.0	46.6	35.1	42.2	1.66	2.02	0.76	5.53	2.13
35	42.5	40.1	45.7	34.3	41.3	1.75	2.11	0.80	5.96	2.25
36	41.6	39.2	44.7	33.5	40.4	1.85	2.22	0.85	6.39	2.37
37	40.7	38.3	43.7	32.7	39.5	1.94	2.32	0.91	6.79	2.53
38	39.8	37.4	42.8	32.0	38.6	2.04	2.42	0.99	7.11	2.71
39	38.8	36.5	41.8	31.2	37.7	2.14	2.52	1.09	7.40	2.92
40	37.9	35.6	40.9	30.4	36.8	2.25	2.63	1.20	7.69	3.16
41	37.0	34.7	39.9	29.7	35.9	2.38	2.76	1.33	8.02	3.40
42	36.1	33.8	39.0	28.9	35.0	2.53	2.93	1.46	8.38	3.65
43	35.2	32.9	38.0	28.1	34.1	2.71	3.13	1.59	8.78	3.90
44	34.3	32.0	37.1	27.4	33.3	2.92	3.38	1.73	9.23	4.15
45	33.4	31.1	36.1	26.6	32.4	3.15	3.66	1.89	9.69	4.43
46	32.5	30.2	35.2	25.9	31.5	3.41	3.98	2.07	10.19	4.74
47	31.6	29.3	34.3	25.1	30.7	3.71	4.33	2.29	10.80	5.07
48	30.7	28.4	33.4	24.4	29.8	4.05	4.71	2.54	11.53	5.43
49	29.8	27.5	32.4	23.7	29.0	4.43	5.12	2.84	12.37	5.83
50	28.9	26.7	31.5	23.0	28.2	4.85	5.58	3.16	13.30	6.27
51	28.1	25.8	30.6	22.3	27.3	5.31	6.10	3.51	14.25	6.75
52	27.2	25.0	29.7	21.6	26.5	5.84	6.73	3.90	15.21	7.30
53	26.4	24.2	28.8	20.9	25.7	6.43	7.49	4.31	16.14	7.91
54	25.6	23.3	28.0	20.3	24.9	7.08	8.35	4.76	17.07	8.59
55	24.7	22.5	27.1	19.6	24.1	7.79	9.29	5.24	18.04	9.31
56	23.9	21.7	26.2	18.9	23.4	8.55	10.29	5.77	19.09	10.09
57	23.1	21.0	25.4	18.3	22.6	9.37	11.37	6.34	20.27	11.01
58	22.3	20.2	24.6	17.7	21.8	10.27	12.55	6.97	21.61	12.12
59	21.6	19.4	23.7	17.1	21.1	11.23	13.81	7.64	23.10	13.38
60	20.8	18.7	22.9	16.4	20.4	12.27	15.18	8.39	24.68	14.76
61	20.1	18.0	22.1	15.9	19.7	13.37	16.63	9.18	26.36	16.17
62	19.3	17.3	21.3	15.3	19.0	14.52	18.12	10.02	28.15	17.51
63	18.6	16.6	20.5	14.7	18.3	15.69	19.62	10.91	30.07	18.72
64	17.9	15.9	19.7	14.1	17.7	16.91	21.18	11.84	32.12	19.85
65	17.2	15.2	19.0	13.6	17.0	18.20	22.80	12.85	34.31	21.00
70	13.9	12.1	15.3	11.0	13.9	27.31	34.77	20.03	47.63	29.38
75	10.9	9.4	11.9	8.8	11.0	41.31	53.66	31.61	65.79	42.53
80	8.3	7.1	8.9	6.9	8.5	63.71	82.84	51.62	94.32	65.05
85 and over	6.2	5.3	6.5	5.6	6.7	1,000.00	1,000.00	1,000.00	1,000.00	1,000.00

[1] Based on the proportion of the cohort who are alive at the beginning of an indicated age interval who will die before reaching the end of that interval. For example, out of every 1,000 people alive and exactly 50 years old at the beginning of the period, between 4 and 5 (4.85) will die before reaching their 51st birthdays.

Source: U.S. National Center for Health Statistics, *Vital Statistics of the United States,* annual; and unpublished data.

A2-2. Expectation of Life at Birth, 1970 to 1990, and Projections, 1995 to 2010

YEAR	TOTAL			WHITE			BLACK AND OTHER			BLACK		
	Total	Male	Female	Total	Male	Female	Total	Male	Female	Total	Male	Female
1970	70.8	67.1	74.7	71.7	68.0	75.6	65.3	61.3	69.4	64.1	60.0	68.3
1975	72.6	68.8	76.6	73.4	69.5	77.3	68.0	63.7	72.4	66.8	62.4	71.3
1976	72.9	69.1	76.8	73.6	69.9	77.5	68.4	64.2	72.7	67.2	62.9	71.6
1977	73.3	69.5	77.2	74.0	70.2	77.9	68.9	64.7	73.2	67.7	63.4	72.0
1978	73.5	69.6	77.3	74.1	70.4	78.0	69.3	65.0	73.5	68.1	63.7	72.4
1979	73.9	70.0	77.8	74.6	70.8	78.4	69.8	65.4	74.1	68.5	64.0	72.9
1980	73.7	70.0	77.4	74.4	70.7	78.1	69.5	65.3	73.6	68.1	63.8	72.5
1981	74.2	70.4	77.8	74.8	71.1	78.4	70.3	66.1	74.4	68.9	64.5	73.2
1982	74.5	70.9	78.1	75.1	71.5	78.7	71.0	66.8	75.0	69.4	65.1	73.7
1983	74.6	71.0	78.1	75.2	71.7	78.7	71.1	67.2	74.9	69.6	65.4	73.6
1984	74.7	71.2	78.2	75.3	71.8	78.7	71.3	67.4	75.0	69.7	65.6	73.7
1985	74.7	71.2	78.2	75.3	71.9	78.7	71.2	67.2	75.0	69.5	65.3	73.5
1986	74.8	71.3	78.3	75.4	72.0	78.8	71.2	67.2	75.1	69.4	65.2	73.5
1987	75.0	71.5	78.4	75.6	72.2	78.9	71.3	67.3	75.2	69.4	65.2	73.6
1988	74.9	71.5	78.3	75.6	72.3	78.9	71.2	67.1	75.1	69.2	64.9	73.4
1989	75.3	71.8	78.6	76.0	72.7	79.2	71.2	67.1	75.2	69.2	64.8	73.5
1990, prel.	75.4	72.0	78.8	76.0	72.6	79.3	72.4	68.4	76.3	70.3	66.0	74.5
Projections:[1] 1995 . .	76.3	72.8	79.7	76.8	73.4	80.2	(NA)	(NA)	(NA)	72.4	68.8	76.0
2000 . .	77.0	73.5	80.4	77.5	74.0	80.9	(NA)	(NA)	(NA)	73.5	69.9	77.1
2005 . .	77.6	74.2	81.0	78.1	74.6	81.5	(NA)	(NA)	(NA)	74.6	71.0	78.1
2010 . .	77.9	74.4	81.3	78.3	74.9	81.7	(NA)	(NA)	(NA)	75.0	71.4	78.5

NA Not available.   [1] Based on middle mortality assumptions; for details, see source. Source: U.S. Bureau of the Census, *Current Population Reports*, series P-25, No. 1018.

Source: Except as noted, U.S. National Center for Health Statistics, *Vital Statistics of the United States*, annual; *Monthly Vital Statistics Report*; and unpublished data.

A2-3. Life Expectancy by Sex: United States, 1970 to 1990

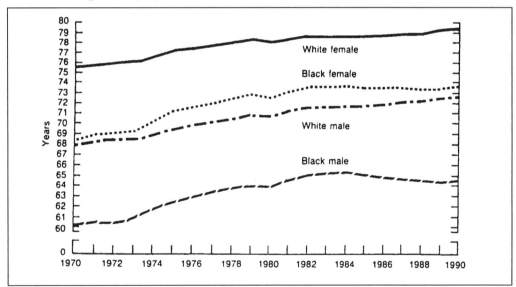

A2-4. Life Expectancy at Birth and at 65 Years of Age, by Race and Sex: Selected Years 1900 to 1989

Specified age and year	All races			White		Black	
	Both sexes	Male	Female	Male	Female	Male	Female
At Birth							
1900[1][2]	47.3	46.3	48.3	46.6	48.7	[3]32.5	[3]33.5
1950[2]	68.2	65.6	71.1	66.5	72.2	58.9	62.7
1960[2]	69.7	66.6	73.1	67.4	74.1	60.7	65.9
1970	70.9	67.1	74.8	68.0	75.6	60.0	68.3
1980	73.7	70.0	77.4	70.7	78.1	63.8	72.5
1989	75.3	71.8	78.6	72.7	79.2	64.8	73.5
At 65 Years							
1900–1902[1][2]	11.9	11.5	12.2	11.5	12.2	10.4	11.4
1950[2]	13.9	12.8	15.0	12.8	15.1	12.9	14.9
1960[2]	14.3	12.8	15.8	12.9	15.9	12.7	15.1
1970	15.2	13.1	17.0	13.1	17.1	12.5	15.7
1980	16.4	14.1	18.3	14.2	18.4	13.0	16.8
1989	17.2	15.2	18.8	15.2	19.0	13.6	17.0

[1]Death registration area only. The death registration area increased from 10 States and the District of Columbia in 1900 to the coterminous United States in 1933.
[2]Includes deaths of nonresidents of the United States.
[3]Figure is for the all other population.

Source: National Center for Health Statistics, *Health, United States, 1990,* Hyattsville, MD: Public Health Service 1991. Table 15 1989 "At birth" data from *Monthly Vital Statistics Report,* Vol. 40, No. 8(s)2, January 7, 1992. 1989 "At 65 years" data unpublished final data from Mortality Statistics Branch.

A2-5. Life Expectancy at 65 Years of Age, According to Race and Sex: 1986 to 1990

Remaining life expectancy in years

Year	All races			White			Black		
	Both sexes	Male	Female	Both sexes	Male	Female	Both sexes	Male	Female
1986	16.8	14.7	18.6	16.9	14.8	18.7	15.4	13.4	17.0
1987	16.9	14.8	18.7	17.0	14.9	18.8	15.4	13.5	17.1
1988	16.9	14.9	18.6	17.0	14.9	18.7	15.4	13.4	16.9
1989	17.2	15.2	18.8	17.3	15.2	19.0	15.5	13.6	17.0
Provisional data:									
1988/a	16.9	14.8	18.6	17.0	14.9	18.7	15.5	13.6	17.1
1989/a	17.2	15.2	18.8	17.3	15.2	18.9	15.8	13.8	17.4
1990/a	17.3	15.3	19.0	17.3	15.3	19.0	16.1	14.2	17.6

/a Includes deaths of nonresidents of the United States.
Data are based on the National Vital Statistics System)

A2-6. Expectation of Life at Selected Ages, by Race and Sex: United States, 1900–02 to 1990

Age	White						All Other Total						Black					
	1900-02	1949-51	1979-81	1988	1989	1990*	1900-02	1949-51	1979-81	1988	1989	1990*	1900-02	1949-51	1979-81	1988	1989	1990*
Expectation of Life (in Years)																		
Male																		
0	48.2	66.3	70.8	72.3	72.7	72.6	58.9	65.6	67.1	67.1	68.4		32.5		64.1	64.9	64.8	66.0
15	46.3	54.2	57.1	58.3	58.6	58.7	48.2	52.5	53.7	53.8	54.8		38.3		51.1	51.6	51.6	52.6
25	38.5	44.9	47.9	49.0	49.4	49.4	39.5	43.5	44.7	44.8	45.9		32.2		42.1	42.7	42.7	43.8
35	31.3	35.7	38.7	39.8	40.1	40.2	31.2	34.8	36.1	36.2	37.4		26.2		33.6	34.3	34.3	35.4
45	24.2	26.9	29.6	30.7	31.1	31.1	23.6	26.6	28.0	28.2	29.3	N/A	20.1	N/A	25.6	26.5	26.6	27.6
55	17.4	19.1	21.3	22.2	22.5	22.6	17.4	19.6	20.5	20.8	21.7		14.7		18.8	19.4	19.6	20.5
65	11.5	12.8	14.3	14.9	15.2	15.3	12.8	13.8	14.3	14.5	15.1		10.4		13.3	13.4	13.6	14.2
75	6.8	7.8	8.9	9.1	9.4	9.3	8.8	9.2	9.2	9.4	9.8		6.6		8.9	8.6	8.8	9.1
85	3.8	4.4	5.1	5.1	5.3	5.3	5.4	5.7	5.8	5.8	6.2		4.0		5.6	5.5	5.6	5.8
Female																		
0	51.1	72.0	78.2	78.9	79.2	79.3	62.7	74.0	75.1	75.2	76.3		35.0		72.9	73.4	73.5	74.5
15	47.8	59.4	64.3	64.8	65.1	65.1	51.4	60.7	61.5	61.7	62.6		39.8		59.7	60.0	60.2	60.9
25	40.1	49.8	54.6	55.0	55.3	55.4	42.4	51.1	51.9	52.1	52.9		33.9		50.1	50.4	50.6	51.3
35	32.8	40.3	44.9	45.4	45.7	45.7	33.8	41.7	42.5	42.7	43.5		27.5		40.8	41.1	41.3	42.0
45	25.5	31.1	35.5	35.8	36.1	36.2	26.1	32.8	33.5	33.7	34.5	N/A	21.4	N/A	31.9	32.2	32.4	33.1
55	18.4	22.6	26.6	26.8	27.1	27.2	19.6	24.7	25.1	25.3	25.9		15.9		24.0	24.0	24.1	24.7
65	12.2	15.0	18.6	18.7	19.0	19.0	14.5	17.6	17.8	17.9	18.6		11.4		17.1	16.9	17.0	17.6
75	7.3	8.9	11.6	11.7	11.9	12.0	10.2	11.7	11.5	11.6	12.2		7.9		11.4	10.9	11.0	11.5
85	4.1	4.8	6.3	6.3	6.5	6.6	6.2	7.2	6.8	6.9	7.4		5.1		7.1	6.6	6.7	7.1
Chances per 1,000 of Surviving From Birth to Specific Age																		
Male																		
15	780	957	982	986	986	986	930	971	977	976	979		597		968	973	973	976
25	739	943	966	972	973	972	903	952	957	955	957		533		948	952	950	950
35	682	925	950	956	957	955	859	919	924	922	924		.465		911	913	910	912
45	614	890	925	931	932	930	787	866	871	867	873		392		850	847	844	850
55	525	805	863	879	881	879	651	760	781	778	792	N/A	300	N/A	734	744	740	754
65	392	635	724	754	759	760	452	585	626	626	654		190		551	579	578	605
75	214	381	477	523	535	538	255	362	406	409	445		89		327	355	357	392
85	53	120	185	214	226	226	99	145	160	168	190		20		124	126	132	149
Female																		
15	807	968	986	989	989	989	943	977	981	980	983		624		975	978	977	980
25	766	961	981	984	985	984	923	970	975	974	977		558		968	971	971	974
35	710	950	974	978	979	978	888	957	961	960	964		496		953	956	955	959
45	647	927	961	966	967	967	823	930	937	936	941		423		923	926	926	931
55	565	877	926	936	937	937	702	870	886	887	897	N/A	331	N/A	857	869	870	881
65	438	768	848	859	863	863	524	754	778	783	793		220		733	749	753	762
75	254	544	687	700	706	705	330	565	598	603	622		111		538	557	561	579
85	71	213	388	403	413	417	156	305	322	329	352		36		280	279	284	306

*Provisional.
Source: Various reports by the National Center for Health Statistics.

A2-7. Percent Surviving from Birth to Age 65 and 85, by Sex and Race: 1900–02 and 1987

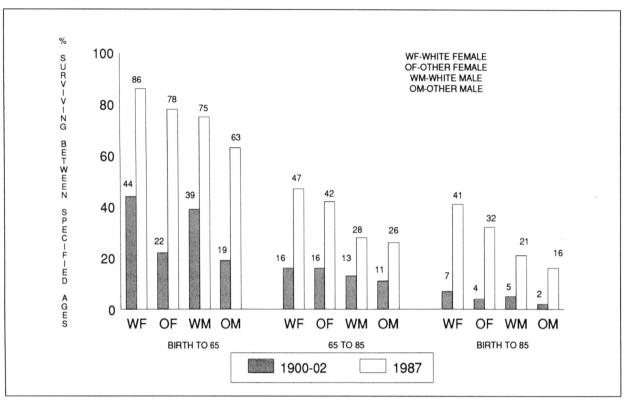

Source: National Center for Health Statistics, "Life Tables," *Vital Statistics of the United States, 1987,* Vol. II, Section 6 (February 1990).

A2-8. Life Expectancy for Black Persons at Individual Ages 65 to 85 Years, by Sex: United States, 1986

Age	Remaining life expectancy in years	
	Male	Female
65 years	13.4	17.0
66 years	12.9	16.4
67 years	12.3	15.7
68 years	11.8	15.1
69 years	11.3	14.5
70 years	10.8	13.9
71 years	10.4	13.3
72 years	9.9	12.7
73 years	9.5	12.1
74 years	9.1	11.6
75 years	8.7	11.1
76 years	8.3	10.5
77 years	7.9	10.0
78 years	7.5	9.5
79 years	7.2	9.0
80 years	6.8	8.5
81 years	6.5	8.1
82 years	6.2	7.7
83 years	5.9	7.3
84 years	5.7	7.0
85 years	5.5	6.7

[Data are based on the National Vital Statistics System]

A2-9. Projected Life Expectancy at Birth and Age 65, by Sex, 1990 to 2050

(in years)

Year	At birth			At age 65		
	Men	Women	Difference	Men	Women	Difference
1990	72.1	79.0	6.9	15.0	19.4	4.4
2000	73.5	80.4	6.9	15.7	20.3	4.6
2010	74.4	81.3	6.9	16.2	21.0	4.8
2020	74.9	81.8	6.9	16.6	21.4	4.8
2030	75.4	82.3	6.9	17.0	21.8	4.8
2040	75.9	82.8	6.9	17.3	22.3	5.0
2050	76.4	83.3	6.9	17.7	22.7	5.0

Source: U.S. Bureau of the Census, "Projections of the Population of the United States, by Age, Sex, and Race: 1988 to 2080," by Gregory Spencer. *Current Population Reports,* Series P-25, No. 1018 (January 1989).

A3. Race and Ethnicity

A3-1. Persons 65 Years and Over, by Age, Sex, Race, and Hispanic Origin: 1990

Race and Sex	Total, 65 and Over	65 to 69	70 to 74	Total, 75 and Over	75 to 79	Total, 80 and Over	80 to 84	Total, 85 and Over	85 to 89	90 to 94	95 to 99	Total, 100 and Over
All races												
Total	31,078,895	10,065,835	7,979,660	13,033,400	6,102,929	6,930,471	3,909,046	3,021,425	2,034,661	747,979	202,977	35,808
Male	12,492,766	4,507,539	3,399,275	4,585,952	2,388,895	2,197,057	1,355,830	841,227	605,936	184,048	43,544	7,699
Female	18,586,129	5,558,296	4,580,385	8,447,448	3,714,034	4,733,414	2,553,216	2,180,198	1,428,725	563,931	159,433	28,109
Males per 100 females	67.2	81.1	74.2	54.3	64.3	46.4	53.1	38.6	42.4	32.6	27.3	27.4
White												
Total	28,020,562	8,983,978	7,191,013	11,845,571	5,518,341	6,327,230	3,566,268	2,760,962	1,858,176	689,928	183,505	29,353
Male	11,284,407	4,047,535	3,079,801	4,157,071	2,165,061	1,992,010	1,232,184	759,826	547,832	167,568	38,559	5,867
Female	16,736,155	4,936,443	4,111,212	7,688,500	3,353,280	4,335,220	2,334,084	2,001,136	1,310,344	522,360	144,946	23,486
Males per 100 females	67.4	82.0	74.9	54.1	64.6	45.9	52.8	38.0	41.8	32.1	26.6	25.0
Black												
Total	2,492,221	859,694	638,077	994,450	483,535	510,915	288,283	222,632	150,294	49,599	17,049	5,690
Male	956,936	360,653	252,967	343,316	178,695	164,621	98,351	66,270	46,949	13,485	4,277	1,559
Female	1,535,285	499,041	385,110	651,134	304,840	346,294	189,932	156,362	103,345	36,114	12,772	4,131
Males per 100 females	62.3	72.3	65.7	52.7	58.6	47.5	51.8	42.4	45.4	37.3	33.5	37.7
American Indian, Eskimo or Aleut												
Total	116,153	43,374	29,831	42,948	21,522	21,426	12,236	9,190	6,287	1,982	659	262
Male	48,874	19,658	12,759	16,457	8,552	7,905	4,641	3,264	2,265	680	222	97
Female	67,279	23,716	17,072	26,491	12,970	13,521	7,595	5,926	4,022	1,302	437	165
Males per 100 females	72.6	82.9	74.7	62.1	65.9	58.5	61.1	55.1	56.3	52.2	50.8	58.8
Asian or Pacific Islander												
Total	449,959	178,789	120,739	150,431	79,531	70,900	42,259	28,641	19,904	6,470	1,764	503
Male	202,549	79,693	53,748	69,108	36,587	32,521	20,654	11,867	8,890	2,315	486	176
Female	247,410	99,096	66,991	81,323	42,944	38,379	21,605	16,774	11,014	4,155	1,278	327
Males per 100 females	81.9	80.4	80.2	85.0	85.2	84.7	95.6	70.7	80.7	55.7	38.0	53.8
Hispanic origin 1/												
Total	1,146,223	431,000	284,085	431,138	211,432	219,706	128,302	91,404	64,945	19,257	5,616	1,586
Male	474,830	192,949	118,696	163,185	82,364	80,821	48,430	32,391	23,695	6,405	1,726	565
Female	671,393	238,051	165,389	267,953	129,068	138,885	79,872	59,013	41,250	12,852	3,890	1,021
Males per 100 females	70.7	81.1	71.8	60.9	63.8	58.2	60.6	54.9	57.4	49.8	44.4	55.3

1/ Hispanic origin may be of any race.

Source: U.S. Bureau of the Census, *1990 Census of Population and Housing, Series CPH-L-74, "Modified and Actual Age, Sex, Race, and Hispanic Origin Data."* U.S. Bureau of the Census, 1990 Census of Population and Housing, Series CPH-L-74, "Modified and Actual Age, Sex, Race, and Hispanic Origin Data."

A3-2. Persons 65 Years and Over for Regions, by Age, Race, and Hispanic Origin: 1990

Age, Race and Hispanic origin	United States	Northeast	Midwest	South	West
All persons, 65 and over	31,241,831	6,995,156	7,749,130	10,724,182	5,773,363
65 to 84 years	28,161,666	6,285,347	6,909,267	9,732,160	5,234,892
85 years and over	3,080,165	709,809	839,863	992,022	538,471
White, 65 and over	27,851,973	6,409,025	7,205,491	9,172,048	5,065,409
65 to 84 years	25,063,921	5,744,880	6,412,420	8,326,660	4,579,961
85 years and over	2,788,052	664,145	793,071	845,388	485,448
Black, 65 and over	2,508,551	454,809	474,957	1,386,175	192,610
65 to 84 years	2,278,368	417,408	432,595	1,251,232	177,133
85 years and over	230,183	37,401	42,362	134,943	15,477
American Indian, Eskimo and Aleut, 65 and over	114,453	8,575	17,461	40,379	48,038
65 to 84 years	105,248	7,872	16,258	37,167	43,951
85 years and over	9,205	703	1,203	3,212	4,087
Asian and Pacific Islander, 65 and over	454,458	64,960	30,427	39,525	319,546
65 to 84 years	424,720	61,132	28,681	37,491	297,416
85 years and over	29,738	3,828	1,746	2,034	22,130
Other races, 65 and over	312,396	57,787	20,794	86,055	147,760
65 to 84 years	289,409	54,055	19,313	79,610	136,431
85 years and over	22,987	3,732	1,481	6,445	11,329
Hispanic origin 1/, 65 and over	1,161,283	199,502	71,169	446,984	443,628
65 to 84 years	1,066,719	183,808	65,525	409,681	407,705
85 years and over	94,564	15,694	5,644	37,303	35,923

1/ Hispanic origin may be of any race.

Source: U.S. Bureau of the Census, 1990 Census of Population and Housing.

A3-3. Persons 65 Years and Over, by Specific Race and Hispanic Origin: 1980 and 1990

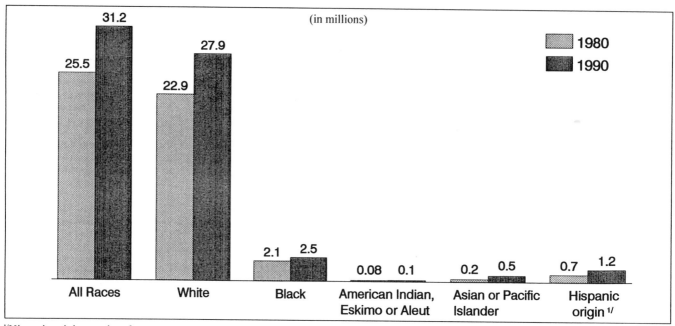

[1]/Hispanic origin may be of any race.

Source: U.S. Bureau of the Census, 1980 Census of Population, "General Social and Economic Characteristics," PC80-1-C1, U.S. Summary, U.S. Government Printing Office, Washington DC: 1983, tables 120 and 130; 1990 Census of Population and Housing.

A3-4. Percent of Elderly Persons, by Race, Hispanic Origin, and Place of Residence: 1990

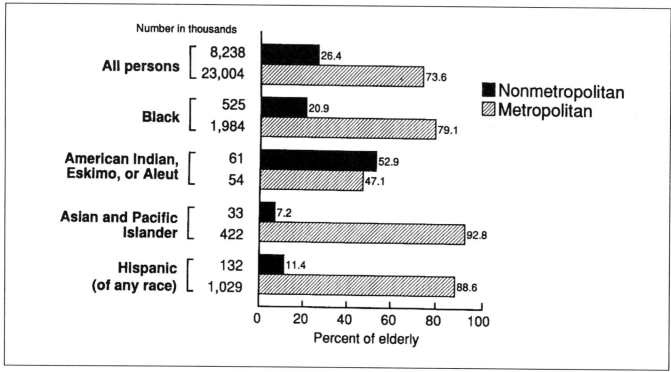

Source: Bureau of the Census, 1990 Census of Population and Housing.

A3-5. Black Population 65 and 85 Years and Over, Ranked by State: 1990

State	65 Years and Over
Total, U.S.	2,508,551
New York	225,303
California	159,313
Texas	156,952
North Carolina	138,791
Georgia	134,404
Illinois	134,137
Florida	129,825
Pennsylvania	113,829
Michigan	112,356
Louisiana	111,655
Alabama	109,280
Ohio	107,684
Virginia	107,564
South Carolina	93,860
Mississippi	91,028
Maryland	80,040
New Jersey	77,384
Tennessee	73,648
District of Columbia	52,263
Missouri	50,312
Arkansas	42,235
Indiana	37,891
Kentucky	26,924
Oklahoma	20,134
Massachusetts	18,626
Connecticut	16,956
Kansas	11,177
Wisconsin	10,657
West Virginia	8,802
Delaware	8,770
Washington	8,208
Colorado	7,119
Arizona	6,852
Nevada	3,874
Minnesota	3,750
Nebraska	3,652
Iowa	3,233
Oregon	3,183
Rhode Island	2,230
New Mexico	2,115
Utah	626
Alaska	493
Hawaii	376
New Hampshire	238
Wyoming	214
Maine	170
Idaho	138
Montana	99
South Dakota	80
Vermont	73
North Dakota	28

State	85 Years and Over
Total, U.S.	230,183
New York	17,973
Texas	16,564
California	12,887
Georgia	12,691
North Carolina	12,454
Alabama	11,787
Louisiana	11,413
Illinois	11,378
Florida	11,207
Mississippi	10,752
Pennsylvania	9,976
Michigan	9,933
Ohio	9,214
Virginia	9,154
South Carolina	7,877
Tennessee	7,673
Maryland	6,415
New Jersey	6,289
Arkansas	5,535
Missouri	5,266
District of Columbia	4,253
Indiana	3,492
Kentucky	2,975
Oklahoma	2,457
Massachusetts	1,608
Connecticut	1,304
Kansas	1,263
West Virginia	1,009
Wisconsin	797
Delaware	727
Colorado	630
Arizona	628
Washington	547
Nebraska	358
Minnesota	335
Iowa	312
Nevada	244
New Mexico	208
Oregon	199
Rhode Island	197
Utah	42
Hawaii	30
New Hampshire	26
Wyoming	22
Maine	21
Alaska	18
Montana	13
Idaho	9
South Dakota	9
Vermont	7
North Dakota	5

Source: U.S. Bureau of the Census, 1990 Census of Population and Housing.

A3-6. Hispanic Origin Population 65 and 85 Years and Over, Ranked by State: 1990

State	65 Years and Over
Total, U.S.	1,161,283
California	314,707
Texas	231,051
Florida	176,174
New York	127,838
New Mexico	'42,232
New Jersey	38,565
Arizona	35,276
Illinois	31,263
Colorado	24,387
Pennsylvania	11,146
Massachusetts	10,453
Michigan	10,051
Connecticut	8,647
Louisiana	7,940
Ohio	7,452
Washington	6,319
Maryland	5,464
Nevada	5,341
Virginia	5,334
Indiana	5,193
Hawaii	4,220
Kansas	4,191
Georgia	3,933
Oregon	3,898
Missouri	3,808
Utah	3,404
Wisconsin	3,362
Oklahoma	3,232
North Carolina	2,806
Minnesota	1,957
Rhode Island	1,873
Tennessee	1,764
Nebraska	1,763
Iowa	1,741
Idaho	1,599
District of Columbia	1,585
Alabama	1,571
Wyoming	1,407
Mississippi	1,261
South Carolina	1,259
Kentucky	1,247
Arkansas	935
West Virginia	830
Delaware	598
Montana	577
New Hampshire	416
Maine	310
Alaska	261
South Dakota	255
Vermont	254
North Dakota	133

State	85 Years and Over
Total, U.S.	94,564
California	25,455
Texas	18,564
Florida	15,491
New York	10,142
New Mexico	3,753
New Jersey	2,943
Arizona	2,639
Illinois	2,207
Colorado	2,170
Pennsylvania	894
Michigan	870
Massachusetts	812
Louisiana	684
Connecticut	667
Ohio	607
Washington	454
Maryland	410
Virginia	407
Indiana	393
Missouri	374
Kansas	374
Georgia	323
Nevada	320
Hawaii	311
Oregon	288
Wisconsin	272
Utah	243
Oklahoma	242
North Carolina	230
Minnesota	199
Iowa	168
Tennessee	168
District of Columbia	149
Rhode Island	147
Nebraska	145
Alabama	140
Idaho	111
Kentucky	110
Wyoming	104
Mississippi	93
South Carolina	92
West Virginia	75
Arkansas	71
Delaware	54
Montana	52
New Hampshire	36
Maine	27
Vermont	26
Alaska	23
South Dakota	20
North Dakota	15

Source: U.S. Bureau of the Census, 1990 Census of Population and Housing.

A3-7. Asian and Pacific Islander Population 65 and 85 Years and Over, Ranked by State: 1990

State	65 Years and Over
Total, U.S.	454,458
California	202,395
Hawaii	89,096
New York	39,650
Illinois	15,198
Washington	12,923
New Jersey	11,353
Texas	10,443
Maryland	6,411
Florida	6,298
Virginia	5,919
Massachusetts	5,813
Pennsylvania	5,381
Michigan	3,732
Oregon	3,645
Ohio	3,270
Colorado	3,262
Arizona	2,421
Minnesota	2,206
Georgia	2,069
Nevada	1,938
Connecticut	1,634
Utah	1,583
Wisconsin	1,578
Louisiana	1,414
Missouri	1,351
North Carolina	1,303
Indiana	1,114
Oklahoma	911
Kansas	874
Tennessee	862
Alaska	855
District of Columbia	785
South Carolina	650
Idaho	619
Rhode Island	596
Iowa	583
Alabama	572
Mississippi	507
New Mexico	482
Kentucky	480
Nebraska	390
Arkansas	381
Delaware	309
New Hampshire	257
West Virginia	211
Maine	206
Montana	190
Wyoming	137
Vermont	70
North Dakota	68
South Dakota	63

State	85 Years and Over
Total, U.S.	29,738
California	12,722
Hawaii	7,653
New York	2,465
Washington	828
Illinois	821
New Jersey	515
Texas	448
Florida	387
Massachusetts	372
Maryland	350
Pennsylvania	305
Oregon	257
Virginia	236
Michigan	233
Ohio	220
Colorado	184
Arizona	158
Utah	117
Minnesota	114
Connecticut	107
Louisiana	106
Missouri	94
Georgia	86
Wisconsin	76
Nevada	72
District of Columbia	69
Indiana	67
Oklahoma	57
North Carolina	57
Mississippi	56
Kansas	54
Idaho	52
Tennessee	51
Iowa	43
Alaska	39
Rhode Island	35
Kentucky	33
South Carolina	31
New Mexico	24
Alabama	22
Arkansas	19
Delaware	19
Nebraska	17
Montana	14
New Hampshire	13
Maine	11
Wyoming	10
West Virginia	7
Vermont	5
North Dakota	5
South Dakota	2

Source: U.S. Bureau of the Census, 1990 Census of Population and Housing.

A3-8. American Indian, Eskimo, or Aleut Population 65 and 85 Years and Over, Ranked by State: 1990

State	65 Years and Over
Total, U.S.	114,453
Oklahoma	21,042
California	14,092
Arizona	10,164
New Mexico	7,250
North Carolina	5,194
Alaska	4,137
New York	4,136
Texas	3,954
Washington	3,812
Michigan	2,810
Florida	2,445
South Dakota	2,423
Montana	2,220
Oregon	2,031
Wisconsin	2,011
Minnesota	1,953
Missouri	1,471
Kansas	1,373
Ohio	1,339
Colorado	1,220
Illinois	1,217
Pennsylvania	1,214
Nevada	1,143
New Jersey	1,121
North Dakota	1,078
Louisiana	1,075
Arkansas	1,017
Alabama	881
Massachusetts	848
Indiana	848
Virginia	848
Utah	745
Tennessee	715
Georgia	683
Idaho	668
Maryland	653
Nebraska	597
Connecticut	479
Mississippi	418
Kentucky	417
South Carolina	413
Wyoming	407
Rhode Island	345
Iowa	341
West Virginia	260
Maine	254
District of Columbia	184
Delaware	180
Hawaii	149
New Hampshire	102
Vermont	76

State	85 Years and Over
Total, U.S.	9,205
Oklahoma	1,840
Arizona	1,060
California	1,023
New Mexico	777
New York	328
North Carolina	326
Alaska	303
Texas	276
Washington	262
Florida	175
Montana	169
South Dakota	167
Michigan	160
Minnesota	141
Oregon	140
Wisconsin	137
Pennsylvania	109
Missouri	109
Colorado	102
Ohio	101
New Jersey	91
Kansas	90
Illinois	89
Arkansas	88
Nevada	84
Utah	84
North Dakota	78
Louisiana	74
Massachusetts	69
Tennessee	57
Virginia	57
Alabama	56
Indiana	55
Maryland	53
Idaho	53
Georgia	50
Nebraska	47
Mississippi	45
Rhode Island	45
Connecticut	36
South Carolina	36
Kentucky	29
Iowa	29
Wyoming	24
West Virginia	19
Delaware	17
District of Columbia	14
Maine	12
New Hampshire	8
Hawaii	6
Vermont	5

Source: U.S. Bureau of the Census, 1990 Census of Population and Housing.

A3-9. Growth of the Minority Elderly Population: 1990 to 2050

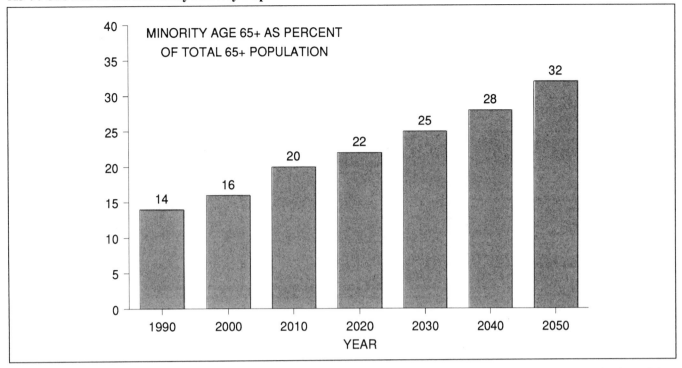

Sources: Figures computed by Donald G. Fowles, U.S. Administration on Aging, from data in U.S. Bureau of the Census, "Projections of the Hispanic Population: 1983–2080," by Gregory Spencer, *Current Population Reports* Series P-25, No. 995 (November 1986) and in U.S. Bureau of the Census, "Projections of the Population of the United States, by Age, Sex, and Race: 1988 to 2080," by Gregory Spencer, *Current Population Reports* Series P-25, No. 1018 (January 1989).

A3-10. Persons 65 Years and Over, by Age, Race, and Hispanic Origin: 2050

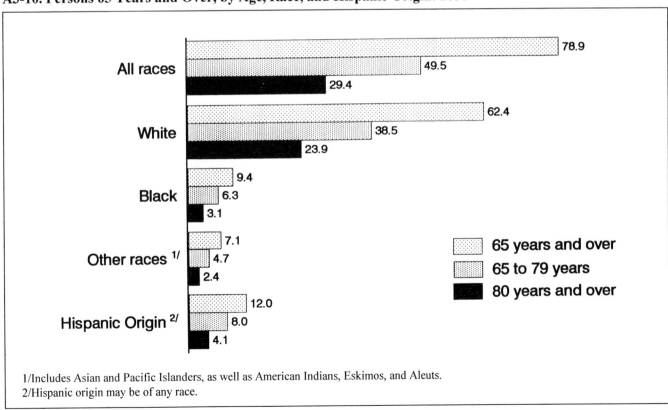

1/Includes Asian and Pacific Islanders, as well as American Indians, Eskimos, and Aleuts.
2/Hispanic origin may be of any race.

Source: U.S. Bureau of the Census, Jennifer C. Day, "Population Projections of the United States, by Age, Sex, Race, and Hispanic Origin: 1992 to 2050," *Current Population Reports,* P25-1092, U.S. Government Printing Office, Washington, DC, 1992 (middle series projections).

A3-11. Percent of the Population 65 Years and Over, by Race and Hispanic Origin: 1990 and 2050

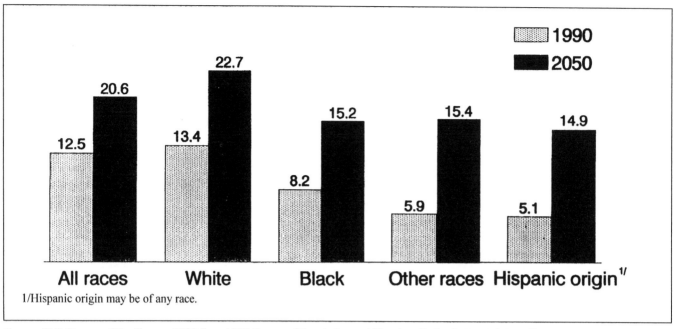

1/Hispanic origin may be of any race.

Source: U.S. Bureau of the Census, 1990 from 1990 Census of Population and Housing, Series CPH-L-74, "Modified and Actual Age, Sex, Race, and Hispanic Origin Data"; 2050 from Jennifer C. Day, "Projections of the Population of the United States by Age, Sex, and Race: 1992 to 2050," *Current Population Reports,* P25-1092, U.S. Government Printing Office, Washington, DC, 1992 (middle series projections).

A3-12. Black Population Aged 65 Years and Over: 1980 to 2050

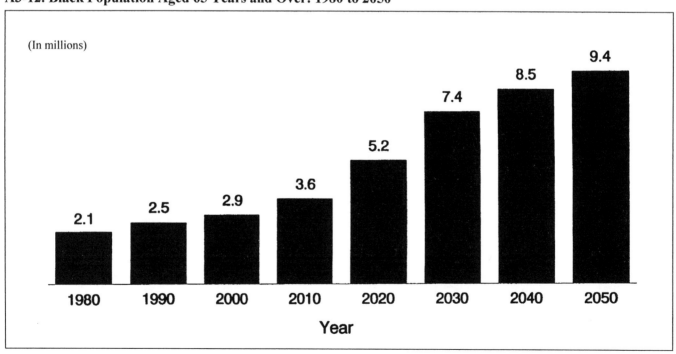

Source: U.S. Bureau of the Census, 1980 from 1980 Census of Population; 1990 from 1990 Census of Population and Housing, Series CPH-L-74, "Modified and Actual Age, Sex, Race, and Hispanic Origin Data," 2000 to 2050 from Jennifer C. Day, "Projections of Projections of the United States, by Age, Sex, Race, and Hispanic Origin: 1992 to 2050," *Current Population Reports*, P25-1092, U.S. Government Printing Office, Washington, DC, 1992 (middle series projections)

A3-13. Black Population Aged 85 Years and Over: 1980 to 2050

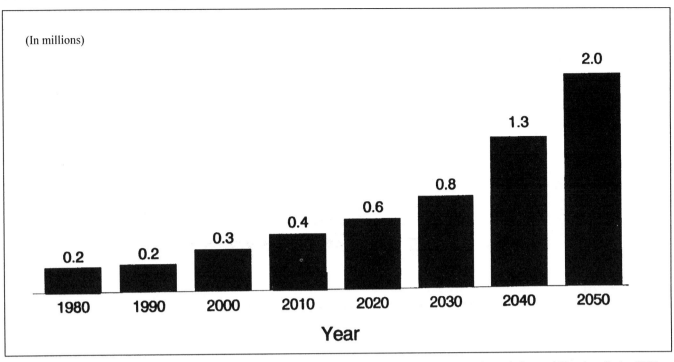

Source: U.S. Bureau of the Census, 1980 from 1980 Census of Population; 1990 from 1990 Census of Population and Housing, Series CPH-L-74, "Modified and Actual Age, Sex, Race, and Hispanic Origin Data," 2000 to 2050 from Jennifer C. Day, "Projections of Projections of the United States by Age, Sex, Race, and Hispanic Origin: 1992 to 2050," *Current Population Reports,* P25-1092, U.S. Government Printing Office, Washington, DC, 1992 (middle series projections).

A3-14. Hispanic Origin Population 65 Years and Over: 1980 to 2050

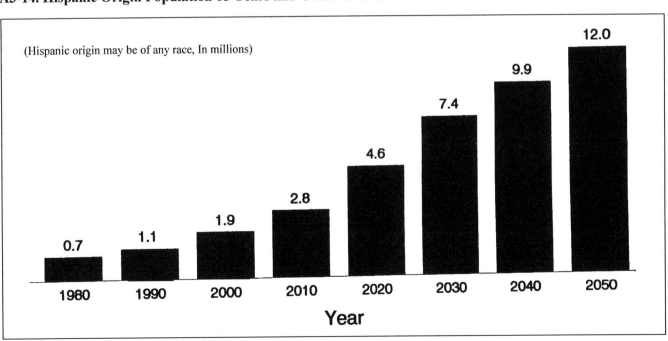

Source: U.S. Bureau of the Census, 1980 from 1980 Census of Population; 1990 from 1990 Census of Population and Housing, Series CPH-L-74, "Modified and Actual Age, Sex, Race, and Hispanic Origin Data," 2000 to 2050 from Jennifer C. Day, "Projections of Projections of the United States, by Age, Sex, Race, and Hispanic Origin: 1992 to 2050," *Current Population Reports*, P25-1092, U.S. Government Printing Office, Washington, DC, 1992 (middle series projections).

A3-15. Hispanic Origin Population 85 Years and Over: 1980 to 2050

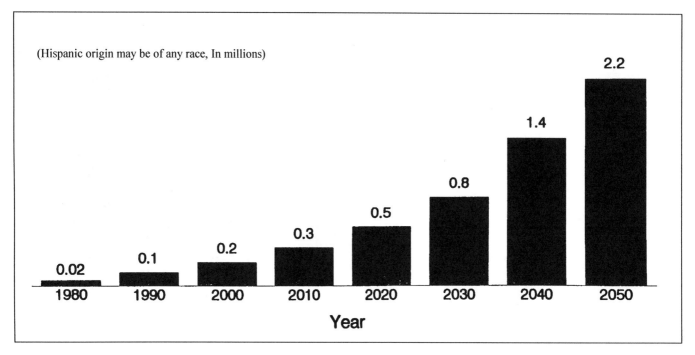

(Hispanic origin may be of any race, In millions)

Source: U.S. Bureau of the Census, 1980 from 1980 Census of Population; 1990 from 1990 Census of Population and Housing Series CPH-L-74, "Modified and Actual Age, Sex, Race, and Hispanic Origin Data," 2000 to 2050 from Jennifer C. Day, "Projections of Projections of the United States, by Age, Sex, Race, and Hispanic Origin: 1992 to 2050," *Current Population Reports*, P25-1092, U.S. Government Printing Office, Washington, DC, 1992 (middle series projections).

A4. Geographic Distribution and Mobility

A4-1. Persons 65 Years and Over for Regions, by Age, Race, and Hispanic Origin: 1990

Age, race, and Hispanic origin	United States	Northeast	Midwest	South	West
All Persons					
65 years and over	31,241,831	6,995,156	7,749,130	10,724,182	5,773,363
65 to 84 years	28,161,666	6,285,347	6,909,267	9,732,160	5,234,892
85 years and over	3,080,165	709,809	839,863	992,022	538,471
White					
65 years and over	27,851,973	6,409,025	7,205,491	9,172,048	5,065,409
65 to 84 years	25,063,921	5,744,880	6,412,420	8,326,660	4,579,961
85 years and over	2,788,052	664,145	793,071	845,388	485,448
Black					
65 years and over	2,508,551	454,809	474,957	1,386,175	192,610
65 to 84 years	2,278,368	417,408	432,595	1,251,232	177,133
85 years and over	230,183	37,401	42,362	134,943	15,477
American Indian, Eskimo, and Aleut					
65 years and over	114,453	8,575	17,461	40,379	48,038
65 to 84 years	105,248	7,872	16,258	37,167	43,951
85 years and over	9,205	703	1,203	3,212	4,087
Asian and Pacific Islander					
65 years and over	454,458	64,960	30,427	39,525	319,546
65 to 84 years	424,720	61,132	28,681	37,491	297,416
85 years and over	29,738	3,828	1,746	2,034	22,130
Other Races					
65 years and over	312,396	57,787	20,794	86,055	147,760
65 to 84 years	289,409	54,055	19,313	79,610	136,431
85 years and over	22,987	3,732	1,481	6,445	11,329
Hispanic Origin[1]					
65 years and over	1,161,283	199,502	71,169	446,984	443,628
65 to 84 years	1,066,719	183,808	65,525	409,681	407,705
85 years and over	94,564	15,694	5,644	37,303	35,923

[1]Hispanic origin may be of any race.

Source: U.S. Bureau of the Census, 1990 Census of Population and Housing, Summary Tape File 1A.

A4-2. Percent Change of U.S. Population 65 Years and Over, by Region, Division, and State: 1980 and 1990

Region, division, and State	Number 1990	Number 1980	Change 1980 to 1990	Percent change, 1980 to 1990	Region, division, and State	Number 1990	Number 1980	Change 1980 to 1990	Percent change, 1980 to 1990
United States	31,241,831	25,549,427	5,692,404	22.3	South Dakota	102,331	91,019	11,312	12.4
					Nebraska..........	223,068	205,684	17,384	8.5
Northeast ......:.....	6,995,156	6,071,839	923,317	15.2	Kansas...........	342,571	306,263	36,308	11.9
New England	1,770,303	1,520,368	249,935	16.4					
Middle Atlantic	5,224,853	4,551,471	673,382	14.8	South Atlantic.......	5,834,408	4,367,060	1,467,348	33.6
					Delaware..........	80,735	59,179	21,556	36.4
Midwest............	7,749,130	6,691,869	1,057,261	15.8	Maryland ...:......	517,482	395,609	121,873	30.8
East North Central .	5,299,384	4,493,184	806,200	17.9	District of Columbia.	77,847	74,287	3,560	4.8
West North Central.	2,449,746	2,198,685	251,061	11.4	Virginia...........	664,470	505,304	159,166	31.5
					West Virginia	268,897	237,868	31,029	13.0
South	10,724,182	8,487,891	2,236,291	26.3	North Carolina	804,341	603,181	201,160	33.3
South Atlantic......	5,834,408	4,367,060	1,467,348	33.6	South Carolina	396,935	287,328	109,607	38.1
East South Central .	1,929,936	1,656,788	273,148	16.5	Georgia	654,270	516,731	137,539	26.6
West South Central.	2,959,838	2,464,043	495,795	20.1	Florida	2,369,431	1,687,573	681,858	40.4
West...............	5,773,363	4,297,828	1,475,535	34.3	East South Central ...	1,929,936	1,656,788	273,148	16.5
Mountain	1,523,825	1,060,983	462,842	43.6	Kentucky..........	466,845	409,828	57,017	13.9
Pacific	4,249,538	3,236,845	1,012,693	31.3	Tennessee	618,818	517,588	101,230	19.6
					Alabama	522,989	440,015	82,974	18.9
New England	1,770,303	1,520,368	249,935	16.4	Mississippi.........	321,284	289,357	31,927	11.0
Maine..............	163,373	140,918	22,455	15.9					
Vermont...........	66,163	58,166	7,997	13.7	West South Central...	2,959,838	2,464,043	495,795	20.1
New Hampshire....	125,029	102,967	22,062	21.4	Arkansas.........	350,058	312,477	37,581	12.0
Massachusetts.....	819,284	726,531	92,753	12.8	Louisiana..........	468,991	404,279	64,712	16.0
Rhode Island	150,547	126,922	23,625	18.6	Oklahoma	424,213	376,126	48,087	12.8
Connecticut.......	445,907	364,864	81,043	22.2	Texas.............	1,716,576	1,371,161	345,415	25.2
Middle Atlantic	5,224,853	4,551,471	673,382	14.8	Mountain	1,523,825	1,060,983	462,842	43.6
New York	2,363,722	2,160,767	202,955	9.4	Montana	106,497	84,559	21,938	25.9
New Jersey........	1,032,025	859,771	172,254	20.0	Idaho	121,265	93,680	27,585	29.4
Pennsylvania	1,829,106	1,530,933	298,173	19.5	Wyoming	47,195	37,175	10,020	27.0
					Colorado	329,443	247,325	82,118	33.2
East North Central ...	5,299,384	4,493,184	806,200	17.9	New Mexico	163,062	115,906	47,156	40.7
Ohio	1,406,961	1,169,460	237,501	20.3	Arizona	478,774	307,362	171,412	55.8
Indiana............	696,196	585,384	110,812	18.9	Utah.............	149,958	109,220	40,738	37.3
Illinois.............	1,436,545	1,261,885	174,660	13.8	Nevada	127,631	65,756	61,875	94.1
Michigan	1,108,461	912,258	196,203	21.5					
Wisconsin	651,221	564,197	87,024	15.4	Pacific	4,249,538	3,236,845	1,012,693	31.3
					Washington........	575,288	431,562	143,726	33.3
West North Central ...	2,449,746	2,198,685	251,061	11.4	Oregon............	391,324	303,336	87,988	29.0
Minnesota	546,934	479,564	67,370	14.0	California..........	3,135,552	2,414,250	721,302	29.9
Iowa	426,106	387,584	38,522	9.9	Alaska	22,369	11,547	10,822	93.7
Missouri...........	717,681	648,126	69,555	10.7	Hawaii	125,005	76,150	48,855	64.2
North Dakota	91,055	80,445	10,610	13.2					

Source: U.S. Bureau of the Census, 1980 and 1990 Censuses of Population: for 1980, *General Population Characteristics*, PC80-1-B1, table 67; for 1990, Summary Tape File 1A.

A4-3. Percent Change of U.S. Population 85 Years and Over, by Region, Division, and State: 1980 and 1990

Region, division, and State	Number		Change 1980 to 1990	Percent change, 1980 to 1990
	1990	1980		
United States	3,080,165	2,240,067	840,098	37.5
Northeast	709,809	546,545	163,264	29.9
New England	194,253	151,371	42,882	28.3
Middle Atlantic	515,556	395,174	120,382	30.5
Midwest	839,863	649,375	190,488	29.3
East North Central	538,530	414,808	123,722	29.8
West North Central	301,333	234,567	66,766	28.5
South	992,022	663,741	328,281	49.5
South Atlantic	514,717	326,842	187,875	57.5
East South Central	186,003	134,007	51,996	38.8
West South Central	291,302	202,892	88,410	43.6
West	538,471	380,406	158,065	41.6
Mountain	132,600	86,302	46,298	53.6
Pacific	405,871	294,104	111,767	38.0
New England	194,253	151,371	42,882	28.3
Maine	18,226	14,099	4,127	29.3
Vermont	7,523	6,007	1,516	25.2
New Hampshire	13,286	9,650	3,636	37.7
Massachusetts	92,209	73,908	18,301	24.8
Rhode Island	16,016	11,978	4,038	33.7
Connecticut	46,993	35,729	11,264	31.5
Middle Atlantic	515,556	395,174	120,382	30.5
New York	248,173	192,983	55,190	28.6
New Jersey	95,547	72,231	23,316	32.3
Pennsylvania	171,836	129,960	41,876	32.2
East North Central	538,530	414,808	123,722	29.8
Ohio	138,030	108,426	29,604	27.3
Indiana	71,751	54,410	17,341	31.9
Illinois	147,549	114,682	32,867	28.7
Michigan	106,907	81,653	25,254	30.9
Wisconsin	74,293	55,637	18,656	33.5
West North Central	301,333	234,567	66,766	28.5
Minnesota	68,835	52,789	16,046	30.4
Iowa	55,255	44,940	10,315	23.0
Missouri	81,217	61,072	20,145	33.0
North Dakota	11,240	8,140	3,100	38.1

Region, division, and State	Number		Change 1980 to 1990	Percent change, 1980 to 1990
	1990	1980		
South Dakota	13,343	10,427	2,916	28.0
Nebraska	29,202	23,744	5,458	23.0
Kansas	42,241	33,455	8,786	26.3
South Atlantic	514,717	326,842	187,875	57.5
Delaware	7,142	5,269	1,873	35.5
Maryland	46,496	32,665	13,831	42.3
District of Columbia	7,847	6,385	1,462	22.9
Virginia	59,709	41,131	18,578	45.2
West Virginia	25,451	19,409	6,042	31.1
North Carolina	69,969	45,203	24,766	54.8
South Carolina	30,749	20,004	10,745	53.7
Georgia	57,244	39,434	17,810	45.2
Florida	210,110	117,342	92,768	79.1
East South Central	186,003	134,007	51,996	38.8
Kentucky	46,367	35,036	11,331	32.3
Tennessee	58,794	41,443	17,351	41.9
Alabama	48,507	34,019	14,488	42.6
Mississippi	32,335	23,509	8,826	37.5
West South Central	291,302	202,892	88,410	43.6
Arkansas	35,216	26,354	8,862	33.6
Louisiana	43,633	30,535	13,098	42.9
Oklahoma	45,848	33,981	11,867	34.9
Texas	166,605	112,022	54,583	48.7
Mountain	132,600	86,302	46,298	53.6
Montana	10,676	8,837	1,839	20.8
Idaho	11,398	8,476	2,922	34.5
Wyoming	4,550	3,473	1,077	31.0
Colorado	32,953	24,363	8,590	35.3
New Mexico	14,232	8,783	5,449	62.0
Arizona	37,717	19,878	17,839	89.7
Utah	13,611	8,852	4,759	53.8
Nevada	7,463	3,640	3,823	105.0
Pacific	405,871	294,104	111,767	38.0
Washington	56,301	41,476	14,825	35.7
Oregon	38,815	28,431	10,384	36.5
California	299,107	218,017	81,090	37.2
Alaska	1,251	619	632	102.1
Hawaii	10,397	5,561	4,836	87.0

Source: U.S. Bureau of the Census, 1980 and 1990 Censuses of Population: for 1980, *General Population Characteristics*, PC80-1-B1, table 67; for 1990, Summary Tape File 1A.

A4-4. Population of the United States for Metropolitan/Nonmetropolitan Areas, by Age, Sex, Race, and Hispanic Origin: 1990

Area, race, Hispanic origin, and sex	65 years and over	65 to 69 years	70 to 74 years	75 to 79 years	80 years and over	80 to 84 years	85 years and over over
Metropolitan							
Total	23,004,177	7,558,466	5,892,987	4,463,816	5,088,908	2,855,256	2,233,652
Male	9,160,888	3,362,778	2,490,975	1,726,348	1,580,787	971,978	608,809
Female	13,843,289	4,195,688	3,402,012	2,737,468	3,508,121	1,883,278	1,624,843
White	20,270,085	6,552,823	5,188,426	3,960,211	4,568,625	2,559,144	2,009,481
Male	8,074,947	2,932,036	2,205,054	1,533,836	1,404,021	865,502	538,519
Female	12,195,138	3,620,787	2,983,372	2,426,375	3,164,604	1,693,642	1,470,962
Black	1,983,740	704,538	509,664	372,955	396,583	223,160	173,423
Male	760,891	297,024	201,922	136,754	125,191	74,877	50,314
Female	1,222,849	407,514	307,742	236,201	271,392	148,283	123,109
American Indian, Eskimo, and Aleut	53,909	21,030	13,900	9,567	9,412	5,495	3,917
Male	21,943	9,349	5,846	3,628	3,120	1,858	1,262
Female	31,966	11,681	8,054	5,939	6,292	3,637	2,655
Asian and Pacific Islander	421,806	166,601	113,880	74,272	67,053	40,233	26,820
Male	188,569	74,014	50,385	33,731	30,439	19,363	11,076
Female	233,237	92,587	63,495	40,541	36,614	20,870	15,744
Other	274,637	113,474	67,117	46,811	47,235	27,224	20,011
Male	114,538	50,355	27,768	18,399	18,016	10,378	7,638
Female	160,099	63,119	39,349	28,412	29,219	16,846	12,373
Hispanic origin[1]	1,029,247	388,641	254,220	188,280	198,106	114,726	83,380
Male	421,722	172,993	104,961	72,498	71,270	42,328	28,942
Female	607,525	215,648	149,259	115,782	126,836	72,398	54,438
Nonmetropolitan							
Total	8,237,654	2,553,269	2,101,836	1,657,553	1,924,996	1,078,483	846,513
Male	3,404,285	1,169,529	918,331	673,420	643,005	394,116	248,889
Female	4,833,369	1,383,740	1,183,505	984,133	1,281,991	684,367	597,624
White	7,581,888	2,346,814	1,938,138	1,524,814	1,772,122	993,551	778,571
Male	3,139,962	1,081,193	850,675	620,563	587,531	361,600	225,931
Female	4,441,926	1,265,621	1,087,463	904,251	1,184,591	631,951	552,640
Black	524,811	158,507	130,751	108,315	127,238	70,478	56,760
Male	204,541	65,918	52,777	41,786	44,060	25,782	18,278
Female	320,270	92,589	77,974	66,529	83,178	44,696	38,482
American Indian, Eskimo, and Aleut	60,544	21,680	15,370	11,585	11,909	6,621	5,288
Male	26,146	9,949	6,654	4,832	4,711	2,699	2,012
Female	34,398	11,731	8,716	6,753	7,198	3,922	3,276
Asian and Pacific Islander	32,652	11,896	8,354	5,867	6,535	3,617	2,918
Male	15,878	5,504	3,915	3,070	3,389	2,066	1,323
Female	16,774	6,392	4,439	2,797	3,146	1,551	1,595
Other	37,759	14,372	9,223	6,972	7,192	4,216	2,976
Male	17,758	6,965	4,310	3,169	3,314	1,969	1,345
Female	20,001	7,407	4,913	3,803	3,878	2,247	1,631
Hispanic origin[1]	132,036	47,616	32,552	24,985	26,883	15,699	11,184
Male	59,687	22,585	14,844	10,857	11,401	6,846	4,555
Female	72,349	25,031	17,708	14,128	15,482	8,853	6,629

[1]Hispanic origin may be of any race.

Source: U.S. Bureau of the Census, 1990 Census of Population and Housing, Summary Tape File 1A.

A4-5. Age Distribution of the Elderly, by Area of Residence: 1990

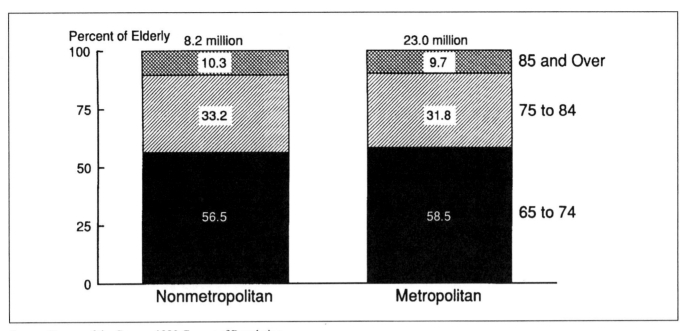

Source: Bureau of the Census, 1990 Census of Population.

A4-6. Age Composition for the Elderly and Children, by Area of Residence: 1980 and 1990

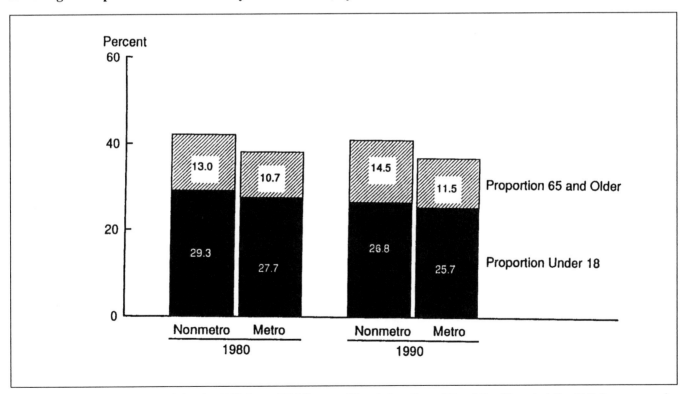

Source: USDA Economic Research Service 1980 data—1980 Census of Population, General Population Characteristics, U.S. Summary; and 1990 data—Public Use File of the Current Population Survey: March 1990.

A4-7. Percent Who Moved, by Type of Move and Age: March 1990 to March 1991

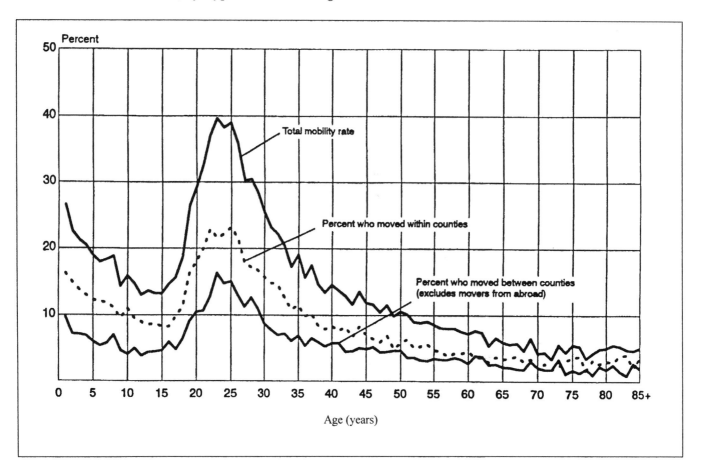

A4-8. Selected Characteristics of Persons, by Mobility Status and Type of Move: 1990 to 1991

(Numbers in thousands)

Characteristic	Total, 1 year old and older	Total movers	Residing in the United States at beginning of the period					Residing outside the United States at beginning of the period
			Total	Different house, same county	Different county			
					Total	Same state	Different state	
NUMBER								
All persons	244,884	41,539	40,154	25,151	15,003	7,881	7,122	1,385
Age:								
1-4 years	15,297	3,474	3,393	2,221	1,171	601	570	81
5-9 years	18,466	3,256	3,154	2,102	1,051	588	464	102
10-14 years	17,601	2,483	2,400	1,647	753	374	379	83
15-19 years	16,839	2,999	2,851	1,817	1,033	518	516	148
20-24 years	17,986	6,353	6,083	3,757	2,326	1,280	1,047	270
25-29 years	20,767	6,766	6,563	3,967	2,596	1,467	1,129	203
30-34 years	22,138	4,786	4,647	3,033	1,614	842	771	139
35-39 years	20,379	3,272	3,162	1,954	1,208	617	591	110
40-44 years	18,286	2,425	2,354	1,425	929	496	433	71
45-49 years	14,129	1,565	1,528	869	659	277	382	37
50-54 years	11,557	1,097	1,053	638	415	215	199	44
55-59 years	10,692	850	812	459	354	178	175	38
60-64 years	10,654	721	701	380	321	143	178	20
65-69 years	10,123	570	555	340	215	117	98	15
70-74 years	8,114	348	342	185	156	53	103	6
75-79 years	5,835	271	260	171	89	59	30	11
80-84 years	3,629	182	178	113	65	33	33	4
85 years and over	2,391	119	118	72	46	21	25	1
Median age	33.5	26.5	26.6	26.3	27.2	27.0	27.6	25.2
Sex:								
Male	119,152	20,815	20,077	12,417	7,660	4,021	3,639	738
Female	125,732	20,724	20,077	12,734	7,343	3,859	3,484	647
Race:								
White	205,514	34,023	33,035	20,296	12,739	6,872	5,867	988
Black	30,307	5,573	5,464	3,817	1,647	722	925	109
Hispanic origin:								
Hispanic	20,907	4,884	4,447	3,482	965	569	396	437
Not Hispanic	223,977	36,655	35,707	21,669	14,038	7,312	6,726	948
Tenure:								
Owner-occupied	164,173	14,450	14,171	8,207	5,964	3,155	2,809	279
Renter-occupied	80,711	27,088	25,983	16,944	9,039	4,726	4,313	1,105
Total 25 years and over	158,694	22,973	22,273	13,606	8,667	4,520	4,147	700
Elementary: 0 to 8 years	16,849	1,941	1,787	1,289	498	297	202	154
High school: 1 to 3 years	17,379	2,654	2,595	1,725	871	499	372	59
4 years	61,272	8,432	8,272	5,229	3,043	1,662	1,381	160
College: 1 to 3 years	29,169	4,624	4,519	2,729	1,790	908	882	105
4 years	20,101	3,343	3,225	1,668	1,558	754	803	118
5 years or more	13,925	1,979	1,874	967	907	400	508	105
Median years of school completed	12.7	12.8	12.8	12.7	13.0	12.9	13.3	12.9
Labor force status:								
Total 16 years and over	190,216	31,892	30,786	18,910	11,876	6,248	5,628	1,106
Civilian labor force	124,074	23,490	22,917	14,248	8,669	4,803	3,866	573
Employed	115,187	20,940	20,463	12,810	7,653	4,253	3,400	477
Unemployed	8,887	2,551	2,454	1,437	1,017	550	466	97
Armed Forces	977	418	353	178	175	32	143	65
Not in the labor force	65,164	7,984	7,516	4,485	3,031	1,412	1,619	468

A4-8. Selected Characteristics of Persons, by Mobility Status and Type of Move: 1990 to 1991 (continued)

(Numbers in thousands)

Characteristic	Total, 1 year old and older	Total movers	Residing in the United States at beginning of the period						Residing outside the United States at beginning of the period
			Total	Different house, same county	Different county				
					Total	Same state	Different state		
PERCENT									
All persons	100.0	17.0	16.4	10.3	6.1	3.2	2.9		0.6
Age:									
1-4 years	100.0	22.7	22.2	14.5	7.7	3.9	3.7		0.5
5-9 years	100.0	17.6	17.1	11.4	5.7	3.2	2.5		0.6
10-14 years	100.0	14.1	13.6	9.4	4.3	2.1	2.2		0.5
15-19 years	100.0	17.8	16.9	10.8	6.1	3.1	3.1		0.9
20-24 years	100.0	35.3	33.8	20.9	12.9	7.1	5.8		1.5
25-29 years	100.0	32.6	31.6	19.1	12.5	7.1	5.4		1.0
30-34 years	100.0	21.6	21.0	13.7	7.3	3.8	3.5		0.6
35-39 years	100.0	16.1	15.5	9.6	5.9	3.0	2.9		0.5
40-44 years	100.0	13.3	12.9	7.8	5.1	2.7	2.4		0.4
45-49 years	100.0	11.1	10.8	6.2	4.7	2.0	2.7		0.3
50-54 years	100.0	9.5	9.1	5.5	3.6	1.9	1.7		0.4
55-59 years	100.0	7.9	7.6	4.3	3.3	1.7	1.6		0.4
60-64 years	100.0	6.8	6.6	3.6	3.0	1.3	1.7		0.2
65-69 years	100.0	5.6	5.5	3.4	2.1	1.2	1.0		0.1
70-74 years	100.0	4.3	4.2	2.3	1.9	0.7	1.3		0.1
75-79 years	100.0	4.6	4.5	2.9	1.5	1.0	0.5		0.2
80-84 years	100.0	5.0	4.9	3.1	1.8	0.9	0.9		0.1
85 years and over	100.0	5.0	4.9	3.0	1.9	0.9	1.0		0.0
Sex:									
Male	100.0	17.5	16.8	10.4	6.4	3.4	3.1		0.6
Female	100.0	16.5	16.0	10.1	5.8	3.1	2.8		0.5
Race:									
White	100.0	16.6	16.1	9.9	6.2	3.3	2.9		0.5
Black	100.0	18.4	18.0	12.6	5.4	2.4	3.1		0.4
Hispanic origin:									
Hispanic	100.0	23.4	21.3	16.7	4.6	2.7	1.9		2.1
Not Hispanic	100.0	16.4	15.9	9.7	6.3	3.3	3.0		0.4
Tenure:									
Owner-occupied	100.0	8.8	8.6	5.0	3.6	1.9	1.7		0.2
Renter-occupied	100.0	33.6	32.2	21.0	11.2	5.9	5.3		1.4
Years of school completed:									
Total 25 years and over	100.0	14.5	14.0	8.6	5.5	2.8	2.6		0.4
Elementary: 0 to 8 years	100.0	11.5	10.6	7.7	3.0	1.8	1.2		0.9
High school: 1 to 3 years	100.0	15.3	14.9	9.9	5.0	2.9	2.1		0.3
4 years	100.0	13.8	13.5	8.5	5.0	2.7	2.3		0.3
College: 1 to 3 years	100.0	15.9	15.5	9.4	6.1	3.1	3.0		0.4
4 years	100.0	16.6	16.0	8.3	7.8	3.8	4.0		0.6
5 years or more	100.0	14.2	13.5	6.9	6.5	2.9	3.6		0.8
Labor force status:									
Total 16 years and over	100.0	16.8	16.2	9.9	6.2	3.3	3.0		0.6
Civilian labor force	100.0	18.9	18.5	11.5	7.0	3.9	3.1		0.5
Employed	100.0	18.2	17.8	11.1	6.6	3.7	3.0		0.4
Unemployed	100.0	28.7	27.6	16.2	11.4	6.2	5.2		1.1
Armed Forces	100.0	42.8	36.1	18.2	17.9	3.3	14.6		6.7
Not in the labor force	100.0	12.3	11.5	6.9	4.7	2.2	2.5		0.7

A4-9. General Mobility, by Race and Hispanic Origin, Sex, and Age: 1990 to 1991

(Mobility data from March 1990 to March 1991. Numbers in thousands)

| Characteristic | Total | Same house (non-movers) | Different house in United States | | Different county | | Different State | | Same region | | | Movers from abroad |
			Total	Same county	Total	Same State	Total	Total	Same division	Different division	Different region	
ALL RACES												
Both Sexes												
Total, 1 year and over	244 884	203 345	40 154	25 151	15 003	7 881	7 122	3 738	2 534	1 205	3 384	1 385
1 to 4 years	15 297	11 824	3 393	2 221	1 171	601	570	279	189	90	291	102
5 to 9 years	18 466	15 210	3 154	2 102	1 051	588	464	248	158	90	216	83
10 to 14 years	17 601	15 118	2 400	1 647	753	374	379	172	121	51	207	148
15 to 19 years	16 839	13 840	2 851	1 817	1 033	518	516	272	190	82	243	74
15 to 17 years	9 924	8 489	1 362	863	499	243	256	137	88	33	119	75
18 and 19 years	6 915	5 351	1 489	955	534	274	260	136	102	33	124	270
20 to 24 years	17 986	11 633	6 083	3 757	2 326	1 280	1 047	545	361	184	502	203
25 to 29 years	20 767	14 001	6 563	3 967	2 596	1 467	1 129	638	423	215	491	139
30 to 34 years	22 138	17 352	4 647	3 033	1 614	842	771	391	263	128	381	110
35 to 39 years	20 379	17 107	3 162	1 954	1 208	617	591	321	195	126	270	71
40 to 44 years	18 286	15 861	2 354	1 425	929	496	433	206	145	61	228	37
45 to 49 years	14 129	12 565	1 528	869	659	277	382	206	167	39	176	44
50 to 54 years	11 557	10 460	1 053	638	415	215	199	107	84	23	92	38
55 to 59 years	10 692	9 841	812	459	354	178	175	111	83	27	65	20
60 to 64 years	10 654	9 932	701	380	321	143	178	96	69	27	82	8
60 and 61 years	4 398	4 073	316	174	142	58	84	50	34	16	34	8
62 to 64 years	6 256	5 859	384	206	179	85	93	46	35	11	48	12
65 to 69 years	10 123	9 554	555	340	215	117	98	64	40	23	34	15
70 to 74 years	8 114	7 767	342	185	156	53	103	51	21	29	53	6
75 to 79 years	5 835	5 564	260	171	89	59	30	9	5	4	21	11
80 to 84 years	3 629	3 446	178	113	65	33	33	14	10	3	19	4
85 years and over	2 391	2 271	118	72	46	21	25	11	10	1	14	1
Median age	33.5	35.8	26.7	26.3	27.2	27.0	27.6	27.8	27.9	27.5	27.4	25.2
Male												
Total, 1 year and over	119 152	98 337	20 077	12 417	7 660	4 021	3 639	1 933	1 320	613	1 706	738
1 to 4 years	7 834	6 042	1 748	1 133	615	313	302	154	102	52	148	44
5 to 9 years	9 465	7 747	1 666	1 101	565	320	245	143	77	65	102	53
10 to 14 years	9 013	7 739	1 224	834	389	186	203	97	71	26	106	51
15 to 19 years	8 513	7 096	1 337	839	498	242	256	118	85	32	139	81
15 to 17 years	5 077	4 370	664	421	243	112	131	58	40	18	74	44
18 and 19 years	3 436	2 726	673	418	255	130	125	60	45	15	65	37
20 to 24 years	8 839	5 864	2 836	1 703	1 133	635	499	274	199	75	225	138
25 to 29 years	10 331	6 802	3 421	2 021	1 399	800	599	338	231	107	261	109
30 to 34 years	10 988	8 477	2 435	1 582	853	432	421	217	143	74	204	75
35 to 39 years	10 066	8 362	1 642	1 002	640	320	321	178	108	70	143	62
40 to 44 years	8 966	7 807	1 111	672	439	228	211	98	69	29	112	48
45 to 49 years	6 904	6 110	778	435	343	156	187	100	83	17	88	16
50 to 54 years	5 524	4 960	543	328	215	114	101	59	45	15	42	21
55 to 59 years	5 179	4 722	436	239	197	110	87	50	42	8	37	21
60 to 64 years	4 982	4 654	324	176	148	59	89	41	32	9	48	4
60 and 61 years	2 077	1 930	145	81	64	23	41	19	15	4	22	3
62 to 64 years	2 905	2 725	179	95	84	36	48	23	17	5	25	2
65 to 69 years	4 586	4 338	240	146	95	51	43	26	14	12	17	7
70 to 74 years	3 570	3 422	144	78	66	22	44	15	5	4	10	3
75 to 79 years	2 275	2 174	98	62	36	21	15	5	4	1	6	–
80 to 84 years	1 322	1 265	56	37	19	8	11	5	3	–	2	–
85 years and over	794	757	37	28	9	4	4	3	3			
Median age	32.5	34.7	26.8	26.5	27.3	27.0	27.6	27.7	27.7	27.5	27.6	25.1
Female												
Total, 1 year and over	125 732	105 008	20 077	12 734	7 343	3 859	3 484	1 806	1 214	592	1 678	647
1 to 4 years	7 463	5 781	1 645	1 088	556	289	268	125	87	37	143	37
5 to 9 years	9 000	7 463	1 488	1 001	486	268	219	105	80	24	114	50
10 to 14 years	8 588	7 380	1 176	812	364	188	176	75	51	25	100	32
15 to 19 years	8 326	6 744	1 514	978	535	276	259	155	105	50	105	68
15 to 17 years	4 847	4 119	698	442	256	131	125	79	49	31	45	30
18 and 19 years	3 479	2 625	816	537	279	145	135	76	57	19	59	132
20 to 24 years	9 148	5 768	3 247	2 054	1 193	645	548	271	162	109	230	94
25 to 29 years	10 436	7 199	3 142	1 946	1 197	667	530	300	192	108	177	64
30 to 34 years	11 150	8 875	2 212	1 451	761	410	351	174	119	54	127	48
35 to 39 years	10 313	8 745	1 520	953	568	297	271	143	88	55	115	23
40 to 44 years	9 320	8 054	1 243	753	490	268	223	107	84	23	88	21
45 to 49 years	7 225	6 455	750	434	316	121	195	106	84	8	50	23
50 to 54 years	6 033	5 500	509	310	199	101	98	48	40	19	28	17
55 to 59 years	5 512	5 120	376	220	157	68	88	61	41	18	34	16
60 to 64 years	5 671	5 278	377	204	173	85	88	55	37	12	11	5
60 and 61 years	2 320	2 144	171	93	78	35	43	32	19	6	22	11
62 to 64 years	3 351	3 135	205	111	95	49	45	23	26	11	17	8
65 to 69 years	5 537	5 215	314	194	120	66	54	37	11	11	36	8
70 to 74 years	4 544	4 345	197	107	90	31	59	23	12	3	11	4
75 to 79 years	3 560	3 390	162	109	53	38	15	4	2	3	13	8
80 to 84 years	2 307	2 181	122	76	46	24	22	9	6	3	13	1
85 years and over	1 597	1 514	82	44	38	17	21	8	7	1	13	4
Median age	34.4	36.9	26.5	26.1	27.2	27.0	27.6	27.9	28.2	27.4	27.2	25.3

See footnote at end of table.

A4-9. General Mobility, by Race and Hispanic Origin, Sex, and Age: 1990 to 1991 (continued)

(Mobility data from March 1990 to March 1991. Numbers in thousands)

Characteristic	Total	Same house (non-movers)	Different house in United States		Different county							Movers from abroad
			Total	Same county	Total	Same State	Different State				Different region	
							Total	Same region				
								Total	Same division	Different division		
WHITE												
Both Sexes												
Total, 1 year and over	205 514	171 492	33 035	20 296	12 739	6 872	5 867	3 062	1 962	1 100	2 805	988
1 to 4 years	12 118	9 442	2 624	1 659	965	525	440	212	130	82	228	53
5 to 9 years	14 794	12 317	2 419	1 560	859	495	364	195	121	74	169	58
10 to 14 years	14 036	12 161	1 813	1 226	588	307	281	121	78	43	160	62
15 to 19 years	13 440	11 085	2 252	1 429	823	429	394	229	150	78	166	103
15 to 17 years	7 885	6 795	1 049	646	403	200	202	116	71	45	87	42
18 and 19 years	5 555	4 290	1 203	783	420	229	192	113	80	33	79	61
20 to 24 years	14 828	9 435	5 193	3 161	2 032	1 139	893	451	284	166	442	200
25 to 29 years	17 252	11 577	5 530	3 291	2 239	1 301	938	531	334	197	407	145
30 to 34 years	18 650	14 669	3 886	2 466	1 420	758	662	332	216	116	330	95
35 to 39 years	17 227	14 473	2 667	1 660	1 007	534	473	257	143	114	216	87
40 to 44 years	15 678	13 689	1 932	1 132	800	439	362	163	106	58	198	57
45 to 49 years	12 150	10 831	1 288	743	545	234	311	166	128	38	145	32
50 to 54 years	9 880	8 965	885	530	355	185	170	86	63	23	84	30
55 to 59 years	9 248	8 530	691	392	299	143	157	96	70	26	61	27
60 to 64 years	9 316	8 707	596	317	278	125	153	85	58	27	68	13
60 and 61 years	3 767	3 488	273	147	125	51	74	48	32	16	26	7
62 to 64 years	5 549	5 220	323	170	153	74	79	37	26	11	42	6
65 to 69 years	8 961	8 481	470	271	199	107	92	58	35	23	34	10
70 to 74 years	7 247	6 947	295	152	143	47	96	49	20	29	47	6
75 to 79 years	5 276	5 036	233	151	82	58	24	7	5	1	17	7
80 to 84 years	3 275	3 110	162	97	65	33	33	14	10	3	19	3
85 years and over	2 139	2 038	100	60	39	14	25	11	10	1	14	1
Median age	34.4	36.8	27.0	26.7	27.5	27.1	28.0	28.1	28.2	27.7	27.9	25.6
Male												
Total, 1 year and over	100 555	83 272	16 747	10 193	6 555	3 528	3 027	1 610	1 037	573	1 417	536
1 to 4 years	6 210	4 800	1 383	864	519	282	237	115	67	48	122	27
5 to 9 years	7 588	6 287	1 274	804	469	269	201	118	62	56	82	27
10 to 14 years	7 202	6 236	929	624	305	151	155	74	50	24	81	37
15 to 19 years	6 813	5 703	1 057	656	401	205	196	103	71	32	93	53
15 to 17 years	4 040	3 508	511	319	192	90	102	51	33	18	51	21
18 and 19 years	2 773	2 196	545	337	209	114	94	52	38	15	42	32
20 to 24 years	7 348	4 772	2 471	1 476	994	565	429	224	157	67	205	105
25 to 29 years	8 684	5 664	2 935	1 731	1 203	705	498	285	180	105	213	85
30 to 34 years	9 371	7 247	2 068	1 316	751	390	361	187	120	67	175	56
35 to 39 years	8 634	7 161	1 422	872	550	289	261	148	82	66	113	51
40 to 44 years	7 800	6 816	948	552	396	208	187	86	56	29	102	37
45 to 49 years	5 988	5 323	650	372	278	129	149	79	64	15	70	14
50 to 54 years	4 760	4 287	460	272	188	101	88	50	35	15	38	13
55 to 59 years	4 525	4 133	376	211	165	85	80	43	35	8	36	16
60 to 64 years	4 398	4 110	284	154	131	55	76	37	28	9	39	4
60 and 61 years	1 788	1 654	131	73	58	22	36	19	15	4	17	3
62 to 64 years	2 610	2 456	153	80	73	33	40	18	13	5	22	1
65 to 69 years	4 092	3 879	208	117	91	49	41	24	12	12	17	6
70 to 74 years	3 175	3 050	121	64	57	16	42	25	7	18	16	4
75 to 79 years	2 067	1 981	86	54	32	21	11	5	4	1	6	1
80 to 84 years	1 198	1 146	52	33	19	8	11	5	4	1	6	-
85 years and over	703	678	25	20	5	1	4	3	3	-	2	-
Median age	33.4	35.7	27.2	26.9	27.5	27.1	28.0	28.0	28.1	27.8	28.0	26.1
Female												
Total, 1 year and over	104 959	88 220	16 288	10 103	6 184	3 344	2 840	1 452	925	527	1 388	451
1 to 4 years	5 908	4 641	1 241	795	445	243	203	97	63	34	106	26
5 to 9 years	7 206	6 030	1 145	755	390	226	164	77	59	18	87	31
10 to 14 years	6 834	5 925	884	602	282	156	127	47	28	19	80	25
15 to 19 years	6 626	5 382	1 195	773	422	224	198	125	80	46	73	50
15 to 17 years	3 845	3 287	537	327	211	110	101	65	38	27	36	20
18 and 19 years	2 781	2 094	658	446	212	114	98	61	42	19	37	29
20 to 24 years	7 481	4 663	2 722	1 685	1 038	574	464	227	128	99	237	95
25 to 29 years	8 568	5 913	2 596	1 560	1 036	596	440	246	154	92	193	60
30 to 34 years	9 279	7 422	1 818	1 149	669	368	301	145	96	49	155	39
35 to 39 years	8 593	7 313	1 245	787	457	246	212	109	61	48	103	35
40 to 44 years	7 878	6 872	985	580	405	230	174	78	49	29	97	21
45 to 49 years	6 163	5 508	637	371	267	105	162	87	65	23	74	17
50 to 54 years	5 120	4 678	426	258	167	85	83	37	28	8	46	16
55 to 59 years	4 723	4 397	315	181	134	58	77	52	34	18	25	11
60 to 64 years	4 918	4 597	311	164	148	71	77	49	30	18	28	9
60 and 61 years	1 979	1 834	142	74	68	29	39	29	17	12	9	4
62 to 64 years	2 939	2 764	170	90	80	42	38	19	13	6	19	5
65 to 69 years	4 869	4 602	262	154	108	58	51	33	23	11	17	5
70 to 74 years	4 073	3 897	174	88	85	31	54	23	12	11	31	2
75 to 79 years	3 209	3 055	148	98	50	37	13	2	2	-	11	6
80 to 84 years	2 077	1 964	110	64	46	24	22	9	6	3	13	3
85 years and over	1 436	1 360	74	41	34	13	21	8	7	1	13	1
Median age	35.3	37.8	26.8	26.4	27.5	27.1	28.0	28.1	28.4	27.6	27.9	25.0

See footnote at end of table.

A4-9. General Mobility, by Race and Hispanic Origin, Sex, and Age: 1990 to 1991 (continued)

(Mobility data from March 1990 to March 1991. Numbers in thousands)

Characteristic	Total	Same house (non-movers)	Different house in United States — Total	Same county	Different county — Total	Same State	Different State — Total	Same region — Total	Same division	Different division	Different region	Movers from abroad
BLACK												
Both Sexes												
Total, 1 year and over	30 307	24 733	5 464	3 817	1 647	722	925	504	437	66	421	109
1 to 4 years	2 481	1 843	632	472	160	55	105	51	44	7	54	5
5 to 9 years	2 829	2 202	608	460	148	69	79	44	28	16	35	19
10 to 14 years	2 799	2 328	461	353	107	40	68	35	32	3	33	10
15 to 19 years	2 622	2 158	459	310	150	71	79	31	28	3	48	4
15 to 17 years	1 553	1 311	240	180	60	31	30	12	9	3	18	3
18 and 19 years	1 068	847	219	130	89	41	49	19	19	–	30	2
20 to 24 years	2 481	1 761	698	475	223	113	110	71	63	8	39	22
25 to 29 years	2 730	1 934	782	518	264	126	138	77	68	9	61	14
30 to 34 years	2 705	2 145	546	426	120	46	74	37	28	9	37	14
35 to 39 years	2 365	1 986	366	220	146	56	90	48	42	5	42	14
40 to 44 years	1 907	1 580	324	226	98	45	53	34	31	3	18	3
45 to 49 years	1 433	1 268	166	80	86	27	59	36	35	2	23	–
50 to 54 years	1 261	1 146	114	77	37	14	23	18	18	–	6	–
55 to 59 years	1 115	1 023	92	53	39	29	10	6	6	–	4	–
60 to 64 years	1 033	957	71	42	28	9	19	7	7	–	12	6
60 and 61 years	485	457	27	16	11	3	8	1	1	–	7	–
62 to 64 years	549	499	43	26	17	6	11	7	7	–	4	6
65 to 69 years	891	827	64	51	13	8	5	5	5	–	–	–
70 to 74 years	690	665	25	11	14	6	7	2	2	–	6	–
75 to 79 years	466	439	27	20	7	1	6	2	2	–	4	–
80 to 84 years	290	279	11	11	–	–	–	–	–	–	–	–
85 years and over	210	192	18	11	7	7	–	–	–	–	–	–
Median age	28.6	30.3	24.1	23.3	25.7	25.5	25.8	26.4	26.8	(B)	25.1	23.8
Male												
Total, 1 year and over	14 202	11 628	2 509	1 720	789	339	450	247	222	25	203	65
1 to 4 years	1 255	966	285	219	66	19	47	28	23	4	19	4
5 to 9 years	1 451	1 113	328	251	77	41	36	22	12	9	14	10
10 to 14 years	1 421	1 189	224	178	46	15	31	16	16	–	15	9
15 to 19 years	1 299	1 078	218	150	68	27	41	10	10	–	30	3
15 to 17 years	780	662	115	82	33	15	18	4	4	–	14	3
18 and 19 years	519	416	103	68	35	12	23	7	7	–	16	–
20 to 24 years	1 149	866	268	165	103	56	47	37	36	1	10	16
25 to 29 years	1 269	905	360	214	146	68	78	42	41	1	36	5
30 to 34 years	1 227	975	246	188	57	17	41	16	10	6	24	7
35 to 39 years	1 074	900	165	93	72	24	48	25	23	2	24	9
40 to 44 years	857	726	128	96	32	12	20	12	12	–	7	3
45 to 49 years	640	553	87	41	46	18	28	18	17	2	10	–
50 to 54 years	557	499	58	42	16	5	11	9	9	–	2	–
55 to 59 years	505	457	48	19	28	24	5	4	4	–	1	–
60 to 64 years	465	436	29	16	13	3	10	3	3	–	7	–
60 and 61 years	232	223	9	4	5	–	5	–	–	–	5	–
62 to 64 years	233	213	20	12	8	3	5	3	3	–	2	–
65 to 69 years	379	354	24	23	2	–	2	2	2	–	–	–
70 to 74 years	315	302	13	4	9	6	2	2	2	–	1	–
75 to 79 years	163	151	13	9	4	–	4	–	–	–	4	–
80 to 84 years	100	96	4	4	–	–	–	–	–	–	–	–
85 years and over	74	62	12	8	3	3	–	–	–	–	–	–
Median age	27.1	28.3	23.7	21.9	26.2	25.8	26.6	26.2	26.5	(B)	27.0	(B)
Female												
Total, 1 year and over	16 105	13 105	2 955	2 097	858	383	475	257	215	42	218	45
1 to 4 years	1 225	877	348	253	94	36	58	23	21	3	35	1
5 to 9 years	1 378	1 089	280	209	72	28	44	22	16	6	21	8
10 to 14 years	1 378	1 139	237	175	62	25	37	19	16	3	19	1
15 to 19 years	1 323	1 080	241	160	82	44	38	21	18	3	17	2
15 to 17 years	773	649	125	98	27	15	12	8	5	3	3	–
18 and 19 years	549	431	117	62	55	28	26	12	12	–	14	2
20 to 24 years	1 331	895	430	310	120	57	63	34	27	7	30	6
25 to 29 years	1 460	1 030	422	305	117	58	59	34	27	8	25	9
30 to 34 years	1 478	1 171	300	237	63	30	33	21	18	3	13	7
35 to 39 years	1 292	1 086	201	128	73	32	41	23	19	4	18	5
40 to 44 years	1 049	854	196	130	66	33	33	22	19	3	11	–
45 to 49 years	793	714	79	39	40	9	31	18	18	–	13	–
50 to 54 years	703	647	56	35	21	8	13	8	8	–	4	–
55 to 59 years	610	566	44	33	11	5	5	4	4	–	3	–
60 to 64 years	569	521	42	27	15	7	9	4	4	–	4	6
60 and 61 years	253	234	18	12	6	3	3	1	1	–	2	–
62 to 64 years	316	287	23	14	9	3	6	4	4	–	2	6
65 to 69 years	512	473	39	28	11	8	3	3	3	–	–	–
70 to 74 years	375	363	12	7	5	–	5	–	–	–	5	–
75 to 79 years	303	288	15	11	3	1	2	2	–	2	–	–
80 to 84 years	190	183	7	7	–	–	–	–	–	–	–	–
85 years and over	136	129	6	3	4	4	–	–	–	–	–	–
Median age	29.9	31.9	24.3	24.1	25.0	25.2	24.8	26.5	27.1	(B)	22.8	(B)

See footnote at end of table.

A4-9. General Mobility, by Race and Hispanic Origin, Sex, and Age: 1990 to 1991 (continued)

(Mobility data from March 1990 to March 1991. Numbers in thousands)

Characteristic	Total	Same house (non-movers)	Different house in United States									Movers from abroad
			Total	Same county	Different county							
					Total	Same State	Different State					
							Total	Same region			Different region	
								Total	Same division	Different division		
HISPANIC[1]												
Both Sexes												
Total, 1 year and over	20 907	16 022	4 447	3 482	965	569	396	207	136	72	189	437
1 to 4 years	1 840	1 341	471	391	81	47	34	21	13	8	12	28
5 to 9 years	2 059	1 650	392	319	73	40	33	22	16	6	11	17
10 to 14 years	1 947	1 580	341	272	69	42	27	7	6	1	20	26
15 to 19 years	1 823	1 387	375	278	96	51	46	29	17	13	16	62
15 to 17 years	1 113	899	187	133	54	30	24	11	7	4	13	27
18 and 19 years	710	488	188	146	42	20	22	18	9	9	4	35
20 to 24 years	2 030	1 223	722	573	149	87	62	29	19	9	34	85
25 to 29 years	2 124	1 363	698	545	152	109	44	26	17	8	18	63
30 to 34 years	2 096	1 572	479	375	104	56	48	20	13	7	27	46
35 to 39 years	1 598	1 251	317	231	86	44	42	22	13	9	20	30
40 to 44 years	1 322	1 086	211	155	56	33	22	10	7	3	12	25
45 to 49 years	948	793	136	108	29	15	14	7	7	-	6	19
50 to 54 years	788	662	117	90	27	18	9	5	4	2	4	9
55 to 59 years	658	574	70	54	16	11	5	-	-	-	4	14
60 to 64 years	582	530	46	35	11	7	4	4	2	2	1	6
60 and 61 years	233	217	14	10	4	1	3	3	2	1	-	2
62 to 64 years	349	313	32	25	7	6	1	1	-	1	1	4
65 to 69 years	441	397	42	30	12	9	3	3	1	2	1	2
70 to 74 years	296	277	15	13	2	-	2	1	-	1	1	4
75 to 79 years	185	177	6	5	1	1	-	-	-	-	-	2
80 to 84 years	116	108	7	5	2	-	2	2	2	-	-	1
85 years and over	53	51	2	1	1	-	1	-	-	-	1	-
Median age	26.8	28.1	24.5	24.2	25.5	25.8	24.7	24.3	24.3	(B)	25.2	25.1
Male												
Total, 1 year and over	10 494	7 896	2 345	1 822	524	326	198	108	76	32	90	253
1 to 4 years	940	670	252	206	45	25	20	13	7	7	7	18
5 to 9 years	1 057	848	197	168	29	18	11	7	6	1	4	12
10 to 14 years	996	812	168	135	32	24	9	1	1	-	8	16
15 to 19 years	927	711	184	129	54	27	27	15	13	2	12	32
15 to 17 years	569	464	94	66	28	14	14	6	5	1	8	12
18 and 19 years	357	248	90	64	26	13	13	9	8	1	4	20
20 to 24 years	1 066	648	370	275	95	61	34	14	12	2	20	48
25 to 29 years	1 110	683	393	305	88	63	25	13	9	4	12	34
30 to 34 years	1 080	775	279	218	61	38	23	13	7	7	9	26
35 to 39 years	809	620	167	125	42	18	24	13	7	6	10	22
40 to 44 years	665	540	111	88	23	14	9	5	4	1	4	14
45 to 49 years	434	352	71	53	18	10	8	7	7	-	1	10
50 to 54 years	377	306	63	45	18	11	7	4	3	1	3	7
55 to 59 years	318	269	42	35	8	6	1	-	-	-	1	6
60 to 64 years	255	237	16	14	2	2	-	-	-	-	-	1
60 and 61 years	96	90	6	6	-	-	-	-	-	-	-	-
62 to 64 years	159	147	10	8	2	2	-	-	-	-	-	1
65 to 69 years	179	163	15	10	5	5	-	-	-	-	-	1
70 to 74 years	145	130	10	10	1	-	1	1	-	1	-	4
75 to 79 years	64	61	2	1	1	1	-	-	-	-	-	1
80 to 84 years	47	44	2	2	-	-	-	-	-	-	-	-
85 years and over	27	26	1	1	-	-	-	-	-	-	-	-
Median age	26.2	26.9	25.0	24.9	25.3	25.6	24.8	26.2	24.8	(B)	23.8	25.1
Female												
Total, 1 year and over	10 413	8 126	2 102	1 661	441	243	198	100	60	40	98	185
1 to 4 years	900	671	220	185	35	22	13	8	6	1	6	10
5 to 9 years	1 002	802	194	151	43	21	22	14	10	5	8	6
10 to 14 years	951	768	174	137	37	19	18	6	5	1	12	9
15 to 19 years	896	675	191	149	42	23	19	14	4	10	5	30
15 to 17 years	543	435	93	67	26	16	10	6	3	3	5	15
18 and 19 years	353	240	98	82	16	7	9	9	1	7	-	15
20 to 24 years	964	576	352	298	54	26	28	14	7	7	14	36
25 to 29 years	1 013	680	304	240	64	46	19	13	8	5	6	29
30 to 34 years	1 016	796	200	157	43	18	25	7	6	1	18	20
35 to 39 years	789	631	150	106	44	26	18	8	5	3	10	8
40 to 44 years	656	545	100	67	32	19	13	5	2	2	8	11
45 to 49 years	514	441	65	55	10	5	5	1	1	-	5	8
50 to 54 years	411	356	54	45	9	6	2	1	1	1	1	2
55 to 59 years	340	305	28	19	8	5	3	-	-	-	3	8
60 to 64 years	327	293	30	21	9	4	4	4	2	2	1	5
60 and 61 years	137	127	8	4	4	1	3	3	2	1	-	2
62 to 64 years	190	166	22	17	5	3	1	1	-	1	1	3
65 to 69 years	262	235	26	20	6	4	3	3	1	2	-	1
70 to 74 years	152	147	5	4	1	-	1	-	-	-	1	-
75 to 79 years	121	116	4	4	-	-	-	-	-	-	-	1
80 to 84 years	69	64	5	3	2	-	2	2	2	-	-	1
85 years and over	26	25	1	-	1	-	1	-	-	-	1	-
Median age	27.4	29.2	23.9	23.5	25.7	26.2	24.7	22.6	(B)	(B)	29.4	25.2

[1]Persons of Hispanic origin may be of any race.

A5. Aging Around the World

A5-1. World's Population, by Age and Sex: 1991 and 2000

Year and age	Population (millions)			Percentage			Males per 100 females
	Both sexes	Male	Female	Both sexes	Male	Female	
1991							
All ages	5,422	2,730	2,692	100.0	100.0	100.0	101.4
Under 15 years	1,750	894	856	32.3	32.7	31.8	104.4
15 to 64 years	3,340	1,693	1,646	61.6	62.0	61.2	102.9
65 years and over ...	332	142	190	6.1	5.2	7.0	75.0
2000							
All ages	6,283	3,163	3,120	100.0	100.0	100.0	101.4
Under 15 years	1,953	996	957	31.1	31.5	30.7	104.1
15 to 64 years	3,904	1,980	1,924	62.1	62.6	61.7	102.9
65 years and over ...	426	187	240	6.8	5.9	7.7	77.9

Source: U.S. Bureau of the Census, Kevin Kinsella, Center for International Research, International Data Base.

A5-2. Average Annual Percent Growth of Elderly Population in Developed and Developing Countries

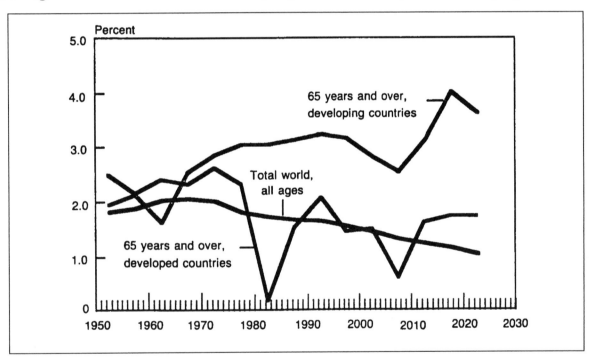

A5-3. Countries with More Than Five Million Elderly (65+) and One Million Oldest Old (80+): 1990

Age and country	Aged population (in thousands)
Age 65+	
China	63,398
United States	31,560
India	29,518
Soviet Union	27,461
Japan	14,655
Germany*	11,779
United Kingdom	8,977
Italy	8,472
France	7,928
Brazil	6,430
Indonesia	5,655
Spain	5,246
Age 80+	
China	7,716
United States	7,082
Soviet Union	6,398
Germany*	2,938
Japan	2,824
India	2,389
France	2,119
United Kingdom	2,087
Italy	1,770
Spain	1,116

*Figures are for a unified Germany.

Source: U.S. Bureau of the Census, International Data Base.

A5-4. Elderly Population, by Age: 1985

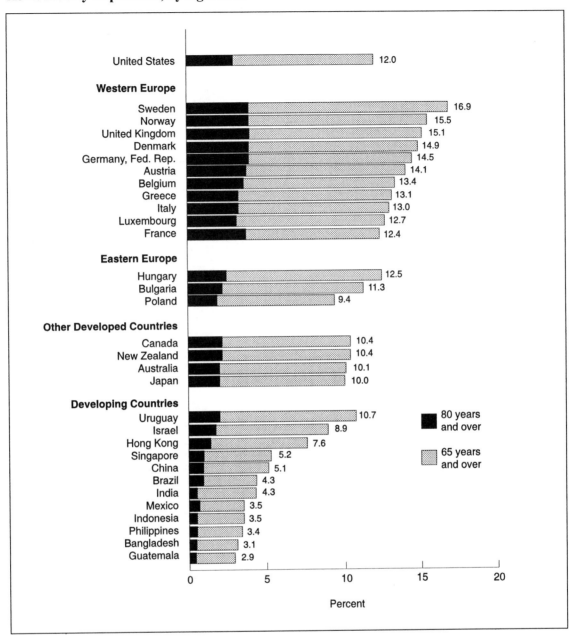

A5-5. Speed of Population Aging in Selected Countries

Country	Year in which percent of population 65 years and over reached or will reach		Number of years required
	7 percent	14 percent	
Japan	1970	1996	26
United Kingdom	1930	1975	45
United States	1944	2010	66
Sweden	1890	1975	85
France	1865	1980	115

Source: U.S. Bureau of the Census, 1984, Projections of the *Population of the United States by Age, Sex, and Race: 1983 to 2080; Current Population Reports,* Series P-25, No. 952, Washington, D.C., table 6; and Japan Ministry of Health and Welfare, 1983, *Annual Report on Health and Welfare for 1983: The Trend of a New Era and Social Security,* Tokyo, p. 141.

A5-6. Countries with More Than Two Million Elderly Persons: 1991

(In thousands) Country	Population aged 65 and over
China, Mainland	67,967
India	32,780
United States	**32,045**
Japan	15,253
Germany	12,010
United Kingdom	9,025
Italy	8,665
France	8,074
Brazil	6,680
Indonesia	5,962
Spain	5,378
Pakistan	4,734
Poland	3,851
Mexico	3,522
Bangladesh	3,492
Vietnam	3,196
Canada	3,140
Argentina	3,012
Turkey	2,789
Nigeria	2,676
Romania	2,489
Philippines	2,380
Thailand	2,350
Yugoslavia	2,328
South Korea	2,135
Egypt	2,077
Iran	2,052

Source: U.S. Bureau of the Census, Kevin Kinsella, Center for International Research, International Data Base.

A5-7. Countries with More Than Two Million Elderly Persons: 2020

(In thousands) Country	Population aged 65 and over
China, Mainland	179,561
India	88,495
United States	**52,067**
Japan	33,421
Indonesia	22,183
Brazil	18,800
Germany	18,396
Italy	13,078
France	12,119
United Kingdom	12,108
Mexico	10,857
Pakistan	9,678
Nigeria	9,152
Bangladesh	9,057
Spain	8,162
Turkey	7,990
Thailand	7,828
Poland	7,243
Vietnam	6,707
Philippines	6,646
South Korea	6,550
Canada	6,404
Egypt	5,680
Iran	5,235
Yugoslavia	4,933
Argentina	4,862
Romania	4,588
Colombia	4,464
South Africa	4,084
Australia	3,956
Ethiopia	3,920
China, Taiwan	3,500
Netherlands	3,461
Burma	3,425
Czechoslovakia	3,149
Morocco	2,972
Venezuela	2,912
Saudi Arabia	2,867
North Korea	2,734
Zaire	2,643
Peru	2,580
Sri Lanka	2,527
Algeria	2,450
Greece	2,237
Hungary	2,186
Malaysia	2,139
Chile	2,133
Belgium	2,071
Portugal	2,053

Source: U.S. Bureau of the Census, Kevin Kinsella, Center for International Research, International Data Base.

A5-8. Countries with More Than One Million Octogenarians: 1991 (Projection)

(In thousands)

Country	Population aged 80 and over
China, Mainland	9,173
United States	**7,310**
India	3,578
Japan	3,089
Germany	3,081
France	2,170
United Kingdom	2,130
Italy	1,853
Spain	1,164

Source: U.S. Bureau of the Census, Kevin Kinsella, Center for International Research, International Data Base and United Nations Department of Economic and Social Affairs.

A5-9. Countries with More Than One Million Octogenarians: 2020 (Projection)

(In thousands)

Country	Population aged 80 and over
China, Mainland	34,535
India	12,719
United States	**12,113**
Japan	10,261
Germany	5,893
Italy	4,119
Indonesia	3,683
United Kingdom	3,497
Brazil	3,319
France	3,136
Mexico	2,449
Turkey	1,888
Canada	1,627
Thailand	1,496
Poland	1,494
Pakistan	1,394
Yugoslavia	1,384
Romania	1,307
South Korea	1,285
Vietnam	1,112

Source: U.S. Bureau of the Census, Kevin Kinsella, Center for International Research, International Data Base and United Nations Department of Economic and Social Affairs.

A5-10. Population, by Age and Sex for Japan: 1991, 2000, and 2020

(In thousands)

Age	1991	2000	2020
0 to 24 years	41,444	36,370	31,818
25 to 54 years	52,698	53,950	47,538
55 to 59 years	7,802	8,808	7,672
60 to 64 years	6,820	7,628	7,266
65 to 69 years	5,243	7,007	8,165
70 to 74 years	3,871	5,758	8,495
75 to 79 years	3,050	3,933	6,501
80 years and over	3,089	4,692	10,261

Source: U.S. Bureau of the Census, Kevin Kinsella, Center for International Research, International Data Base.

A5-11. Projections of Elderly Population, by Age: 1985 to 2025

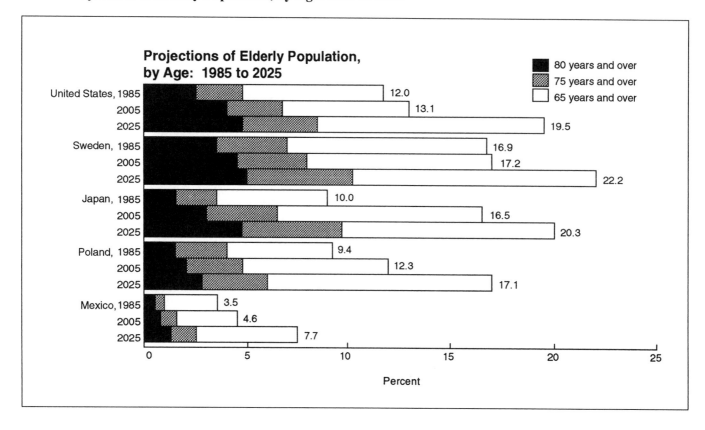

B. Social Characteristics

B1. LIVING ARRANGEMENTS AND MARITAL STATUS

In the last few decades, there has been an increase in the proportion of older people, especially women, who live alone. In 1990, over 80% of men, but only 55% of women, over 65 lived with their spouses or other relatives. In the oldest old group, only 10% of women live with their spouses; they are more likely to live with relatives than their surviving male counterparts. Almost 50% of women in this age group, but only 15% of men, were widowed. Elderly widowed men remarry about seven times more often than women.

B2. HOUSEHOLDS, HOUSING, AND INFORMAL SUPPORTS

In the last 20 years, there has been a substantial increase in nonfamily households in the general population. Older people without spouses live alone more frequently today compared to 30 or 40 years ago. As the population ages, fewer younger persons are available to be caregivers.

In urban areas, three-quarters of the elderly own homes, while one-quarter rents. In rural areas, home ownership and percentage of houses owned free and clear is greater than in urban areas; however, the homes are often old and in poor condition.

B3. EDUCATION

The educational attainment of the elderly population will increase significantly in the coming years because younger cohorts were more likely to have completed high school and attended college than the elderly of today. Between 1960 and 1990 the median level of education among the elderly increased from 8.3 to 12.1 years; by the year 2000, it is expected to reach 12.4 years. Elderly blacks and Hispanics are much less likely to have finished high school than younger blacks and Hispanics. This difference is especially pronounced in the 75-year-old and above group.

B4. SOCIAL ATTITUDES AND ACTIVITIES

The young old have become pacesetters in new ways to spend the retirement years; two-thirds enjoy good to excellent health and are very satisfied with their lives. Travel ranks high among favorite activities. Approximately 75% of the older population belong to religious organizations that play an important role in their lives and serve many of their spiritual and social needs, including counseling, transportation, education, and recreation. Almost 20% regularly perform unpaid volunteer work, and many provide direct help to their children and grandchildren.

Older people maintain a strong interest in the election process and have a high voting record, possibly because they have more leisure time than younger people. During the 1990 congressional elections, 77% of the elderly were registered and more than 60% voted, compared to 40% registered and 20% voting among the 18 to 24 age group. Presidential election years always have higher registration and voting records; in 1992, 78% of the elderly registered and 70% voted, compared to 52% registered and 43% voting for the 18 to 24 age group.

B5. VICTIMIZATION AND ABUSE OF THE ELDERLY

A 1992 Bureau of Justice Statistics special report on elderly victims concludes that the elderly are less likely than those who are younger to sustain victimization by crime, but, when victimized, are more likely to be harmed by strangers and sustain grievous injuries. Victimization rates for crimes of violence are considerably lower than those for younger people and actually decreased from a high of 9 per thousand in 1974 to a low of 3.5 per thousand in 1990. The elderly are most susceptible to crimes motivated by economic gain such as robbery and theft.

The number of cases of elder abuse in domestic settings, both physical abuse and neglect, increased over the past few years; it is not clear whether this increase indicates an actual rise in the incidence of domestic elder abuse or more frequent reporting of such abuse due to education and awareness efforts. The oldest old are most subject to abuse.

B6. OTHER SOCIAL PROBLEMS

Alcohol abuse, alcohol dependence, and adverse consequences of drinking are less prevalent among the elderly than among the younger population. However, heavy drinking is a problem among elderly males living in rural areas, and alcohol related hospitalizations among elderly people are common. In the last 20 years, blood alcohol concentration of elderly drivers involved in fatal crashes and the percent of heavy smokers has decreased, especially among white males. Difficulties in driving, involvement in crashes, and driver fatality rates increase dramatically after age 70.

B1. Living Arrangements and Marital Status

B1-1. Living Arrangements of Adults, by Age: 1991

Living arrangement	Total, 15 years and over	15 to 19 years	20 to 24 years	25 to 29 years	30 to 34 years	35 to 39 years	40 to 44 years	45 to 64 years	65 years and over
Total persons	193,519	16,839	17,986	20,767	22,138	20,379	18,286	47,031	30,093
Married.	112,771	514	4,731	11,257	14,912	14,849	13,779	35,881	16,847
Percent.	58.3	3.1	26.3	54.2	67.4	72.9	75.4	76.3	56.0
Maintains own household.	108,744	367	4,171	10,535	14,276	14,409	13,457	35,088	16,445
Unmarried	80,748	16,325	13,255	9,510	7,226	5,530	4,507	11,150	13,246
Percent.	41.7	96.9	73.7	45.8	32.6	27.1	24.6	23.7	44.0
Total unmarried	80,748	16,325	13,255	9,510	7,226	5,530	4,507	11,150	13,246
Percent	100.0	100.0	100.0	100.0	100.0	100.0	100.0	100.0	100.0
Maintains own household.	46.7	2.0	20.6	44.1	55.0	63.1	72.3	77.7	83.5
Alone	27.0	0.6	7.4	20.0	26.3	28.0	32.4	44.0	68.2
Shares with relatives	14.5	0.9	6.3	14.3	20.0	27.9	32.3	27.9	13.6
Shares with nonrelatives only. . . .	5.2	0.5	6.9	9.8	8.7	7.3	7.6	5.8	1.8
Lives with others	53.3	98.0	79.4	55.9	45.0	36.9	27.7	22.3	16.5
With parents	35.9	88.2	59.4	30.5	22.5	16.6	13.0	6.1	0.4
With other relatives	7.3	5.9	6.6	6.5	5.8	5.2	3.7	7.5	13.2
With nonrelatives only.	10.0	3.9	13.4	18.9	16.7	15.1	11.0	8.7	2.9

B1-2. Living Arrangements of the Elderly, by Sex, Race, and Hispanic Origin: 1992

[Numbers in thousands. Noninstitutional population]

Living arrangements and age	All races			White			Black			Hispanic*		
	Total	Men	Women	Total	Men	Women	Total	Men	Women	Total	Men	Women
65 years and over.	**30,590**	**12,800**	**17,790**	**27,297**	**11,431**	**15,866**	**2,607**	**1,058**	**1,549**	**1,143**	**466**	**677**
Living—												
Alone	9,523	2,086	7,437	8,463	1,741	6,722	938	312	626	219	50	169
With spouse	16,537	9,448	7,089	15,220	8,664	6,556	956	572	384	585	342	243
With other relatives	3,814	897	2,917	2,998	723	2,275	638	124	514	309	63	246
With nonrelatives only	716	369	347	616	303	313	75	50	25	30	11	19
65 to 74 years	**18,440**	**8,266**	**10,174**	**16,315**	**7,323**	**8,992**	**1,665**	**739**	**926**	**732**	**310**	**422**
Living—												
Alone	4,561	1,100	3,461	3,918	867	3,051	567	210	357	121	29	92
With spouse	11,606	6,372	5,234	10,626	5,808	4,818	722	425	297	428	237	191
With other relatives	1,837	516	1,321	1,405	418	987	319	68	251	162	35	127
With nonrelatives only	436	278	158	366	230	136	57	36	21	21	9	12
75 years and over . . .	**12,149**	**4,533**	**7,616**	**10,983**	**4,108**	**6,875**	**941**	**318**	**623**	**412**	**157**	**255**
Living—												
Alone	4,962	986	3,976	4,546	875	3,671	371	102	269	98	21	77
With spouse	4,931	3,076	1,855	4,594	2,856	1,738	235	147	88	157	105	52
With other relatives	1,976	380	1,596	1,594	305	1,289	310	54	256	147	29	118
With nonrelatives only	280	91	189	249	72	177	25	15	10	10	2	8

*Persons of Hispanic origin may be of any race.

B1-3. Living Arrangements of the Elderly: 1991

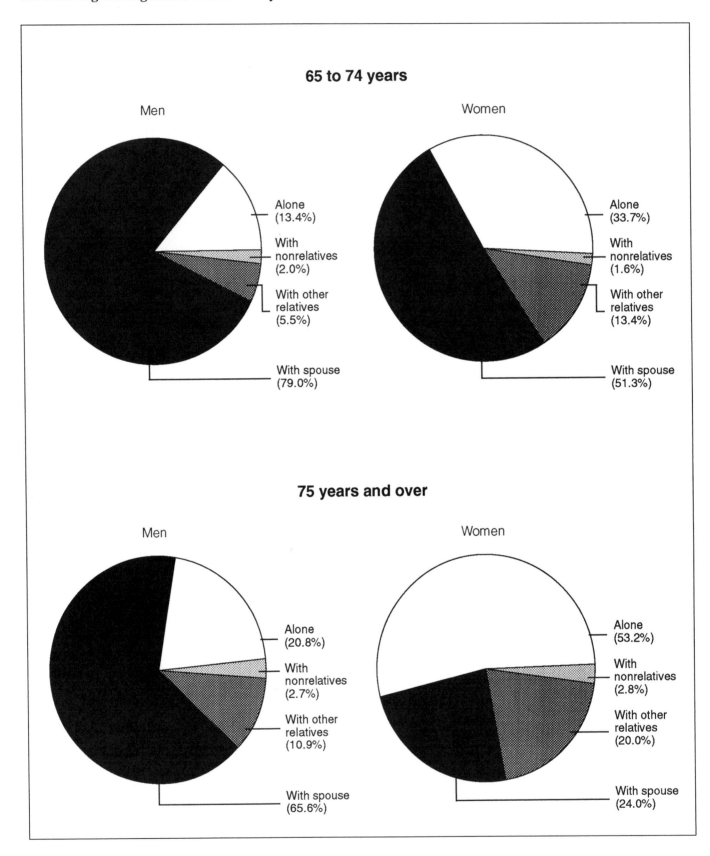

B1-4. Living Arrangements of the Elderly: 1980 and 1990

(Numbers in thousands)

Living arrangement and age	1990			Percent distribution			1980			Percent distribution		
	Total	Men	Women	Total	Men	Women	Total	Men	Women	Total	Men	Women
65 years and over.....	29,566	12,334	17,232	100.0	100.0	100.0	24,157	9,889	14,268	100.0	100.0	100.0
Living—												
Alone...................	9,176	1,942	7,233	31.0	15.7	42.0	7,067	1,447	5,620	29.3	14.6	39.4
With spouse............	16,003	9,158	6,845	54.1	74.3	39.7	12,781	7,441	5,340	52.9	75.2	37.4
With other relatives.......	3,734	953	2,782	12.6	7.7	16.1	3,892	832	3,060	16.1	8.4	21.4
With nonrelatives only[1] ...	653	281	372	2.2	2.3	2.2	417	169	248	1.7	1.7	1.7
65 to 74 years..........	17,979	8,013	9,966	100.0	100.0	100.0	15,302	6,621	8,681	100.0	100.0	100.0
Living—												
Alone...................	4,350	1,042	3,309	24.2	13.0	33.2	3,750	797	2,953	24.5	12.0	34.0
With spouse............	11,353	6,265	5,089	63.1	78.2	51.1	9,436	5,285	4,151	61.7	79.8	47.8
With other relatives.......	1,931	528	1,401	10.7	6.6	14.1	1,890	436	1,454	12.4	6.6	16.7
With nonrelatives only[1] ...	345	178	167	1.9	2.2	1.7	226	103	123	1.5	1.6	1.4
. 75 to 84 years..........	9,354	3,562	5,792	100.0	100.0	100.0	7,172	2,708	4,464	100.0	100.0	100.0
Living—												
Alone...................	3,774	688	3,086	40.3	19.3	53.3	2,664	505	2,159	37.1	18.6	48.4
With spouse............	4,145	2,537	1,607	44.3	71.2	27.7	2,977	1,882	1,095	41.5	69.5	24.5
With other relatives.......	1,237	264	974	13.2	7.4	16.8	1,394	271	1,123	19.4	10.0	25.2
With nonrelatives only[1] ...	198	73	125	2.1	2.0	2.2	137	50	87	1.9	1.8	1.9
85 years and over.......	2,233	758	1,475	100.0	100.0	100.0	1,683	560	1,123	100.0	100.0	100.0
Living—												
Alone...................	1,051	213	838	47.1	28.1	56.8	653	145	508	38.8	25.9	45.2
With spouse............	505	356	150	22.6	47.0	10.2	368	274	94	21.9	48.9	8.4
With other relatives.......	567	160	406	25.4	21.1	27.5	608	125	483	36.1	22.3	43.0
With nonrelatives only[1] ...	110	29	81	4.9	3.8	5.5	54	16	38	3.2	2.9	3.4

[1]1980 data include a small number of persons in unrelated subfamilies.
Source of 1980 data: U.S. Bureau of the Census, 1980 Census of Population, Chapter D, Detailed Population Characteristics, tables 264, 265, and 266.

B1-5. Living Arrangements of Elderly Persons, by Residence: 1990

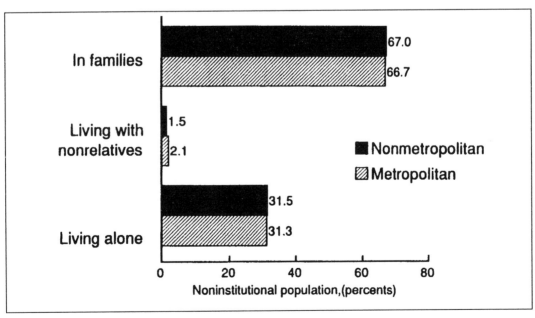

NOTE: For information about sampling error, see "Marital Status and Living Arrangements: March 1990," *Current Population Reports*, Series P-20, No. 450, Appendix B.
Source: Bureau of the Census, 1990 Current Population Survey, unpublished tabulations.

B1-6. Percent Distribution of Black Persons 65 Years of Age and Over, by Living Arrangement, According to Sex and Age: United States 1986

(Data are based on household interviews of the civilian noninstitutionalized population)

	Living arrangement		
Sex and age	Lives alone	Lives with others [1]	Lives with spouse
Both sexes	Percent distribution[2]		
65 years and over..............	32.1	28.5	39.4
75 years and over..............	38.5	35.6	25.9
85 years and over..............	44.9	45.7	9.4
Male			
65 years and over..............	22.2	18.2	59.6
75 years and over..............	28.0	27.5	44.5
85 years and over..............	22.7	53.6	23.6
Female			
65 years and over..............	38.7	35.4	25.9
75 years and over..............	44.5	40.3	15.2
85 years and over..............	51.6	43.3	5.1

[1]Lives with a nonrelative or a relative other than a spouse.
[2]May not add to 100 percent because of rounding.
Source: National Center for Health Statistics: Data from the National Health Interview Survey 1986 Functional Limitations Supplement.

B1-7. Percent of Persons 65 Years and Over Living Alone, by State: 1990

State	Number	Percent
United States	**8,824,845**	**28.2**
Alabama	154,191	29.5
Alaska	5,737	25.6
Arizona	119,287	24.9
Arkansas	103,386	29.5
California	818,520	26.1
Colorado	95,849	29.1
Connecticut	121,918	27.3
Delaware	21,566	26.7
District of Columbia	27,237	35.0
Florida	591,468	25.0
Georgia	185,027	28.3
Hawaii	20,933	16.7
Idaho	32,939	27.2
Illinois	423,740	29.5
Indiana	208,437	29.9
Iowa	130,964	30.7
Kansas	104,297	30.4
Kentucky	142,045	30.4
Louisiana	137,596	29.3
Maine	48,257	29.5
Maryland	135,318	26.1
Massachusetts	243,334	29.7
Michigan	317,659	28.7
Minnesota	167,001	30.5
Mississippi	98,180	30.6
Missouri	221,516	30.9
Montana	32,208	30.2
Nebraska	69,640	31.2
Nevada	33,244	26.0
New Hampshire	34,522	27.6
New Jersey	273,736	26.5
New Mexico	42,964	26.3
New York	700,016	29.6
North Carolina	226,384	28.1
North Dakota	28,021	30.8
Ohio	416,352	29.6
Oklahoma	131,237	30.9
Oregon	108,579	27.7
Pennsylvania	526,264	28.8
Rhode Island	44,627	29.6
South Carolina	109,012	27.5
South Dakota	31,560	30.8
Tennessee	178,077	28.8
Texas	472,029	27.5
Utah	38,320	25.6
Vermont	19,648	29.7
Virginia	178,575	26.9
Washington	162,520	28.3
West Virginia	84,405	31.4
Wisconsin	192,072	29.5
Wyoming	14,431	30.6

Source: U.S. Bureau of the Census, 1990 Census of Population and Housing, Summary Tape File 1A.

B1-8. Persons Living Alone, by Age and Sex: 1990, 1980, 1970, and 1960

(Numbers in thousands)

Age	1990	1980	1970[1]	1960[1]	Percent distribution			
					1990	1980	1970[1]	1960[1]
Both sexes	22,999	18,296	10,851	7,063	100.0	100.0	100.0	100.0
15 to 24 years	1,210	1,726	556	234	5.3	9.4	5.1	3.3
25 to 34 years	3,972	3,259	893	} 1,212	17.3	17.8	8.2	} 17.2
35 to 44 years	3,138	1,470	711		13.6	8.0	6.6	
45 to 54 years	2,422	1,705	1,303	} 2,720	10.5	9.3	12.0	} 38.5
55 to 64 years	3,080	2,809	2,319		13.4	15.4	21.4	
65 to 74 years	4,350	3,851	2,815	1,834	18.9	21.0	25.9	26.0
75 years and over	4,825	3,477	2,256	1,064	21.0	19.0	20.8	15.1
Median age	57.5	58.5	63.5	60.3	(X)	(X)	(X)	(X)
Men	9,049	6,966	3,532	2,628	100.0	100.0	100.0	100.0
15 to 24 years	674	947	274	124	7.4	13.6	7.8	4.7
25 to 34 years	2,395	1,975	535	} 686	26.5	28.4	15.1	} 26.1
35 to 44 years	1,836	945	398		20.3	13.6	11.3	
45 to 54 years	1,167	804	513	} 965	12.9	11.5	14.5	} 36.7
55 to 64 years	1,036	809	639		11.4	11.6	18.1	
65 to 74 years	1,042	775	611	527	11.5	11.1	17.3	20.1
75 years and over	901	711	563	326	10.0	10.2	15.9	12.4
Median age	42.5	40.9	55.7	55.4	(X)	(X)	(X)	(X)
Women	13,950	11,330	7,319	4,436	100.0	100.0	100.0	100.0
15 to 24 years	536	779	282	110	3.8	6.9	3.9	2.5
25 to 34 years	1,578	1,284	358	} 526	11.3	11.3	4.9	} 11.9
35 to 44 years	1,303	525	313		9.3	4.6	4.3	
45 to 54 years	1,256	901	790	} 1,755	9.0	8.0	10.8	} 39.6
55 to 64 years	2,044	2,000	1,680		14.7	17.7	23.0	
65 to 74 years	3,309	3,076	2,204	1,307	23.7	27.1	30.1	29.5
75 years and over	3,924	2,766	1,693	738	28.1	24.4	23.1	16.6
Median age	65.8	65.6	66.1	63.0	(X)	(X)	(X)	(X)

X Not applicable.

[1] 1970 and 1960 data are for persons 14 years and over.

NOTE: Medians are calculated using detailed age distribution not shown.

Source of 1960 data: U.S. Bureau of the Census, 1960 Census of Population, PC(2)-4B, Persons by Family Characteristics, table 15.

B1-9. Marital Status of Persons 15 Years Old and Over, by Age, Sex, Region, and Race: March 1991

(Numbers in thousands. For meaning of symbols, see text)

Race, region, and marital status	Total, 15 years and over Male	Female	15 to 24 years Male	Female	25 to 34 years Male	Female	35 to 44 years Male	Female	45 to 54 years Male	Female	55 to 64 years Male	Female	65 years and over Male	Female
BLACK														
United States														
Total................	10,074	12,124	2,448	2,654	2,496	2,938	1,931	2,341	1,198	1,496	970	1,178	1,031	1,516
Percent............	100.0	100.0	100.0	100.0	100.0	100.0	100.0	100.0	100.0	100.0	100.0	100.0	100.0	100.0
Never married..........	44.8	38.7	93.9	89.8	53.4	48.6	25.5	23.7	15.1	10.4	16.0	7.5	5.2	5.1
Married, spouse present..	36.7	29.8	5.4	6.8	33.0	32.8	50.2	40.4	58.7	43.8	51.9	39.5	55.2	26.4
Married, spouse absent..	6.4	8.6	0.3	2.6	7.5	9.7	9.9	11.9	8.0	14.3	8.2	10.5	8.1	4.7
Widowed................	3.3	11.9	0.1	0.1	0.2	1.0	0.9	3.7	1.5	10.2	5.9	28.4	22.5	55.4
Divorced..............	8.8	11.0	0.4	0.7	5.9	7.9	13.4	20.3	16.6	21.3	18.1	14.0	9.1	8.3
South														
Total................	5,615	6,637	1,349	1,430	1,427	1,599	1,085	1,256	628	797	555	677	570	877
Percent............	100.0	100.0	100.0	100.0	100.0	100.0	100.0	100.0	100.0	100.0	100.0	100.0	100.0	100.0
Never married..........	43.7	36.3	92.4	87.7	51.8	43.2	26.1	21.3	13.9	10.9	13.5	8.7	4.4	5.3
Married, spouse present..	38.7	32.5	6.4	8.3	35.6	38.7	50.2	42.2	62.8	47.7	53.2	40.6	59.9	26.6
Married, spouse absent..	6.2	7.7	0.5	3.0	6.5	9.1	10.8	9.6	7.9	12.7	9.6	9.4	5.2	4.7
Widowed................	3.7	12.5	-	0.1	0.2	1.1	0.8	4.2	1.1	8.9	8.5	28.7	24.4	55.7
Divorced..............	7.7	11.1	0.7	0.9	5.9	7.9	12.2	22.7	14.2	19.8	15.1	12.6	6.1	7.7
North and West														
Total................	4,459	5,487	1,100	1,224	1,069	1,339	846	1,085	569	699	414	501	461	638
Percent............	100.0	100.0	100.0	100.0	100.0	100.0	100.0	100.0	100.0	100.0	100.0	100.0	100.0	100.0
Never married..........	46.2	41.6	95.7	92.1	55.5	54.9	24.8	26.5	16.5	9.8	19.2	5.9	6.2	4.9
Married, spouse present..	34.3	26.6	4.1	5.0	29.6	25.8	50.2	38.4	54.0	39.4	50.1	38.0	49.4	26.2
Married, spouse absent..	6.6	9.7	-	2.2	8.8	10.4	8.9	14.6	8.2	16.2	6.2	12.1	11.7	4.8
Widowed................	2.8	11.2	0.2	-	0.2	0.8	1.2	3.1	2.0	11.6	2.3	28.0	20.0	54.9
Divorced..............	10.1	11.0	-	0.6	5.9	8.0	14.9	17.4	19.3	23.0	22.2	15.9	12.7	9.2
WHITE														
United States														
Total................	79,555	85,012	14,161	14,107	18,054	17,848	16,434	16,471	10,748	11,282	8,923	9,641	11,235	15,663
Percent............	100.0	100.0	100.0	100.0	100.0	100.0	100.0	100.0	100.0	100.0	100.0	100.0	100.0	100.0
Never married..........	28.0	20.8	87.9	76.5	34.0	21.3	12.6	8.6	6.7	4.8	4.8	3.2	4.3	5.2
Married, spouse present..	60.1	56.1	10.6	19.8	56.2	64.9	72.5	72.5	78.1	72.2	82.0	70.8	76.2	41.0
Married, spouse absent..	2.3	2.9	0.9	1.9	2.8	4.4	3.2	4.2	3.0	3.1	2.2	2.2	1.5	1.2
Widowed................	2.5	11.2	-	-	0.1	0.5	0.3	1.2	1.0	4.5	2.9	13.4	13.9	47.6
Divorced..............	7.1	8.9	0.6	1.7	6.9	8.9	11.4	13.5	11.3	15.4	8.0	10.4	4.2	5.0
South														
Total................	25,430	27,456	4,420	4,650	5,708	5,738	5,219	5,193	3,526	3,712	2,943	3,141	3,613	5,023
Percent............	100.0	100.0	100.0	100.0	100.0	100.0	100.0	100.0	100.0	100.0	100.0	100.0	100.0	100.0
Never married..........	24.8	18.3	83.8	72.3	28.7	17.1	10.6	6.3	5.2	3.2	3.9	1.7	2.6	3.5
Married, spouse present..	63.0	58.1	14.0	22.9	60.0	68.0	74.5	74.5	79.6	74.5	84.0	71.2	77.7	42.2
Married, spouse absent..	2.4	3.2	1.2	2.7	3.1	4.7	3.5	4.4	2.8	3.4	1.9	2.3	1.5	0.9
Widowed................	2.3	11.5	-	0.1	0.1	0.6	0.1	1.3	0.9	4.4	2.5	14.6	13.1	48.7
Divorced..............	7.5	8.9	1.0	2.1	8.1	9.6	11.3	13.4	11.5	14.5	7.7	10.2	5.1	4.8
North and West														
Total................	54,125	57,556	9,741	9,457	12,346	12,109	11,215	11,278	7,222	7,571	5,979	6,501	7,622	10,640
Percent............	100.0	100.0	100.0	100.0	100.0	100.0	100.0	100.0	100.0	100.0	100.0	100.0	100.0	100.0
Never married..........	29.5	22.0	89.7	78.6	36.5	23.3	13.5	9.6	7.5	5.7	5.2	3.9	5.0	6.0
Married, spouse present..	58.7	55.2	9.0	18.4	54.4	63.4	71.5	71.5	77.3	71.1	80.9	70.7	75.5	40.5
Married, spouse absent..	2.3	2.8	0.8	1.6	2.7	4.2	3.1	4.1	3.1	2.9	2.4	2.1	1.5	1.4
Widowed................	2.6	11.1	-	-	0.1	0.5	0.5	1.2	1.0	4.5	3.2	12.8	14.2	47.1
Divorced..............	6.8	8.9	0.5	1.4	6.3	8.6	11.5	13.6	11.1	15.9	8.2	10.5	3.8	5.0

B1-10. Marital Status of Older People, by Age, Sex, Race, and Hispanic Origin: March 1989

(Excludes people in institutions) Marital status	65+		65 to 74		75 to 84		85+	
	Men	Women	Men	Women	Men	Women	Men	Women
ALL RACES								
Total (thousands)	12,078	16,944	7,880	9,867	3,506	5,669	693	1,408
Percent	100.0	100.0	100.0	100.0	100.0	100.0	100.0	100.0
Never married	4.7	5.0	4.9	4.5	4.6	5.8	3.2	5.6
Married, spouse present	74.3	40.1	78.4	51.4	70.4	28.1	48.2	9.1
Married, spouse absent .	2.7	1.6	2.7	1.8	2.3	1.5	4.4	0.9
Widowed	14.0	48.7	8.9	36.6	19.7	61.5	42.1	82.3
Divorced........................	4.3	4.5	5.1	5.7	2.9	3.0	2.1	2.1
WHITE								
Total (thousands)	10,798	15,204	7,050	8,767	3,136	5,174	612	1,263
Percent	100.0	100.0	100.0	100.0	100.0	100.0	100.0	100.0
Never married	4.6	5.1	4.8	4.5	4.5	6.0	3.1	5.7
Married, spouse present	76.3	41.2	80.6	53.3	72.3	28.7	47.9	8.8
Married, spouse absent .	2.1	1.2	2.0	1.3	1.6	1.1	4.8	0.6
Widowed	13.2	48.1	8.1	35.5	19.2	61.0	41.8	82.7
Divorced........................	3.8	4.4	4.5	5.4	2.4	3.2	2.4	2.2
BLACK								
Total (thousands)	981	1,455	619	913	300	416	62	126
Percent	100.0	100.0	100.0	100.0	100.0	100.0	100.0	100.0
Never married	4.5	4.5	4.0	4.3	6.0	4.6	(B)	5.7
Married, spouse present	56.0	27.9	58.6	33.4	50.9	20.8	(B)	12.2
Married, spouse absent .	8.3	5.8	8.6	6.0	9.2	5.9	(B)	4.2
Widowed	21.4	55.3	17.6	47.1	24.7	66.9	(B)	76.3
Divorced........................	9.8	6.5	11.1	9.2	9.2	1.9	(B)	1.6
HISPANIC ORIGIN*								
Total (thousands)	447	558	301	350	120	176	26	31
Percent	100.0	100.0	100.0	100.0	100.0	100.0	100.0	100.0
Never married	6.6	8.2	6.4	6.8	6.0	11.0	(B)	(B)
Married, spouse present	65.6	37.6	69.7	47.5	62.8	23.1	(B)	(B)
Married, spouse absent .	7.7	2.5	8.5	2.4	6.6	2.9	(B)	(B)
Widowed	15.1	43.6	9.3	33.6	21.4	57.8	(B)	(B)
Divorced........................	5.0	8.1	6.1	9.7	3.2	5.2	(B)	(B)

(B) Base less than 75,000

*People of Hispanic origin may be of any race.

NOTE: Percentage distributions may not add to 100.0 due to rounding.

Source: U.S. Bureau of the Census, "Marital Status and Living Arrangements: March 1989," *Current Population Reports,* Series P-20, No. 445 (June 1990).

B1-11. Marital Status of Persons 65 Years and Over, by Age and Sex: 1960 to 2040

(Percentage distribution; civilian noninstitutional population for March 1960 to 1990;
Social Security Area population January 1, 2000 to 2040)

Age and year	Male				Female			
	Never married	Married[1]	Widowed	Divorced	Never married	Married[1]	Widowed	Divorced
65 Years and Over								
1960.........................	7.1	72.5	18.8	1.6	8.5	37.1	52.9	1.5
1970.........................	7.5	73.1	17.1	2.3	7.7	35.4	54.4	2.3
1980.........................	4.9	78.0	13.5	3.6	5.9	39.5	51.2	3.4
1990.........................	4.2	76.5	14.2	5.0	4.9	41.5	48.6	5.1
2000.........................	4.5	75.0	14.5	6.0	4.2	41.2	46.6	8.0
2020.........................	6.1	74.2	11.9	7.8	5.0	43.9	36.7	14.3
2040.........................	10.4	69.2	12.9	7.4	7.3	42.2	37.2	13.2
65 to 74 Years								
1960.........................	6.7	78.9	12.7	1.7	8.4	45.6	44.4	1.7
1970.........................	8.0	78.0	11.3	2.7	7.8	45.2	44.0	3.0
1980.........................	5.2	82.1	8.4	4.3	5.6	50.0	40.4	4.0
1990.........................	4.7	80.2	9.2	6.0	4.6	53.2	36.1	6.2
2000.........................	5.2	79.5	8.5	6.8	3.9	55.6	30.1	10.4
2020.........................	7.8	76.5	6.9	8.8	6.0	55.9	21.8	16.3
2040.........................	12.6	72.9	6.4	8.1	7.7	57.9	21.5	12.9
75 Years and Over								
1960.........................	7.8	59.1	31.6	1.5	8.6	21.8	68.3	1.2
1970.........................	6.6	64.3	27.7	1.4	7.5	20.6	70.3	1.3
1980.........................	4.2	69.8	23.7	2.2	6.4	23.4	67.9	2.4
1990.........................	3.4	69.9	23.7	3.1	5.4	25.4	65.6	3.6
2000.........................	3.5	68.7	22.9	4.9	4.4	27.7	62.1	5.8
2020.........................	3.1	69.9	21.0	5.9	3.9	28.9	55.5	11.7
2040.........................	8.2	65.4	19.6	6.7	7.0	30.8	48.7	13.5

[1]Includes separated.

Source: Data for 1960: U.S. Bureau of the Census, "Marital Status and Family Status: March 1960," *Current Population Reports,* Series P-20, No. 105, U.S. Government Office, Washington DC, November 1960, table 1. Data for 1970 and 1980: unpublished revised data that replaces data published in appropriate P-20 report. Data for 1990: Arlene F. Sauter, U.S. Bureau of the Census, "Marital Status and Living Arrangements: March 1990," *Current Population Reports,* Series P-20, No. 450, U.S. Government Printing Office, Washington, DC, May 1991, table 1. Projections for 1990-2040: Social Security Administration, Alice Wade, "Social Security Area Population Projections: 1989," Actuarial Study No. 105, SSA Pub. No. 11-11552, June 1989, Alternative II (intermediate projections), pp. 33-35.

B1-12. Percent of Older Men and Women Widowed, by Age, Race, and Hispanic Origin: 1989

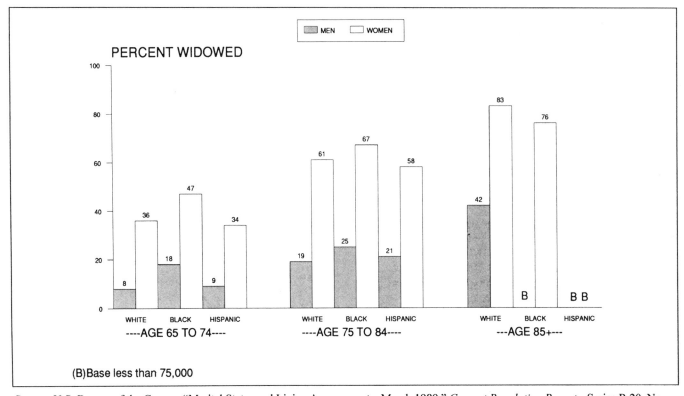

Source: U.S. Bureau of the Census, "Marital Status and Living Arrangements: March 1989," *Current Population Reports,* Series P-20, No. 445 (June 1990).

B1-13. Percent Never Married, by Age, Sex, Race, and Hispanic Origin: 1992, 1980, and 1970

Age	Women			Men		
	1992	1980	1970	1992	1980	1970
ALL RACES						
20 to 24 years	65.7	50.2	35.8	80.3	68.8	54.7
25 to 29 years	33.2	20.9	10.5	48.7	33.1	19.1
30 to 34 years	18.8	9.5	6.2	29.4	15.9	9.4
35 to 39 years	12.6	6.2	5.4	18.4	7.8	7.2
40 to 44 years	8.4	4.8	4.9	9.2	7.1	6.3
45 to 54 years	5.3	4.7	4.9	7.3	6.1	7.5
55 to 64 years	4.0	4.5	6.8	5.6	5.3	7.8
65 years and over........................	4.9	5.9	7.7	4.2	4.9	7.5
White						
20 to 24 years	62.7	47.2	34.6	78.5	67.0	54.4
25 to 29 years	28.5	18.3	9.2	45.8	31.4	17.8
30 to 34 years	15.1	8.1	5.5	26.8	14.2	9.2
35 to 39 years ....'...............	9.7	5.2	4.6	16.3	6.6	6.1
40 to 44 years ....,.....	7.3	4.3	4.8	8.7	6.7	5.7
45 to 54 years	4.5	4.4	4.9	6.7	5.6	7.1
55 to 64 years	3.5	4.4	7.0	4.9	5.2	7.6
65 years and over........................	4.8	6.1	8.0	4.0	4.8	7.4
Black						
20 to 24 years	80.3	68.5	43.5	88.3	79.3	56.1
25 to 29 years	60.4	37.2	18.8	65.2	44.2	28.4
30 to 34 years	41.0	19.0	10.8	47.8	30.0	9.2
35 to 39 years	32.1	12.2	12.1	36.0	18.5	15.8
40 to 44 years	16.5	9.0	6.9	13.9	10.8	11.2
45 to 54 years	11.5	7.7	4.4	14.4	11.7	10.4
55 to 64 years	8.2	5.7	4.7	12.0	5.9	9.1
65 years and over........................	5.7	4.5	4.2	6.5	5.5	5.7
HISPANIC ORIGIN*						
20 to 24 years	57.2	42.8	33.4	71.8	61.8	49.9
25 to 29 years	28.5	22.5	13.7	45.7	28.9	19.4
30 to 34 years	20.2	11.2	8.4	27.0	12.1	11.0
35 to 39 years	13.7	6.6	6.9	20.8	5.8	7.6
40 to 44 years	8.8	7.9	6.3	10.9	6.5	7.1
45 to 54 years	8.4	7.1	6.1	10.7	6.4	6.2
55 to 64 years	5.0	7.8	6.7	5.9	4.3	6.0
65 years and over........................	7.3	5.4	7.7	3.7	9.7	8.8

*Persons of Hispanic origin may be of any race.
Source of Hispanic data for 1970: 1970 Census of Population, *U.S. Summary*, table 203.

B1-14. Ratio of Unmarried Men Per 100 Unmarried Women, by Age: 1992, 1980, and 1970

[Numbers in thousands. Unmarried includes never married, widowed, and divorced]

Sex and age	1992	1980	1970
Men, unmarried...............................	**37,583**	**30,134**	**23,450**
15 to 24 years........................	15,477	17,282	15,212
25 to 29 years........................	5,380	3,657	1,423
30 to 34 years........................	4,109	2,036	692
35 to 39 years........................	3,027	1,082	557
40 to 44 years........................	2,030	906	586
45 to 64 years........................	4,477	2,983	2,740
65 years and over	3,083	2,188	2,239
Women, unmarried	**44,283**	**36,950**	**29,618**
15 to 24 years........................	13,964	15,166	13,576
25 to 29 years........................	4,193	2,900	1,043
30 to 34 years........................	3,404	1,925	678
35 to 39 years........................	2,787	1,337	713
40 to 44 years........................	2,438	1,088	831
45 to 64 years........................	7,047	5,923	5,342
65 years and over	10,449	8,610	7,432
Ratio.....................................	**85**	**82**	**79**
15 to 24 years........................	111	114	112
25 to 29 years........................	128	126	136
30 to 34 years........................	121	106	102
35 to 39 years........................	109	81	78
40 to 44 years........................	83	83	71
45 to 64 years........................	64	50	51
65 years and over	30	25	30

B2. Households, Housing, and Informal Supports

B2-1. Adults in Unmarried-Couple Households, by Age, Sex, and Marital Status: 1990

(Numbers in thousands)

Male partner		Female partner				
	Total	Under 25 years	25-34 years	35-44 years	45-64 years	65 years and over
Total.......................	2,856	788	1,170	494	320	83
Under 25 years	530	381	141	8	3	-
25 to 34 years	1,189	333	726	113	15	3
35 to 44 years	618	55	236	270	55	2
45 to 64 years	390	19	54	100	195	24
65 years and over	129	4	13	4	55	54
Percent	100.0	27.6	41.0	17.3	11.2	2.9
Under 25 years	18.6	13.3	4.9	0.3	0.1	-
25 to 34 years	41.6	11.7	25.4	4.0	0.5	0.1
35 to 44 years	21.6	1.9	8.3	9.5	1.9	0.1
45 to 64 years	13.7	0.7	1.9	3.5	6.8	0.8
65 years and over	4.5	0.1	0.5	0.1	1.9	1.9

Male partner	Total	Never married	Married		Widowed	Divorced
			Separated	Other		
Total.......................	2,856	1,595	149	8	142	963
Never married	1,584	1,178	62	3	30	311
Married: Separated....................	184	70	43	-	18	55
Other	20	7	-	3	1	8
Widowed	95	27	1	2	34	32
Divorced	973	285	44	-	60	555
Percent	100.0	55.8	5.2	0.3	5.0	33.7
Never married	55.5	41.2	2.2	0.1	1.1	10.9
Married: Separated....................	6.4	2.5	1.5	-	0.6	1.9
Other	0.7	0.2	-	0.1	-	0.3
Widowed	3.3	0.9	-	0.1	1.2	1.1
Divorced	34.1	10.0	1.5	-	2.1	19.4

- Represents zero.

B2-2. Size of Households for Householders 65 Years and Over, by Age, Race, and Hispanic Origin: March 1990

(In thousands; noninstitutional population)

Size of household	All ages	Number				Percent			
		65 years and over	65 to 74 years	75 to 84 years	85 years and over	65 years and over	65 to 74 years	75 to 84 years	85 years and over
All Races									
All households	93,347	20,156	11,733	6,856	1,567	100.0	100.0	100.0	100.0
One-person household	22,999	9,175	4,350	3,774	1,051	45.5	37.1	55.0	67.1
Two-person households	30,114	8,927	5,847	2,641	439	44.3	49.8	38.5	28.0
Three-person households	16,128	1,328	971	310	47	6.6	8.3	4.5	3.0
Four-or-more-person households ..	24,107	728	566	131	31	3.6	4.8	1.9	2.0
Persons per household	2.63	1.75	1.89	1.57	1.44	(X)	(X)	(X)	(X)
White									
All households	80,163	18,144	10,477	6,244	1,423	100.0	100.0	100.0	100.0
One-person household	19,879	8,290	3,841	3,475	974	45.7	36.7	55.7	68.4
Two-person households	26,714	8,235	5,411	2,431	393	45.4	51.6	38.9	27.6
Three-person households	13,585	1,108	809	261	38	6.1	7.7	4.2	2.7
Four-or-more-person households ..	19,985	511	417	77	17	2.8	4.0	1.2	1.2
Persons per household	2.58	1.71	1.85	1.54	1.4	(X)	(X)	(X)	(X)
Black									
All households	10,486	1,696	1,028	543	125	100.0	100.0	100.0	100.0
One-person household	2,610	776	435	274	67	45.8	42.3	50.5	53.6
Two-person households	2,721	559	335	183	41	33.0	32.6	33.7	32.8
Three-person households	2,043	179	130	41	8	10.6	12.6	7.6	6.4
Four-or-more-person households ..	3,113	182	129	45	8	10.7	12.5	8.3	6.4
Persons per household	2.88	2.08	2.24	1.86	1.78	(X)	(X)	(X)	(X)
Hispanic Origin[1]									
All households	5,933	671	463	168	40	100.0	100.0	100.0	(B)
One-person household	856	222	125	76	21	33.1	27.0	45.2	(B)
Two-person households	1,292	278	204	64	10	41.4	44.1	38.1	(B)
Three-person households	1,139	84	67	13	4	12.5	14.5	7.7	(B)
Four-or-more-person households ..	2,646	88	68	14	6	13.1	14.7	8.3	(B)
Persons per household	3.47	2.21	2.32	1.95	(B)	(X)	(X)	(X)	(X)

Source: Steve Rawlings, U.S. Bureau of the Census, "Household and Family Characteristics: March 1990 and 1989," *Current Population Reports*, Series P-20, No. 447. U.S. Government Printing Office, Washington, DC, 1990, table 17.

B2-3. Grandparents Maintaining Families with Grandchildren Present: 1991

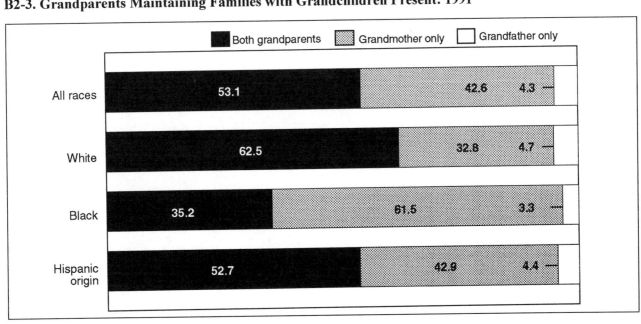

B2-4. Support Ratios of Elderly Persons, by Age, Race, and Hispanic Origin: 1990 and 2050

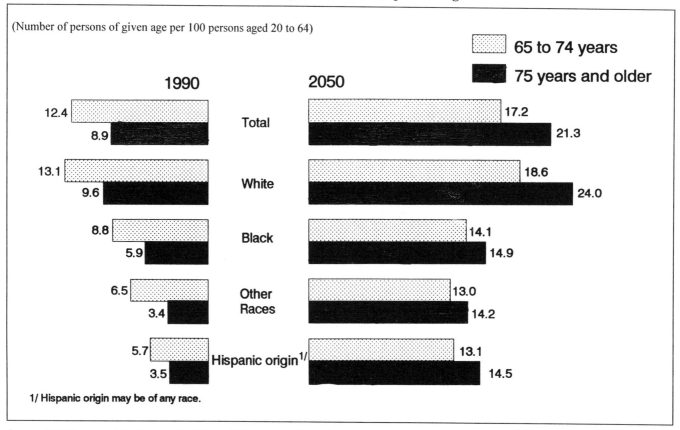

(Number of persons of given age per 100 persons aged 20 to 64)

65 to 74 years
75 years and older

1990   **2050**

	65 to 74 (1990)	75+ (1990)	65 to 74 (2050)	75+ (2050)
Total	12.4	8.9	17.2	21.3
White	13.1	9.6	18.6	24.0
Black	8.8	5.9	14.1	14.9
Other Races	6.5	3.4	13.0	14.2
Hispanic origin[1]	5.7	3.5	13.1	14.5

1/ Hispanic origin may be of any race.

Source: U.S. Bureau of the Census, 1990 from 1990 Census of Population and Housing, Series CPH-L-74, "Modified and Actual Age, Sex, Race, and Hispanic Origin Data"; 2050 from Jennifer C. Day, "Projections of the Population of the United States by Age, Sex, and Race: 1992 to 2050," *Current Population Reports*, P25-1092, U.S. Government Printing Office, Washington, DC, 1992 (middle series projections).

B2-5. Percent Distributions of Caregivers, by Relationship to 65+ Individual with Activity Limitations: 1985

Age of recipient and relationship of caregiver	Care recipient	
	Male	Female
65 to 74:		
Spouse	45	18
Offspring	21	29
Other relative	21	33
Formal	13	20
75 to 84:		
Spouse	35	8
Offspring	23	35
Other relative	25	36
Formal	19	23
85 +:		
Spouse	20	2
Offspring	34	39
Other relative	27	36
Formal	19	23
All 65 +:		
Spouse	37	10
Offspring	24	34
Other relative	23	35
Formal	16	21

B2-6. Homeownership Rate for the Elderly, by Residence: 1989

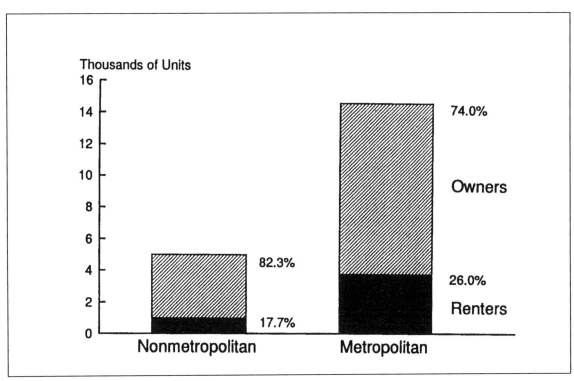

Source: Department of Housing and Urban Development, 1989 American Housing Survey.

B2-7. Percent of Owned Houses Owned Free and Clear (Nonmortgaged) for the Elderly, by Residence: 1989

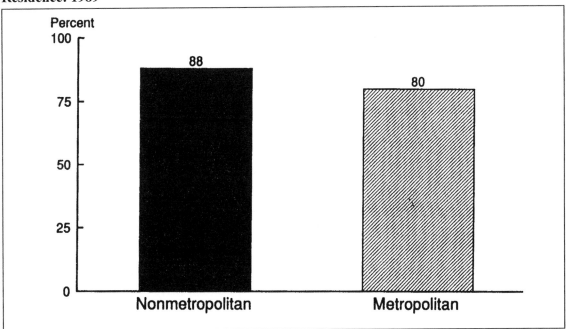

Source: Department of Housing and Urban Development, 1989 American Housing Survey.

B2-8. Housing Tenure of Aged Families and Unrelated Individuals, by Poverty Status: 1988

Family and poverty status	Total (thousands)	Percent distribution					
		Total	Own housing	No cash rent	Rent housing		
					Total	Publicly supported	Not publicly supported
Families with any member age 65+	12,365	100.0	86.4	1.1	12.5	1.9	10.6
Below poverty level in 1987....	874	100.0	67.8	3.6	28.6	8.7	19.9
Above poverty level in 1987 ...	11,492	100.0	87.8	1.0	11.2	1.3	9.9
Unrelated individuals..................	9,330	100.0	60.8	3.6	35.6	11.9	23.7
Below poverty level in 1987....	2,241	100.0	50.5	4.9	44.6	23.3	21.4
Above poverty level in 1987 ...	7,089	100.0	64.0	3.2	32.8	8.3	24.5

Source: March 1988 Current Population Survey, unpublished data.

B3. Education

B3-1. Years of School Completed, by Selected Characteristic: 1991

(For persons 25 years old and over. As of March. In percent, except number of persons.)

CHARACTERISTIC	Population (1,000)	PERCENT OF POPULATION WITH—		
		4 years of high school or more	1 or more years of college	4 or more years of college
Total persons.	158,694	78.4	39.8	21.4
Age:				
25 to 34 years old.	42,905	86.1	45.3	23.7
35 to 44 years old.	38,665	87.7	50.2	27.5
45 to 54 years old.	25,686	81.2	41.1	23.2
55 to 64 years old.	21,346	71.9	31.4	16.9
65 to 74 years old.	18,237	63.5	25.3	13.2
75 years old or over	11,855	49.0	20.8	10.5
Sex: Male.	75,487	78.5	42.5	24.3
Female.	83,207	78.3	37.4	18.8
Race: White	136,299	79.9	40.8	22.2
Black	17,096	66.7	29.0	11.5
Other	5,299	78.7	49.0	33.5
Hispanic origin: Hispanic.	11,208	51.3	22.0	9.7
Non-Hispanic.	147,486	80.5	41.2	22.3
Region: Northeast	33,293	80.3	39.7	23.7
Midwest	38,230	80.7	38.0	20.0
South	54,217	74.2	36.9	19.4
West	32,954	80.9	46.9	24.3
Marital Status:				
Never married	22,091	81.8	47.4	27.7
Married, spouse present.	101,706	81.4	41.7	23.0
Married, spouse absent	5,820	66.8	28.8	12.3
Separated	4,349	68.2	27.8	10.9
Widowed	13,665	53.6	19.6	8.3
Divorced	15,413	80.5	38.7	17.1
Civilian labor force status:				
Employed	97,874	87.3	48.4	27.3
Unemployed	6,203	73.1	30.0	12.6
Not in the labor force	53,844	62.6	25.1	11.7

Source: U.S. Bureau of the Census, *Current Population Reports,* Series P-20, No. 462

B3-2. Selected Measures of Educational Attainment for People Age 25+ and 65+: 1950 to 1989

Year and age group	Percent with:		Median years of school
	High school education	Four or more years of college	
1989*			
25+ years	76.9	21.1	12.7
65+ years	54.9	11.1	12.1
1980			
25+ years	66.5	16.2	12.5
65+ years	38.8	8.2	10.0
1970			
25+ years	52.3	10.7	12.1
65+ years	27.1	5.5	8.7
1960			
25+ years	41.1	7.7	10.5
65+ years	19.1	3.7	8.3
1950			
25+ years	33.4	6.0	9.3
65+ years	17.0	3.4	8.3

*Excludes people in institutions.

Sources: U.S. Bureau of the Census, unpublished data from the March 1989 Current Population Survey; U.S. Bureau of the Census, "Detailed Population Characteristics," *1980 Census of Population,* PC80-1-D1, United States Summary (March 1984); U.S. Bureau of the Census, "Detailed Characteristics," *1970 Census of Population,* PC(1)-D1, United States Summary (February 1973); U.S. Bureau of the Census, "Characteristics of the Population," *1960 Census of Population,* Volume 1, Part 1, United States Summary, Chapter D (1964).

B3-3. Median Years of School for People 25+ and 65+: 1950 to 1989

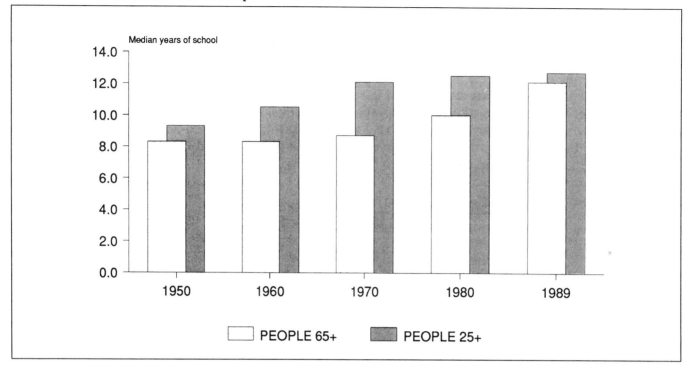

Sources: U.S. Bureau of the Census, unpublished data from the March 1989 Current Population Survey; U.S. Bureau of the Census, "Detailed Population Characteristics," *1980 Census of Population,* PC80-1-D1, United States Summary (March 1984); U.S. Bureau of the Census, "Detailed Characteristics," *1970 Census of Population,* PC (1)-D1, United States Summary (February 1973); U.S. Bureau of the Census, "Characteristics of the Population," *1960 Census of Population,* Volume 1, Part 1, United States Summary, Chapter D (1964).

B3-4. Educational Attainment of People Age 65+ in the United States, by Regions: 1987

Area	Median school years completed	High school graduates (percent)	Four or more years of college (percent)
United States	12.0	51	10
Regions:....................................			
Northeast	12.0	50	10
Midwest.................................	12.0	50	8
South.....................................	11.4	47	10
West......................................	12.3	62	13

Source: U.S. Bureau of the Census, "Educational Attainment in the United States: March 1987 and 1986," *Current Population Reports,* Series P-20, No. 428 (August 1988) and errata sheet.

B3-5. Educational Attainment of Elderly Persons, by Residence: 1989

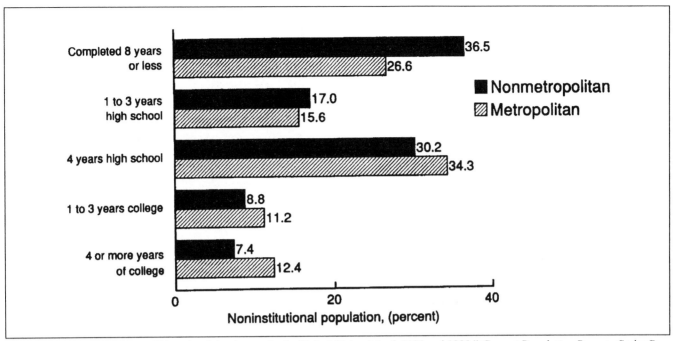

Source: Bureau of the Census, "Educational Attainment in the United States: March 1989 and 1988," *Current Population Reports*, Series P-20, No. 451.

B3-6. Measures of Educational Attainment, by Age Group, Sex, Race, and Hispanic Origin: March 1989

(excludes people in institutions)

Measure of educational attainment and age	Sex			White			Black			Hispanic origin*		
	Total	Men	Women	Total	Men	Women	Total	Men	Women	Total	Men	Women
Median years of school completed:												
25+	12.7	12.8	12.6	12.7	12.8	12.7	12.4	12.4	12.4	12.0	12.0	12.0
60 to 64	12.4	12.5	12.4	12.5	12.5	12.4	10.7	10.6	10.7	9.3	9.6	8.9
65+	12.1	12.1	12.2	12.2	12.2	12.2	8.5	8.1	8.7	8.0	8.1	8.0
65 to 69	12.3	12.3	12.3	12.4	12.4	12.4	9.5	9.1	9.8	8.4	8.5	8.3
70 to 74	12.2	12.2	12.2	12.3	12.3	12.3	8.4	8.2	8.6	8.0	8.1	7.9
75+	10.9	10.5	11.3	11.6	11.1	11.9	7.8	7.0	8.2	7.1	7.0	7.1
Percent with a high school education:												
25+	77	77	77	78	79	78	65	64	65	51	51	51
60 to 64	66	65	67	69	68	71	39	43	37	34	37	31
65+	55	54	56	58	57	59	25	22	26	28	26	29
65 to 69	63	61	65	67	65	68	31	28	33	33	31	35
70 to 74	57	56	58	60	59	62	21	20	22	25	21	29
75+	46	44	48	49	47	50	21	18	23	23	21	24
Percent with four or more years of college:												
25+	21	25	18	22	25	19	12	12	12	10	11	9
60 to 64	14	19	10	15	21	10	5	7	4	6	5	7
65+	11	14	9	12	15	10	5	4	5	6	7	5
65 to 69	13	16	10	13	17	10	5	3	6	9	9	9
70 to 74	11	13	9	11	13	10	3	3	3	3	3	3
75+	10	12	9	11	13	9	6	4	6	4	7	3

*People of Hispanic origin may be of any race.
Source: U.S. Bureau of the Census, unpublished data from the March 1989 Current Population Survey.

B3-7. Years of School Completed, by Age, Race, and Hispanic Origin: March 1989

(In thousands; noninstitutional population)

Age, race, and Hispanic origin	Total	0 to 8 years	High school, 1 to 3 years	High school, 4 years	College, 1 to 3 years	College, 4 years or more	Percent high school graduates
ALL RACES							
Number							
25 years and over..................	154,155	17,922	17,719	59,336	26,614	32,565	76.9
25 to 64 years.........................	125,133	9,451	13,093	49,701	23,546	29,342	82.0
65 years and over.....................	29,022	8,471	4,626	9,635	3,068	3,223	54.9
65 to 69 years.....................	10,018	2,161	1,548	3,837	1,210	1,262	63.0
70 to 74 years.....................	7,729	1,937	1,386	2,747	838	821	57.0
75 years and over..................	11,276	4,374	1,691	3,051	1,019	1,140	46.2
Percent							
25 years and over..................	100.0	11.6	11.5	38.5	17.3	21.1	(X)
25 to 64 years.........................	100.0	7.6	10.5	39.7	18.8	23.4	(X)
65 years and over.....................	100.0	29.2	15.9	33.2	10.6	11.1	(X)
65 to 69 years.....................	100.0	21.6	15.5	38.3	12.1	12.6	(X)
70 to 74 years.....................	100.0	25.1	17.9	35.5	10.8	10.6	(X)
75 years and over..................	100.0	38.8	15.0	27.1	9.0	10.1	(X)
BLACK							
Number							
25 years and over..................	16,395	2,839	2,959	5,988	2,679	1,929	64.6
25 to 64 years.........................	13,959	1,443	2,518	5,602	2,578	1,816	71.6
65 years and over.....................	2,436	1,396	441	386	101	113	24.6
65 to 69 years.....................	908	414	214	192	43	44	30.8
70 to 74 years.....................	624	359	131	84	31	18	21.3
75 years and over..................	904	623	95	111	25	49	20.6
Percent							
25 years and over..................	100.0	17.3	18.0	36.5	16.3	11.8	(X)
25 to 64 years.........................	100.0	10.3	18.0	40.1	18.5	13.0	(X)
65 years and over.....................	100.0	57.3	18.1	15.8	4.1	4.6	(X)
65 to 69 years.....................	100.0	45.6	23.6	21.1	4.7	4.8	(X)
70 to 74 years.....................	100.0	57.5	21.0	13.5	5.0	2.9	(X)
75 years and over..................	100.0	68.9	10.5	12.3	2.8	5.4	(X)
HISPANIC ORIGIN[1]							
Number							
25 years and over..................	10,438	3,589	1,539	2,907	1,373	1,030	50.9
25 to 64 years.........................	9,433	2,947	1,455	2,732	1,329	971	53.3
65 years and over.....................	1,005	642	84	175	44	59	27.7
65 to 69 years.....................	419	247	34	69	33	37	33.0
70 to 74 years.....................	232	149	24	46	5	7	25.3
75 years and over..................	354	246	28	59	7	16	23.0
Percent							
25 years and over..................	100.0	34.4	14.7	27.9	13.2	9.9	(X)
25 to 64 years.........................	100.0	31.2	15.4	29.0	14.1	10.3	(X)
65 years and over.....................	100.0	63.9	8.4	17.4	4.4	5.9	(X)
65 to 69 years.....................	100.0	58.9	8.1	16.5	7.9	8.8	(X)
70 to 74 years.....................	100.0	64.2	10.3	19.8	2.2	3.0	(X)
75 years and over..................	100.0	69.5	7.9	16.7	2.0	4.5	(X)

[1]Hispanic origin may be of any race.

X Not applicable.

Source: Robert Kominski, U.S. Bureau of the Census, "Educational Attainment in the United States: March 1989 and 1988," *Current Population Reports,* Series P-20, No. 451, U.S. Government Printing Office, Washington, DC, 1991, table 1.

B3-8. Highest Degree Earned, by Selected Characteristic: 1987

(For persons 18 years old and over. Based on the Survey of Income and Program Participation; see source for details)

CHARACTERISTIC	Total persons	LEVEL OF DEGREE								
		Not a high school graduate	High school graduate only	Some college, no degree	Vocational	Associate	Bachelor's	Master's	Professional	Doctorate
NUMBER (1,000)										
All persons [1]	176,405	39,679	64,636	31,045	3,743	7,393	21,018	6,192	1,723	977
Age: 18 to 24 years old	28,148	4,203	10,596	8,043	389	928	1,912	77	-	-
25 to 34 years old	42,858	5,032	16,202	8,248	987	2,574	7,623	1,575	499	117
35 to 44 years old	34,352	4,921	12,101	5,931	862	2,208	5,359	2,114	509	347
45 to 54 years old	23,052	5,394	9,048	3,208	478	763	2,508	1,211	232	210
55 to 64 years old	21,726	6,668	8,364	2,690	457	473	1,928	656	285	205
65 years old and over	28,268	13,462	8,324	2,924	571	446	1,687	558	198	98
Sex: Male	84,106	19,341	28,494	15,160	1,273	3,376	10,909	3,416	1,344	792
Female	92,299	20,338	36,141	15,884	2,471	4,017	10,109	2,776	379	184
Race: White	151,882	31,875	56,240	26,981	3,415	6,538	18,850	5,486	1,605	891
Male	72,862	15,552	24,687	13,404	1,211	3,028	9,982	2,978	1,307	713
Female	79,020	16,323	31,553	13,577	2,205	3,510	8,868	2,508	298	178
Black	19,290	6,406	6,911	3,069	245	706	1,445	440	37	33
Male	8,696	3,127	3,176	1,252	41	261	583	221	8	26
Female	10,594	3,279	3,735	1,817	203	445	861	219	29	7
MEAN MONTHLY INCOME [2] (dol.)										
All persons [1]	1,325	761	1,135	1,283	1,417	1,630	2,109	2,776	4,323	4,118
Age: 18 to 24 years old	649	422	683	573	1,249	859	1,033	(B)	(B)	(B)
25 to 34 years old	1,360	741	1,126	1,391	1,166	1,581	1,836	2,294	3,449	4,703
35 to 44 years old	1,695	876	1,298	1,624	1,534	1,947	2,319	2,834	5,725	4,703
45 to 54 years old	1,778	962	1,494	1,999	1,744	2,033	2,838	3,786	4,781	3,178
55 to 64 years old	1,433	847	1,262	1,439	1,618	1,547	2,753	2,678	4,639	5,901
65 years old and over	993	708	971	1,310	1,354	1,337	2,079	2,064	(B)	(B)
Sex: Male	1,810	1,046	1,578	1,693	1,917	2,133	2,777	3,327	4,840	4,493
Female	883	489	785	892	1,159	1,206	1,388	2,098	2,494	(B)
Race: White	1,382	799	1,174	1,318	1,474	1,654	2,159	2,825	4,370	4,224
Black	915	559	877	1,072	835	1,361	1,596	2,181	(B)	(B)

[1]Includes other races, not shown separately.

-Less than .05 percent. B Base figure too small to meet statistical standards for reliability of a derived figure.

Source: U.S. Bureau of the Census, *Current Population Reports,* Series P-70, No. 21.

B3-9. Percent Literate for Persons 65 Years and Over and 14 Years and Over, by Race, Nativity, and Parentage: 1979

(Percentages are based on persons reporting on literacy and, hence, it is assumed that persons not reporting on literacy are distributed in the same proportion as persons who did report on literacy)

Age and literacy	Total[1]	Race		Nativity and parentage		
		White	Black	Native of native parentage	Foreign birth or parentage	
					Native of foreign parentage	Foreign born
65 years and over[2]	100.0	100.0	100.0	100.0	100.0	100.0
Reported able to read and write	98.3	98.9	93.1	98.3	99.4	95.9
Reported unable to read and write	1.7	1.1	6.8	1.7	0.6	4.1
14 years old and over[2]	100.0	100.0	100.0	100.0	100.0	100.0
Reported able to read and write	99.4	99.6	98.4	99.5	99.5	98.2
Reported unable to read and write	0.6	0.4	1.6	0.5	0.5	1.8

[1]Includes other races and persons not reporting nativity, not shown separately.

[2]About 4 percent of the population 65 years and over and about 3½ percent of the population 14 years and over did not report on literacy.

Source: U.S. Bureau of the Census, *Ancestry and Language,* Current Population Reports, Series P-23, No. 116, table 8.

B3-10. Undergraduate Enrollment in Institutions of Higher Education, by Type of Institution, Sex, Attendance Status, and Age: 50 States and D.C., Fall 1989

Attendance status and age	All institutions			4-year			2-year 1/		
	Total	Men	Women	Total	Men	Women	Total	Men	Women
Total............	11,665,643	5,277,774	6,387,869	6,582,182	3,090,917	3,491,265	5,083,461	2,186,857	2,896,604
Under 18..........	219,488	91,802	127,686	111,648	46,476	65,172	107,840	45,326	62,514
18-19.............	2,644,409	1,206,234	1,438,175	1,863,122	850,790	1,012,332	781,287	355,444	425,843
20-21.............	2,344,076	1,120,468	1,223,608	1,829,663	869,267	960,396	514,413	251,201	263,212
22-24.............	1,556,058	816,372	739,686	1,118,947	611,349	507,598	437,111	205,023	232,088
25-29.............	1,178,040	557,660	620,380	629,863	325,765	304,098	548,177	231,895	316,282
30-34.............	812,290	329,037	483,253	371,426	160,760	210,666	440,864	168,277	272,587
35-39.............	598,160	211,965	386,195	266,790	97,230	169,560	331,370	114,735	216,635
40-49.............	617,052	194,341	422,711	250,371	77,689	172,682	366,681	116,652	250,029
50-64.............	189,015	63,112	125,903	56,872	17,035	39,837	132,143	46,077	86,066
65 and over.......	66,325	24,978	41,347	14,366	5,809	8,557	51,959	19,169	32,790
Age unknown	1,440,730	661,805	778,925	69,114	28,747	40,367	1,371,616	633,058	738,558
Full-time..........	6,808,366	3,266,721	3,541,645	4,976,524	2,406,029	2,570,495	1,831,842	860,692	971,150
Under 18..........	137,771	56,840	80,931	85,954	35,066	50,888	51,817	21,774	30,043
18-19.............	2,321,216	1,062,989	1,258,227	1,764,225	806,131	958,094	556,991	256,858	300,133
20-21.............	1,929,882	930,752	999,130	1,662,791	791,871	870,920	267,091	138,881	128,210
22-24.............	973,359	543,636	429,723	826,498	468,518	357,980	146,861	75,118	71,743
25-29.............	442,310	229,202	213,108	305,858	171,977	133,881	136,452	57,225	79,227
30-34.............	229,353	93,330	136,023	134,370	59,343	75,027	94,983	33,987	60,996
35-39.............	148,062	51,685	96,377	85,988	30,851	55,137	62,074	20,834	41,240
40-49.............	125,292	41,910	83,382	68,738	22,031	46,707	56,554	19,879	36,675
50-64.............	24,159	8,683	15,476	10,825	3,449	7,376	13,334	5,234	8,100
65 and over.......	5,127	2,314	2,813	2,049	854	1,195	3,078	1,460	1,618
Age unknown	471,835	245,380	226,455	29,228	15,938	13,290	442,607	229,442	213,165
Part-time..........	4,857,277	2,011,053	2,846,224	1,605,658	684,888	920,770	3,251,619	1,326,165	1,925,454
Under 18..........	81,717	34,962	46,755	25,694	11,410	14,284	56,023	23,552	32,471
18-19.............	323,193	143,245	179,948	98,897	44,659	54,238	224,296	98,586	125,710
20-21.............	414,194	189,716	224,478	166,872	77,396	89,476	247,322	112,320	135,002
22-24.............	582,699	272,736	309,963	292,449	142,831	149,618	290,250	129,905	160,345
25-29.............	735,730	328,458	407,272	324,005	153,788	170,217	411,725	174,670	237,055
30-34.............	582,937	235,707	347,230	237,056	101,417	135,639	345,881	134,290	211,591
35-39.............	450,098	160,280	289,818	180,802	66,379	114,423	269,296	93,901	175,395
40-49.............	491,760	152,431	339,329	181,633	55,658	125,975	310,127	96,773	213,354
50-64.............	164,856	54,429	110,427	46,047	13,586	32,461	118,809	40,843	77,966
65 and over.......	61,198	22,664	38,534	12,317	4,955	7,362	48,881	17,709	31,172
Age unknown	968,895	416,425	552,470	39,886	12,809	27,077	929,009	403,616	525,393

1/ Includes students enrolled in less-than-2-year institutions of higher education.

B3-11. Enrollment in All Institutions of Higher Education, by Level of Study, Sex, Attendance Status, and Age: 50 States and D.C., Fall 1989

Attendance status and age	Total			Undergraduate			First-professional			Graduate		
	Total	Men	Women	Total	Men	Women	Total	Men	Women	Total	Men	Women
Total	13,457,855	6,155,484	7,302,371	11,665,643	5,277,774	6,387,869	273,728	168,480	105,248	1,518,484	709,230	809,254
Under 18	220,098	92,120	127,978	219,488	91,802	127,686	45	37	8	565	281	284
18-19	2,645,031	1,206,530	1,438,501	2,644,409	1,206,234	1,438,175	231	126	105	391	170	221
20-21	2,361,749	1,129,182	1,232,567	2,344,076	1,120,468	1,223,608	8,148	4,279	3,869	9,525	4,435	5,090
22-24	1,860,154	973,168	886,986	1,556,058	816,372	739,686	98,775	59,843	38,932	205,321	96,953	108,368
25-29	1,711,589	851,350	860,239	1,178,040	557,660	620,380	94,743	62,040	32,703	438,806	231,650	207,156
30-34	1,131,246	498,808	632,438	812,290	329,037	483,253	32,035	20,176	11,859	286,921	149,595	137,326
35-39	836,156	316,966	519,190	598,160	211,965	386,195	16,819	9,627	7,192	221,177	95,374	125,803
40-49	876,567	287,531	589,036	617,052	194,341	422,711	12,161	6,132	6,029	247,354	87,058	160,296
50-64	248,103	83,428	164,675	189,015	63,112	125,903	2,429	1,260	1,169	56,659	19,056	37,603
65 and over	72,645	27,884	44,761	66,325	24,978	41,347	510	259	251	5,810	2,647	3,163
Age unknown*	1,494,517	688,517	806,000	1,440,730	661,805	778,925	7,832	4,701	3,131	45,955	22,011	23,944
Full-time	7,627,172	3,727,823	3,899,349	6,808,366	3,266,721	3,541,645	247,434	152,419	95,015	571,372	308,683	262,689
Under 18	137,958	56,952	81,006	137,771	56,840	80,931	42	35	7	145	77	68
18-19	2,321,636	1,063,225	1,258,411	2,321,216	1,062,989	1,258,227	229	124	105	191	112	79
20-21	1,945,008	938,439	1,006,569	1,929,882	930,752	999,130	8,086	4,242	3,844	7,040	3,445	3,595
22-24	1,196,848	666,177	530,671	973,359	543,636	429,723	95,904	58,113	37,791	127,585	64,428	63,157
25-29	724,036	401,482	322,554	442,310	229,202	213,108	86,649	56,870	29,779	195,077	115,410	79,667
30-34	356,350	169,633	186,717	229,353	93,330	136,023	26,233	16,359	9,874	100,764	59,944	40,820
35-39	221,486	89,333	132,153	148,062	51,685	96,377	12,650	7,220	5,430	60,774	30,428	30,346
40-49	189,020	68,713	120,307	125,292	41,910	83,382	8,207	4,019	4,188	55,521	22,784	32,737
50-64	36,047	13,342	22,705	24,159	8,683	15,476	1,532	755	777	10,356	3,904	6,452
65 and over	6,404	2,934	3,470	5,127	2,314	2,813	396	190	206	881	430	451
Age unknown*	492,379	257,593	234,786	471,835	245,380	226,455	7,506	4,492	3,014	13,038	7,721	5,317
Part-time	5,830,683	2,427,661	3,403,022	4,857,277	2,011,053	2,846,224	26,294	16,061	10,233	947,112	400,547	546,565
Under 18	82,140	35,168	46,972	81,717	34,962	46,755	3	2	1	420	204	216
18-19	323,395	143,305	180,090	323,193	143,245	179,948	2	2	0	200	58	142
20-21	416,741	190,743	225,998	414,194	189,716	224,478	62	37	25	2,485	990	1,495
22-24	663,306	306,991	356,315	582,699	272,736	309,963	2,871	1,730	1,141	77,736	32,525	45,211
25-29	987,553	449,868	537,685	735,730	328,458	407,272	8,094	5,170	2,924	243,729	116,240	127,489
30-34	774,896	329,175	445,721	582,937	235,707	347,230	5,802	3,817	1,985	186,157	89,651	96,506
35-39	614,670	227,633	387,037	450,098	160,280	289,818	4,169	2,407	1,762	160,403	64,946	95,457
40-49	687,547	218,818	468,729	491,760	152,431	339,329	3,954	2,113	1,841	191,833	64,274	127,559
50-64	212,056	70,086	141,970	164,856	54,429	110,427	897	505	392	46,303	15,152	31,151
65 and over	66,241	24,950	41,291	61,198	22,664	38,534	114	69	45	4,929	2,217	2,712
Age unknown*	1,002,138	430,924	571,214	968,895	416,425	552,470	326	209	117	32,917	14,290	18,627

*Note the high proportion of "age unknown" data.

B3-12. Educational Attainment—Persons 18 Years Old and Over, by Total Money Earnings in 1991, Age, Work Experience in 1991, and Sex

[Persons 18 years old and over as of March 1992.

Age	Total	Less than 9th grade	High school 9th to 12th grade (no diploma)	High school graduate (includes equivalency)	Some college, no degree	Associate degree	College / Bachelor's degree or more Total	Bachelor's degree	Master's degree	Professional degree	Doctorate degree
MALE											
Total											
Number with Earnings (thousands)											
Total	70 145	3 635	7 044	24 110	14 062	4 014	17 280	11 126	3 929	1 398	827
Under 65 years	67 364	3 211	6 697	23 338	13 697	3 911	16 511	10 697	3 796	1 277	741
18 to 24 years	10 097	292	1 737	3 540	3 433	351	744	710	30	4	-
25 to 34 years	19 746	751	1 768	7 612	3 653	1 232	4 731	3 545	836	279	71
25 to 29 years	9 383	347	841	3 606	1 823	561	2 206	1 771	299	117	18
30 to 34 years	10 363	404	927	4 006	1 830	671	2 525	1 774	536	162	53
35 to 44 years	18 255	658	1 274	5 903	3 516	1 435	5 469	3 411	1 320	490	248
35 to 39 years	9 720	323	746	3 439	1 785	732	2 694	1 770	551	254	119
40 to 44 years	8 536	335	527	2 464	1 731	704	2 775	1 641	769	236	129
45 to 54 years	11 970	706	1 001	3 952	2 042	580	3 689	2 015	1 112	307	256
45 to 49 years	6 748	342	482	2 164	1 236	361	2 163	1 164	681	172	146
50 to 54 years	5 222	364	519	1 788	806	218	1 526	851	432	134	110
55 to 64 years	7 296	805	917	2 331	1 053	312	1 877	1 015	498	198	166
55 to 59 years	4 161	483	437	1 333	628	196	1 104	595	298	114	96
60 to 64 years	3 135	342	480	998	426	116	773	420	200	83	70
65 years and over	2 780	424	347	772	365	103	789	430	133	121	86
65 to 74 years	2 351	346	303	652	303	95	653	384	106	87	75
65 to 69 years	1 602	234	206	427	209	68	458	276	79	51	51
70 to 74 years	749	112	96	225	94	26	195	108	27	37	24
75 years and over	429	77	44	120	62	8	117	46	27	34	10
Mean Earnings (dollars)											
Total	27 494	14 023	15 589	22 663	24 075	29 793	44 169	38 484	47 053	72 411	59 224
Under 65 years	27 845	14 880	15 923	22 927	24 215	29 949	44 669	38 880	47 990	74 413	59 977
18 to 24 years	9 803	8 961	6 944	11 805	8 108	12 712	13 730	13 762	(B)	(B)	(B)
25 to 34 years	24 285	12 148	14 963	21 175	24 105	26 087	34 368	31 701	39 016	52 854	(B)
25 to 29 years	21 075	13 245	14 052	18 974	21 105	23 473	27 782	27 014	37 412	39 715	(B)
30 to 34 years	27 191	11 206	15 789	23 156	27 092	28 273	40 122	36 380	45 494	62 358	(B)
35 to 44 years	33 551	15 295	19 270	25 912	30 411	34 919	48 977	43 490	50 089	77 827	61 516
35 to 39 years	31 435	13 526	18 791	25 371	28 202	32 598	46 655	41 197	47 828	76 060	59 830
40 to 44 years	35 960	17 003	19 948	26 669	32 889	37 331	51 231	45 964	51 709	79 731	63 253
45 to 54 years	37 333	16 837	22 091	28 955	37 423	36 929	54 375	48 489	55 075	85 402	60 658
45 to 49 years	37 504	15 823	22 038	28 960	36 333	36 771	53 716	48 300	54 227	81 471	61 742
50 to 54 years	37 112	17 789	22 141	28 949	39 093	37 189	55 310	48 700	56 413	90 455	59 221
55 to 64 years	32 611	17 517	23 399	27 752	30 801	28 780	51 271	47 005	43 736	80 586	65 053
55 to 59 years	34 469	17 634	24 709	28 647	32 733	29 592	54 279	47 814	46 652	92 800	72 488
60 to 64 years	30 146	17 358	22 205	26 556	27 952	27 409	46 977	45 858	39 385	64 155	(B)
65 years and over	18 979	7 529	9 153	14 686	18 836	23 865	33 438	28 627	20 290	51 309	52 703
65 to 74 years	19 815	7 700	9 640	15 600	19 493	24 081	34 697	29 192	23 635	55 632	54 135
65 to 69 years	20 613	8 642	11 444	16 524	19 722	(B)	34 002	30 296	26 825	(B)	(B)
70 to 74 years	18 107	5 738	5 773	13 848	18 982	(B)	36 331	26 362	(B)	(B)	(B)
75 years and over	14 400	6 767	(B)	9 732	(B)	(B)	26 394	(B)	(B)	(B)	(B)
Standard Error of Mean (dollars)											
Total	148	357	287	163	274	517	414	432	849	2 195	2 382
Under 65 years	150	386	296	163	276	522	419	439	861	2 241	2 422
18 to 24 years	132	631	248	224	213	756	585	602	(B)	(B)	(B)
25 to 34 years	196	534	389	232	368	789	543	507	1 691	3 529	(B)
25 to 29 years	228	922	555	287	445	1 263	574	590	1 680	3 941	(B)
30 to 34 years	304	589	542	350	560	973	848	790	2 361	5 065	(B)
35 to 44 years	301	1 097	697	316	527	915	716	778	1 325	3 371	4 567
35 to 39 years	393	802	1 007	435	594	1 143	1 030	1 048	1 950	5 033	7 548
40 to 44 years	459	2 002	894	453	871	1 426	993	1 149	1 789	4 424	5 342
45 to 54 years	424	876	745	443	918	1 548	987	1 174	1 741	4 929	3 438
45 to 49 years	560	870	990	591	1 213	1 924	1 254	1 513	2 226	6 313	4 193
50 to 54 years	650	1 487	1 104	671	1 392	2 597	1 590	1 856	2 793	7 764	5 742
55 to 64 years	569	768	1 283	692	1 280	1 455	1 565	1 928	2 437	6 715	6 049
55 to 59 years	763	960	1 551	887	1 761	1 729	2 065	2 365	2 871	10 081	8 125
60 to 64 years	849	1 258	1 999	1 098	1 795	2 593	2 379	3 235	4 264	7 077	(B)
65 years and over	833	761	903	1 174	1 882	3 467	2 304	2 269	3 516	8 639	9 388
65 to 74 years	909	857	993	1 319	2 099	3 695	2 463	2 381	4 246	9 924	10 209
65 to 69 years	1 011	1 076	1 341	1 689	2 657	(B)	2 434	2 851	5 325	(B)	(B)
70 to 74 years	1 859	1 361	980	2 072	3 290	(B)	5 941	4 284	(B)	(B)	(B)
75 years and over	2 048	1 613	(B)	2 264	(B)	(B)	6 316	(B)	(B)	(B)	(B)

(B) Base less than 75,000

B3-12. Educational Attainment—Persons 18 Years Old and Over, by Total Money Earnings in 1991, Age, Work Experience in 1991, and Sex (continued)

[Persons 18 years old and over as of March 1992.

Age	Total	Educational Attainment									
		High school			College						
									Bachelor's degree or more		
		Less than 9th grade	9th to 12th grade (no diploma)	High school graduate (includes equivalency)	Some college, no degree	Associate degree	Total	Bachelor's degree	Master's degree	Professional degree	Doctorate degree
MALE—Con.											
Year-Round, Full-Time Workers											
Number with Earnings (thousands)											
Total	47 844	1 956	3 549	16 791	8 868	3 067	13 613	8 710	3 082	1 147	674
Under 65 years	46 874	1 837	3 449	16 531	8 735	3 024	13 297	8 513	3 049	1 101	634
18 to 24 years	3 649	149	466	1 788	834	167	264	255	9	-	-
25 to 34 years	14 087	394	916	5 548	2 665	933	3 631	2 739	608	226	58
25 to 29 years	6 389	201	430	2 560	1 240	420	1 538	1 255	179	85	18
30 to 34 years	7 699	194	486	2 988	1 425	513	2 094	1 484	429	141	40
35 to 44 years	14 451	386	818	4 475	2 786	1 213	4 775	2 971	1 141	443	219
35 to 39 years	7 547	193	464	2 558	1 397	609	2 326	1 526	481	219	100
40 to 44 years	6 904	193	354	1 916	1 389	604	2 448	1 445	660	225	119
45 to 54 years	9 602	426	678	3 087	1 708	466	3 238	1 778	944	283	233
45 to 49 years	5 483	216	342	1 704	1 028	287	1 907	1 035	576	157	138
50 to 54 years	4 119	210	336	1 383	680	180	1 331	743	368	126	95
55 to 64 years	5 084	482	571	1 654	742	245	1 389	770	347	148	124
55 to 59 years	3 100	285	311	1 010	461	156	878	476	226	100	76
60 to 64 years	1 984	198	261	644	281	89	511	294	121	46	47
65 years and over	970	119	100	260	133	42	316	197	33	37	37
65 to 74 years	869	101	87	238	114	42	287	185	28	23	31
65 to 69 years	656	84	67	168	81	36	221	142	24	14	5
70 to 74 years	213	17	20	70	33	7	66	43	4	10	3
75 years and over	101	18	13	22	19	-	29	12	5	10	3
Mean Earnings (dollars)											
Total	34 378	19 075	22 442	27 001	32 133	34 605	50 198	43 890	53 760	80 061	64 603
Under 65 years	34 358	19 243	22 544	26 998	32 160	34 574	50 057	43 842	53 874	79 390	64 211
18 to 24 years	16 544	12 327	13 694	16 559	16 479	19 114	22 437	22 479	(B)	(B)	(B)
25 to 34 years	28 742	15 853	19 596	24 045	28 135	29 923	39 765	36 198	47 934	61 038	(B)
25 to 29 years	25 156	16 852	18 649	21 630	25 027	26 662	33 619	32 292	36 528	47 369	(B)
30 to 34 years	31 718	14 820	20 434	26 115	30 840	32 593	44 280	39 500	52 706	69 331	(B)
35 to 44 years	37 882	19 972	23 770	28 984	34 377	37 887	52 130	46 238	51 818	81 462	85 384
35 to 39 years	35 899	17 187	23 565	28 475	32 210	35 598	50 369	44 376	55 278	79 997	66 820
40 to 44 years	40 051	22 766	24 038	29 664	36 555	40 195	53 802	48 203	58 532	86 440	64 168
45 to 54 years	41 676	20 713	25 277	32 468	41 121	41 796	56 918	50 715	58 532	81 291	61 837
45 to 49 years	41 849	18 972	25 415	32 336	40 569	41 497	56 630	50 843	58 682	92 890	83 337
50 to 54 years	41 445	22 505	25 137	32 631	41 956	42 272	57 330	50 537	52 603	89 933	59 659
55 to 64 years	38 868	22 274	29 491	32 484	35 291	32 695	59 089	53 008	53 388	97 030	78 126
55 to 59 years	39 336	22 118	29 479	31 858	33 373	35 373	60 192	51 858	51 137	(B)	84 238
60 to 64 years	38 137	22 498	29 506	33 467	35 157	31 899	57 195	54 871	(B)	(B)	(B)
65 years and over	35 303	16 479	18 926	27 165	30 365	(B)	56 164	45 954	(B)	(B)	(B)
65 to 74 years	35 555	16 800	19 710	27 039	32 711	(B)	54 993	45 611	(B)	(B)	(B)
65 to 69 years	34 898	16 132	(B)	26 091	32 771	(B)	52 510	44 919	(B)	(B)	(B)
70 to 74 years	37 584	(B)	(B)	(B)	(B)	(B)	(B)	(B)	(B)	(B)	(B)
75 years and over	33 137	(B)	(B)	(B)	(B)	(B)	(B)	(B)	(B)	(B)	(B)
Standard Error of Mean (dollars)											
Total	185	545	448	188	330	584	469	484	961	2 418	2 543
Under 65 years	185	565	457	188	332	588	470	488	967	2 412	2 635
18 to 24 years	220	810	492	305	484	1 018	891	907	(B)	(B)	(B)
25 to 34 years	235	776	521	263	398	913	618	554	2 030	3 884	(B)
25 to 29 years	274	1 290	721	319	484	1 566	667	662	2 163	4 685	(B)
30 to 34 years	356	828	741	396	594	1 022	926	833	2 658	5 287	4 952
35 to 44 years	341	1 723	912	336	573	992	766	821	1 423	3 533	8 472
35 to 39 years	451	996	1 381	461	628	1 245	1 106	1 100	2 052	5 499	6 666
40 to 44 years	514	3 276	1 080	485	952	1 535	1 058	1 221	1 950	4 467	3 507
45 to 54 years	481	1 156	851	497	998	1 651	1 061	1 257	1 929	5 125	4 320
45 to 49 years	631	1 102	1 101	652	1 338	2 046	1 342	1 621	2 460	6 521	5 867
50 to 54 years	744	2 038	1 300	765	1 479	2 773	1 724	1 988	3 111	8 075	7 089
55 to 64 years	702	1 030	1 867	794	1 161	1 544	1 884	2 248	3 005	8 198	8 948
55 to 59 years	887	1 273	1 950	977	1 402	1 822	2 365	2 608	3 360	11 106	(B)
60 to 64 years	1 146	1 719	3 369	1 342	2 029	2 798	3 113	4 097	5 899	(B)	(B)
65 years and over	1 693	2 034	2 046	2 172	2 883	(B)	3 971	3 555	(B)	(B)	(B)
65 to 74 years	1 704	2 191	2 250	2 226	3 223	(B)	3 866	3 539	(B)	(B)	(B)
65 to 69 years	1 716	2 297	(B)	2 208	3 964	(B)	3 629	4 133	(B)	(B)	(B)
70 to 74 years	4 516	(B)	(B)	(B)	(B)	(B)	(B)	(B)	(B)	(B)	(B)
75 years and over	7 016	(B)	(B)	(B)	(B)	(B)	(B)	(B)	(B)	(B)	(B)

(B) Base less than 75,000

B3-12. Educational Attainment—Persons 18 Years Old and Over, by Total Money Earnings in 1991, Age, Work Experience in 1991, and Sex (continued)

[Persons 18 years old and over as of March 1992.

Age	Total	Less than 9th grade	High school 9th to 12th grade (no diploma)	High school graduate (includes equivalency)	Some college, no degree	Associate degree	College Bachelor's degree or more Total	Bachelor's degree	Master's degree	Professional degree	Doctorate degree
FEMALE											
Total											
Number with Earnings (thousands)											
Total	60 214	1 863	5 012	22 393	13 092	4 560	13 294	9 346	3 172	474	30
Under 65 years	58 262	1 597	4 758	21 602	12 821	4 478	13 007	9 166	3 087	465	290
18 to 24 years	9 440	135	1 168	3 121	3 712	460	844	810	32	3	
25 to 34 years	16 712	341	1 115	6 041	3 300	1 495	4 420	3 506	689	184	61
25 to 29 years	7 986	120	549	2 882	1 520	690	2 225	1 876	264	66	19
30 to 34 years	8 726	221	566	3 159	1 780	805	2 195	1 630	405	118	42
35 to 44 years	15 978	394	969	5 673	3 152	1 459	4 330	2 829	1 231	170	99
35 to 39 years	8 296	192	521	2 991	1 610	769	2 213	1 509	555	96	53
40 to 44 years	7 682	203	449	2 682	1 542	690	2 117	1 320	676	74	46
45 to 54 years	10 422	380	883	4 180	1 802	796	2 400	1 420	821	77	83
45 to 49 years	5 977	161	397	2 287	1 133	472	1 526	914	526	36	51
50 to 54 years	4 445	219	486	1 894	669	324	874	506	295	41	32
55 to 64 years	5 710	346	641	2 586	854	268	1 014	601	334	32	46
55 to 59 years	3 290	186	339	1 478	526	166	595	343	209	15	28
60 to 64 years	2 419	160	302	1 108	328	102	419	259	125	17	19
65 years and over	1 951	266	254	791	272	82	287	180	86	9	12
65 to 74 years	1 616	212	206	685	215	71	226	142	72	6	7
65 to 69 years	1 129	148	165	492	137	49	142	84	48	5	5
70 to 74 years	487	66	42	193	78	23	85	58	24	1	2
75 years and over	335	54	48	106	56	10	61	39	14	4	5
Mean Earnings (dollars)											
Total	16 320	8 155	9 065	13 523	14 364	19 317	25 810	22 802	30 591	44 999	38 564
Under 65 years	16 564	8 510	9 132	13 717	14 493	19 415	26 058	22 983	31 017	45 614	39 140
18 to 24 years	8 227	5 160	4 984	8 915	7 094	11 575	13 820	13 884	(B)	(B)	(B)
25 to 34 years	16 672	8 514	8 536	13 183	15 849	18 529	24 109	22 761	28 503	34 179	(B)
25 to 29 years	15 979	7 740	7 773	12 942	14 952	18 134	22 416	22 262	23 547	(B)	(B)
30 to 34 years	17 306	8 933	9 277	13 403	16 615	18 868	25 824	23 335	31 732	40 032	(B)
35 to 44 years	19 496	8 530	10 390	15 297	18 512	21 782	27 990	24 672	31 347	51 242	41 093
35 to 39 years	19 118	8 006	10 701	14 652	18 208	21 568	27 911	24 879	30 471	52 275	(B)
40 to 44 years	19 908	9 024	10 029	16 015	18 830	22 021	28 074	24 435	32 064	(B)	(B)
45 to 54 years	19 690	9 593	12 855	15 970	18 841	20 666	30 540	25 841	34 983	51 353	47 774
45 to 49 years	20 092	9 736	12 608	16 217	18 305	20 094	30 270	26 253	34 477	(B)	(B)
50 to 54 years	19 149	9 487	13 066	15 671	19 750	21 502	31 011	25 097	35 885	(B)	(B)
55 to 64 years	16 117	8 602	10 810	13 656	17 410	21 196	25 883	21 835	26 912	(B)	(B)
55 to 59 years	17 187	9 615	11 414	14 372	17 819	21 906	27 972	23 294	28 792	(B)	(B)
60 to 64 years	14 661	7 420	10 134	12 702	16 753	20 040	22 918	19 904	23 783	(B)	(B)
65 years and over	9 039	6 021	7 808	8 211	8 269	13 981	14 527	13 562	15 284	(B)	(B)
65 to 74 years	9 211	5 776	8 336	8 408	8 389	(B)	15 289	13 844	(B)	(B)	(B)
65 to 69 years	9 550	6 400	8 351	8 878	8 769	(B)	15 977	15 817	(B)	(B)	(B)
70 to 74 years	8 425	(B)	(B)	7 212	7 722	(B)	14 138	(B)	(B)	(B)	(B)
75 years and over	8 207	(B)	(B)	6 939	(B)	(B)	(B)	(B)	(B)	(B)	(B)
Standard Error of Mean (dollars)											
Total	91	234	190	109	158	314	263	258	583	2 643	2 372
Under 65 years	92	253	195	111	160	316	265	261	589	2 672	2 403
18 to 24 years	119	516	340	187	163	650	513	521	(B)	(B)	(B)
25 to 34 years	156	588	355	202	280	440	386	364	1 440	2 598	(B)
25 to 29 years	197	804	428	294	378	623	401	433	1 186	(B)	(B)
30 to 34 years	239	792	559	277	405	619	658	604	2 217	3 513	(B)
35 to 44 years	193	487	404	224	371	638	475	506	840	4 777	3 154
35 to 39 years	264	620	543	289	484	821	681	738	1 154	6 333	(B)
40 to 44 years	283	690	601	347	564	993	661	683	1 200	(B)	(B)
45 to 54 years	241	572	515	286	424	670	700	744	1 190	6 593	6 124
45 to 49 years	321	670	644	410	529	862	843	961	1 404	(B)	(B)
50 to 54 years	365	758	781	391	708	1 061	1 234	1 157	2 167	(B)	(B)
55 to 64 years	304	522	535	305	684	1 827	1 126	1 215	1 524	(B)	(B)
55 to 59 years	416	729	753	398	882	1 820	1 596	1 691	1 939	(B)	(B)
60 to 64 years	436	721	755	470	1 079	3 770	1 488	1 704	2 406	(B)	(B)
65 years and over	374	570	786	492	908	2 505	1 493	1 578	3 140	(B)	(B)
65 to 74 years	391	564	846	479	883	(B)	1 737	1 726	(B)	(B)	(B)
65 to 69 years	443	719	877	556	1 145	(B)	1 977	2 243	(B)	(B)	(B)
70 to 74 years	789	(B)	(B)	928	1 363	(B)	3 249	(B)	(B)	(B)	(B)
75 years and over	1 090	(B)	(B)	1 959	(B)	(B)	(B)	(B)	(B)	(B)	(B)

(B) Base less than 75,000

B3-12. Educational Attainment—Persons 18 Years Old and Over, by Total Money Earnings in 1991, Age, Work Experience in 1991, and Sex (continued)

[Persons 18 years old and over as of March 1992.

Age	Total	Less than 9th grade	High school 9th to 12th grade (no diploma)	High school graduate (includes equivalency)	Some college, no degree	Associate degree	College — Bachelor's degree or more: Total	Bachelor's degree	Master's degree	Professional degree	Doctorate degree
FEMALE—Con.											
Year-Round, Full-Time Workers											
Number with Earnings (thousands)											
Total	32 420	770	2 009	12 262	6 505	2 712	8 162	5 613	2 031	313	206
Under 65 years	31 921	717	1 932	12 081	6 448	2 683	8 062	5 555	1 997	309	200
18 to 24 years	2 998	37	189	1 326	884	190	372	362	8	2	-
25 to 34 years	9 538	143	408	3 287	1 891	934	2 876	2 296	430	111	39
25 to 29 years	4 652	46	184	1 608	841	468	1 503	1 287	171	33	12
30 to 34 years	4 887	97	223	1 678	1 050	466	1 372	1 008	260	77	27
35 to 44 years	9 703	173	495	3 460	1 987	904	2 684	1 687	808	118	72
35 to 39 years	4 935	82	258	1 762	1 019	483	1 352	877	367	71	37
40 to 44 years	4 769	91	237	1 699	968	441	1 333	809	441	48	35
45 to 54 years	6 655	214	535	2 657	1 185	495	1 569	892	561	61	55
45 to 49 years	3 824	92	244	1 475	713	297	1 003	576	371	30	25
50 to 54 years	2 831	122	291	1 182	472	199	567	316	190	31	30
55 to 64 years	3 026	150	305	1 351	500	160	561	319	190	18	34
55 to 59 years	1 904	100	182	857	315	108	344	195	125	6	17
60 to 64 years	1 122	50	123	494	185	52	217	124	65	11	17
65 years and over	500	53	77	182	59	30	100	57	33	4	6
65 to 74 years	439	44	68	169	49	28	81	50	24	1	8
65 to 69 years	344	36	58	131	31	25	63	39	19	1	4
70 to 74 years	96	8	10	38	19	3	18	11	5	-	2
75 years and over	60	9	9	13	9	2	19	7	9	3	-
Mean Earnings (dollars)											
Total	22 956	12 376	14 966	18 711	21 749	25 024	32 573	29 390	36 693	54 683	45 099
Under 65 years	23 024	12 333	14 931	18 725	21 782	25 014	32 688	29 469	36 912	55 037	45 312
18 to 24 years	14 884	(B)	11 253	13 558	14 850	17 979	20 800	20 556	(B)	(B)	(B)
25 to 34 years	22 429	12 521	13 849	18 269	20 993	23 120	29 614	28 021	34 596	43 429	(B)
25 to 29 years	21 383	(B)	13 704	17 948	19 758	21 644	27 102	26 866	28 158	(B)	(B)
30 to 34 years	23 424	12 542	13 968	18 577	21 983	24 604	32 366	29 497	38 830	47 917	(B)
35 to 44 years	25 277	12 255	15 037	19 824	24 100	27 329	35 214	32 192	36 753	61 484	(B)
35 to 39 years	25 041	11 800	15 446	19 058	23 851	27 248	35 577	32 886	36 349	(B)	(B)
40 to 44 years	25 520	12 661	14 592	20 619	24 363	27 309	34 845	31 439	37 088	(B)	(B)
45 to 54 years	24 521	12 319	16 854	20 342	23 369	26 035	36 264	31 586	39 579	(B)	(B)
45 to 49 years	24 931	12 206	16 204	20 535	23 061	25 217	35 942	32 000	38 849	(B)	(B)
50 to 54 years	23 968	12 405	17 401	20 101	23 836	27 257	36 833	30 832	41 003	(B)	(B)
55 to 64 years	22 451	13 201	15 116	18 914	24 049	28 168	34 363	29 684	35 601	(B)	(B)
55 to 59 years	22 665	13 638	14 480	19 020	23 961	27 568	35 968	31 511	36 404	(B)	(B)
60 to 64 years	22 067	(B)	16 053	18 729	24 200	(B)	31 827	26 808	(B)	(B)	(B)
65 years and over	18 590	(B)	15 833	17 757	(B)	(B)	23 332	(B)	(B)	(B)	(B)
65 to 74 years	18 197	(B)	(B)	17 585	(B)	(B)	24 458	(B)	(B)	(B)	(B)
65 to 69 years	17 869	(B)	(B)	17 749	(B)	(B)	(B)	(B)	(B)	(B)	(B)
70 to 74 years	19 374	(B)	(B)	(B)	(B)	(B)	(B)	(B)	(B)	(B)	(B)
75 years and over	(B)	(B)	(B)	(B)	(B)	(B)	(B)	(B)	(B)	(B)	(B)
Standard Error of Mean (dollars)											
Total	125	377	285	144	209	391	330	314	729	3 187	2 840
Under 65 years	126	391	290	145	209	392	331	316	730	3 206	2 869
18 to 24 years	192	(B)	508	242	310	963	685	678	(B)	(B)	(B)
25 to 34 years	204	1 067	502	270	323	485	467	425	1 940	3 202	(B)
25 to 29 years	240	(B)	733	386	452	672	425	457	1 234	(B)	(B)
30 to 34 years	326	1 476	689	377	451	686	846	622	3 048	4 180	(B)
35 to 44 years	248	694	578	274	435	799	590	717	967	5 983	(B)
35 to 39 years	344	957	777	343	551	1 036	859	943	1 286	(B)	(B)
40 to 44 years	358	994	859	429	678	1 226	808	797	1 411	(B)	(B)
45 to 54 years	304	749	646	357	473	740	868	889	1 484	(B)	(B)
45 to 49 years	402	994	726	507	596	949	1 038	1 172	1 692	(B)	(B)
50 to 54 years	464	1 080	1 019	494	772	1 167	1 547	1 312	2 870	(B)	(B)
55 to 64 years	421	756	738	386	841	2 568	1 427	1 696	1 670	(B)	(B)
55 to 59 years	527	871	983	485	1 081	2 020	1 878	2 152	2 164	(B)	(B)
60 to 64 years	697	(B)	1 097	635	1 335	(B)	2 154	2 709	(B)	(B)	(B)
65 years and over	886	(B)	1 421	954	(B)	(B)	3 031	(B)	(B)	(B)	(B)
65 to 74 years	900	(B)	(B)	987	(B)	(B)	3 514	(B)	(B)	(B)	(B)
65 to 69 years	849	(B)	(B)	985	(B)	(B)	(B)	(B)	(B)	(B)	(B)
70 to 74 years	2 783	(B)	(B)	(B)	(B)	(B)	(B)	(B)	(B)	(B)	(B)
75 years and over	(B)	(B)	(B)	(B)	(B)	(B)	(B)	(B)	(B)	(B)	(B)

(B) Base less than 75,000

B3-13. Years of School Completed by Persons 25 Years and Over, by Age, Race, Household Relationship, and Poverty Status in 1991

[Numbers in thousands. Persons, families and unrelated individuals as of March of the following year.

Characteristic	All races			White			Black			Hispanic Origin[1]		
		Below poverty level			Below poverty level			Below poverty level			Below poverty level	
	Total	Number	Percent of total	Total	Number	Percent of total	Total	Number	Percent of total	Total	Number	Percent of total
ALL EDUCATION LEVELS												
Both Sexes												
Total	160 827	17 247	10.7	137 646	12 109	8.8	17 445	4 364	25.0	11 623	2 475	21.3
25 to 34 years	42 493	5 568	13.1	35 318	3 870	11.0	5 423	1 428	26.3	4 249	1 026	24.1
35 to 54 years	66 594	5 759	8.6	56 752	3 925	6.9	7 250	1 532	21.1	4 980	983	19.7
55 to 64 years	21 150	2 139	10.1	18 280	1 511	8.3	2 166	524	24.2	1 250	226	18.2
65 years and over	30 590	3 781	12.4	27 297	2 802	10.3	2 606	880	33.8	1 143	237	20.8
65 to 74 years	18 441	1 961	10.6	16 315	1 345	8.2	1 665	547	32.9	732	137	18.8
75 years and over	12 149	1 820	15.0	10 983	1 457	13.3	941	333	35.3	411	100	24.3
Male												
Total	76 579	6 244	8.2	66 063	4 491	6.8	7 803	1 421	18.2	5 744	996	17.3
25 to 34 years	21 124	2 049	9.7	17 736	1 505	8.5	2 505	432	17.2	2 227	400	18.0
35 to 54 years	32 620	2 387	7.3	28 165	1 729	6.1	3 263	536	16.4	2 454	422	17.2
55 to 64 years	10 036	793	7.9	8 731	564	6.5	978	182	18.6	597	102	17.1
65 years and over	12 800	1 015	7.9	11 431	693	6.1	1 058	271	25.6	466	72	15.4
65 to 74 years	8 266	632	7.6	7 323	407	5.6	739	193	26.1	310	42	13.4
75 years and over	4 533	383	8.5	4 108	286	7.0	319	78	24.6	157	30	19.3
Female												
Total	84 248	11 003	13.1	71 583	7 618	10.6	9 641	2 943	30.5	5 878	1 479	25.2
25 to 34 years	21 369	3 519	16.5	17 581	2 365	13.5	2 918	996	34.1	2 022	626	31.0
35 to 54 years	33 975	3 372	9.9	28 587	2 196	7.7	3 987	997	25.0	2 526	561	22.2
55 to 64 years	11 114	1 346	12.1	9 549	947	9.9	1 188	342	28.7	654	126	19.3
65 years and over	17 790	2 766	15.5	15 866	2 109	13.3	1 549	609	39.3	677	166	24.5
65 to 74 years	10 174	1 329	13.1	8 992	939	10.4	926	355	38.3	422	96	22.7
75 years and over	7 616	1 436	18.9	6 874	1 171	17.0	623	254	40.8	255	70	27.4
Household Relationship												
In families	127 957	10 804	8.4	109 846	7 294	6.6	13 303	2 946	22.1	9 801	1 960	20.0
Householder	64 531	6 775	10.5	55 154	4 445	8.1	7 226	2 015	27.9	4 785	1 191	24.9
In families with related children under 18 years	61 080	7 776	12.7	50 625	5 110	10.1	7 660	2 237	29.2	6 413	1 705	26.6
Householder	33 089	5 303	16.0	27 084	3 357	12.4	4 700	1 697	36.1	3 329	1 061	31.9
In married couple families	107 241	6 000	5.6	95 660	4 811	5.0	7 665	806	10.5	7 409	1 214	16.4
Householder	50 965	2 921	5.7	45 786	2 373	5.2	3 533	375	10.6	3 310	592	17.9
Husband	51 086	2 939	5.8	45 860	2 375	5.2	3 548	390	11.0	3 360	603	17.9
Wife	49 826	2 755	5.5	44 652	2 226	5.0	3 367	350	10.4	3 246	539	16.6
In married couple families with related children under 18 years	50 525	3 870	7.7	43 897	3 103	7.1	4 286	489	11.4	4 985	1 045	21.0
Householder	24 530	1 910	7.8	21 483	1 547	7.2	2 049	239	11.7	2 282	510	22.3
Husband	24 590	1 926	7.8	21 524	1 554	7.2	2 057	247	12.0	2 312	521	22.5
Wife	23 801	1 753	7.4	20 819	1 414	6.8	1 920	213	11.1	2 201	460	20.9
In families with female householder, no spouse present	15 859	4 282	27.0	10 582	2 172	20.5	4 693	1 956	41.7	1 743	660	37.9
Householder	10 782	3 511	32.6	7 206	1 851	25.7	3 215	1 539	47.9	1 149	541	47.1
In families with female householder, no spouse present, with related children under 18 years	8 720	3 589	41.2	5 361	1 809	33.7	3 045	1 652	54.3	1 152	594	51.5
Householder	7 162	3 134	43.8	4 509	1 640	36.4	2 417	1 386	57.3	870	502	57.7
In unrelated subfamilies	578	226	39.2	470	178	38.0	79	39	49.4	101	39	38.3
Unrelated individuals	32 293	6 216	19.2	27 330	4 636	17.0	4 062	1 379	33.9	1 721	476	27.7
Male	15 028	2 271	15.1	12 356	1 565	12.7	2 174	599	27.5	1 051	232	22.1
Householder	11 196	1 423	12.7	9 410	996	10.6	1 498	384	25.7	553	115	20.8
Female	17 265	3 945	22.9	14 974	3 071	20.5	1 888	780	41.3	670	244	36.4
Householder	15 082	3 303	21.9	13 131	2 571	19.6	1 656	674	40.7	485	159	32.8
NO HIGH SCHOOL DIPLOMA												
Both Sexes												
Total	33 110	8 340	25.2	26 337	5 749	21.8	5 642	2 276	40.3	5 510	1 761	32.0
25 to 34 years	5 754	2 103	36.5	4 572	1 525	33.4	988	507	51.3	1 765	675	38.2
35 to 54 years	9 352	2 420	25.9	7 197	1 654	23.0	1 737	654	37.7	2 185	689	31.5
55 to 64 years	5 677	1 230	21.7	4 385	796	18.1	1 075	365	34.0	710	185	26.1
65 years and over	12 328	2 587	21.0	10 182	1 774	17.4	1 842	750	40.7	850	213	25.0
65 to 74 years	6 449	1 266	19.6	5 174	772	14.9	1 083	449	41.5	531	124	23.3
75 years and over	5 879	1 321	22.5	5 008	1 002	20.0	759	300	39.6	319	89	27.9
Male												
Total	15 547	2 955	19.0	12 498	2 071	16.6	2 574	745	28.9	2 660	697	26.2
25 to 34 years	2 970	776	26.1	2 429	591	24.3	446	154	34.6	926	261	28.2
35 to 54 years	4 591	965	21.0	3 609	712	19.7	818	210	25.7	1 071	290	27.1
55 to 64 years	2 797	474	16.9	2 176	304	14.0	527	141	26.8	328	82	25.0
65 years and over	5 189	740	14.3	4 284	464	10.8	783	240	30.6	335	63	18.8
65 to 74 years	2 991	440	14.7	2 409	248	10.3	509	168	32.9	217	36	16.7
75 years and over	2 198	300	13.6	1 875	216	11.5	274	72	26.3	117	27	22.7
Female												
Total	17 563	5 386	30.7	13 839	3 678	26.6	3 068	1 531	49.9	2 850	1 065	37.4
25 to 34 years	2 784	1 327	47.7	2 144	935	43.6	542	352	65.1	839	413	49.2
35 to 54 years	4 761	1 455	30.6	3 588	942	26.2	919	444	48.3	1 114	398	35.7
55 to 64 years	2 880	757	26.3	2 210	491	22.2	548	224	40.9	382	103	27.0
65 years and over	7 138	1 847	25.9	5 898	1 310	22.2	1 060	510	48.1	515	150	29.1
65 to 74 years	3 458	826	23.9	2 764	524	19.0	574	282	49.0	313	87	27.9
75 years and over	3 680	1 021	27.8	3 134	786	25.1	485	229	47.1	202	62	30.9

See footnote at end of table.

B3-13. Years of School Completed by Persons 25 Years and Over, by Age, Race, Household Relationship, and Poverty Status in 1991 (continued)

[Numbers in thousands. Persons, families and unrelated individuals as of March of the following year.

Characteristic	All races			White			Black			Hispanic Origin[1]		
		Below poverty level			Below poverty level			Below poverty level			Below poverty level	
	Total	Number	Percent of total	Total	Number	Percent of total	Total	Number	Percent of total	Total	Number	Percent of total
NO HIGH SCHOOL DIPLOMA—Con.												
Household Relationship												
In families	25 111	5 156	20.5	20 047	3 458	17.2	4 099	1 439	35.1	4 676	1 411	30.2
Householder	13 094	3 171	24.2	10 395	2 081	20.0	2 307	954	41.4	2 326	840	36.1
In families with related children under 18 years	10 263	3 532	34.4	7 748	2 349	30.3	1 979	996	50.3	3 168	1 223	38.6
Householder	5 652	2 331	41.2	4 187	1 499	35.8	1 240	734	59.2	1 644	742	45.1
In married couple families	18 956	2 976	15.7	16 017	2 303	14.4	2 187	476	21.8	3 355	918	27.4
Householder	9 319	1 456	15.6	7 958	1 147	14.4	1 075	219	20.4	1 505	436	29.0
Husband	9 459	1 468	15.5	8 068	1 153	14.3	1 113	225	20.2	1 549	444	28.6
Wife	7 887	1 334	16.9	6 695	1 025	15.3	856	222	25.9	1 437	418	29.1
In married couple families with related children under 18 years	7 306	1 831	25.1	5 992	1 461	24.4	898	241	26.8	2 362	779	33.0
Householder	3 408	883	25.9	2 835	712	25.1	426	117	27.4	1 060	368	34.7
Husband	3 466	883	25.5	2 877	713	24.8	446	113	25.4	1 086	375	34.6
Wife	3 060	826	27.0	2 539	659	25.9	353	112	31.6	999	353	35.3
In families with female householder, no spouse present	4 636	1 911	41.2	2 947	1 003	34.0	1 552	855	55.1	945	436	46.1
Householder	3 017	1 549	51.3	1 875	831	44.3	1 060	678	64.0	653	369	56.5
In families with female householder, no spouse present, with related children under 18 years	2 463	1 548	62.8	1 397	792	56.7	974	705	72.4	646	397	61.5
Householder	1 902	1 325	69.7	1 100	708	64.3	744	580	77.9	496	341	68.8
In unrelated subfamilies	181	93	51.3	147	78	53.1	29	14	(B)	60	20	(B)
Unrelated individuals	7 819	3 091	39.5	6 143	2 213	36.0	1 514	824	54.4	774	329	42.5
Male	3 138	968	30.9	2 315	631	27.3	742	311	41.9	464	154	33.1
Householder	2 328	648	27.8	1 736	407	23.5	556	231	41.6	229	75	32.9
Female	4 681	2 123	45.4	3 828	1 582	41.3	771	513	66.5	310	176	56.7
Householder	4 296	1 913	44.5	3 524	1 421	40.3	706	469	66.4	224	125	55.8
HIGH SCHOOL DIPLOMA, NO COLLEGE												
Both Sexes												
Total	57 860	5 541	9.6	50 045	3 883	7.8	6 220	1 467	23.6	3 176	481	15.2
25 to 34 years	16 021	2 211	13.8	13 168	1 460	11.1	2 367	666	28.1	1 269	238	18.8
35 to 54 years	23 441	1 890	8.1	20 024	1 241	6.2	2 747	580	21.1	1 432	196	13.7
55 to 64 years	8 031	600	7.5	7 133	474	6.6	666	113	17.0	317	32	10.0
65 years and over	10 367	842	8.1	9 720	707	7.3	441	108	24.5	157	15	9.3
65 to 74 years	6 852	503	7.3	6 360	398	6.3	346	87	25.1	106	9	8.7
75 years and over	3 515	338	9.6	3 361	310	9.2	95	21	22.4	52	6	(B)
Male												
Total	25 774	1 917	7.4	22 261	1 397	6.3	2 842	460	16.2	1 557	210	13.5
25 to 34 years	8 113	766	9.4	6 726	554	8.2	1 161	188	16.2	695	99	14.3
35 to 54 years	10 671	779	7.3	9 130	542	5.9	1 274	218	17.1	665	92	13.8
55 to 64 years	3 244	195	6.0	2 889	157	5.4	272	29	10.8	135	14	10.1
65 years and over	3 746	178	4.7	3 516	144	4.1	135	25	18.7	62	6	(B)
65 to 74 years	2 584	131	5.1	2 401	101	4.2	116	24	20.9	42	4	(B)
75 years and over	1 161	47	4.0	1 115	43	3.9	19	1	(B)	20	2	(B)
Female												
Total	32 086	3 624	11.3	27 784	2 486	8.9	3 379	1 007	29.8	1 618	271	16.8
25 to 34 years	7 908	1 445	18.3	6 442	906	14.1	1 206	478	39.6	574	139	24.3
35 to 54 years	12 770	1 111	8.7	10 894	699	6.4	1 473	363	24.6	767	105	13.7
55 to 64 years	4 786	405	8.5	4 244	317	7.5	394	84	21.3	182	18	9.9
65 years and over	6 622	664	10.0	6 205	563	9.1	306	83	27.1	95	9	9.5
65 to 74 years	4 268	373	8.7	3 959	297	7.5	230	63	27.2	63	5	(B)
75 years and over	2 354	291	12.4	2 246	266	11.9	76	20	26.6	32	4	(B)
Household Relationship												
In families	47 523	3 733	7.9	41 238	2 475	6.0	4 932	1 125	22.8	2 716	382	14.1
Householder	22 160	2 337	10.5	19 012	1 489	7.8	2 587	777	30.0	1 243	234	18.8
In families with related children under 18 years	22 333	2 795	12.5	18 515	1 772	9.6	3 076	922	30.0	1 721	330	19.2
Householder	11 598	1 922	16.6	9 410	1 165	12.4	1 858	702	37.8	872	212	24.3
In married couple families	39 941	1 943	4.9	36 128	1 616	4.5	2 766	251	9.1	2 076	205	9.9
Householder	17 202	908	5.3	15 610	753	4.8	1 195	124	10.4	858	105	12.2
Husband	17 124	918	5.4	15 528	753	4.8	1 211	134	11.1	863	111	12.8
Wife	20 305	945	4.7	18 546	807	4.4	1 223	93	7.6	967	85	8.8
In married couple families with related children under 18 years	18 343	1 295	7.1	16 064	1 048	6.5	1 676	186	11.1	1 349	183	13.6
Householder	8 378	618	7.4	7 366	502	6.8	776	94	12.1	596	95	15.9
Husband	8 390	636	7.6	7 368	509	6.9	794	106	13.3	601	101	16.8
Wife	9 126	617	6.8	8 077	506	6.3	745	73	9.8	619	74	12.0
In families with female householder, no spouse present	5 896	1 607	27.3	3 840	742	19.3	1 854	814	43.9	468	155	33.1
Householder	4 005	1 303	32.5	2 637	648	24.6	1 245	620	49.8	289	113	39.2
In families with female householder, no spouse present, with related children under 18 years	3 319	1 382	41.6	1 936	646	33.4	1 284	701	54.6	302	133	43.9
Householder	2 704	1 206	44.6	1 628	596	36.6	999	582	58.2	221	105	47.6
In unrelated subfamilies	223	85	37.9	189	67	35.4	24	14	(B)	32	17	(B)
Unrelated individuals	10 114	1 724	17.0	8 618	1 341	15.6	1 265	329	26.0	428	83	19.3
Male	4 620	644	13.9	3 739	461	12.3	776	163	21.0	270	49	18.0
Householder	3 239	398	12.3	2 704	295	10.9	476	91	19.1	131	24	18.1
Female	5 494	1 081	19.7	4 879	880	18.0	490	166	34.0	158	34	21.5
Householder	4 779	853	17.9	4 300	708	16.5	399	127	31.8	109	18	16.7

See footnote at end of table.

B3-13. Years of School Completed by Persons 25 Years and Over, by Age, Race, Household Relationship, and Poverty Status in 1991 (continued)

[Numbers in thousands. Persons, families and unrelated individuals as of March of the following year.

Characteristic	All races Total	Below poverty level Number	Below poverty level Percent of total	White Total	Below poverty level Number	Below poverty level Percent of total	Black Total	Below poverty level Number	Below poverty level Percent of total	Hispanic Origin[1] Total	Below poverty level Number	Below poverty level Percent of total
SOME COLLEGE, LESS THAN BACHELOR'S DEGREE												
Both Sexes												
Total	35 520	2 307	6.5	30 912	1 687	5.5	3 502	512	14.6	1 853	164	8.8
25 to 34 years	10 859	906	8.3	9 035	655	7.3	1 418	216	15.2	805	83	10.3
35 to 54 years	16 657	979	5.9	14 489	676	4.7	1 652	244	14.8	856	69	8.0
55 to 64 years	3 701	206	5.6	3 357	157	4.7	252	39	15.6	122	7	6.1
65 years and over	4 304	215	5.0	4 030	198	4.9	180	12	6.9	69	5	(B)
65 to 74 years	2 784	122	4.4	2 577	109	4.2	145	8	5.5	53	3	(B)
75 years and over	1 520	93	6.1	1 453	89	6.1	35	4	(B)	17	2	(B)
Male												
Total	16 631	840	5.1	14 653	644	4.4	1 462	157	10.7	944	62	6.6
25 to 34 years	5 114	330	6.5	4 315	255	5.9	591	61	10.4	406	29	7.1
35 to 54 years	7 968	387	4.9	7 062	284	4.0	684	83	12.2	443	27	6.0
55 to 64 years	1 732	76	4.4	1 588	62	3.9	99	10	10.6	65	5	(B)
65 years and over	1 817	47	2.6	1 688	43	2.5	88	2	2.0	30	2	(B)
65 to 74 years	1 227	34	2.8	1 126	31	2.7	76	1	1.1	22	1	(B)
75 years and over	590	13	2.2	563	12	2.1	12	1	(B)	8	1	(B)
Female												
Total	18 889	1 467	7.8	16 258	1 043	6.4	2 041	355	17.4	909	102	11.2
25 to 34 years	5 744	576	10.0	4 720	400	8.5	826	155	18.7	399	54	13.6
35 to 54 years	8 689	592	6.8	7 427	392	5.3	968	161	16.6	414	42	10.1
55 to 64 years	1 969	130	6.6	1 769	95	5.3	154	29	18.9	57	3	(B)
65 years and over	2 487	169	6.8	2 342	155	6.6	92	11	11.5	40	3	(B)
65 to 74 years	1 557	88	5.7	1 451	79	5.4	70	7	(B)	31	2	(B)
75 years and over	930	80	8.6	890	77	8.6	23	3	(B)	9	1	(B)
Household Relationship												
In families	28 490	1 415	5.0	24 835	1 000	4.0	2 740	337	12.3	1 535	119	7.7
Householder	14 441	944	6.5	12 524	652	5.2	1 520	246	16.2	755	89	11.8
In families with related children under 18 years	15 070	1 110	7.4	12 802	768	6.0	1 727	282	16.3	1 030	110	10.7
Householder	8 137	813	10.0	6 819	542	7.9	1 062	228	21.5	533	82	15.4
In married couple families	24 080	720	3.0	21 743	617	2.8	1 622	66	4.1	1 240	59	4.8
Householder	11 360	346	3.0	10 335	312	3.0	745	25	3.4	569	36	6.3
Husband	11 194	339	3.0	10 186	303	3.0	723	24	3.3	573	33	5.7
Wife	11 686	348	3.0	10 551	294	2.8	772	30	3.9	533	22	4.2
In married couple families with related children under 18 years	12 569	509	4.1	11 105	434	3.9	1 046	50	4.7	842	55	6.6
Householder	6 022	264	4.4	5 355	234	4.4	496	22	4.4	393	33	8.4
Husband	5 935	262	4.4	5 285	230	4.4	473	21	4.4	396	30	7.5
Wife	6 310	233	3.7	5 588	196	3.5	518	24	4.6	393	22	5.6
In families with female householder, no spouse present	3 446	650	18.8	2 386	354	14.8	933	263	28.2	238	55	23.3
Householder	2 494	563	22.6	1 737	316	18.2	672	217	32.3	154	49	31.6
In families with female householder, no spouse present, with related children under 18 years	2 096	566	27.0	1 397	314	22.5	619	224	36.2	158	52	32.6
Householder	1 802	518	28.8	1 215	289	23.8	523	202	38.6	119	46	38.5
In unrelated subfamilies	129	36	27.9	106	26	24.4	21	10	(B)	5	1	(B)
Unrelated individuals	6 901	857	12.4	5 971	661	11.1	741	165	22.3	312	44	14.1
Male	3 412	387	11.3	2 901	287	9.9	394	82	20.7	201	22	10.8
Householder	2 591	233	9.0	2 228	175	7.9	289	47	16.2	112	12	10.5
Female	3 489	470	13.5	3 070	374	12.2	347	84	24.0	111	22	19.9
Householder	2 993	352	11.7	2 628	275	10.5	306	66	21.7	84	9	11.0
BACHELOR'S DEGREE OR MORE												
Both Sexes												
Total	34 337	1 058	3.1	30 352	790	2.6	2 080	109	5.2	1 084	68	6.3
25 to 34 years	9 860	348	3.5	8 542	229	2.7	650	39	6.0	410	30	7.4
35 to 54 years	17 144	469	2.7	15 041	353	2.3	1 114	54	4.8	506	30	5.8
55 to 64 years	3 741	103	2.8	3 404	84	2.5	173	6	3.3	101	4	3.5
65 years and over	3 591	137	3.8	3 365	123	3.7	143	10	7.0	67	5	(B)
65 to 74 years	2 356	70	3.0	2 204	66	3.0	90	3	3.7	43	1	(B)
75 years and over	1 235	67	5.5	1 161	57	4.9	53	7	(B)	23	4	(B)
Male												
Total	18 628	531	2.9	16 651	379	2.3	926	59	6.3	583	27	4.7
25 to 34 years	4 927	177	3.6	4 266	105	2.5	306	28	9.2	200	11	5.5
35 to 54 years	9 390	255	2.7	8 364	191	2.3	488	25	5.1	275	14	5.0
55 to 64 years	2 262	49	2.1	2 078	40	1.9	80	1	1.7	68	2	(B)
65 years and over	2 048	51	2.5	1 943	43	2.2	52	5	(B)	40	1	(B)
65 to 74 years	1 464	27	1.9	1 387	27	2.0	39	–	(B)	28	–	(B)
75 years and over	584	24	4.1	556	15	2.8	14	5	(B)	12	1	(B)
Female												
Total	15 709	526	3.4	13 701	411	3.0	1 154	50	4.3	500	41	8.2
25 to 34 years	4 933	172	3.5	4 276	124	2.9	344	11	3.2	210	19	9.2
35 to 54 years	7 754	214	2.8	6 677	162	2.4	627	29	4.6	231	16	6.9
55 to 64 years	1 479	54	3.7	1 327	44	3.3	93	4	4.8	33	2	(B)
65 years and over	1 543	86	5.6	1 422	81	5.7	91	5	6.0	27	4	(B)
65 to 74 years	892	43	4.8	818	39	4.8	51	3	(B)	15	1	(B)
75 years and over	651	44	6.7	604	41	6.9	39	2	(B)	11	3	(B)

See footnote at end of table.

B3-13. Years of School Completed by Persons 25 Years and Over, by Age, Race, Household Relationship, and Poverty Status in 1991 (continued)

[Numbers in thousands. Persons, families and unrelated individuals as of March of the following year.

Characteristic	All races			White			Black			Hispanic Origin[1]		
		Below poverty level			Below poverty level			Below poverty level			Below poverty level	
	Total	Number	Percent of total	Total	Number	Percent of total	Total	Number	Percent of total	Total	Number	Percent of total
BACHELOR'S DEGREE OR MORE —Con.												
Household Relationship												
In families	26 833	501	1.9	23 726	361	1.5	1 532	46	3.0	875	48	5.5
Householder	14 837	323	2.2	13 222	224	1.7	813	38	4.6	461	28	6.0
In families with related children under 18 years	13 414	339	2.5	11 559	221	1.9	878	37	4.2	494	42	8.4
Householder	7 703	237	3.1	6 668	152	2.3	540	32	5.8	280	25	8.9
In married couple families	24 264	361	1.5	21 773	275	1.3	1 090	13	1.2	737	32	4.3
Householder	13 105	211	1.6	11 884	161	1.4	517	7	1.3	378	15	4.0
Husband	13 310	214	1.6	12 079	165	1.4	501	7	1.4	374	16	4.2
Wife	9 948	128	1.3	8 860	100	1.1	516	5	1.0	309	14	4.4
In married couple families with related children under 18 years	12 307	234	1.9	10 736	161	1.5	666	12	1.8	432	28	6.5
Householder	6 724	145	2.2	5 928	100	1.7	352	7	1.9	232	14	6.1
Husband	6 799	145	2.1	5 995	102	1.7	345	7	2.0	230	15	6.4
Wife	5 304	76	1.4	4 614	54	1.2	304	5	1.7	190	11	5.7
In families with female householder, no spouse present	1 881	114	6.1	1 408	73	5.2	355	24	6.8	93	14	14.9
Householder	1 267	96	7.6	958	56	5.8	238	24	10.2	53	11	(B)
In families with female householder, no spouse present, with related children under 18 years	842	94	11.1	631	56	8.9	169	22	13.2	45	12	(B)
Householder	753	85	11.3	566	48	8.5	151	22	14.8	34	10	(B)
In unrelated subfamilies	45	13	(B)	28	8	(B)	6	2	(B)	3	–	(B)
Unrelated individuals	7 459	544	7.3	6 598	421	6.4	542	61	11.2	206	20	9.7
Male	3 858	272	7.1	3 400	186	5.5	263	43	16.5	115	8	6.8
Householder	3 038	144	4.8	2 743	119	4.4	177	15	8.7	81	4	5.2
Female	3 600	272	7.5	3 198	235	7.4	280	18	6.3	91	12	13.4
Householder	3 014	185	6.1	2 679	168	6.3	245	12	4.7	69	7	(B)

[1]Persons of Hispanic origin may be of any race.

(B) Base less than 75,000

B4. Social Attitudes and Activities

B4-1. How Older Americans Feel About Themselves and Their Lives

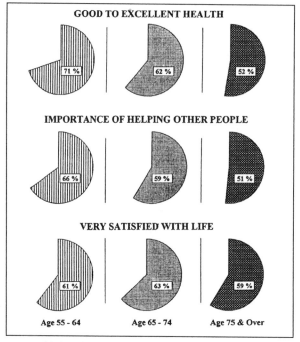

Source: The Commonwealth Fund, 1992 Graphics: U.S. House Select Committee on Aging.

B4-2. Percent of Persons 65 and Older Reporting Specific Leisure-Time Activities: 1980

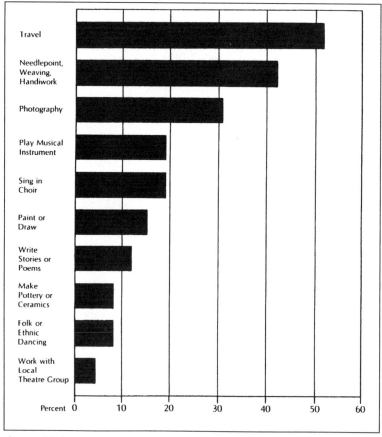

Source: National Council on Aging.

B4-3. Percent of Adults Who Are Church or Synagogue Members, by Age Group: 1979

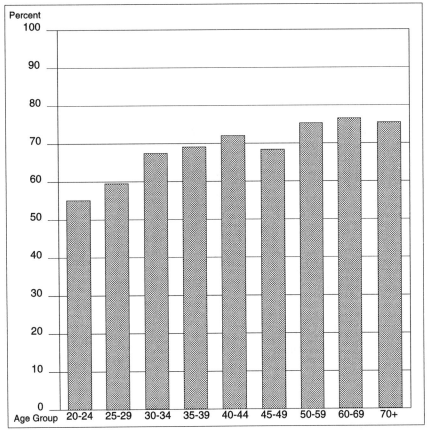

Source: Princeton Religion Research Center.

B4-4. Social Activities and Religious Attendance of the Elderly, by Residence: 1987

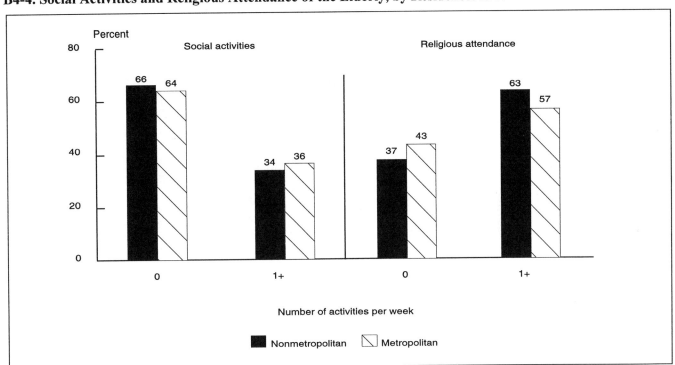

Source: National Center for Health Statistics, 1987 National Health Interview Survey.

B4-5. Number of Friends/Relatives the Elderly Talked with in the Past Month, by Residence: 1987

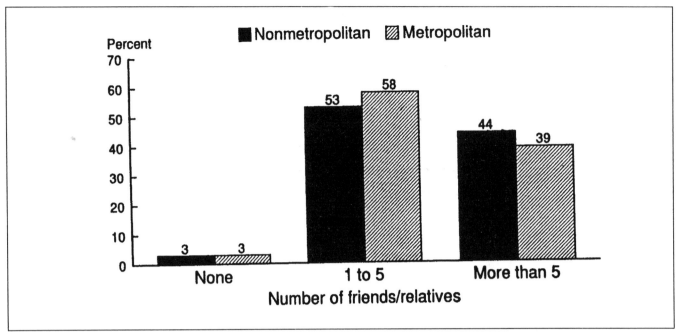

Source: National Center for Health Statistics, 1987 National Health Interview Survey.

B4-6. Number of Relatives the Elderly Can Call for Help, by Residence: 1987

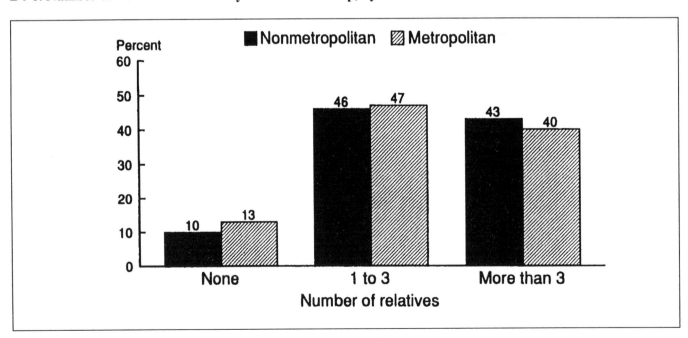

Source: National Center for Health Statistics, 1987 National Health Interview Survey.

B4-7. Number of Friends the Elderly Can Call for Help, by Residence: 1987

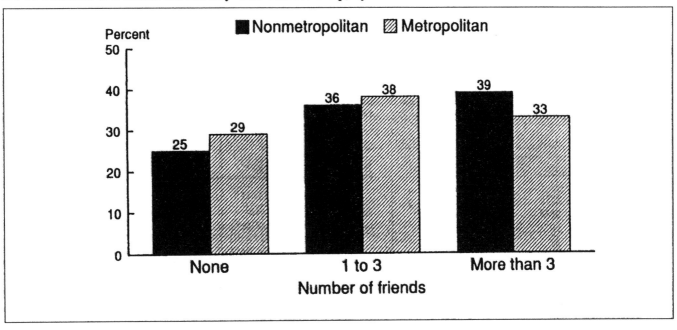

Source: National Center for Health Statistics, 1987 National Health Interview Survey.

B4-8. Percent of Adult Population Doing Volunteer Work: 1989

(For year ending in May. Covers civilian noninstitutional population, 16 years old and over. A volunteer is a person who performed unpaid work for an organization such as a church, the Boy or Girl Scouts, a school, Little League, etc., during the year. Persons who did work on their own such as helping out neighbors or relatives are excluded. Based on Current Population Survey.)

CHARACTERISTIC	VOLUNTEER WORKERS		PERCENT DISTRIBUTION OF VOLUNTEERS, BY TYPE OF ORGANIZATION [1]							
	Number (1,000)	Per-cent of popu-lation	Total	Churches, other religious organi-zations	Schools, other educa-tional insti-tutions	Civic or political organi-zations	Hospi-tals, other health organi-zations	Social or welfare organi-zations	Sport or recrea-tional organi-zations	Other organi-zations
Total [2]	**38,042**	**20.4**	**100.0**	**37.4**	**15.1**	**13.2**	**10.4**	**9.9**	**7.8**	**6.3**
16 to 19 years old	1,902	13.4	100.0	34.4	26.8	8.9	9.2	7.0	8.2	5.5
20 to 24 years old	2,064	11.4	100.0	30.5	18.5	12.7	11.9	11.6	8.0	6.8
25 to 34 years old	8,680	20.2	100.0	34.9	18.3	13.3	9.1	9.3	8.9	6.1
35 to 44 years old	10,337	28.9	100.0	33.1	20.3	12.6	7.4	8.5	12.1	6.1
45 to 54 years old	5,670	23.0	100.0	40.8	11.8	15.1	10.1	8.8	7.1	6.3
55 to 64 years old	4,455	20.8	100.0	45.7	6.7	16.1	12.4	10.9	2.5	5.7
65 years old and over	4,934	16.9	100.0	43.3	4.3	11.1	17.8	14.5	1.8	7.2
Male	16,681	18.8	100.0	35.9	10.5	17.2	7.0	10.1	11.8	7.5
Female	21,361	21.9	100.0	38.5	18.8	10.1	13.1	9.7	4.6	5.3
White	34,823	21.9	100.0	36.6	15.1	13.5	10.7	9.8	8.0	6.3
Black	2,505	11.9	100.0	50.4	12.4	9.6	7.0	10.4	4.6	5.6
Hispanic origin [3]	1,289	9.4	100.0	42.2	18.3	9.6	8.5	8.9	6.9	5.6
Educational attainment: [4]										
Less than 4 years of high school	2,939	8.3	100.0	48.4	6.6	10.0	10.0	13.1	4.8	7.0
4 years of high school	11,105	18.8	100.0	41.5	12.5	11.2	11.1	8.8	8.2	6.7
1 to 3 years of college	7,572	28.1	100.0	36.8	14.7	13.3	10.8	10.1	8.0	6.3
4 years of college or more .	12,459	38.4	100.0	32.9	17.4	16.4	9.7	10.1	7.8	5.7

[1]Organization for which most of the work was done.

[2]Includes other races, not shown separately.

[3]Persons of Hispanic origin may be of any race.

[4]Persons 25 years old and over.

Source: U.S. Bureau of Labor Statistics, News, USDL 90-154, March 29, 1990.

B4-9. Characteristics of Unpaid Volunteer Workers, by Age Group: May 1989

(numbers of people in thousands)	Age		
Characteristic	16+	55-64	65+
Both sexes, total...	186,181	21,373	29,153
Unpaid volunteers..	38,042	4,455	4,934
As % of total	20.4	20.8	16.9
Men, total..	88,656	10,053	12,135
Unpaid volunteers..	16,681	1,987	1,917
As % of total	18.8	19.8	15.8
Women, total	97,525	11,320	17,017
Unpaid volunteers..	21,361	2,468	3,016
As % of total	21.9	21.8	17.7
Unpaid volunteers, total.......................................	38,042	4,455	4,934
Percent	100.0	100.0	100.0
Type of organization for which work was performed:			
Hospital or other health organization............................	10.4	12.4	17.8
School or other educational institution.........................	15.1	6.7	4.3
Social or welfare organization	9.9	10.9	14.5
Civic or political organization	13.2	16.1	11.1
Sport or recreation organization	7.8	2.5	1.8
Church or other religious organization..........................	/37.4	45.7	43.3
Other organizations	6.3	5.7	7.2
Hours worked per week:			
Less than 5 hours...	60.0	58.9	53.6
5 to 9 hours...	19.9	19.9	23.8
10 to 19 hours..	10.8	11.7	11.0
20 to 34 hours..	5.8	6.1	7.4
35 hours and over...	3.6	3.4	4.2
Median hours worked	4.3	4.4	4.7
Weeks worked per year:			
Less than 5 weeks..	20.2	17.5	14.4
5 to 14 weeks	21.2	18.8	16.6
15 to 26 weeks	14.4	12.8	14.8
27 to 49 weeks	15.9	15.9	16.9
50 to 52 weeks	28.3	35.1	37.2
Median weeks worked...	25.2	30.5	34.9

NOTE: Data exclude people in institutions.

Source: U.S. Department of Labor, Bureau of Labor Statistics, "Thirty-Eight Million Persons Do Volunteer Work," Press Release, USDL 90-154 (March 29, 1990). Data are from May 1989 Current Population Survey.

B4-10. Type of Organization for Which Volunteer Work Was Performed, by Age Group: May 1989

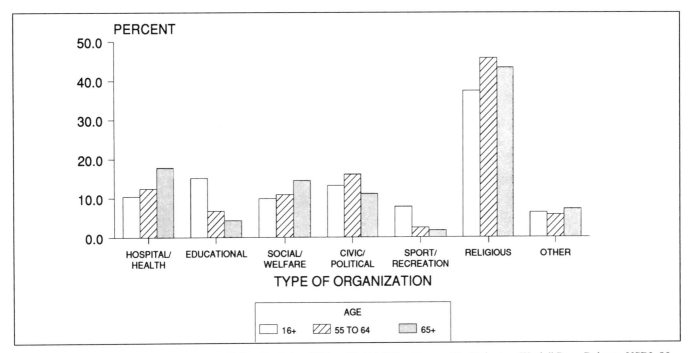

Source: U.S. Department of Labor, Bureau of Labor Statistics, "Thirty-Eight Million Persons Do Volunteer Work," Press Release, USDL 90-154 (March 29, 1990). Data are from May 1989 Current Population Survey.

B4-11. Persons Who Performed Unpaid Volunteer Work at Some Time During the Year Ended May 1989, by Sex and Selected Characteristics

[Numbers in thousands]

Characteristic	Both sexes		Men		Women	
	Volunteer workers	Volunteers as percent of population	Volunteer workers	Volunteers as percent of population	Volunteer workers	Volunteers as percent of population
Total	38,042	20.4	16,681	18.8	21,361	21.9
Age						
16 to 24 years old	3,966	12.3	1,814	11.4	2,152	13.1
16 to 19	1,902	13.4	879	12.3	1,023	14.4
20 to 24	2,064	11.4	935	10.6	1,129	12.1
25 to 34 years old	8,680	20.2	3,678	17.4	5,002	23.0
35 to 44 years old	10,337	28.9	4,683	26.8	5,655	30.9
45 to 54 years old	5,670	23.0	2,601	21.8	3,069	24.1
55 to 64 years old	4,455	20.8	1,987	19.8	2,468	21.8
65 years old and over	4,934	16.9	1,917	15.8	3,016	17.7
Race and Hispanic origin						
White	34,823	21.9	15,273	20.0	19,550	23.6
Black	2,505	11.9	1,082	11.5	1,423	12.3
Hispanic origin	1,289	9.4	587	8.6	702	10.1
Marital status						
Never married	6,327	13.7	3,102	12.4	3,225	15.3
Married, spouse present ...	26,344	24.8	12,131	22.8	14,213	26.9
Married, spouse absent ...	765	13.2	275	12.1	489	14.0
Divorced	2,510	17.3	908	15.3	1,602	18.6
Widowed	2,096	15.3	266	11.9	1,831	16.0
Years of school completed by persons 25 years old and over						
0 to 11 years	2,939	8.3	1,295	7.8	1,644	8.8
12 years only	11,105	18.8	4,120	16.0	6,985	20.9
13 to 15 years	7,572	28.1	3,042	24.0	4,531	31.6
16 years or more	12,459	38.4	6,410	36.0	6,049	41.4
Employment status						
In labor force	27,284	22.1	14,094	20.9	13,190	23.6
Employed	26,439	22.6	13,734	21.4	12,705	24.0
Full time	21,182	21.9	12,541	21.8	8,641	22.0
Part time	5,257	26.0	1,193	18.0	4,064	29.9
Unemployed	845	13.8	360	11.1	485	16.8
Not in labor force	10,758	17.1	2,587	12.2	8,171	19.6

B4-12. Volunteers Helping Younger Generations

- 22.6 million Americans age 55 and older provide direct help to children or grandchildren/great grandchildren.

- Those receiving assistance include:

	Number	Typical amount each week
-- Children	17.6 million	5 hours
-- Grandchildren/great grandchildren	14.2 million	8 hours

- The total amount of help to children and grandchildren is equivalent to the hours of 4.4 million full-time workers.

B4-13. Productive Engagement: Contributions by Those 75+

- 6.3 million Americans age 75 and older -- nearly one-half of all -- are actively engaged in helping American society:

    -- 23% volunteer through organizations.

    -- 22% give care to the sick or disabled.

    -- 19% help younger generations.

    -- 4% are in paid employment.

B4-14. Volunteers Providing Direct Care

- 15.1 million Americans age 55 and older provide direct volunteer care to sick or disabled family members, friends, or neighbors.

Those receiving assistance include:	Number	Typical amount each week
-- Spouses	3.4 million	20 hours
-- Parents	3.1 million	6 hours
-- Other relatives	4.6 million	5 hours
-- Friends and neighbors	5.2 million	3 hours
	16.3 million	

- The total amount of direct volunteer care to the sick or disabled is equivalent to the hours of 2.7 million full-time workers.

B4-15. Voting-Age Population, Percent Reporting Registered, and Voted: 1976 to 1990

(As of November. Covers civilian noninstitutional population 18 years old and over. Includes aliens. Figures are based on Current Population Survey)

CHARACTERISTIC	VOTING-AGE POPULATION (mil.) 1976	1978	1980	1982	1984	1986	1988	1990	REGISTERED Presidential 1976	1980	1984	1988	REGISTERED Congressional 1978	1982	1986	1990	VOTED Presidential 1976	1980	1984	1988	VOTED Congressional 1978	1982	1986	1990
Total [1]	146.5	151.6	157.1	165.5	170.0	173.9	178.1	182.1	66.7	66.9	68.3	66.6	62.6	64.1	64.3	62.2	59.2	59.2	59.9	57.4	45.9	48.5	46.0	45.0
18 to 20 years old	12.1	12.2	12.3	12.1	11.2	10.7	10.7	10.8	47.1	44.7	47.0	44.9	34.7	35.0	35.4	35.4	38.0	35.7	36.7	33.2	20.1	19.8	18.6	18.4
21 to 24 years old	14.8	15.5	15.9	16.7	16.7	15.7	14.8	14.0	54.8	52.7	54.3	50.6	45.1	47.8	46.6	43.3	45.6	43.1	43.5	38.3	26.2	28.4	24.2	22.0
25 to 34 years old	31.7	33.4	35.7	38.8	40.3	41.9	42.7	42.7	62.3	62.0	63.3	57.8	55.5	57.1	55.8	52.0	55.4	54.6	54.5	48.0	38.0	40.4	35.1	33.8
35 to 44 years old	22.8	24.2	25.6	28.1	30.7	33.0	35.2	37.9	69.8	70.6	70.9	69.3	66.7	67.5	67.9	65.5	63.3	64.4	63.5	61.3	50.1	52.2	49.3	48.4
45 to 64 years old	43.3	43.4	43.6	44.2	44.3	44.8	45.9	46.9	75.5	75.8	76.6	75.5	74.3	75.6	74.8	71.4	68.7	69.3	69.8	67.9	58.5	62.2	58.7	55.8
65 years old and over	22.0	23.0	24.1	25.6	26.7	27.7	28.8	29.9	71.4	74.6	76.9	78.4	72.6	75.2	76.9	78.5	62.2	65.1	67.7	68.8	55.9	59.9	60.9	60.3
Male	69.0	71.5	74.1	78.0	80.3	82.4	84.5	86.6	67.1	66.6	67.3	65.2	62.6	63.7	63.4	61.2	59.6	59.1	59.0	56.4	46.6	48.7	45.8	44.6
Female	77.6	80.2	83.0	87.4	89.6	91.5	93.6	95.5	66.4	67.1	69.3	67.8	62.5	64.4	65.0	63.1	58.8	59.4	60.8	58.3	45.3	48.4	46.1	45.4
White	129.3	133.4	137.7	143.6	146.8	149.9	152.9	155.6	68.3	68.4	69.6	67.9	63.8	65.6	65.3	63.8	60.9	60.9	61.4	59.1	47.3	49.9	47.0	46.7
Black	14.9	15.6	16.4	17.6	18.4	19.0	19.7	20.4	58.5	60.0	66.3	64.5	57.1	59.1	64.0	58.8	48.7	50.5	55.8	51.5	37.2	43.0	43.2	39.2
Hispanic [2]	6.6	6.8	8.2	8.8	9.5	11.8	12.9	13.8	37.8	36.3	40.1	35.5	32.9	35.3	35.9	32.3	31.8	29.9	32.6	28.8	23.5	25.3	24.2	21.0
Region:																								
Northeast	33.9	35.1	35.5	36.4	36.9	37.3	37.9	38.1	65.9	64.6	66.6	64.8	62.3	62.5	62.0	61.0	59.5	58.5	59.7	57.4	48.1	49.8	44.4	45.2
Midwest	39.2	40.3	41.5	41.9	42.1	42.8	43.3	43.9	72.3	73.8	74.6	72.5	68.2	71.1	70.7	68.2	65.1	65.8	65.7	62.9	50.5	54.7	49.5	48.6
South	47.1	48.8	50.6	55.4	57.6	59.2	60.7	62.4	64.6	64.8	66.9	65.6	60.1	61.7	63.0	61.3	54.9	55.6	56.8	54.5	39.6	41.8	43.0	42.4
West	26.2	27.5	29.5	31.9	33.4	34.6	36.2	37.7	63.2	63.3	64.7	63.0	59.1	60.6	60.8	57.7	57.5	57.2	58.5	55.6	47.5	50.7	48.4	45.0
School years completed:																								
8 years or less	24.9	23.6	22.7	22.4	20.8	19.6	19.1	17.7	54.4	53.0	53.4	47.5	53.2	52.3	50.5	44.0	44.1	42.6	42.9	36.7	34.6	35.7	32.7	27.7
High school:																								
1 to 3 years	22.2	22.3	22.5	22.3	22.1	21.4	21.1	21.0	55.6	54.6	54.9	52.8	52.9	53.3	52.4	47.9	47.2	45.6	44.4	41.3	35.1	37.7	33.8	30.9
4 years	55.7	58.4	61.2	65.2	67.8	68.6	70.0	71.5	66.9	66.4	67.3	64.6	62.0	62.9	62.9	60.0	59.4	58.9	58.7	54.7	45.3	47.1	44.1	42.2
College:																								
1 to 3 years	23.6	25.1	26.7	28.8	30.9	33.0	34.3	36.3	75.2	74.4	75.7	73.5	68.7	70.0	70.0	68.7	68.1	67.2	67.5	64.5	51.5	53.3	49.9	50.0
4 years or more	20.2	22.2	24.0	26.9	28.6	31.3	33.6	35.6	83.7	84.3	83.8	83.1	76.9	79.4	77.8	77.3	79.8	79.9	79.1	77.6	63.9	66.5	62.5	62.5
Employed	86.0	93.2	95.0	97.2	104.2	106.1	113.6	115.5	66.8	66.7	68.4	67.1	63.0	65.5	64.4	62.6	62.0	61.8	61.6	58.4	46.7	50.0	45.7	45.1
Unemployed	6.4	4.9	6.9	10.8	7.4	6.6	5.8	6.7	52.1	50.3	54.3	50.4	44.1	49.8	50.6	44.8	43.7	41.2	44.0	38.6	27.4	34.1	31.2	27.9
Not in labor force	54.1	53.5	55.2	57.5	58.4	58.8	58.5	59.9	65.2	65.8	68.1	67.2	63.4	64.3	65.4	63.4	56.5	57.0	58.9	57.3	46.2	48.7	48.2	46.7

[1] Includes other races not shown separately.

[2] Hispanic persons may be of any race.

Source: U.S. Bureau of the Census, *Current Population Reports,* series P-20, No. 453, and earlier reports.

B4-16. Percent Reported Voting in Congressional Election Years, by Region, Race, Hispanic Origin, Sex, and Age: November 1966 to 1990

(Numbers in thousands)

Region, race, Hispanic origin, sex, and age	Congressional elections of— 1990	1986	1982	1978	1974	1970	1966
UNITED STATES							
Total, voting age	182,118	173,890	165,483	151,646	141,299	120,701	112,800
Percent voted	45.0	46.0	48.5	45.9	44.7	54.6	55.4
White	46.7	47.0	49.9	47.3	46.3	56.0	57.0
Black	39.2	43.2	43.0	37.2	33.8	43.5	41.7
Hispanic origin [1]	21.0	24.2	25.3	23.5	22.9	(NA)	(NA)
Male	44.6	45.8	48.7	46.6	46.2	56.8	58.2
Female	45.4	46.1	48.4	45.3	43.4	52.7	53.0
18 to 24 years	20.4	21.9	24.8	23.5	23.8	2/30.4	2/31.1
25 to 44 years	40.7	41.4	45.4	43.1	42.2	51.9	53.1
45 to 64 years	55.8	58.7	62.2	58.5	56.9	64.2	64.5
65 years and over	60.3	60.9	59.9	55.9	51.4	57.0	56.1
NORTH AND WEST							
Total, voting age	119,740	114,689	110,126	102,894	96,505	83,515	78,355
Percent voted	46.4	47.5	51.9	48.9	48.8	59.0	60.9
White	48.2	48.7	53.1	50.0	50.0	59.8	61.7
Black	38.4	44.2	48.5	41.3	37.9	51.4	52.1
Hispanic origin [1]	20.5	23.8	25.8	23.9	(NA)	(NA)	(NA)
SOUTH							
Total, voting age	62,378	59,201	55,357	48,752	44,794	37,186	34,445
Percent voted	42.4	43.0	41.8	39.6	36.0	44.7	43.0
White	43.5	43.5	42.9	41.1	37.4	46.4	45.1
Black	39.8	42.5	38.3	33.5	30.0	36.8	32.9
Hispanic origin [1]	22.1	25.0	24.2	22.5	(NA)	(NA)	(NA)

[1] Persons of Hispanic origin may be of any race.

[2] Prior to 1972, includes persons 17 to 20 years old in Georgia and Kentucky, 19 and 20 in Alaska, and 20 years old in Hawaii.

NA Not available.

Source: Current Population Reports, Series P-20, Nos. 174, 228, 293, 344, 383, 414.

B4-17. Percent of Persons 65 Years and Over Reported Voting in Congressional Elections, by Race and Hispanic Origin: November 1966 to 1990

(Numbers in thousands)

Race and Hispanic origin	1990	1986	1982	1978	1974	1970	1966
White							
Total, 65 years and over	26,807	24,982	23,139	20,798	19,058	17,583	16,413
Voted	16,550	15,464	14,135	11,892	10,058	10,307	9,504
Percent	61.7	61.9	61.1	57.2	52.8	58.6	57.9
Black							
Total, 65 years and over...........	2,528	2,318	2,132	1,943	1,710	1,413	1,316
Voted............................	1,296	1,236	1,083	886	659	556	464
Percent	51.3	53.3	50.8	45.6	38.5	39.3	35.3
Hispanic[1]							
Total, 65 years and over..........	1,072	881	599	511	413	(NA)	(NA)
Voted............................	434	322	177	127	116	(NA)	(NA)
Percent	40.5	36.5	29.5	24.9	28.1	(NA)	(NA)

[1]Hispanics may be of any race.
NA Not available
Source: Current Population Reports, Series P-20, Nos. 174, 228, 293, 344, 393, 414.

B4-18. Percent Reported Voting in Presidential Election Years, by Region, Race, Hispanic Origin, Sex, and Age: November 1964 to 1992

(Numbers in thousands. Civilian noninstitutional population)

Region, race, Hispanic origin, sex, and age	Presidential elections of—							
	1992	1988	1984	1980	1976	1972	1968	1964
UNITED STATES								
Total, voting age	185,684	178,098	169,963	157,085	146,548	136,203	116,535	110,604
Percent voted.................	61.3	57.4	59.9	59.2	59.2	63.0	67.8	69.3
White	63.6	59.1	61.4	60.9	60.9	64.5	69.1	70.7
Black	54.0	51.5	55.8	50.5	48.7	52.1	57.6	[2]58.5
Hispanic origin[1]	28.9	28.8	32.6	29.9	31.8	37.5	(NA)	(NA)
Male............................	60.2	56.4	59.0	59.1	59.6	64.1	69.8	71.9
Female..........................	62.3	58.3	60.8	59.4	58.8	62.0	66.0	67.0
18 to 24 years	42.8	36.2	40.8	39.9	42.2	49.6	[3]50.4	[3]50.9
25 to 44 years	58.3	54.0	58.4	58.7	58.7	62.7	66.6	69.0
45 to 64 years	70.0	67.9	69.8	69.3	68.7	70.8	74.9	75.9
65 years and over	70.1	68.8	67.7	65.1	62.2	63.5	65.8	66.3
NORTH AND WEST								
Total, voting age	122,025	117,373	112,376	106,524	99,403	93,653	81,594	78,174
Percent voted.................	62.5	58.9	61.6	61.0	61.2	66.4	71.0	74.6
White	64.9	60.4	63.0	62.4	62.6	67.5	71.8	74.7
Black	53.8	55.6	58.9	52.8	52.2	56.7	64.8	[2]72.0
SOUTH								
Total, voting age	63,659	60,725	57,587	50,561	47,145	42,550	34,941	32,429
Percent voted.................	59.0	54.5	56.8	55.6	54.9	55.4	60.1	56.7
White	60.8	56.4	58.1	57.4	57.1	57.0	61.9	59.5
Black	54.3	48.0	53.2	48.2	45.7	47.8	51.6	[2]44.0

[1]Persons of Hispanic origin may be of any race.
[2]Black and other races in 1964.
[3]Prior to 1972, includes persons 18 to 20 years old in Georgia and Kentucky, 19 and 20 in Alaska, and 20 years old in Hawaii.
NA Not available.
Source: Current Population Reports, Series P-20, Nos. 174, 228, 293, 344, 393, 414, 440, and table 2 of this report.

B4-19. Percent Reported Registered in Congressional Election Years, by Region, Race, Hispanic Origin, Sex, and Age: November 1966 to 1990

(Numbers in thousands)

Region, race, Hispanic origin, sex, and age	Congressional elections of —						
	1990	1986	1982	1978	1974	1970	1966
UNITED STATES							
Total, voting age	182,118	173,890	165,483	151,646	141,299	120,701	112,800
Percent registered	62.2	64.3	64.1	62.6	62.2	68.1	70.3
White	63.8	65.3	65.6	63.8	63.5	69.1	71.6
Black	58.8	64.0	59.1	57.1	54.9	60.8	60.2
Hispanic origin[1]	32.3	35.9	35.3	32.9	34.9	(NA)	(NA)
Male	61.2	63.4	63.7	62.6	62.8	69.6	72.2
Female	63.1	65.0	64.4	62.5	61.7	66.8	68.6
18 to 24 years	39.9	42.0	42.4	40.5	41.3	[2]40.9	2/44.1
25 to 44 years	58.4	61.1	61.5	60.2	59.9	65.0	67.6
45 to 64 years	71.4	74.8	75.6	74.3	73.6	77.5	78.9
65 years and over	76.5	76.9	75.2	72.8	70.2	73.7	73.5
NORTH AND WEST							
Total, voting age	119,740	114,689	110,126	102,894	96,505	83,515	78,355
Percent registered	62.6	64.9	65.2	63.8	63.3	70.0	73.8
White	64.4	66.2	66.7	64.9	64.6	70.8	74.5
Black	58.4	63.1	61.7	58.0	54.2	64.5	68.8
Hispanic origin[1]	30.4	33.2	33.9	32.0	(NA)	(NA)	(NA)
SOUTH							
Total, voting age	62,378	59,201	55,357	48,752	44,794	37,186	34,445
Percent registered	61.3	63.0	61.7	60.1	59.8	63.8	62.2
White	62.5	63.2	63.2	61.2	61.0	65.1	64.3
Black	59.0	64.6	56.9	56.2	55.5	57.5	52.9
Hispanic origin[1]	36.1	41.0	38.3	34.9	(NA)	(NA)	(NA)

NA Not available. [1]Persons of Hispanic origin may be of any race. [2]Prior to 1972, includes persons 18 to 20 years old in Georgia and Kentucky, 19 and 20 in Alaska, and 20 years old in Hawaii.

B4-20. Reported Registration, by Region, Race, Hispanic Origin, Sex, and Age: November 1968 to 1992

(Numbers in thousands. Civilian noninstitutional population)

Region, race, Hispanic origin, sex, and age	Presidential elections of—						
	1992	1988	1984	1980	1976	1972	1968
UNITED STATES							
Total, voting age	185,684	178,098	169,963	157,085	146,548	136,203	116,535
Percent registered	68.2	66.6	68.3	66.9	66.7	72.3	74.3
White	70.1	67.9	69.6	68.4	68.3	73.4	75.4
Black	63.9	64.5	66.3	60.0	58.5	65.5	66.2
Hispanic origin[1]	35.0	35.5	40.1	36.3	37.8	44.4	(NA)
Male	66.9	65.2	67.3	66.6	67.1	73.1	76.0
Female	69.3	67.8	69.3	67.1	66.4	71.6	72.8
18 to 24 years	52.5	48.2	51.3	49.2	51.3	58.9	[2]56.0
25 to 44 years	64.8	63.0	66.6	65.6	65.5	71.3	72.4
45 to 64 years	75.3	75.5	76.6	75.8	75.5	79.7	81.1
65 years and over	78.0	78.4	76.9	74.6	71.4	75.6	75.6
NORTH AND WEST							
Total, voting age	122,025	117,373	112,376	106,524	99,403	93,653	81,594
Percent registered	68.7	67.1	69.0	67.9	67.7	73.9	76.5
White	70.9	68.5	70.5	69.3	69.0	74.9	77.2
Black	63.0	65.9	67.2	60.6	60.9	67.0	71.8
SOUTH							
Total, voting age	63,659	60,725	57,587	50,561	47,145	42,550	34,941
Percent registered	67.2	65.6	66.9	64.8	64.6	68.7	69.2
White	68.5	66.6	67.8	66.2	66.7	69.8	70.8
Black	64.7	63.3	65.6	59.3	56.4	64.0	61.6

NA Not available. [1]Persons of Hispanic origin may be of any race. [2]Prior to 1972, includes persons 18 to 20 years old in Georgia and Kentucky, 19 and 20 in Alaska, and 20 years old in Hawaii.
Source: Current Population Reports, Series P-20, Nos. 192, 253, 293, 322, 344, 370, 383, 405, 414, 440.

B4-21. Average Annual Miles Per Licensed Driver, by Driver Age and Sex: 1969, 1977, 1983, and 1990 NPTS

(miles)					Percent Change	
Age	1969	1977	1983	1990	69-90[1]	69-90[2]
MALE						
16 - 19	5,461	7,045	5,908	9,543	2.7	75
20 - 34	13,133	15,222	15,844	18,310	1.6	39
35 - 54	12,841	16,097	17,808	18,871	1.9	47
55 - 64	10,696	12,455	13,431	15,224	1.7	42
65+	5,919	6,795	7,198	9,162	2.1	55
Average	**11,352**	**13,397**	**13,962**	**16,536**	**1.8**	**46**
FEMALE						
16 - 19	3,586	4,036	3,874	7,387	3.5	106
20 - 34	5,512	6,571	7,121	11,174	3.4	103
35 - 54	6,003	6,534	7,347	10,539	2.7	76
55 - 64	5,375	5,097	5,432	7,211	1.4	34
65+	3,664	3,572	3,308	4,750	1.2	30
Average	**5,411**	**5,940**	**6,382**	**9,528**	**2.7**	**76**

[1]Compounded annual rate of percentage change.
[2]Percentage change rate.
Source: Data obtained from driver's estimate of annual miles driven, including driving in all vehicles (personal and commercial).

B4-22. Distribution of Estimated Annual Miles, by Driver Age and Sex: 1969, 1977, 1983, and 1990 NPTS

(percentage) Age	1969	1977	1983	1990
MALE				
16 - 19	3.1	3.2	2.0	2.0
20 - 34	27.0	29.7	28.6	24.3
35 - 54	30.1	27.2	27.0	27.1
55 - 64	9.3	8.5	9.3	6.8
65+	3.7	3.7	3.8	4.4
Total	**73.2**	**72.3**	**70.7**	**64.6**
FEMALE				
16 - 19	1.5	1.6	1.1	1.5
20 - 34	9.9	11.9	12.4	14.6
35 - 54	11.3	10.1	10.9	14.3
55 - 64	2.9	2.8	3.4	2.9
65+	1.2	1.3	1.5	2.1
Total	**26.8**	**27.7**	**29.3**	**35.4**

Source: Data obtained from driver's estimate of annual miles driven, including driving in all vehicles (personal and commercial).

B4-23. Travel by Individuals 65 Years and Older Compared to All Age Groups: 1983 and 1990 NPTS

Age	Average Annual Person Trips			Average Annual Person Miles of Travel			Average Trip Length		
	1983	1990	Percent Change[1]	1983	1990	Percent Change[1]	1983	1990	Percent Change[1]
65 and older	672.3	713.5	6.1	4,447.5	5,596.4	25.8	6.7	8.0	19.4
All ages	977.9	1,042.4	6.6	8,483.9	9,670.6	14.0	8.7	9.5	9.2

[1]Percentage change rate.

B5. Victimization and Abuse of the Elderly

B5-1. Victimization Rates for Personal Crimes of Violence and Theft, Persons Age 65 or Older: 1973 to 1990

B5-2. Victimization Rates for Household Crimes, Head of Households Age 65 or Older: 1973 to 1990

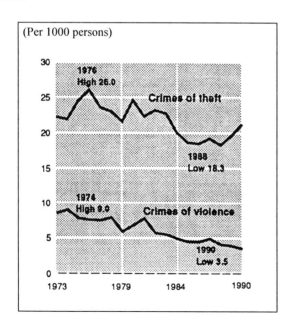

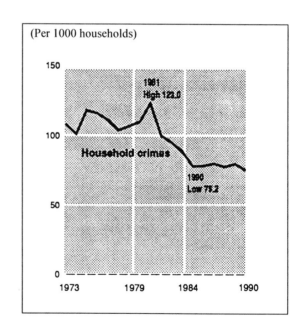

B5-3. Average Annual Victimization Rates, by Age of Victim and Type of Crime: 1987 to 1990

	Number of victimizations per 1,000 persons or households			
	12-24	25-49	50-64	65 or older
Crimes of violence	64.6	27.2	8.5	4.0
Rape	1.5	.6	.1*	.9*
Robbery	10.0	5.3	2.4	1.5
Assault	53.1	21.2	5.9	2.3
Aggravated	18.4	7.5	2.2	1.1
Simple	34.6	13.7	3.7	1.3
Crimes of theft	112.7	71.2	38.3	19.5
Personal larceny with contact	3.6	2.4	2.2	2.6
Personal larceny without contact	109.0	68.8	36.1	16.9
Average annual population	45,983,893	92,550,343	32,787,706	28,577,225
Household crimes[a]	309.3	200.2	133.0	78.5
Burglary	121.3	66.6	43.3	32.4
Household larceny	153.4	111.9	73.3	39.5
Motor vehicle theft	34.6	21.7	16.4	6.6
Average annual number of households	6,534,240	48,597,483	19,026,720	19,803,345

Note: The victimization rate is the annual average of the number of victimizations for 1987-90 per 1,000 persons in each age group. Detail may not add to total because of rounding.
*Estimated is based on 10 or fewer sample cases.
[a]Household crimes are categorized by age of head of household.

B5-4. Relationship of Offenders to Victims of Violent Crime, by Age of Victim and Type of Crime: 1987 to 1990

	Percent of violent crime victims whose offenders were:			
	Relatives	Acquaintances	Strangers	Relationship not ascertained
Crimes of violence				
Under 65	8%	33%	56%	3%
65 or older	8	20	64	8
Robbery				
Under 65	5	17	74	4
65 or older	3	5	83	9
Assault				
Under 65	9	36	52	3
65 or older	13	32	47	8

B5-5. Place of Occurrence of Crimes of Violence, by Age of Victim and Type of Crime: 1987 to 1990

	Place of occurrence				
	Total	At home	Near home	On the street	In commercial or public establishment	Else- where
Crimes of violence					
Under 65	100%	14%	11%	39%	21%	15%
65 or older	100	25	25	31	9	10
Robbery					
Under 65	100	13	9	52	16	10
65 or older	100	20	21	37	13	10
Assault					
Under 65	100	14	12	36	21	15
65 or older	100	27	29	27	7	10

B5-6. Average Annual Victimization Rates of Persons Age 65 or Older, by Sex, Race, Marital Status, and Type of Crime: 1987 to 1990

| | Number of victimizations per 1,000 persons or households | | | | | | | |
| | Sex | | Race | | Marital status | | | |
	Male	Female	White	Black	Never married	Widowed	Married	Divorced/ separated
Crimes of violence	4.9	3.4	3.6	7.6	3.0	4.2	7.6	11.3
Robbery	2.0	1.2	1.2	4.4	1.2	1.7	5.1	1.7
Aggravated assault	1.4	.8	1.1	1.4	.8	.9	1.5	4.8
Simple assault	1.4	1.2	1.2	1.4	.9	1.4	.7	4.4
Crimes of theft	19.8	19.4	19.5	19.6	18.2	4.2	26.3	35.4
Personal larceny with contact	1.8	3.2	2.3	5.7	1.8	2.9	6.1	6.4
Personal larceny without contact	17.9	16.2	17.2	13.9	16.4	15.1	20.2	30.0
Household crimes*	82.2	74.3	70.9	154.1	77.6	75.1	71.1	110.4
Burglary	32.8	31.9	29.1	63.8	28.7	33.7	35.2	46.3
Household larceny	41.6	37.1	36.5	71.9	41.6	35.7	34.1	37.8
Motor vehicle theft	7.7	5.2	5.3	18.3	7.2	5.7	1.8	10.5

*Household crimes are categorized by sex, race, and marital status of head of household.

B5-7. Average Annual Victimization Rates of Persons Age 65 or Over, by Location of Residence, Home Ownership, and Type of Crime: 1987 to 1990

| | Number of victimizations per 1,000 persons or households | | | | |
| | Locality of residence | | | Tenure | |
	City	Suburb	Rural	Own	Rent
Crimes of violence	7.1	2.9	2.2	3.1	7.7
Robbery	3.5	.9	.4	1.1	3.6
Aggravated assault	1.4	.8	1.0	1.0	1.6
Simple assault	1.9	1.1	.7	1.0	2.2
Crimes of theft	26.4	19.6	11.4	17.8	26.7
Personal larceny with contact	6.5	1.2	.4	1.9	5.5
Personal larceny without contact	19.9	18.4	10.9	16.0	21.1
Household crimes	112.6	61.2	64.5	82.0	66.8
Burglary	42.4	25.6	30.7	33.6	28.3
Household larceny	57.3	31.2	31.3	42.1	30.9
Motor vehicle theft	12.8	4.3	2.5	6.2	7.5

B5-8. Average Annual Victimization Rates of Persons Age 65 or Older, by Family Income and Type of Crime: 1987 to 1990

	Number of victimizations per 1,000 persons or households			
	Less than $7,500	$7,500-14,999	$15,000-24,999	$25,000 or more
Crimes of violence	12.0	8.4	6.5	6.1
Robbery	4.4	2.6	1.5	3.9
Aggravated assault	3.4	3.3	1.5	.6
Simple assault	3.9	2.3	3.3	1.5
Crimes of theft	29.1	30.4	40.3	60.8
Personal larceny with contact	7.1	4.2	5.7	4.3
Personal larceny without contact	22.0	26.2	34.6	56.5
Household crimes	76.3	70.2	81.3	96.0
Burglary	37.9	29.3	30.7	34.2
Household larceny	35.1	35.0	43.0	51.6
Motor vehicle theft	3.3	5.8	7.5	10.2

NOTE: It should be remembered that this measure represents only annual family income, not total assets.

B5-9. Average Annual Victimization Rates, by Age of Victim and Type of Crime: 1987 to 1990

	Number of victimizations per 1,000 persons or households	
	65-74	75 or older
Crimes of violence	4.7	3.0
Rape	.1*	.1*
Robbery	1.5	1.6
Assault	3.0	1.3
Aggravated	1.3	.7
Simple	1.7	.6
Crimes of theft	22.9	14.2
Personal larceny with contact	2.5	2.8
Personal larceny without contact	20.4	11.1
Average annual population	17,774,054	11,351,210
Household crimes[a]	85.4	68.9
Burglary	33.7	30.5
Household larceny	43.2	34.4
Motor vehicle theft	8.4	4.0
Average annual number of households	11,557,918	8,245,427

Note: The victimization rates are the annual average of the number of victimizations for 1987-90 per 1,000 persons or households in that age group. Detail may not add to total because of rounding.
* Estimate is based on about 10 or fewer cases.
[a]Household crimes are categorized by age of head of household.

B5-10. Average Annual Victimization Rates of Persons Age 65 to 74 and 75 or Older for Crimes of Violence, Crimes of Theft, and Household Crimes

| | Number of victimizations per 1,000 persons or households | | | | | |
| | Crimes of violence | | Crimes of theft | | Household crimes | |
	65-74	75+	65-74	75+	65-74	75+
Sex						
Male	5.2	4.4	22.4	14.8	86.9	73.1
Female	4.2	2.2	23.4	13.9	82.9	65.6
Race						
White	4.2	2.6	23.1	14.2	77.6	61.4
Black	13.9	6.5	36.7	16.1	156.8	149.6
Marital status						
Married	3.3	2.2	20.5	12.9	82.7	66.5
Widowed	5.6	3.1	24.6	13.0	83.3	68.5
Never married	8.1	7.0	30.8	20.2	73.3	67.7
Divorced/separated	13.1	6.2	34.9	36.5	116.6	92.2
Family Income						
Less than $7,500	9.7	3.3	19.1	12.0	83.3	70.7
$7,500-$14,999	4.5	4.1	18.2	12.0	49.4	64.6
$15,000-$24,999	3.6	2.2	21.1	15.9	86.5	70.6
$25,000 or over	3.2	1.7	30.6	20.9	78.5	78.6

B5-11. Injuries, Medical Treatment, and Hospital Care Received by Violent Crime Victims, by Age of Victim: 1987 to 1990

| | Percent of violent crime victims | |
Outcome	Under 65	65 or older
Injured	31%	33%
Serious	5	9
Minor	26	24
Received medical care	15	19
Hospital care	8	14

Note: Serious injuries are broken bones, loss of teeth, internal injuries, loss of consciousness, rape or attempted rape injuries, or undetermined injuries requiring 2 or more days of hospitalization. Minor injuries are bruises, black eyes, cuts, scratches, swelling, or undetermined injuries requiring less than 2 days of hospitalization.

B5-12. Self-Protective Measures Taken in Violent Crimes, by Age of Victim: 1987 to 1990

| | Percent of violent crime victims | |
	Under 65	65 or older
Did not take any action	27%	42%
Took some form of action	73	58
Type of action taken		
Physical action, including attacking offender with weapon, chasing offender, or physically resisting	34	23
Nonphysical action, including arguing or reasoning with offender, screaming, or running away	39	34

B5-13. Percent of Victimizations Reported to the Police, by Type of Crime and Age of Victims

Type of crime	Percent of victimizations reported to the police				
	12–19	20–34	35–49	50–64	65 and over
All personal crimes	**23.9 %**	**39.7 %**	**39.4 %**	**37.9 %**	**32.5 %**
Crimes of violence	35.6	53.3	56.8	58.0	64.0
Completed	48.6	61.4	65.3	66.2	88.7
Attempted	28.1	47.6	52.3	53.6	45.4
Rape	43.9	64.3	81.7 *	29.1 *	0.0 *
Robbery	38.7	56.8	64.9	44.2	72.2
Completed	52.1	63.4	67.0	50.8 *	95.2
With injury	78.9	67.6	75.1	81.7 *	100.0 *
From serious assault	75.7 *	65.2	66.2 *	100.0 *	100.0 *
From minor assault	80.3	71.4	83.5 *	76.9 *	0.0 *
Without injury	36.1	61.2	62.3	43.0 *	93.3 *
Attempted	19.6 *	42.0	61.3	24.3 *	41.2 *
With injury	24.4 *	35.3 *	79.1	100.0 *	0.0 *
From serious assault	14.9 *	43.0 *	83.3 *	0.0 *	0.0 *
From minor assault	29.2 *	25.5 *	71.8 *	100.0 *	0.0 *
Without injury	17.6 *	44.6	42.6 *	14.6 *	48.2 *
Assault	34.8	52.0	53.7	62.0	55.3
Aggravated	44.7	63.9	65.3	79.1	52.1 *
Completed with injury	55.4	67.9	63.0	100.0 *	59.9 *
Attempted with weapon	39.1	61.2	66.6	73.8	48.1 *
Simple	30.7	45.6	49.7	54.0	58.7 *
Completed with injury	45.4	54.6	66.2	69.2	100.0 *
Attempted without weapon	23.8	41.8	44.6	48.0	47.9 *
Crimes of theft	14.7	32.2	33.2	32.5	26.4
Completed	14.8	32.5	34.1	33.4	26.6
Attempted	12.3 *	29.7	21.1	21.3 *	18.3 *
Personal larceny with contact	26.5 *	41.3	33.5	43.6	44.5
Purse snatching	33.3 *	58.6 *	45.1 *	65.4 *	56.8 *
Completed	39.6 *	60.2 *	63.8 *	83.9 *	58.6 *
Attempted	0.0 *	50.2 *	18.0 *	0.0 *	44.6 *
Pocket picking	25.2 *	35.8	27.8 *	26.7 *	38.6 *
Personal larceny without contact	14.3	31.9	33.2	31.9	23.5
Completed	14.4	32.1	34.1	32.6	23.9
Less than $50	5.8	15.3	15.4	13.8	9.9 *
$50 or more	27.6	41.9	45.0	45.4	35.9
Amount not available	6.0 *	20.7	28.3	18.2 *	17.6 *
Attempted	12.5 *	29.4	21.3	22.8 *	12.4 *

* Estimate is based on about 10 or fewer sample cases.

B5-14. Percent of Victimizations Reported to the Police, by Age of Victims and Victim-Offender Relationship

Age	Percent of all victimizations reported to the police		
	All victimizations	Involving strangers	Involving nonstrangers
All ages	**48.6 %**	**48.9 %**	**48.0 %**
12–19	35.6	37.0	34.1
20–34	53.3	52.6	54.4
35–49	56.8	54.4	60.5
50–64	58.0	55.5	62.8
65 and over	64.0	61.9	77.1 *

* Estimate is based on about 10 or fewer sample cases.

B5-15. Average Annual Homicide Rates, by Age of Victim and Victim-Offender Relationship: 1980 to 1987

	Average annual number of homi-cides per 100,000 persons when the victim/offender relationship was:		
	Family	Acquaintance	Stranger
Age			
0-34	2.5	7.2	2.8
35-54	2.0	4.0	1.7
55-64	1.9	2.6	1.5
65+	1.0	1.1	1.0

B5-16. Average Annual Homicide Rates, by Age of Victim and Precipitating Circumstances: 1980 to 1987

	Average annual number of homi-cides per 100,000 persons where the incident occurred in:		
	Conflict	Felony	Other
Age			
0-34	5.9	.7	2.4
35-54	6.5	.7	2.5
55-64	2.1	1.5	.8
65+	.9	1.7	.6

B5-17. Types of Elder Abuse: 1990 and 1991 (Reports from 29 and 30 States)

	Percentage	
Type of Maltreatment*	**FY90 (N=29)**	**FY91 (N=30)**
Physical Abuse	20.3%	19.1%
Sexual Abuse	0.6%	0.6%
Psychological/emotional abuse	11.6%	13.8%
Neglect	46.6%	45.2%
Financial/material exploitation	17.4%	17.1%
All other types	3.3%	4.0%
Unknown/missing data	0.2%	0.2%
Totals:	100.0%	100.0%

* This analysis includes <u>only</u> the substantiated reports involving abuse victims and does <u>not</u> include self-neglect reports.

States reporting for 1990: Arizona, California, Delaware, the District of Columbia, Florida, Hawaii, Idaho, Illinois, Iowa, Kentucky, Maryland, Massachusetts, Missouri, Montana, Nebraska, Nevada, New Hampshire, New Jersey, New York, Ohio, Pennsylvania, Rhode Island, South Carolina, South Dakota, Texas, Utah, Virginia, Wisconsin, and Wyoming.

States reporting for 1991: Arizona, Arkansas, California, Delaware, the District of Columbia, Florida, Hawaii, Idaho, Illinois, Kentucky, Maryland, Massachusetts, Missouri, Montana, Nebraska, Nevada, New Hampshire, New Jersey, New Mexico, New York, Ohio, Oklahoma, Pennsylvania, Puerto Rico, Rhode Island, South Carolina, South Dakota, Texas, Utah, and Virginia.

B5-18. Effectiveness of Nine Factors in Identifying Elder Abuse

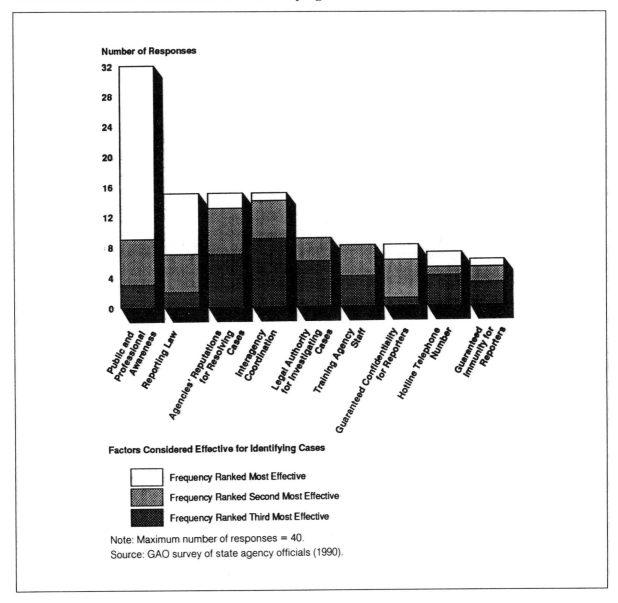

Number of Responses

Factors Considered Effective for Identifying Cases

Frequency Ranked Most Effective

Frequency Ranked Second Most Effective

Frequency Ranked Third Most Effective

Note: Maximum number of responses = 40.

Source: GAO survey of state agency officials (1990).

B5-19. Effectiveness of Eight Factors in Preventing a First Occurrence of Elder Abuse

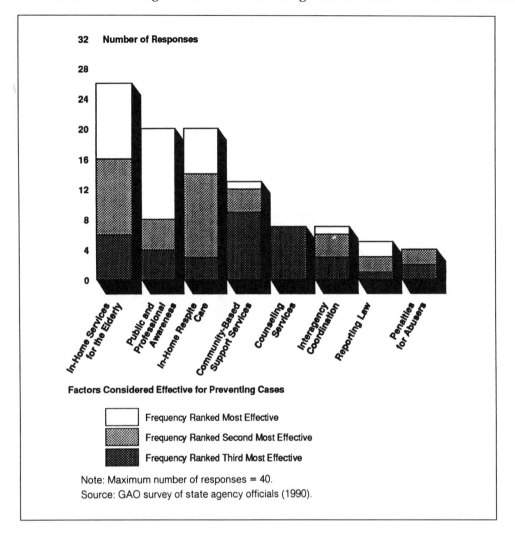

32   Number of Responses

Factors Considered Effective for Preventing Cases

☐ Frequency Ranked Most Effective

▨ Frequency Ranked Second Most Effective

■ Frequency Ranked Third Most Effective

Note: Maximum number of responses = 40.
Source: GAO survey of state agency officials (1990).

B5-20. Sex of Elder Abuse Victims: 1990 and 1991 (Reports from 28 and 29 States)

		Percentage	
Sex of Victim		**FY90 (N=28)**	**FY91 (N=29)**
Male		31.3%	32.0%
Female		68.6%	67.8%
Unknown/missing data		0.2%	0.2%
	Totals:	100.1%*	100.0%

*Due to rounding errors, the totals are not exactly 100.0%.

States Reporting for 1990: Arizona, California, Colorado, the District of Columbia, Florida, Georgia, Hawaii, Illinois, Iowa, Kentucky, Maine, Massachusetts, Michigan, Mississippi, Missouri, Montana, Nebraska, New Hampshire, New Jersey, New York, North Carolina, Ohio, Pennsylvania, Rhode Island, South Carolina, Texas, Virginia, and Wisconsin.

States Reporting for 1991: Arizona, Arkansas, California, Colorado, the District of Columbia, Florida, Georgia, Hawaii, Illinois, Kentucky, Maine, Massachusetts, Michigan, Mississippi, Missouri, Montana, Nebraska, New Hampshire, New Jersey, New York, North Carolina, Ohio, Oklahoma, Pennsylvania, Puerto Rico, Rhode Island, South Carolina, Texas, and Virginia.

B5-21. Age of Elder Abuse Victims: 1990 and 1991 (Reports from 22 and 25 States)

	Percentage	
Age Category	**FY90 (N=22)**	**FY91 (N=25)**
60-64	7.8%	7.6%
65-69	11.2%	10.5%
70-74	15.0%	15.5%
75-79	17.4%	17.1%
80-84	19.2%	19.4%
85 and up	22.2%	23.1%
Missing data	7.2%	6.8%
Totals:	100.0%	100.0%

States reporting for 1990: Arizona, Colorado, the District of Columbia, Florida, Georgia, Hawaii, Iowa, Kentucky, Maine, Michigan, Missouri, Nebraska, New Hampshire, New Jersey, New York, Ohio, Oregon, Pennsylvania, Rhode Island, Texas, Utah, and Wisconsin.

States reporting for 1991: Arizona, Arkansas, Colorado, the District of Columbia, Florida, Georgia, Hawaii, Illinois, Kentucky, Maine, Massachusetts, Michigan, Missouri, Nebraska, New Hampshire, New Jersey, New York, Ohio, Oklahoma, Oregon, Pennsylvania, Puerto Rico, Rhode Island, Texas, and Utah.

B5-22. Abusers of the Elderly: 1990 and 1991 (Reports from 21 States)

	Percentage	
Type of Abuser	**FY90 (N=21)**	**FY91 (N=21)**
Adult children	31.9%	32.5%
Grandchildren	4.0%	4.2%
Spouse	15.4%	14.4%
Sibling	2.6%	2.5%
Other relatives	13.0%	12.5%
Service provider	6.6%	6.3%
Friend/neighbor	7.3%	7.5%
All other categories	16.7%	18.2%
Unknown/missing data	2.5%	2.0%
Totals:	100.0%	100.1%*

* Due to rounding errors, the total is not exactly 100.0%.

States reporting for 1990: Arizona, California, the District of Columbia, Florida, Illinois, Iowa, Kentucky, Michigan, Missouri, Montana, Nebraska, New Hampshire, New Jersey, New York, Pennsylvania, Rhode Island, South Dakota, Texas, Utah, Wisconsin, and Wyoming.

States reporting for 1991: Arizona, Arkansas, California, Delaware, the District of Columbia, Florida, Illinois, Kentucky, Michigan, Missouri, Montana, Nebraska, New Hampshire, New Jersey, New York, Pennsylvania, Rhode Island, South Dakota, Texas, and Utah.

B5-23. Effectiveness of Eight Factors in Treating Elder Abuse

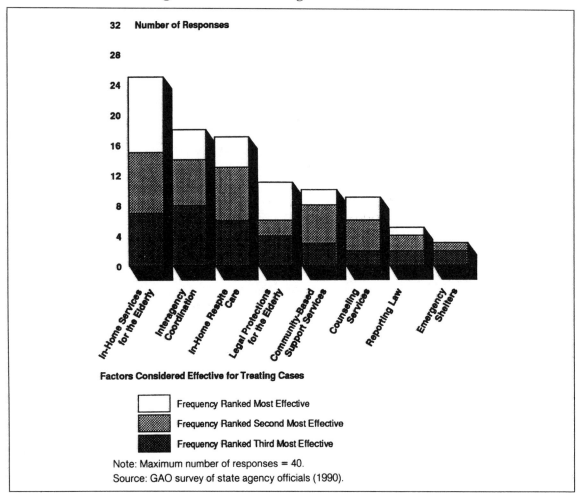

Factors Considered Effective for Treating Cases

☐ Frequency Ranked Most Effective

▒ Frequency Ranked Second Most Effective

■ Frequency Ranked Third Most Effective

Note: Maximum number of responses = 40.

Source: GAO survey of state agency officials (1990).

B6. Other Social Problems

B6-1. Alcohol Abuse or Dependence in the Past Year, by Age, Sex, and Ethnicity: Data from ECA (DSM-III) and 1988 NHIS (DSM-III-R), in Percentages (standard error shown in parentheses)*

| | Age | Men (%) | | Women (%) | |
		ECA (DSM-III)	1988 NHIS (DSM-III-R)	ECA (DSM-III)	1988 NHIS (DSM-III-R)
White					
	18+	11.69 (0.53)	13.99 (0.34)	2.11 (0.23)	4.68 (0.17)
	18-29	18.10 (1.13)	26.14 (0.91)	4.54 (0.62)	11.45 (0.53)
	30-44	13.52 (1.08)	14.87 (0.54)	1.96 (0.43)	4.33 (0.27)
	45-64	7.20 (0.80)	7.14 (0.42)	0.81 (0.27)	1.77 (0.22)
	65+	2.85 (0.75)	2.73 (0.35)	0.47 (0.25)	0.34 (0.10)
ECA Black/ NHIS Nonwhite					
	18+	11.51 (1.53)	9.29 (0.69)	2.50 (0.68)	2.50 (0.26)
	18-29	7.92 (2.11)	10.50 (1.26)	2.37 (1.12)	3.86 (0.55)
	30-44	16.30 (3.30)	10.79 (1.19)	3.37 (1.49)	2.66 (0.46)
	45-64	15.24 (3.52)	7.98 (1.31)	2.56 (1.39)	1.47 (0.39)
	65+	2.93 (2.55)	3.15 (1.27)	0.60 (0.96)	0.62 (0.33)
Hispanics					
	18+	15.97 (2.33)		2.46 (0.97)	
	18-29	19.29 (3.81)		3.59 (1.87)	
	30-44	19.16 (4.63)		1.84 (1.51)	
	45-64	7.69 (3.67)		2.65 (2.15)	
	65+	6.57 (6.31)		0.00 --	
Total					
	18+	11.90 (0.49)	13.35 (0.31)	2.16 (0.21)	4.36 (0.15)
	18-29	17.03 (0.98)	23.50 (0.78)	4.14 (0.53)	10.10 (0.45)
	30-44	14.10 (1.10)	14.30 (0.49)	2.12 (0.40)	4.07 (0.24)
	45-64	7.85 (0.77)	7.24 (0.40)	1.04 (0.28)	1.73 (0.19)
	65+	3.10 (0.73)	2.77 (0.34)	0.46 (0.24)	0.37 (0.10)

*ECA = Epidemiologic Catchment Area; DSM-III = *Diagnostic and Statistical Manual of Mental Disorders,* Third Edition; NHIS = National Health Interview Survey; DSM-III-R = *Diagnostic and Statistical Manual of Mental Disorders*, Third Edition, Revised.
Source: ECA data from Helzer et al. 1991 (Reprinted with the permission of The Free Press, a division of Macmillan, Inc. from *Psychiatric Disorders in America: The Epidemiologic Catchment Area Study* by Lee N. Robins and Davis A. Regier. Copyright 1991 by Lee N. Robins and David A. Regier.), pp. 85 and 88; 1988 NHIS data from Grant, Harford et al. 1991.

B6-2. Elderly Drinkers Who Are Heavy Current Drinkers, by Sex: 1990

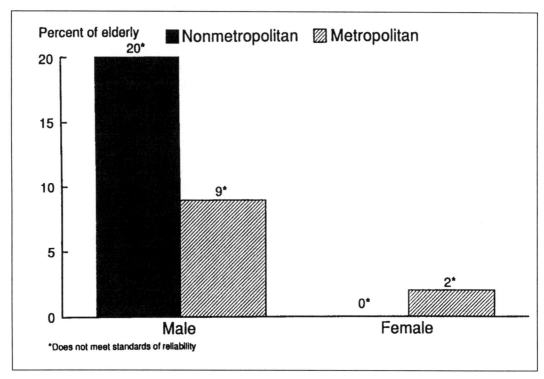

Source: National Center for Health Statistics, 1990 National Health Interview Survey.

B6-3. Blood Alcohol Content for Drivers Involved in Fatal Crashes, by Age

Year	16-20			21-24			25-44			45-64			65+		
	Total	0.01+	0.10+	Total	0.01+	0.10+	Total	0.01+	0.10+	Total	0.01+	0.10+	Total	0.01+	0.10+
1982	9,858	44.0	31.1	9,018	51.6	40.0	22,771	40.8	32.6	8,921	26.4	20.7	3,894	13.7	9.9
1983	9,334	42.2	29.7	8,432	50.7	39.1	22,538	40.2	32.2	8,854	24.6	19.4	4,026	12.1	8.6
1984	9,804	39.6	26.6	8,963	49.0	37.3	23,796	38.3	30.4	9,143	22.7	17.7	4,316	12.5	8.8
1985	9,386	35.5	23.9	9,046	45.9	35.3	24,149	37.1	29.4	9,262	21.6	16.7	4,479	11.1	7.6
1986	10,163	36.5	23.7	9,129	47.3	36.1	25,419	37.5	29.9	9,096	21.4	16.2	4,881	10.5	6.8
1987	9,910	33.3	21.0	8,808	45.4	34.1	26,340	37.8	30.1	9,693	20.6	15.9	5,078	10.1	6.7
1988	10,171	32.3	20.7	8,555	46.1	35.2	26,475	37.4	29.9	10,081	21.2	16.5	5,376	10.9	7.0
1989	9,442	29.9	19.5	7,723	45.0	34.5	26,034	36.6	29.3	10,240	21.5	16.8	5,431	10.0	6.6
1990	8,808	31.7	21.2	7,179	44.9	34.7	25,882	37.8	30.3	9,917	20.2	15.6	5,487	9.8	6.4

B6-4. Elderly Smokers Who Smoke Heavily,* by Sex: 1990

*Heavy smoking is defined as at least 25 cigarettes per day.
Source: National Center for Health Statistics, 1990 National Health Interview Survey.

B6-5. Percent of Persons 65 Years and Over Who Smoked Cigarettes at Time of Survey, by Sex and Race: 1965 to 1987

Year	Male			Female		
	Total	White	Black	Total	White	Black
1987	17.2	16.0	30.3	13.7	13.9	11.7
1979	20.9	20.5	26.2	13.2	13.8	8.5
1974	24.8	24.3	29.7	12.0	12.3	8.9
1965	28.5	27.7	36.4	9.6	9.8	7.1

*Heavy smoking is defined as at least 25 cigarettes per day.
Source: National Center for Health Statistics, *Health, United States, 1990*, Hyattsville, MD: Public Health Service, 1991, Table 55.

B6-6. Crash Involvements Per Million V.M. of Travel, by Age

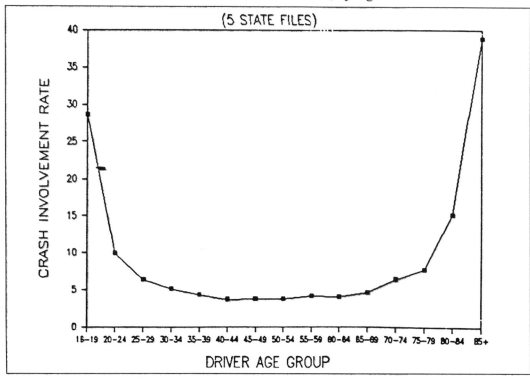

B6-7. Self-Reported Driving Difficulties of Older and Younger Drivers

Reported Difficulty	Percentage by Driver's Age (N = 446)	
	55+	35–44
Reading traffic signs	27	12
Seeing while driving at night	40	32
Turning head while backing	23	5
Reading instrument panel	9	3
Reaching seat belt	22	10
Merging and exiting in high-speed traffic	32	15

B6-8. Driver Fatality Rate, 1986

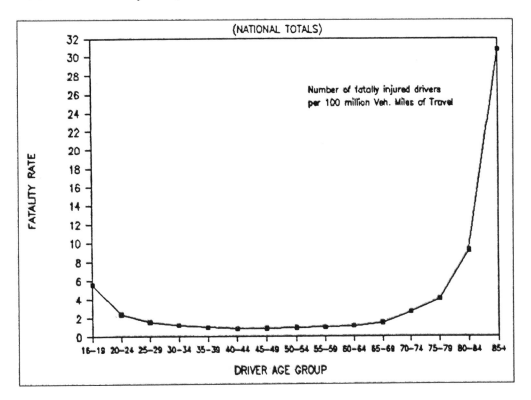

B6-9. Fatalities as a Percent of Serious Injuries, 1986

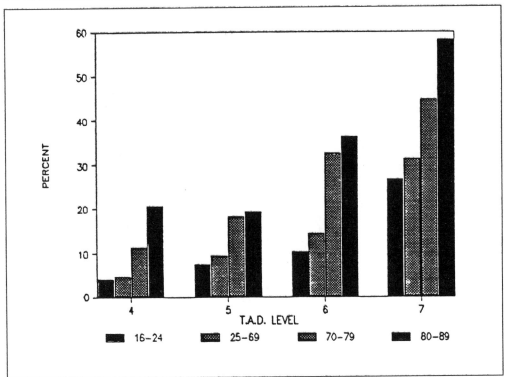

B6-10. Nonmotorist Fatality Rate Per 100,000 Population, by Age, 1975 to 1990

Year				Age				
	0-4	5-15	16-24	25-44	45-64	65-79	80+	Total
1975	3.64	4.76	3.45	2.54	3.40	7.06	11.12	3.99
1976	3.52	4.52	3.43	2.51	3.44	6.39	11.12	3.87
1977	2.99	4.39	3.64	2.67	3.60	6.76	11.14	3.97
1978	3.14	4.48	3.81	2.85	3.54	6.01	9.68	3.96
1979	2.87	4.31	4.29	3.08	3.50	6.21	9.78	4.08
1980	2.67	4.09	4.40	3.02	3.54	6.03	10.38	4.03
1981	2.14	3.76	4.20	3.14	3.32	5.54	9.70	3.87
1982	2.14	3.41	4.20	3.03	3.04	5.13	7.49	3.58
1983	2.02	3.31	3.77	2.81	2.95	4.30	8.61	3.31
1984	1.91	3.32	3.62	2.78	3.11	4.57	8.80	3.37
1985	2.03	3.28	3.38	2.67	3.00	4.48	8.29	3.26
1986	1.87	3.36	3.55	2.73	2.90	4.29	8.23	3.26
1987	1.64	3.39	3.30	2.75	2.98	4.35	8.13	3.21
1988	1.66	3.21	3.20	2.81	2.87	4.60	8.57	3.22
1989	1.52	2.74	2.80	2.85	2.84	4.12	7.92	3.02
1990	1.65	2.48	2.67	2.86	2.83	4.23	7.88	2.99

B6-11. State Prison Inmates—Selected Characteristics: 1979 and 1986

[Based on a sample survey of about 13,711 inmates in 1986 and 11,397 inmates in 1979; subject to sampling variability]

CHARACTERISTIC	NUMBER		PERCENT OF PRISON INMATES		CHARACTERISTIC	NUMBER		PERCENT OF PRISON INMATES	
	1979	1986	1979	1986		1979	1986	1979	1986
Total [1]	274,564	450,416	100.0	100.0	Never married	142,414	241,707	51.9	53.7
					Married	61,420	91,492	22.4	20.3
Under 18 years old	2,220	2,057	0.8	0.5	Widowed	6,248	8,343	2.3	1.9
18 to 24 years old	97,860	120,384	35.6	26.7	Divorced	46,314	81,263	16.9	18.1
25 to 34 years old	116,284	205,817	42.4	45.7	Separated	18,168	26,985	6.6	6.0
35 to 44 years old	37,926	87,502	13.8	19.4	Years of school:				
45 to 54 years old	13,987	23,524	5.1	5.2	Less than 12 years	144,771	276,309	52.7	61.6
55 to 64 years old	4,786	8,267	1.7	1.8	12 years or more	129,792	172,385	47.3	38.4
65 years old and over	1,499	2,808	0.5	0.6	Pre-arrest employment status:				
Male	263,484	430,604	96.0	95.6	Employed	192,800	309,364	70.5	69.0
Female	11,080	19,812	4.0	4.4	Not employed	80,663	138,773	29.5	31.0
White	136,295	223,648	49.6	49.7	Looking for work	38,230	80,508	14.0	18.0
Black	131,329	211,021	47.8	46.9	Not looking for work	42,433	58,265	15.5	13.0
Other races	6,939	15,412	2.6	3.4					

[1] For 1986, includes data not reported for all characteristics except sex.

Source: U.S. Bureau of Justice Statistics, *Profile of State Prison Inmates, 1986*, January 1988.

C. Health Status

HEALTH ASSESSMENT

As more elderly survive to the oldest ages they also face more illness and disability. Issues surrounding the care of the frail elderly are becoming more prevalent. During the twentieth century, the health status of the population in general and the elderly in particular has significantly improved due to the great advances in public health, medical research, and medical care. At the turn of the century, acute and infectious diseases were the main health problems; today, the main health problems are chronic diseases and disabilities. In spite of the fact that 20% of the elderly suffer from at least a mild degree of disability, and 80% have at least one chronic condition, almost 1 in 4 assess their health as good or excellent.

DISEASES AND DISABILITIES

The most prevalent chronic conditions affecting the elderly are arthritis, hypertension, heart conditions, hearing and visual impairments, cancer, and diabetes. With increasing age, restrictions in activities and difficulties in performing activities of daily living increase greatly. Psychiatric problems are less common among the older than the younger population, but cognitive impairments, disorientation, and senility are common problems of the elderly.

DEATH RATES AND CAUSES OF DEATH

About 75% of all deaths are caused by heart disease, cancer, and stroke. Overall death rates have been declining significantly during the past 30 years. Due to new medical advances and modifications in eating, smoking, and exercise habits, death rates from heart disease declined during the last 20 years while death rates from cancer increased.

HEALTH CARE ACCESS AND UTILIZATION

The average annual number of physician visits per person increases significantly with increasing age; the oldest old in fair or poor health average one physician visit per month. As contact with physicians becomes more frequent, the need for support services, nursing homes, hospitals, and medications increases greatly with age, particularly after age 85; only dentists are seen less frequently.

HOSPITALS AND NURSING HOMES

The elderly are hospitalized more frequently, and they stay longer than younger people. However, over the last decade, length of hospital stay has decreased in general, as well as for the elderly, due to improvements in technology, more stringent criteria for hospitalization brought about by attempts to control costs, and increasing availability of home health services. The nursing home population increased by 24% between 1980 and 1990, from 1.4 million to almost 1.8 million. The rate of nursing home use has almost doubled since the introduction of Medicare and Medicaid in 1966. About 55% of the elderly who are confined in nursing homes suffer from chronic mental conditions, memory impairment, and senile dementia; among those living in the community, 15% to 25% have at least mild symptoms of mental illness such as depression and disorientation.

HEALTH INSURANCE COVERAGE

Almost all elderly are covered by Medicare or Medicaid; between 1980 and 1990 increasing numbers of the elderly also carried private supplemental insurance. Health insurance premiums per elderly family have more than tripled since 1961, before the introduction of Medicare.

C1. Health Assessment

C1-1. Number of Persons and Percent Distribution, by Respondent-Assessed Health Status, According to Sociodemographic Characteristics: United States, 1990

(Data are based on household interviews of the civilian noninstitutionalized population.)

Characteristic	All persons[1]	All health statuses[2]	Excellent	Very good	Good	Fair	Poor
	Number in thousands			Percent distribution			
All persons[3]	246,098	100.0	39.5	28.6	22.5	6.9	2.6
Age							
Under 5 years	19,084	100.0	53.2	28.1	15.8	2.6	0.3
5–17 years	45,567	100.0	52.3	28.0	17.4	2.0	0.3
18–24 years	25,023	100.0	44.6	31.1	20.3	3.5	0.6
25–44 years	80,059	100.0	41.6	31.2	21.0	4.9	1.3
45–64 years	46,585	100.0	29.2	27.1	27.7	10.9	5.1
65 years and over	29,780	100.0	17.1	22.9	32.3	18.7	8.9
Sex and age							
Male:							
All ages	119,364	100.0	42.2	28.4	20.9	6.0	2.5
Under 5 years	9,768	100.0	52.4	28.0	16.5	2.7	0.4
5–17 years	23,319	100.0	52.5	28.2	17.1	2.0	0.2
18–24 years	12,242	100.0	49.9	28.7	18.1	2.8	0.4
25–44 years	39,299	100.0	44.9	31.0	18.9	4.1	1.2
45–64 years	22,324	100.0	31.7	27.4	25.5	10.3	5.2
65 years and over	12,414	100.0	18.4	22.3	32.0	18.1	9.3
Female:							
All ages	126,734	100.0	36.8	28.8	24.0	7.7	2.7
Under 5 years	9,317	100.0	54.0	28.3	15.0	2.4	*0.2
5–17 years	22,248	100.0	52.2	27.8	17.6	2.1	0.3
18–24 years	12,781	100.0	39.5	33.3	22.4	4.1	0.7
25–44 years	40,760	100.0	38.5	31.5	23.0	5.8	1.3
45–64 years	24,261	100.0	26.9	26.9	29.7	11.5	5.0
65 years and over	17,367	100.0	16.3	23.3	32.6	19.2	8.7
Race and age							
White:							
All ages	207,125	100.0	40.6	29.0	21.6	6.4	2.4
Under 5 years	15,387	100.0	54.5	28.9	14.2	2.1	0.3
5–17 years	36,674	100.0	54.9	28.0	15.3	1.6	0.2
18–24 years	20,362	100.0	45.7	31.8	18.8	3.2	0.5
25–44 years	67,571	100.0	43.2	31.7	19.7	4.3	1.1
45–64 years	40,339	100.0	30.6	27.7	27.1	10.0	4.6
65 years and over	26,791	100.0	17.4	23.2	32.8	18.2	8.3
Black:							
All ages	30,371	100.0	32.1	25.7	28.4	10.1	3.8
Under 5 years	2,986	100.0	46.8	24.8	23.0	5.1	*0.3
5–17 years	7,137	100.0	39.8	27.8	27.5	4.4	*0.5
18–24 years	3,535	100.0	38.2	26.3	29.2	5.6	*0.8
25–44 years	9,422	100.0	31.6	27.8	28.8	9.5	2.2
45–64 years	4,786	100.0	18.0	21.9	31.8	18.8	9.5
65 years and over	2,505	100.0	13.0	18.6	28.3	24.0	16.1

See footnotes at end of table.

C1-1. Number of Persons and Percent Distribution, by Respondent-Assessed Health Status, According to Sociodemographic Characteristics: United States, 1990 (continued)

[Data are based on household interviews of the civilian noninstitutionalized population. The survey design, general qualifications, and information on the reliability of the estimates are given in appendix I. Definitions of terms are given in appendix II]

Characteristic	All persons[1]	All health statuses[2]	Respondent-assessed health status				
			Excellent	Very good	Good	Fair	Poor
Family income and age	Number in thousands	Percent distribution					
Under $10,000:							
All ages	24,255	100.0	25.8	23.4	29.2	14.2	7.4
Under 5 years	2,338	100.0	40.3	26.4	27.3	5.3	*0.6
5–17 years	4,376	100.0	34.3	25.9	33.4	5.6	0.9
18–24 years	4,342	100.0	37.8	32.2	24.1	5.2	*0.7
25–44 years	5,045	100.0	24.1	22.6	31.0	16.5	5.8
45–64 years	3,068	100.0	12.4	13.0	26.4	24.9	23.3
65 years and over	5,086	100.0	11.2	19.4	30.6	24.7	14.0
$10,000–$19,999:							
All ages	39,731	100.0	30.4	27.6	27.9	10.3	3.8
Under 5 years	3,380	100.0	46.6	29.6	20.4	3.1	*0.3
5–17 years	7,152	100.0	42.9	29.6	23.9	3.2	*0.4
18–24 years	4,604	100.0	36.7	32.1	24.9	5.6	*0.7
25–44 years	11,075	100.0	31.9	30.9	28.0	7.4	1.8
45–64 years	5,965	100.0	17.5	22.4	31.5	19.3	9.3
65 years and over	7,555	100.0	15.5	21.4	34.2	20.0	9.0
$20,000–$34,999:							
All ages	53,026	100.0	39.2	30.5	22.3	6.2	1.8
Under 5 years	4,427	100.0	52.0	30.0	15.4	2.2	*0.5
5–17 years	10,142	100.0	50.5	31.0	16.5	1.7	*0.3
18–24 years	4,962	100.0	46.6	31.9	18.4	2.6	*0.6
25–44 years	18,932	100.0	40.3	33.3	21.0	4.5	1.0
45–64 years	9,118	100.0	26.9	27.3	29.5	12.4	3.8
65 years and over	5,445	100.0	18.0	24.6	34.4	16.6	6.4
$35,000 or more:							
All ages	88,525	100.0	49.7	29.3	17.2	3.1	0.8
Under 5 years	6,461	100.0	63.3	26.3	8.7	1.5	*0.2
5–17 years	17,599	100.0	62.2	26.2	10.6	0.9	*0.1
18–24 years	7,184	100.0	54.6	28.2	15.4	1.5	*0.3
25–44 years	33,623	100.0	49.2	31.7	16.3	2.4	0.4
45–64 years	19,233	100.0	38.1	30.2	25.1	5.1	1.5
65 years and over	4,426	100.0	25.8	25.4	29.9	13.3	5.5
Geographic region							
Northeast	49,901	100.0	41.1	28.3	22.5	6.1	2.0
Midwest	59,788	100.0	40.3	29.5	21.7	6.4	2.1
South	84,223	100.0	36.4	27.8	24.1	8.3	3.5
West	52,187	100.0	41.9	29.2	20.8	5.9	2.2
Place of residence							
MSA[4]	192,826	100.0	40.7	28.6	21.8	6.5	2.4
Central city	75,490	100.0	37.5	28.4	23.7	7.6	2.9
Not central city	117,336	100.0	42.8	28.8	20.7	5.7	2.0
Not MSA[4]	53,272	100.0	35.0	28.4	24.8	8.4	3.4

[1]Includes unknown health status.

[2]Excludes unknown health status.

[3]Includes other races and unknown family income.

[4]MSA is metropolitan statistical area.

C1-2. Self-Assessment of Health, According to Selected Characteristics: United States, 1985 and 1990

Characteristic	Total	Excellent		Very good		Good		Fair or poor	
		1985	*1990*	*1985*	*1990*	*1985*	*1990*	*1985*	*1990*
		Percent distribution[1]							
Total[2,3]	100.0	40.4	40.5	27.1	28.5	22.8	22.0	9.8	8.9
Age									
Under 15 years	100.0	53.1	52.8	26.3	28.1	18.2	16.6	2.5	2.4
Under 5 years	100.0	54.7	53.2	25.8	28.1	17.2	15.8	2.3	2.9
5–14 years	100.0	52.2	52.6	26.5	28.1	18.7	17.1	2.5	2.2
15–44 years	100.0	43.9	43.1	30.1	30.9	20.6	20.6	5.4	5.4
45–64 years	100.0	27.0	29.2	25.3	27.1	29.2	27.7	18.6	16.0
65 years and over	100.0	15.9	17.1	20.2	22.9	32.5	32.3	31.4	27.7
65–74 years.	100.0	17.1	18.9	20.7	23.5	32.9	32.6	29.3	25.1
75 years and over	100.0	13.9	14.5	19.5	21.9	31.9	31.9	34.7	31.7
Sex[2]									
Male.	100.0	42.8	42.5	26.2	28.3	21.5	20.8	9.5	8.4
Female.	100.0	38.0	38.7	27.9	28.8	24.1	23.2	10.0	9.3
Race[2]									
White.	100.0	42.1	42.1	27.5	29.0	21.5	20.8	8.9	8.1
Black	100.0	29.1	31.1	23.9	25.3	30.0	28.5	17.0	15.1
Family income[2,4]									
Less than $14,000.	100.0	28.3	28.1	24.0	24.3	28.4	28.9	19.3	18.6
$14,000–$24,999.	100.0	35.0	34.6	27.9	29.6	25.6	25.0	11.6	10.8
$25,000–$34,999.	100.0	41.0	40.6	28.3	30.2	22.7	21.7	8.0	7.5
$35,000–$49,999.	100.0	44.5	45.9	28.8	29.7	20.2	19.1	6.4	5.3
$50,000 or more	100.0	53.3	52.1	27.1	28.0	15.3	16.0	4.2	4.0
Geographic region[2]									
Northeast	100.0	40.5	43.1	27.9	28.1	23.1	21.6	8.5	7.2
Midwest	100.0	41.2	41.7	27.9	29.3	21.9	21.1	9.0	7.9
South.	100.0	37.3	37.3	26.5	27.8	24.3	23.8	11.9	11.2
West	100.0	44.5	42.2	25.8	29.1	21.3	20.6	8.5	8.1
Location of residence[2]									
Within MSA.	100.0	41.3	41.6	27.3	28.5	22.3	21.5	9.0	8.5
Outside MSA.	100.0	37.1	36.7	26.3	28.7	24.5	24.1	12.1	10.4

[1]Denominator excludes unknown health status.

[2]Age adjusted.

[3]Includes all other races not shown separately and unknown family income.

[4]Family income categories for 1990. Income categories for 1985 are less than $11,000; $11,000-$19,999; $20,000-$29,999; $30,000-$39,000; and $40,000 or more.

Source: Division of Health Interview Statistics, National Center for Health Statistics; data from the National Health Interview Survey.

C1-3. Average Annual Percent Distribution of Persons 55 Years of Age and Over, by Respondent-Assessed Health Status, According to Sex, Race, and Age: United States, 1985 to 1987

(Data are based on household interviews of the civilian noninstitutionalized population.)

Sex, race, and age	Total	Respondent-assessed health status[1]				
		Excellent	Very good	Good	Fair	Poor
Total [2]	Number of persons in thousands	Percent distribution [3]				
55–59 years...................	11,105	24.3	24.9	30.5	13.3	7.0
60-64 years...................	10,779	19.8	23.5	32.2	16.0	8.6
65–69 years...................	9,456	17.8	21.3	33.9	18.9	8.2
70–74 years...................	7,444	16.0	21.2	32.8	20.9	9.0
75–79 years...................	5,312	14.0	19.7	32.4	23.0	11.0
80–84 years...................	3,161	13.9	19.2	31.7	23.3	12.0
55–64 years...................	21,884	22.1	24.2	31.3	14.6	7.8
65–74 years...................	16,900	17.0	21.3	33.4	19.8	8.5
75–84 years...................	8,473	14.0	19.6	32.1	23.1	11.3
65 years and over.............	27,405	15.9	20.7	32.8	20.9	9.7
75 years and over.............	10,505	14.2	19.7	31.8	22.8	11.7
85 years and over.............	2,032	14.9	20.2	30.4	21.5	13.0
White male						
55–64 years...................	9,144	24.7	25.2	29.5	12.7	7.9
65–74 years...................	6,721	18.3	21.5	32.5	19.1	8.7
75–84 years...................	2,868	14.3	19.6	32.4	21.9	11.8
65 years and over.............	10,201	17.0	20.8	32.4	20.0	9.8
75 years and over.............	3,480	14.5	19.5	32.4	21.7	12.0
85 years and over.............	612	15.6	19.0	32.0	20.3	13.1
Black male						
55–64 years...................	929	16.1	16.8	28.6	23.6	14.9
65 years and over.............	921	10.6	16.2	28.5	27.7	17.0
White female						
55–64 years...................	10,227	21.6	24.8	33.1	14.1	6.4
65–74 years...................	8,470	17.1	21.9	35.0	18.9	7.1
75–84 years...................	4,794	14.6	20.2	32.7	22.6	10.0
65 years and over.............	14,509	16.1	21.3	33.8	20.3	8.5
75 years and over.............	6,038	14.7	20.3	32.2	22.3	10.6
85 years and over.............	1,244	15.0	21.0	30.2	21.2	12.6
Black female						
55–64 years...................	1,141	10.7	17.5	30.2	27.1	14.5
65 years and over.............	1,372	8.6	16.9	27.6	29.4	17.5

[1]Excludes unknown respondent-assessed health status.
[2]Includes races other than white and black.
[3]May not add to 100 percent because of rounding.
Source: National Center for Health Statistics: Data from the National Health Interview Survey.

C1-4. Percent Distribution of Persons 65 Years of Age and Over, by Number of Activities of Daily Living for Which Difficulty Was Reported, According to Sex, Age, and Respondent-Assessed Health Status: United States, 1986

[Data are based on household interviews of the civilian noninstitutionalized population]

Sex, age, and respondent-assessed health status[1]	Total	Number of activities of daily living causing difficulty			
		None	1	2	3 or more
Male, 65–69 years	Number of persons in thousands[2]	Percent distribution[3]			
All health statuses..............	4,092	85.0	5.3	3.5	6.2
Excellent and very good.........	1,615	96.0	*1.5	*1.7	*0.7
Good.......................	1,392	92.3	3.4	*1.0	3.3
Fair and poor	1,085	59.3	13.5	9.2	18.1
Male, 70–74 years					
All health statuses..............	3,223	84.7	7.6	3.1	4.6
Excellent and very good.........	1,313	94.8	3.0	*0.6	*1.6
Good.......................	1,007	89.2	4.6	*3.5	*2.7
Fair and poor	904	65.1	17.8	6.2	10.9
Male, 75–79 years					
All health statuses..............	2,115	80.5	9.4	3.7	6.4
Excellent and very good.........	724	94.0	*4.4	*1.0	*0.6
Good.......................	666	85.8	8.7	*3.3	*2.2
Fair and poor	724	62.1	15.1	*6.8	16.0
Male, 80–84 years					
All health statuses..............	1,081	74.6	11.8	*2.4	11.1
Excellent and very good.........	341	88.1	*5.6	*2.2	*4.2
Good.......................	379	80.8	11.6	*1.0	*6.7
Fair and poor	362	55.4	18.0	*4.2	22.4
Male, 85 years and over					
All health statuses..............	587	64.6	11.7	5.9	17.8
Excellent and very good.........	241	77.6	*9.4	*2.1	*10.9
Good.......................	178	70.5	*9.8	*7.2	*12.6
Fair and poor	168	39.9	*17.2	*10.0	33.0
Female, 65–69 years					
All health statuses..............	5,095	84.3	6.1	3.5	6.1
Excellent and very good.........	1,935	96.4	2.4	*0.9	*0.4
Good.......................	1,757	90.4	4.9	*1.9	*2.7
Fair and poor	1,403	59.9	12.7	9.2	18.2
Female, 70–74 years					
All health statuses..............	4,169	78.8	8.7	4.7	7.9
Excellent and very good.........	1,516	92.0	5.0	*1.8	*1.3
Good.......................	1,481	85.5	5.8	4.3	4.3
Fair and poor	1,172	53.3	17.0	8.7	20.9

See notes at end of table.

C1-4. Percent Distribution of Persons 65 Years of Age and Over, by Number of Activities of Daily Living for Which Difficulty Was Reported, According to Sex, Age, and Respondent-Assessed Health Status: United States, 1986 (continued)

[Data are based on household interviews of the civilian noninstitutionalized population]

Sex, age, and respondent-assessed health status[1]	Total	Number of activities of daily living causing difficulty			
		None	1	2	3 or more
Female, 75–79 years	Number of persons in thousands[2]	Percent distribution[3]			
All health statuses.............	3,147	70.3	9.1	5.5	15.1
Excellent and very good.........	1,083	87.1	4.5	*3.6	*4.8
Good.......................	1,018	77.0	11.5	4.0	7.4
Fair and poor	1,047	46.5	11.5	8.9	33.1
Female, 80–84 years					
All health statuses.............	2,037	60.3	10.4	8.8	20.5
Excellent and very good.........	703	80.8	5.4	7.1	*6.7
Good.......................	649	64.7	10.4	9.2	15.7
Fair and poor	685	35.1	15.6	10.0	39.3
Female, 85 years and over					
All health statuses.............	1,351	51.6	12.0	9.2	27.2
Excellent and very good.........	492	70.3	13.2	9.8	6.8
Good.......................	384	49.4	14.5	13.5	22.6
Fair and poor	475	34.1	8.6	5.2	52.1

[1]Excludes unknown respondent-assessed health status.
[2]Excludes those for whom information was missing on all activities of daily living (ADLs).
[3]May not add to 100 percent because of rounding.
*Figure does not meet standard of reliability.
NOTES: Persons reported as not performing an ADL were classified with those reported as having difficulty with that ADL. ADLs include eating, toileting, dressing, bathing, walking, getting in and out of a bed or chair, and getting outside.
Source: National Center for Health Statistics; data from the National Health Interview Survey 1986 Functional Limitations Supplement.

C1-5. Percent of Elderly in Fair or Poor Health, by Race and Residence: 1985 to 1987

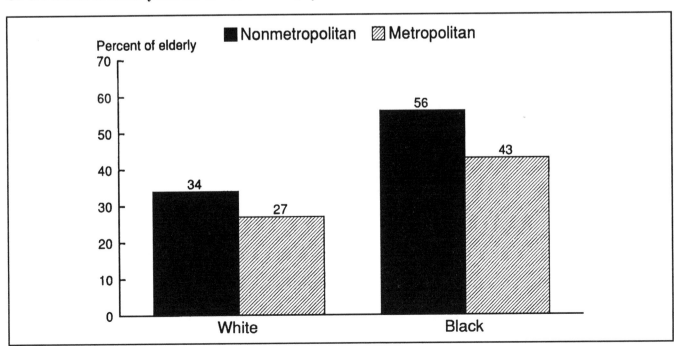

Source: National Center for Health Statistics, 1985-87 National Health Interview Survey.

C2. Diseases and Disabilities

C2-1. Number of Acute Conditions, by Age and Type of Condition: United States, 1990

Type of acute condition	All ages	Under 5 years	5–17 years	18–24 years	25–44 years	45 years and over		
						Total	45–64 years	65 years and over
	Number of acute conditions in thousands							
All acute conditions	423,027	69,664	108,640	43,731	116,169	84,823	53,308	31,515
Infective and parasitic diseases	51,662	10,454	19,737	5,316	10,195	5,960	3,820	2,140
Common childhood diseases	4,255	2,173	1,850	70	162	–	–	–
Intestinal virus, unspecified	12,398	1,896	5,116	1,330	2,749	1,307	882	425
Viral infections, unspecified	15,415	3,020	5,157	1,226	3,504	2,506	1,777	73
Other	19,594	3,364	7,614	2,689	3,780	2,147	1,162	985
Respiratory conditions	209,825	32,122	55,341	22,070	59,435	40,857	26,796	14,061
Common cold	61,450	12,561	14,673	6,811	16,291	11,114	6,535	4,579
Other acute upper respiratory infections	22,413	3,573	9,012	1,942	4,868	3,018	1,852	1,166
Influenza	106,807	11,517	28,150	11,591	34,458	21,091	15,357	5,734
Acute bronchitis	10,372	2,226	2,097	1,004	2,139	2,905	1,824	1,081
Pneumonia	3,862	976	377	57	950	1,502	794	708
Other respiratory conditions	4,920	1,269	1,032	664	727	1,227	434	793
Digestive system conditions	13,023	805	3,340	1,661	3,909	3,307	1,982	1,325
Dental conditions	2,107	340	158	127	952	531	478	52
Indigestion, nausea, and vomiting	6,875	165	2,795	988	1,709	1,218	570	648
Other digestive conditions	4,041	300	387	546	1,249	1,559	933	626
Injuries	60,123	5,261	13,527	7,202	20,140	13,994	9,265	4,729
Fractures and dislocations	6,756	373	1,976	968	1,932	1,507	951	556
Sprains and strains	12,722	264	2,061	1,892	5,719	2,787	1,853	934
Open wounds and lacerations	12,751	1,595	3,912	1,959	3,446	1,839	1,232	608
Contusions and superficial injuries	10,033	817	2,417	866	3,476	2,457	1,443	1,015
Other current injuries	17,861	2,212	3,162	1,517	5,567	5,403	3,786	1,617
Selected other acute conditions	62,176	16,781	12,662	5,728	15,275	11,730	6,638	5,093
Eye conditions	2,439	506	366	276	473	818	416	402
Acute ear infections	21,256	12,795	4,874	751	1,702	1,134	781	353
Other ear conditions	3,423	598	1,341	235	467	781	436	345
Acute urinary conditions	6,518	410	358	825	2,035	2,890	1,393	1,497
Disorders of menstruation	1,281	...	513	270	440	58	58	–
Other disorders of female genital tract	2,499	–	–	392	1,707	400	237	162
Delivery and other conditions of pregnancy and puerperium	4,994	...	257	1,382	3,356	–	–	...
Skin conditions	4,598	957	1,116	240	1,092	1,193	458	735
Acute musculoskeletal conditions	7,606	–	911	635	2,570	3,490	2,233	1,258
Headache, excluding migraine	3,200	–	894	485	1,119	702	515	187
Fever, unspecified	4,363	1,514	2,031	238	315	264	110	154
All other acute conditions	26,218	4,242	4,032	1,755	7,215	8,975	4,807	4,168

NOTE: Excluded from these estimates are conditions involving neither medical attention nor activity restriction.

C2-2. Number of Acute Conditions Per 100 Persons Per Year, by Age and Type of Condition: United States, 1990

(Data are based on household interviews of the civilian noninstitutionalized population.)

Type of acute condition	All ages	Under 5 years	5–17 years	18–24 years	25–44 years	45 years and over		
						Total	45–64 years	65 years and over
	Number of acute conditions per 100 persons per year							
All acute conditions	171.9	365.0	238.4	174.8	145.1	111.1	114.4	105.8
Infective and parasitic diseases	21.0	54.8	43.3	21.2	12.7	7.8	8.2	7.2
Common childhood diseases	1.7	11.4	4.1	*0.3	*0.2	*–	*–	*–
Intestinal virus, unspecified	5.0	9.9	11.2	5.3	3.4	1.7	1.9	*1.4
Viral infections, unspecified	6.3	15.8	11.3	4.9	4.4	3.3	3.8	*2.5
Other	8.0	17.6	16.7	10.7	4.7	2.8	2.5	3.3
Respiratory conditions	85.3	168.3	121.4	88.2	74.2	53.5	57.5	47.2
Common cold	25.0	65.8	32.2	27.2	20.3	14.6	14.0	15.4
Other acute upper respiratory infections	9.1	18.7	19.8	7.8	6.1	4.0	4.0	3.9
Influenza	43.4	60.3	61.8	46.3	43.0	27.6	33.0	19.3
Acute bronchitis	4.2	11.7	4.6	4.0	2.7	3.8	3.9	3.6
Pneumonia	1.6	5.1	*0.8	*0.2	1.2	2.0	*1.7	*2.4
Other respiratory conditions	2.0	6.6	2.3	*2.7	*0.9	1.6	*0.9	*2.7
Digestive system conditions	5.3	4.2	7.3	6.6	4.9	4.3	4.3	4.4
Dental conditions	0.9	*1.8	*0.3	*0.5	1.2	*0.7	*1.0	*0.2
Indigestion, nausea, and vomiting	2.8	*0.9	6.1	3.9	2.1	1.6	*1.2	*2.2
Other digestive conditions	1.6	*1.6	*0.8	*2.2	1.6	2.0	2.0	*2.1
Injuries	24.4	27.6	29.7	28.8	25.2	18.3	19.9	15.9
Fractures and dislocations	2.7	*2.0	4.3	3.9	2.4	2.0	2.0	*1.9
Sprains and strains	5.2	*1.4	4.5	7.6	7.1	3.6	4.0	3.1
Open wounds and lacerations	5.2	8.4	8.6	7.8	4.3	2.4	2.6	*2.0
Contusions and superficial injuries	4.1	4.3	5.3	3.5	4.3	3.2	3.1	3.4
Other current injuries	7.3	11.6	6.9	6.1	7.0	7.1	8.1	5.4
Selected other acute conditions	25.3	87.9	27.8	22.9	19.1	15.4	14.2	17.1
Eye conditions	1.0	*2.7	*0.8	*1.1	*0.6	1.1	*0.9	*1.3
Acute ear infections	8.6	67.0	10.7	*3.0	2.1	1.5	*1.7	*1.2
Other ear conditions	1.4	*3.1	2.9	*0.9	*0.6	*1.0	*0.9	*1.2
Acute urinary conditions	2.6	*2.1	*0.8	3.3	2.5	3.8	3.0	5.0
Disorders of menstruation	0.5	...	*1.1	*1.1	*0.5	*0.1	*0.1	*–
Other disorders of female genital tract	1.0	*–	*–	*1.6	2.1	*0.5	*0.5	*0.5
Delivery and other conditions of pregnancy and puerperium	2.0	...	*0.6	5.5	4.2	*–	*–	...
Skin conditions	1.9	5.0	2.4	*1.0	1.4	1.6	*1.0	*2.5
Acute musculoskeletal conditions	3.1	*–	2.0	*2.5	3.2	4.6	4.8	4.2
Headache, excluding migraine	1.3	*–	2.0	*1.9	1.4	*0.9	*1.1	*0.6
Fever, unspecified	1.8	7.9	4.5	*1.0	*0.4	*0.3	*0.2	*0.5
All other acute conditions	10.7	22.2	8.8	7.0	9.0	11.8	10.3	14.0

*Figure does not meet standards of reliability.

NOTE: Excluded from these estimates are conditions involving neither medical attention nor activity restriction.

C2-3. Average Annual Number of Selected Reported Chronic Conditions Per 1,000 Persons 55 Years of Age and Over, by Type of Chronic Condition, Sex, and Age: United States, 1979 to 1981, 1982 to 1984, and 1985 to 1987

[Data are based on household interviews of the civilian noninstitutionalized population]

| | Type of chronic condition | | | | | | | | |
| | Ischemic heart disease | | | Hypertension | | | Diabetes | | |
Sex and age	*1979–81*	*1982–84*	*1985–87*	*1979–81*	*1982–84*	*1985–87*	*1979–81*	*1982–84*	*1985–87*
Both sexes	Number per 1,000 persons								
55–64 years............	58.8	75.7	70.1	286.4	306.5	302.7	66.1	71.6	76.1
65–74 years............	105.0	115.7	114.1	365.6	392.5	400.8	87.7	92.8	99.0
65 years and over.......	103.7	116.2	121.5	376.6	393.8	392.5	85.9	89.7	99.7
75 years and over.......	101.3	117.1	133.6	395.8	396.1	379.3	82.8	84.7	100.8
Male									
55–64 years............	77.6	107.5	98.9	275.2	291.2	287.6	65.3	72.1	79.1
65–74 years............	133.9	149.9	150.7	305.6	335.7	359.3	84.8	79.9	101.9
65 years and over.......	125.0	142.8	152.6	297.3	318.6	331.1	82.8	83.0	102.5
75 years and over.......	106.6	128.9	156.3	280.4	285.6	276.6	78.6	88.7	103.6
Female									
55–64 years............	42.1	47.9	44.7	296.4	320.0	316.1	66.9	71.3	73.4
65–74 years............	82.8	89.4	85.3	411.7	436.0	433.4	90.0	102.7	96.7
65 years and over.......	88.8	97.9	99.8	431.9	445.8	435.7	88.1	94.3	97.7
75 years and over.......	98.2	110.4	120.4	463.7	460.0	438.9	85.3	82.3	99.1

NOTE: These rates are based on unduplicated counts; a person was counted only once for each condition regardless of the number of mentions of that condition.
Source: National Center for Health Statistics; data from the National Health Interview Survey.

C2-4. Number of Selected Reported Chronic Conditions Per 1,000 Persons, by Age: United States, 1990

(Data are based on household interviews of the civilian noninstitutionalized population.)

Type of chronic condition	All ages	Under 45 years			45–64 years	65 years and over		
		Total	Under 18 years	18–44 years		Total	65–74 years	75 years and over
Selected skin and musculoskeletal conditions				Number of chronic conditions per 1,000 persons				
Arthritis	125.3	30.8	3.0	47.9	249.1	470.1	428.1	535.2
Gout, including gouty arthritis	9.1	2.1	*–	3.5	19.4	32.8	33.0	32.6
Intervertebral disc disorders	19.5	11.8	*0.5	18.8	42.9	27.1	31.7	19.9
Bone spur or tendinitis, unspecified	8.7	5.6	*0.8	8.5	15.2	16.6	19.7	*11.6
Disorders of bone or cartilage	5.6	2.9	*1.3	3.9	8.5	16.0	16.4	15.3
Trouble with bunions	13.2	5.5	*0.6	8.5	27.4	34.6	32.9	37.3
Bursitis, unclassified	18.0	8.2	*0.8	12.8	37.6	43.0	43.4	42.3
Sebaceous skin cyst	5.1	4.3	*1.2	6.2	6.3	7.4	8.8	*5.1
Trouble with acne	18.8	26.1	25.8	26.3	3.9	*0.3	*0.6	*–
Psoriasis	9.3	6.7	2.9	9.1	14.6	16.0	15.3	17.0
Dermatitis	35.3	35.2	31.0	37.7	37.0	33.1	33.2	33.1
Trouble with dry (itching) skin, unclassified . .	20.5	16.8	9.4	21.4	22.6	38.1	39.3	36.1
Trouble with ingrown nails	24.5	17.5	8.2	23.2	34.0	50.0	46.4	55.7
Trouble with corns and calluses	20.0	11.8	*1.3	18.3	32.7	47.1	46.3	48.3
Impairments								
Visual impairment	30.6	21.0	8.7	28.5	38.5	73.1	51.4	106.5
Color blindness	10.0	9.5	4.6	12.5	12.1	9.9	12.5	*5.9
Cataracts	24.1	1.9	*0.9	2.5	22.1	153.9	112.2	218.4
Glaucoma	9.1	0.9	*–	1.5	11.9	51.0	42.7	63.9
Hearing impairment[1]	94.7	39.6	21.0	51.1	150.0	321.8	264.1	411.0
Tinnitus[1]	29.0	11.2	2.7	16.5	53.7	92.2	94.2	89.1
Speech impairment	9.3	9.9	14.1	7.2	6.2	10.8	12.5	*8.2
Absence of extremities (excludes tips of fingers or toes only)	5.0	2.8	*1.0	3.8	8.4	12.6	14.5	*9.7
Paralysis of extremities, complete or partial . .	5.9	3.0	2.4	3.4	7.8	19.2	20.2	17.6
Deformity or orthopedic impairment	117.4	95.3	28.8	136.3	161.5	174.4	168.2	183.9
Back	70.3	58.0	9.7	87.6	101.0	92.9	88.6	99.5
Upper extremities	14.2	10.2	2.5	14.9	21.3	25.8	27.0	23.8
Lower extremities	47.4	38.2	17.8	50.8	57.0	85.1	79.5	93.9
Selected digestive conditions								
Ulcer	18.1	12.6	*1.6	19.5	28.6	33.2	33.3	32.9
Hernia of abdominal cavity	17.0	6.6	*1.8	9.5	29.3	57.1	50.3	67.4
Gastritis or duodenitis	12.3	9.1	2.4	13.2	17.9	21.6	22.0	20.9
Frequent indigestion	23.4	17.8	*1.7	27.6	32.7	41.4	44.6	36.5
Enteritis or colitis	9.4	7.1	3.6	9.3	12.9	17.2	14.7	21.0
Spastic colon	7.0	4.6	*1.1	6.8	11.2	14.4	11.2	19.4
Diverticula of intestines	8.3	1.1	*0.1	1.8	12.9	41.7	42.0	41.2
Frequent constipation	16.2	10.2	6.7	12.4	14.3	53.4	33.9	83.5

*Figure does not meet standards of reliability.

C2-4. Number of Selected Reported Chronic Conditions Per 1,000 Persons, by Age: United States, 1990 (continued)

(Data are based on household interviews of the civilian noninstitutionalized population.)

Type of chronic condition	All ages	Under 45 years			45–64 years	65 years and over		
		Total	Under 18 years	18–44 years		Total	65–74 years	75 years and over
Selected conditions of the genitourinary, nervous, endocrine, metabolic, and blood and blood-forming systems				Number of chronic conditions per 1,000 persons				
Goiter or other disorders of the thyroid	13.9	7.1	*0.7	11.0	27.9	30.7	34.9	24.2
Diabetes	25.3	6.5	*0.6	10.1	50.4	93.4	102.2	79.7
Anemias	15.5	15.3	9.8	18.6	12.9	21.2	19.6	23.7
Epilepsy	4.8	5.2	4.1	5.8	4.1	*3.5	*2.5	*5.0
Migraine headache	39.8	38.4	13.7	53.5	56.9	21.0	22.6	18.3
Neuralgia or neuritis, unspecified	1.9	*0.2	*–	*0.3	4.6	7.3	*6.0	*9.3
Kidney trouble	12.4	8.4	3.8	11.3	19.6	24.1	27.2	19.2
Bladder disorders	12.4	8.1	3.7	10.8	14.5	33.9	25.4	47.1
Diseases of prostate	7.0	1.4	*–	2.3	10.9	32.7	30.3	36.4
Diseases of female genital organs	20.7	23.3	5.9	34.0	18.0	10.5	10.6	*10.4
Selected circulatory conditions								
Rheumatic fever with or without heart disease	7.0	4.3	*0.5	6.6	15.7	8.9	*8.2	*10.0
Heart disease	78.5	30.8	18.9	38.1	118.7	287.3	257.1	333.9
Ischemic heart disease	31.1	3.0	*–	4.8	58.6	148.2	136.3	166.7
Heart rhythm disorders	28.8	20.6	13.2	25.2	35.9	64.4	60.2	70.9
Tachycardia or rapid heart	6.6	3.2	*0.3	4.9	8.1	23.8	24.9	22.1
Heart murmurs	15.7	15.0	12.6	16.5	18.3	15.9	15.0	17.2
Other and unspecified heart rhythm disorders	6.5	2.4	*0.2	3.8	9.5	24.7	20.3	31.6
Other selected diseases of heart, excluding hypertension	18.5	7.2	5.8	8.0	24.1	74.6	60.6	96.4
High blood pressure (hypertension)	110.2	35.2	*1.8	55.7	218.3	369.0	354.1	392.0
Cerebrovascular disease	11.7	1.4	*0.7	1.7	16.7	63.0	49.7	83.5
Hardening of the arteries	8.4	*0.2	*–	*0.4	10.8	51.0	43.9	62.0
Varicose veins of lower extremities	28.3	15.3	*0.2	24.6	46.8	74.0	67.4	84.2
Hemorrhoids	38.4	25.8	*1.2	41.0	70.9	58.9	64.4	50.4
Selected respiratory conditions								
Chronic bronchitis	51.1	46.0	53.3	41.5	57.4	70.4	76.3	61.4
Asthma	41.9	43.8	57.6	35.2	38.6	36.3	32.5	42.4
Hay fever or allergic rhinitis without asthma	90.2	92.7	56.5	115.0	95.1	67.7	75.3	55.9
Chronic sinusitis	131.3	113.8	56.7	149.0	181.9	151.7	154.1	148.1
Deviated nasal septum	6.2	4.7	*0.9	7.0	8.4	11.0	13.8	*6.9
Chronic disease of tonsils or adenoids	11.0	14.8	22.5	10.0	3.8	*0.5	*0.8	*–
Emphysema	8.2	*0.4	*–	*0.7	12.8	45.4	44.3	47.1

*Figure does not meet standards of reliability.

C2-5. Number of Selected Reported Chronic Conditions Per 1,000 Persons, by Sex and Age: United States, 1990

(Data are based on household interviews of the civilian noninstitutionalized population.)

Type of chronic condition	Male					Female				
			65 years and over					65 years and over		
	Under 45 years	45–64 years	Total	65–74 years	75 years and over	Under 45 years	45–64 years	Total	65–74 years	75 years and over
Selected skin and musculoskeletal conditions	Number of chronic conditions per 1,000 persons									
Arthritis	25.8	204.9	374.5	373.3	376.8	35.8	289.7	538.4	472.2	628.6
Gout, including gouty arthritis	3.2	26.5	44.6	48.3	37.8	*1.1	12.8	24.4	20.8	29.4
Intervertebral disc disorders	12.2	51.3	30.7	40.9	*11.8	11.5	35.1	24.5	24.4	24.8
Bone spur or tendinitis, unspecified	5.0	13.3	14.3	20.2	*3.2	6.1	16.9	18.2	19.4	*16.5
Disorders of bone or cartilage	2.1	*5.9	*3.1	*4.8	*–	3.7	10.9	25.2	25.8	24.4
Trouble with bunions	2.1	10.4	*6.0	*3.2	*11.1	8.9	43.1	55.0	56.8	52.7
Bursitis, unclassified	7.9	26.7	37.1	39.2	*33.0	8.6	47.5	47.2	46.7	47.8
Sebaceous skin cyst	4.8	6.9	*10.3	*9.7	*11.5	3.8	*5.8	*5.3	*8.3	*1.4
Trouble with acne	24.7	*2.2	*–	*–	*–	27.6	*5.4	*0.6	*1.0	*–
Psoriasis	6.4	17.0	18.3	*18.4	*18.0	7.0	12.4	14.3	*12.7	*16.5
Dermatitis	28.2	21.9	23.4	22.7	*24.4	42.1	50.9	40.1	41.6	38.2
Trouble with dry (itching) skin, unclassified	12.9	19.7	30.4	30.6	*30.4	20.7	25.3	43.5	46.4	39.5
Trouble with ingrown nails	20.1	33.0	38.3	34.3	45.7	14.9	35.0	58.4	56.2	61.6
Trouble with corns and calluses	10.0	22.7	25.0	23.0	*28.6	13.7	41.9	62.9	65.1	59.9
Impairments										
Visual impairment	30.3	49.5	86.0	73.3	109.8	11.7	28.4	63.8	33.9	104.5
Color blindness	17.4	23.7	23.8	28.1	*15.9	*1.7	*1.4	*–	*–	*–
Cataracts	*1.2	17.4	98.0	81.2	129.4	2.5	26.3	193.8	137.2	271.0
Glaucoma	*1.1	11.5	53.7	44.1	71.7	*0.7	12.3	49.1	41.5	59.5
Hearing impairment	49.7	197.8	395.5	350.1	480.2	29.6	106.0	269.1	194.9	370.3
Tinnitus	12.6	59.6	98.1	101.3	92.3	9.8	48.2	87.9	88.4	87.2
Speech impairment	12.6	6.8	*11.9	*16.5	*3.5	7.1	*5.7	10.1	*9.3	*11.2
Absence of extremities (excludes tips of fingers or toes only)	4.2	13.3	18.6	23.3	*9.9	*1.3	*3.8	*8.3	*7.4	*9.5
Paralysis of extremities, complete or partial	3.6	9.6	25.6	29.3	*18.7	2.4	*6.2	14.6	*12.9	*17.1
Deformity or orthopedic impairment	92.4	151.4	141.5	152.3	121.1	98.2	170.8	197.9	181.0	220.9
Back	50.5	87.0	63.7	74.3	44.0	65.4	113.8	113.7	100.1	132.3
Upper extremities	12.0	25.3	30.6	34.2	*24.0	8.3	17.7	22.3	21.3	23.7
Lower extremities	40.8	57.0	73.7	69.8	81.0	35.7	56.9	93.3	87.1	101.5
Selected digestive conditions										
Ulcer	11.0	31.6	38.2	38.3	38.1	14.3	25.8	29.6	29.2	29.9
Hernia of abdominal cavity	6.7	35.1	55.5	42.7	79.3	6.4	24.0	58.2	56.5	60.4
Gastritis or duodenitis	7.6	14.6	17.6	*15.8	*20.8	10.6	20.9	24.5	27.1	21.1
Frequent indigestion	16.6	36.5	35.2	29.2	46.4	18.9	29.1	45.8	57.0	30.6
Enteritis or colitis	5.5	7.9	*9.1	*9.9	*7.6	8.7	17.5	23.0	18.7	28.9
Spastic colon	1.9	*3.2	*9.3	*9.3	*9.5	7.2	18.5	18.0	*12.7	25.2
Diverticula of intestines	*0.8	*5.6	28.4	39.1	*8.3	*1.4	19.6	51.2	44.3	60.7
Frequent constipation	4.9	*5.6	30.5	*17.3	55.1	15.5	22.3	69.7	47.3	100.2

*Figure does not meet standards of reliability.

C2-5. Number of Selected Reported Chronic Conditions Per 1,000 Persons, by Sex and Age: United States, 1990 (continued)

(Data are based on household interviews of the civilian noninstitutionalized population.)

Type of chronic condition	Male					Female				
			65 years and over					65 years and over		
	Under 45 years	45–64 years	Total	65–74 years	75 years and over	Under 45 years	45–64 years	Total	65–74 years	75 years and over
Selected conditions of the genitourinary, nervous, endocrine, metabolic, and blood and blood-forming systems	Number of chronic conditions per 1,000 persons									
Goiter or other disorders of the thyroid	2.0	9.5	*10.8	*8.8	*14.5	12.2	44.9	45.0	56.0	29.9
Diabetes	5.6	48.6	96.5	102.0	86.3	7.4	52.1	91.1	102.3	75.9
Anemias	4.6	*2.5	*9.5	*8.9	*10.8	25.9	22.5	29.5	28.1	31.4
Epilepsy	5.1	*3.4	*1.9	*–	*5.5	5.3	*4.7	*4.7	*4.6	*4.8
Migraine headache	20.9	23.9	*3.3	*4.7	*0.7	55.8	87.3	33.6	37.0	28.9
Neuralgia or neuritis, unspecified	*–	*1.9	*7.7	*9.9	*3.5	*0.4	7.0	*7.1	*2.9	*12.8
Kidney trouble	6.0	19.6	17.6	*18.6	*15.9	10.9	19.7	28.7	34.2	21.2
Bladder disorders	*1.7	*3.4	13.9	*4.5	*31.8	14.5	24.6	48.2	42.3	56.1
Diseases of prostate	2.9	22.8	78.5	68.0	98.0	. . .	. . .	. . .	. . .	. . .
Diseases of female genital organs	. . .	. . .	. . .	. . .	. . .	46.4	34.6	18.0	19.2	*16.6
Selected circulatory conditions										
Rheumatic fever with or without heart disease	3.2	10.8	*2.5	*3.8	*–	5.3	20.2	13.5	*11.8	*15.9
Heart disease	27.3	137.4	320.4	275.2	404.8	34.2	101.5	263.5	242.5	292.3
Ischemic heart disease	4.2	84.3	199.5	173.2	248.6	1.8	34.9	111.5	106.5	118.4
Heart rhythm disorders	17.5	26.7	55.3	48.3	68.3	23.7	44.4	70.9	69.8	72.5
Tachycardia or rapid heart	2.6	7.9	17.5	20.4	*12.0	3.8	8.2	28.3	28.3	28.2
Heart murmurs	12.6	10.6	*11.7	*10.3	*14.3	17.4	25.3	18.9	18.9	*19.1
Other and unspecified heart rhythm disorders . .	2.3	8.1	26.1	*17.5	42.0	2.6	10.8	23.8	22.6	25.4
Other selected diseases of heart, excluding hypertension	5.6	26.3	65.7	53.7	87.9	8.7	22.1	81.0	66.2	101.4
High blood pressure (hypertension)	38.1	221.9	291.7	285.0	304.2	32.3	215.1	424.3	409.8	444.1
Cerebrovascular disease	*1.6	19.0	73.5	60.9	96.9	*1.1	14.5	55.5	40.8	75.5
Hardening of the arteries	*0.4	11.6	57.0	40.6	87.4	*–	10.1	46.8	46.6	47.0
Varicose veins of lower extremities	4.8	17.6	38.7	27.5	59.7	25.8	73.6	99.2	99.5	98.7
Hemorrhoids	22.7	71.1	46.2	53.4	*32.7	28.9	70.8	68.1	73.4	60.8
Selected respiratory conditions										
Chronic bronchitis	40.4	31.6	58.0	62.0	50.5	51.7	81.1	79.3	87.8	67.8
Asthma	43.4	28.8	34.1	28.6	44.3	44.1	47.7	38.0	35.6	41.2
Hay fever or allergic rhinitis without asthma	89.1	80.6	66.0	65.1	67.6	96.3	108.4	68.9	83.5	49.0
Chronic sinusitis	99.9	162.7	136.9	132.2	145.5	127.7	199.5	162.3	171.7	149.6
Deviated nasal septum	5.0	11.9	14.8	20.1	*5.1	4.3	*5.1	*8.3	*8.6	*8.0
Chronic disease of tonsils or adenoids	10.7	*1.0	*0.9	*1.4	*–	18.8	6.3	*0.2	*0.4	*–
Emphysema	*0.4	16.1	71.0	67.4	77.7	*0.4	9.7	27.1	25.8	29.0

*Figure does not meet standards of reliability.

C2-6. Percent of Persons 55 Years of Age and Over Who Reported Joint Pain or Physician-Diagnosed Arthritis, by Sex, Race, and Age: United States, Selected Time Periods

(Data for 1960-84 are based on interviews of samples of the civilian noninstitutionalized population.)

Sex, race, and age	Joint pain[1]		Physician-diagnosed arthritis[2]		
	1960–62	1976–80	1960–62	1976–80	1984
Total	41.5	48.9	37.2	44.3	47.7
55–59 years	37.9	49.9	34.7	38.9	38.4
60-64 years	45.1	50.0	37.0	44.2	44.6
65–69 years	37.7	47.5	35.9	48.4	48.8
70–74 years	49.1	47.6	42.1	48.0	55.5
75–79 years	38.8	...	39.7	...	54.2
80 years and over	...	...	...	...	55.6
Male	33.9	49.3	28.3	37.2	38.9
55–59 years	29.1	50.0	24.4	32.6	29.2
60–64 years	37.0	50.3	28.8	38.2	37.0
65–69 years	34.7	48.4	32.1	40.9	42.2
70–74 years	41.3	47.2	28.4	38.7	47.8
75–79 years	26.4	...	29.7	...	43.3
80 years and over	...	...	...	...	45.1
White male	33.1	49.7	28.1	37.3	38.2
55–59 years	27.2	50.5	22.8	33.5	28.2
60–64 years	36.0	50.0	28.8	38.0	36.1
65–69 years	34.9	49.1	32.0	40.3	41.3
70–74 years	40.8	48.4	29.2	38.9	47.4
75–79 years	26.8	...	30.5	...	42.4
80 years and over	...	...	...	...	44.8
Black male	41.4	44.7	30.2	36.4	47.5
55–64 years	45.5	49.1	33.6	31.9	43.3
65–74 years	38.9	38.4	26.8	42.8	51.7
75 years and over	*21.4	...	*18.8	...	51.1
Female	48.2	48.7	45.1	50.2	54.0
55–59 years	45.6	49.9	43.7	44.1	45.5
60–64 years	53.0	49.6	45.1	50.0	50.9
65–69 years	40.2	46.8	39.0	54.2	54.0
70–74 years	55.5	47.9	53.3	54.9	60.7
75–79 years	51.3	...	49.8	...	61.3
80 years and over	...	...	...	...	60.4
White female	47.3	48.5	45.1	49.2	53.2
55–59 years	47.5	49.4	43.1	42.2	45.5
60–64 years	49.1	50.2	44.5	49.6	50.4
65–69 years	38.5	46.2	39.4	52.8	52.9
70–74 years	54.8	47.9	53.1	55.2	59.3
75–79 years	50.7	...	53.0	...	60.2
80 years and over	...	...	...	...	59.3
Black female	58.4	50.0	45.0	59.7	61.2
55–64 years	55.8	49.9	49.9	58.5	50.1
65–74 years	62.8	50.2	44.5	61.3	69.9
75 years and over	57.0	...	*19.7	...	73.6

[1]Specific questions concerned "joint pains" and "pain in back, neck, or other joint."

[2]Specific question: "Doctor confirm or ever told sample person that he/she had arthritis?"

*Figure does not meet standard of reliability.

Sources: National Center for Health Statistics: 1960-62 data from the Health Examination Survey; 1976-80 data from the second National Health and Nutrition Examination Survey; 1984 data from the National Health Interview Survey Supplement on Aging.

C2-7. Average Annual Number of Selected Reported Chronic Conditions Per 1,000 Black Persons 55 Years of Age and Over, by Type of Chronic Condition, Sex, and Age: United States, 1985 to 1987

(Data are based on household interviews of the civilian noninstitutionalized population.)

Sex and age	Type of chronic condition		
	Ischemic heart disease	Hypertension	Diabetes
Both sexes			
55-64 years	44.6	418.2	143.2
65-74 years	59.8	509.7	157.4
65 years and over	47.4	474.4	166.8
75 years and over	26.2	413.4	182.9
Male			
55-64 years	47.2	425.1	117.1
65-74 years	55.3	384.0	143.3
65 years and over	49.8	324.1	135.3
75 years and over	39.1	205.4	119.5
Female			
55-64 years	42.5	412.6	164.6
65-74 years	63.0	601.3	167.7
65 years and over	45.8	575.1	187.9
75 years and over	18.7	534.0	219.7

NOTE: These rates are based on unduplicated counts; a person was counted only once for each condition regardless of the number of mentions of that condition.

C2-8. Selected Chronic Conditions Among Adult Males and Females: Percent in the SAIAN and General U.S. Population with at Least One Condition, by Age and Sex: United States, 1987

Condition and age in years	SAIAN population				U.S. population		
	Total	Male	Female		Total	Male	Female
Number (in thousands)	505	240	265		169,054	79,900	89,154
				Percent			
Cardiovascular disease							
19-44	2.1	*1.9	*2.3		2.0	1.9	2.0
45-64	14.8	20.5	10.1		13.4	16.2	10.8
65 or older	28.7	34.7	23.8		35.0	38.0	32.9
Cancer							
19-44	1.5	*0.5	*2.5		1.6	1.1	2.2
45-64	3.0	*1.9	4.0		7.4	5.6	9.1
65 or older	8.2	*11.3	5.6		13.6	13.5	13.7
Emphysema							
19-44	0.3	*0.2	*0.4		0.5	0.6	0.4
45-64	2.6	2.7	*2.5		4.0	4.8	3.3
65 or older	6.0	*9.4	*3.2		7.6	10.8	5.3
Gallbladder disease							
19-44	4.1	0.9	7.1		2.2	0.4	3.9
45-64	9.2	5.1	12.6		8.6	4.5	12.2
65 or older	16.7	12.4	20.4		14.3	8.7	18.2
Hypertension							
19-44	11.6	12.6	10.6		12.6	13.2	12.0
45-64	37.8	38.1	37.5		36.1	35.2	36.9
65 or older	36.7	35.6	37.6		49.3	44.2	52.9
Rheumatism							
19-44	*0.8	*0.6	*1.0		0.9	0.7	1.1
45-64	5.9	6.9	*5.1		7.0	6.3	7.6
65 or older	*16.3	19.5	*13.6		16.3	15.4	17.0
Arthritis							
19-44	6.4	5.4	7.3		7.0	5.6	8.4
45-64	31.5	28.5	34.0		33.8	26.5	40.4
65 or older	48.6	44.3	52.2		55.1	46.3	61.4
Diabetes							
19-44	3.7	3.2	4.2		1.9	1.3	2.5
45-64	21.5	21.2	21.8		8.1	7.9	8.2
65 or older	27.4	22.2	31.8		14.2	15.2	13.5

*Figure does not meet standards of reliability.

C2-9. Number of Restricted-Activity Days Associated with Acute Conditions, by Age and Type of Condition: United States, 1990

(Data are based on household interviews of the civilian noninstitutionalized population.)

Type of acute condition	All ages	Under 5 years	5–17 years	18–24 years	25–44 years	45 years and over		
						Total	45–64 years	65 years and over
					Number of restricted-activity days in thousands			
All acute conditions	1,734,705	181,964	298,876	193,574	532,028	528,263	270,557	257,706
Infective and parasitic diseases	180,025	34,758	65,129	16,478	33,600	30,060	15,278	14,782
Common childhood diseases	31,991	12,686	15,471	2,174	1,660	–	–	–
Intestinal virus, unspecified	32,506	5,082	9,995	5,473	6,731	5,226	2,431	2,794
Viral infections, unspecified	52,373	10,536	15,562	2,153	13,728	10,394	6,214	4,180
Other	63,154	6,453	24,101	6,678	11,482	14,441	6,633	7,808
Respiratory conditions	713,662	96,551	147,037	61,303	194,049	214,722	111,328	103,394
Common cold	144,811	25,994	28,314	14,130	37,312	39,061	19,107	19,955
Other acute upper respiratory infections	60,521	11,357	18,308	5,684	11,230	13,941	6,036	7,905
Influenza	383,361	37,969	85,909	33,572	114,228	111,684	64,747	46,937
Acute bronchitis	50,131	7,860	8,503	3,505	12,903	17,360	7,793	9,567
Pneumonia	56,808	9,794	3,443	3,070	15,320	25,181	11,429	13,752
Other respiratory conditions	18,030	3,577	2,559	1,343	3,056	7,495	2,217	5,278
Digestive system conditions	58,450	3,490	8,037	5,670	16,605	24,648	15,786	8,862
Dental conditions	10,908	1,219	1,749	1,139	2,509	4,292	3,293	999
Indigestion, nausea, and vomiting	14,627	358	3,615	2,500	4,672	3,482	1,055	2,427
Other digestive conditions	32,915	1,913	2,673	2,031	9,424	16,873	11,437	5,436
Injuries	403,955	7,862	41,610	59,340	161,311	133,831	69,782	64,049
Fractures and dislocations	115,818	2,649	15,942	12,758	37,568	46,900	16,934	29,966
Sprains and strains	106,091	253	7,447	13,628	55,183	29,581	22,219	7,362
Open wounds and lacerations	42,423	1,245	5,453	14,643	12,221	8,860	4,208	4,652
Contusions and superficial injuries	43,888	91	3,408	7,269	17,291	15,829	5,849	9,981
Other current injuries	95,735	3,624	9,360	11,042	39,048	32,660	20,572	12,088
Selected other acute conditions	278,107	32,704	28,940	41,368	99,177	75,919	34,996	40,922
Eye conditions	5,596	681	874	54	846	3,141	921	2,219
Acute ear infections	48,320	23,851	11,638	2,585	4,336	5,911	4,733	1,178
Other ear conditions	6,134	1,668	1,275	66	2,041	1,084	281	803
Acute urinary conditions	30,581	1,251	884	2,581	8,220	17,646	5,622	12,024
Disorders of menstruation	5,002	. . .	770	582	2,915	735	735	–
Other disorders of female genital tract	15,429	–	2,046	1,530	7,596	4,256	4,256	–
Delivery and other conditions of pregnancy and puerperium	72,632	. . .	1,314	27,279	44,039	–	–	. . .
Skin conditions	12,716	1,242	1,344	1,052	1,122	7,957	2,064	5,893
Acute musculoskeletal conditions	63,589	–	2,609	3,338	24,578	33,062	15,462	17,600
Headache, excluding migraine	7,437	–	1,590	1,431	3,142	1,274	760	515
Fever, unspecified	10,671	4,013	4,595	870	340	852	162	691
All other acute conditions	100,507	6,599	8,122	9,415	27,286	49,084	23,387	25,697

C2-10. Number of Restricted-Activity Days Associated with Acute Conditions Per 100 Persons Per Year, by Age and Type of Condition: United States, 1990

(Data are based on household interviews of the civilian noninstitutionalized population.)						45 years and over		
Type of acute condition	All ages	Under 5 years	5–17 years	18–24 years	25–44 years	Total	45–64 years	65 years and over
	Number of restricted-activity days per 100 persons per year							
All acute conditions	704.9	953.5	655.9	773.6	664.5	691.8	580.8	865.4
Infective and parasitic diseases	73.2	182.1	142.9	65.9	42.0	39.4	32.8	49.6
Common childhood diseases	13.0	66.5	34.0	*8.7	*2.1	*–	*–	*–
Intestinal virus, unspecified	13.2	*26.6	21.9	*21.9	8.4	*6.8	*5.2	*9.4
Viral infections, unspecified	21.3	55.2	34.2	*8.6	17.1	13.6	13.3	*14.0
Other	25.7	33.8	52.9	26.7	14.3	18.9	14.2	26.2
Respiratory conditions	290.0	505.9	322.7	245.0	242.4	281.2	239.0	347.2
Common cold	58.8	136.2	62.1	56.5	46.6	51.2	41.0	67.0
Other acute upper respiratory infections	24.6	59.5	40.2	*22.7	14.0	18.3	13.0	26.5
Influenza	155.8	199.0	188.5	134.2	142.7	146.3	139.0	157.6
Acute bronchitis	20.4	41.2	18.7	*14.0	16.1	22.7	16.7	32.1
Pneumonia	23.1	51.3	*7.6	*12.3	19.1	33.0	24.5	46.2
Other respiratory conditions	7.3	*18.7	*5.6	*5.4	*3.8	9.8	*4.8	*17.7
Digestive system conditions	23.8	*18.3	17.6	*22.7	20.7	32.3	33.9	29.8
Dental conditions	4.4	*6.4	*3.8	*4.6	*3.1	*5.6	*7.1	*3.4
Indigestion, nausea, and vomiting	5.9	*1.9	*7.9	*10.0	*5.8	*4.6	*2.3	*8.1
Other digestive conditions	13.4	*10.0	*5.9	*8.1	11.8	22.1	24.6	*18.3
Injuries	164.1	41.2	91.3	237.1	201.5	175.3	149.8	215.1
Fractures and dislocations	47.1	*13.9	35.0	51.0	46.9	61.4	36.4	100.6
Sprains and strains	43.1	*1.3	16.3	54.5	68.9	38.7	47.7	24.7
Open wounds and lacerations	17.2	*6.5	*12.0	58.5	15.3	11.6	*9.0	*15.6
Contusions and superficial injuries	17.8	*0.5	*7.5	29.0	21.6	20.7	*12.6	33.5
Other current injuries	38.9	*19.0	20.5	44.1	48.8	42.8	44.2	40.6
Selected other acute conditions	113.0	171.4	63.5	165.3	123.9	99.4	75.1	137.4
Eye conditions	*2.3	*3.6	*1.9	*0.2	*1.1	*4.1	*2.0	*7.5
Acute ear infections	19.6	125.0	25.5	*10.3	*5.4	7.7	*10.2	*4.0
Other ear conditions	2.5	*8.7	*2.8	*0.3	*2.5	*1.4	*0.6	*2.7
Acute urinary conditions	12.4	*6.6	*1.9	*10.3	10.3	23.1	*12.1	40.4
Disorders of menstruation	*2.0	...	*1.7	*2.3	*3.6	*1.0	*1.6	*–
Other disorders of female genital tract	6.3	*–	*4.5	*6.1	9.5	*5.6	*9.1	*–
Delivery and other conditions of pregnancy and puerperium	29.5	...	*2.9	109.0	55.0	*–	*–	...
Skin conditions	5.2	*6.5	*2.9	*4.2	*1.4	10.4	*4.4	*19.8
Acute musculoskeletal conditions	25.8	*–	*5.7	13.3	30.7	43.3	33.2	59.1
Headache, excluding migraine	3.0	*–	*3.5	*5.7	*3.9	*1.7	*1.6	*1.7
Fever, unspecified	4.3	*21.0	*10.1	*3.5	*0.4	*1.1	*0.3	*2.3
All other acute conditions	40.8	34.6	17.8	37.6	34.1	64.3	50.2	86.3

*Figure does not meet standards of reliability.

C2-11. Number of Days Per Person Per Year and Number of Days of Activity Restriction Due to Acute and Chronic Conditions, by Type of Restriction and Sociodemographic Characteristics: United States, 1990

(Data are based on household inteviews of the civilian noninstitutionalized population.)

Characteristic	Type of restriction					
	All types	Bed disability	Work or school loss[1]	All types	Bed disability	Work or school loss[1]
	Number of days per person			Number of days in thousands		
All persons[2]	14.9	6.2	5.1	3,669,240	1,521,141	833,258
Age						
Under 5 years	11.0	5.3	. . .	209,599	100,817	. . .
5–17 years	8.4	3.7	4.6	383,383	167,751	211,787
18 years and over	17.0	6.9	5.3	3,076,258	1,252,573	621,471
18–24 years	10.0	4.1	5.4	250,514	102,200	91,590
25–44 years	12.1	4.7	4.9	970,935	372,780	321,226
45–64 years	19.7	8.0	5.8	919,089	371,663	184,072
65 years and over	31.4	13.6	6.1	935,720	405,930	24,582
Sex and age						
Male:						
All ages	13.1	5.2	4.6	1,558,060	625,349	402,381
Under 5 years	11.1	5.6	. . .	108,513	54,287	. . .
5–17 years	8.1	3.3	4.3	188,176	77,790	99,772
18 years and over	14.6	5.7	4.7	1,261,371	493,272	302,609
18–24 years	7.9	3.1	4.2	96,930	38,230	37,266
25–44 years	10.4	3.6	4.2	407,221	142,909	150,257
45–64 years	18.2	6.9	5.6	405,204	153,624	98,219
65 years and over	28.4	12.8	7.4	352,015	158,508	16,867
Female:						
All ages	16.7	7.1	5.7	2,111,180	895,792	430,878
Under 5 years	10.8	5.0	. . .	101,086	46,530	. . .
5–17 years	8.8	4.0	5.0	195,207	89,961	112,016
18 years and over	19.1	8.0	5.9	1,814,887	759,302	318,862
18–24 years	12.0	5.0	6.6	153,584	63,970	54,324
25–44 years	13.8	5.6	5.8	563,714	229,871	170,969
45–64 years	21.2	9.0	6.0	513,885	218,038	85,853
65 years and over	33.6	14.2	4.5	583,705	247,423	7,716
Race and age						
White:						
All ages	14.8	6.0	4.9	3,056,745	1,235,051	684,611
Under 5 years	11.3	5.1	. . .	174,608	78,078	. . .
5–17 years	8.7	3.8	4.7	318,747	139,247	173,771
18 years and over	16.5	6.6	5.0	2,563,389	1,017,725	510,840
18–24 years	10.3	4.1	5.3	209,532	84,146	76,569
25–44 years	11.8	4.4	4.7	794,868	294,277	262,596
45–64 years	18.7	7.4	5.5	752,606	296,581	152,880
65 years and over	30.1	12.8	5.2	806,383	342,721	18,794
Black:						
All ages	17.7	8.2	6.4	536,079	248,277	125,267
Under 5 years	10.3	6.7	. . .	30,785	19,938	. . .
5–17 years	7.4	3.3	4.5	52,892	23,206	32,015
18 years and over	22.3	10.1	7.5	452,402	205,133	93,252
18–24 years	9.8	4.2	6.2	34,640	14,859	12,298
25–44 years	15.9	7.0	6.9	150,001	65,639	48,943
45–64 years	31.3	14.3	9.2	149,584	68,254	28,146
65 years and over	47.2	22.5	*11.2	118,177	56,381	3,864

See footnotes at end of table.

*Figure does not meet standards of reliability.

C2-11. Number of Days Per Person Per Year and Number of Days of Activity Restriction Due to Acute and Chronic Conditions, by Type of Restriction and Sociodemographic Characteristics: United States, 1990 (continued)

(Data are based on household interviews of the civilian noninstitutionalized population.)

	Type of restriction					
Characteristic	All types	Bed disability	Work or school loss[1]	All types	Bed disability	Work or school loss[1]
Family income and age	Number of days per person			Number of days in thousands		
Less than $10,000:						
All ages	27.3	12.2	5.6	662,211	296,207	57,615
Under 5 years	13.7	6.8	...	32,074	15,925	...
5–17 years	8.4	3.4	5.0	36,733	14,782	21,718
18 years and over	33.8	15.1	6.1	593,404	265,499	35,897
18–24 years	13.1	5.8	4.6	57,015	24,979	9,773
25–44 years	25.5	11.8	6.6	128,465	59,338	15,308
45–64 years	61.6	28.6	*7.8	188,863	87,871	7,576
65 years and over	43.1	18.3	*7.7	219,061	93,311	3,239
$10,000–$19,999:						
All ages	19.1	8.1	6.4	758,090	321,300	144,261
Under 5 years	13.1	7.3	...	44,310	24,765	...
5–17 years	9.3	4.5	5.6	66,239	32,299	39,855
18 years and over	22.2	9.0	6.8	647,541	264,236	104,406
18–24 years	11.6	4.8	6.7	53,434	22,194	20,735
25–44 years	15.6	6.1	6.4	173,177	67,279	53,467
45–64 years	30.5	11.5	8.5	182,121	68,326	26,648
65 years and over	31.6	14.1	*4.3	238,809	106,437	3,556
$20,000–$34,999:						
All ages	13.5	5.5	5.6	714,685	289,652	206,436
Under 5 years	10.4	5.3	...	45,946	23,523	...
5–17 years	8.5	4.2	4.8	86,070	42,817	49,134
18 years and over	15.2	5.8	5.9	582,668	223,311	157,302
18–24 years	9.6	3.6	6.0	47,729	17,865	22,640
25–44 years	11.4	4.5	5.3	215,538	85,518	84,484
45–64 years	19.3	7.1	6.9	176,245	64,926	43,351
65 years and over	26.3	10.1	*8.1	143,157	55,003	6,827
$35,000 or more:						
All ages	10.3	3.8	4.6	911,756	339,261	317,201
Under 5 years	10.6	4.4	...	68,492	28,450	...
5–17 years	8.5	3.3	4.4	149,319	57,271	76,659
18 years and over	10.8	3.9	4.7	693,944	253,539	240,543
18–24 years	7.7	3.1	4.8	55,056	22,119	26,519
25–44 years	9.6	3.1	4.4	323,567	105,796	131,245
45–64 years	11.2	4.2	5.0	215,284	79,884	76,790
65 years and over	22.6	10.3	*6.0	100,037	45,739	5,988
Geographic region						
Northeast	13.2	5.4	5.1	656,228	268,324	166,184
Midwest	14.0	5.5	5.2	835,979	330,457	207,581
South	16.7	7.2	4.9	1,404,429	609,175	271,750
West	14.8	6.0	5.3	772,605	313,186	187,744
Place of residence						
MSA[3]	14.7	6.0	5.1	2,826,360	1,166,450	664,680
Central city	15.8	7.1	5.5	1,191,104	536,048	267,853
Not central city	13.9	5.4	4.9	1,635,257	630,402	396,827
Not MSA[3]	15.8	6.7	4.9	842,880	354,691	168,578

[1]Sum of school-loss days for children 5-17 years of age and work-loss days for currently employed persons 17 years of age and over. School-loss days are shown for the age group 5-17 years; work-loss days are shown for the age group 18 years and over and each older age group.
[2]Includes other races and unknown family income.
[3]MSA is metropolitan statistical area.

C2-12. Percent Distribution of Persons with Difficulty in Activities of Daily Living and Instrumental Activities of Daily Living, by Sex and Age

| Sex and age | Difficulties in ADL's and IADL's | | | |
	None	ADL difficulty only	IADL difficulty only	Both
Total........................	66.6	5.2	10.9	17.3
Sex				
Male........................	74.7	6.6	7.4	11.3
Female......................	60.9	4.3	13.4	21.5
Age				
65–74 years.................	74.1	4.7	9.2	12.0
75–84 years.................	58.7	6.5	12.5	22.4
85 years or over	37.1	4.8	18.3	39.8

NOTE: ADL is activities of daily living. IADL is instrumental activities of daily living.

C2-13. Difficulties of the Elderly with ADLs and IADLs, by Residence: 1986

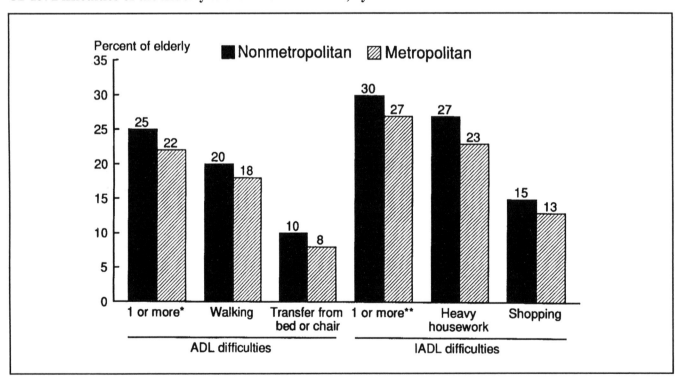

*Includes walking, transferring, bathing, dressing, toileting, and eating.
**Includes heavy and light housework, shopping, preparing meals, managing money.
Source: National Center for Health Statistics, 1986 National Health Interview Survey.

C2-14. Percent of Persons 65 Years of Age and Over Who Reported Receiving the Help of Another Person with Performing Activities of Daily Living, by Race, Sex, and Age: United States, 1986

(Data are based on household interviews of the civilian noninstitutionalized population.)

Race, sex, and age	Total	ADL for which help of another person received						
		Eating	Toileting	Dressing	Bathing	Trans-ferring[1]	Walking	Getting outside
Race	Number of persons in thousands	Percent						
White	24,753	1.1	2.3	4.2	5.6	3.0	4.5	6.1
All other	2,784	*0.6	3.5	6.1	9.4	5.2	5.8	7.8
Sex								
Male.	11,357	1.0	1.9	3.9	4.3	2.6	3.1	3.8
Female.	16,181	1.1	2.8	4.7	7.2	3.7	5.8	8.0
Age								
65–74 years.	16,987	0.8	1.4	2.9	3.2	2.1	2.6	3.2
75–84 years.	8,552	1.1	3.3	5.4	8.6	4.0	6.4	9.2
65 years and over.	27,538	1.1	2.4	4.4	6.0	3.2	4.6	6.3
75 years and over.	10,551	1.6	4.1	6.8	10.6	5.0	8.0	11.3
85 years and over.	1,999	4.1	7.5	12.6	19.0	9.4	14.8	20.6
Male								
65–74 years.	7,490	0.9	1.5	3.2	3.3	2.3	2.3	2.7
75–84 years.	3,251	*0.6	1.9	4.2	4.9	2.3	3.7	4.8
65 years and over.	11,357	1.0	1.9	3.9	4.3	2.6	3.1	3.8
75 years and over.	3,866	1.3	2.5	5.2	6.4	3.2	4.5	6.0
85 years and over.	615	*4.7	*5.9	10.0	14.1	7.8	8.3	12.8
Female								
65–74 years.	9,496	0.6	1.3	2.6	3.1	2.0	2.8	3.5
75–84 years.	5,301	1.3	4.1	6.1	10.9	5.0	8.0	11.9
65 years and over.	16,181	1.1	2.8	4.7	7.2	3.7	5.8	8.0
75 years and over.	6,685	1.8	5.0	7.7	13.0	6.1	10.0	14.4
85 years and over.	1,384	*3.9	8.3	13.8	21.2	10.1	17.8	24.1

[1]Transferring means getting in and out of a bed or chair.

*Figure does not meet standards of reliability.

NOTE: Persons reported as not performing an activity of daily living (ADL) were classified with those reported as receiving help with that ADL.

Source: National Center for Health Statistics; data from the National Health Interview Survey 1986 Functional Limitations Supplement.

C3. Death Rates and Causes of Death

C3-1. Provisional Death Rates for All Causes, According to Race, Sex, and Age: 1988 to 1990

(Data are based on a 10-percent sample of death certificates from the National Vital Statistics Systems.)

Sex and age	All races 1988	All races 1990	White 1988	White 1990	Black 1988	Black 1990
Both sexes	Deaths per 100,000 resident population					
65–74 years..................	2,731.2	2,607.4	2,679.4	2,565.7	3,587.3	3,319.7
75–84 years..................	6,324.4	6,084.5	6,305.2	6,081.0	7,257.6	6,873.2
85 years and over.............	15,577.7	14,784.4	15,888.0	15,087.7	13,206.1	12,707.3
Male						
65–74 years..................	3,583.2	3,358.5	3,533.8	3,316.2	4,527.3	4,172.9
75–84 years..................	8,243.2	7,950.2	8,234.6	7,976.4	9,360.3	8,731.4
85 years and over.............	18,475.2	17,521.6	18,933.7	17,973.3	15,342.9	14,743.2
Female						
65–74 years..................	2,051.4	2,002.1	1,993.0	1,956.9	2,887.1	2,673.9
75–84 years..................	5,166.6	4,941.7	5,145.3	4,921.1	5,997.8	5,763.7
85 years and over.............	14,451.7	13,727.5	14,727.8	13,993.7	12,259.5	11,831.4

NOTE: Includes deaths of nonresidents of the United States.

C3-2. Crude and Age-Adjusted Death Rates: United States, 1940 to 1990

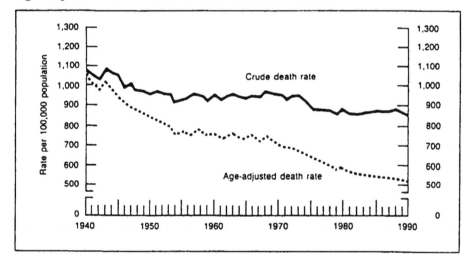

C3-3. Deaths and Death Rates, by Age, Race, and Sex: United States, 1990

(Rates per 100,000 population in specified group)

Age	All races			White			All other — Total			All other — Black		
	Both sexes	Male	Female	Both sexes	Male	Female	Both sexes	Male	Female	Both sexes	Male	Female
Number												
All ages	2,150,466	1,114,190	1,036,276	1,853,841	950,852	902,989	296,625	163,338	133,287	267,642	146,393	121,249
Under 1 year	39,655	22,361	17,294	25,794	14,760	11,034	13,861	7,601	6,260	12,527	6,842	5,685
1–4 years	7,292	4,110	3,182	5,133	2,910	2,223	2,159	1,200	959	1,830	1,021	809
5–9 years	4,313	2,510	1,803	3,187	1,864	1,323	1,126	646	480	953	559	394
10–14 years	4,601	2,914	1,687	3,467	2,211	1,256	1,134	703	431	967	603	364
15–19 years	15,570	11,263	4,307	11,945	8,450	3,495	3,625	2,813	812	3,120	2,456	664
20–24 years	20,918	15,902	5,016	15,232	11,560	3,672	5,686	4,342	1,344	5,037	3,846	1,191
25–29 years	26,930	19,932	6,998	19,514	14,640	4,874	7,416	5,292	2,124	6,685	4,772	1,913
30–34 years	33,594	24,222	9,372	23,876	17,498	6,378	9,718	6,724	2,994	8,947	6,203	2,744
35–39 years	37,862	26,742	11,120	26,885	19,234	7,651	10,977	7,508	3,469	10,050	6,938	3,112
40–44 years	43,057	28,586	14,471	32,046	21,376	10,670	11,011	7,210	3,801	10,025	6,583	3,442
45–49 years	50,857	32,718	18,139	38,963	25,166	13,797	11,894	7,552	4,342	10,781	6,857	3,924
50–54 years	67,409	42,105	25,304	52,670	32,966	19,704	14,739	9,139	5,600	13,329	8,317	5,012
55–59 years	101,474	62,981	38,493	82,414	51,499	30,915	19,060	11,482	7,578	17,258	10,446	6,812
60–64 years . . . . . , .	158,584	96,628	61,956	133,021	81,919	51,102	25,563	14,709	10,854	23,262	13,340	9,922
65–69 years	219,097	129,847	89,250	187,834	112,194	75,640	31,263	17,653	13,610	28,452	16,031	12,421
70–74 years	262,127	148,559	113,568	230,704	131,599	99,105	31,423	16,960	14,463	28,507	15,209	13,298
75–79 years	301,225	157,090	144,135	268,221	140,663	127,558	33,004	16,427	16,577	29,815	14,555	15,260
80–84 years	297,981	135,580	162,401	270,882	123,249	147,633	27,099	12,331	14,768	24,205	10,644	13,561
85 years and over . . .	457,358	149,735	307,623	421,669	136,813	284,856	35,689	12,922	22,767	31,725	11,056	20,669
Not stated	562	405	157	384	281	103	178	124	54	167	115	52
Rate												
All ages [1]	866.3	921.0	814.3	887.2	930.2	846.0	755.2	870.8	649.5	872.9	1,006.5	752.4
Under 1 year [2]	1,005.2	1,107.0	898.4	815.5	909.4	716.0	1,772.5	1,914.6	1,626.0	2,023.7	2,179.0	1,863.9
1–4 years	49.2	54.2	44.0	43.2	47.8	38.4	73.9	80.8	66.8	80.6	88.4	72.5
5–9 years	23.7	26.9	20.3	21.8	24.8	18.6	31.4	35.6	27.2	34.0	39.3	28.6
10–14 years	27.1	33.5	20.4	25.5	31.7	19.0	33.6	41.0	26.0	36.1	44.3	27.6
15–19 years	87.4	123.9	49.4	83.3	115.3	49.8	104.5	159.5	47.6	113.1	176.2	48.6
20–24 years	111.8	169.7	53.7	99.2	149.5	48.1	170.1	265.2	78.8	190.0	300.7	86.8
25–29 years	124.1	183.5	64.6	107.8	160.1	54.4	206.2	307.1	113.3	236.5	355.6	128.8
30–34 years	151.8	218.6	84.8	128.6	186.4	69.5	272.4	397.2	159.7	326.1	481.2	188.6
35–39 years	193.0	274.8	112.4	161.7	230.6	92.4	366.4	540.5	216.0	444.7	670.3	254.0
40–44 years	255.0	344.7	168.5	220.2	295.7	145.7	472.4	677.6	300.0	580.8	841.8	364.2
45–49 years	376.1	495.7	262.1	333.8	437.1	233.3	643.3	895.8	431.6	772.8	1,095.4	510.3
50–54 years	592.6	764.3	431.4	538.1	688.1	394.2	929.3	1,271.1	645.2	1,089.9	1,528.9	738.1
55–59 years	946.1	1,229.9	686.8	885.2	1,149.5	640.1	1,346.0	1,791.3	977.8	1,546.4	2,056.3	1,120.4
60–64 years	1,459.3	1,902.5	1,070.4	1,390.1	1,821.2	1,007.7	1,969.4	2,531.7	1,511.7	2,247.5	2,856.5	1,749.9
65–69 years	2,154.3	2,803.9	1,611.6	2,080.3	2,716.6	1,544.0	2,740.0	3,516.5	2,129.9	3,106.1	3,987.8	2,411.8
70–74 years	3,271.7	4,288.7	2,496.5	3,207.3	4,217.9	2,432.6	3,836.8	4,930.2	3,044.8	4,312.7	5,550.7	3,445.1
75–79 years	4,993.0	6,586.6	3,951.1	4,939.6	6,551.6	3,886.6	5,473.3	6,902.1	4,541.6	6,134.8	7,783.4	5,103.7
80–84 years	7,993.1	10,381.3	6,705.2	7,946.1	10,365.8	6,650.1	8,495.0	10,539.3	7,347.3	9,455.1	11,696.7	8,218.8
85 years and over	15,034.8	17,615.9	14,033.9	15,272.3	17,978.1	14,242.8	12,700.7	14,519.1	11,857.8	13,442.8	15,355.6	12,526.7

[1]Figures for age not stated are included in All ages but not distributed among age groups.
[2]Death rates under 1 year (based on population estimates) differ from infant mortality rates (based on live births).
Source: National Center for Health Statistics, *Monthly Vital Statistics Report*, vol. 40, No. 8 Supplement, January 7, 1992, p. 15.

C3-4. Percent Change in Death Rates Between 1989 and 1990, by Age, Race, and Sex: United States

Age	Total	White	Black	Male	Female
Percent change					
All ages	-0.9	-0.6	-1.9	-0.9	-0.8
Under 1 year [1]	-5.4	-5.6	-4.1	-4.5	-6.7
1–4 years	-6.0	-5.9	-5.9	-4.4	-7.9
5–14 years	-6.6	-6.3	-5.2	-6.6	-6.3
15–24 years.	1.6	0.2	6.1	3.5	-3.7
25–34 years.	-0.6	-1.1	0.6	0.0	-2.0
35–44 years.	0.5	1.0	-1.7	0.9	-0.7
45–54 years.	-1.4	-1.0	-2.5	-1.9	-0.5
55–64 years.	-2.2	-2.1	-2.6	-2.6	-1.7
65–74 years.	-1.7	-1.5	-3.1	-1.9	-1.4
75–84 years.	-1.3	-1.1	-2.5	-0.9	-1.7
85 years and over	-0.5	-0.5	-0.2	0.2	-0.8

[1]Death rates under 1 year (based on population estimates) differ from infant mortality rates (based on live births).

C3-5. Deaths, by Selected Cause and Selected Characteristics: 1989

(In thousands. Excludes deaths of nonresidents of the U.S. Deaths classified according to ninth revision of *International Classification of Diseases.*)

AGE, SEX, AND RACE	Total [1]	Diseases of heart	Malignant neoplasms	Accidents and adverse effects	Cerebrovascular diseases	Chronic obstructive pulmonary diseases [2]	Pneumonia, flu	Suicide	Chronic liver disease, cirrhosis	Diabetes mellitus	Homicide and legal intervention
ALL RACES [3]											
Both sexes, total [4]	2,150.5	733.9	496.2	95.0	145.8	84.3	76.6	30.2	26.7	46.8	22.9
Under 15 years old	55.9	1.4	1.8	7.9	0.3	0.2	1.0	0.2	(Z)	0.1	1.2
15 to 24 years old	36.5	0.9	1.9	16.7	0.2	0.2	0.3	4.9	0.1	0.1	6.2
25 to 34 years old	60.5	3.5	5.3	16.6	0.9	0.3	0.9	6.6	1.0	0.7	7.1
35 to 44 years old	80.9	11.8	15.7	11.9	2.4	0.6	1.4	6.3	3.6	1.4	4.0
45 to 54 years old	118.3	30.9	39.1	7.5	4.6	2.3	1.7	3.6	4.7	2.8	1.9
55 to 64 years old	260.1	81.4	96.1	7.8	10.5	10.7	3.9	3.3	6.8	6.9	1.1
65 to 74 years old	481.2	165.8	155.0	8.8	26.3	27.1	10.4	3.3	6.5	13.2	0.7
75 to 84 years old	599.2	234.3	130.6	10.3	50.7	30.6	24.0	2.3	3.3	14.2	0.4
85 years old and over	457.4	203.9	50.6	7.8	49.6	12.3	33.0	0.7	0.7	7.5	0.1
Male, total [4]	1,114.2	388.2	263.3	63.9	57.3	48.2	35.7	24.1	17.3	19.7	17.7
Under 15 years old	31.9	0.7	1.0	4.9	0.1	0.1	0.6	0.2	(Z)	(Z)	0.7
15 to 24 years old	27.2	0.6	1.1	12.6	0.1	0.1	0.1	4.1	(Z)	0.1	5.1
25 to 34 years old	44.2	2.4	2.6	12.9	0.5	0.2	0.5	5.3	0.7	0.4	5.6
35 to 44 years old	55.3	8.8	6.9	9.0	1.3	0.3	0.9	4.1	2.7	0.9	3.1
45 to 54 years old	74.8	23.1	19.7	5.5	2.4	1.1	1.1	2.7	3.4	1.6	1.5
55 to 64 years old	159.6	56.2	53.6	5.3	5.7	6.0	2.5	2.5	4.5	3.4	0.8
65 to 74 years old	278.4	101.6	87.4	5.3	13.3	15.8	6.4	2.7	3.9	5.9	0.5
75 to 84 years old	292.7	112.3	69.3	5.2	20.8	18.0	12.1	1.9	1.7	5.4	0.2
85 years old and over	149.7	62.4	21.8	3.0	13.1	8.6	11.5	0.6	0.3	2.0	0.1
Female, total [4]	1,036.3	345.7	232.9	31.1	88.2	36.2	40.9	6.1	9.4	27.1	5.2
Under 15 years old	24.0	0.6	0.8	2.9	0.1	0.1	0.4	0.1	(Z)	(Z)	0.6
15 to 24 years old	9.3	0.3	0.8	4.1	0.1	0.1	0.1	0.8	(Z)	0.1	1.1
25 to 34 years old	16.4	1.1	2.7	3.7	0.5	0.1	0.4	1.2	0.3	0.3	1.5
35 to 44 years old	25.6	2.9	8.8	2.8	1.1	0.3	0.5	1.2	0.9	0.5	0.9
45 to 54 years old	43.4	7.9	19.4	2.0	2.2	1.1	0.6	0.9	1.3	1.2	0.4
55 to 64 years old	100.4	25.1	42.5	2.3	4.8	4.8	1.4	0.8	2.2	3.6	0.3
65 to 74 years old	202.8	64.2	67.7	3.5	13.0	11.3	4.1	0.6	2.6	7.2	0.3
75 to 84 years old	306.5	122.0	61.3	5.0	29.9	12.7	11.9	0.4	1.6	8.7	0.2
85 years old and over	307.6	141.5	28.8	4.8	36.5	5.7	21.4	0.1	0.4	5.4	0.1
WHITE											
Both sexes, total [4]	1,853.8	648.9	434.2	79.1	125.5	77.9	67.9	27.4	22.2	38.1	11.3
Under 15 years old	37.8	0.9	1.4	5.7	0.2	0.1	0.8	0.2	(Z)	(Z)	0.6
15 to 24 years old	27.2	0.6	1.5	14.3	0.2	0.1	0.2	4.1	(Z)	0.1	2.5
25 to 34 years old	43.4	2.3	4.3	13.8	0.6	0.2	0.5	5.7	0.6	0.5	3.3
35 to 44 years old	58.9	8.6	12.6	9.4	1.5	0.4	0.8	4.8	2.5	1.1	2.1
45 to 54 years old	91.6	23.9	31.9	6.0	3.0	1.9	1.2	3.4	3.7	2.0	1.2
55 to 64 years old	215.4	67.1	82.1	6.2	7.8	9.6	3.0	3.2	5.7	5.1	0.7
65 to 74 years old	418.5	144.4	136.6	7.6	21.8	25.1	8.9	3.1	5.8	10.6	0.5
75 to 84 years old	539.1	211.8	117.6	9.2	44.9	28.9	21.8	2.2	3.1	12.0	0.3
85 years old and over	421.7	189.1	46.0	7.1	45.9	11.6	30.8	0.7	0.7	6.6	0.1
BLACK											
Both sexes, total [4]	267.6	77.6	55.6	13.4	18.9	5.7	7.6	2.2	3.9	8.0	11.0
Under 15 years old	16.3	0.4	0.3	1.8	0.1	0.1	0.3	(Z)	(Z)	(Z)	0.5
15 to 24 years old	8.2	0.3	0.3	1.9	0.1	0.1	0.1	0.5	(Z)	(Z)	3.5
25 to 34 years old	15.6	1.1	0.9	2.5	0.3	0.1	0.3	0.7	0.3	0.1	3.6
35 to 44 years old	20.1	3.0	2.7	2.1	0.8	0.2	0.6	0.4	0.9	0.3	1.7
45 to 54 years old	24.1	6.4	6.4	1.3	1.4	0.4	0.5	0.2	0.9	0.7	0.7
55 to 64 years old	40.5	13.1	12.6	1.2	2.5	1.0	0.8	0.1	0.9	1.8	0.4
65 to 74 years old	57.0	19.6	16.8	1.1	4.3	1.8	1.4	0.1	0.6	2.3	0.3
75 to 84 years old	54.0	20.3	11.7	0.9	5.2	1.5	1.9	(Z)	0.2	1.9	0.1
85 years old and over	31.7	13.2	4.1	0.6	3.3	0.5	1.8	(Z)	0.3	0.8	0.1

[1]Includes other causes, not shown separately.
[2]Includes allied conditions.
[3]Includes other races, not shown separately.
[4]Includes those deaths with age not stated.
Z Fewer than 50.
Source: U.S. National Center for Health Statistics, *Vital Statistics of the United States,* annual.

C3-6. Deaths and Death Rates for the 10 Leading Causes of Death in Specified Age Groups: United States, 1990

(Rates per 100,000 population in specified groups.)

1–4 years

...	All causes		6,931	46.8
1	Accidents and adverse effects	E800–E949	2,566	17.3
...	Motor vehicle accidents	E810–E825	928	6.3
...	All other accidents and adverse effects	E800–E807,E826–E949	1,638	11.1
2	Congenital anomalies	740–759	896	6.0
3	Malignant neoplasms, including neoplasms of lymphatic and hematopoietic tissues	140–208	513	3.5
4	Homicide and legal intervention	E960–E978	378	2.6
5	Diseases of heart	390–398,402,404–429	282	1.9
6	Pneumonia and influenza	480–487	171	1.2
7	Certain conditions originating in the perinatal period	760–779	134	0.9
8	Human immunodeficiency virus infection	*042–*044	123	0.8
9	Septicemia	038	100	0.7
10	Meningitis	320–322	81	0.5
...	All other causes	Residual	1,687	11.4

5–14 years

...	All causes		8,436	24.0
1	Accidents and adverse effects	E800–E949	3,650	10.4
...	Motor vehicle accidents	E810–E825	2,059	5.9
...	All other accidents and adverse effects	E800–E807,E826–E949	1,591	4.5
2	Malignant neoplasms, including neoplasms of lymphatic and hematopoietic tissues	140–208	1,094	3.1
3	Homicide and legal intervention	E960–E978	512	1.5
4	Congenital anomalies	740–759	468	1.3
5	Diseases of heart	390–398,402,404–429	308	0.9
6	Suicide	E950–E959	264	0.8
7	Pneumonia and influenza	480–487	134	0.4
8	Chronic obstructive pulmonary diseases and allied conditions	490–496	115	0.3
9	Benign neoplasms, carcinoma in situ, and neoplasms of uncertain behavior and of unspecified nature	210–239	100	0.3
10	Human immunodeficiency virus infection	*042–*044	84	0.2
...	All other causes	Residual	1,707	4.9

15–24 years

...	All causes		36,733	99.2
1	Accidents and adverse effects	E800–E949	16,241	43.9
...	Motor vehicle accidents	E810–E825	12,607	34.1
...	All other accidents and adverse effects	E800–E807,E826–E949	3,634	9.8
2	Homicide and legal intervention	E960–E978	7,354	19.9
3	Suicide	E950–E959	4,869	13.2
4	Malignant neoplasms, including neoplasms of lymphatic and hematopoietic tissues	140–208	1,819	4.9
5	Diseases of heart	390–398,402,404–429	917	2.5
6	Human immunodeficiency virus infection	*042–*044	541	1.5
7	Congenital anomalies	740–759	491	1.3
8	Cerebrovascular diseases	430–438	234	0.6
9	Pneumonia and influenza	480–487	231	0.6
10	Chronic obstructive pulmonary diseases and allied conditions	490–496	178	0.5
..	All other causes	Residual	3,858	10.4

25–44 years

...	All causes		143,653	178.2
1	Accidents and adverse effects	E800–E949	27,663	34.3
...	Motor vehicle accidents	E810–E825	16,488	20.5
...	All other accidents and adverse effects	E800–E807,E826–E949	11,175	13.9
2	Malignant neoplasms, including neoplasms of lymphatic and hematopoietic tissues	140–208	21,650	26.9
3	Human immunodeficiency virus infection	*042–*044	18,748	23.3
4	Diseases of heart	390–398,402,404–429	15,045	18.7
5	Suicide	E950–E959	12,267	15.2
6	Homicide and legal intervention	E960–E978	12,060	15.0
7	Chronic liver disease and cirrhosis	571	4,505	5.6
8	Cerebrovascular diseases	430–438	3,352	4.2
9	Diabetes mellitus	250	2,184	2.7
10	Pneumonia and influenza	480–487	2,178	2.7
...	All other causes	Residual	24,001	29.8

45–64 years

...	All causes		371,304	804.2
1	Malignant neoplasms, including neoplasms of lymphatic and hematopoietic tissues	140–208	134,742	291.8
2	Diseases of heart	390–398,402,404–429	107,750	233.4
3	Cerebrovascular diseases	430–438	14,814	32.1
4	Accidents and adverse effects	E800–E949	14,607	31.6
...	Motor vehicle accidents	E810–E825	7,282	15.8
...	All other accidents and adverse effects	E800–E807,E826–E949	7,325	15.9
5	Chronic obstructive pulmonary diseases and allied conditions	490–496	12,605	27.3
6	Chronic liver disease and cirrhosis	571	10,806	23.4
7	Diabetes mellitus	250	9,803	21.2
8	Suicide	E950–E959	7,101	15.4
9	Pneumonia and influenza	480–487	5,673	12.3
10	Human immunodeficiency virus infection	*042–*044	5,126	11.1
...	All other causes	Residual	48,277	104.6

65 years and over

...	All causes		1,542,493	4,963.2
1	Diseases of heart	390–398,402,404–429	594,858	1,914.0
2	Malignant neoplasms, including neoplasms of lymphatic and hematopoietic tissues	140–208	345,387	1,111.3
3	Cerebrovascular diseases	430–438	125,409	403.5
4	Chronic obstructive pulmonary diseases and allied conditions	490–496	72,755	234.1
5	Pneumonia and influenza	480–487	70,485	226.8
6	Diabetes mellitus	250	35,523	114.3
7	Accidents and adverse effects	E800–E949	26,213	84.3
...	Motor vehicle accidents	E810–E825	7,210	23.2
...	All other accidents and adverse effects	E800–E807,E826–E949	19,003	61.1
8	Nephritis, nephrotic syndrome, and nephrosis	580–589	17,306	55.7
9	Atherosclerosis	440	17,158	55.2
10	Septicemia	038	15,351	49.4
...	All other causes	Residual	222,048	2,045.9

[1]Rank based on number of deaths.

C3-7. Provisional Death Rates for the Three Leading Causes of Death, According to Age: United States, 1988 to 1990

(Data are based on a 10-percent sample of death certificates from the National Vital Statistics System.)

Cause of death and age	1988	1989	1990
Diseases of heart	Deaths per 100,000 resident population		
All ages, age adjusted	166.7	155.9	150.3
All ages, crude	312.2	296.3	289.0
Under 1 year	23.6	18.8	17.9
1–14 years	1.4	1.1	1.1
15–24 years	2.8	2.1	2.4
25–34 years	7.3	7.5	7.6
35–44 years	33.0	30.8	30.2
45–54 years	131.4	124.6	117.9
55–64 years	405.6	377.8	357.2
65–74 years	985.6	910.1	885.8
75–84 years	2,554.4	2,412.5	2,344.3
85 years and over	7,119.1	6,742.6	6,451.4
Malignant neoplasms			
All ages, age adjusted	133.3	133.7	133.0
All ages, crude	198.6	200.3	201.7
Under 1 year	1.3	1.5	2.2
1–14 years	3.5	3.2	3.0
15–24 years	5.0	5.3	4.8
25–34 years	10.8	13.3	12.7
35–44 years	44.3	45.0	43.2
45–54 years	157.2	158.5	155.7
55–64 years	456.5	451.4	440.7
65–74 years	845.4	843.5	857.3
75–84 years	1,324.8	1,338.4	1,348.7
85 years and over	1,664.5	1,655.2	1,702.1
Cerebrovascular diseases			
All ages, age adjusted	29.8	28.5	27.6
All ages, crude	61.1	59.4	57.9
Under 1 year	1.0	2.8	2.5
1–14 years	0.1	0.3	0.3
15–24 years	0.9	0.4	0.8
25–34 years	2.1	1.9	1.9
35–44 years	7.1	6.7	6.6
45–54 years	20.4	18.1	19.7
55–64 years	51.9	50.6	46.5
65–74 years	155.7	147.6	144.5
75–84 years	544.4	530.2	501.5
85 years and over	1,710.3	1,632.8	1,573.9

NOTES: Includes deaths of nonresidents of the United States. Code numbers for cause of death are based on the International Classification of Diseases. Ninth Revision.

Sources: National Center for Health Statistics: Annual summary of births, marriages, divorces, and deaths, United States, 1988. *Monthly Vital Statistics Report,* Vol. 37, No. 13, DHHS Pub No. (PHS) 89-1120, July 26, 1989; and Annual summary of births, marriages, divorces, and deaths, United States, 1990. *Monthly Vital Statistics Report,* Vol. 39, No. 13, DHHS Pub. No. (PHS) 91-1120, 1991. Public Health Service, Hyattsville, MD.

C3-8. Death Rates for All Causes Among Black Persons 55 Years of Age and Over, by Sex and Age: United States, Selected Years 1960 to 1986

(Data are based on the National Vital Statistics System.)

Sex and age	1960 [1]	1970	1980	1986
Male	Number of deaths per 100,000 resident population			
55–59 years.	2,664.5	2,825.8	2,457.2	2,075.4
60–64 years.	4,199.6	3,778.7	3,377.1	3,075.6
65–69 years.	5,226.5	5,051.3	4,484.0	4,074.1
70–74 years.	6,664.5	6,936.6	6,047.7	5,797.0
75–79 years.	7,653.7	8,827.8	8,092.2	8,038.1
80–84 years.	10,757.1	10,629.9	11,554.2	11,854.7
65 years and over.	6,979.0	7,151.7	6,919.8	6,760.8
75 years and over.	9,695.2	10,047.9	10,530.5	10,552.9
85 years and over.	14,844.8	12,222.2	16,098.8	15,488.1
Female				
55–59 years.	2,051.1	1,688.5	1,305.8	1,148.2
60–64 years.	3,113.2	2,335.8	1,860.7	1,822.3
65–69 years.	3,551.9	3,285.3	2,538.4	2,402.1
70–74 years.	4,832.6	4,728.5	3,759.6	3,514.8
75–79 years.	5,931.2	6,059.7	5,243.8	5,032.1
80–84 years.	8,437.3	7,761.0	8,030.1	8,170.6
65 years and over.	5,287.3	5,151.1	4,766.7	4,842.7
75 years and over.	7,943.4	7,642.8	7,612.3	7,753.0
85 years and over.	13,052.6	10,706.6	12,367.2	12,510.3

[1]Includes deaths of nonresidents of the United States.
Source: National Center for Health Statistics. Vital Statistics of the United States, Vol. II, Mortality, Part A. Washington: Public Health Service. Selected years.

C3-9. Death Rates for Diseases of the Heart for Persons 65 Years and Over, by Age, Sex, and Race: 1988

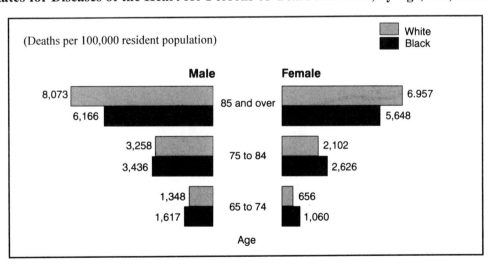

Source: National Center for Health Statistics, Health, United States, 1990, Hyattsville, MD: Public Health Service, 1991, Table 27.

C3-10. Death Rates for Malignant Neoplasms for Persons 65 Years and Over, by Age, Sex, and Race: 1988

(Deaths per 100,000 resident population.)

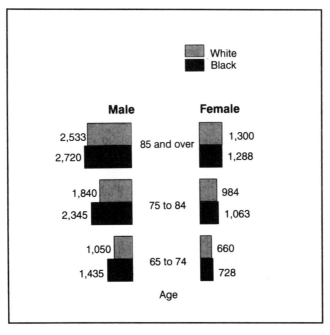

Source: National Center for Health Statistics, *Health, United States, 1990,* Hyattsville, MD: Public Health Service, 1991, Table 29.

C3-11. Death Rates for Cerebrovascular Diseases for Persons 65 Years and Over, by Age, Sex, and Race: 1988

(Deaths per 100,000 resident population.)

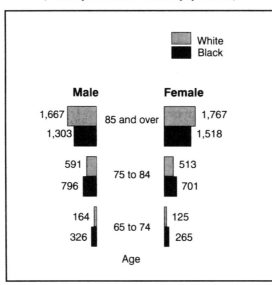

Source: National Center for Health Statistics, *Health, United States, 1990,* Hyattsville, MD: Public Health Service, 1991, Table 28.

C3-12. Death Rates for Diseases of Heart, According to Sex, Race, and Age: United States, Selected Years 1950 to 1989

(Data are based on the National Vital Statistics System)

Sex, race, and age	1950[1]	1960[1]	1970	1980	1985	1986	1987	1988	1989
All races	Deaths per 100,000 resident population								
All ages, age adjusted	307.2	286.2	253.6	202.0	180.5	175.0	169.6	166.3	155.9
All ages, crude	355.5	369.0	362.0	336.0	323.0	317.5	312.4	311.3	295.6
Under 1 year	3.5	6.6	13.1	22.8	24.5	26.1	25.2	22.6	19.7
1–4 years	1.3	1.3	1.7	2.6	2.1	2.5	2.2	2.4	1.9
5–14 years	2.1	1.3	0.8	0.9	0.9	0.9	0.9	0.9	0.8
15–24 years	6.8	4.0	3.0	2.9	2.8	2.8	2.8	2.9	2.6
25–34 years	19.4	15.6	11.4	8.3	8.2	8.6	8.4	8.2	7.9
35–44 years	86.4	74.6	66.7	44.6	38.0	37.5	35.6	34.2	32.3
45–54 years	308.6	271.8	238.4	180.2	152.9	144.6	140.5	131.4	124.2
55–64 years	808.1	737.9	652.3	494.1	439.1	424.2	408.8	400.9	376.7
65–74 years	1,839.8	1,740.5	1,558.2	1,218.6	1,080.6	1,043.0	1,007.9	984.1	911.8
75–84 years	4,310.1	4,089.4	3,683.8	2,993.1	2,712.6	2,637.5	2,560.0	2,542.7	2,400.6
85 years and over	9,150.6	9,317.8	7,891.3	7,777.1	7,275.0	7,178.7	7,074.2	7,098.1	6,701.6
White male									
All ages, age adjusted	381.1	375.4	347.6	277.5	244.5	234.8	225.9	220.5	205.9
All ages, crude	433.0	454.6	438.3	384.0	358.9	348.6	340.1	336.8	318.3
Under 1 year	4.1	6.9	12.0	22.5	23.8	26.0	24.8	21.2	18.4
1–4 years	1.1	1.0	1.5	2.1	1.7	2.1	1.8	1.9	1.7
5–14 years	1.7	1.1	0.8	0.9	0.8	0.9	0.9	1.0	0.7
15–24 years	5.8	3.6	3.0	2.9	3.0	3.0	3.0	3.1	2.7
25–34 years	20.1	17.6	12.3	9.1	9.2	9.5	9.3	9.2	8.9
35–44 years	110.6	107.5	94.6	61.8	52.4	51.7	48.7	46.2	43.1
45–54 years	423.6	413.2	365.7	269.8	224.4	208.8	201.6	186.3	174.8
55–64 years	1,081.7	1,056.0	979.3	730.6	635.6	610.3	582.7	565.1	531.5
65–74 years	2,308.3	2,297.9	2,177.2	1,729.7	1,501.0	1,440.9	1,378.0	1,348.9	1,243.8
75–84 years	4,907.3	4,839.9	4,617.6	3,883.2	3,532.9	3,405.2	3,291.0	3,257.6	3,066.1
85 years and over	9,950.5	10,135.8	8,818.0	8,958.0	8,396.3	8,138.4	8,030.6	8,072.5	7,549.9
Black male									
All ages, age adjusted	415.5	381.2	375.9	327.3	301.0	294.3	287.1	286.2	272.6
All ages, crude	348.4	330.6	330.3	301.0	285.0	281.3	276.1	276.3	263.5
Under 1 year	- - -	13.9	33.5	42.8	46.7	49.8	45.7	43.0	34.4
1–4 years	- - -	3.8	3.9	6.3	4.4	5.3	5.1	4.5	4.6
5–14 years	6.4	3.0	1.4	1.3	1.5	1.4	1.6	1.8	1.4
15–24 years	18.0	8.7	8.3	8.3	7.2	6.7	6.9	7.9	6.3
25–34 years	51.9	43.1	41.6	30.3	29.1	29.3	26.9	27.6	25.3
35–44 years	198.1	168.1	189.2	136.6	122.0	123.6	118.8	113.0	108.3
45–54 years	624.1	514.0	512.8	433.4	382.4	365.1	362.8	352.9	359.4
55–64 years	1,434.0	1,236.8	1,135.4	987.2	882.6	864.9	814.7	833.0	795.8
65–74 years	2,140.1	2,281.4	2,237.8	1,847.2	1,738.4	1,673.1	1,659.7	1,616.7	1,531.5
75–84 years	- - -	3,533.6	3,783.4	3,578.8	3,450.0	3,407.3	3,371.6	3,435.7	3,157.2
85 years and over	- - -	6,037.9	5,367.6	6,819.5	6,098.5	6,268.7	6,050.7	6,165.7	5,837.5
White female									
All ages, age adjusted	223.6	197.1	167.8	134.6	121.7	119.0	116.3	114.2	106.6
All ages, crude	289.4	306.5	313.8	319.2	320.7	319.0	317.1	318.0	303.0
Under 1 year	2.7	4.3	7.0	15.7	18.3	19.1	19.4	16.8	14.2
1–4 years	1.1	0.9	1.2	2.1	1.6	2.1	1.7	2.2	1.3
5–14 years	1.9	0.9	0.7	0.8	0.9	0.7	0.7	0.7	0.6
15–24 years	5.3	2.8	1.7	1.7	1.7	1.6	1.7	1.7	1.5
25–34 years	12.2	8.2	5.5	3.9	3.8	4.1	4.1	3.9	3.8
35–44 years	40.5	28.6	23.9	16.4	14.3	13.8	13.1	12.5	11.9
45–54 years	141.9	103.4	91.4	71.2	62.1	59.8	58.8	54.5	50.4
55–64 years	460.2	383.0	317.7	248.1	225.8	221.4	217.1	213.3	196.1
65–74 years	1,400.9	1,229.8	1,044.0	796.7	713.7	693.9	675.1	656.2	604.4
75–84 years	3,925.2	3,629.7	3,143.5	2,493.6	2,233.3	2,180.2	2,120.7	2,101.5	1,990.7
85 years and over	9,084.7	9,280.8	7,839.9	7,501.6	7,089.3	7,021.3	6,924.6	6,957.3	6,580.4
Black female	Deaths per 100,000 resident population								
All ages, age adjusted	349.5	292.6	251.7	201.1	186.8	185.1	180.8	181.1	172.9
All ages, crude	289.9	268.5	261.0	249.7	248.1	250.8	248.3	251.2	242.7
Under 1 year	- - -	12.0	31.3	43.6	39.5	42.8	36.4	39.9	39.7
1–4 years	- - -	2.8	4.2	4.4	5.2	4.8	4.4	4.1	3.2
5–14 years	8.8	3.0	1.8	1.7	1.7	1.5	1.4	1.0	1.6
15–24 years	19.8	10.0	6.0	4.6	4.6	4.6	4.4	4.4	4.2
25–34 years	52.0	35.9	24.7	15.7	13.1	15.3	14.8	13.2	13.1
35–44 years	185.0	125.3	99.8	61.7	50.4	50.1	46.5	50.8	47.1
45–54 years	526.8	360.7	290.9	202.4	172.6	172.5	165.7	167.8	153.7
55–64 years	1,210.7	952.3	710.5	530.1	500.4	479.0	469.9	471.4	453.1
65–74 years	1,659.4	1,680.5	1,553.2	1,210.3	1,133.6	1,108.3	1,090.2	1,060.0	1,024.9
75–84 years	- - -	2,926.9	2,964.1	2,707.2	2,606.0	2,623.5	2,566.3	2,625.6	2,492.9
85 years and over	- - -	5,650.0	5,003.8	5,796.5	5,441.0	5,698.6	5,627.6	5,648.1	5,469.7

[1]Includes deaths of nonresidents of the United States.

Sources: National Center for Health Statistics: Vital Statistics of the United States, Vol. II, Mortality, Part A, for data years 1950-89. Public Health Service. Washington. U.S. Government Printing Office; Data computed by the Division of Analysis from data compiled by the Division of Vital Statistics.

C3-13. Death Rates for Malignant Neoplasms, According to Sex, Race, and Age: United States, Selected Years 1950 to 1989

(Data are based on the National Vital Statistics System)

Sex, race, and age	1950[1]	1960[1]	1970	1980	1985	1986	1987	1988	1989
All races	Deaths per 100,000 resident population								
All ages, age adjusted.	125.3	125.8	129.8	132.8	133.6	133.2	132.9	132.7	133.0
All ages, crude.	139.8	149.2	162.8	183.9	193.3	194.7	195.9	197.3	199.9
Under 1 year	8.7	7.2	4.7	3.2	3.0	2.6	2.7	2.3	2.7
1–4 years.	11.7	10.9	7.5	4.5	3.8	4.0	3.8	3.7	3.4
5–14 years.	6.7	6.8	6.0	4.3	3.5	3.4	3.3	3.2	3.3
15–24 years.	8.6	8.3	8.3	6.3	5.4	5.4	5.1	5.1	5.1
25–34 years.	20.0	19.5	16.5	13.7	13.1	13.1	12.4	11.9	12.1
35–44 years.	62.7	59.7	59.5	48.6	45.7	45.3	43.5	44.2	43.1
45–54 years.	175.1	177.0	182.5	180.0	169.1	165.7	164.3	160.4	157.2
55–64 years.	392.9	396.8	423.0	436.1	450.5	444.4	447.0	447.3	445.1
65–74 years.	692.5	713.9	751.2	817.9	838.3	847.0	843.6	842.7	852.6
75–84 years.	1,153.3	1,127.4	1,169.2	1,232.3	1,281.0	1,287.3	1,298.4	1,313.3	1,338.1
85 years and over.	1,451.0	1,450.0	1,320.7	1,594.6	1,591.5	1,612.0	1,618.0	1,638.9	1,662.3
White male									
All ages, age adjusted.	130.9	141.6	154.3	160.5	159.2	158.8	158.4	157.6	157.2
All ages, crude.	147.2	166.1	185.1	208.7	217.2	218.8	220.5	221.4	223.3
Under 1 year	9.6	7.9	4.3	3.5	3.1	3.0	2.7	2.3	2.8
1–4 years.	13.1	13.1	8.5	5.4	4.4	4.7	4.1	3.9	3.9
5–14 years.	7.6	8.0	7.0	5.2	4.0	3.9	4.1	3.7	3.7
15–24 years.	9.9	10.3	10.6	7.8	6.5	6.8	6.0	5.9	5.7
25–34 years.	17.7	18.8	16.2	13.6	13.0	13.5	11.9	11.5	11.4
35–44 years.	44.5	46.3	50.1	41.1	39.5	37.7	36.7	36.9	35.6
45–54 years.	150.8	164.1	172.0	175.4	161.2	158.5	157.1	153.5	149.6
55–64 years.	409.4	450.9	498.1	497.4	508.4	504.3	509.8	508.6	505.7
65–74 years.	798.7	887.3	997.0	1,070.7	1,061.2	1,063.3	1,061.1	1,050.4	1,054.3
75–84 years.	1,367.6	1,413.7	1,592.7	1,779.7	1,820.1	1,827.0	1,826.6	1,839.7	1,853.0
85 years and over.	1,732.7	1,791.4	1,772.2	2,375.6	2,424.5	2,462.3	2,475.5	2,533.0	2,566.1
Black male									
All ages, age adjusted.	126.1	158.5	198.0	229.9	231.6	229.0	227.9	227.0	230.6
All ages, crude.	106.6	136.7	171.6	205.5	212.2	211.4	212.2	211.7	216.2
Under 1 year	- - -	*6.8	*5.3	*4.5	*2.4	*1.7	*2.1	*2.7	*1.6
1–4 years.	- - -	7.9	7.6	5.1	3.3	3.1	4.3	3.4	2.9
5–14 years.	5.8	4.4	4.8	3.7	3.6	3.8	2.7	3.1	3.3
15–24 years.	7.9	9.7	9.4	8.1	6.4	6.3	6.5	6.2	6.9
25–34 years.	18.0	18.4	18.8	14.1	14.7	14.2	14.3	14.0	14.9
35–44 years.	55.7	72.9	81.3	73.8	71.2	71.4	64.9	68.0	65.3
45–54 years.	211.7	244.7	311.2	333.0	313.6	303.6	296.7	302.2	304.6
55–64 years.	490.8	579.7	689.2	812.5	803.3	776.0	767.3	749.8	759.5
65–74 years.	636.4	938.5	1,168.9	1,417.2	1,448.7	1,455.1	1,453.6	1,434.5	1,460.7
75–84 years.	- - -	1,053.3	1,624.8	2,029.6	2,238.3	2,249.2	2,329.5	2,344.5	2,410.4
85 years and over.	- - -	1,155.2	1,387.0	2,393.9	2,507.7	2,620.9	2,659.4	2,720.0	2,787.5
White female									
All ages, age adjusted.	119.4	109.5	107.6	107.7	110.3	110.1	109.7	110.1	110.7
All ages, crude.	139.9	139.8	149.4	170.3	183.7	185.6	186.9	189.3	192.9
Under 1 year	7.8	6.8	5.4	2.7	3.0	2.4	3.0	2.2	3.0
1–4 years.	11.3	9.7	6.9	3.6	3.5	3.4	3.6	3.7	3.0
5–14 years.	6.3	6.2	5.4	3.7	3.1	3.1	2.8	2.6	3.0
15–24 years.	7.5	6.5	6.2	4.7	4.3	4.2	3.9	4.2	4.3
25–34 years.	20.9	18.8	16.3	13.5	12.6	12.1	12.3	11.5	12.0
35–44 years.	74.5	66.6	62.4	50.9	47.0	47.4	45.1	46.2	45.5
45–54 years.	185.8	175.7	177.3	166.4	160.6	155.6	154.9	151.3	148.1
55–64 years.	362.5	329.0	338.6	355.5	374.1	369.4	370.1	372.5	370.9
65–74 years.	616.5	562.1	554.7	605.2	645.3	658.7	654.0	660.0	670.8
75–84 years.	1,026.6	939.3	903.5	905.4	949.2	956.4	968.6	984.4	1,013.9
85 years and over.	1,348.3	1,304.9	1,126.6	1,266.8	1,270.9	1,283.6	1,291.0	1,300.1	1,322.0

See footnote at end of table.

C3-13. Death Rates for Malignant Neoplasms, According to Sex, Race, and Age: United States, Selected Years 1950 to 1989 (continued)

Sex, race, and age	1950[1]	1960[1]	1970	1980	1985	1986	1987	1988	1989
Black female				Deaths per 100,000 resident population					
All ages, age adjusted.	131.9	127.8	123.5	129.7	130.4	132.1	132.0	131.2	130.9
All ages, crude	111.8	113.8	117.3	136.5	143.9	146.7	147.8	148.9	149.6
Under 1 year	- - -	*6.7	*3.3	*3.0	*4.3	*2.8	*1.8	*3.4	*3.3
1–4 years	- - -	6.9	5.7	3.9	2.5	4.3	2.6	3.8	3.7
5–14 years	3.9	4.8	4.0	3.4	3.0	2.9	3.0	2.8	2.8
15–24 years	8.8	6.9	6.4	5.7	4.3	4.7	5.3	4.9	4.9
25–34 years	34.3	31.0	20.9	18.3	17.0	17.8	15.8	17.5	15.8
35–44 years	119.8	102.4	94.6	73.5	69.5	72.2	72.9	71.2	67.4
45–54 years	277.0	254.8	228.6	230.2	208.1	215.3	214.5	196.2	197.8
55–64 years	484.6	442.7	404.8	450.4	465.4	451.6	457.3	454.1	442.3
65–74 years	477.3	541.6	615.8	662.4	694.2	717.5	703.4	728.3	748.1
75–84 years	- - -	696.3	763.3	923.9	1,014.6	1,017.9	1,045.5	1,062.6	1,078.7
85 years and over	- - -	728.9	791.5	1,159.9	1,228.8	1,254.5	1,256.6	1,288.0	1,282.4

[1]Includes deaths of nonresidents of the United States.

*Based on fewer than 20 deaths.

NOTE: For data years shown, the code numbers for cause of death are based on the then current International Classification of Diseases.

Sources: National Center for Health Statistics: Vital Statistics of the United States, Vol. II, Mortality, Part A, for data years 1950-89. Public Health Service. Washington. U.S. Government Printing Office; Data computed by the Division of Analysis from data compiled by the Division of Vital Statistics and from table 1.

C3-14. Death Rates for Cerebrovascular Diseases, According to Sex, Race, and Age: United States, Selected Years 1950 to 1989

(Data are based on the National Vital Statistics System)

Sex, race, and age	1950[1]	1960[1]	1970	1980	1985	1986	1987	1988	1989
All races				Deaths per 100,000 resident population					
All ages, age adjusted...............	88.6	79.7	66.3	40.8	32.3	31.0	30.3	29.7	28.0
All ages, crude.....................	104.0	108.0	101.9	75.1	64.1	62.1	61.6	61.2	58.6
Under 1 year......................	5.1	4.1	5.0	4.4	3.6	2.9	3.4	3.9	3.2
1–4 years.........................	0.9	0.8	1.0	0.5	0.3	0.3	0.4	0.4	0.3
5–14 years........................	0.5	0.7	0.7	0.3	0.2	0.2	0.2	0.2	0.2
15–24 years.......................	1.6	1.8	1.6	1.0	0.8	0.7	0.6	0.7	0.6
25–34 years.......................	4.2	4.7	4.5	2.6	2.1	2.2	2.2	2.2	2.1
35–44 years.......................	18.7	14.7	15.6	8.5	7.2	7.1	7.0	6.9	6.4
45–54 years.......................	70.4	49.2	41.6	25.2	21.1	20.4	20.1	19.2	18.4
55–64 years.......................	195.3	147.3	115.8	65.2	54.3	53.0	52.2	51.3	48.8
65–74 years.......................	549.7	469.2	384.1	219.5	171.3	164.1	157.2	154.7	144.7
75–84 years.......................	1,499.6	1,491.3	1,254.2	788.6	605.8	573.8	562.6	553.6	519.8
85 years and over..................	2,990.1	3,680.5	3,014.3	2,288.9	1,837.5	1,762.6	1,733.1	1,707.4	1,631.0
White male									
All ages, age adjusted...............	87.0	80.3	68.8	41.9	32.8	31.1	30.3	30.0	28.0
All ages, crude.....................	100.5	102.7	93.5	63.3	52.5	50.5	49.9	50.0	47.5
Under 1 year......................	5.9	4.3	4.5	3.8	3.7	2.5	3.6	3.1	2.8
1–4 years.........................	1.1	0.8	1.2	0.4	*0.3	*0.2	0.5	0.3	*0.2
5–14 years........................	0.5	0.7	0.8	0.2	0.2	0.2	0.2	0.2	0.3
15–24 years.......................	1.6	1.7	1.6	1.0	0.7	0.7	0.6	0.7	0.6
25–34 years.......................	3.4	3.5	3.2	2.0	1.8	1.8	1.8	1.8	1.7
35–44 years.......................	13.1	11.3	11.8	6.5	5.4	5.7	5.4	5.5	5.0
45–54 years.......................	53.7	40.9	35.6	21.7	18.0	16.5	16.7	16.0	14.8
55–64 years.......................	182.2	139.0	119.9	64.2	54.2	51.4	50.7	50.4	47.4
65–74 years.......................	569.7	501.0	420.0	240.4	183.7	171.4	165.4	163.5	152.2
75–84 years.......................	1,556.3	1,564.8	1,361.6	854.8	651.1	617.3	601.2	590.8	554.6
85 years and over..................	3,127.1	3,734.8	3,018.1	2,236.9	1,747.8	1,697.0	1,663.1	1,667.1	1,568.3
Black male									
All ages, age adjusted...............	146.2	141.2	122.5	77.5	60.8	58.9	57.1	57.8	54.1
All ages, crude.....................	122.0	122.9	108.8	73.1	58.5	57.1	55.7	56.5	53.2
Under 1 year......................	- - -	8.5	12.3	11.2	9.8	8.0	*5.9	9.3	7.6
1–4 years.........................	- - -	1.9	*1.4	*0.6	*0.8	*0.5	*0.5	*0.5	*0.3
5–14 years........................	*0.7	*0.9	0.8	*0.5	*0.1	*0.2	*0.3	*0.2	*0.4
15–24 years.......................	3.3	3.7	3.0	2.1	1.3	1.1	0.9	0.9	1.0
25–34 years.......................	12.0	12.8	14.6	7.7	5.7	6.1	5.4	6.7	4.8
35–44 years.......................	59.3	47.4	52.7	29.2	25.9	27.2	27.1	25.9	24.9
45–54 years.......................	211.9	166.1	136.1	82.1	70.6	68.2	67.5	66.6	66.8
55–64 years.......................	522.8	439.9	343.4	189.8	151.6	144.3	143.9	146.4	135.6
65–74 years.......................	783.6	899.2	780.1	472.8	358.9	337.8	318.5	325.8	301.8
75–84 years.......................	- - -	1,475.2	1,445.7	1,067.6	817.6	809.9	777.6	796.3	715.5
85 years and over..................	- - -	2,700.0	1,963.1	1,873.2	1,363.1	1,350.7	1,339.1	1,302.9	1,333.3
White female									
All ages, age adjusted...............	79.7	68.7	56.2	35.2	27.9	27.1	26.3	25.5	24.1
All ages, crude.....................	103.3	110.1	109.8	88.8	78.1	76.2	75.8	74.9	72.1
Under 1 year......................	2.9	2.6	3.2	3.3	2.2	1.8	2.0	2.8	2.5
1–4 years.........................	0.6	0.5	0.6	0.4	*0.3	*0.2	*0.3	*0.3	*0.3
5–14 years........................	0.4	0.6	0.6	0.3	0.3	0.2	0.2	0.2	0.2
15–24 years.......................	1.2	1.4	1.1	0.7	0.7	0.6	0.6	0.6	0.5
25–34 years.......................	2.9	3.4	3.4	2.0	1.6	1.6	1.7	1.6	1.5
35–44 years.......................	13.6	10.1	11.5	6.7	5.3	5.0	5.1	4.6	4.3
45–54 years.......................	55.0	33.8	30.5	18.7	15.4	15.5	14.5	13.9	13.2
55–64 years.......................	156.9	103.0	78.1	48.7	39.7	40.1	38.7	37.0	35.6
65–74 years.......................	498.1	383.3	303.2	172.8	138.0	136.3	129.3	125.3	117.8
75–84 years.......................	1,471.3	1,444.7	1,176.8	730.3	559.4	530.7	524.0	512.7	479.7
85 years and over..................	3,017.9	3,795.7	3,167.6	2,367.8	1,923.0	1,837.3	1,807.8	1,767.0	1,695.9

See footnote at end of table.

C3-14. Death Rates for Cerebrovascular Diseases, According to Sex, Race, and Age: United States, Selected Years 1950 to 1989 (continued)

(Data are based on the National Vital Statistics System)

Sex, race, and age	1950[1]	1960[1]	1970	1980	1985	1986	1987	1988	1989
Black female				Deaths per 100,000 resident population					
All ages, age adjusted	155.6	139.5	107.9	61.7	50.3	47.6	46.7	46.6	44.9
All ages, crude	128.3	127.7	112.2	77.9	68.0	65.0	64.3	65.4	63.5
Under 1 year	- - -	*6.7	9.1	*6.4	*5.3	*5.3	7.8	8.2	*4.6
1–4 years	- - -	*1.3	*1.4	*0.5	*0.5	*0.4	*0.6	*0.7	*0.4
5–14 years	*0.6	1.0	0.8	*0.3	*0.3	*0.3	*0.2	*0.4	*0.3
15–24 years	4.2	3.4	3.0	1.7	1.5	1.0	1.1	1.1	1.3
25–34 years	15.9	17.4	14.3	7.0	5.6	6.0	5.8	5.3	5.7
35–44 years	75.0	57.4	49.1	21.6	19.3	18.5	17.5	18.5	16.9
45–54 years	248.9	166.2	119.4	61.9	49.8	46.4	47.2	43.0	44.1
55–64 years	567.7	452.0	272.4	138.7	111.3	109.4	108.7	105.7	99.5
65–74 years	754.4	830.5	673.5	362.2	281.5	268.5	261.2	264.7	248.1
75–84 years	- - -	1,413.1	1,338.3	918.6	775.4	710.7	685.7	700.7	701.1
85 years and over	- - -	2,578.9	2,210.5	1,896.3	1,585.6	1,504.1	1,480.9	1,517.7	1,419.4

[1]Includes deaths of nonresidents of the United States.
*Based on fewer than 20 deaths.
NOTE: For data years shown, the code numbers for cause of death are based on the current International Classification of Diseases.
Sources: National Center for Health Statistics: Vital Statistics of the United States, Vol. II, Mortality, Part A, for data years 1950-89. Public Health Service. Washington. U.S. Government Printing Office; Data computed by the Division of Analysis from data compiled by the Division of Vital Statistics.

C3-15. Percent Change in Death Rates for Persons 55 Years of Age and Over, According to Age, Sex, and Race: 1960 to 1986

Age	Male			Female		
	Total	White	Black	Total	White	Black
55–59 years	−29.7	−31.6	−28.4	−24.7	−21.6	−44.0
60–64 years	−30.0	−29.5	−36.5	−26.4	−22.6	−41.5
65–69 years	−27.7	−28.2	−28.3	−26.2	−25.4	−32.4
70–74 years	−22.1	−22.1	−11.5	−29.2	−29.2	−27.3
75–79 years	−18.2	−19.7	+5.0	−32.9	−34.3	−15.2
80–84 years	−19.8	−20.1	+10.2	−35.6	−36.2	−3.2
85 years and over	−14.2	−14.6	+4.3	−24.8	−25.5	−4.2

C3-16. Percent Change in Death Rates for Diseases of the Heart for Persons 55 Years of Age and Over, According to Age, Sex, and Race: 1980 to 1986

Age	Male			Female		
	Total	White	Black	Total	White	Black
55–59 years	−18.9	−19.1	−16.9	−13.8	−14.2	−15.0
60–64 years	−16.5	−16.4	−10.0	−10.7	−11.5	−7.1
65–69 years	−18.2	−18.8	−10.9	−13.3	−13.6	−9.1
70–74 years	−14.9	−15.3	−8.0	−12.7	−13.0	−9.0
75–79 years	−13.0	−13.3	−6.5	−12.8	−13.3	−5.4
80–84 years	−10.3	−10.7	−2.4	−11.4	−12.0	−1.4
85 years and over	−9.6	−9.1	−8.1	−6.3	−6.4	−1.7

C3-17. Percent Change in Death Rates for Malignant Neoplasms for Persons 55 Years of Age and Over, According to Age, Sex, and Race: 1980 to 1986

Age	Male			Female		
	Total	White	Black	Total	White	Black
55–59 years.....................	−2.0	−0.3	−12.4	−1.2	−0.5	−6.1
60–64 years.....................	+0.4	+0.3	+0.8	+5.0	+5.3	+4.8
65–69 years.....................	−2.4	−2.2	−1.1	+6.8	+6.9	+11.6
70–74 years.....................	+0.9	+0.4	+6.9	+9.4	+10.3	+4.2
75–79 years.....................	+1.4	+0.8	+11.0	+6.6	+6.9	+7.8
80–84 years.....................	+5.9	+5.8	+10.6	+4.5	+4.1	+13.0
85 years and over..............	+3.8	+3.6	+9.5	+1.7	+1.3	+8.2

C3-18. Percent Change in Death Rates for Cerebrovascular Disease for Persons 55 Years of Age and Over, According to Age, Sex, and Race: 1980 to 1986

Age	Male			Female		
	Total	White	Black	Total	White	Black
55–59 years.....................	−18.5	−20.0	−19.4	−18.8	−17.2	−27.3
60–64 years.....................	−22.7	−22.1	−28.2	−18.9	−20.1	−17.8
65–69 years.....................	−28.6	−28.9	−28.1	−21.8	−20.1	−28.4
70–74 years.....................	−29.1	−29.1	−29.1	−22.6	−22.4	−25.0
75–79 years.....................	−29.2	−29.5	−25.5	−27.2	−27.3	−25.6
80–84 years.....................	−25.3	−25.5	−22.2	−27.0	−27.4	−19.9
85 years and over..............	−24.7	−24.1	−27.9	−22.5	−22.4	−20.7

C4. Health Care Access and Utilization

C4-1. Annual Movement of Persons 65-74 Through the Health Care System

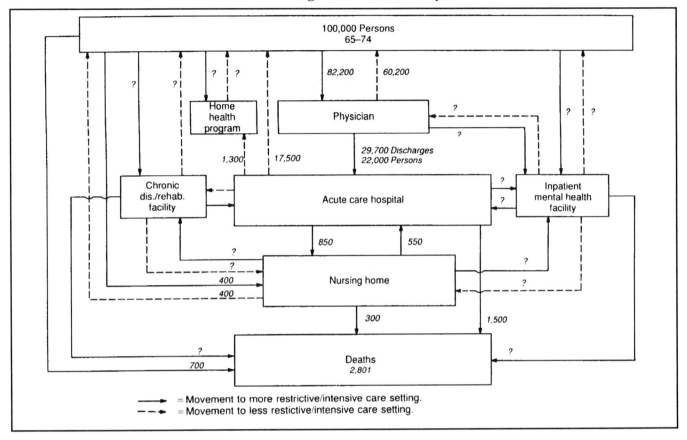

C4-2. Annual Movement of Persons 75 and Over Through the Health Care System

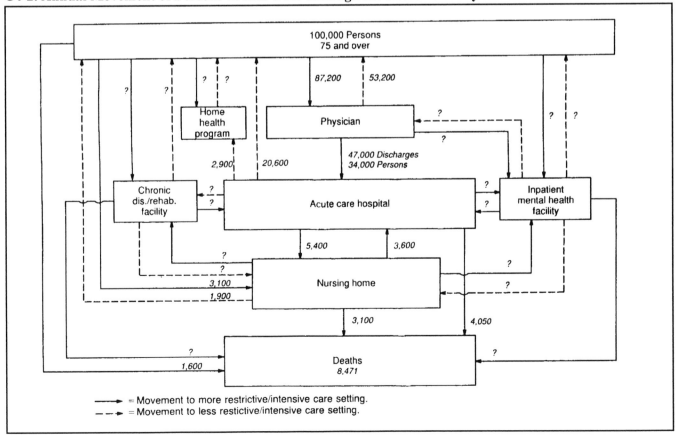

C4-3. Professionally Active Physicians Per 100,000 Residents, by Type of County and Population Size: 1987 to 1988

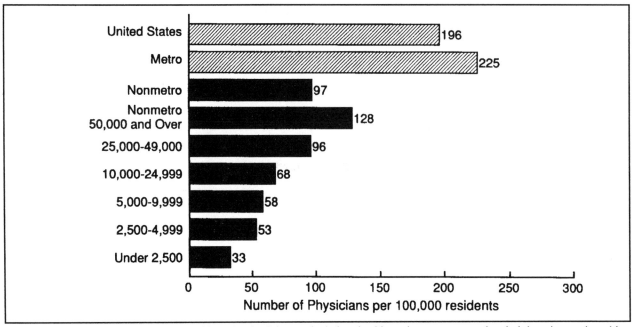

NOTE: Includes allopathic (MD) and osteopathic (DO) physicians actively involved in patient care, research, administration, and teaching. Includes physicians in federal service. MD data as of Jan. 1, 1988. DO data as of 1987.
Source: Health Resources and Services Administration Area Resource File.

C4-4. Number of Dentists Per 100,000 Residents, by Type of County: 1987

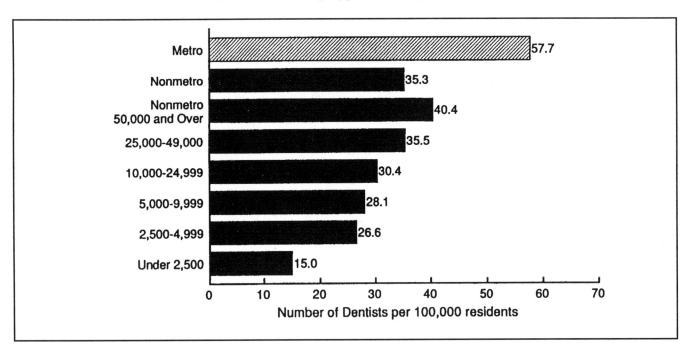

NOTE: Includes both full-time and part-time dentists.
Source: Health Resources and Services Administration Area Resource File.

C4-5. Dental Care/Visits and Toothlessness of the Elderly: 1989

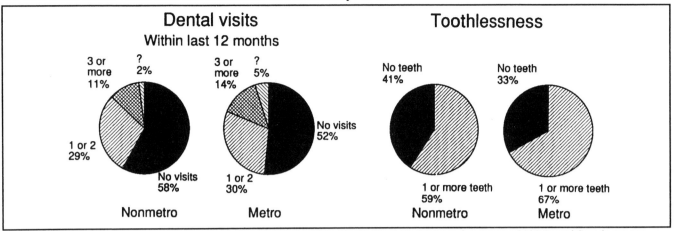

Source: National Institute of Dental Research, National Institute of Health; National Health Interview Survey-1989 Dental Supplement; National Center for Health Statistics.

C4-6. Average Annual Number of Physician Visits Per Person, by Race, Sex, Respondent-Assessed Health Status, and Age: United States, 1985 to 1987

Respondent-assessed health status and age	All races[1]		White		Black	
	Male	Female	Male	Female	Male	Female
All health statuses[2]	Number of visits per person per year					
55–59 years	4.2	4.7	4.1	4.5	4.8	6.2
60–64 years	4.8	5.2	4.7	5.1	5.9	6.5
65–69 years	4.9	5.4	4.8	5.3	6.0	7.0
70–74 years	5.4	5.8	5.3	5.5	5.7	8.4
75–79 years	5.5	5.9	5.5	5.8	5.5	6.6
80–84 years	5.9	6.3	5.9	6.3	6.5	7.4
65 years and over	5.4	5.8	5.4	5.7	5.9	7.4
75 years and over	6.0	6.2	6.0	6.1	6.1	6.9
85 years and over	7.5	6.6	7.5	6.6	7.7	6.9
Good or excellent health						
55–59 years	2.7	3.1	2.7	3.2	1.9	3.0
60–64 years	3.2	3.3	3.2	3.3	2.9	3.6
65–69 years	3.4	3.9	3.4	3.9	2.7	4.5
70–74 years	3.5	4.0	3.6	4.1	2.9	3.6
75–79 years	3.9	4.5	3.9	4.5	3.6	4.7
80–84 years	4.4	4.5	4.5	4.4	3.8	4.8
65 years and over	3.7	4.2	3.8	4.2	3.1	4.3
75 years and over	4.3	4.6	4.3	4.6	3.9	4.8
85 years and over	5.1	5.2	5.1	5.2	5.6	4.9
Fair or poor health						
55–59 years	10.5	10.6	10.2	10.6	10.6	11.1
60–64 years	9.8	11.0	9.7	11.2	10.0	10.4
65–69 years	8.9	9.6	8.8	9.5	9.7	10.0
70–74 years	9.5	10.1	9.5	9.4	9.8	*14.2
75–79 years	8.5	8.6	8.7	8.6	7.3	8.8
80–84 years	8.6	9.9	8.6	10.0	9.3	9.6
65 years and over	9.2	9.5	9.2	9.3	9.2	10.8
75 years and over	9.2	9.2	9.3	9.2	8.2	9.2
85 years and over	12.1	9.3	12.3	9.4	9.9	9.5

[1]Includes races other than white and black. [2]Includes unknown respondent-assessed health status. *Figure does not meet standards of reliability.
Source: National Center for Health Statistics; data from the National Health Interview Survey.

C4-7. Number of Mentions of Most Common Patient Reasons for a Physician Visit for Ambulatory Patients 55 Years of Age and Over and Rank of Males and Females, by Age: United States, 1985

[Data are based on reporting by a sample of office-based physicians]

Rank	Age and most common patient reason for a physician visit	Number of mentions per 1,000 visits	Rank Male	Rank Female
	55–59 years			
1	Hypertension	56	1	2
2	General medical examination	50	4	1
3	Postoperative visit	49	2	3
4	Blood pressure test	41	3	4
5	Cough	37	6	5
6	Progress visit	27	5	12
7	Diabetes mellitus	26	7	9
8	Back pain	22	9	11
9	Shoulder pain	20	8	19
10	Headache	20	21	7
	60–64 years			
1	General medical examination	60	3	1
2	Postoperative visit	55	1	2
3	Hypertension	53	2	3
4	Blood pressure test	39	5	4
5	Diabetes mellitus	38	4	7
6	Progress visit	37	6	6
7	Cough	30	12	5
8	Back pain	25	10	9
9	Anxiety	25	19	8
10	Chest pain (excluding heart pain)	24	8	15
	65–69 years			
1	General medical examination	60	3	1
2	Postoperative visit	54	1	3
3	Hypertension	53	2	2
4	Blood pressure test	40	5	4
5	Progress visit	39	4	5
6	Diabetes mellitus	30	6	7
7	Cough	29	9	6
8	Vertigo	28	8	8
9	Chest pain (excluding heart pain)	25	7	10
10	Shortness of breath	21	13	11
	70–74 years			
1	Postoperative visit	78	1	1
2	General medical examination	60	2	2
3	Hypertension	46	3	4
4	Progress visit	39	4	5
5	Blood pressure test	38	7	3
6	Diabetes mellitus	33	6	6
7	Cough	32	5	9
8	Diminished vision	26	10	7
9	Vertigo	24	16	8
10	Back pain	23	9	12

C4-8. Office Visits to Physicians, According to Selected Patient and Visit Characteristics and Physician Specialty: United States, 1985 and 1989

(Data are based on reporting by a sample of office-based physicians)

Characteristic	Patient's first visit		Visit lasted 10 minutes or less[1]		Return visit scheduled	
	1985	1989	1985	1989	1985	1989
	Percent of visits					
Total[2]	17.7	17.5	42.6	41.3	58.8	58.1
Age						
Under 15 years	17.8	15.8	50.8	52.2	49.2	45.0
15–44 years	20.8	21.8	41.6	39.9	58.9	59.2
45–64 years	14.8	15.1	36.3	32.9	65.6	66.7
65 years and over	10.5	9.7	35.6	32.3	72.8	74.6
65–74 years	11.2	11.0	34.6	32.2	72.6	74.1
75 years and over	9.6	8.2	36.9	32.4	73.1	75.3
Sex[2]						
Male	19.5	20.1	43.3	41.6	56.7	56.1
Female	16.9	16.3	42.2	41.1	59.8	59.0
Race[2]						
White	17.4	16.8	42.3	41.0	58.4	57.8
Black	20.1	22.0	45.0	41.1	62.2	61.5

Characteristic	All specialties		General and family practice		Internal medicine		Pediatrics[3]		General surgery	
	1985	1989	1985	1989	1985	1989	1985	1989	1985	1989
	Percent of visits with drug administered or prescribed									
Total[2]	60.4	59.8	71.2	69.3	72.7	67.9	...	...	37.2	32.8
Age										
Under 15 years	62.0	63.0	68.1	64.9	68.1	56.6	67.0	67.3	37.9	36.2
15–44 years	55.9	55.3	68.6	68.5	70.6	69.0	63.1	61.7	35.6	30.6
45–64 years	63.4	61.9	76.1	73.7	79.3	75.4	...	...	35.3	29.2
65 years and over	68.2	64.2	81.2	76.1	81.7	81.2	...	...	46.1	39.7
65–74 years	67.1	62.6	80.2	75.3	81.0	78.7	...	...	43.5	39.3
75 years and over	69.7	66.3	82.5	77.1	82.7	83.9	...	...	49.9	40.2
Sex[2]										
Male	59.0	58.2	69.2	67.5	67.9	66.9	67.0	65.5	39.2	32.0
Female	61.3	60.9	72.5	70.3	76.1	69.1	67.0	69.2	35.2	33.8
Race[2]										
White	59.7	59.4	70.1	69.8	72.6	68.1	66.6	66.0	36.7	31.0
Black	67.0	63.9	78.7	73.1	75.0	83.9	70.5	73.5	42.0	45.7

[1]Time spent in face-to-face contact between physician and patient.

[2]Age adjusted.

[3]Data shown by sex and race are for children under 15 years of age.

NOTE: Rates are based on the civilian noninstitutionalized population. In 1985 the survey exluced Alaska and Hawaii. In 1989, the survey was redesigned and included all 50 states.

Source: Division of Health Care Statistics, National Center for Health Statistics; data from the National Ambulatory Medical Care Survey.

C4-9. Number and Percent of Persons 55 Years of Age and Over Currently Using Vitamin or Mineral Supplements, by Selected Characteristics: United States, 1986

(Data are based on household interviews of the civilian noninstitutionalized population)

Characteristic	Total number in thousands	Percent
Sex		
Male...	21,652	35.0
Female.......................................	27,807	47.2
Age		
55–64 years..................................	22,073	41.9
65–74 years..................................	16,906	42.7
75–84 years..................................	8,652	40.6
65 years and over............................	27,386	41.8
75 years and over............................	10,480	40.3
85 years and over............................	1,828	38.8
Race		
White..	44,160	43.9
Black..	4,360	21.6
All other....................................	939	40.1
Education		
High school or less..........................	37,543	39.0
More than high school	11,916	50.7
Income		
Less than $20,000............................	25,676	38.1
$20,000 or more	21,632	46.5
Respondent-assessed health status		
Excellent or very good	20,751	44.8
Good...	15,944	21.8
Fair or poor.................................	12,502	36.7

NOTE: Current usage includes those reporting nonprescription and prescription vitamin or mineral supplement use in the past 2 weeks.

Source: National Center for Health Statistics; data from the 1986 National Health Interview Survey Supplement on Vitamins and Minerals.

C4-10. Number and Percent of Black Persons 55 Years of Age and Over Currently Using Vitamin or Mineral Supplements, by Selected Characteristics: United States, 1986

(Data are based on household interviews of the civilian noninstitutionalized population)

Characteristic	Total number in thousands	Percent
Total.	4,360	21.6
Sex		
Male.	1,851	18.2
Female.	2,509	24.1
Age		
55–64 years.	2,074	24.5
65 years and over.	2,286	18.9
Education		
High school or less.	3,695	20.3
More than high school	665	28.6
Family income		
Less than $20,000.	3,283	19.6
$20,000 or more	880	32.6
Respondent-assessed health status		
Excellent or very good	1,213	20.3
Good.	1,179	28.3
Fair or poor.	1,954	18.5

NOTE: Current usage includes those reporting nonprescription and prescription vitamin or mineral supplement use in the past 2 weeks.
Source: National Center for Health Statistics; data from the 1986 National Health Interview Survey Supplement on Vitamins and Minerals.

C5. Hospitals and Nursing Homes

C5-1. Average Length of Stay by Race, Sex, and Selected First-Listed Diagnosis for Persons 65 Years of Age and Over: United States, 1981 and 1987

Sex and first-listed diagnosis	Black		White	
	1981	1987	1981	1987
Both sexes	Average length of stay in days			
Heart disease	12.3	8.0	10.0	7.5
Malignant neoplasm	15.3	11.8	12.6	9.2
Cerebrovascular disease	14.6	14.0	12.7	9.7
Male				
Heart disease	11.8	8.3	9.7	7.3
Malignant neoplasm	15.3	12.6	12.6	8.9
Cerebrovascular disease	15.4	12.8	12.1	8.6
Female				
Heart disease	12.7	7.7	10.3	7.7
Malignant neoplasm	15.3	10.8	12.7	9.5
Cerebrovascular disease	14.2	14.7	13.3	10.4

C5-2. Percent of Elderly Hospitalized Persons Discharged Home and Percent Discharged to a Nursing Home, by Age: 1986

Discharge destination	Age		
	65 and over	65 - 74	75 and over
Home	77.5	85.7	69.2
Informal care	70.2	80.0	60.7
Home care program	7.3	5.7	8.5
Nursing home	10.2	3.9	15.9

C5-3. Discharge Destination of Persons Discharged from Nursing Homes Expressed as a Percent of Persons Admitted, by Age: 1986

Age group	Persons admitted[1]	Persons discharged to			Discharges as percent of persons admitted[2]		
		Community	Acute-care hospitals	Death	Community	Acute-care hospitals	Death
65 and over	4,100	1,000	1,800	1,500	24.4	43.9	36.6
65 - 74	1,250	400	600	300	32.0	48.0	24.0
75 and over	8,500	1,900	3,600	3,100	22.4	42.4	36.5

[1]From a population of 100,000 exclusive of persons admitted from rehabilitation and mental health facilities.
[2]Percentages differ from 100 percent because of rounding and because of footnote 1.

C5-4. Discharges and Average Length of Stay in Nonfederal Short-Stay, Hospitals, According to Sex, Age, and Selected First-Listed Diagnosis: United States, 1980, 1988, 1989, and 1990

(Data are based on a sample of hospital records)

Sex, age, and first-listed diagnosis	Discharges				Average length of stay			
	1980[1]	1988	1989	1990	1980[1]	1988	1989	1990
Both sexes	Number in thousands				Number of days			
Total[2]	37,832	31,146	30,947	30,788	7.3	6.5	6.5	6.4
Females with delivery	3,762	3,781	3,937	4,025	3.8	2.9	2.9	2.8
Diseases of heart	3,201	3,641	3,534	3,556	9.5	7.1	7.0	6.9
Malignant neoplasms	1,829	1,670	1,608	1,571	12.0	9.4	9.2	9.4
Pneumonia, all forms	782	924	1,033	1,052	8.3	8.4	8.1	8.3
Fracture, all sites	1,163	1,014	1,021	1,017	10.8	8.4	8.5	8.3
Male								
All ages[2]	15,145	12,642	12,583	12,280	7.7	7.1	7.0	6.9
Diseases of heart	1,688	1,955	1,892	1,913	9.1	6.9	6.8	6.7
Malignant neoplasms	875	772	770	730	12.0	9.4	9.2	9.5
Pneumonia, all forms	414	472	544	530	8.2	8.3	7.8	8.2
Fracture, all sites	582	506	480	466	9.0	7.2	7.5	6.7
Cerebrovascular diseases	371	336	344	359	12.1	9.8	10.3	9.2
Inguinal hernia	458	232	193	149	4.7	2.5	2.6	2.2
Under 15 years[2]	2,063	1,486	1,521	1,362	4.3	5.0	4.9	4.8
Acute respiratory infection	154	103	137	111	3.8	3.1	3.4	3.2
Pneumonia, all forms	136	105	126	119	4.9	4.4	4.1	4.4
Bronchitis, emphysema, and asthma	105	111	115	115	4.0	2.7	2.9	2.8
Congenital anomalies	106	95	83	74	5.5	5.4	4.8	5.6
Fracture, all sites	97	71	77	54	6.2	5.2	5.4	4.0
Chronic disease of tonsils and adenoids	141	64	46	29	1.7	1.4	1.2	1.3
Otitis media and eustachian tube disorders	118	55	47	41	2.5	2.1	2.0	2.5
15–44 years[2]	4,687	3,485	3,405	3,330	6.3	6.3	6.2	6.1
Fracture, all sites	320	257	241	238	8.0	6.0	6.1	5.5
Psychoses	155	219	217	220	12.9	13.4	13.5	13.6
Diseases of heart	149	159	146	166	7.5	5.7	5.4	5.3
Lacerations and open wounds	176	124	124	134	5.2	4.3	3.7	4.1
Intervertebral disc disorders	120	139	122	138	8.8	5.1	4.4	4.2
Alcohol dependence syndrome	180	118	109	118	9.5	11.9	11.1	9.8
45–64 years[2]	4,127	3,221	3,179	3,115	8.1	6.8	6.7	6.7
Diseases of heart	712	751	730	704	8.5	6.2	6.0	5.8
Malignant neoplasms	304	215	240	236	11.6	9.7	9.0	9.3
Cerebrovascular diseases	99	93	88	91	10.6	8.5	8.7	10.0
Fracture, all sites	85	79	80	74	9.0	7.4	9.0	7.2
Pneumonia, all forms	68	65	77	75	9.3	8.4	8.4	8.0
Inguinal hernia	146	72	53	42	5.3	2.3	2.5	2.3
Alcohol dependence syndrome	134	49	44	51	10.7	8.4	8.5	9.5
65 years and over[2]	4,268	4,450	4,478	4,472	10.3	8.6	8.6	8.3
Diseases of heart	814	1,038	1,007	1,036	10.0	7.6	7.6	7.5
Malignant neoplasms	479	457	447	411	12.7	9.5	9.5	9.9
Pneumonia, all forms	156	248	271	264	11.1	10.0	9.4	10.0
Cerebrovascular diseases	253	226	238	247	12.3	10.5	11.0	9.2
Hyperplasia of prostate	188	191	193	195	9.8	6.0	5.5	5.2
Female								
All ages[2]	22,686	18,504	18,364	18,508	7.0	6.2	6.1	6.1
Delivery	3,762	3,781	3,937	4,025	3.8	2.9	2.9	2.8
Diseases of heart	1,513	1,686	1,642	1,643	10.0	7.4	7.2	7.1
Malignant neoplasms	954	898	838	841	12.0	9.4	9.3	9.2
Fracture, all sites	580	508	541	551	12.6	9.7	9.4	9.7
Pneumonia, all forms	368	452	489	522	8.4	8.6	8.4	8.4
Pregnancy with abortive outcome	531	266	229	208	2.1	2.3	2.3	2.1

See footnotes at end of table.

C5-4. Discharges and Average Length of Stay in Nonfederal Short-Stay Hospitals, According to Sex, Age, and Selected First-Listed Diagnosis: United States, 1980, 1988, 1989, and 1990 (continued)

(Data are based on a sample of hospital records)

Sex, age, and first-listed diagnosis	Discharges				Average length of stay			
	1980[1]	1988	1989	1990	1980[1]	1988	1989	1990
Female — Con.	Number in thousands				Number of days			
Under 15 years[2]	1,609	1,125	1,077	1,049	4.5	4.9	4.9	4.9
Pneumonia, all forms	91	79	95	92	4.9	4.9	4.6	4.6
Acute respiratory infection	115	65	78	75	3.5	3.5	3.5	3.4
Bronchitis, emphysema, and asthma	63	66	64	68	3.8	2.9	2.8	3.1
Congenital anomalies	80	55	53	46	6.1	6.8	6.2	5.8
Chronic disease of tonsils and adenoids	160	61	48	38	1.8	1.1	1.2	1.2
Noninfectious enteritis and colitis	92	52	39	43	4.6	2.7	3.8	3.0
15–44 years[2]	10,949	8,448	8,443	8,469	4.8	4.1	4.1	4.0
Delivery	3,741	3,768	3,926	4,008	3.7	2.9	2.9	2.8
Pregnancy with abortive outcome	525	264	227	205	2.1	2.3	2.3	2.1
Psychoses	129	210	197	228	15.1	15.9	14.3	14.6
Benign neoplasms	253	176	161	163	5.4	4.4	4.2	4.0
Inflammatory disease of female pelvic organs	268	145	137	130	5.1	4.6	4.4	4.1
Disorders of menstruation	347	88	66	70	3.3	3.6	3.5	3.3
45–64 years[2]	4,533	3,235	3,092	3,129	8.3	6.8	6.6	6.8
Diseases of heart	415	411	386	397	8.6	6.2	6.0	6.1
Malignant neoplasms	387	351	273	309	11.5	8.3	8.2	8.4
Benign neoplasms	156	116	108	107	6.7	5.1	4.8	4.9
Cholelithiasis	109	97	107	114	9.2	6.0	5.4	5.7
Psychoses	72	99	104	103	16.3	14.9	14.9	14.6
Diabetes	148	67	78	70	10.0	7.8	6.9	8.9
65 years and over[2]	5,596	5,696	5,752	5,861	11.0	9.1	9.1	8.9
Diseases of heart	995	1,185	1,170	1,164	10.8	7.9	7.8	7.6
Malignant neoplasms	437	422	431	401	13.5	11.0	10.6	10.2
Cerebrovascular diseases	331	352	368	362	13.3	9.9	10.2	9.7
Fracture, all sites	295	300	329	350	16.1	11.6	11.5	11.3
Pneumonia, all forms	150	242	261	283	11.2	10.3	9.8	10.4
Eye diseases and conditions	251	105	73	58	4.1	2.1	2.7	2.0

[1]Comparisons of 1980 with later years should be made with caution as estimates of change may reflect improvements in the design rather than true changes in hospital use.

[2]Includes discharges with first-listed diagnoses not shown in table.

NOTE: Excludes newborn infants. In each sex and age group, data are shown for diagnoses with the five highest discharge rates in 1980 and 1989. Diagnostic categories are based on the International Classification of Diseases, 9th Revision, Clinical Modification.

Source: Division of Health Care Statistics, National Center for Health Statistics; data from the National Hospital Discharge Survey.

C5-5. Patients Discharged from Short-Stay Hospitals, Days of Care, and Average Lengths of Stay, by Sex, Age, Race, and Income: 1989

	Hospital discharges		Hospital days	
	Number per 100 persons	Number in thousands	Average length of stay	Number in thousands
All persons	11.3	27,423	6.5	179,332
Age				
Under 5 years	7.7	1,438	6.6	9,501
5–17 years	3.4	1,531	5.6	8,561
18–24 years	11.5	2,926	4.1	121
25–44 years	9.8	7,746	4.8	37,022
45–64 years	13.1	6,020	7.2	43,233
65–74 years	23.7	4,219	8.5	34,733
75 years and more	31.1	3,543	9.4	33,246
Sex and age				
Male				
All ages	9.6	11,298	7.3	82,595
Under 18 years	4.7	1,543	6.0	9,200
18–44 years	6.0	3,044	5.8	17,526
45–64 years	13.9	3,076	7.2	22,284
65 years and more	29.9	3,635	9.2	33,585
Female				
All ages	12.8	16,125	6.0	96,737
Under 18 years	4.6	1,426	6.2	8,862
18–44 years	14.4	7,628	4.1	31,531
45–64 years	12.2	2,944	7.1	20,949
65 years and more	24.2	4,127	8.6	35,394
Race and age				
White				
All ages	11.4	23,311	6.5	152,323
Under 18 years	4.7	2,403	6.3	15,091
18–44 years	40.2	8,882	4.6	40,499
45–64 years	12.9	5,154	7.1	36,669
65 years and more	26.1	6,873	8.7	60,065
Black				
All ages	11.5	3,442	6.8	23,260
Under 18 years	5.1	504	5.5	2,795
18–44 years	11.5	1,468	5.0	7,294
45–64 years	15.2	715	8.2	5,841
65 years and more	30.8	755	9.7	7,329
Family income and age				
Under $10,000				
All ages	18.0	4,704	7.3	34,432
Under 18 years	7.4	550	6.0	3,273
18–44 years	16.9	1,654	4.8	7,958
45–64 years	24.2	814	9.5	7,767
65 years and more	30.0	1,686	9.2	15,434
$10,000–$19,999				
All ages	13.7	5,641	6.9	38,672
Under 18 years	4.7	504	6.3	3,154
18–44 years	12.4	1,967	4.6	8,951
45–64 years	15.6	1,011	6.9	6,944
65 years and more	27.0	2,158	9.1	19,624
$20,000–$34,000				
All ages	10.3	5,848	6.2	35,966
Under 18 years	4.3	679	6.6	4,461
18–44 years	10.4	2,700	4.6	12,548
45–64 years	13.3	1,313	6.3	8,242
65 years and more	22.1	1,156	9.3	10,715
$35,000 and more				
All ages	7.8	6,264	5.7	355,686
Under 18 years	3.9	829	6.6	5,430
18–44 years	7.8	2,910	4.5	13,150
45–64 years	9.8	1,756	5.8	10,242
65 years and more	22.1	769	8.9	6,864

Source: National Center for Health Statistics.

C5-6. Patients Discharged from Short-Stay Hospitals, by Category of First-Listed Diagnosis, Sex, and Age: 1988

(Thousands)

First-listed diagnostic category	Total	Sex Male	Female	Under 15 years	Age 15–44 years	45–64 years	65 years or more
All conditions	31,146	12,642	18,504	2,610	11,934	6,456	10,146
Heart disease	3,641	1,955	1,686	14	243	1,162	2,223
Malignant neoplasms and carcinoma-in-situ	1,670	772	898	37	187	566	880
Benign neoplasms and neoplasms of uncertain behavior	428	78	350	16	191	142	79
Fractures, all sites	1,014	506	508	107	356	154	398
Diseases of the genito-urinary system	2,204	828	1,376	71	922	512	700
Pneumonia, all forms	924	472	452	184	111	139	490
Chronic disease of tonsils and adenoids	197	87	110	125	70	—	—
Cerebrovascular disease	784	336	448	—	32	171	578
Diabetes mellitus	454	209	245	28	125	134	166
Inguinal hernia	257	232	25	30	65	78	84
Cholelithiasis	484	132	352	—	183	146	154
Appendicitis	242	141	101	52	145	24	20
Mental disorders	1,559	765	793	58	962	288	251
Infectious and parasitic diseases	693	333	359	191	211	104	187
Hyperplasia of the prostate	247	247	—	—	—	56	191
Females with obstetrical deliveries	3,781	—	3,781	10	3,768	—	—

Source: National Center for Health Statistics. Advance Data. 1989.

C5-7. Procedures Provided to Patients Discharged from Short-Stay Hospitals, by Sex and Age: 1988

(Thousands)

Procedure	Total	Sex Male	Female	Under 15 years	Age 15–44 years	45–64 years	65 years or more
All procedures	39,192	15,735	23,457	2,050	15,520	8,939	12,682
Operations on the nervous system	896	467	429	216	279	200	201
Operations on the endocrine system	111	31	79	—	43	39	26
Operations on the eye	547	243	304	33	80	126	308
Operations on the ear	198	109	88	107	46	25	19
Operations on the nose, mouth, and pharynx	820	436	385	220	372	135	94
Operations on the respiratory system	991	561	430	69	190	291	441
Operations on the cardiovascular system	3,626	2,220	1,406	169	422	1,358	1,676
Operations on the hemic and lymphatic systems	392	192	200	24	91	106	172
Operations on the digestive system	5,257	2,277	2,981	233	1,244	1,335	2,145
Operations on the urinary system	1,706	1,018	688	48	398	426	833
Operations on the male genital organs	633	633	—	50	54	128	400
Operations on the female genital organs	2,501	—	2,501	10	1,773	516	202
Obstetrical procedures	6,042	—	6,042	16	6,024	—	—
Operations on the musculoskeletal system	3,143	1,648	1,496	203	1,325	747	868
Operations on the integumentary system	1,475	639	836	105	537	393	440
Miscellaneous diagnostic and therapeutic procedures	10,854	5.262	5,593	544	2,342	3,112	4,856

NOTE: Details may not add to total due to rounding.
Source: National Center for Health Statistics. Advance Data, 1989.

C5-8. Nursing Home Residents 65 Years of Age and Over Per 1,000 Population, According to Age, Sex, and Race: United States, 1963, 1973 to 1974, 1977, and 1985

Age, sex, and race	Residents per 1,000 population[1]			
	1963	*1973–74*[2]	*1977*[3]	*1985*
Age				
All ages	25.4	44.7	47.1	46.2
65–74 years	7.9	12.3	14.4	12.5
75–84 years	39.6	57.7	64.0	57.7
85 years and over	148.4	257.3	225.9	220.3
Sex				
Male	18.1	30.0	30.3	29.0
65–74 years	6.8	11.3	12.6	10.8
75–84 years	29.1	39.9	44.9	43.0
85 years and over	105.6	182.7	146.3	145.7
Female	31.1	54.9	58.6	57.9
65–74 years	8.8	13.1	15.8	13.8
75–84 years	47.5	68.9	75.4	66.4
85 years and over	175.1	294.9	262.4	250.1
Race[4]				
White	26.6	46.9	48.9	47.7
65–74 years	8.1	12.5	14.2	12.3
75–84 years	41.7	60.3	67.0	59.1
85 years and over	157.7	270.8	234.2	228.7
Black	10.3	22.0	30.7	5.0
65–74 years	5.9	11.1	17.6	15.4
75–84 years	13.8	26.7	33.4	45.3
85 years and over	41.8	105.7	133.6	141.5

[1]Residents per 1,000 population for 1973-74 and 1977 differ from those presented in the original source reports because the rates have been recomputed using revised census estimates for these years.
[2]Excludes residents in personal care or domiciliary care homes.
[3]Includes residents in domiciliary care homes.
[4]For data years 1973-74 and 1977, all people of Hispanic origin were included in the white category. For 1963, "black" includes all other races.

C5-9. Nursing Home and Personal Care Home Residents 65 Years of Age and Over and Rate Per 1,000 Population, According to Age, Sex, and Race: United States, 1963, 1973 to 1974, 1977, and 1985

[Data are based on a sample of nursing homes]

Age, sex, and race	Residents				Residents per 1,000 population[1]			
	1963	1973–74[2]	1977[3]	1985	1963	1973–74[2]	1977[3]	1985
Age								
All ages.	445,600	961,500	1,126,000	1,318,300	25.4	44.7	47.1	46.2
65–74 years	89,600	163,100	211,400	212,100	7.9	12.3	14.4	12.5
75–84 years	207,200	384,900	464,700	509,000	39.6	57.7	64.0	57.7
85 years and over	148,700	413,600	449,900	597,300	148.4	257.3	225.9	220.3
Sex								
Male.	141,000	265,700	294,000	334,400	18.1	30.0	30.3	29.0
65–74 years	35,100	65,100	80,200	80,600	6.8	11.3	12.6	10.8
75–84 years	65,200	102,300	122,100	141,300	29.1	39.9	44.9	43.0
85 years and over	40,700	98,300	91,700	112,600	105.6	182.7	146.3	145.7
Female	304,500	695,800	832,000	983,900	31.1	54.9	58.6	57.9
65–74 years	54,500	98,000	131,200	131,500	8.8	13.1	15.8	13.8
75–84 years	142,000	282,600	342,600	367,700	47.5	68.9	75.4	66.4
85 years and over	108,000	315,300	358,200	484,700	175.1	294.9	262.4	250.1
Race[4]								
White	431,700	920,600	1,059,900	1,227,400	26.6	46.9	48.9	47.7
65–74 years	84,400	150,100	187,500	187,800	8.1	12.5	14.2	12.3
75–84 years	202,000	369,700	443,200	473,600	41.7	60.3	67.0	59.1
85 years and over	145,400	400,800	429,100	566,000	157.7	270.8	234.2	228.7
Black	13,800	37,700	60,800	82,000	10.3	22.0	30.7	35.0
65–74 years	5,200	12,200	22,000	22,500	5.9	11.1	17.6	15.4
75–84 years	5,300	13,400	19,700	30,600	13.8	26.7	33.4	45.3
85 years and over	3,300	12,100	19,100	29,000	41.8	105.7	133.6	141.5

[1]Residents per 1,000 population for 1973-74 and 1977 will differ from those presented in the sources because the rates have been recomputed using revised census estimates for these years

[2]Excludes residents in personal care or domiciliary care homes.

[3]Includes residents in domiciliary care homes.

[4]For data years 1973-74 and 1977, all Hispanics were included in the white category. For 1963, "black" includes all other races.

C5-10. Nursing Home Population, by Region, Division, and State: 1980 and 1990

Region, Division, and State	Nursing Homes			Percent change 1980-1990	1990 Percent of Population
	1990	1980	Change 1980-1990		
UNITED STATES	1,772,032	1,426,371	345,661	24.2	0.7
Northeast	399,329	327,319	72,010	22.0	0.8
New England	119,646	106,344	13,302	12.5	0.9
Middle Atlantic	279,683	220,975	58,708	26.6	0.7
Midwest	544,650	472,568	72,082	15.3	0.9
East North Central	346,243	296,088	50,155	16.9	0.8
West North Central	198,407	176,480	21,927	12.4	1.1
South	558,382	396,554	161,828	40.8	0.7
South Atlantic	270,930	163,080	107,850	66.1	0.6
East South Central	102,900	77,060	25,840	33.5	0.7
West South Central	184,552	156,414	28,138	18.0	0.7
West	269,671	229,930	39,741	17.3	0.5
Mountain	65,842	47,139	18,703	39.7	0.5
Pacific	203,829	182,791	21,038	11.5	0.5
New England	119,646	106,344	13,302	12.5	0.9
Maine	9,855	9,570	285	3.0	0.8
Vermont	4,809	4,354	455	10.5	0.9
New Hampshire	8,202	6,673	1,529	22.9	0.7
Massachusetts	55,662	49,728	5,934	11.9	0.9
Rhode Island	10,156	8,146	2,010	24.7	1.0
Connecticut	30,962	27,873	3,089	11.1	0.9
Middle Atlantic	279,683	220,975	58,708	26.6	0.7
New York	126,175	114,276	11,899	10.4	0.7
New Jersey	47,054	34,414	12,640	36.7	0.6
Pennsylvania	106,454	72,285	34,169	47.3	0.9
East North Central	346,243	296,088	50,155	16.9	0.8
Ohio	93,769	71,479	22,290	31.2	0.9
Indiana	50,845	40,112	10,733	26.8	0.9
Illinois	93,662	80,410	13,252	16.5	0.8
Michigan	57,622	55,805	1,817	3.3	0.6
Wisconsin	50,345	48,282	2,063	4.3	1.0
West North Central	198,407	176,480	21,927	12.4	1.1
Minnesota	47,051	44,553	2,498	5.6	1.1
Iowa	36,455	36,217	238	0.7	1.3
Missouri	52,060	37,942	14,118	37.2	1.0
North Dakota	8,159	7,486	673	9.0	1.3
South Dakota	9,356	8,087	1,269	15.7	1.3
Nebraska	19,171	17,650	1,521	8.6	1.2
Kansas	26,155	24,545	1,610	6.6	1.1
South Atlantic	270,930	163,080	107,850	66.1	0.6
Delaware	4,596	2,771	1,825	65.9	0.7
Maryland	26,884	19,821	7,063	35.6	0.6
District of Columbia	7,008	2,866	4,142	144.5	1.2
Virginia	37,762	24,323	13,439	55.3	0.6
West Virginia	12,591	6,355	6,236	98.1	0.7
North Carolina	47,014	29,596	17,418	58.9	0.7
South Carolina	18,228	11,666	6,562	56.2	0.5
Georgia	36,549	29,376	7,173	24.4	0.6
Florida	80,298	36,306	43,992	121.2	0.6
East South Central	102,900	77,060	25,840	33.5	0.7
Kentucky	27,874	23,591	4,283	18.2	0.8
Tennessee	35,192	22,014	13,178	59.9	0.7
Alabama	24,031	18,702	5,329	28.5	0.6
Mississippi	15,803	12,753	3,050	23.9	0.6
West South Central	184,552	156,414	28,138	18.0	0.7
Arkansas	21,809	18,631	3,178	17.1	0.9
Louisiana	32,072	22,776	9,296	40.8	0.8
Oklahoma	29,666	25,732	3,934	15.3	0.9
Texas	101,005	89,275	11,730	13.1	0.6
Mountain	65,842	47,139	18,703	39.7	0.5
Montana	7,764	5,479	2,285	41.7	1.0
Idaho	6,318	5,084	1,234	24.3	0.6
Wyoming	2,679	2,198	481	21.9	0.6
Colorado	18,506	16,109	2,397	14.9	0.6
New Mexico	6,276	2,585	3,691	142.8	0.4
Arizona	14,472	8,424	6,048	71.8	0.4
Utah	6,222	4,921	1,301	26.4	0.4
Nevada	3,605	2,339	1,266	54.1	0.3
Pacific	203,829	182,791	21,038	11.5	0.5
Washington	32,840	27,970	4,870	17.4	0.7
Oregon	18,200	16,052	2,148	13.4	0.6
California	148,362	134,756	13,606	10.1	0.5
Alaska	1,202	854	348	40.7	0.2
Hawaii	3,225	3,159	66	2.1	0.3

Source: U.S. Bureau of the Census, 1990 from 1980 Census of Population "Persons in Institutions and Other Group Quarters," PC80-2-4D; 1990 from 1990 Census of Population and Housing.

C5-11. Percent Change in Nursing Home Population: 1980 to 1990

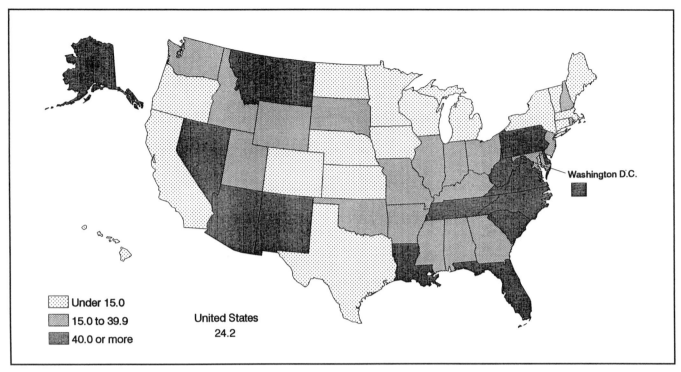

Source: U.S. Bureau of the Census, 1980 and 1990 Censuses of Population, 1980 from "Persons in Institutions and Other Group Quarters," PC80-2-4D.

C5-12. Nursing Home Residents Who Required Assistance, by Age and Activity: 1985

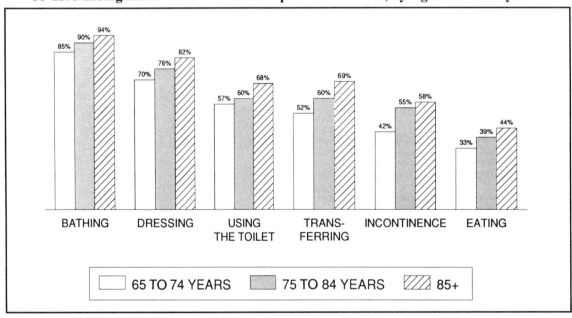

Source: National Center for Health Statistics. Esther Hing. "Use of Nursing Homes by the Elderly, Preliminary Data From the 1985 National Nursing Home Survey." Advance Data From Vital and Health Statistics, No. 135, Pub. No. (PHS)87-1250 (May 14, 1987).

C5-13. Selected Characteristics of Nursing Home and Community Residents Age 65+: 1985 and 1984

Subject	Living in nursing homes 1985	Living in community 1984
Total 65+		
Number (thousands)	1,318	26,343
Percent	100.0	100.0
Age:		
65 to 74	16.1	61.7
75 to 84	38.6	30.7
85+	45.3	7.6
Sex:		
Men	25.4	40.8
Women	74.6	59.2
Race:		
White:	93.1	90.4
Black	6.2	8.3
Other	0.7	1.3
Marital Status[1]		
Widowed	67.8	34.1
Married	12.8	54.7
Never married	13.5	4.4
Divorced or separated	5.9	6.3
With living children	63.1	81.3
Requires assistance in:		
Bathing	91.0	6.0
Dressing	77.6	4.3
Using toilet room	63.2	2.2
Transferring[2]	62.6	2.8
Eating	40.3	1.1
Difficulty with bowel and/or bladder control	54.5	(NA)[3]
Disorientation or memory impairment	62.6	(NA)
Senile dementia or chronic organic brain syndrome	46.9	(NA)

[1] For nursing home residents, marital status at time of admission.

[2] Getting in or out of bed or chair.

[3] Although comparable data are not available, the 1984 SOA (see source) found that 6 percent of the community-resident older population had difficulty with urinary control or had urinary catheters.

(NA) Not available.

Source: National Center for Health Statistics; data from the National Health Interview Survey, Supplement on Aging, 1984, and the 1985 National Nursing Home Survey, Advance Data Nos. 115, 121, 133, and 135; Series 13, No. 102; and unpublished data.

C5-14. Nursing Home Length of Stay Probabilities, by Age of Entry and Marital Status

(in percent) Length of stay in days	Married			Unmarried		
	65 to 74	75 to 84	85+	65 to 74	75 to 84	85+
1 to 29	29	32	30	21	20	19
30 to 59	13	14	14	12	11	10
60 to 89	8	5	5	7	5	6
90 to 179	14	10	9	10	10	12
180 to 364	11	9	10	9	12	12
365 to 729	8	10	10	9	11	13
730 to 1,094	6	4	5	7	7	8
1,095 to 1,469	3	3	4	4	6	6
1,470 to 1,824	3	2	5	3	4	4
1,825 to 2,189	2	3	2	3	3	3
2,190+	4	7	6	15	10	9
TOTAL	100	100	100	100	100	100

Source: Brookings Institution and Lewin/CF calculations using data from the *1985 Nursing Home Survey.*

C5-15. Inpatient and Residential Treatment Episodes in Mental Health Organizations, Rate Per 100,000 Civilian Population, and Inpatient Days, According to Type of Organization: United States, Selected Years 1969 to 1988.

(Data are based on inventories of mental health organizations)

Organization	1969	1975	1981[1]	1983	1986	1988[2]
	Episodes in thousands					
All organizations	1,710	1,817	1,720	1,861	2,055	2,234
State and county mental hospitals.	767	599	499	459	445	408
Private psychiatric hospitals	103	137	177	181	258	411
Non-Federal general hospital psychiatric services.	535	566	677	820	883	914
Veterans Administration psychiatric services[3].	187	214	206	171	204	266
Federally funded community mental health centers.	65	247	. . .	. . .	. . .	. . .
Residential treatment centers for emotionally disturbed children.	21	28	34	33	47	47
All other[4,5].	32	26	127	197	218	188
	Episodes per 100,000 civilian population					
All organizations	859.1	859.6	755.6	799.1	858.9	914.4
State and county mental hospitals.	385.3	283.3	219.3	197.7	186.0	167.0
Private psychiatric hospitals	51.5	64.8	77.5	77.8	107.9	168.3
Non-Federal general hospital psychiatric services	269.0	267.6	297.3	351.3	369.0	374.4
Veterans Administration psychiatric services[3].	93.9	101.4	90.3	73.4	85.2	108.8
Federally funded community mental health centers.	32.6	116.8	. . .	. . .	. . .	. . .
Residential treatment centers for emotionally disturbed children.	10.7	13.4	15.1	14.0	19.7	19.1
All other[4,5].	16.1	12.3	56.1	84.9	91.1	76.8
	Days in thousands					
All organizations	168,934	104,970	77,053	81,821	83,413	83,167
State and county mental hospitals.	134,185	70,584	44,558	42,427	39,075	36,310
Private psychiatric hospitals	4,237	4,401	5,578	6,010	8,568	10,857
Non-Federal general hospital psychiatric services.	6,500	8,349	10,727	12,529	12,570	13,126
Veterans Administration psychiatric services[3].	17,206	11,725	7,591	7,425	7,753	7,155
Federally funded community mental health centers.	1,924	3,718	. . .	. . .	. . .	. . .
Residential treatment centers for emotionally disturbed children	4,528	5,900	6,127	5,776	8,267	8,464
All other[4,5].	354	293	2,472	7,654	7,180	7,255

[1]In 1981, some organizations were reclassified and data for some organization types were not available, resulting in a particularly large increase for the "all other" category in 1981.

[2]Data for 1977 are provisional.

[3]Includes Veterans Administration neuropsychiatric hospitals and Veterans Administration general hospitals with separate psychiatric services.

[4]Includes other multiservice mental health organizations with inpatient and residential treatment services that are not elsewhere classified.

[5]Beginning in 1983 a definitional change sharply increased the number of multiservice mental health organizations.

NOTE: Changes in reporting procedures in 1981 affect the comparability of data with those from previous years.

Sources: Survey and Reports Branch, Division of Biometry and Applied Sciences, National Institute of Mental Health: R. W. Manderscheid and S. A. Barrate: Mental Health, United States, 1987. DHHS Pub. No. (ADM) 87-1518 U.S. Government Printing Office, 1987; Unpublished data.

C5-16. Admissions to Selected Inpatient Psychiatric Organizations and Rate Per 100,000 Civilian Population, According to Sex, Age, and Race: United States, 1975, 1980, and 1986

Sex, age, and race	State and county mental hospitals			Private psychiatric hospitals			Non-Federal general hospitals[1]		
	1975	1980	1986	1975	1980	1986	1975	1980	1986
Both sexes	*Number in thousands*								
Total	385	369	326	130	141	207	516	564	794
Under 18 years	25	17	16	15	17	42	43	44	46
18–24 years	72	77	58	19	23	22	93	98	120
25–44 years	166	177	189	47	56	91	220	249	405
45–64 years	102	78	48	35	32	34	121	123	142
65 years and over	21	20	15	13	14	18	38	50	82
White	296	265	217	119	123	177	451	469	607
All other	89	104	109	10	18	30	65	95	187
Male									
Total	249	239	205	56	67	107	212	255	379
Under 18 years	16	11	10	8	9	23	20	20	21
18–24 years	52	56	39	10	13	14	45	52	57
25–44 years	107	119	125	20	27	50	85	115	215
45–64 years	61	43	25	14	13	14	48	46	60
65 years and over	13	11	7	5	5	6	14	21	26
White	191	171	135	51	58	89	184	213	274
All other	58	68	69	5	9	18	27	42	105
Female									
Total	136	130	121	74	74	101	304	309	415
Under 18 years	9	5	6	8	7	20	23	23	25
18–24 years	20	22	19	9	10	8	48	45	63
25–44 years	59	58	64	28	29	41	135	135	190
45–64 years	41	35	24	21	18	20	74	77	81
65 years and over	8	9	8	8	9	12	24	29	56
White	105	94	82	69	65	88	267	256	333
All other	31	36	40	5	9	13	37	53	82
Both sexes	*Rate per 100,000 civilian population*								
Total	182.2	163.6	136.1	61.4	62.6	86.7	243.8	250.0	331.7
Under 18 years	38.1	26.1	25.2	23.3	26.3	67.1	64.4	68.5	72.0
18–24 years	271.8	264.6	215.6	73.7	79.6	81.3	352.8	334.2	443.7
25–44 years	314.1	282.9	251.9	89.3	89.1	121.6	416.8	399.0	540.4
45–64 years	233.5	175.7	107.0	80.1	71.0	75.2	278.5	276.4	314.9
65 years and over	91.8	78.0	50.9	57.7	54.1	61.9	170.3	195.4	281.5
White	161.1	136.8	106.7	64.9	63.4	87.3	245.4	241.8	299.0
All other	321.9	328.0	299.8	37.9	57.5	83.1	233.3	300.0	514.3
Male									
Total	243.7	219.8	176.6	54.5	61.9	92.1	207.1	233.8	327.6
Under 18 years	48.3	35.4	30.1	22.5	28.9	69.8	59.1	62.6	63.7
18–24 years	409.0	387.9	292.6	78.0	92.2	103.2	350.8	365.3	428.5
25–44 years	418.4	388.1	338.4	76.6	86.8	136.1	332.8	374.7	584.2
45–64 years	291.5	202.3	114.4	66.8	63.2	65.5	228.6	219.1	281.1
65 years and over	136.4	105.3	57.1	50.3	47.3	52.1	152.0	203.4	223.1
White	214.2	182.2	137.1	57.0	61.7	90.3	206.9	226.3	278.3
All other	444.5	457.8	403.0	38.1	62.7	102.8	209.1	281.1	610.3
Female									
Total	124.7	111.1	98.1	67.8	63.3	81.5	278.1	265.1	335.5
Under 18 years	27.5	16.4	20.0	24.1	23.6	64.3	70.0	74.6	80.7
18–24 years	143.1	145.8	141.0	69.6	67.4	60.2	354.6	304.4	458.3
25–44 years	215.9	182.3	168.1	101.2	91.2	107.6	495.8	422.2	498.1
45–64 years	180.5	151.7	100.2	92.3	78.1	84.0	324.3	328.2	345.8
65 years and over	60.8	59.6	46.7	62.8	58.8	68.6	182.9	190.0	321.3
White	111.2	94.1	78.1	72.5	65.0	84.5	281.7	256.4	318.6
All other	212.0	212.6	207.2	37.7	52.8	65.5	254.9	316.7	428.0

[1]Non-Federal general hospitals include public and nonpublic facilities.

Sources: National Institute of Mental Health: C. A. Taube and S. A. Barrett: Mental Health, United States, 1985. DHHS Pub. No. (ADM) 85-1378. U.S. Government Printing Office, 1985; R. W. Manderscheid and M. A. Sonnenschein: Mental Health, United States, 1990. DHHS Pub. No. (ADM) 90-1708. U.S. Government Printing Office, 1990: Unpublished data.

C5-17. Admissions to Selected Inpatient Psychiatric Organizations, According to Selected Primary Diagnoses and Age: United States, 1975, 1980, and 1986

Primary diagnosis and age	State and county mental hospitals			Private psychiatric hospitals			Non-Federal general hospitals[1]		
	1975	1980	1986	1975	1980	1986	1975	1980	1986
All diagnoses[2]				Rate per 100,000 civilian population					
All ages	182.2	163.6	136.1	61.4	62.6	86.7	243.8	250.0	331.7
Under 25 years	104.8	101.2	82.1	37.7	43.1	71.4	146.7	152.2	183.1
25–44 years	314.1	282.9	251.9	89.3	89.1	121.6	416.8	399.0	540.4
45–64 years	233.5	175.7	107.0	80.1	71.0	75.2	278.5	276.4	314.9
65 years and over	91.8	78.0	50.9	57.7	54.1	61.9	170.3	195.4	281.5
Alcohol related									
All ages	50.4	35.5	22.5	5.1	5.8	6.6	17.0	18.8	41.4
Under 25 years	10.7	12.4	15.5	0.4	1.4	2.2	2.4	4.4	13.4
25–44 years	86.2	64.0	42.6	7.6	9.3	10.0	31.0	34.3	92.6
45–64 years	110.0	57.7	15.3	12.5	10.9	11.0	34.5	30.6	31.8
65 years and over	14.8	11.5	*3.2	4.3	4.4	4.5	10.2	12.8	11.3
Drug related									
All ages	6.8	7.8	8.7	1.5	1.8	6.1	8.4	7.4	20.2
Under 25 years	7.2	9.4	5.8	1.5	1.8	7.5	7.7	7.8	18.4
25–44 years	12.6	12.9	14.2	2.3	3.0	9.3	13.8	9.3	41.2
45–64 years	*0.6	1.4	10.5	0.1	1.0	*1.8	6.5	7.1	*2.1
65 years and over	*3.5	*0.7	*0.8	0.4	0.6	- - -	*2.6	*2.0	*0.1
Organic disorders[3]									
All ages	9.6	6.8	4.3	2.5	2.2	2.0	9.0	7.4	9.8
Under 25 years	2.2	1.2	*0.2	0.7	0.5	*0.5	1.1	*0.8	1.7
25–44 years	6.4	4.7	2.6	1.1	0.9	*0.3	5.4	5.6	6.1
45–64 years	12.2	8.1	7.3	1.7	2.7	*1.5	9.3	6.9	5.7
65 years and over	43.3	30.0	17.2	14.5	10.8	11.7	49.3	36.4	50.7
Affective disorders									
All ages	21.3	22.0	22.8	26.0	26.8	41.9	91.9	79.2	121.9
Under 25 years	7.5	9.1	9.6	9.5	13.5	28.5	35.3	32.2	49.2
25–44 years	40.6	36.9	43.2	39.4	38.9	63.4	160.9	123.7	176.8
45–64 years	29.4	32.4	25.0	43.3	36.3	38.5	135.6	113.8	147.3
65 years and over	16.8	14.3	7.9	29.6	29.2	33.4	78.5	81.0	166.3
Schizophrenia									
All ages	61.2	62.1	49.7	13.4	13.3	9.9	58.9	59.9	63.3
Under 25 years	35.9	36.6	18.6	11.1	10.6	5.7	42.0	38.3	30.4
25–44 years	125.8	125.0	107.5	23.8	22.5	18.9	118.0	114.5	118.6
45–64 years	63.5	54.8	35.9	11.3	11.6	8.5	50.3	53.6	68.9
65 years and over	9.3	13.9	18.3	2.7	3.6	*1.8	5.6	16.3	14.0

[1]Non-Federal general hospitals include public and nonpublic facilities.

[2]Includes all other diagnoses not listed separately.

[3]Excludes alcohol- and drug-related diagnoses.

*Based on 5 or fewer sample admissions.

NOTE: Primary diagnosis categories are based on the then current International Classification of Diseases and Diagnostic and Statistical Manual of Mental Disorders.

C6. Health Insurance Coverage

C6-1. Percent without Health Insurance for at Least One Month: February 1987 to May 1989

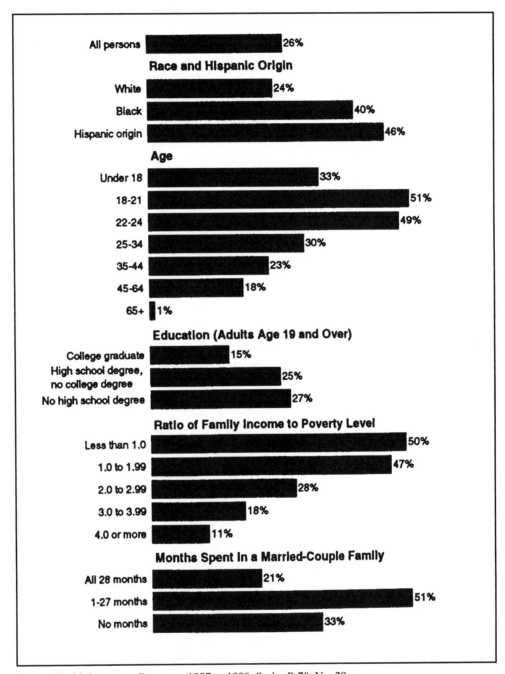

Source: Health Insurance Coverage: 1987 to 1990, Series P-70, No. 29.

C6-2. Health Insurance Coverage Status—Persons, by Age: 1990 and 1991

(Persons as of March of the following year)

Year and age	Total (thous.)	Percent covered by:							Not covered
		Private or government health insurance							
		Total	Private health insurance		Government health insurance				
			Total	Group health	Total	Medicaid	Medicare	CHAMPUS	
1991									
All Persons	251,434	85.9	72.1	59.7	25.4	10.7	13.1	3.9	14.1
Under 18 years...............	66,173	87.3	69.7	60.0	23.9	20.4	0.1	3.7	12.7
Under 15 years..............	56,191	87.9	69.5	60.2	24.8	21.6	-	3.5	12.1
18 to 24 years	24,434	73.1	62.1	47.0	13.9	10.1	0.7	3.8	26.9
25 to 34 years	42,493	79.9	70.1	63.8	11.8	8.3	1.2	3.1	20.1
35 to 44 years	39,571	85.7	78.6	71.6	9.4	5.1	1.4	3.6	14.3
45 to 54 years	27,023	87.7	81.3	73.1	10.3	4.4	2.5	4.3	12.3
55 to 64 years	21,150	87.6	77.9	64.4	17.4	5.8	7.5	6.4	12.4
65 years and over	30,590	99.1	67.7	33.1	96.3	9.5	96.0	3.9	0.9
1990									
All Persons	248,886	86.0	73.2	60.4	24.5	9.7	13.0	4.0	14.0
Under 18 years...............	65,290	87.0	71.1	61.2	21.9	18.5	0.1	3.7	13.0
Under 15 years..............	55,366	87.4	71.0	61.5	22.7	19.6	-	3.5	12.6
18 to 24 years	24,901	73.9	63.9	48.2	13.1	8.9	0.6	4.4	26.1
25 to 34 years	42,905	80.6	72.0	65.1	10.8	7.4	1.1	3.0	19.4
35 to 44 years	38,665	86.7	80.3	72.8	9.2	4.9	1.5	3.5	13.3
45 to 54 years	25,686	87.1	80.6	72.0	10.3	4.4	2.5	4.5	12.9
55 to 64 years	21,345	87.4	77.7	64.1	17.2	5.5	7.1	6.8	12.6
65 years and over	30,093	99.1	68.3	33.2	96.0	8.6	95.7	3.8	0.9

C6-3. Health Insurance Premiums Per Elderly Family: 1961 and 1991

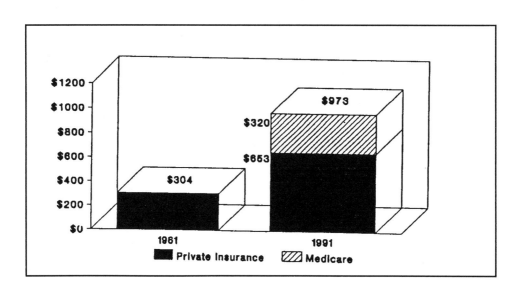

C6-4. Health Care Coverage for Persons 65 Years and Over, by Type of Coverage: 1980 and 1989

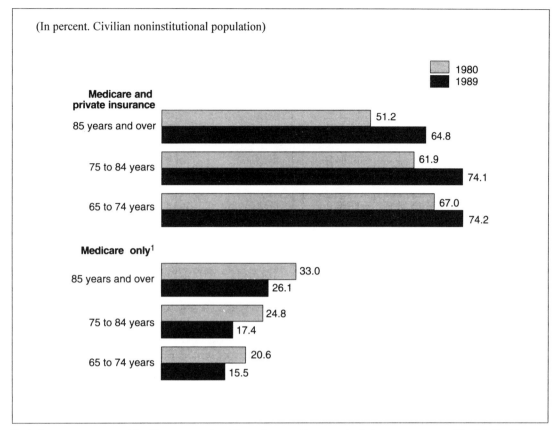

[1]Includes persons covered by Champus and public assistance. Does not include persons covered by Medicaid.
Source: National Center for Health Statistics, Health United States, 1990, Hyattsville, MD: Public Health Service, 1991, Table 125.

C6-5. Health Insurance Coverage, by Age and Race: 1986 to 1989

(Percent)

Status	1986	1987	1988	1989
Total population	**238,179,000**	**240,493,000**	**243,094,000**	**244,900,000**
Private or government health insurance				
Total	85.9	86.8	87.0	87.1
Age:				
Less than 16 years	83.6	84.3	84.7	85.6
16 to 24 years	76.2	78.0	78.0	79.5
25 to 34 years	83.2	84.0	83.8	82.7
35 to 44 years	87.9	88.4	88.8	88.1
45 to 54 years	88.6	88.8	89.5	89.4
55 to 64 years	89.7	90.6	90.7	89.2
65 years and more	99.5	99.6	99.7	99.7
Race and Hispanic origin:				
White	87.1	87.8	88.3	87.8
Black	79.4	81.0	79.8	82.5
Hispanic	69.2	70.4	73.5	68.8
Covered by private health insurance				
Total	75.4	76.5	77.5	77.0
Age:				
Less than 16 years	69.2	69.7	71.2	71.9
16 to 24 years	68.9	70.9	71.4	72.3
25 to 34 years	75.8	77.0	77.6	75.9
35 to 44 years	82.3	82.6	83.2	82.4
45 to 54 years	82.8	83.6	84.6	83.6
55 to 64 years	82.1	83.3	83.6	80.9
65 years and more	75.8	77.9	79.0	78.4
Race and Hispanic origin:				
White	78.7	79.9	81.0	80.2
Black	54.9	56.1	55.3	58.4
Hispanic origin	50.8	53.9	57.4	53.3
Private health insurance (related to employment)				
Total	61.1	62.0	63.1	62.8
Age:				
Less than 16 years	59.7	60.8	61.9	61.5
16 to 24 years	53.9	54.6	55.7	56.5
25 to 34 years	67.7	69.1	70.1	69.0
35 to 44 years	74.5	74.4	75.2	75.3
45 to 54 years	72.4	73.3	74.7	74.9
55 to 64 years	66.5	66.9	68.0	64.8
65 years and more	33.3	34.3	35.0	35.5
Race and Hispanic origin:				
White	63.7	64.6	65.7	65.1
Black	45.4	46.2	46.8	49.8
Hispanic origin	43.5	45.9	48.6	45.9
Percent covered by Medicaid				
Total	7.2	7.3	7.1	7.4
Age:				
Less than 16 years	13.1	13.4	12.5	13.3
16 to 24 years	6.3	6.4	6.6	6.8
25 to 34 years	5.9	5.5	5.0	5.5
35 to 44 years	4.1	4.2	4.4	4.2
45 to 54 years	3.3	3.5	3.7	4.1
55 to 64 years	4.4	4.6	4.2	4.5
65 years and more	7.9	8.1	8.3	8.0
Race and Hispanic origin:				
White	5.2	5.1	4.9	4.9
Black	20.5	21.7	20.6	21.6
Hispanic	15.9	14.3	14.1	14.0

Source: Health Insurance Coverage 1986-88 by Charles Nelson and Kathleen Short; *Current Population Reports*, Household Economic Studies, Survey of Income Participation, U.S. Department of Commerce, Bureau of the Census.

C6-6. Firms That Offer Health Benefits and Firms That Do Not Offer Health Benefits, by Size: 1990

(Percent)

Firm size	Offer health benefits	Do not offer health benefits
Total	**42**	**58**
Fewer than 10 employees	27	73
10 to 24 employees	73	27
25 to 99 employees	87	13
25 to 49 employees	85	15
50 to 99 employees	89	11
100 or more employees	98	2

NOTE: Total may not add to 100% because of rounding.
Source: HIAA, Critical Distinctions: How Firms That Offer Health Benefits Differ from Those That Do Not.

C6-7. Percent Distribution of Persons 70 Years of Age and Over, by Type of Private Health Insurance Coverage, According to Age and Sex: United States, 1984

(Data are based on household interviews of the civilian noninstitutionalized population)

Type of private health insurance coverage	Total	70 years and over		70–79 years		80 years and over	
		Male	Female	Male	Female	Male	Female
Private health insurance	Number in thousands	Percent distribution					
Hospital only	289	1.6	1.7	1.6	1.6	1.8	2.0
Hospital and physician	11,468	67.5	65.3	69.3	68.9	61.5	57.4
Physician only	24	*0.1	*0.2	*0.1	*0.1	*0.1	*0.3
No private health insurance coverage	4,961	28.4	28.8	26.9	25.3	33.3	36.5
Other	580	2.4	3.9	2.0	4.0	3.3	3.7
Unknown	13	*0.0	*0.1	*0.1	*0.1	–	*0.1

*Figure does not meet standards of reliability. NOTE: Column percents may not add to 100 because of rounding.
Source: National Center for Health Statistics; data from the National Health Interview Survey Longitudinal Study on Aging, 1986.

C6-8. Percent Distribution of Persons 70 Years of Age and Over, by Health Care Coverage, According to Age and Sex: United States, 1984

(Data are based on household interviews of the civilian noninstitutionalized population)

Health care coverage	Total	70 years and over		70–79 years		80 years and over	
		Male	Female	Male	Female	Male	Female
Medicare and/or private health insurance	Number in thousands	Percent distribution					
Covered by one or both	17,081	98.4	98.6	98.1	99.0	99.3	97.8
Not covered by either	239	1.5	1.3	1.8	1.0	*0.7	2.0
Unknown	15	*0.1	*0.1	*0.1	*0.0	–	*0.2
Other public assistance program[1]							
Covered	51	*0.1	*0.4	*0.1	*0.5	*0.1	*0.3
Not covered	17,277	99.9	99.5	99.9	99.5	99.9	99.7
Unknown	7	–	*0.1	–	*0.1	–	*0.1

NOTE: Column percents may not add to 100 because of rounding.
[1]Specific survey questions ask about coverage by public assistance programs other than Medicaid that pay for health care.
Source: National Center for Health Statistics; data from the National Health Interview Survey Longitudinal Study on Aging, 1986.

C6-9. Percent Distribution of Persons 70 Years of Age and Over, by Type of Medicare and/or Private Health Insurance Coverage, According to Age and Sex: United States, 1984

(Data are based on household interviews of the civilian noninstitutionalized population)

Medicare and/or private health insurance coverage	Total	70 years and over		70–79 years		80 years and over	
		Male	Female	Male	Female	Male	Female
	Number in thousands	Percent distribution					
Hospital only	149	0.8	0.9	0.9	0.9	*0.6	0.9
Hospital and physician	16,709	96.4	96.4	96.4	96.8	96.5	95.3
Physician only	21	*0.1	*0.1	*0.2	*0.1	–	*0.1
No Medicare or private health insurance coverage.	239	1.5	1.3	1.8	1.0	*0.7	2.0
Unknown[1]	216	1.2	1.3	*0.7	1.2	2.2	1.7

[1]Unknown category includes those for whom Medicare and/or private health coverage breakdown is unknown.
NOTE: Column percents may not add to 100 because of rounding.
Source: National Center for Health Statistics; data from the National Health Interview Survey Longitudinal Study on Aging, 1986.

C6-10. Health Insurance Coverage for the Elderly, by Residence: 1987

Source: Agency for Health Care Policy and Research, National Medical Expenditure Survey-Household Survey, 1987.

C6-11. Selected Characteristics of Persons, by Health Insurance Coverage Status and Poverty Status: 1991

(Numbers in thousands)

Age, race, and Hispanic origin	Total	Covered by some form of health insurance all or part of year					Not covered
		Total	Private insurance[1]	Medicaid[1]	Medicare[1]	CHAMPUS, VA or military health plan[1]	
ALL INCOME LEVELS							
Total	251,179	215,821	181,331	26,739	32,907	9,807	35,358
Under 18 years	65,918	57,625	46,075	13,374	52	2,425	8,293
18 to 44 years	106,498	85,682	76,090	8,055	1,217	3,670	20,816
Men	52,713	40,593	37,226	2,281	636	1,859	12,122
Women	53,785	45,090	38,865	5,775	582	1,810	8,695
45 to 64 years	48,173	42,213	38,450	2,420	2,260	2,535	5,961
65 years and over	30,590	30,301	20,715	2,891	29,377	1,178	289
White	210,121	183,033	159,596	16,990	28,940	7,855	27,088
Black	31,312	24,850	15,454	8,282	3,248	1,481	6,462
Hispanic origin[2]	22,068	15,106	10,336	4,577	1,309	521	6,962
INCOME BELOW POVERTY LEVEL							
Total	35,708	25,488	7,941	16,888	4,586	644	10,220
Under 18 years	14,341	11,406	2,864	9,388	24	219	2,935
18 to 44 years	13,280	7,717	2,720	5,011	385	227	5,562
Men	5,175	2,344	1,143	824	168	101	2,831
Women	8,105	5,373	1,577	3,885	217	126	2,731
45 to 64 years	4,306	2,688	1,128	1,301	557	127	1,618
65 years and over	3,781	3,677	1,229	1,187	3,619	71	104
White	23,747	16,333	6,035	9,782	3,307	463	7,414
Black	10,242	7,927	1,513	6,241	1,169	144	2,315
Hispanic origin	6,339	3,773	836	3,022	319	56	2,566
PERCENT DISTRIBUTION							
All Income Levels							
Total	100.0	85.9	72.2	10.6	13.1	3.9	14.1
Under 18 years	100.0	87.4	69.9	20.3	0.1	3.7	12.6
18 to 44 years	100.0	80.5	71.4	7.6	1.1	3.4	19.5
Men	100.0	77.0	70.6	4.3	1.2	3.5	23.0
Women	100.0	83.8	72.3	10.7	1.1	3.4	16.2
45 to 64 years	100.0	87.6	79.8	5.0	4.7	5.3	12.4
65 years and over	100.0	99.1	67.7	9.5	96.0	3.9	0.9
White	100.0	87.1	76.0	8.1	13.8	3.7	12.9
Black	100.0	79.4	49.4	26.4	10.4	4.7	20.6
Hispanic origin	100.0	68.5	46.8	20.7	5.9	2.4	31.5
INCOME BELOW POVERTY LEVEL							
Total	100.0	71.4	22.2	47.3	12.8	1.8	28.6
Under 18 years	100.0	79.5	20.0	65.5	0.2	1.5	20.5
18 to 44 years	100.0	58.1	20.5	37.7	2.9	1.7	41.9
Men	100.0	45.3	22.1	15.9	3.2	2.0	54.7
Women	100.0	66.3	19.5	47.9	2.7	1.6	33.7
45 to 64 years	100.0	62.4	26.2	30.2	12.9	2.9	37.6
65 years and over	100.0	97.2	32.5	31.4	95.7	1.9	2.7
White	100.0	68.8	25.4	41.2	13.9	1.9	31.2
Black	100.0	77.4	14.8	60.9	11.4	1.4	22.6
Hispanic origin	100.0	59.5	13.2	47.7	5.0	0.9	40.5

[1]Includes those also covered by other insurance.
[2]Persons of Hispanic origin may be of any race.

D. Employment

LABOR FORCE PARTICIPATION

The dramatic change in the population's age distribution since the turn of the century is reflected by the change in labor force participation of the 65+ population. At the turn of the century, the average man basically worked until he died; he spent only 3% of his lifetime in retirement. Today, he is spending one-fifth of his life in retirement. While life expectancy has increased, labor force participation drops rapidly with increasing age and almost two-thirds of older workers retire before age 65. About 15% of older men and 9% of older women remain in the labor force; three-quarters of this group is employed in white collar occupations.

UNEMPLOYMENT

Unemployment creates great problems for elderly people who want to work; older workers who lose their jobs suffer greater earning losses than do younger workers because they tend to stay unemployed longer, become discouraged more easily, and give up looking for other jobs sooner. If they do find other work it is usually at a much lower salary and with fewer fringe benefits.

RETIREMENT TRENDS AND PENSIONS

The financial support of Social Security and corporate and personal pension funds makes retirement at an earlier age financially more feasible today than 50 years ago when people had to rely on their personal savings during retirement. In the future, retirement age may go up because more people are healthy enough to work longer and because government budget conditions are such that the minimum age for nondisability social security payments may have to be raised.

Many workers are forced to retire due to ill health, mandatory retirement, or failure to find employment. Voluntary retirees indicate that they wanted to retire to do things they had not been able to do before. The most satisfactory situation for the physically fit elderly seems to be part-time employment or volunteering in activities related to their skills and interests.

D1. Labor Force Participation

D1-1. Labor Force Participation for Older People, by Age and Sex: 1989
(annual averages)

Labor force status	55 to 59			60 to 64			65+		
	Total	Men	Women	Total	Men	Women	Total	Men	Women
Civilian labor force (in thousands)......................	7,088	4,033	3,055	4,789	2,750	2,039	3,446	2,017	1,429
Labor force participation rate (percent).............................	66.6	79.5	54.8	44.5	54.8	35.5	11.8	16.6	8.4
Number employed (in thousands)......................	6,854	3,890	2,964	4,644	2,658	1,986	3,355	1,968	1,388

NOTE: The U.S. labor force includes workers who are employed or unemployed but actively seeking employment. The participation rate is the percentage of individuals in a given group (e.g., age group) who are in the labor force.
Source: U.S. Department of Labor, Bureau of Labor Statistics, *Employment and Earnings,* Vol. 37, No. 1 (January 1990).

D1-2. Labor Force Participation Rates for Older People, by Age, Sex, and Race: 1989

(annual averages in percent) Sex & race	50 to 54 years	55 to 59 years	60 to 64 years	65 to 69 years	70+ years
Total men..............................	89.3	79.5	54.8	26.1	10.9
Total women..........................	65.9	54.8	35.5	16.4	4.6
White men	90.4	81.0	55.7	26.6	11.0
White women........................	65.6	55.1	35.7	16.4	4.5
Black men.............................	79.9	66.4	43.6	20.7	10.3
Black women	68.2	51.5	32.7	16.4	5.9

NOTE: The U.S. labor force includes workers who are employed or unemployed by actively seeking employment. The participation rate is the percentage of individuals in a given group (e.g., age group) who are in the labor force.
Source: U.S. Department of Labor, Bureau of Labor Statistics, *Employment and Earnings,* Vol. 37, No. 1 (January 1990).

D1-3. Percent of Civilian Noninstitutional Population in the Labor Force, by Age and Sex: 1950 and 1990

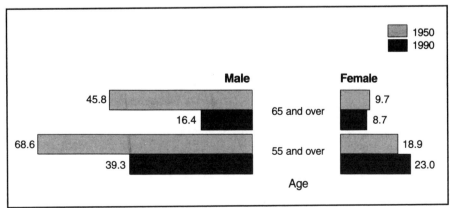

Source: U.S. Bureau of Labor Statistics, Data for 1990, *Employment and Earnings,* Vol. 38, No. 1, January 1991, Table 3; data for 1950, unpublished tabulations from 1950 Current Population Survey, available from the Bureau of Labor Statistics.

D1-4. Labor Force Participation Rates for Persons Aged 45 to 49 Through 75 Years or Older, by Sex: Selected Years, 1950 to 2005

Sex and year	Age group						
	45 to 49 years	50 to 54 years	55 to 59 years	60 to 64 years	65 to 69 years	70 to 74 years	75 years and over
Men							
1950	96.5	95.0	89.9	83.4	63.9	43.2	21.3
1955	97.1	95.7	92.5	82.6	57.0	37.1	19.4
1960	96.9	94.7	91.6	81.1	46.8	31.6	17.5
1965	96.1	95.0	90.2	78.0	43.0	24.8	14.1
1970	95.3	93.0	89.5	75.0	41.6	25.2	12.0
1975	94.1	90.1	84.4	65.5	31.7	21.1	10.1
1980	93.2	89.2	81.7	60.8	28.5	17.9	8.8
1985	93.3	88.6	79.6	55.6	24.5	14.9	7.0
1990	92.3	88.8	79.8	55.5	26.0	15.4	7.1
Projected:[1]							
1995	92.0	88.8	79.4	54.7	26.6	15.4	7.4
2000	91.8	89.0	79.2	54.2	27.3	15.6	7.3
2005	91.6	88.8	78.8	53.3	27.9	15.5	7.2
Women							
1950	39.9	35.7	29.7	23.8	15.5	7.9	3.2
1955	45.8	41.5	35.6	29.0	17.8	9.2	4.0
1960	50.7	48.7	42.2	31.4	17.6	9.5	4.4
1965	51.7	50.1	47.1	34.0	17.4	9.1	3.7
1970	55.0	53.8	49.0	36.1	17.3	9.1	3.4
1975	55.9	53.3	47.9	33.2	14.5	7.6	3.0
1980	62.1	57.8	48.5	33.2	15.1	7.5	2.5
1985	67.8	60.8	50.3	33.4	13.5	7.6	2.2
1990	74.8	66.9	55.3	35.5	17.0	8.2	2.7
Projected:[1]							
1995	79.1	71.0	58.4	37.9	18.2	8.4	2.5
2000	82.7	74.8	61.9	39.5	19.7	8.5	2.7
2005	85.1	77.6	64.5	40.9	20.7	8.5	2.6

[1]Projected rates are unpublished 1991 middle-scenario estimates from the Bureau of Labor Statistics economic projections program.
Source: Data for 1990 are from the Bureau of Labor Statistics monthly publication, *Employment and Earnings,* January 1991.

D1-5. Civilian Labor Force and Participation Rates, by Race, Hispanic Origin, Sex, and Age, 1970 to 1991, and Projections, 2000 and 2005

RACE, SEX, AND AGE	CIVILIAN LABOR FORCE (millions)							PARTICIPATION RATE (percent)						
	1970	1980	1985	1990	1991	2000	2005	1970	1980	1985	1990	1991	2000	2005
Total[1]	82.8	106.9	115.5	124.8	125.3	142.9	150.7	60.4	63.8	64.8	66.4	66.0	69.0	69.0
White	73.6	93.6	99.9	107.2	107.5	120.3	125.8	60.2	64.1	65.0	66.8	66.6	69.3	69.7
Male	46.0	54.5	56.5	59.3	59.3	64.5	66.8	80.0	78.2	77.0	76.9	76.4	76.7	76.2
Female	27.5	39.1	43.5	47.9	48.2	55.8	58.9	42.6	51.2	54.1	57.5	57.4	62.3	63.5
Black[2]	9.2	10.9	12.4	13.5	13.5	16.5	17.8	61.8	61.0	62.9	63.3	62.6	65.7	65.6
Male	5.2	5.6	6.2	6.7	6.8	8.1	8.7	76.5	70.3	70.8	70.1	69.5	71.0	70.2
Female	4.0	5.3	6.1	6.8	6.8	8.4	9.1	49.5	53.1	56.5	57.8	57.0	61.2	61.7
Hispanic[3]	(NA)	6.1	7.7	9.6	9.8	14.2	16.8	(NA)	64.0	64.6	67.0	66.1	69.3	69.9
Male	(NA)	3.8	4.7	5.8	5.9	8.4	9.9	(NA)	81.4	80.3	81.2	80.1	81.8	81.6
Female	(NA)	2.3	3.0	3.8	3.9	5.8	6.9	(NA)	47.4	49.3	53.0	52.3	56.6	58.0
Male	51.2	61.5	64.4	68.2	68.4	75.9	79.3	79.7	77.4	76.3	76.1	75.5	76.0	75.4
16 to 19 years	4.0	5.0	4.1	3.9	3.6	4.4	4.6	56.1	60.5	56.8	55.7	53.2	57.4	57.7
16 and 17 years	1.8	2.1	1.7	1.5	1.4	1.8	1.9	47.0	50.1	45.1	43.7	41.2	47.3	47.9
18 and 19 years	2.2	2.9	2.5	2.4	2.2	2.6	2.6	66.7	71.3	68.9	67.0	65.3	68.0	68.0
20 to 24 years	5.7	8.6	8.3	7.3	7.2	7.2	8.0	83.3	85.9	85.0	84.3	83.4	85.5	86.1
25 to 34 years	11.3	17.0	18.8	19.8	19.6	17.3	17.0	96.4	95.2	94.7	94.2	93.7	93.9	93.6
35 to 44 years	10.5	11.6	14.5	17.3	17.9	20.4	19.2	96.9	95.5	95.0	94.4	94.2	93.7	93.4
45 to 54 years	10.4	9.9	9.9	11.2	11.5	16.5	18.6	94.3	91.2	91.0	90.7	90.5	90.5	90.3
55 to 64 years	7.1	7.2	7.1	6.8	6.7	7.8	9.7	83.0	72.1	67.9	67.7	66.9	68.2	67.9
65 years and over	2.2	1.9	1.8	2.0	2.0	2.2	2.3	26.8	19.0	15.8	16.4	15.8	15.8	16.0
Female	31.5	45.5	51.1	56.6	56.9	67.0	71.4	43.3	51.5	54.5	57.5	57.3	62.0	63.0
16 to 19 years	3.2	4.4	3.8	3.5	3.3	4.1	4.2	44.0	52.9	52.1	51.8	50.2	54.1	54.3
16 and 17 years	1.3	1.8	1.5	1.4	1.3	1.7	1.7	34.9	43.6	42.1	41.9	40.1	45.3	45.4
18 and 19 years	1.9	2.6	2.3	2.2	2.0	2.4	2.5	53.6	61.9	61.7	60.5	59.8	62.9	63.2
20 to 24 years	4.9	7.3	7.4	6.6	6.4	6.6	7.3	57.7	68.9	71.8	71.6	70.4	74.3	75.3
25 to 34 years	5.7	12.3	14.7	16.0	15.8	14.8	14.7	45.0	65.5	70.9	73.6	73.3	78.2	79.7
35 to 44 years	6.0	8.6	11.6	14.6	15.1	18.4	17.7	51.1	65.5	71.8	76.5	76.6	83.3	85.3
45 to 54 years	6.5	7.0	7.5	9.3	9.7	15.0	17.2	54.4	59.9	64.4	71.2	72.0	79.0	81.5
55 to 64 years	4.2	4.7	4.9	5.1	5.1	6.5	8.4	43.0	41.3	42.0	45.3	45.3	51.9	54.3
65 years and over	1.1	1.2	1.2	1.5	1.5	1.6	1.8	9.7	8.1	7.3	8.7	8.6	8.6	8.8

[1]Beginning 1980, includes other races not shown separately.
[2]For 1970, Black and other.
[3]Persons of Hispanic origin may be of any race.
NA No available.
Source: U.S. Bureau of Labor Statistics, Bulletin 2307; *Employment and Earnings*, monthly, January issues; *Monthly Labor Review*, November 1991; and unpublished data.

D1-6. Civilian Labor Force—Employment Status, by Sex, Race, and Age: 1991

(For civilian noninstitutional population 16 years old and over. Annual averages of monthly figures.)

AGE AND RACE	CIVILIAN LABOR FORCE Total (1,000)	Percent by age Male	Percent by age Female	MALE (1,000) Total	MALE (1,000) Employed	MALE (1,000) Unemployed	FEMALE (1,000) Total	FEMALE (1,000) Employed	FEMALE (1,000) Unemployed	PERCENT OF LABOR FORCE Employed Male	Employed Female	Unemployed Male	Unemployed Female
All workers[1]	125,303	100.0	100.0	68,411	63,593	4,817	56,893	53,284	3,609	93.0	93.7	7.0	6.3
16 to 19 years . . .	6,918	5.2	5.9	3,588	2,879	709	3,330	2,749	581	80.2	82.6	19.8	17.4
20 to 24 years . . .	13,710	10.6	11.3	7,270	6,421	849	6,440	5,812	628	88.3	90.2	11.7	9.8
25 to 34 years . . .	35,330	28.6	27.7	19,548	18,188	1,360	15,782	14,726	1,057	93.0	93.3	7.0	6.7
35 to 44 years . . .	32,975	26.1	26.6	17,854	16,883	971	15,121	14,402	718	94.6	95.3	5.4	4.7
45 to 54 years . . .	21,118	16.8	17.0	11,461	10,909	552	9,657	9,255	402	95.2	95.8	4.8	4.2
55 to 64 years . . .	11,752	9.8	8.9	6,699	6,389	310	5,052	4,879	173	95.4	96.6	4.6	3.4
65 years and over .	3,500	2.9	2.7	1,990	1,923	66	1,511	1,461	50	96.7	96.7	3.3	3.3
White	107,486	100.0	100.0	59,332	55,557	3,775	48,154	45,482	2,672	93.6	94.5	6.4	5.5
16 to 19 years . . .	5,966	5.2	6.0	3,094	2,552	542	2,872	2,436	436	82.5	84.8	17.5	15.2
20 to 24 years . . .	11,575	10.4	11.3	6,148	5,522	626	5,427	4,990	436	89.8	92.0	10.2	8.0
25 to 34 years . . .	29,896	28.2	27.3	16,754	15,695	1,059	13,142	12,403	740	93.7	94.4	6.3	5.6
35 to 44 years . . .	28,293	26.2	26.5	15,547	14,769	777	12,747	12,195	551	95.0	95.7	5.0	4.3
45 to 54 years . . .	18,288	16.9	17.1	10,035	9,593	442	8,253	7,928	325	95.6	96.1	4.4	3.9
55 to 64 years . . .	10,314	10.0	9.1	5,940	5,667	272	4,375	4,231	143	95.4	96.7	4.6	3.3
65 years and over .	3,154	3.1	2.8	1,815	1,758	57	1,339	1,298	41	96.9	96.9	3.1	3.1
Black	13,542	100.0	100.0	6,754	5,880	874	6,788	5,983	805	87.1	88.1	12.9	11.9
16 to 19 years . . .	744	5.8	5.2	390	247	142	354	227	128	63.5	63.9	36.5	36.1
20 to 24 years . . .	1,673	12.9	11.8	870	675	195	802	636	166	77.6	79.3	22.4	20.7
25 to 34 years . . .	4,199	31.2	30.8	2,110	1,858	252	2,089	1,809	280	88.1	86.6	11.9	13.4
35 to 44 years . . .	3,507	24.9	26.9	1,680	1,519	162	1,827	1,688	139	90.4	92.4	9.6	7.6
45 to 54 years . . .	2,057	14.9	15.5	1,003	917	86	1,054	989	65	91.4	93.8	8.6	6.2
55 to 64 years . . .	1,087	8.4	7.7	565	537	28	522	502	20	95.0	96.2	5.0	3.8
65 years and over .	275	2.0	2.1	135	127	8	140	133	6	94.1	95.7	5.9	4.3
Hispanic[2] . . .	9,762	100.0	100.0	5,873	5,278	595	3,890	3,521	368	89.9	90.5	10.1	9.5
16 to 19 years . . .	653	6.5	7.0	379	290	90	273	213	60	76.3	78.0	23.7	22.0
20 to 24 years . . .	1,476	16.0	13.8	939	830	109	537	474	63	88.4	88.3	11.6	11.7
25 to 34 years . . .	3,204	33.9	31.2	1,991	1,807	185	1,213	1,102	111	90.7	90.8	9.3	9.2
35 to 44 years . . .	2,363	23.5	25.3	1,379	1,261	118	984	909	75	91.4	92.4	8.6	7.6
45 to 54 years . . .	1,307	12.5	14.7	736	678	58	571	525	46	92.1	91.9	7.9	8.1
55 to 64 years . . .	653	6.5	6.9	383	352	31	270	259	11	91.9	95.9	8.1	4.1
65 years and over .	107	1.1	1.1	65	60	5	42	39	3	92.3	92.9	7.7	7.1

[1]Includes other races not shown separately.

[2]Persons of Hispanic origin may be of any race.

Source: U.S. Bureau of Labor Statistics, *Employment and Earnings*, monthly, January 1992.

D1-7. Employed Civilians and Weekly Hours, by Selected Characteristics: 1970 to 1991

(In thousands, except as indicated. For civilian noninstitutional population 16 years old and over. Annual averages of monthly figures.)

AGE, SEX, AND MARITAL STATUS	1970	1980	1985	1986	1987	1988	1989	1990	1991
Total employed	78,678	99,303	107,150	109,597	112,440	114,968	117,342	117,914	116,877
Age:									
16 to 19 years	6,144	7,710	6,434	6,472	6,640	6,805	6,759	6,261	5,628
20 to 24 years.	9,731	14,087	13,980	13,790	13,524	13,244	12,962	12,622	12,233
25 to 34 years.	16,318	27,204	31,208	32,201	33,105	33,574	34,045	33,831	32,914
35 to 44 years.	15,922	19,523	24,732	25,861	27,179	28,269	29,443	30,543	31,286
45 to 54 years.	16,473	16,234	16,509	16,949	17,487	18,447	19,279	19,765	20,164
55 to 64 years.	10,974	11,586	11,474	11,405	11,465	11,433	11,499	11,464	11,268
65 years and over	3,118	2,960	2,813	2,919	3,041	3,197	3,355	3,428	3,384
Sex: Male	48,990	57,186	59,891	60,892	62,107	63,273	64,315	64,435	63,593
Female	29,688	42,117	47,259	48,706	50,334	51,696	53,027	53,479	53,284
Marital status:									
Married, spouse present	55,554	62,536	65,584	66,802	68,372	69,228	70,164	70,624	70,196
Single (never married).	15,039	24,082	26,780	27,478	28,355	29,500	30,111	29,761	29,278
Widowed, divorced, separated	8,087	12,684	14,786	15,318	15,713	16,242	17,066	17,531	17,403
Class of worker:									
Nonagriculture.	75,215	95,938	103,971	106,434	109,232	111,800	114,142	114,728	113,644
Wage and salary worker.	69,491	88,525	95,871	98,299	100,771	103,021	105,259	105,715	104,520
Self-employed	5,221	7,000	7,811	7,881	8,201	8,519	8,605	8,760	8,899
Unpaid family workers	502	413	289	255	260	260	279	252	225
Agriculture	3,463	3,364	3,179	3,163	3,208	3,169	3,199	3,186	3,233
Wage and salary worker.	1,154	1,425	1,535	1,547	1,632	1,621	1,665	1,679	1,673
Self-employed	1,810	1,642	1,458	1,447	1,423	1,398	1,403	1,400	1,442
Unpaid family workers	499	297	185	169	153	150	131	107	118
Weekly hours:									
Nonagriculture:									
Wage and salary workers	38.3	38.1	38.7	38.8	38.7	39.1	39.3	39.2	39.0
Self-employed	45.0	41.2	41.1	41.2	41.0	41.0	41.1	40.8	40.4
Unpaid family workers	37.9	34.7	35.1	35.5	36.3	36.0	35.1	33.9	35.4
Agriculture:									
Wage and salary workers	40.0	41.6	40.8	40.9	40.6	41.3	41.8	41.3	41.0
Self-employed	51.0	49.3	48.2	48.4	47.8	47.5	47.9	46.9	46.8
Unpaid family workers	40.0	38.6	38.5	39.7	39.9	39.7	39.4	38.5	40.3

Source: U.S. Bureau of Labor Statistics, *Employment and Earnings,* monthly, January issues; and unpublished data.

D1-8. Percent Change in Labor Force Participation of Men 55 Years and Over, by Age: 1970 to 2005

Period	55 years and over	55 to 59 years	60 to 64 years	65 to 69 years	70 to 74 years
Historical					
1970 to 1975	−6.4	−5.1	−9.5	−9.9	−5.9
1975 to 1980	−3.7	−2.7	−4.7	−3.2	−2.9
1980 to 1985	−4.6	−2.1	−5.2	−4.1	−3.3
1985 to 1990	−1.7	0.2	−0.1	1.6	0.6
Projected					
1990 to 1995	−0.9	−0.3	−0.8	0.6	0.0
1995 to 2000	1.2	−0.3	−0.5	0.7	0.2
2000 to 2005	2.2	−0.4	−0.9	0.6	0.1

Source: Howard Fullerton, Jr., Bureau of Labor Statistics, "Labor Force Projections: The Baby Boom Moves On," *Monthly Labor Review*, Vol. 114, No. 11 (November 1991), pp. 37-38.

D1-9. Occupation of Employed Older Workers, by Age: 1989

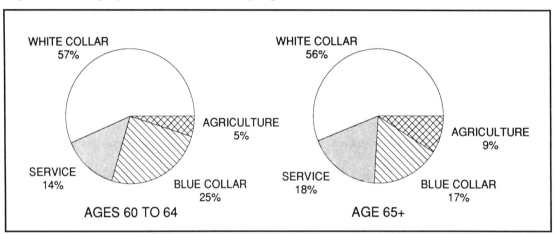

NOTE: May add to more than 100 percent due to rounding. White collar includes (1) managerial and professional specialty and (2) technical, sales, and administrative support. Blue collar includes (1) precision production, craft, and repair and (2) operators, fabricators, and laborers.
Source: U.S. Department of Labor, Bureau of Labor Statistics, unpublished data from the 1989 Current Population Survey.

D1-10. Industry of Employed Older Workers, by Age: 1989

(annual averages) Industry	Age		
	55 to 59	60 to 64	65+
Employed workers (in thousands)	6,854	4,644	3,355
Distribution (in percent)	100	100	100
Agriculture..	3	5	9
Mining	1	0	0
Construction...	6	6	4
Manufacturing-durables	12	11	6
Manufacturing-nondurables	9	7	5
Transportation/public utilities	7	6	3
Trade-wholesale and retail.............................	16	18	21
Finance, insurance, and real estate...............	7	7	8
Services	34	35	40
Public administration....................................	5	5	4

Source: U.S. Department of Labor, Bureau of Labor Statistics, unpublished data from the 1989 Current Population Survey.

D1-11. Occupation of Employed Older Workers, by Age: 1989

(annual averages)

Occupation	Age 55 to 59	Age 60 to 64	Age 65+
Employed workers (in thousands)................	6,854	4,644	3,355
Distribution (in percent)*...............................	100	100	100
Managerial and professional specialty......	28	27	26
Technical, sales, administrative support...	28	30	30
Service..	13	14	18
Precision production, craft, repair............	12	11	7
Operators, fabricators, laborers...............	15	14	10
Farming, forestry, fishing	3	5	9

*May not add to 100 due to rounding.

Source: U.S. Department of Labor, Bureau of Labor Statistics, unpublished data from the 1989 Current Population Survey.

D1-12. Civilian Labor Force Participation Rate, by Age and Sex: 1950-1988, and Projected for 2000

(in percent)

Age and sex	Actual 1950	Actual 1960	Actual 1970	Actual 1980	Actual 1988	Projected* 2000
Total, 16+	59.2	59.4	60.4	63.8	65.9	69.0
Men, 16+	86.4	83.3	79.7	77.4	76.2	75.9
16 to 24	77.3	71.7	69.4	74.4	72.4	73.2
25 to 54	96.5	97.0	95.8	94.2	93.6	93.0
55+	68.6	60.9	55.7	45.6	39.9	38.9
55 to 64	86.9	86.8	83.0	72.1	67.0	68.1
65+	45.8	33.1	26.8	19.0	16.5	14.7
Women, 16+	33.9	37.7	43.3	51.5	56.6	62.6
16 to 24	43.9	42.8	51.3	61.9	64.5	69.4
25 to 54	36.8	42.9	50.1	64	72.7	81.4
55+	18.9	23.6	25.3	22.8	22.3	24.0
55 to 64	27.0	37.2	43.0	41.3	43.5	49.0
65+	9.7	10.8	9.7	8.1	7.9	7.6

*Moderate growth assumptions.

Source: Howard N. Fullerton. "New Labor Force Projections, Spanning 1988 to 2000," *Monthly Labor Review,* Vol. 112, No. 11 (November 1989). Bureau of Labor Statistics, U.S. Department of Labor. Handbook of Labor Statistics. Bulletin 2217 (June 1985).

D1-13. Employment Status of the Civilian Noninstitutional Population, by Age, Sex, and Race: 1992

Age, sex, and race	Civilian noninstitutional population	December 1992									
		Civilian labor force					Not in labor force				
					Unemployed						
		Total	Percent of population	Employed	Number	Percent of labor force	Total	Keeping house	Going to school	Unable to work	Other reasons
TOTAL											
16 years and over	192,509	126,902	65.9	118,073	8,829	7.0	65,607	24,454	9,397	3,838	27,918
16 to 19 years	13,181	6,396	48.5	5,260	1,136	17.8	6,785	455	5,860	23	446
16 to 17 years	6,646	2,512	37.8	2,007	505	20.1	4,134	72	3,891	8	162
18 to 19 years	6,535	3,884	59.4	3,253	631	16.2	2,651	383	1,969	15	284
20 to 24 years	17,735	13,545	76.4	12,110	1,435	10.6	4,190	1,283	2,171	91	645
25 to 54 years	109,631	91,639	83.6	86,029	5,609	6.1	17,993	11,057	1,305	1,663	3,969
25 to 34 years	41,600	34,829	83.7	32,328	2,501	7.2	6,771	4,259	848	391	1,273
25 to 29 years	19,437	16,263	83.7	15,042	1,221	7.5	3,173	1,877	529	141	626
30 to 34 years	22,164	18,566	83.8	17,286	1,280	6.9	3,598	2,382	319	249	647
35 to 44 years	39,839	33,889	85.1	31,875	2,014	5.9	5,950	3,753	326	574	1,297
35 to 39 years	21,117	17,823	84.4	16,667	1,155	6.5	3,295	2,171	199	294	631
40 to 44 years	18,722	16,066	85.8	15,208	859	5.3	2,656	1,582	127	280	667
45 to 54 years	28,192	22,920	81.3	21,826	1,094	4.8	5,272	3,044	131	698	1,398
45 to 49 years	15,607	13,067	83.7	12,460	607	4.6	2,541	1,485	77	358	620
50 to 54 years	12,584	9,853	78.3	9,366	487	4.9	2,731	1,559	53	340	778
55 to 64 years	21,052	11,796	56.0	11,252	544	4.6	9,256	3,783	43	899	4,532
55 to 59 years	10,659	7,114	66.7	6,792	322	4.5	3,545	1,646	35	476	1,388
60 to 64 years	10,393	4,682	45.0	4,460	222	4.7	5,711	2,137	8	422	3,144
65 years and over	30,910	3,527	11.4	3,422	105	3.0	27,383	7,877	19	1,162	18,326
65 to 69 years	10,065	2,128	21.1	2,065	63	3.0	7,936	2,412	8	284	5,233
70 to 74 years	8,470	902	10.7	875	27	3.0	7,567	2,149	2	236	5,180
75 years and over	12,375	496	4.0	481	15	3.0	11,880	3,316	9	642	7,912
Men											
16 years and over	92,060	68,867	74.8	63,809	5,058	7.3	23,193	608	4,662	2,107	15,817
16 to 19 years	6,692	3,358	50.2	2,683	675	20.1	3,334	30	3,050	17	237
16 to 17 years	3,415	1,290	37.8	1,001	289	22.4	2,125	13	2,031	4	77
18 to 19 years	3,276	2,068	63.1	1,682	386	18.7	1,209	17	1,019	13	160
20 to 24 years	8,697	7,129	82.0	6,320	809	11.4	1,568	35	1,134	60	339
25 to 54 years	53,706	49,733	92.6	46,570	3,163	6.4	3,973	315	463	1,062	2,133
25 to 34 years	20,478	19,105	93.3	17,721	1,384	7.2	1,373	111	311	265	685
25 to 29 years	9,545	8,806	92.3	8,132	675	7.7	739	61	229	103	347
30 to 34 years	10,933	10,299	94.2	9,589	710	6.9	634	50	83	162	338
35 to 44 years	19,565	18,279	93.4	17,159	1,120	6.1	1,286	117	122	384	664
35 to 39 years	10,410	9,774	93.9	9,108	666	6.8	636	68	76	184	309
40 to 44 years	9,154	8,505	92.9	8,050	455	5.3	649	48	46	200	355
45 to 54 years	13,663	12,348	90.4	11,690	658	5.3	1,315	87	30	414	784
45 to 49 years	7,591	6,988	92.1	6,631	357	5.1	603	40	22	221	321
50 to 54 years	6,072	5,361	88.3	5,059	301	5.6	712	47	9	193	463
55 to 64 years	9,988	6,624	66.3	6,260	364	5.5	3,364	69	11	518	2,766
55 to 59 years	5,120	3,970	77.5	3,759	211	5.3	1,149	34	8	269	839
60 to 64 years	4,869	2,654	54.5	2,502	152	5.7	2,215	35	3	249	1,928
65 years and over	12,978	2,023	15.6	1,976	48	2.4	10,954	159	4	449	10,342
65 to 69 years	4,604	1,193	25.9	1,159	33	2.8	3,411	44	2	154	3,211
70 to 74 years	3,708	542	14.6	536	6	1.1	3,166	56	–	86	3,024
75 years and over	4,666	289	6.2	280	8	2.9	4,377	58	2	210	4,107
Women											
16 years and over	100,449	58,035	57.8	54,264	3,771	6.5	42,414	23,846	4,735	1,731	12,101
16 to 19 years	6,489	3,038	46.8	2,577	461	15.2	3,451	425	2,810	6	210
16 to 17 years	3,231	1,222	37.8	1,006	216	17.7	2,009	59	1,861	4	85
18 to 19 years	3,258	1,816	55.7	1,571	245	13.5	1,443	366	950	3	125
20 to 24 years	9,038	6,416	71.0	5,791	625	9.7	2,622	1,248	1,037	31	306
25 to 54 years	55,925	41,906	74.9	39,459	2,446	5.8	14,020	10,742	841	600	1,836
25 to 34 years	21,122	15,724	74.4	14,607	1,117	7.1	5,399	4,148	537	126	589
25 to 29 years	9,691	7,457	75.4	6,910	547	7.3	2,435	1,816	300	39	279
30 to 34 years	11,231	8,267	73.6	7,697	570	6.9	2,964	2,331	236	87	309
35 to 44 years	20,275	15,610	77.0	14,716	894	5.7	4,665	3,636	204	190	634
35 to 39 years	10,707	8,049	75.2	7,559	490	6.1	2,658	2,102	123	110	322
40 to 44 years	9,568	7,562	79.0	7,157	404	5.3	2,006	1,534	81	80	311
45 to 54 years	14,528	10,572	72.8	10,136	436	4.1	3,956	2,958	100	284	614
45 to 49 years	8,016	6,079	75.8	5,829	250	4.1	1,937	1,445	56	137	299
50 to 54 years	6,512	4,493	69.0	4,307	186	4.1	2,019	1,512	44	147	315
55 to 64 years	11,064	5,172	46.7	4,992	180	3.5	5,892	3,714	32	381	1,765
55 to 59 years	5,539	3,144	56.8	3,033	111	3.5	2,396	1,612	27	208	549
60 to 64 years	5,525	2,028	36.7	1,959	69	3.4	3,497	2,102	5	173	1,216
65 years and over	17,932	1,503	8.4	1,446	57	3.8	16,429	7,718	15	713	7,984
65 to 69 years	5,461	936	17.1	906	30	3.2	4,525	2,368	6	130	2,022
70 to 74 years	4,762	360	7.6	339	21	5.8	4,401	2,092	2	151	2,156
75 years and over	7,709	207	2.7	200	7	3.2	7,502	3,258	7	432	3,805

D1-13. Employment Status of the Civilian Noninstitutional Population, by Age, Sex, and Race: 1992 (continued)

(Numbers in thousands)

Age, sex, and race	December 1992										
	Civilian noninsti-tutional population	Civilian labor force					Not in labor force				
		Total	Percent of population	Employed	Unemployed		Total	Keeping house	Going to school	Unable to work	Other reasons
					Number	Percent of labor force					
WHITE											
16 years and over	163,259	108,390	66.4	101,847	6,543	6.0	54,869	20,804	7,059	2,917	24,088
16 to 19 years	10,517	5,436	51.7	4,640	796	14.6	5,080	349	4,416	22	293
16 to 17 years	5,301	2,187	41.2	1,822	364	16.7	3,114	53	2,941	7	113
18 to 19 years	5,216	3,250	62.3	2,818	432	13.3	1,966	296	1,475	15	180
20 to 24 years	14,452	11,309	78.3	10,369	940	8.3	3,142	992	1,652	57	441
25 to 54 years	92,454	78,167	84.5	73,916	4,251	5.4	14,287	9,085	932	1,235	3,035
25 to 34 years	34,591	29,386	85.0	27,525	1,861	6.3	5,205	3,415	599	278	912
25 to 29 years	16,085	13,687	85.1	12,780	907	6.6	2,398	1,477	371	108	442
30 to 34 years	18,506	15,699	84.8	14,746	954	6.1	2,807	1,939	228	170	470
35 to 44 years	33,702	28,953	85.9	27,431	1,522	5.3	4,749	3,100	234	429	985
35 to 39 years	17,821	15,184	85.2	14,302	881	5.8	2,637	1,800	141	209	487
40 to 44 years	15,881	13,769	86.7	13,129	640	4.7	2,112	1,300	93	221	498
45 to 54 years	24,162	19,828	82.1	18,960	868	4.4	4,334	2,570	98	528	1,138
45 to 49 years	13,452	11,372	84.5	10,889	483	4.2	2,080	1,243	58	286	493
50 to 54 years	10,710	8,456	79.0	8,071	385	4.6	2,254	1,327	40	242	645
55 to 64 years	18,202	10,287	56.5	9,826	461	4.5	7,915	3,263	42	689	3,922
55 to 59 years	9,159	6,180	67.5	5,900	280	4.5	2,979	1,415	34	353	1,177
60 to 64 years	9,043	4,107	45.4	3,926	181	4.4	4,936	1,848	8	336	2,745
65 years and over	27,634	3,190	11.5	3,095	95	3.0	24,444	7,115	18	914	16,397
65 to 69 years	8,873	1,908	21.5	1,853	56	2.9	6,965	2,157	8	207	4,593
70 to 74 years	7,536	827	11.0	802	24	3.0	6,709	1,914	2	178	4,616
75 years and over	11,225	455	4.1	440	15	3.2	10,770	3,044	8	530	7,188
Men											
16 years and over	78,705	59,562	75.7	55,714	3,848	6.5	19,143	406	3,515	1,619	13,603
16 to 19 years	5,333	2,827	53.0	2,355	472	16.7	2,506	20	2,307	15	164
16 to 17 years	2,717	1,102	40.6	901	201	18.2	1,614	10	1,545	4	55
18 to 19 years	2,616	1,724	65.9	1,453	271	15.7	892	10	762	12	108
20 to 24 years	7,130	5,967	83.7	5,411	556	9.3	1,163	24	887	37	215
25 to 54 years	45,920	43,074	93.8	40,611	2,463	5.7	2,846	189	306	798	1,553
25 to 34 years	17,265	16,347	94.7	15,295	1,052	6.4	917	63	197	183	473
25 to 29 years	8,004	7,500	93.7	6,990	510	6.8	505	32	150	75	248
30 to 34 years	9,260	8,847	95.5	8,305	542	6.1	413	31	48	109	225
35 to 44 years	16,784	15,868	94.5	14,991	877	5.5	916	75	89	295	457
35 to 39 years	8,905	8,452	94.9	7,943	510	6.0	453	51	52	130	219
40 to 44 years	7,879	7,415	94.1	7,048	367	5.0	464	23	37	165	238
45 to 54 years	11,872	10,860	91.5	10,325	534	4.9	1,012	52	19	319	622
45 to 49 years	6,631	6,171	93.1	5,882	289	4.7	460	23	14	182	241
50 to 54 years	5,240	4,689	89.5	4,443	245	5.2	552	28	5	137	382
55 to 64 years	8,704	5,845	67.1	5,530	315	5.4	2,860	51	11	408	2,389
55 to 59 years	4,415	3,481	78.8	3,296	185	5.3	934	24	8	205	697
60 to 64 years	4,289	2,363	55.1	2,234	129	5.5	1,926	27	3	204	1,692
65 years and over	11,617	1,850	15.9	1,807	42	2.3	9,767	121	5	360	9,282
65 to 69 years	4,059	1,074	26.5	1,046	28	2.6	2,985	36	2	115	2,832
70 to 74 years	3,332	502	15.1	496	6	1.2	2,830	42	–	67	2,721
75 years and over	4,226	273	6.5	265	8	3.0	3,952	43	2	178	3,729
Women											
16 years and over	84,555	48,828	57.7	46,133	2,695	5.5	35,726	20,398	3,545	1,298	10,485
16 to 19 years	5,184	2,610	50.3	2,285	324	12.4	2,574	329	2,109	6	129
16 to 17 years	2,584	1,084	41.9	921	163	15.1	1,500	43	1,396	4	58
18 to 19 years	2,599	1,526	58.7	1,365	161	10.6	1,074	286	713	3	71
20 to 24 years	7,321	5,342	73.0	4,958	384	7.2	1,979	968	765	20	226
25 to 54 years	46,534	35,093	75.4	33,305	1,788	5.1	11,441	8,896	626	437	1,482
25 to 34 years	17,326	13,039	75.3	12,230	809	6.2	4,287	3,352	402	95	439
25 to 29 years	8,080	6,187	76.6	5,790	397	6.4	1,893	1,444	222	33	194
30 to 34 years	9,246	6,852	74.1	6,440	412	6.0	2,394	1,908	180	62	245
35 to 44 years	16,918	13,085	77.3	12,440	645	4.9	3,832	3,026	145	134	528
35 to 39 years	8,916	6,731	75.5	6,360	372	5.5	2,184	1,749	89	78	268
40 to 44 years	8,002	6,354	79.4	6,081	273	4.3	1,648	1,277	56	56	259
45 to 54 years	12,290	8,969	73.0	8,634	334	3.7	3,322	2,518	79	209	516
45 to 49 years	6,821	5,201	76.3	5,007	194	3.7	1,620	1,219	44	103	252
50 to 54 years	5,469	3,768	68.9	3,628	140	3.7	1,702	1,299	35	105	263
55 to 64 years	9,498	4,443	46.8	4,296	146	3.3	5,055	3,212	31	280	1,533
55 to 59 years	4,744	2,699	56.9	2,604	95	3.5	2,044	1,391	25	148	480
60 to 64 years	4,754	1,744	36.7	1,692	51	2.9	3,011	1,821	5	132	1,053
65 years and over	16,017	1,341	8.4	1,288	53	3.9	14,677	6,994	13	554	7,115
65 to 69 years	4,815	835	17.3	807	28	3.3	3,980	2,121	6	92	1,761
70 to 74 years	4,203	324	7.7	306	18	5.6	3,879	1,872	2	111	1,894
75 years and over	7,000	182	2.6	175	7	3.6	6,818	3,001	6	352	3,459

D1-13. Employment Status of the Civilian Noninstitutional Population, by Age, Sex, and Race: 1992 (continued)

(Numbers in thousands)

Age, sex, and race	Civilian noninstitutional population	December 1992								
		Civilian labor force					Not in labor force			
		Total	Percent of population	Employed	Unemployed		Total	Keeping house	Going to school	Unable to work	Other reasons
					Number	Percent of labor force					
BLACK										
16 years and over	22,131	13,852	62.6	11,959	1,893	13.7	8,279	2,752	1,633	831	3,062
16 to 19 years	2,081	742	35.7	461	281	37.8	1,339	96	1,102	1	140
16 to 17 years	1,058	254	24.0	142	112	44.2	804	18	744	–	41
18 to 19 years	1,023	488	47.7	320	168	34.5	535	77	358	1	99
20 to 24 years	2,500	1,723	68.9	1,301	422	24.5	777	246	326	32	172
25 to 54 years	12,743	10,016	78.6	8,892	1,124	11.2	2,727	1,399	204	382	742
25 to 34 years	5,317	4,168	78.4	3,616	552	13.2	1,149	611	137	100	301
25 to 29 years	2,575	2,003	77.8	1,724	279	13.9	572	314	82	26	150
30 to 34 years	2,742	2,165	79.0	1,892	273	12.6	577	297	55	74	151
35 to 44 years	4,529	3,628	80.1	3,230	398	11.0	901	468	52	129	251
35 to 39 years	2,486	1,985	79.9	1,751	234	11.8	501	266	35	76	124
40 to 44 years	2,043	1,643	80.4	1,479	164	10.0	400	202	18	53	127
45 to 54 years	2,897	2,220	76.6	2,046	174	7.9	677	320	15	153	190
45 to 49 years	1,543	1,212	78.6	1,125	87	7.2	331	161	11	61	99
50 to 54 years	1,354	1,008	74.4	920	88	8.7	346	159	4	92	91
55 to 64 years	2,158	1,119	51.9	1,060	59	5.3	1,038	378	1	186	474
55 to 59 years	1,134	669	59.0	646	23	3.4	466	181	2	112	171
60 to 64 years	1,023	450	44.0	414	36	8.0	573	197	–	74	303
65 years and over	2,650	252	9.5	245	7	2.9	2,398	633	–	230	1,534
65 to 69 years	950	161	17.0	156	5	3.2	789	214	–	70	505
70 to 74 years	743	59	7.9	56	3	(¹)	684	184	–	55	444
75 years and over	957	32	3.4	33	–	(¹)	925	235	–	105	586
Men										
16 years and over	9,978	6,823	68.4	5,838	985	14.4	3,155	172	767	433	1,783
16 to 19 years	1,036	403	38.9	239	164	40.7	633	9	556	1	67
16 to 17 years	536	142	26.6	78	64	45.3	393	2	372	–	18
18 to 19 years	500	260	52.1	161	100	38.2	240	7	183	1	49
20 to 24 years	1,163	877	75.4	671	207	23.5	286	12	147	22	105
25 to 54 years	5,716	4,841	84.7	4,264	577	11.9	876	109	64	239	464
25 to 34 years	2,411	2,074	86.0	1,791	283	13.6	337	41	47	72	178
25 to 29 years	1,166	999	85.6	854	145	14.5	168	28	32	23	85
30 to 34 years	1,245	1,076	86.4	938	138	12.8	170	13	15	49	94
35 to 44 years	2,034	1,725	84.8	1,527	198	11.5	309	39	16	82	172
35 to 39 years	1,120	965	86.1	834	131	13.5	155	16	10	51	78
40 to 44 years	914	760	83.2	693	66	8.9	154	23	6	30	94
45 to 54 years	1,271	1,041	81.9	945	96	9.2	230	29	1	85	114
45 to 49 years	683	574	84.0	522	51	8.9	110	13	1	32	63
50 to 54 years	588	468	79.6	423	45	9.6	120	15	–	53	51
55 to 64 years	985	577	58.6	543	35	6.0	408	12	–	91	305
55 to 59 years	535	352	65.8	335	17	4.9	183	8	–	54	121
60 to 64 years	450	225	50.0	207	18	7.8	225	4	–	36	185
65 years and over	1,077	125	11.6	122	3	2.1	952	30	–	80	842
65 to 69 years	427	83	19.4	80	3	3.9	344	5	–	35	305
70 to 74 years	300	31	10.5	31	–	(¹)	269	12	–	17	240
75 years and over	349	10	2.9	11	–	(¹)	339	14	–	28	297
Women										
16 years and over	12,153	7,030	57.8	6,122	908	12.9	5,124	2,580	866	398	1,279
16 to 19 years	1,045	339	32.5	223	116	34.3	706	87	546	–	73
16 to 17 years	522	112	21.4	64	48	42.6	410	16	372	–	23
18 to 19 years	523	227	43.5	159	69	30.2	296	71	174	–	50
20 to 24 years	1,336	846	63.3	630	215	25.5	491	235	179	10	67
25 to 54 years	7,026	5,175	73.7	4,628	547	10.6	1,851	1,290	140	143	278
25 to 34 years	2,906	2,094	72.1	1,825	269	12.8	812	570	90	28	123
25 to 29 years	1,409	1,005	71.3	870	134	13.4	404	285	50	3	65
30 to 34 years	1,497	1,089	72.8	955	135	12.4	408	285	40	25	57
35 to 44 years	2,495	1,903	76.3	1,703	200	10.5	592	429	36	48	79
35 to 39 years	1,366	1,021	74.7	917	104	10.2	346	250	25	25	46
40 to 44 years	1,128	882	78.2	786	96	10.9	246	179	11	23	33
45 to 54 years	1,626	1,178	72.5	1,100	78	6.6	448	291	14	67	76
45 to 49 years	860	638	74.3	603	35	5.6	221	147	9	28	36
50 to 54 years	766	540	70.5	497	43	7.9	226	144	4	39	39
55 to 64 years	1,172	542	46.2	518	24	4.5	630	366	1	95	168
55 to 59 years	599	316	52.8	311	6	1.8	283	173	2	57	50
60 to 64 years	573	225	39.3	207	19	8.3	348	193	–	37	118
65 years and over	1,573	128	8.1	123	5	3.6	1,445	603	–	150	692
65 to 69 years	523	78	14.9	76	2	2.6	445	210	–	36	200
70 to 74 years	442	27	6.2	25	3	(¹)	415	173	–	38	204
75 years and over	608	22	3.6	22	–	(¹)	586	220	–	76	289

¹Data not shown where base is less than 75,000.

D1-14. Employed Civilians, by Age, Sex, and Class of Worker: 1992

(In thousands)

Age and sex	December 1992								
	Nonagricultural industries						Agriculture		
	Wage and salary workers				Self-employed workers	Unpaid family workers	Wage and salary workers	Self-employed workers	Unpaid family workers
	Total	Private household workers	Government	Other					
Total, 16 years and over	106,221	1,067	18,334	86,820	8,715	206	1,572	1,279	80
16 to 19 years	4,986	146	219	4,621	67	12	161	10	24
16 to 17 years	1,905	103	53	1,748	18	8	57	5	14
18 to 19 years	3,081	43	166	2,873	48	4	105	5	10
20 to 24 years	11,551	155	1,108	10,289	255	9	250	45	2
25 to 34 years	29,803	187	4,169	25,448	1,748	36	499	229	14
35 to 44 years	28,562	205	5,700	22,657	2,663	58	318	269	5
45 to 54 years	19,153	135	4,688	14,331	2,172	57	174	257	13
55 to 64 years	9,607	148	2,040	7,418	1,217	27	122	270	9
55 to 59 years	5,879	81	1,307	4,491	699	13	76	120	5
60 to 64 years	3,728	68	733	2,927	519	14	46	149	4
65 years and over	2,559	92	411	2,056	593	7	49	200	13
Men, 16 years and over	55,754	120	8,194	47,439	5,673	43	1,229	1,079	31
16 to 19 years	2,492	25	97	2,370	28	8	127	10	18
16 to 17 years	923	22	16	884	6	6	49	5	13
18 to 19 years	1,569	3	80	1,486	23	2	78	5	5
20 to 24 years	5,915	33	488	5,393	154	6	205	41	–
25 to 34 years	15,978	22	1,946	14,010	1,154	11	389	185	5
35 to 44 years	14,982	17	2,401	12,564	1,701	9	248	217	1
45 to 54 years	9,950	11	2,134	7,806	1,411	3	122	201	3
55 to 64 years	5,081	8	933	4,140	835	2	100	243	–
55 to 59 years	3,113	2	565	2,546	477	1	63	105	–
60 to 64 years	1,968	5	368	1,595	358	1	37	138	–
65 years and over	1,357	6	195	1,156	390	4	38	182	5
Women, 16 years and over	50,467	947	10,140	39,381	3,042	163	344	200	49
16 to 19 years	2,494	121	122	2,251	38	4	34	–	6
16 to 17 years	982	81	37	864	13	2	8	–	1
18 to 19 years	1,512	40	85	1,386	26	2	27	–	4
20 to 24 years	5,636	121	620	4,895	101	3	45	3	2
25 to 34 years	13,825	165	2,222	11,438	593	25	110	44	9
35 to 44 years	13,580	188	3,299	10,094	962	49	70	51	4
45 to 54 years	9,203	124	2,554	6,525	762	53	51	57	10
55 to 64 years	4,526	141	1,107	3,278	382	25	22	27	10
55 to 59 years	2,766	79	742	1,945	222	12	13	15	5
60 to 64 years	1,760	62	365	1,332	161	13	9	12	5
65 years and over	1,202	86	217	900	203	4	11	18	8

D1-15. Employed Civilians in Agriculture and Nonagricultural Industries, by Age and Sex: 1991 and 1992

(In thousands)

Industry and age	Total		Men		Women	
	Dec. 1991	Dec. 1992	Dec. 1991	Dec. 1992	Dec. 1991	Dec. 1992
All industries	116,549	118,073	63,025	63,809	53,524	54,264
16 to 19 years	5,186	5,260	2,557	2,683	2,628	2,577
16 to 17 years	1,945	2,007	930	1,001	1,015	1,006
18 to 19 years	3,240	3,253	1,627	1,682	1,613	1,571
20 to 24 years	12,024	12,110	6,265	6,320	5,759	5,791
25 to 54 years	84,800	86,029	46,009	46,570	38,791	39,459
25 to 34 years	32,731	32,328	18,010	17,721	14,720	14,607
35 to 44 years	31,530	31,875	16,887	17,159	14,643	14,716
45 to 54 years	20,539	21,826	11,112	11,690	9,428	10,136
55 to 64 years	11,264	11,252	6,350	6,260	4,913	4,992
55 to 59 years	6,741	6,792	3,770	3,759	2,970	3,033
60 to 64 years	4,523	4,460	2,580	2,502	1,943	1,959
65 years and over	3,276	3,422	1,843	1,976	1,432	1,446
Agriculture	2,862	2,931	2,239	2,339	623	592
16 to 19 years	131	195	106	155	26	40
16 to 17 years	64	76	44	67	20	9
18 to 19 years	67	119	61	88	6	31
20 to 24 years	275	296	233	245	42	51
25 to 54 years	1,743	1,777	1,320	1,371	423	406
25 to 34 years	709	741	548	579	161	163
35 to 44 years	587	592	439	466	148	125
45 to 54 years	447	444	333	326	114	118
55 to 64 years	461	401	366	342	95	59
55 to 59 years	251	201	187	168	65	33
60 to 64 years	209	200	179	175	30	25
65 years and over	252	262	214	225	38	37
Nonagricultural industries	113,687	115,142	60,785	61,470	52,901	53,672
16 to 19 years	5,054	5,064	2,452	2,528	2,602	2,537
16 to 17 years	1,881	1,931	886	934	995	997
18 to 19 years	3,173	3,133	1,566	1,594	1,607	1,540
20 to 24 years	11,749	11,814	6,032	6,074	5,718	5,740
25 to 54 years	83,057	84,252	44,688	45,199	38,368	39,053
25 to 34 years	32,021	31,586	17,463	17,142	14,559	14,444
35 to 44 years	30,943	31,283	16,447	16,692	14,495	14,591
45 to 54 years	20,093	21,382	10,778	11,364	9,314	10,018
55 to 64 years	10,803	10,851	5,984	5,918	4,819	4,933
55 to 59 years	6,489	6,591	3,583	3,591	2,906	3,000
60 to 64 years	4,314	4,261	2,401	2,327	1,913	1,934
65 years and over	3,024	3,160	1,629	1,751	1,394	1,409

D1-16. Persons at Work in Nonagricultural Industries, by Sex, Age, Race, Marital Status, and Full- or Part-Time Status: 1992

(Numbers in thousands)

Sex, age, race, and marital status	December 1992							
	Total at work	On part time for economic reasons	On voluntary part time	On full-time schedules			Average hours, total at work	Average hours, workers on full-time schedules
				Total	40 hours or less	41 hours or more		
TOTAL								
Total, 16 years and over	111,288	5,935	15,609	89,744	55,956	33,788	39.2	43.8
16 to 19 years	4,953	418	3,344	1,191	915	276	22.6	39.7
16 to 17 years	1,886	43	1,725	119	105	14	16.2	35.9
18 to 19 years	3,067	375	1,620	1,072	810	262	26.5	40.1
20 years and over	106,335	5,518	12,264	88,553	55,041	33,512	40.0	43.8
20 to 24 years	11,492	942	2,608	7,942	5,512	2,430	35.4	42.1
25 years and over	94,843	4,576	9,656	80,611	49,529	31,082	40.5	44.0
25 to 44 years	60,916	3,043	5,073	52,800	31,965	20,835	41.1	44.1
45 to 64 years	30,957	1,399	3,126	26,432	16,619	9,813	40.6	43.9
65 years and over	2,971	134	1,459	1,378	943	435	28.9	42.1
Men, 16 years and over	59,546	2,842	4,860	51,843	28,626	23,217	42.0	45.3
16 to 19 years	2,468	205	1,587	676	521	156	23.5	39.2
16 to 17 years	906	20	815	71	65	6	16.8	(¹)
18 to 19 years	1,562	186	771	605	455	150	27.4	39.7
20 years and over	57,077	2,637	3,273	51,167	28,106	23,061	42.8	45.4
20 to 24 years	5,924	480	1,107	4,338	2,824	1,514	37.0	43.0
25 years and over	51,153	2,158	2,166	46,829	25,282	21,548	43.5	45.6
25 to 44 years	32,941	1,489	732	30,720	16,190	14,530	44.1	45.7
45 to 64 years	16,578	619	689	15,270	8,527	6,743	43.5	45.5
65 years and over	1,635	49	745	841	567	273	30.4	42.3
Women, 16 years and over	51,742	3,093	10,749	37,901	27,330	10,571	36.0	41.7
16 to 19 years	2,485	212	1,757	515	394	121	21.7	40.4
16 to 17 years	979	23	909	47	39	8	15.6	(¹)
18 to 19 years	1,505	190	848	467	355	112	25.6	40.7
20 years and over	49,258	2,880	8,991	37,386	26,936	10,451	36.7	41.7
20 to 24 years	5,568	462	1,501	3,605	2,688	917	33.6	41.0
25 years and over	43,690	2,418	7,490	33,782	24,248	9,534	37.1	41.8
25 to 44 years	27,975	1,554	4,340	22,081	15,778	6,303	37.5	41.9
45 to 64 years	14,379	779	2,435	11,165	8,097	3,068	37.2	41.7
65 years and over	1,336	85	714	537	376	161	27.2	41.8
RACE								
White, 16 years and over	95,831	4,755	13,941	77,135	46,492	30,643	39.3	44.0
Men	51,901	2,313	4,240	45,349	24,063	21,286	42.3	45.6
Women	43,930	2,442	9,702	31,787	22,429	9,357	35.8	41.8
Black, 16 years and over	11,394	927	1,123	9,344	7,224	2,120	38.2	41.9
Men	5,499	420	403	4,676	3,404	1,272	39.6	42.9
Women	5,895	507	720	4,668	3,820	848	36.8	40.9
MARITAL STATUS								
Men, 16 years and over:								
Married, spouse present	38,113	1,293	1,551	35,269	18,542	16,727	44.0	45.9
Widowed, divorced, or separated	6,243	416	280	5,548	3,180	2,368	42.1	44.8
Single (never married)	15,190	1,134	3,029	11,026	6,904	4,122	37.1	43.7
Women, 16 years and over:								
Married, spouse present	28,937	1,540	6,039	21,358	15,738	5,619	36.0	41.4
Widowed, divorced, or separated	10,275	674	1,288	8,313	5,801	2,511	38.3	42.2
Single (never married)	12,530	878	3,421	8,231	5,790	2,441	34.1	42.0

¹Data not shown where base is less than 75,000.

D1-17. Labor Force Participation Rates for Men Age 60 to 64 and 65+ in Selected Countries: 1988

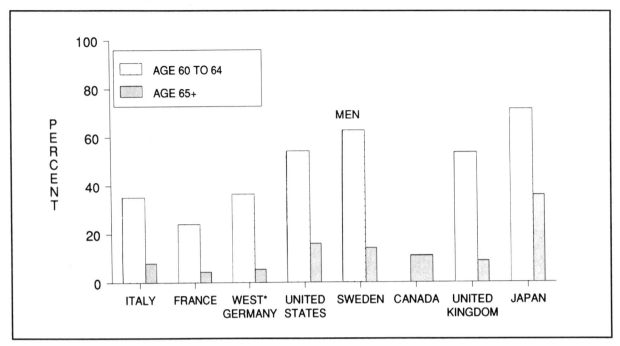

*Rates for West Germany are for 1987.
Source: Organization for Economic Co-operation and Development (OECD) Labor Force Statistics, 1988. Paris: OECD (1990).

D1-18. Labor Force Participation Rates for Women Age 60 to 64 and 65+ in Selected Countries: 1988

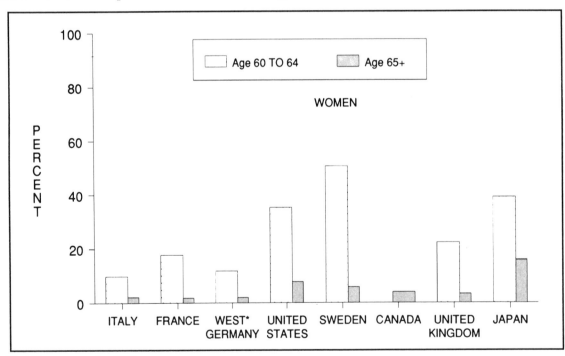

*Rates for West Germany are for 1987.
Source: Organization for Economic Co-operation and Development (OECD) Labor Force Statistics, 1988. Paris: OECD (1990).

D1-19. Work Experience During Year, by Selected Characteristics and Poverty Status in 1991 of Civilians 16 Years Old and Over

[Numbers in thousands. Persons as of March of the following year.

Characteristic	Worked during year									Did not work during year		
	All workers			Worked year-round full-time			Not year-round full-time					
	Total	Below poverty level		Total	Below poverty level		Total	Below poverty level		Total	Below poverty level	
		Number	Percent of total		Number	Percent of total		Number	Percent of total		Number	Percent of total
ALL PERSONS												
Both Sexes												
Total	132 571	9 175	6.9	79 574	2 076	2.6	52 997	7 099	13.4	58 450	13 323	22.8
16 to 17 years	2 868	286	10.0	57	10	(B)	2 811	277	9.8	3 733	877	23.5
18 to 64 years	124 953	8 674	6.9	78 040	2 010	2.6	46 913	6 665	14.2	28 877	8 879	30.7
18 to 24 years	19 417	2 235	11.5	6 532	293	4.5	12 885	1 942	15.1	4 886	1 868	38.2
25 to 34 years	36 072	2 970	8.2	23 237	701	3.0	12 835	2 269	17.7	6 011	2 585	43.0
35 to 54 years	56 426	2 916	5.2	40 153	882	2.2	16 273	2 034	12.5	9 872	2 841	28.8
55 to 64 years	13 038	553	4.2	8 118	134	1.6	4 920	419	8.5	8 107	1 586	19.6
65 years and over	4 750	214	4.5	1 477	57	3.8	3 273	158	4.8	25 840	3 567	13.8
Male												
Total	70 900	4 469	6.3	47 124	1 228	2.6	23 776	3 241	13.6	20 337	3 902	19.2
16 to 17 years	1 533	147	9.6	42	4	(B)	1 491	143	9.6	1 842	380	20.6
18 to 64 years	66 581	4 228	6.3	46 109	1 197	2.6	20 472	3 031	14.8	8 481	2 601	30.7
18 to 24 years	9 980	1 049	10.5	3 539	173	4.9	6 442	876	13.6	1 977	566	28.6
25 to 34 years	19 358	1 417	7.3	13 708	425	3.1	5 650	992	17.6	1 374	619	45.1
35 to 54 years	29 951	1 492	5.0	23 782	533	2.2	6 169	959	15.5	2 392	894	37.4
55 to 64 years	7 293	270	3.7	5 081	66	1.3	2 212	205	9.3	2 738	523	19.1
65 years and over	2 786	94	3.4	972	28	2.8	1 813	66	3.7	10 014	921	9.2
Female												
Total	61 670	4 706	7.6	32 450	848	2.6	29 221	3 858	13.2	38 113	9 421	24.7
16 to 17 years	1 335	139	10.5	15	6	(B)	1 320	134	10.1	1 891	498	26.3
18 to 64 years	58 372	4 446	7.6	31 931	813	2.5	26 441	3 633	13.7	20 396	6 278	30.8
18 to 24 years	9 437	1 187	12.6	2 993	120	4.0	6 444	1 066	16.5	2 909	1 300	44.7
25 to 34 years	16 714	1 553	9.3	9 529	276	2.9	7 185	1 277	17.8	4 638	1 966	42.4
35 to 54 years	26 476	1 424	5.4	16 371	349	2.1	10 105	1 075	10.6	7 481	1 948	26.0
55 to 64 years	5 745	283	4.9	3 037	68	2.2	2 708	214	7.9	5 369	1 064	19.8
65 years and over	1 964	120	6.1	505	29	5.8	1 460	91	6.2	15 826	2 646	16.7
Household Relationship												
Persons 16 to 64 years old	127 821	8 961	7.0	78 097	2 019	2.6	49 724	6 941	14.0	32 610	9 756	29.9
In families	104 344	5 952	5.7	62 744	1 551	2.5	41 600	4 401	10.6	28 750	7 230	25.1
Householder	48 322	3 765	7.8	36 350	1 188	3.3	11 973	2 577	21.5	7 019	3 187	45.4
In families with related children under 18 years	58 885	4 944	8.4	34 194	1 328	3.9	24 691	3 616	14.6	16 893	5 719	33.9
Householder	29 695	3 301	11.1	22 210	1 052	4.7	7 485	2 249	30.0	3 986	2 681	67.2
In families with related children under 6 years	25 549	2 770	10.8	15 336	745	4.9	10 213	2 025	19.8	8 101	3 451	42.6
Householder	14 035	1 934	13.8	10 278	610	5.9	3 756	1 324	35.2	2 287	1 725	75.4
In married couple families	86 709	3 194	3.7	53 354	1 020	1.9	33 355	2 174	6.5	21 391	3 315	15.5
Husband	39 076	1 811	4.6	30 955	758	2.4	8 121	1 053	13.0	3 342	833	24.9
Wife	32 886	999	3.0	17 881	192	1.1	15 005	807	5.4	12 541	1 804	14.4
Related children[1]	13 519	318	2.4	3 890	47	1.2	9 629	272	2.8	4 988	591	11.9
Other	1 228	66	5.4	627	24	3.8	601	42	7.0	521	87	16.7
In married couple families with related children under 18 years	49 164	2 562	5.2	29 263	859	2.9	19 901	1 704	8.6	11 909	2 391	20.1
Husband	23 341	1 504	6.4	18 804	670	3.6	4 537	834	18.4	1 145	528	46.1
Wife	18 383	761	4.1	8 916	137	1.5	9 468	625	6.6	6 793	1 318	19.4
Related children[1]	6 662	238	3.6	1 118	29	2.6	5 544	210	3.8	3 590	477	13.3
Other	777	59	7.6	425	24	5.6	353	35	10.0	380	69	18.1
In married couple families with related children under 6 years	21 815	1 537	7.0	13 526	493	3.6	8 289	1 044	12.6	5 638	1 472	26.1
Husband	11 614	991	8.5	9 255	415	4.5	2 359	575	24.4	546	314	57.5
Wife	8 446	417	4.9	3 663	51	1.4	4 783	366	7.7	4 088	913	22.3
Other	530	50	9.5	288	21	7.3	242	29	12.1	248	61	24.7
In families with female householder, no spouse present	13 263	2 413	18.2	6 788	451	6.6	6 475	1 961	30.3	6 215	3 644	58.6
Householder	7 273	1 748	24.0	4 443	390	8.8	2 831	1 358	48.0	2 871	2 191	76.3
Other	5 990	665	11.1	2 346	61	2.6	3 644	604	16.6	3 344	1 453	43.5
In families with female householder, no spouse present, with related children under 18 years	7 866	2 129	27.1	3 793	409	10.8	4 073	1 720	42.2	4 458	3 163	70.9
Householder	5 370	1 642	30.6	3 062	359	11.7	2 308	1 283	55.6	2 356	2 028	86.1
Related children[1]	1 938	387	19.9	473	29	6.1	1 466	358	24.4	1 767	947	53.6
Other	557	101	18.1	258	21	8.3	299	79	26.5	334	187	55.9
In families with female householder, no spouse present, with related children under 6 years	2 957	1 099	37.2	1 339	225	16.8	1 618	874	54.0	2 278	1 884	82.7
Householder	2 073	868	41.9	1 008	188	18.7	1 065	680	63.8	1 450	1 320	91.0
Related children[1]	555	160	28.8	179	21	11.6	376	139	37.0	599	427	71.2
Other	329	71	21.7	152	16	10.3	177	56	31.5	228	137	60.1
In unrelated subfamilies	565	185	32.7	270	22	8.2	294	163	55.3	240	170	70.7
Unrelated individuals	22 911	2 824	12.3	15 083	446	3.0	7 829	2 378	30.4	3 620	2 356	65.1
Male	13 311	1 627	12.2	8 710	282	3.2	4 600	1 345	29.2	1 587	917	57.8
Householder	9 167	770	8.4	6 381	145	2.3	2 786	625	22.4	1 049	531	50.6
Female	9 601	1 197	12.5	6 372	164	2.6	3 229	1 033	32.0	2 032	1 439	70.8
Householder	7 029	607	8.6	4 909	96	2.0	2 120	511	24.1	1 436	922	64.2

See footnote at end of table.

D1-19. Work Experience During Year, by Selected Characteristics and Poverty Status in 1991 of Civilians 16 Years Old and Over (continued)

[Numbers in thousands. Persons as of March of the following year.

Characteristic	Worked during year									Did not work during year		
	All workers			Worked year-round full-time			Not year-round full-time					
	Total	Below poverty level		Total	Below poverty level		Total	Below poverty level		Total	Below poverty level	
		Number	Percent of total		Number	Percent of total		Number	Percent of total		Number	Percent of total
WHITE												
Both Sexes												
Total	113 900	6 734	5.9	68 745	1 621	2.4	45 154	5 113	11.3	48 296	8 858	18.3
16 to 17 years	2 559	207	8.1	54	10	(B)	2 505	197	7.9	2 704	506	18.7
18 to 64 years	107 116	6 379	6.0	67 380	1 576	2.3	39 736	4 803	12.1	22 519	5 698	25.3
18 to 24 years	16 529	1 682	10.2	5 748	240	4.2	10 781	1 442	13.4	3 312	1 098	33.2
25 to 34 years	30 463	2 175	7.1	19 811	548	2.8	10 652	1 628	15.3	4 527	1 685	37.2
35 to 54 years	48 712	2 134	4.4	34 676	697	2.0	14 036	1 437	10.2	7 816	1 790	22.9
55 to 64 years	11 412	387	3.4	7 145	91	1.3	4 267	296	6.9	6 864	1 124	16.4
65 years and over	4 225	148	3.5	1 312	35	2.7	2 914	113	3.9	23 072	2 654	11.5
Male												
Total	61 538	3 427	5.6	41 464	1 032	2.5	20 074	2 396	11.9	16 499	2 490	15.1
16 to 17 years	1 375	99	7.2	40	4	(B)	1 335	96	7.2	1 322	215	16.3
18 to 64 years	57 666	3 269	5.7	40 562	1 013	2.5	17 104	2 256	13.2	6 244	1 640	26.3
18 to 24 years	8 505	824	9.7	3 109	152	4.9	5 396	672	12.5	1 297	298	23.0
25 to 34 years	16 519	1 115	6.7	11 894	361	3.0	4 625	754	16.3	907	380	41.9
35 to 54 years	26 228	1 144	4.4	21 029	451	2.1	5 199	693	13.3	1 728	584	33.8
55 to 64 years	6 414	186	2.9	4 530	49	1.1	1 884	137	7.3	2 312	378	16.3
65 years and over	2 497	59	2.4	863	15	1.8	1 635	43	2.7	8 934	634	7.1
Female												
Total	52 362	3 306	6.3	27 281	589	2.2	25 081	2 717	10.8	31 796	6 368	20.0
16 to 17 years	1 184	107	9.1	14	6	(B)	1 170	102	8.7	1 383	291	21.0
18 to 64 years	49 450	3 110	6.3	26 818	563	2.1	22 632	2 546	11.3	16 275	4 057	24.9
18 to 24 years	8 024	858	10.7	2 639	88	3.3	5 385	770	14.3	2 015	801	39.7
25 to 34 years	13 944	1 061	7.6	7 917	187	2.4	6 027	874	14.5	3 621	1 305	36.0
35 to 54 years	22 484	990	4.4	13 647	246	1.8	8 837	744	8.4	6 088	1 205	19.8
55 to 64 years	4 998	201	4.0	2 615	42	1.6	2 383	158	6.7	4 551	746	16.4
65 years and over	1 728	89	5.2	449	20	4.4	1 279	69	5.4	14 138	2 020	14.3
Household Relationship												
Persons 16 to 64 years old	109 674	6 586	6.0	67 434	1 585	2.4	42 241	5 000	11.8	25 223	6 204	24.6
In families	89 783	4 207	4.7	54 349	1 217	2.2	35 434	2 990	8.4	22 399	4 443	19.8
Householder	41 602	2 653	6.4	31 727	923	2.9	9 875	1 730	17.5	5 124	1 880	36.7
In families with related children under 18 years	49 752	3 457	6.9	29 007	1 028	3.5	20 745	2 429	11.7	12 536	3 420	27.3
Householder	24 996	2 289	9.2	19 086	814	4.3	5 910	1 475	25.0	2 543	1 520	59.8
In families with related children under 6 years	21 263	1 938	9.1	12 908	569	4.4	8 355	1 369	16.4	5 925	2 056	34.7
Householder	11 740	1 352	11.5	8 809	467	5.3	2 931	885	30.2	1 399	967	69.1
In married couple families	77 292	2 689	3.5	47 485	898	1.9	29 807	1 791	6.0	18 338	2 569	14.0
Husband	35 107	1 545	4.4	27 932	677	2.4	7 175	868	12.1	2 854	634	22.2
Wife	29 293	843	2.9	15 635	162	1.0	13 658	681	5.0	11 213	1 464	13.1
Related children[1]	11 960	249	2.1	3 435	38	1.1	8 526	211	2.5	3 878	406	10.5
Other	932	52	5.6	483	22	4.5	448	31	6.9	390	65	16.8
In married couple families with related children under 18 years	43 167	2 179	5.0	25 524	753	2.9	17 643	1 426	8.1	9 944	1 832	18.4
Husband	20 690	1 287	6.2	16 760	594	3.5	3 930	692	17.6	871	385	44.2
Wife	16 087	647	4.0	7 522	114	1.5	8 565	533	6.2	5 969	1 059	17.7
Related children[1]	5 804	195	3.4	923	23	2.5	4 881	173	3.5	2 814	338	12.0
Other	586	49	8.4	319	22	6.8	267	27	10.3	290	50	17.2
In married couple families with related children under 6 years	18 962	1 314	6.9	11 750	436	3.7	7 212	878	12.2	4 737	1 121	23.7
Husband	10 278	855	8.3	8 258	370	4.5	2 020	485	24.0	389	216	55.5
Wife	7 346	352	4.8	3 026	42	1.4	4 320	311	7.2	3 622	739	20.4
Other	401	42	10.5	218	19	8.7	183	23	12.6	191	42	22.2
In families with female householder, no spouse present	9 077	1 277	14.1	4 824	256	5.3	4 253	1 021	24.0	3 320	1 722	51.9
Householder	4 940	952	19.3	3 115	216	6.9	1 825	736	40.3	1 622	1 148	70.8
Other	4 137	325	7.9	1 709	40	2.3	2 428	285	11.7	1 698	574	33.8
In families with female householder, no spouse present, with related children under 18 years	5 099	1 096	21.5	2 568	228	8.9	2 531	868	34.3	2 236	1 488	66.6
Householder	3 534	880	24.9	2 099	197	9.4	1 435	682	47.5	1 280	1 062	83.0
Related children[1]	1 251	168	13.4	315	16	5.1	936	152	16.2	815	355	43.5
Other	313	48	15.4	154	14	9.1	160	34	21.6	142	71	50.4
In families with female householder, no spouse present, with related children under 6 years	1 675	525	31.4	784	110	14.1	891	415	46.6	1 068	881	82.5
Householder	1 201	439	36.5	583	89	15.3	619	350	56.5	773	695	89.9
Related children[1]	283	52	18.5	109	8	7.4	174	44	25.5	199	133	66.7
Other	190	34	17.9	92	13	14.4	99	21	21.2	95	53	55.7
In unrelated subfamilies	472	146	30.9	237	19	8.2	235	126	53.8	178	128	71.6
Unrelated individuals	19 420	2 233	11.5	12 848	349	2.7	6 572	1 884	28.7	2 646	1 633	61.7
Male	11 141	1 235	11.1	7 373	211	2.9	3 768	1 024	27.2	1 123	612	54.5
Householder	7 836	595	7.6	5 482	118	2.2	2 354	477	20.3	805	373	46.4
Female	8 279	998	12.1	5 475	138	2.5	2 804	860	30.7	1 523	1 021	67.0
Householder	6 016	490	8.1	4 187	77	1.8	1 829	412	22.5	1 091	648	59.4

See footnote at end of table.

D1-19. Work Experience During Year, by Selected Characteristics and Poverty Status in 1991 of Civilians 16 Years Old and Over (continued)

[Numbers in thousands. Persons as of March of the following year.]

Characteristic	Worked during year									Did not work during year		
	All workers			Worked year-round full-time			Not year-round full-time					
		Below poverty level			Below poverty level			Below poverty level			Below poverty level	
	Total	Number	Percent of total	Total	Number	Percent of total	Total	Number	Percent of total	Total	Number	Percent of total
BLACK												
Both Sexes												
Total	13 933	2 022	14.5	8 018	383	4.8	5 916	1 638	27.7	7 921	3 837	48.4
16 to 17 years	221	59	26.5	3	–	(B)	218	59	26.9	823	320	38.9
18 to 64 years	13 324	1 910	14.3	7 907	366	4.6	5 417	1 544	28.5	4 879	2 690	55.1
18 to 24 years	2 262	458	20.3	632	48	7.5	1 630	410	25.2	1 118	746	66.7
25 to 34 years	4 229	679	16.1	2 593	142	5.5	1 637	537	32.8	1 583	895	56.6
35 to 54 years	5 607	637	11.4	3 960	144	3.6	1 647	494	30.0	940	389	41.4
55 to 64 years	1 226	135	11.0	723	32	4.5	503	103	20.4	1 239	660	53.3
65 years and over	388	53	13.7	107	17	16.1	280	36	12.8	2 219	827	37.3
Male												
Total	6 800	815	12.0	4 014	154	3.8	2 786	660	23.7	3 037	1 165	38.4
16 to 17 years	118	35	29.3	2	–	(B)	115	35	29.9	410	137	33.4
18 to 64 years	6 475	756	11.7	3 941	144	3.7	2 534	611	24.1	1 777	782	44.0
18 to 24 years	1 114	167	15.0	339	19	5.6	776	148	19.1	523	223	42.6
25 to 34 years	2 064	242	11.7	1 312	55	4.2	753	187	24.9	365	187	51.3
35 to 54 years	2 640	275	10.4	1 896	59	3.1	744	216	29.0	567	261	46.1
55 to 64 years	656	72	10.9	395	11	2.9	261	60	23.1	322	111	34.3
65 years and over	206	25	11.8	71	10	(B)	137	14	10.5	850	246	29.0
Female												
Total	7 133	1 207	16.9	4 003	229	5.7	3 130	978	31.2	4 884	2 672	54.7
16 to 17 years	104	24	23.3	1	–	(B)	103	24	23.4	413	183	44.4
18 to 64 years	6 850	1 154	16.8	3 966	222	5.6	2 884	932	32.3	3 102	1 908	61.5
18 to 24 years	1 147	291	25.4	293	29	9.8	855	262	30.7	716	437	61.1
25 to 34 years	2 165	437	20.2	1 281	88	6.8	884	350	39.6	753	558	74.2
35 to 54 years	2 967	363	12.2	2 064	85	4.1	903	278	30.8	1 016	634	62.4
55 to 64 years	571	63	11.1	328	21	6.4	243	42	17.4	617	278	45.1
65 years and over	180	29	15.9	37	7	(B)	143	22	15.1	1 369	580	42.4
Household Relationship												
Persons 16 to 64 years old	13 546	1 968	14.5	7 910	366	4.6	5 636	1 602	28.4	5 703	3 010	52.8
In families	10 763	1 471	13.7	6 123	278	4.5	4 640	1 193	25.7	4 886	2 390	48.9
Householder	5 020	952	19.0	3 393	228	6.7	1 626	724	44.5	1 599	1 154	72.2
In families with related children under 18 years	6 823	1 265	18.5	3 800	248	6.5	3 023	1 016	33.6	3 411	1 966	57.6
Householder	3 601	879	24.4	2 332	204	8.8	1 269	675	53.1	1 238	1 027	83.0
In families with related children under 6 years	3 190	722	22.6	1 735	153	8.8	1 455	569	39.1	1 723	1 197	69.5
Householder	1 743	510	29.3	1 081	126	11.7	662	384	58.0	766	678	88.6
In married couple families	6 319	337	5.3	3 950	80	2.0	2 369	256	10.8	1 931	487	25.2
Husband	2 596	180	6.9	1 956	54	2.8	642	126	19.7	343	131	38.0
Wife	2 412	100	4.1	1 563	20	1.3	849	79	9.4	755	221	29.2
Related children[1]	1 115	49	4.4	336	6	1.9	779	42	5.4	770	123	15.9
Other	194	8	4.4	95	–	–	99	8	8.6	63	13	(B)
In married couple families with related children under 18 years	4 048	250	6.2	2 522	68	2.7	1 525	181	11.9	1 235	347	28.1
Husband	1 755	147	8.4	1 337	51	3.8	418	96	23.0	183	88	48.2
Wife	1 561	75	4.8	967	15	1.5	595	60	10.1	470	165	35.0
Related children[1]	620	23	3.7	154	3	2.0	466	20	4.3	544	84	15.4
Other	111	5	4.4	65	–	(B)	46	5	(B)	38	11	(B)
In married couple families with related children under 6 years	1 918	156	8.1	1 153	43	3.7	765	112	14.7	533	215	40.4
Husband	857	95	11.1	611	34	5.5	245	61	24.9	99	61	61.9
Wife	768	46	6.0	453	10	2.1	315	37	11.6	232	106	45.7
Other	67	5	(B)	35	–	(B)	32	5	(B)	28	11	(B)
In families with female householder, no spouse present	3 731	1 050	28.2	1 745	185	10.6	1 986	865	43.6	2 669	1 801	67.5
Householder	2 087	736	35.3	1 196	165	13.8	891	572	64.2	1 149	971	84.5
Other	1 644	314	19.1	549	21	3.8	1 095	293	26.8	1 520	830	54.6
In families with female householder, no spouse present, with related children under 18 years	2 517	964	38.3	1 117	172	15.4	1 400	792	56.6	2 068	1 568	75.8
Householder	1 670	711	42.6	884	152	17.2	785	559	71.1	997	898	90.1
Related children[1]	631	202	32.0	144	13	8.8	487	189	38.9	900	565	62.8
Other	217	51	23.5	89	7	7.5	128	44	34.6	172	105	61.2
In families with female householder, no spouse present, with related children under 6 years	1 158	539	46.6	507	106	21.0	651	433	66.5	1 134	946	83.4
Householder	798	403	50.5	398	92	23.1	400	311	77.7	635	589	92.7
Related children[1]	247	101	40.9	64	13	(B)	182	88	48.4	377	279	73.8
Other	114	36	31.5	45	2	(B)	69	34	(B)	121	78	64.3
In unrelated subfamilies	74	35	(B)	24	3	(B)	50	32	(B)	44	30	(B)
Unrelated individuals	2 709	462	17.1	1 763	85	4.8	946	377	39.8	773	590	76.3
Male	1 684	311	18.5	1 058	63	6.0	626	248	39.6	356	236	66.3
Householder	1 053	141	13.4	731	23	3.2	322	118	36.6	199	137	68.8
Female	1 025	151	14.7	705	22	3.2	320	129	40.3	417	354	84.9
Householder	824	98	11.9	585	16	2.7	239	82	34.5	309	256	82.9

See footnote at end of table.

D1-19. Work Experience During Year, by Selected Characteristics and Poverty Status in 1991 of Civilians 16 Years Old and Over (continued)

[Numbers in thousands. Persons as of March of the following year.

Characteristic	All workers Total	Below poverty level Number	Percent of total	Worked year-round full-time Total	Below poverty level Number	Percent of total	Not year-round full-time Total	Below poverty level Number	Percent of total	Did not work during year Total	Below poverty level Number	Percent of total
HISPANIC ORIGIN[2]												
Both Sexes												
Total	10 166	1 565	15.4	5 822	490	8.4	4 343	1 075	24.7	4 940	1 926	39.0
16 to 17 years	206	50	24.3	9	2	(B)	198	48	24.4	535	203	38.0
18 to 64 years	9 806	1 499	15.3	5 765	486	8.4	4 042	1 013	25.1	3 415	1 501	44.0
18 to 24 years	1 950	362	18.5	805	75	9.3	1 146	286	25.0	834	403	48.2
25 to 34 years	3 323	538	16.2	1 969	188	9.5	1 354	350	25.9	912	488	53.5
35 to 54 years	3 840	541	14.1	2 545	208	8.2	1 295	333	25.7	1 111	442	39.7
55 to 64 years	693	59	8.5	446	15	3.4	247	44	17.8	558	169	30.3
65 years and over	153	15	10.1	49	2	(B)	104	13	12.9	990	222	22.4
Male												
Total	6 005	903	15.0	3 701	335	9.1	2 304	568	24.6	1 494	527	35.2
16 to 17 years	126	21	17.0	7	2	(B)	119	19	16.4	258	89	34.4
18 to 64 years	5 781	875	15.1	3 661	333	9.1	2 120	542	25.6	868	373	42.9
18 to 24 years	1 136	206	18.2	509	55	10.7	627	152	24.2	277	118	42.6
25 to 34 years	2 058	317	15.4	1 289	131	10.1	769	186	24.2	154	83	53.7
35 to 54 years	2 164	314	14.5	1 565	138	8.8	599	175	29.3	262	108	41.1
55 to 64 years	422	38	9.0	298	9	3.2	124	28	22.9	175	64	36.7
65 years and over	98	7	6.8	33	–	(B)	65	7	(B)	368	65	17.6
Female												
Total	4 161	662	15.9	2 122	155	7.3	2 039	507	24.9	3 446	1 400	40.6
16 to 17 years	81	29	35.7	2	–	(B)	79	29	36.5	277	114	41.3
18 to 64 years	4 025	624	15.5	2 104	153	7.3	1 922	471	24.5	2 547	1 128	44.3
18 to 24 years	814	155	19.1	296	20	6.9	518	135	26.0	557	284	51.1
25 to 34 years	1 265	221	17.5	680	57	8.3	585	164	28.1	757	405	53.5
35 to 54 years	1 676	227	13.5	980	70	7.1	696	157	22.6	850	334	39.3
55 to 64 years	271	21	7.8	148	6	3.8	123	16	12.6	383	105	27.3
65 years and over	55	9	(B)	16	2	(B)	39	7	(B)	622	157	25.2
Household Relationship												
Persons 16 to 64 years old	10 013	1 549	15.5	5 774	488	8.4	4 239	1 061	25.0	3 950	1 704	43.2
In families	8 326	1 205	14.5	4 788	413	8.6	3 538	791	22.4	3 607	1 441	40.0
Householder	3 836	759	19.8	2 622	312	11.9	1 214	447	36.8	870	542	62.4
In families with related children under 18 years	5 726	1 092	19.1	3 191	391	12.2	2 535	702	27.7	2 764	1 296	46.9
Householder	2 831	695	24.5	1 912	299	15.6	919	396	43.1	679	499	73.5
In families with related children under 6 years	2 987	705	23.6	1 666	267	16.0	1 321	437	33.1	1 525	847	55.5
Householder	1 559	460	29.5	1 020	206	20.2	539	254	47.1	421	344	81.7
In married couple families	6 336	798	12.6	3 748	300	8.0	2 588	498	19.2	2 449	752	30.7
Husband	2 943	507	17.2	2 129	244	11.4	814	264	32.4	276	121	43.9
Wife	2 019	191	9.5	1 040	33	3.2	980	158	16.1	1 372	430	31.4
Related children[1]	1 007	62	6.1	378	6	1.6	629	56	8.8	644	155	24.1
Other	367	38	10.3	201	17	8.5	166	21	12.4	157	45	28.5
In married couple families with related children under 18 years	4 583	739	16.1	2 603	286	11.0	1 979	453	22.9	1 856	664	35.8
Husband	2 220	470	21.2	1 595	233	14.6	625	238	38.0	170	97	57.3
Wife	1 434	173	12.1	655	30	4.6	779	143	18.3	1 016	380	37.4
Related children[1]	642	59	9.2	184	6	3.2	458	53	11.7	527	146	27.7
Other	286	37	12.9	169	17	10.1	117	20	16.9	143	41	28.6
In married couple families with related children under 6 years	2 457	506	20.6	1 404	201	14.3	1 054	305	29.0	1 065	472	44.3
Husband	1 312	343	26.2	904	167	18.5	408	176	43.1	97	69	71.2
Wife	760	108	14.3	319	16	5.0	441	92	20.9	669	296	44.3
Other	208	30	14.4	119	14	12.1	89	15	17.4	109	35	32.4
In families with female householder, no spouse present	1 324	332	25.1	686	96	13.9	638	236	37.0	981	641	65.4
Householder	676	221	32.7	387	69	17.9	289	152	52.6	484	390	80.6
Other	648	111	17.1	299	26	8.9	349	84	24.1	497	251	50.5
In families with female householder, no spouse present, with related children under 18 years	859	288	33.6	433	87	20.1	427	201	47.2	788	595	75.6
Householder	518	202	39.0	288	66	22.9	231	136	59.1	426	373	87.5
Related children[1]	223	61	27.4	82	9	10.5	141	52	37.1	288	177	61.5
Other	118	25	21.3	63	13	(B)	55	12	(B)	73	45	(B)
In families with female householder, no spouse present, with related children under 6 years	388	157	40.5	185	55	29.6	204	103	50.4	412	353	85.7
Householder	221	109	49.2	109	37	33.9	112	72	64.0	266	247	93.0
Related children[1]	90	28	31.0	36	6	(B)	54	22	(B)	99	73	74.2
Other	78	21	26.8	40	12	(B)	38	9	(B)	47	32	(B)
In unrelated subfamilies	102	38	37.3	49	10	(B)	52	28	(B)	43	23	(B)
Unrelated individuals	1 585	307	19.3	936	64	6.9	649	242	37.3	300	240	80.0
Male	1 088	202	18.5	635	45	7.1	453	156	34.5	137	103	75.1
Householder	527	69	13.2	343	14	4.0	184	56	30.3	76	56	73.6
Female	498	105	21.1	301	19	6.4	196	86	43.7	163	137	84.0
Householder	280	28	9.9	196	6	3.1	84	22	25.8	83	59	71.4

[1]Includes related children 16 and 17 years of age and own children 18 years and over.

[2]Persons of Hispanic origin may be of any race.

(B) Base less than 75,000

D2. Unemployment

D2-1. Unemployed Workers—Summary: 1980 to 1991

(In thousands, except as indicated. For civilian noninstitutional population: 16 years old and over. Annual averages of monthly figures.)

ITEM AND CHARACTERISTIC	1980	1984	1985	1986	1987	1988	1989	1990	1991
UNEMPLOYED									
Total [1]	7,637	8,539	8,312	8,237	7,425	6,701	6,528	6,874	8,426
Labor force time lost [2] (percent)	7.9	8.6	8.1	7.9	7.1	6.3	5.9	6.2	7.6
16 to 19 years old	1,669	1,499	1,468	1,454	1,347	1,226	1,194	1,149	1,290
20 to 24 years old	1,835	1,838	1,738	1,651	1,453	1,261	1,218	1,221	1,477
25 to 44 years old	2,964	3,709	3,681	3,761	3,410	3,095	3,010	3,273	4,106
45 to 64 years old	1,075	1,384	1,331	1,279	1,135	1,032	1,016	1,124	1,437
65 years and over	94	97	93	91	78	87	91	107	116
Male	4,267	4,744	4,521	4,530	4,101	3,655	3,525	3,799	4,817
16 to 19 years old	913	812	806	779	732	667	658	629	709
20 to 24 years old	1,076	1,023	944	899	779	676	660	666	849
25 to 44 years old	1,619	2,050	1,950	2,054	1,858	1,657	1,572	1,774	2,331
45 to 64 years old	600	806	766	741	684	606	585	668	862
65 years and over	58	53	55	58	49	49	49	61	66
Female	3,370	3,794	3,791	3,707	3,324	3,046	3,003	3,075	3,609
16 to 19 years old	755	687	661	675	616	558	536	519	581
20 to 24 years old	760	815	794	752	674	585	558	555	628
25 to 44 years old	1,345	1,659	1,732	1,708	1,552	1,439	1,437	1,498	1,775
45 to 64 years old	473	589	566	539	453	427	430	456	575
65 years and over	36	45	39	33	30	38	41	46	50
White [3]	5,884	6,372	6,191	6,140	5,501	4,944	4,770	5,091	6,447
16 to 19 years old	1,291	1,116	1,074	1,070	995	910	863	858	977
20 to 24 years old	1,364	1,282	1,235	1,149	1,017	874	858	844	1,063
Black [3]	1,553	1,914	1,864	1,840	1,684	1,547	1,544	1,527	1,679
16 to 19 years old	343	353	357	347	312	288	300	258	270
20 to 24 years old	426	504	455	453	397	349	322	335	362
Hispanic [3][4]	620	800	811	857	751	732	750	769	963
16 to 19 years old	145	149	141	141	138	148	132	131	149
20 to 24 years old	138	164	171	183	152	145	158	135	172
Full-time workers	6,269	7,057	6,793	6,708	5,979	5,357	5,211	5,541	6,932
Part-time workers	1,369	1,481	1,519	1,529	1,446	1,343	1,317	1,332	1,494
UNEMPLOYMENT RATE (percent) [5]									
Total [1]	7.1	7.5	7.2	7.0	6.2	5.5	5.3	5.5	6.7
16 to 19 years old	17.8	18.9	18.6	18.3	16.9	15.3	15.0	15.5	18.6
20 to 24 years old	11.5	11.5	11.1	10.7	9.7	8.7	8.6	8.8	10.8
25 to 44 years old	6.0	6.4	6.2	6.1	5.4	4.8	4.5	4.8	6.0
45 to 64 years old	3.7	4.8	4.5	4.3	3.8	3.3	3.2	3.5	4.4
65 years and over	3.1	3.3	3.2	3.0	2.5	2.7	2.6	3.0	3.3
Male	6.9	7.4	7.0	6.9	6.2	5.5	5.2	5.6	7.0
16 to 19 years old	18.3	19.6	19.5	19.0	17.8	16.0	15.9	16.3	19.8
20 to 24 years old	12.5	11.9	11.4	11.0	9.9	8.9	8.8	9.1	11.7
25 to 44 years old	5.6	6.3	5.9	6.0	5.3	4.6	4.3	4.8	6.2
45 to 64 years old	3.5	4.8	4.5	4.4	4.0	3.5	3.3	3.7	4.7
65 years and over	3.1	3.0	3.1	3.2	2.6	2.5	2.4	3.0	3.3
Female	7.4	7.6	7.4	7.1	6.2	5.6	5.4	5.4	6.3
16 to 19 years old	17.2	18.0	17.6	17.6	15.9	14.4	14.0	14.7	17.4
20 to 24 years old	10.4	10.9	10.7	10.3	9.4	8.5	8.3	8.5	9.8
25 to 44 years old	6.4	6.6	6.6	6.2	5.5	4.9	4.8	4.9	5.7
45 to 64 years old	4.0	4.9	4.6	4.2	3.5	3.2	3.1	3.2	3.9
65 years and over	3.1	3.8	3.3	2.8	2.4	2.9	2.9	3.1	3.3
White [3]	6.3	6.5	6.2	6.0	5.3	4.7	4.5	4.7	6.0
16 to 19 years old	15.5	16.0	15.7	15.6	14.4	13.1	12.7	13.4	16.4
20 to 24 years old	9.9	9.3	9.2	8.7	8.0	7.1	7.2	7.2	9.2
Black [3]	14.3	15.9	15.1	14.5	13.0	11.7	11.4	11.3	12.4
16 to 19 years old	38.5	42.7	40.2	39.3	34.7	32.4	32.4	31.1	36.3
20 to 24 years old	23.6	26.1	24.5	24.1	21.8	19.6	18.0	19.9	21.6
Hispanic [3][4]	10.1	10.7	10.5	10.6	8.8	8.2	8.0	8.0	9.9
16 to 19 years old	22.5	24.1	24.3	24.7	22.3	22.0	19.4	19.5	22.9
20 to 24 years old	12.1	12.4	12.6	12.9	10.6	9.8	10.7	9.1	11.6
Experienced workers [6]	6.9	7.1	6.8	6.6	5.8	5.2	5.0	5.3	6.5
Women maintaining families [1]	9.2	10.4	10.5	9.9	9.3	8.2	8.1	8.2	9.1
White	7.3	7.8	8.1	7.8	6.8	6.0	6.1	6.3	7.2
Black	14.0	16.7	16.7	15.4	15.4	13.7	13.0	13.1	13.9
Married men, wife present [1]	4.2	4.6	4.3	4.4	3.9	3.3	3.0	3.4	4.4
White	3.9	4.3	4.0	4.0	3.6	3.0	2.8	3.1	4.2
Black	7.4	8.1	8.0	8.0	6.5	5.8	5.8	6.2	6.5
Percent without work for—									
Less than 5 weeks	43.1	39.2	42.1	41.9	43.7	46.0	48.6	46.1	40.1
5 to 10 weeks	23.4	20.6	22.2	22.6	21.6	22.2	22.2	23.5	22.9
11 to 14 weeks	9.0	8.1	8.0	8.4	7.9	7.8	8.1	8.6	9.5
15 to 26 weeks	13.8	12.9	12.9	12.7	12.7	12.0	11.2	11.8	14.5
27 weeks and over	10.7	19.1	15.4	14.4	14.0	12.1	9.9	10.1	13.0
Unemployment duration, average (weeks)	11.9	18.2	15.6	15.0	14.5	13.5	11.9	12.1	13.8

[1] Includes other races, not shown separately.

[2] Aggregate hours lost by the unemployed and persons on part time for economic reasons as a percent of potentially available labor force hours.

[3] Includes other ages, not shown separately.

[4] Persons of Hispanic origin may be of any race.

[5] Unemployed as percent of civilian labor force in specified group. [6] Wage and salary workers.

Source: U.S. Bureau of Labor Statistics, *Employment and Earnings,* monthly, January issues; and unpublished data.

D2-2. Unemployed Persons, by Sex, Age, Race, Marital Status, and Duration of Unemployment: 1991 and 1992

Sex, age, race, and marital status	Thousands of persons					Weeks		Percent of unemployed in group			
	Total	Less than 5 weeks	5 to 14 weeks	15 to 26 weeks	27 weeks and over	Average (mean) duration	Median duration	Unemployed less than 5 weeks		Unemployed 15 weeks and over	
	December 1992							Dec. 1991	Dec. 1992	Dec. 1991	Dec. 1992
Total, 16 years and over	8,829	2,757	2,736	1,434	1,901	19.2	9.5	35.7	31.2	31.3	37.8
16 to 19 years	1,136	506	397	146	87	11.0	5.6	45.4	44.6	15.3	20.5
20 to 24 years	1,435	542	479	255	158	13.4	7.2	44.0	37.8	20.8	28.8
25 to 34 years	2,501	766	809	400	526	18.7	9.4	34.7	30.6	32.8	37.0
35 to 44 years	2,014	544	584	350	536	22.4	12.1	29.8	27.0	36.7	44.0
45 to 54 years	1,094	247	311	172	365	25.4	14.0	28.7	22.6	42.7	49.0
55 to 64 years	544	116	135	100	193	28.1	17.0	29.3	21.3	45.3	53.8
65 years and over	105	36	21	11	37	28.4	13.2	28.1	34.2	49.3	45.9
Men, 16 years and over	5,058	1,458	1,566	805	1,229	21.0	10.2	34.5	28.8	32.7	40.2
16 to 19 years	675	305	233	80	57	11.3	5.6	46.7	45.3	14.9	20.2
20 to 24 years	809	282	290	141	97	14.3	7.9	40.4	34.8	21.4	29.4
25 to 34 years	1,384	393	445	226	320	20.4	9.9	31.7	28.4	35.4	39.5
35 to 44 years	1,120	255	332	179	355	25.4	13.6	28.9	22.7	38.5	47.6
45 to 54 years	658	136	176	103	243	27.4	16.5	30.1	20.7	45.6	52.6
55 to 64 years	364	65	84	73	141	30.7	19.8	34.1	18.0	41.1	58.8
65 years and over	48	22	6	4	16	(¹)	(¹)	(¹)	(¹)	(¹)	(¹)
Women, 16 years and over	3,771	1,299	1,170	629	672	16.8	8.5	37.3	34.5	29.3	34.5
16 to 19 years	461	201	164	67	30	10.5	5.5	43.7	43.5	15.8	21.0
20 to 24 years	625	261	189	114	61	12.3	6.3	48.9	41.7	20.0	28.1
25 to 34 years	1,117	374	363	174	206	16.6	8.5	38.9	33.4	29.2	34.0
35 to 44 years	894	289	253	172	181	18.7	10.3	31.0	32.3	34.0	39.4
45 to 54 years	436	111	135	69	121	22.3	11.7	26.7	25.4	38.8	43.6
55 to 64 years	180	50	51	27	52	23.0	12.0	21.0	27.9	52.7	43.7
65 years and over	57	14	15	7	22	(¹)	(¹)	(¹)	(¹)	(¹)	(¹)
White, 16 years and over	6,543	2,145	2,028	1,012	1,357	18.7	9.1	36.0	32.8	30.7	36.2
Men	3,848	1,157	1,176	589	925	20.9	10.0	35.0	30.1	32.3	39.4
Women	2,695	988	853	423	432	15.6	7.7	37.4	36.7	28.2	31.7
Black, 16 years and over	1,893	501	587	341	464	20.9	11.1	35.6	26.5	33.0	42.5
Men	985	245	314	166	260	22.1	10.9	32.8	24.9	34.3	43.2
Women	908	256	273	175	204	19.7	11.2	38.6	28.2	31.7	41.8
Men, 16 years and over:											
Married, spouse present	2,061	489	615	322	635	24.6	12.7	32.9	23.7	37.9	46.4
Widowed, divorced, or separated	746	210	210	139	186	22.8	11.9	31.2	28.2	36.4	43.7
Single (never married)	2,252	759	741	344	408	17.1	8.5	37.1	33.7	26.8	33.4
Women, 16 years and over:											
Married, spouse present	1,498	520	485	245	247	16.3	8.0	38.0	34.7	30.4	32.8
Widowed, divorced, or separated	887	265	274	150	197	19.1	10.2	32.9	29.9	35.4	39.1
Single (never married)	1,386	513	410	234	228	16.0	7.8	39.4	37.0	24.2	33.4

¹Data not shown where base is less than 75,000.

D2-3. Persons Not in the Labor Force, by Reason, Race, Hispanic Origin, Age, and Sex: 1992

(In thousands)

Reason, race, and Hispanic origin	Total		Age						Sex			
			16 to 24 years		25 to 59 years		60 years and over		Men		Women	
	IV 1991	IV 1992	IV 1991	IV 1992	IV 1991	IV 1992	IV 1991	IV 1992	IV 1991	IV 1992	IV 1991	IV 1992
WHITE												
Total not in labor force	54,488	54,714	8,194	8,216	17,190	17,202	29,104	29,295	18,860	19,020	35,628	35,694
Do not want a job now	50,312	50,310	6,922	6,952	14,850	14,778	28,540	28,580	17,338	17,440	32,973	32,870
Current activity:												
Going to school	6,222	6,370	5,419	5,554	789	799	14	17	3,147	3,095	3,075	3,275
Ill, disabled	3,944	4,044	92	80	2,186	2,252	1,667	1,712	2,078	2,099	1,866	1,945
Keeping house	19,802	18,261	1,053	904	9,384	8,883	9,365	8,473	314	223	19,489	18,038
Retired	17,375	18,383	—	—	395	528	16,980	17,855	10,265	10,440	7,111	7,943
Other activity	2,967	3,253	358	415	2,096	2,316	513	522	1,534	1,582	1,433	1,671
Want a job now	4,186	4,356	1,273	1,249	2,317	2,422	596	685	1,531	1,570	2,656	2,785
Reason for not looking:												
School attendance	935	1,081	739	838	193	235	3	8	482	506	454	575
Ill health, disability	762	872	68	51	518	647	175	174	391	399	370	474
Home responsibility	881	837	197	175	636	616	47	46	—	—	881	837
Think cannot get a job	781	710	125	77	482	457	173	175	288	292	492	417
Other reasons[1]	828	856	143	108	488	467	197	281	369	373	459	483
BLACK												
Total not in labor force	8,214	8,200	2,234	2,141	3,026	3,076	2,954	2,983	3,049	3,094	5,165	5,106
Do not want a job now	6,852	6,807	1,713	1,623	2,289	2,300	2,850	2,884	2,566	2,621	4,286	4,186
Current activity:												
Going to school	1,439	1,337	1,330	1,212	109	124	—	1	668	616	771	721
Ill, disabled	1,016	1,012	18	25	577	642	421	345	501	513	516	499
Keeping house	2,130	1,978	213	197	1,096	1,004	820	777	104	100	2,026	1,878
Retired	1,602	1,793	—	—	47	44	1,555	1,746	931	963	672	830
Other activity	664	687	151	187	459	486	54	15	363	429	301	258
Want a job now	1,362	1,393	521	519	737	775	104	99	483	473	879	920
Reason for not looking:												
School attendance	358	372	271	309	83	63	4	—	179	150	179	222
Ill health, disability	225	244	21	33	161	179	43	33	104	105	121	139
Home responsibility	333	282	107	66	209	214	17	2	—	—	333	282
Think cannot get a job	259	300	77	81	159	211	23	8	120	125	139	175
Other reasons[1]	187	195	45	30	125	109	16	57	81	93	106	102
HISPANIC ORIGIN												
Total not in labor force	5,132	5,265	1,347	1,356	2,399	2,459	1,385	1,450	1,514	1,502	3,618	3,764
Do not want a job now	4,415	4,509	1,075	1,110	1,973	2,006	1,367	1,394	1,271	1,268	3,143	3,241
Current activity:												
Going to school	712	820	637	723	75	97	—	—	328	397	384	423
Ill, disabled	489	433	40	16	292	281	157	136	277	244	211	189
Keeping house	2,192	2,155	331	292	1,401	1,377	461	486	40	22	2,152	2,133
Retired	743	788	—	—	13	23	730	764	450	438	293	350
Other activity	278	314	67	79	191	227	20	8	176	168	103	146
Want a job now	674	749	272	280	363	422	39	48	200	239	474	510
Reason for not looking:												
School attendance	164	192	149	158	15	34	—	—	68	77	96	115
Ill health, disability	99	108	18	6	69	88	12	14	48	28	50	80
Home responsibility	177	139	49	49	125	88	3	2	—	—	177	139
Think cannot get a job	135	178	24	33	104	130	8	14	39	83	97	94
Other reasons[1]	99	132	33	33	50	81	17	18	45	50	54	81

[1]Includes small number of men not looking for work because of "home responsibilities."

NOTE: Detail for the above race and Hispanic-origin groups will not sum to totals because data for the other races are not presented and Hispanics are included in both the white and black population groups.

D2-4. Persons Not in the Labor Force, by Reason, Sex, and Age: 1992

(In thousands)

Reason and sex	Total		Age							
			16 to 19 years		20 to 24 years		25 to 59 years		60 years and over	
	IV 1991	IV 1992	IV 1991	IV 1992	IV 1991	IV 1992	IV 1991	IV 1992	IV 1991	IV 1992
TOTAL										
Total not in labor force	65,091	65,374	6,777	6,783	4,309	4,224	21,264	21,335	32,742	33,032
Do not want a job now	59,273	59,349	5,762	5,724	3,437	3,413	18,041	17,981	32,033	32,231
Current activity:										
Going to school	8,277	8,320	5,236	5,188	1,996	2,054	1,031	1,058	14	20
Ill, disabled	5,086	5,170	24	19	93	90	2,839	2,955	2,132	2,106
Keeping house	22,747	21,100	284	265	1,041	903	11,030	10,456	10,392	9,477
Retired	19,369	20,657	—	—	—	—	451	579	18,918	20,075
Other activity	3,794	4,102	219	252	307	364	2,690	2,933	577	552
Want a job now	5,819	6,025	1,015	1,059	872	811	3,223	3,355	709	801
Reason for not looking:										
School attendance	1,382	1,557	821	894	256	340	297	315	8	8
Ill health, disability	1,009	1,150	17	24	75	61	697	858	220	207
Home responsibility	1,268	1,159	41	36	274	208	888	865	64	50
Think cannot get a job	1,102	1,063	84	54	126	108	693	708	198	193
Job-market factors	741	689	43	28	80	63	531	523	87	75
Personal factors	361	374	42	26	46	45	162	186	112	118
Other reasons[1]	1,060	1,096	51	51	140	94	648	608	220	344
Men										
Total not in labor force	22,764	22,982	3,358	3,304	1,596	1,547	4,828	4,996	12,981	13,135
Do not want a job now	20,645	20,831	2,827	2,748	1,304	1,298	3,892	4,045	12,621	12,741
Current activity										
Going to school	4,152	4,031	2,674	2,592	1,065	1,037	409	395	3	6
Ill, disabled	2,642	2,678	15	16	48	52	1,625	1,637	954	973
Keeping house	436	346	7	7	20	27	210	163	198	149
Retired	11,437	11,677	—	—	—	—	327	409	11,110	11,265
Other activity	1,979	2,099	131	133	171	179	1,320	1,440	356	347
Want a job now	2,119	2,150	531	556	292	249	936	951	360	394
Reason for not looking										
School attendance	712	690	457	472	143	134	111	78	—	7
Ill health, disability	511	528	9	13	37	43	353	375	112	97
Think cannot get a job	424	448	40	39	53	39	222	265	109	105
Other reasons[1]	472	483	25	33	59	33	250	233	139	185
Women										
Total not in labor force	42,327	42,392	3,419	3,479	2,712	2,677	16,436	16,339	19,761	19,897
Do not want a job now	38,628	38,518	2,935	2,977	2,132	2,115	14,149	13,936	19,412	19,490
Current activity										
Going to school	4,125	4,289	2,561	2,596	931	1,017	622	662	11	14
Ill, disabled	2,445	2,492	9	3	45	38	1,213	1,318	1,178	1,133
Keeping house	22,312	20,754	277	257	1,021	876	10,820	10,293	10,194	9,328
Retired	7,932	8,979	—	—	—	—	124	170	7,808	8,810
Other activity	1,815	2,003	88	120	136	185	1,370	1,493	222	205
Want a job now	3,699	3,875	483	502	580	562	2,287	2,403	349	407
Reason for not looking										
School attendance	670	867	363	422	113	206	186	237	8	1
Ill health, disability	497	622	8	10	38	18	344	483	108	110
Home responsibility	1,267	1,158	41	36	274	208	888	865	64	50
Think cannot get a job	678	615	45	15	74	69	471	443	89	88
Other reasons	587	613	26	19	82	61	399	375	81	158

[1]Includes small number of men not looking for work because of "home responsibilities."

NOTE: Detail in tables D2-3 and D2-4 may not add to not-in-labor-force totals because of differences in the weighting patterns used in aggregating these data.

D2-5. Persons Not in the Labor Force Who Desire Work But Think They Cannot Get Jobs, by Reason, Sex, Age, Race, and Hispanic Origin: 1992

(in thousands)

Reason and sex	Total	4th Quarter 1992						
		Age				Race and Hispanic origin		
		16 to 19 years	20 to 24 years	25 to 59 years	60 years and over	White	Black	Hispanic origin
TOTAL								
Personal factors:								
Employers think too young or old	144	11	--	33	100	115	20	21
Lacks education or training	158	10	31	110	7	112	34	37
Other personal handicap	73	5	14	43	11	54	15	12
Job-market factors:								
Could not find work	419	23	59	316	21	222	181	71
Thinks no job available	270	6	4	206	54	206	49	36
Men								
Personal factors:								
Employers think too young or old	72	9	--	11	52	57	9	10
Lacks education or training	63	7	12	42	2	45	11	22
Other personal handicap	28	--	6	16	6	26	3	3
Job-market factors:								
Could not find work	151	19	17	110	6	63	80	24
Thinks no job available	134	4	4	86	39	103	23	25
Women								
Personal factors:								
Employers think too young or old	72	2	--	22	48	58	11	11
Lacks education or training	94	2	19	69	5	68	24	15
Other personal handicap	45	5	8	26	5	29	13	9
Job-market factors:								
Could not find work	268	4	42	207	16	159	101	47
Thinks no job available	136	1	--	120	15	103	26	12

NOTE: Detail for the above race and Hispanic-origin groups will not sum to totals because data for the "other races" group are not presented and Hispanics are included in both the white and black population groups.

D2-6. Unemployed Jobseekers, by Sex, Age, Race, and Jobsearch Methods Used: 1992

Sex, age, and race	December 1992								
	Thousands of persons		Methods used as a percent of total jobseekers						Average number of methods used
	Total unemployed	Total jobseekers	Public employment agency	Private employment agency	Employer directly	Placed or answered ads	Friends or relatives	Other	
Total, 16 years and over	8,829	7,488	23.0	9.4	73.7	43.1	23.8	6.0	1.79
16 to 19 years	1,136	1,099	8.8	4.5	80.9	32.1	17.7	4.0	1.48
20 to 24 years	1,435	1,280	23.6	6.0	73.8	43.4	24.2	4.9	1.76
25 to 34 years	2,501	2,094	27.5	9.3	76.3	44.4	22.8	3.9	1.84
35 to 44 years	2,014	1,664	26.6	13.8	71.0	45.7	26.0	7.7	1.91
45 to 54 years	1,094	844	27.0	13.1	69.7	46.8	28.4	11.2	1.96
55 to 64 years	544	423	17.5	6.8	65.3	48.0	24.6	6.7	1.69
65 years and over	105	84	8.1	16.4	52.7	38.6	25.3	14.8	1.56
Men, 16 years and over	5,058	4,122	26.1	10.2	74.3	43.7	26.2	6.4	1.87
16 to 19 years	675	649	8.7	4.8	82.7	31.3	19.0	4.1	1.51
20 to 24 years	809	711	26.5	6.8	72.6	47.4	29.5	5.1	1.88
25 to 34 years	1,384	1,100	31.1	9.9	78.0	43.4	26.2	3.9	1.92
35 to 44 years	1,120	852	32.6	17.2	68.2	46.9	27.9	8.0	2.01
45 to 54 years	658	504	30.5	11.9	71.8	47.4	29.2	12.9	2.04
55 to 64 years	364	277	19.6	7.9	70.9	47.8	22.3	8.7	1.77
65 years and over	48	29	(¹)	(¹)	(¹)	(¹)	(¹)	(¹)	(¹)
Women, 16 years and over	3,771	3,366	19.3	8.5	73.1	42.4	20.8	5.5	1.70
16 to 19 years	461	450	9.0	4.1	78.4	33.2	15.9	3.9	1.44
20 to 24 years	625	569	20.0	5.0	75.3	38.3	17.5	4.6	1.61
25 to 34 years	1,117	994	23.6	8.7	74.4	45.5	19.0	3.9	1.75
35 to 44 years	894	812	20.3	10.4	73.9	44.5	24.0	7.3	1.80
45 to 54 years	436	340	21.7	15.0	66.6	46.0	27.3	8.7	1.85
55 to 64 years	180	146	13.6	4.5	54.5	48.2	29.1	2.7	1.53
65 years and over	57	54	(¹)	(¹)	(¹)	(¹)	(¹)	(¹)	(¹)
White, 16 years and over	6,543	5,424	21.8	8.9	73.7	44.7	23.7	6.2	1.79
Men	3,848	3,061	25.4	9.9	74.9	45.0	26.1	6.6	1.88
Women	2,695	2,363	17.0	7.7	72.2	44.3	20.7	5.8	1.68
Black, 16 years and over	1,893	1,712	27.7	11.4	74.0	36.5	22.7	5.3	1.78
Men	985	857	30.7	11.8	72.4	38.7	27.1	5.9	1.87
Women	908	855	24.7	10.9	75.6	34.3	18.3	4.8	1.69

¹Data not shown where base is less than 75,000.

NOTE: The jobseeker total is less than the total unemployed because it does not include persons on layoff or waiting to begin a new job within 30 days, groups for whom jobseeking information is not collected. The percent using each method will always total more than 100 because many jobseekers use more than one method.

D2-7. Reason for Not Working or Reason for Spending Time Out of Labor Force, by Poverty Status in 1991 of Persons Who Did Not Work or Who Spent Time Out of Labor Force

[Numbers in thousands. Persons as of March of the following year.

Characteristic	Did not work last year						Worked last year, spent time out of labor force					
		Reason						Reason				
	Total	Ill or disabled	Retired	Home or family reasons	Could not find work	School or other	Total	Ill or disabled	Retired	Home or family reasons	Could not find work	School or other
ALL INCOME LEVELS												
Both Sexes												
Total	58 450	8 385	22 041	17 315	2 301	8 408	28 331	3 169	2 128	6 333	2 235	14 466
16 to 17 years	3 733	25	2	69	100	3 536	2 135	15	2	22	38	2 058
18 to 64 years	28 877	5 633	3 306	13 149	2 133	4 657	24 317	2 979	945	6 169	2 116	12 107
18 to 24 years	4 886	225	7	1 229	467	2 956	7 609	320	-	842	385	6 063
25 to 34 years	6 011	838	17	3 711	632	813	6 314	822	2	2 338	587	2 565
35 to 54 years	9 872	2 595	321	5 460	826	670	7 732	1 389	93	2 551	941	2 758
55 to 64 years	8 107	1 974	2 961	2 748	208	217	2 662	449	850	438	204	722
65 years and over	25 840	2 727	18 733	4 096	68	215	1 880	175	1 181	143	81	300
Male												
Total	20 337	4 006	10 706	251	1 316	4 056	11 601	1 562	1 330	322	1 362	7 025
16 to 17 years	1 842	17	-	8	50	1 767	1 139	10	2	2	23	1 103
18 to 64 years	8 481	3 041	1 742	198	1 236	2 264	9 397	1 459	576	305	1 292	5 764
18 to 24 years	1 977	125	6	25	275	1 547	3 608	146	-	51	257	3 153
25 to 34 years	1 374	525	11	70	366	403	2 182	414	-	107	408	1 253
35 to 54 years	2 392	1 421	179	84	455	252	2 365	622	60	123	517	1 043
55 to 64 years	2 738	971	1 547	19	140	62	1 242	278	517	23	111	315
65 years and over	10 014	948	8 966	46	30	25	1 065	93	752	15	47	158
Female												
Total	38 113	4 379	11 333	17 064	985	4 352	16 730	1 607	798	6 011	873	7 441
16 to 17 years	1 891	8	2	62	50	1 769	996	5	-	19	15	956
18 to 64 years	20 396	2 591	1 564	12 951	897	2 393	14 920	1 520	369	5 864	824	6 343
18 to 24 years	2 909	101	2	1 204	192	1 409	4 002	174	-	791	128	2 910
25 to 34 years	4 638	313	6	3 642	266	411	4 131	408	2	2 231	179	1 311
35 to 54 years	7 481	1 174	142	5 376	371	418	5 367	767	33	2 428	424	1 715
55 to 64 years	5 369	1 003	1 414	2 729	68	155	1 419	171	334	415	93	407
65 years and over	15 826	1 780	9 767	4 051	38	190	814	82	429	127	34	142
Household Relationship												
Persons 16 to 64 years old	32 610	5 658	3 308	13 218	2 233	8 193	26 451	2 994	947	6 191	2 154	14 166
In families	28 750	4 218	2 692	12 620	1 850	7 370	22 579	2 411	815	5 807	1 670	11 875
Householder	7 019	1 903	1 477	2 437	639	564	5 592	1 224	513	1 080	673	2 102
In families with related children under 18 years	16 893	1 573	233	8 436	1 142	5 508	13 809	1 359	55	4 585	894	6 916
Householder	3 966	908	137	2 079	448	415	3 300	745	36	907	414	1 197
In families with related children under 6 years	8 101	595	94	5 471	574	1 367	5 600	610	16	2 682	383	1 908
Householder	2 287	334	58	1 415	236	245	1 687	325	9	570	212	571
In married couple families	21 391	2 808	2 394	10 263	1 093	4 833	18 155	1 833	757	4 928	1 231	9 409
Husband	3 342	1 345	1 304	73	390	229	3 454	861	497	165	518	1 413
Wife	12 541	940	1 029	9 772	305	495	8 542	746	257	4 575	425	2 539
Related children[1]	4 988	427	7	253	337	3 963	5 890	201	2	148	253	5 286
Other	521	96	54	165	61	145	269	24	1	38	35	170
In married couple families with related children under 18 years	11 909	1 026	176	6 440	686	3 582	11 054	997	48	3 824	674	5 511
Husband	1 145	580	97	64	264	140	1 650	466	30	114	322	718
Wife	6 793	275	42	6 054	191	231	5 629	425	15	3 576	239	1 373
Related children[1]	3 590	121	-	186	181	3 102	3 631	95	2	105	101	3 328
Other	380	49	37	136	50	108	144	11	1	29	11	92
In married couple families with related children under 6 years	5 638	360	60	4 064	333	820	4 458	450	16	2 196	277	1 517
Husband	546	214	34	38	156	106	795	215	9	69	160	342
Wife	4 088	93	10	3 779	94	111	3 007	201	8	2 038	83	677
Other	248	25	17	110	28	67	92	7	-	20	6	59
In families with female householder, no spouse present	6 215	1 117	190	2 165	617	2 126	3 595	478	46	803	329	1 940
Householder	2 871	509	120	1 728	227	288	1 535	312	35	620	111	457
Other	3 344	608	70	437	390	1 838	2 060	166	10	183	218	1 482
In families with female householder, no spouse present, with related children under 18 years	4 458	478	37	1 875	410	1 658	2 383	314	6	704	192	1 167
Householder	2 356	318	28	1 569	190	251	1 250	245	6	566	76	358
Related children[1]	1 767	78	-	190	154	1 346	958	48	-	81	82	747
Other	334	82	9	116	66	62	175	21	-	57	34	62
In families with female householder, no spouse present, with related children under 6 years	2 278	206	18	1 341	217	495	988	135	-	455	89	310
Householder	1 450	127	15	1 078	89	141	664	95	-	364	38	166
Related children[1]	599	29	-	167	88	315	212	24	-	48	31	110
Other	228	50	3	97	40	39	112	16	-	43	19	34
In unrelated subfamilies	240	20	2	141	20	59	155	14	-	78	10	53
Unrelated individuals	3 620	1 420	614	458	363	764	3 718	568	131	305	474	2 238
Male	1 587	695	272	25	223	372	2 025	303	61	53	316	1 292
Householder	1 049	506	242	16	145	141	1 221	186	55	25	201	752
Female	2 032	725	343	432	140	392	1 693	266	70	252	158	947
Householder	1 436	619	327	236	79	175	1 084	201	68	133	120	561

D2-7. Reason for Not Working or Reason for Spending Time Out of Labor Force, by Poverty Status in 1991 of Persons Who Did Not Work or Who Spent Time Out of Labor Force (continued)

[Numbers in thousands. Persons as of March of the following year.

Characteristic	Did not work last year						Worked last year, spent time out of labor force					
		Reason						Reason				
	Total	Ill or disabled	Retired	Home or family reasons	Could not find work	School or other	Total	Ill or disabled	Retired	Home or family reasons	Could not find work	School or other
PERCENT BELOW POVERTY LEVEL												
Both Sexes												
Total	22.8	33.7	11.8	24.7	52.0	28.7	14.0	16.6	5.1	17.4	23.1	11.9
16 to 17 years	23.5	(B)	(B)	(B)	31.6	22.5	10.4	(B)	(B)	(B)	(B)	9.8
18 to 64 years	30.7	36.2	13.7	28.0	53.5	33.6	15.0	16.7	5.1	17.7	23.6	12.4
18 to 24 years	38.2	34.0	(B)	56.1	51.0	29.1	16.3	19.7	(B)	34.9	24.6	13.0
25 to 34 years	43.0	40.4	(B)	40.1	59.6	45.8	19.2	20.6	(B)	19.9	28.4	15.9
35 to 54 years	28.8	36.9	15.3	20.5	53.2	41.4	12.5	15.8	5.5	11.2	20.8	9.5
55 to 64 years	19.6	33.8	13.3	14.1	41.1	24.4	8.2	10.3	5.0	10.6	20.2	5.6
65 years and over	13.8	26.6	11.5	13.5	(B)	24.0	6.0	16.3	5.1	2.1	9.2	4.6
Male												
Total	19.2	28.4	8.7	39.0	51.5	26.1	13.4	15.7	3.7	20.7	24.9	12.1
16 to 17 years	20.6	(B)	(B)	(B)	(B)	20.5	9.6	(B)	(B)	(B)	(B)	9.4
18 to 64 years	30.7	31.3	12.4	47.4	53.0	30.2	14.9	16.2	4.0	21.6	25.5	12.9
18 to 24 years	28.6	29.8	(B)	(B)	51.1	24.3	14.0	18.3	(B)	(B)	24.3	12.6
25 to 34 years	45.1	37.1	(B)	(B)	59.7	40.1	18.7	19.4	(B)	21.8	28.3	15.1
35 to 54 years	37.4	33.0	13.0	48.4	53.1	47.1	16.6	15.5	(B)	20.7	24.4	13.5
55 to 64 years	19.1	26.0	11.9	(B)	39.5	(B)	7.5	11.8	3.7	(B)	23.0	5.2
65 years and over	9.2	19.1	8.0	(B)	(B)	(B)	4.1	8.7	3.5	(B)	(B)	2.5
Female												
Total	24.7	38.6	14.8	24.5	52.6	31.1	14.5	17.6	7.3	17.3	20.2	11.6
16 to 17 years	26.3	(B)	(B)	(B)	(B)	24.5	11.4	(B)	(B)	(B)	(B)	10.3
18 to 64 years	30.8	42.0	15.1	27.7	54.0	36.8	15.0	17.2	6.8	17.5	20.5	11.9
18 to 24 years	44.7	39.1	(B)	56.3	51.0	34.4	18.4	20.9	(B)	35.0	25.2	13.4
25 to 34 years	42.4	45.9	(B)	39.9	59.5	51.3	19.4	21.8	(B)	19.8	28.7	16.7
35 to 54 years	26.0	41.7	18.2	20.0	53.4	37.9	10.7	16.1	(B)	10.7	16.5	7.1
55 to 64 years	19.8	41.3	14.9	14.0	(B)	16.8	8.7	7.9	7.1	11.1	16.7	6.0
65 years and over	16.7	33.7	14.7	13.6	(B)	20.8	8.5	24.8	7.8	2.3	(B)	7.1
Household Relationship												
Persons 16 to 64 years old	29.9	36.1	13.7	28.2	52.5	28.8	14.6	16.6	5.1	17.8	23.6	12.0
In families	25.1	26.7	9.5	25.8	45.7	23.8	11.1	14.8	3.5	15.3	18.4	7.7
Householder	45.4	36.3	11.3	66.3	62.1	56.2	23.8	22.8	4.1	45.4	26.1	17.4
In families with related children under 18 years	33.9	42.9	17.8	34.0	56.4	27.1	15.0	21.5	(B)	17.7	26.0	10.5
Householder	67.2	53.4	19.5	74.5	73.3	70.3	34.9	30.7	(B)	51.2	35.0	25.9
In families with related children under 6 years	42.6	53.4	17.0	38.3	67.6	46.3	20.9	24.3	(B)	20.4	38.0	17.1
Householder	75.4	65.9	(B)	78.3	84.4	76.2	41.3	35.8	(B)	54.2	43.0	31.7
In married couple families	15.5	20.5	8.5	15.1	35.8	12.3	6.3	10.3	3.0	7.8	11.9	4.2
Husband	24.9	26.9	10.4	(B)	56.7	34.8	11.9	15.8	3.1	11.8	19.3	9.9
Wife	14.4	16.7	6.3	14.8	23.6	12.4	6.2	6.5	2.9	7.6	6.9	3.8
Related children[1]	11.9	9.9	(B)	15.0	26.8	10.6	3.0	1.0	(B)	12.3	6.1	2.7
Other	16.7	14.8	(B)	17.0	(B)	23.1	6.6	(B)	(B)	(B)	(B)	8.0
In married couple families with related children under 18 years	20.1	30.6	14.3	19.5	43.3	13.9	8.0	14.1	(B)	8.7	16.4	5.3
Husband	46.1	38.8	20.4	(B)	69.0	48.4	18.4	20.8	(B)	16.7	25.7	14.4
Wife	19.4	22.9	(B)	19.1	29.2	16.0	7.4	9.5	(B)	8.3	8.0	4.4
Related children[1]	13.3	19.5	(B)	20.4	28.4	11.7	4.1	2.2	(B)	17.3	6.5	3.6
Other	18.1	(B)	(B)	20.5	(B)	28.6	9.1	(B)	(B)	(B)	(B)	10.5
In married couple families with related children under 6 years	26.1	40.5	(B)	22.3	56.1	27.8	11.9	17.7	(B)	10.3	25.3	10.2
Husband	57.5	53.5	(B)	(B)	82.2	48.2	25.0	30.3	(B)	(B)	31.8	20.8
Wife	22.3	23.0	(B)	22.0	37.0	21.2	8.9	6.0	(B)	9.9	14.8	6.2
Other	24.7	(B)	(B)	24.7	(B)	(B)	12.8	(B)	(B)	(B)	(B)	(B)
In families with female householder, no spouse present	58.6	43.4	20.2	76.3	65.6	50.1	34.0	30.4	(B)	60.6	37.9	23.7
Householder	76.3	60.9	17.5	83.3	85.5	78.8	52.9	41.3	(B)	69.5	56.0	40.9
Other	43.5	28.8	(B)	48.4	54.0	45.6	19.8	10.1	(B)	30.5	28.7	18.5
In families with female householder, no spouse present, with related children under 18 years	70.9	69.1	(B)	83.7	77.5	56.3	45.3	42.1	(B)	65.8	54.8	32.4
Householder	86.1	77.7	(B)	88.8	89.5	85.4	61.1	49.5	(B)	73.7	71.9	47.6
Related children[1]	53.6	47.3	(B)	65.2	64.1	51.1	27.1	(B)	(B)	30.1	43.3	25.6
Other	55.9	56.4	(B)	45.5	(B)	(B)	31.9	(B)	(B)	(B)	(B)	(B)
In families with female householder, no spouse present, with related children under 6 years	82.7	75.8	(B)	86.1	84.2	77.4	58.9	45.1	(B)	69.1	72.9	45.7
Householder	91.0	80.4	(B)	92.5	97.2	91.7	68.0	56.1	(B)	77.3	(B)	49.5
Related children[1]	71.2	(B)	(B)	67.9	73.9	73.7	41.4	(B)	(B)	(B)	(B)	43.7
Other	60.1	(B)	(B)	45.9	(B)	(B)	37.5	(B)	(B)	(B)	(B)	(B)
In unrelated subfamilies	70.7	(B)	(B)	79.6	(B)	(B)	65.5	(B)	(B)	70.4	(B)	(B)
Unrelated individuals	65.1	63.5	31.7	79.6	85.8	76.3	33.9	23.8	14.8	51.7	40.8	33.6
Male	57.8	53.9	22.5	(B)	84.8	73.3	32.0	20.5	(B)	(B)	43.1	31.9
Householder	50.6	54.7	21.0	(B)	77.5	56.9	22.9	14.7	(B)	(B)	34.9	22.2
Female	70.8	72.8	39.0	79.8	87.5	79.2	36.1	27.5	(B)	50.3	36.2	36.0
Householder	64.2	72.9	37.7	68.3	80.0	70.0	26.7	27.4	(B)	39.3	29.9	23.5

[1]Includes related children 16 and 17 years of age and own children 18 years and over.

D2-7. Reason for Not Working or Reason for Spending Time Out of Labor Force, by Poverty Status in 1991 of Persons Who Did Not Work or Who Spent Time Out of Labor Force (continued)

[Numbers in thousands. Persons as of March of the following year.

Characteristic	Did not work last year						Worked last year, spent time out of labor force					
	Total	Reason					Total	Reason				
		Ill or disabled	Retired	Home or family reasons	Could not find work	School or other		Ill or disabled	Retired	Home or family reasons	Could not find work	School or other
BELOW POVERTY LEVEL												
Both Sexes												
Total	13 323	2 825	2 608	4 282	1 196	2 412	3 971	527	108	1 105	516	1 715
16 to 17 years	877	4	-	45	32	797	222	-	-	11	10	202
18 to 64 years	8 879	2 040	452	3 683	1 140	1 564	3 636	498	48	1 091	498	1 499
18 to 24 years	1 866	77	-	690	239	861	1 239	63	-	293	94	788
25 to 34 years	2 585	338	8	1 489	377	372	1 210	169	-	466	167	408
35 to 54 years	2 841	958	49	1 117	440	277	969	220	5	286	196	262
55 to 64 years	1 586	667	394	386	85	53	217	46	43	46	41	41
65 years and over	3 567	780	2 157	554	24	52	113	28	60	3	7	14
Male												
Total	3 902	1 136	932	96	678	1 058	1 552	245	50	67	339	852
16 to 17 years	380	2	-	2	13	363	109	-	-	1	5	103
18 to 64 years	2 601	953	215	94	655	683	1 399	237	23	66	329	744
18 to 24 years	566	37	-	13	140	376	504	27	-	17	62	398
25 to 34 years	619	195	8	36	218	162	409	80	-	23	115	190
35 to 54 years	894	469	23	41	242	119	393	97	4	26	126	141
55 to 64 years	523	252	184	4	55	27	94	33	19	-	25	16
65 years and over	921	181	717	2	9	12	44	8	27	-	5	4
Female												
Total	9 421	1 689	1 676	4 184	518	1 354	2 419	282	58	1 038	176	864
16 to 17 years	498	2	-	43	19	434	113	-	-	10	5	99
18 to 64 years	6 278	1 087	236	3 589	485	881	2 236	262	25	1 025	169	755
18 to 24 years	1 300	39	-	677	98	485	735	36	-	277	32	390
25 to 34 years	1 966	144	-	1 453	158	211	802	89	-	442	51	219
35 to 54 years	1 948	489	26	1 076	198	158	577	123	1	260	70	122
55 to 64 years	1 064	415	211	382	30	26	123	14	24	46	16	24
65 years and over	2 646	599	1 440	552	15	40	69	20	34	3	2	10
Household Relationship												
Persons 16 to 64 years old	9 756	2 045	452	3 727	1 172	2 360	3 858	498	48	1 102	508	1 701
In families	7 230	1 126	255	3 251	846	1 751	2 498	356	29	889	307	917
Householder	3 187	690	167	1 616	397	317	1 332	280	21	491	176	365
In families with related children under 18 years	5 719	675	42	2 865	644	1 493	2 066	292	3	812	233	727
Householder	2 681	485	27	1 549	329	291	1 151	229	3	464	145	310
In families with related children under 6 years	3 451	318	16	2 096	388	633	1 168	148	-	547	146	327
Householder	1 725	220	12	1 107	199	187	697	116	-	309	91	181
In married couple families	3 315	575	204	1 550	392	595	1 137	188	23	386	147	393
Husband	833	362	136	34	221	80	411	136	15	19	100	140
Wife	1 804	157	64	1 449	72	61	529	49	7	347	30	97
Related children[1]	591	42	1	38	90	420	178	2	-	18	16	143
Other	87	14	2	28	8	34	18	1	-	1	2	14
In married couple families with related children under 18 years	2 391	314	25	1 255	297	499	881	141	1	334	111	294
Husband	528	225	20	33	183	68	303	97	1	19	83	103
Wife	1 318	63	5	1 157	56	37	417	40	-	297	19	61
Related children[1]	477	24	-	38	51	364	147	2	-	18	7	120
Other	69	3	-	28	7	31	13	1	-	-	2	10
In married couple families with related children under 6 years	1 472	146	5	906	187	228	530	79	-	226	70	155
Husband	314	114	4	17	128	51	199	65	-	12	51	42
Wife	913	21	1	832	35	24	268	12	-	201	12	8
Other	61	2	-	27	7	24	12	1	-	-	2	8
In families with female householder, no spouse present	3 644	485	38	1 651	405	1 065	1 221	145	3	487	125	461
Householder	2 191	310	21	1 439	194	227	812	129	3	431	62	187
Other	1 453	175	17	212	211	838	409	17	-	56	63	273
In families with female householder, no spouse present, with related children under 18 years	3 163	330	12	1 569	318	934	1 080	132	1	463	105	378
Householder	2 028	247	4	1 393	170	214	765	122	1	417	54	170
Related children[1]	947	37	-	124	99	688	260	9	-	24	36	191
Other	187	46	8	53	49	31	56	2	-	22	15	17
In families with female householder, no spouse present, with related children under 6 years	1 884	156	7	1 155	183	383	581	61	-	315	65	142
Householder	1 320	102	4	997	87	129	452	53	-	281	34	82
Related children[1]	427	16	-	113	65	232	88	7	-	14	19	48
Other	137	38	3	44	31	22	42	2	-	19	11	11
In unrelated subfamilies	170	16	2	112	14	26	101	8	-	55	8	31
Unrelated individuals	2 356	903	195	365	311	583	1 259	135	19	158	193	753
Male	917	375	61	20	189	273	647	62	5	31	136	413
Householder	531	277	51	11	112	80	280	27	1	14	70	167
Female	1 439	528	133	345	122	311	612	73	14	127	57	341
Householder	922	451	124	161	63	123	289	55	14	52	36	132

See footnote at end of table.

[1]Includes related children 16 and 17 years of age and own children 18 years and over.

(B) Base less than 75,000

D3. Retirement Trends and Pensions

D3-1. Pension Plan Coverage of Workers, by Selected Characteristics: 1990

Covers workers as of March of following year who had earnings in year shown.

SEX AND AGE	NUMBER WITH COVERAGE (1,000)				PERCENT OF TOTAL WORKERS			
	Total [1]	White	Black	Hispanic [2]	Total [1]	White	Black	Hispanic [2]
Total	**53,120**	**45,817**	**5,757**	**2,639**	**46**	**46**	**41**	**26**
Male.	30,664	26,887	2,893	1,537	42	43	42	26
Under 65 years old	29,987	26,275	2,838	1,515	43	43	42	26
15 to 24 years old	1,626	1,368	217	162	13	13	17	12
25 to 44 years old.	18,060	15,738	1,786	939	47	48	46	28
45 to 64 years old.	10,301	9,169	835	414	55	55	53	37
65 years old and over.	677	612	55	22	25	24	29	23
Female.	22,456	18,930	2,864	1,102	38	38	40	27
Under 65 years old	21,990	18,524	2,818	1,095	37	38	41	27
15 to 24 years old	1,341	1,119	185	88	12	11	14	10
25 to 44 years old.	13,509	11,266	1,824	691	42	41	46	31
45 to 64 years old.	7,140	6,139	809	316	48	45	50	36
65 years old and over.	466	406	46	7	22	22	22	12

[1]Includes other races, not shown separately.

[2]Hispanic persons may be of any race.

Source: U.S. Bureau of the Census, unpublished data.

D3-2. Beneficiaries Receiving a Retirement Pension from a Private Pension Plan as a Percent of All Persons Age 65 and Over: 1970 to 1989

[Percent]

Year	Australia	Canada	France	Germany (FRG)	Japan	Netherlands	Switzerland	United Kingdom	United States
1970.	—	—	—	—	—	22	18	14	16
1975.	—	—	33	—	—	25	21	14	20
1980.	—	—	46	—	5	28	24	16	23
1981.	—	26	49	—	6	28	25	—	24
1982.	—	26	51	—	6	29	25	—	25
1983.	—	27	53	—	7	30	27	21	27
1984.	—	27	57	—	7	30	27	—	27
1985.	2	28	63	—	8	31	—	—	28
1986.	1	30	67	—	8	32	—	—	29
1987.	—	32	69	—	9	32	30	27	—
1988.	—	33	70	33	9	31	—	—	—
1989.	—	—	71	—	9	32	—	—	29

— Data not available.

D3-3. Demographic Characteristics of Wage-and-Salary Workers Offered an Employer or Union Pension Plan, by Employment Size of Firm, Small Firm Detail: 1988

			(Percent)				
			Employment size of firm				
Demographic characteristic	All firms	1-9	10-24	25-49	50-99	Under 100	100+
Total	57.6	12.6	25.8	40.6	50.6	26.3	79.2
Age:							
16-24	43.1	6.3	18.1	23.0	46.4	17.5	67.1
25-44	61.0	12.7	28.1	42.1	50.8	28.5	81.1
45–64	61.5	15.9	26.5	47.3	50.9	29.4	82.9
65+	39.2	9.5	28.4	51.3	58.2	25.2	66.3
Gender:							
Men	59.6	12.5	27.2	43.0	50.8	27.9	81.5
Women	55.0	11.4	23.7	34.8	49.5	24.3	76.3
Maritial status:							
Married, spouse present	60.9	15.4	28.1	46.6	53.3	30.2	81.0
Other	52.4	7.2	22.3	29.8	46.0	21.0	76.4

D3-4. Percent of Employers Offering Health Care Coverage to Retirees, by Size of Employer

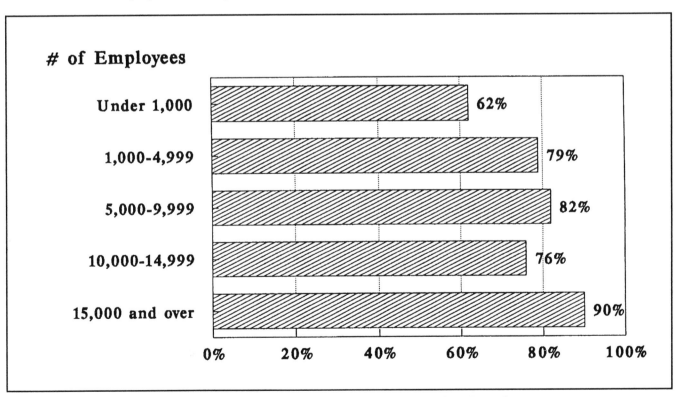

Source: Hewitt Associates Survey of Retiree Medical Benefits, 1990 prepared by AARP Public Policy Institute.

D3-5. Survival Status of New Retired-Worker Beneficiaries to 1989, by Selected Characteristics for Men and Women

Characteristic	Total		Men		Women	
	Alive	Dead	Alive	Dead	Alive	Dead
	Percent—**Continued**					
Year of birth:						
Before 1914	3.9	7.8	5.3	9.0	2.3	4.7
1914	3.0	3.7	3.8	4.1	2.0	2.8
1915	14.3	15.9	16.6	16.8	11.6	13.6
1916	13.3	14.5	15.3	15.8	10.9	11.1
1917	9.6	8.6	10.4	8.5	8.6	8.8
1918	36.5	35.3	31.4	32.8	42.6	41.9
1919	19.3	14.2	17.1	13.1	22.0	17.2
Income:						
Lowest quartile	29.3	39.0	28.8	37.6	30.0	42.6
2nd quartile	26.3	24.2	26.5	25.3	26.0	21.1
3rd quartile	23.5	19.0	22.7	18.8	24.5	19.6
Highest quartile	20.8	17.8	22.0	18.3	19.5	16.6
Education:						
Elementary or less	23.1	28.2	26.4	31.3	19.1	20.0
Some high school	19.7	22.6	19.3	21.3	20.2	26.1
High school	32.2	28.8	28.5	27.1	36.6	33.3
College	24.4	19.7	25.0	19.7	23.6	19.5
Other	.5	.5	.6	.2	.4	1.2
Other health insurance:						
Yes	78.2	69.1	76.3	67.0	80.5	74.6
No	21.5	30.2	23.4	32.4	19.2	24.1
Geographic region:						
South—						
SMSA [2]	21.9	23.0	21.7	24.0	22.0	20.4
Non-SMSA [2]	11.3	12.4	11.7	11.8	10.9	13.9
East—						
SMSA [2]	19.9	19.0	18.5	18.3	21.5	20.8
Non-SMSA [2]	2.2	2.2	2.4	2.3	2.0	2.0
Central—						
SMSA [2]	18.9	17.4	18.7	17.8	19.2	16.3
Non-SMSA [2]	9.4	11.4	9.9	12.4	8.7	8.6
West—						
SMSA [2]	12.1	12.0	12.3	10.9	11.8	15.1
Non-SMSA [2]	4.4	2.7	4.8	2.5	3.9	3.0

D3-5. Survival Status of New Retired-Worker Beneficiaries to 1989, by Selected Characteristics for Men and Women (continued)

Characteristic	Total		Men		Women	
	Alive	Dead	Alive	Dead	Alive	Dead
Number of beneficiaries (in thousands)	1,057.4	156.7	575.5	114.3	482.0	42.5
Average number of health disorders	2.45	3.01	2.52	3.02	2.36	2.9
	Percent					
Health indicators:						
One or more disorders	78.1	87.4	79.3	86.7	76.6	89.4
Two or more disorders	52.4	67.2	54.0	66.6	50.5	68.8
Functional limitation—						
Severe	14.8	25.2	12.5	22.9	17.4	31.5
Moderate	15.4	23.1	15.0	22.4	16.0	24.9
Minor or none	69.8	51.7	72.4	54.7	66.6	43.6
Diagnostic group—						
Musculoskeletal	53.1	57.2	51.9	55.0	54.5	62.9
Circulatory	40.1	53.1	40.7	53.1	39.5	53.1
Digestive	17.8	25.5	18.6	24.0	16.9	29.7
Respiratory	12.4	22.3	14.7	23.5	9.7	19.3
Left job for health reasons	19.5	29.4	19.8	29.0	19.1	30.3
Sociodemographic factor:						
Professional, technical	19.5	19.2	22.5	19.1	16.0	19.4
Sales, administrative	28.0	21.5	18.1	16.4	39.8	35.2
Precision, craft, and repair	13.8	17.5	22.7	22.7	3.2	3.7
Operator, fabricator, and laborer	18.8	18.7	20.3	20.5	16.9	13.9
Services	13.3	14.9	9.1	12.6	18.3	21.3
Self-employment	12.9	13.8	18.5	17.0	6.2	5.4
Black	7.9	11.4	7.9	11.2	7.9	11.9
White	89.7	86.5	89.6	86.4	89.8	86.8
Other	1.7	1.5	1.8	1.8	1.7	.7
Married	78.5	72.7	85.4	77.1	70.4	60.9
Not married	21.5	27.3	14.6	22.9	29.6	39.1
Men	54.4	72.9	100.0	100.0	(1)	(1)
Women	45.6	27.1	(1)	(1)	100.0	100.0

See footnotes at end of table.

[1]Data not available.
[2]Standard Metropolitan Statistical Area (SMSA).
Source: 1982 New Beneficiary Survey.

E. Economic Conditions

SOURCES OF INCOME

Some elderly are economically secure. Others, especially many of the oldest old, those living alone, blacks, Native Americans, some Asian groups, and Hispanics, have relatively high rates of poverty. The elderly rely heavily on Social Security benefits and asset income. In 1990, more than 9 out of 10 elderly persons received Social Security benefits. Social Security makes up 35% of the income of elderly Americans compared to almost 80% in Sweden. Asset income is received by two-thirds of the elderly; less than half receive pensions other than Social Security and 22% have some earnings. Asset income is unevenly divided: One-fourth of the elderly have none, and among the remainder the lower income group derives a much smaller proportion of its income from this source than the more affluent group. Blacks and Hispanics are much less likely to receive income from assets and pensions than whites.

Income from pensions is on the increase as a result of the Employment Retirement Income Security Act (ERISA), which provides strong incentives to invest in IRA, Keogh, 401(k), and other profit-sharing plans. While older persons have substantially less cash income than those under 65, several noncash factors favor the elderly: tax treatment; reduced family size; and in-kind benefits such as Medicare, Medicaid, group health insurance, and food stamps.

INCOME AND ASSETS

In 1990, the median family income of the elderly was $13,500. Social Security income accounts for a larger proportion of single persons' incomes than that of families. Women over 65 account for over half of the elderly population, but for over three-quarters of the poor. The nonwhite elderly population has substantially lower incomes than their white counterparts. The median income of elderly white men is almost twice as much as that of black and Hispanic men. The median income of single elderly men is substantially higher than that of single women.

Among the assets of the elderly are savings accounts, personal property, home and other real estate equity, and annuities. Home equity represents about 40% of the net worth of elderly households.

LIVING COSTS

The Consumer Price Index remained fairly stable between 1981 and 1992, compared to the rapid rise during the previous decade. The steepest rise was in the cost of medical care.

As the average age of the population has increased, not only federal but personal out-of-pocket expenditures of older individuals for health care have risen. Because many elderly are primarily on fixed incomes, price increases are of great concern to them.

POVERTY

While poverty rates among children and young adults increased during the last several years, the rates declined for the elderly, from 24% in 1970 to 11.4% in 1989; they increased slightly to 12.2% in 1990 when about 3.7 million elderly persons were below the poverty level ($7,905 for an older couple household, $6,268 for an older individual living alone). Another 2.1 million were classified as "near poor" at 125% of the poverty level. One of every 10 elderly whites was poor in 1990, compared to about one-third of blacks and one-fifth of Hispanics. Elderly women, especially black women, had a higher poverty rate than older men, and more of the oldest old were poor.

E1. Sources of Income

E1-1. Sources of Income of Persons 65 or Older: 1990

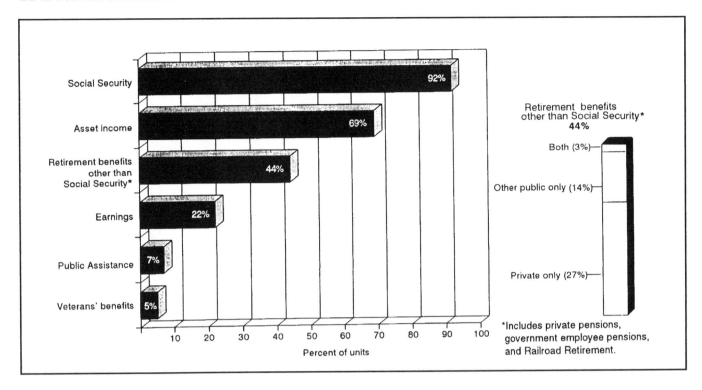

E1-2. Income Sources, by Age, Sex, and Marital Status: Percent of Aged Units 55 or Older with Money Income from Specified Sources: 1990

Unit source of income	Age 55-61	Age 62-64	Aged 65 or older					
			Total	65-69	70-74	75-79	80-84	85 or older
			All units					
Number (in thousands)	10,067	4,120	23,148	6,913	6,165	4,681	3,139	2,249
Percent of units with--								
Earnings	81	61	22	40	22	12	8	3
Wages and salaries..................................	74	56	18	34	19	10	6	2
Self-employment	15	12	5	8	5	3	2	1
Retirement benefits	29	66	95	90	96	97	97	95
Social Security [1]	13	56	92	86	94	95	95	92
Benefits other than Social Security............	20	40	44	48	48	42	37	29
Other public pensions	10	15	17	19	18	16	15	12
Railroad Retirement	0	1	2	2	2	2	2	2
Government employee pensions......................	9	14	15	17	16	14	13	10
Military	4	3	2	3	2	2	1	1
Federal	3	4	5	6	6	6	4	4
State/local	4	8	8	9	9	8	8	6
Private pensions or annuities.....................	11	27	30	33	34	29	24	19
Income from assets	67	70	69	71	70	68	69	65
Interest	64	67	68	69	68	67	67	63
Other income from assets............................	32	31	26	30	27	23	25	19
Dividends	24	24	19	23	19	18	18	13
Rent or royalties....................................	14	13	11	12	12	9	11	8
Estates or trusts....................................	0	0	1	1	1	1	1	0
Veterans' benefits	4	4	5	7	7	4	3	2
Unemployment compensation	7	4	1	1	1	0	0	0
Workers' compensation	3	2	0	1	0	0	0	0
Public assistance	6	6	7	6	7	7	8	8
Supplemental Security Income......................	4	5	6	6	6	7	7	8
Other public assistance............................	3	2	1	1	1	0	1	1
Personal contributions	2	1	1	1	1	0	1	1
See footnote at end of table.								

E1-2. Income Sources, by Age, Sex, and Marital Status: Percent of Aged Units 55 or Older with Money Income from Specified Sources: 1990 (continued)

Unit source of income	Age 55-61	Age 62-64	Aged 65 or older					
			Total	65-69	70-74	75-79	80-84	85 or older
			Married couples					
Number (in thousands)	6,026	2,351	9,343	3,756	2,706	1,610	895	377
Percent of units with--								
Earnings	91	73	34	50	32	19	13	8
Wages and salaries	84	67	29	43	28	16	10	6
Self-employment	20	17	9	12	7	6	4	3
Retirement benefits	30	68	96	92	98	99	99	98
Social Security[1]	11	56	93	88	95	97	97	95
Benefits other than Social Security	23	47	57	57	61	59	51	45
Other public pensions	11	18	22	22	23	23	19	18
Railroad Retirement	0	1	2	1	2	2	2	3
Government employee pensions	11	17	20	20	21	21	17	15
Military	5	4	3	4	4	3	2	1
Federal	3	5	7	7	7	7	6	7
State/local	4	9	11	11	11	13	11	8
Private pensions or annuities	12	32	41	40	45	41	36	32
Income from assets	78	79	79	80	79	79	78	74
Interest	75	76	77	78	77	78	77	72
Other income from assets	41	39	36	38	37	33	35	31
Dividends	31	31	28	30	28	26	25	20
Rent or royalties	19	18	15	15	15	13	14	14
Estates or trusts	0	0	1	0	1	1	1	0
Veterans' benefits	4	5	7	8	8	6	4	2
Unemployment compensation	8	5	1	2	1	0	0	0
Workers' compensation	3	2	1	1	0	0	0	0
Public assistance	2	3	3	3	3	2	2	6
Supplemental Security Income	1	2	2	2	2	2	2	6
Other public assistance	1	1	1	1	1	1	0	1
Personal contributions	1	0	0	0	0	0	0	2

Unit source of income	Age 55-61	Age 62-64	Aged 65 or older					
			Total	65-69	70-74	75-79	80-84	85 or older
			Nonmarried persons					
Number (in thousands)	4,041	1,768	13,805	3,157	3,459	3,072	2,244	1,872
Percent of units with--								
Earnings	65	45	13	27	15	9	6	2
Wages and salaries	59	41	11	24	13	7	4	1
Self-employment	8	5	2	4	3	2	2	0
Retirement benefits	28	64	94	87	96	96	96	95
Social Security[1]	15	56	91	84	93	94	93	92
Benefits other than Social Security	16	30	34	38	37	34	31	26
Other public pensions	7	12	13	15	14	13	14	11
Railroad Retirement	0	1	2	2	1	2	2	2
Government employee pensions	7	11	12	13	13	11	11	9
Military	2	2	1	2	1	1	1	1
Federal	2	3	4	5	5	5	4	3
State/local	3	7	7	6	8	6	7	5
Private pensions or annuities	10	19	22	25	25	23	19	17
Income from assets	50	58	63	60	63	63	65	63
Interest	48	55	61	58	62	61	63	61
Other income from assets	19	20	19	20	20	18	22	17
Dividends	14	15	13	14	13	13	15	12
Rent or royalties	8	8	8	8	9	6	9	7
Estates or trusts	0	0	1	1	1	1	1	1
Veterans' benefits	4	4	4	5	5	3	3	2
Unemployment compensation	5	3	0	1	1	0	0	0
Workers' compensation	2	2	0	1	0	0	0	0
Public assistance	12	10	9	10	10	9	10	8
Supplemental Security Income	8	7	9	9	9	9	9	8
Other public assistance	5	3	1	1	1	0	1	1
Personal contributions	3	3	1	1	1	1	1	1

See footnote at end of table.

E1-2. Income Sources, by Age, Sex, and Marital Status: Percent of Aged Units 55 or Older with Money Income from Specified Sources: 1990 (continued)

Unit source of income	Age 55-61	Age 62-64	Aged 65 or older Total	65-69	70-74	75-79	80-84	85 or older
			Nonmarried men					
Number (in thousands)	1,552	580	3,225	847	865	668	428	417
Percent of units with--								
Earnings	67	50	16	29	17	11	9	3
Wages and salaries	58	42	11	23	12	7	4	2
Self-employment	11	10	5	7	6	5	5	1
Retirement benefits	25	60	93	84	95	96	98	96
Social Security [1]	12	53	89	79	91	92	96	93
Benefits other than Social Security	14	32	41	44	42	42	38	34
Other public pensions	8	12	13	15	16	12	13	7
Railroad Retirement	0	0	2	2	2	3	2	2
Government employee pensions	7	12	11	12	14	9	11	6
Military	3	3	2	3	2	1	0	1
Federal	2	3	5	4	7	3	7	2
State/local	3	6	5	6	7	5	4	4
Private pensions or annuities	7	20	29	31	28	30	27	27
Income from assets	46	55	61	58	61	59	64	62
Interest	45	54	58	56	59	57	61	60
Other income from assets	17	18	21	20	22	17	26	19
Dividends	14	14	15	14	14	13	18	14
Rent or royalties	6	7	8	8	10	6	13	6
Estates or trusts	1	0	0	1	0	1	0	0
Veterans' benefits	4	6	7	10	10	4	5	3
Unemployment compensation	6	5	0	1	1	0	0	0
Workers' compensation	2	2	0	1	0	0	0	0
Public assistance	9	7	8	9	9	7	10	6
Supplemental Security Income	6	5	8	8	9	7	10	6
Other public assistance	4	2	0	1	0	0	0	0
Personal contributions	1	1	0	0	0	0	1	1

See footnote at end of table.

Unit source of income	Age 55-61	Age 62-64	Aged 65 or older Total	65-69	70-74	75-79	80-84	85 or older
			Nonmarried women					
Number (in thousands)	2,489	1,188	10,580	2,310	2,594	2,404	1,816	1,456
Percent of units with--								
Earnings	64	42	12	27	14	8	5	2
Wages and salaries	60	41	11	25	13	7	4	1
Self-employment	6	3	1	2	2	1	1	0
Retirement benefits	29	66	94	89	96	97	96	94
Social Security [1]	17	57	92	85	94	95	93	92
Benefits other than Social Security	17	29	32	36	36	32	29	24
Other public pensions	7	12	14	15	13	13	14	12
Railroad Retirement	0	1	2	2	1	1	2	2
Government employee pensions	7	11	12	14	12	12	11	10
Military	2	1	1	2	1	2	1	2
Federal	2	3	4	6	4	5	3	3
State/local	3	8	7	7	8	6	8	6
Private pensions or annuities	11	18	20	22	24	21	17	14
Income from assets	52	59	63	60	64	64	65	63
Interest	50	56	62	58	62	63	64	61
Other income from assets	20	21	19	20	19	18	21	17
Dividends	13	15	13	14	12	14	14	11
Rent or royalties	9	8	8	8	9	6	8	7
Estates or trusts	0	1	1	2	1	1	1	1
Veterans' benefits	3	3	3	3	4	2	2	2
Unemployment compensation	3	2	0	1	1	0	0	0
Workers' compensation	1	1	0	1	0	0	0	0
Public assistance	13	11	10	10	10	10	10	9
Supplemental Security Income	9	8	10	10	10	10	9	9
Other public assistance	5	3	1	1	1	0	1	1
Personal contributions	4	4	1	2	1	1	1	1

[1]Social Security beneficiaries may be receiving retired-worker benefits, dependents' or survivors' benefits, disability benefits, transitionally insured, or special age-72 benefits.

E1-3. Income Sources, by Age, Sex, Marital Status, and Social Security Beneficiary Status: Percent of Aged Units 55 or Older with Money Income from Specified Sources: 1990

Unit source of income	All units			Married couples			Nonmarried persons Total			Nonmarried persons Men			Nonmarried persons Women		
	55-61	62-64	65 or older	55-61	62-64	65 or older	55-61	62-64	65 or older	55-61	62-64	65 or older	55-61	62-64	65 or older
White															
Number (in thousands)	8,471	3,563	20,489	5,451	2,162	8,579	3,020	1,401	11,910	1,137	473	2,676	1,883	928	9,234
Percent of units with--															
Earnings	83	63	22	91	73	34	69	47	13	71	53	15	67	45	12
Wages and salaries	76	57	18	84	67	29	61	43	11	60	44	10	62	42	11
Self-employment	17	13	5	21	18	9	10	6	2	14	11	6	7	3	1
Retirement benefits	30	68	96	30	69	96	29	68	95	27	64	94	30	70	96
Social Security [1]	12	57	93	11	56	93	15	58	93	12	55	91	16	60	93
Benefits other than soc. security	22	42	46	23	48	59	19	33	36	17	35	44	19	32	34
Other public pensions	10	16	17	11	18	22	8	12	14	9	12	13	7	13	14
Railroad Retirement	0	1	2	0	1	2	0	1	2	1	0	2	0	1	2
Government employee pensions	10	15	15	11	17	20	7	12	12	8	12	11	7	12	12
Military	4	3	2	5	4	3	2	2	1	3	4	2	1	1	1
Federal	3	4	6	3	5	7	2	4	4	2	3	5	2	4	4
State/local	4	8	9	4	9	11	3	7	7	3	6	5	3	8	7
Private pensions or annuities	12	29	32	13	33	43	12	22	24	9	24	32	13	21	22
Income from assets	72	74	74	81	81	82	58	65	68	53	64	67	61	65	69
Interest	70	72	72	78	78	80	55	62	66	51	62	65	58	62	67
Other income from assets	36	34	28	43	41	38	23	24	22	22	21	24	24	25	21
Dividends	27	27	21	33	33	30	17	18	15	17	18	17	17	19	15
Rent or royalties	16	15	11	19	18	15	9	9	9	8	8	10	10	10	8
Estates or trusts	0	0	1	0	0	1	1	1	1	1	0	0	0	1	1
Veterans' benefits	4	4	5	4	5	7	4	4	4	5	5	7	2	3	3
Unemployment compensation	7	4	1	8	5	1	5	3	0	7	5	0	3	2	0
Workers' compensation	3	2	0	3	2	1	2	2	0	2	2	0	1	1	0
Public assistance	4	4	5	2	3	2	9	7	7	7	4	6	10	8	7
Supplemental Security Income	3	4	5	1	2	2	6	5	7	4	4	6	7	6	7
Other public assistance	2	1	0	1	0	0	3	2	1	3	0	0	4	2	1
Personal contributions	2	1	1	1	0	0	4	3	1	1	1	0	5	3	1

See footnotes at end of table.

Unit source of income	All units			Married couples			Nonmarried persons Total			Nonmarried persons Men			Nonmarried persons Women		
	55-61	62-64	65 or older	55-61	62-64	65 or older	55-61	62-64	65 or older	55-61	62-64	65 or older	55-61	62-64	65 or older
Beneficiary units [1]															
Number (in thousands)	1,269	2,301	21,250	668	1,314	8,659	601	987	12,591	185	305	2,873	416	682	9,718
Percent of units with--															
Earnings	45	45	20	68	59	32	20	26	12	15	28	13	22	25	11
Wages and salaries	42	41	17	65	54	28	17	23	10	14	22	9	18	23	10
Self-employment	7	8	5	9	12	8	4	3	2	2	6	5	4	2	1
Retirement benefits	100	100	100	100	100	100	100	100	100	100	100	100	100	100	100
Social Security [1]	100	100	100	100	100	100	100	100	100	100	100	100	100	100	100
Benefits other than soc. security	30	52	44	36	62	59	23	38	35	12	46	42	28	35	32
Other public pensions	9	17	16	11	21	21	6	13	12	3	14	12	8	13	13
Railroad Retirement	1	0	1	0	1	1	1	0	1	2	0	1	1	0	1
Government employee pensions	8	17	15	11	20	20	5	13	11	2	14	11	7	13	12
Military	2	4	2	4	5	3	1	2	1	0	4	2	1	1	1
Federal	2	4	5	3	5	7	1	3	4	0	4	4	2	3	4
State/local	5	10	9	5	12	12	4	8	7	2	7	6	5	9	7
Private pensions or annuities	22	37	32	27	45	44	17	27	24	8	33	32	21	24	22
Income from assets	53	68	70	66	76	80	37	58	64	28	53	61	42	59	65
Interest	51	65	69	64	73	78	36	55	63	25	52	59	41	56	64
Other income from assets	22	27	27	33	34	36	11	18	20	7	13	21	13	20	20
Dividends	14	20	19	22	25	28	6	12	14	5	11	14	7	13	14
Rent or royalties	10	12	11	13	15	15	6	8	8	5	3	8	6	9	8
Estates or trusts	0	0	1	0	0	1	0	0	1	0	0	0	0	0	1
Veterans' benefits	7	5	5	9	5	7	5	5	4	10	9	8	3	4	3
Unemployment compensation	3	3	1	5	4	1	1	1	0	0	2	0	1	0	0
Workers' compensation	4	1	0	6	2	1	1	1	0	1	2	0	1	1	0
Public assistance	14	5	6	7	3	2	23	8	8	16	5	7	26	9	8
Supplemental Security Income	12	4	5	6	3	2	20	6	8	16	5	7	22	6	8
Other public assistance	3	1	0	1	1	0	5	3	1	4	0	0	5	4	1
Personal contributions	1	1	1	1	0	0	1	2	1	2	0	0	1	3	1

See footnote at end of table.

[1] Social Security beneficiaries may be receiving retired-worker benefits, dependents' or survivors' benefits, disability benefits, transitionally insured, or special age-72 benefits.

E1-4. Income Sources, by Age, Sex, Marital Status, Race, and Hispanic Origin: Percent of Aged Units 55 or Older with Money Income from Specified Sources: 1990

	All units			Married couples			Nonmarried persons								
							Total			Men			Women		
Unit source of income	55-61	62-64	65 or older	55-61	62-64	65 or older	55-61	62-64	65 or older	55-61	62-64	65 or older	55-61	62-64	65 or older
Black															
Number (in thousands)	1,277	445	2,147	401	143	569	877	303	1,577	374	92	462	502	211	1,115
Percent of units with--															
Earnings	66	47	20	88	72	37	55	36	14	56	36	18	55	35	12
Wages and salaries	63	45	19	86	69	36	52	34	12	53	34	15	52	34	11
Self-employment	6	4	2	11	4	4	3	3	2	3	7	3	3	2	1
Retirement benefits	26	56	90	31	62	96	24	53	88	19	42	87	27	58	88
Social Security[1]	18	51	87	18	56	91	17	49	85	13	42	83	20	52	85
Benefits other than soc. security	11	23	27	16	38	41	8	16	22	6	13	28	10	18	20
Other public pensions	6	11	13	8	17	19	5	9	11	3	8	13	6	9	11
Railroad Retirement	0	0	1	0	0	1	0	0	1	0	0	2	0	0	1
Government employee pensions	6	11	12	8	17	18	5	9	10	3	8	11	6	9	9
Military	1	3	1	4	7	1	0	1	1	1	2	1	0	0	1
Federal	2	2	4	2	4	6	2	1	4	1	0	6	3	2	3
State/local	3	6	7	2	6	12	3	6	5	2	5	5	4	7	5
Private pensions or annuities	5	13	15	8	23	26	3	8	11	3	5	15	4	9	10
Income from assets	30	34	29	45	49	43	24	27	24	24	13	26	23	33	23
Interest	29	32	27	43	44	40	22	27	23	24	13	26	21	32	21
Other income from assets	8	8	7	16	16	12	5	3	5	4	4	4	5	3	5
Dividends	3	3	3	6	7	5	2	1	2	3	0	3	2	2	1
Rent or royalties	5	4	4	11	9	8	3	2	3	2	4	1	3	2	4
Estates or trusts	0	0	0	0	0	0	0	0	0	0	0	0	0	0	0
Veterans' benefits	3	5	4	4	7	8	3	4	3	2	9	7	3	2	1
Unemployment compensation	5	3	1	7	4	1	4	3	1	5	6	1	3	1	0
Workers' compensation	2	3	0	2	7	0	2	1	1	3	3	1	1	0	0
Public assistance	19	17	21	9	6	10	23	22	25	18	20	20	27	23	27
Supplemental Security Income	12	13	20	6	3	7	15	17	25	11	13	19	18	19	27
Other public assistance	7	5	2	3	3	3	9	7	1	7	7	1	10	7	1
Personal contributions	1	2	1	1	0	1	1	2	1	0	0	0	1	3	1

See footnotes at end of table.

	All units			Married couples			Nonmarried persons								
							Total			Men			Women		
Unit source of income	55-61	62-64	65 or older	55-61	62-64	65 or older	55-61	62-64	65 or older	55-61	62-64	65 or older	55-61	62-64	65 or older
Nonbeneficiary units															
Number (in thousands)	8,798	1,818	1,898	5,358	1,038	684	3,440	781	1,214	1,367	274	352	2,073	506	862
Percent of units with--															
Earnings	86	82	38	94	91	57	73	69	28	74	74	38	73	66	24
Wages and salaries	79	75	34	87	83	50	66	64	25	64	65	33	68	64	22
Self-employment	17	17	8	22	24	15	9	7	4	13	14	8	7	4	2
Retirement benefits	19	24	34	21	27	40	15	19	30	15	16	32	15	21	29
Social Security[1]	—	—	—	—	—	—	—	—	—	—	—	—	—	—	—
Benefits other than soc. security	19	24	34	21	27	40	15	19	30	15	16	32	15	21	29
Other public pensions	10	12	27	11	13	32	7	10	25	8	9	27	7	11	24
Railroad Retirement	0	1	10	0	1	12	0	1	10	0	1	12	0	2	9
Government employee pensions	9	11	18	11	12	21	7	9	16	8	9	15	7	9	16
Military	4	2	2	5	3	3	2	1	1	3	3	1	2	0	2
Federal	3	4	11	3	5	13	2	3	10	2	2	12	3	4	10
State/local	3	5	6	4	5	6	3	5	5	3	4	3	3	6	6
Private pensions or annuities	10	13	8	10	16	12	8	9	7	7	7	6	9	11	7
Income from assets	69	72	54	79	82	70	52	58	45	49	58	56	54	58	41
Interest	66	69	52	77	79	67	50	56	44	47	56	54	51	57	40
Other income from assets	34	36	21	42	46	35	20	23	13	19	24	20	21	22	11
Dividends	25	30	17	32	38	30	15	18	10	15	18	15	15	18	7
Rent or royalties	15	15	8	20	21	14	8	8	5	6	11	7	9	6	4
Estates or trusts	0	1	1	0	1	0	0	1	1	1	0	1	0	2	2
Veterans' benefits	3	3	4	3	4	5	3	3	3	4	2	7	3	3	.2
Unemployment compensation	7	6	1	9	7	2	5	5	1	7	8	1	4	4	1
Workers' compensation	2	2	1	3	3	0	2	2	1	3	2	1	2	2	1
Public assistance	5	7	19	2	3	10	10	12	24	9	9	15	11	13	28
Supplemental Security Income	3	5	19	1	2	9	6	9	24	5	6	15	7	11	27
Other public assistance	3	2	2	1	1	3	5	3	2	4	3	1	5	3	2
Personal contributions	2	2	1	1	1	1	3	3	1	1	1	1	5	4	1

E1-4. Income Sources, by Age, Sex, Marital Status, Race, and Hispanic Origin: Percent of Aged Units 55 or Older with Money Income from Specified Sources: 1990 (continued)

	All units			Married couples			Nonmarried persons								
							Total			Men			Women		
Unit source of income	55-61	62-64	65 or older	55-61	62-64	65 or older	55-61	62-64	65 or older	55-61	62-64	65 or older	55-61	62-64	65 or older
	Hispanic origin [2]														
Number (in thousands)	638	234	860	319	116	345	319	118	515	117	44	120	202	74	395
Percent of units with--															
Earnings	74	56	20	86	70	33	62	43	11	70	(³)	13	57	(³)	10
Wages and salaries	69	53	17	81	63	29	58	43	10	64	(³)	11	54	(³)	9
Self-employment	9	7	4	14	13	8	4	1	1	6	(³)	1	3	(³)	1
Retirement benefits	18	55	83	20	54	91	17	57	78	17	(³)	80	17	(³)	77
Social Security [1]	10	48	80	10	47	87	9	49	76	7	(³)	78	11	(³)	75
Benefits other than soc. security	11	27	24	13	31	37	9	23	15	11	(³)	27	8	(³)	12
Other public pensions	6	9	8	6	10	14	5	8	5	7	(³)	9	4	(³)	4
Railroad Retirement	1	1	1	1	1	1	1	2	1	1	(³)	1	0	(³)	1
Government employee pensions	5	8	8	6	9	13	5	7	4	6	(³)	9	4	(³)	3
Military	1	2	1	1	2	1	0	1	0	0	(³)	0	0	(³)	0
Federal	2	4	4	2	6	7	2	3	2	4	(³)	7	1	(³)	1
State/local	2	2	3	2	1	6	2	3	2	2	(³)	2	2	(³)	2
Private pensions or annuities	6	17	16	8	20	25	5	14	10	4	(³)	17	5	(³)	8
Income from assets	41	41	38	52	50	48	30	32	32	37	(³)	38	26	(³)	30
Interest	38	36	36	48	45	47	28	27	29	35	(³)	33	24	(³)	28
Other income from assets	13	13	9	19	17	12	7	8	7	9	(³)	12	5	(³)	5
Dividends	6	6	4	9	8	6	3	4	2	5	(³)	5	2	(³)	2
Rent or royalties	8	8	5	13	10	7	4	6	4	4	(³)	7	4	(³)	3
Estates or trusts	0	0	0	0	0	0	0	0	0	0	(³)	0	0	(³)	0
Veterans' benefits	3	3	3	2	4	6	3	2	2	3	(³)	4	3	(³)	1
Unemployment compensation	9	5	1	10	7	2	7	2	1	11	(³)	0	4	(³)	1
Workers' compensation	4	1	0	6	1	0	2	1	1	4	(³)	1	2	(³)	0
Public assistance	9	12	24	3	9	13	16	14	31	11	(³)	18	18	(³)	35
Supplemental Security Income	6	8	23	2	7	12	10	10	31	6	(³)	18	11	(³)	34
Other public assistance	5	4	1	2	4	2	8	4	1	5	(³)	1	10	(³)	1
Personal contributions	2	0	2	0	0	1	3	1	2	2	(³)	3	4	(³)	2

[1] Social Security beneficiaries may be receiving retired-worker benefits, dependents' or survivors' benefits, disability benefits, transitionally insured, or special age-72 benefits.

[2] Persons of Hispanic origin may be of any race.
[3] Fewer than 75,000 weighted cases.

E1-5. Income Sources, by Age, Race, Hispanic Origin, and Social Security Beneficiary Status: Percent of Aged Units 55 or Older with Money Income from Specified Sources: 1990

	Beneficiary units [1]			Nonbeneficiary units		
Unit source of income	55-61	62-64	65 or older	55-61	62-64	65 or older
	White					
Number (in thousands)	1,025	2,025	19,048	7,446	1,538	1,442
Percent of units with--						
Earnings	49	47	20	88	85	42
Retirement benefits	100	100	100	20	26	39
Social Security [1]	100	100	100	—	—	—
Benefits other than Social Security	34	54	46	20	26	39
Other public pensions	10	18	16	10	13	31
Railroad Retirement	1	0	1	0	1	13
Government employee pensions	9	17	15	10	12	19
Private pensions or annuities	25	40	34	11	15	11
Income from assets	60	72	75	74	78	63
Veterans' benefits	8	5	5	3	4	4
Public assistance	10	4	4	4	4	15
	Black					
Number (in thousands)	225	227	1,858	1,052	218	288
Percent of units with--						
Earnings	30	31	19	73	64	29
Retirement benefits	100	100	100	10	10	23
Social Security [1]	100	100	100	—	—	—
Benefits other than Social Security	14	36	28	10	10	23
Other public pensions	5	15	12	6	7	21
Railroad Retirement	0	0	1	0	0	5
Government employee pensions	5	15	11	6	7	17
Private pensions or annuities	9	21	17	4	4	2
Income from assets	17	34	30	33	34	25
Veterans' benefits	4	9	4	3	0	4
Public assistance	32	11	19	16	23	33

E1-5. Income Sources, by Age, Race, Hispanic Origin, and Social Security Beneficiary Status: Percent of Aged Units 55 or Older with Money Income from Specified Sources: 1990 (continued)

Unit source of income	Beneficiary units [1]			Nonbeneficiary units		
	55-61	62-64	65 or older	55-61	62-64	65 or older
	Hispanic origin [2]					
Number (in thousands)...............................	63	113	691	575	121	168
Percent of units with--						
Earnings	([3])	35	19	77	76	23
Retirement benefits	([3])	100	100	9	14	13
Social Security [1]	([3])	100	100	—	—	—
Benefits other than Social Security....................	([3])	41	26	9	14	13
Other public pensions.................................	([3])	11	9	6	8	8
Railroad Retirement	([3])	0	0	1	2	3
Government employee pensions....................	([3])	11	8	5	5	5
Private pensions or annuities........................	([3])	30	19	5	6	5
Income from assets......................................	([3])	41	43	41	41	18
Veterans' benefits	([3])	4	4	3	2	2
Public assistance	([3])	11	20	8	12	39

[1]Social Security beneficiaries may be receiving retired-worker benefits, dependents' or survivors' benefits, disability benefits, transitionally insured, or special age-72 benefits.
[2]Persons of Hispanic origin may be of any race.
[3]Fewer than 75,000 weighted cases.

E1-6. Percent Composition of Total Income of Family Units, by Type of Income and Age of Unit Head: 1984 and 1989[1]

Age of unit head	1984					1989				
	Earnings	Social Security	Property	Pension	Other	Earnings	Social Security	Property	Pension	Other
All ages...	75.5	7.7	9.3	4.1	3.3	76.7	7.3	8.3	4.6	3.1
Under 65......	87.3	1.7	5.5	2.2	3.4	88.0	1.6	5.0	2.3	3.2
65 or older....	19.6	36.4	27.5	13.6	2.9	22.1	35.0	24.2	15.8	2.9
Under 25......	89.2	.4	2.0	.1	8.3	89.8	.4	1.6	.2	8.0
25-34	93.6	.4	2.2	.4	3.4	94.0	.4	2.0	.3	3.3
35-44	92.2	.8	3.7	.5	2.9	92.4	.7	3.6	.6	2.7
45-54	87.9	1.4	5.8	2.0	3.0	88.9	1.1	5.5	1.8	2.7
55-64	71.6	5.4	12.7	7.3	2.9	71.1	5.3	11.5	8.9	3.2
65-74	24.4	33.2	25.0	14.6	2.8	27.8	30.4	21.8	17.1	2.8
75 or older....	10.5	42.3	32.3	11.7	3.2	11.6	43.4	28.6	13.3	3.1

[1]Income adjusted for size of family unit and age of head.
Source: Tabulations from March 1985 and March 1990 PS files.

E1-7. Relative Importance of Income Sources, by Age, Sex, and Marital Status: Percent Distribution of Aged Units 55 or Older Receiving Particular Sources of Income: 1990

Proportion of unit income (recipients only) [1]	Age 55-61				Age 62-64				Aged 65 or older			
	Married couples	Nonmarried persons			Married couples	Nonmarried persons			Married couples	Nonmarried persons		
		Total	Men	Women		Total	Men	Women		Total	Men	Women
Retirement benefits [2]												
Number (in thousands)	1,793	1,117	384	733	1,595	1,138	349	788	8,932	12,949	2,984	9,965
Total percent	100	100	100	100	100	100	100	100	100	100	100	100
1-19	32	14	11	16	23	10	8	11	7	3	3	3
20-39	28	15	12	17	17	11	13	10	12	8	8	8
40-59	15	14	13	15	16	15	14	15	17	14	13	15
60-79	10	13	12	13	14	15	9	18	20	18	19	17
80 or more	15	43	52	39	30	49	56	46	44	56	56	56
50 or more	32	64	71	60	51	72	76	71	72	82	83	81
90 or more	12	36	44	32	22	42	49	39	32	46	46	46
100	6	23	29	20	9	22	23	22	12	24	24	24
Mean proportion	39	63	69	60	53	69	72	68	68	76	77	76
Social Security [3]												
Number (in thousands)	668	601	185	416	1,314	987	305	682	8,658	12,584	2,871	9,713
Total percent	100	100	100	100	100	100	100	100	100	100	100	100
1-19	42	10	10	10	39	14	16	13	16	7	8	6
20-39	26	15	9	18	28	21	24	20	25	16	18	16
40-59	15	21	17	23	16	20	20	21	24	19	21	18
60-79	4	13	11	13	9	15	11	16	16	19	20	18
80 or more	13	41	52	37	8	30	28	31	20	40	33	42
50 or more	24	68	73	65	23	54	51	55	47	68	64	69
90 or more	9	34	45	30	6	26	24	26	13	31	25	33
100	8	26	33	22	4	17	16	18	7	18	16	18
Mean proportion	33	65	70	63	33	57	53	59	50	66	62	67
Government employee pension [4]												
Number (in thousands)	653	281	110	172	392	202	67	135	1,865	1,634	362	1,272
Total percent	100	100	100	100	100	100	100	100	100	100	100	100
1-19	24	19	13	23	25	17	([5])	18	28	20	15	21
20-39	40	22	17	25	28	21	([5])	24	28	30	20	33
40-59	15	18	21	15	19	22	([5])	21	22	24	27	23
60-79	10	14	10	17	16	24	([5])	23	15	18	24	16
80 or more	10	27	38	20	11	17	([5])	14	7	9	13	8
50 or more	27	51	58	46	39	53	([5])	49	32	38	52	34
90 or more	7	20	28	15	6	10	([5])	9	4	5	7	5
100	2	9	12	6	3	4	([5])	2	1	2	1	2
Mean proportion	38	52	60	47	42	51	([5])	48	39	43	50	41
Private pension or annuity												
Number (in thousands)	740	388	116	272	758	336	119	217	3,852	3,096	930	2,166
Total percent	100	100	100	100	100	100	100	100	100	100	100	100
1-19	48	33	20	38	35	32	22	38	48	48	33	55
20-39	22	24	18	27	33	31	27	34	36	33	42	29
40-59	13	15	16	15	22	25	32	20	13	15	20	13
60-79	8	9	13	8	6	6	10	3	2	3	4	2
80 or more	9	19	33	12	4	6	8	5	1	1	1	2
50 or more	24	34	52	26	20	21	28	17	7	9	13	7
90 or more	5	15	26	11	3	6	6	5	0	1	1	1
100	2	9	17	5	0	4	2	5	0	1	0	1
Mean proportion	30	41	55	35	30	34	40	31	23	24	30	22

E1-7. Relative Importance of Income Sources, by Age, Sex, and Marital Status: Percent Distribution of Aged Units 55 or Older Receiving Particular Sources of Income: 1990 (continued)

Proportion of unit income (recipients only) [1]	Age 55-61				Age 62-64				Aged 65 or older			
	Married couples	Nonmarried persons			Married couples	Nonmarried persons			Married couples	Nonmarried persons		
		Total	Men	Women		Total	Men	Women		Total	Men	Women
Earnings												
Number (in thousands)	5,450	2,617	1,028	1,588	1,710	786	284	503	3,152	1,775	491	1,284
Total percent	100	100	100	100	100	100	100	100	100	100	100	100
1-19	2	4	4	4	10	7	7	7	24	28	25	29
20-39	4	4	3	5	12	12	12	12	25	21	20	21
40-59	7	6	4	8	13	11	11	11	20	21	20	21
60-79	14	10	9	11	17	14	15	14	18	13	13	12
80 or more	72	76	80	73	48	56	54	56	13	18	22	17
50 or more	90	89	92	87	73	75	75	75	41	40	45	38
90 or more	58	67	70	64	34	43	45	42	8	13	17	11
100	13	32	38	28	7	14	12	16	2	5	6	5
Mean proportion	83	84	87	83	68	71	72	71	43	43	46	41
Income from assets												
Number (in thousands)	4,558	1,981	706	1,275	1,805	1,011	317	694	7,299	8,591	1,942	6,649
Total percent	100	100	100	100	100	100	100	100	100	100	100	100
1-19	79	65	70	63	70	63	71	60	55	49	51	48
20-39	13	13	11	14	17	20	15	22	23	24	25	23
40-59	4	7	6	8	7	9	5	10	13	15	14	16
60-79	2	4	2	5	3	5	6	4	6	9	7	9
80 or more	2	11	11	11	2	4	2	4	3	4	3	4
50 or more	6	18	16	19	8	13	10	14	14	19	15	21
90 or more	2	9	10	9	1	3	1	3	1	2	1	2
100	2	8	8	7	1	2	1	3	0	1	1	1
Mean proportion	10	18	16	19	13	17	13	18	21	24	22	24
Public assistance												
Number (in thousands)	148	481	147	335	68	171	40	131	262	1,307	257	1,049
Total percent	100	100	100	100	100	100	100	100	100	100	100	100
1-19	44	16	12	17	(⁵)	19	(⁵)	18	31	33	32	33
20-39	12	9	7	9	(⁵)	18	(⁵)	19	32	29	37	26
40-59	11	12	8	14	(⁵)	9	(⁵)	11	12	15	9	17
60-79	3	6	6	6	(⁵)	4	(⁵)	5	2	3	3	4
80 or more	30	58	67	54	(⁵)	50	(⁵)	46	23	20	18	20
50 or more	36	67	75	64	(⁵)	57	(⁵)	55	30	30	26	31
90 or more	26	55	65	51	(⁵)	47	(⁵)	43	23	19	17	19
100	25	52	63	48	(⁵)	42	(⁵)	39	19	17	15	18
Mean proportion	44	71	77	68	(⁵)	63	(⁵)	62	42	40	38	41

[1]Units with zero or negative total income are excluded. In addition, units with negative earnings are excluded from the earnings section and units with negative income from assets are excluded from the income from assets section.

[2]Retirement benefits include Social Security benefits, Railroad Retirement, government employee pensions, and private pensions or annuities.

[3]Social Security beneficiaries may be receiving retired-worker benefits, dependents' or survivors' benefits, transitionally insured, or special age-72 benefits.

[4]Government employee pensions include federal, state, local, and military pensions.

[5]Fewer than 75,000 weighted cases.

E1-8. Receipt of Income of Aged Units from Various Sources, by Race and Hispanic Origin: 1990

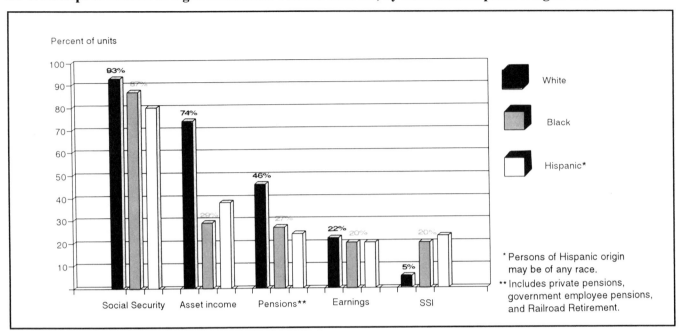

* Persons of Hispanic origin
  may be of any race.
** Includes private pensions,
  government employee pensions,
  and Railroad Retirement.

E1-9. Source of Income—Number with Income and Mean Income of Specified Type—of Persons 65 Years and Over: 1991

(Numbers in Thousands)

Total	30 256	15 130	27 068	15 738	2 546	9 572	1 089	9 991
Earnings	4 732	14 880	4 207	15 470	388	9 893	153	12 462
Wages and salary	3 757	15 192	3 294	15 871	350	10 118	132	12 496
Nonfarm self-employment	923	12 039	861	12 297	38	(B)	22	(B)
Farm self-employment	263	8 422	259	8 523	-	(B)	-	(B)
Unemployment compensation	156	1 915	141	2 010	11	(B)	12	(B)
State or local only	119	1 534	106	1 601	10	(B)	9	(B)
Combinations	37	(B)	36	(B)	1	(B)	3	(B)
Workers' compensation	88	5 741	68	(B)	17	(B)	4	(B)
State payments	36	(B)	24	(B)	8	(B)	1	(B)
Employment insurance	42	(B)	34	(B)	7	(B)	3	(B)
Own insurance	2	(B)	2	(B)	-	(B)	-	(B)
Other	9	(B)	8	(B)	1	(B)	-	(B)
Social Security	27 598	6 465	24 830	6 581	2 271	5 319	870	5 473
SSI (Supplemental Security Income)	1 722	2 517	1 090	2 458	520	2 347	257	3 182
Public assistance, total	153	2 060	100	1 975	46	(B)	20	(B)
AFDC only	48	(B)	25	(B)	18	(B)	6	(B)
Other assistance only	105	1 548	74	(B)	27	(B)	14	(B)
Both	-	(B)	-	(B)	-	(B)	-	(B)
Veterans' benefits	1 299	4 259	1 163	4 281	114	4 060	28	(B)
Disability only	698	3 759	653	3 768	41	(B)	11	(B)
Survivors only	237	3 762	208	3 871	20	(B)	5	(B)
Pension only	280	5 981	228	6 144	43	(B)	10	(B)
Education only	-	(B)	-	(B)	-	(B)	-	(B)
Other only	72	(B)	64	(B)	8	(B)	2	(B)
Combinations	12	(B)	10	(B)	1	(B)	1	(B)
Means-tested	432	4 210	355	4 245	61	(B)	10	(B)
Nonmeans-tested	867	4 283	809	4 297	53	(B)	18	(B)
Survivors benefits	1 996	6 346	1 882	6 386	93	5 011	41	(B)
Company or union	927	4 748	867	4 787	44	(B)	19	(B)
Federal government	254	7 604	237	7 584	18	(B)	4	(B)
Military retirement	136	4 736	134	4 719	2	(B)	5	(B)
State or local government	202	4 768	188	4 674	13	(B)	5	(B)
Railroad retirement	155	6 583	144	6 669	11	(B)	4	(B)
Workers' compensation	13	(B)	13	(B)	-	(B)	2	(B)
Black Lung	63	(B)	61	(B)	2	(B)	-	(B)
Estates or trusts	142	16 359	139	16 219	4	(B)	1	(B)
Annuities	151	3 613	147	3 651	4	(B)	1	(B)
Other or Don't Know	47	(B)	46	(B)	2	(B)	1	(B)
Disability benefits	327	6 511	276	6 770	48	(B)	13	(B)
Workers' compensation	28	(B)	20	(B)	6	(B)	-	(B)
Company or union	77	3 735	57	(B)	20	(B)	4	(B)
Federal government	77	10 093	73	(B)	4	(B)	3	(B)
Military retirement	28	(B)	23	(B)	5	(B)	1	(B)
State or local government	23	(B)	18	(B)	5	(B)	-	(B)
Railroad retirement	13	(B)	13	(B)	-	(B)	-	(B)
Accident insurance	23	(B)	23	(B)	-	(B)	1	(B)
Black Lung	46	(B)	43	(B)	3	(B)	1	(B)
Temporary insurance	-	(B)	-	(B)	-	(B)	-	(B)
Other or Don't Know	17	(B)	12	(B)	6	(B)	3	(B)
Pensions	9 994	8 071	9 329	8 164	556	6 640	190	7 464
Company or union	6 476	5 837	6 092	5 893	322	4 722	103	4 930
Federal government	977	15 888	900	16 396	54	(B)	28	(B)
Military retirement	345	15 322	324	15 524	20	(B)	4	(B)
State or local government	1 765	8 578	1 598	8 605	149	8 014	34	(B)
Railroad retirement	292	9 686	278	9 820	13	(B)	14	(B)
Annuities	219	7 136	213	7 130	5	(B)	3	(B)
IRA, KEOGH, or 401(k)	295	6 215	292	6 240	2	(B)	5	(B)
Other or Don't Know	126	5 483	114	5 805	5	(B)	2	(B)
Interest	20 712	3 399	19 673	3 452	704	2 104	387	2 433
Dividends	5 297	3 566	5 196	3 593	48	(B)	35	(B)
Rents, royalties, estates or trusts	2 787	4 178	2 595	4 165	148	4 502	56	(B)
Education	19	(B)	19	(B)	-	(B)	3	(B)
Pell grant only	1	(B)	1	(B)	-	(B)	1	(B)
Other government only	2	(B)	2	(B)	-	(B)	-	(B)
Scholarships only	2	(B)	2	(B)	-	(B)	2	(B)
Other only	14	(B)	14	(B)	-	(B)	1	(B)
Combinations	-	(B)	-	(B)	-	(B)	-	(B)
Child support	10	(B)	6	(B)	4	(B)	2	(B)
Alimony	32	(B)	31	(B)	1	(B)	1	(B)
Financial assistance	147	3 228	139	3 379	5	(B)	11	(B)
Other income	356	4 089	338	4 144	9	(B)	3	(B)
Combinations of income types:								
Government transfer payments	28 921	8 109	25 882	8 275	2 451	6 691	1 026	6 664
Public assistance or SSI	1 794	2 591	1 136	2 532	541	2 418	265	3 346
Social Security or Railroad retirement	27 897	6 538	25 109	6 659	2 291	5 338	886	5 561
Company or union pension[2]	7 318	5 807	6 867	5 858	378	4 717	123	5 095
Military retirement[2]	505	12 264	476	12 400	27	(B)	10	(B)
Federal government retirement[2]	1 280	14 239	1 182	14 627	75	9 958	36	(B)
State or local retirement[2]	1 947	8 305	1 766	8 311	161	7 984	37	(B)
Property income[3]	21 204	4 870	20 097	4 958	759	2 899	408	3 478
Child support or alimony	42	(B)	37	(B)	5	(B)	3	(B)
Rents, royalties, estates, or trusts[3]	2 905	4 809	2 709	4 820	148	4 502	57	(B)

[1]Persons of Hispanic origin may be of any race.

[2]Includes payments reported as survivor, disability, or retirement benefits.

[3]Includes estates and trusts reported as survivor benefits.

(B) Base less then 75,000

E1-10. Composition of Gross Income of Families with Heads Age 65 to 74 in Selected Countries: 1979 to 1981

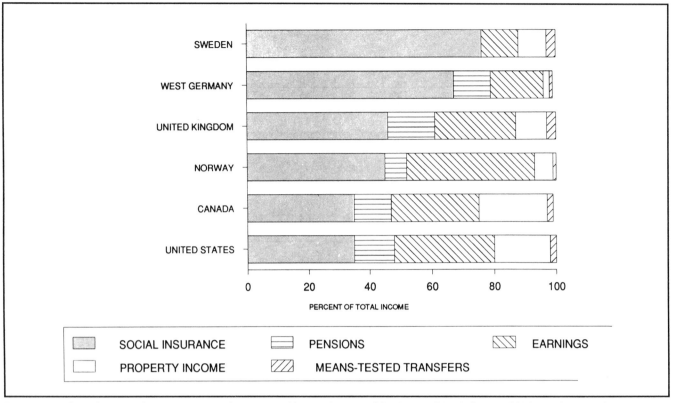

Source: Data from the Luxembourg Income Study as reported in U.S. Bureau of the Census. "An Aging World," by Barbara Boyle Torrey, Keven Kinsella, and Cynthia M. Taeuber. International Population Reports, Series P-95, No. 78 (September 1987).

E1-11. Composition of Gross Income of Elderly Families, by Age of Head and Income Type in Selected Countries: 1979 to 1981

Country	Year	Total income	Social insurance	Pensions	Earnings	Property income	Means-tested transfers	Private transfers
Age 65 to 74								
United States........................	1979	100	35	13	32	18	2	0
West Germany	1981	100	67	12	17	2	1	0
Norway	1979	100	45	7	41	6	0	1
Sweden	1979	100	76	(X)	12	9	3	(X)
United Kingdom...................	1979	100	46	15	26	10	3	0
Canada.................................	1981	100	35	12	28	22	2	0
Age 75+								
United States........................	1979	100	45	12	17	24	2	0
West Germany	1981	100	75	12	8	4	1	(X)
Norway	1979	100	75	10	6	8	1	(X)
Sweden	1979	100	78	(X)	2	13	7	(X)
United Kingdom...................	1979	100	54	12	17	10	7	0
Canada.................................	1981	100	45	8	13	30	2	(X)

(X) Not available.

Source: Data from the Luxembourg Income Study as reported in U.S. Bureau of the Census. "An Aging World," by Barbara Boyle Torrey, Kevin Kinsella, and Cynthia M. Taeuber. International Population Reports, Series P-95, No. 78 (September 1987).

E2. Income and Assets

E2-1. Money Income of Households—Aggregate and Mean Income, by Race and Hispanic Origin of Householder: 1990

CHARACTERISTIC	ALL RACES [1]		WHITE		BLACK		HISPANIC [2]	
	Aggregate money income (bil.dol.)	Mean income (dol.)	Aggregate money income (bil.dol.)	Mean income (dol.)	Aggregate money income (bil.dol.)	Mean income (dol.)	Aggregate money income (bil.dol.)	Mean income (dol.)
Total	**3,528**	**37,403**	**3,151**	**38,912**	**265**	**24,814**	**174**	**27,972**
Age of householder:								
15 to 24 years old	105	21,484	92	22,727	10	14,068	12	20,098
25 to 34 years old	701	34,484	620	36,322	57	22,014	48	26,385
35 to 44 years old	960	45,076	846	46,987	80	30,906	48	31,307
45 to 54 years old	738	50,003	652	52,014	56	33,198	33	34,076
55 to 64 years old	519	41,459	473	43,483	33	24,775	22	32,667
65 years old and over	505	24,586	468	25,363	29	16,286	12	17,900
Region:								
Northeast	789	40,953	717	42,479	53	26,979	30	26,571
Midwest	845	36,387	782	37,628	52	24,310	12	29,245
South	1,104	34,180	954	36,549	134	23,308	53	26,539
West	789	40,443	698	40,547	27	31,184	80	29,411
Size of household:								
One person	487	20,644	433	21,314	42	15,193	15	15,826
Two persons	1,184	39,233	1,094	40,726	67	25,061	36	26,310
Three persons	699	43,436	623	45,837	56	27,820	35	28,884
Four persons	702	48,223	620	50,342	51	30,573	37	31,552
Five persons	291	46,834	251	48,802	25	31,598	27	32,690
Six persons	101	45,251	82	47,331	12	33,395	12	31,372
Seven persons or more	64	43,914	47	47,351	10	29,790	13	36,618

[1]Includes other races not shown separately.

[2]Hispanic persons may be of any race.

Source: U.S. Bureau of the Census, *Current Population Reports*, series P-60, No. 174.

E2-2. Median Family Unit Income, by Age of Head: 1990

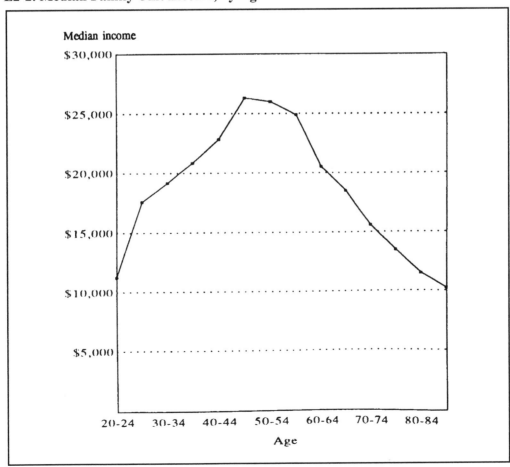

E2-3. Family Net Worth—Mean and Median of Net Worth, by Selected Characteristics: 1983 and 1989

CHARACTERISTIC	1983			1989		
	Percent of families	Net worth		Percent of families	Net worth	
		Mean	Median		Mean	Median
All families	100	149.1	42.7	100	183.7	47.2
White	82	173.0	54.3	87	203.8	58.5
Nonwhite and Hispanic	18	37.6	6.9	13	45.9	4.0
Under 35 years old	31	40.9	8.5	26	46.9	6.8
35 to 44 years old	19	110.5	49.8	23	148.3	52.8
45 to 54 years old	15	215.9	89.4	14	286.4	86.7
55 to 64 years old	15	242.2	84.4	.15	292.5	91.3
65 to 74 years old	12	272.6	76.3	13	278.3	77.6
75 years old and over	7	166.8	49.8	9	194.5	66.1
Under 55 years old:						
Unmarried, no children	11	48.9	6.0	11	47.5	8.4
Married, no children	6	80.1	20.1	5	147.9	27.3
Unmarried, children	13	57.8	10.8	13	54.2	5.7
Married, children	35	140.6	51.3	34	196.9	62.0
55 years and over:						
In labor force	14	363.1	108.0	12	438.3	104.5
Retired	18	153.6	63.9	18	211.6	94.1
Managerial and professional specialties	24	328.5	95.8	25	382.0	104.5
Technical, sales, and administrative support	12	105.1	39.1	12	139.7	32.6
Service occupations	7	33.6	12.1	7	46.1	8.4
Precision production, craft, and repair	12	70.4	40.0	12	91.5	46.0
Operators, fabricators, and laborers	12	49.3	28.6	9	67.3	18.8
Farming, forestry, and fishing	2	343.9	185.0	2	322.3	107.3
Not working	31	110.7	30.0	33	138.9	44.0
Income (1989 dollars):						
Less than $10,000	19	30.0	3.8	20	30.1	2.3
$10,000 to $19,999	23	53.0	19.3	20	63.1	27.1
$20,000 to $29,999	19	69.5	36.9	17	89.6	37.0
$30,000 to $49,999	23	117.6	67.7	23	150.2	69.2
$50,000 and over	17	550.5	176.1	20	586.7	185.6

Source: Board of Governors of the Federal Reserve System, *Federal Reserve Bulletin*, January 1992.

E2-4. Median Net Worth of Households, by Age of Householder: 1988

Age of householder	Total	Excluding home equity
All ages	$35,752	$9,840
Under 35	6,078	3,258
35-44	33,183	8,993
45-54	57,466	15,542
55-64	80,032	26,396
65 or older	73,471	23,856
65-69	83,478	27,482
70-74	82,111	28,172
75 or older	61,491	18,819

Source: Bureau of the Census (1990), table E.

Source: Bureau of the Census (1990).

E2-5. Distribution of Net Worth, by Age and Asset Type: 1988

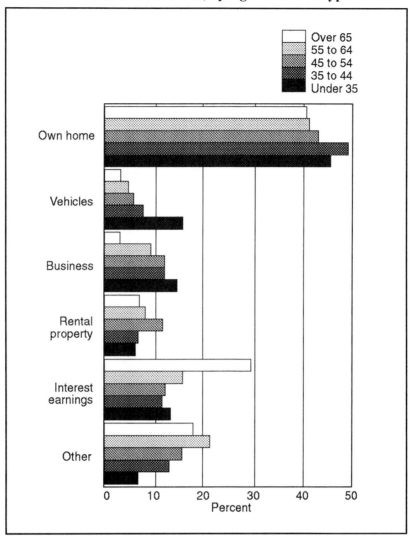

E2-6. Total Income of Aged Units: 1990

Median income for all aged units is $13,499, but there are wide differences within the total group. About 10% have an income of under $5,000 (an income level that is about 20% below the 1990 poverty threshold of $6,268 for one person aged 65 or older), and 7% have an income of $50,000 or more.

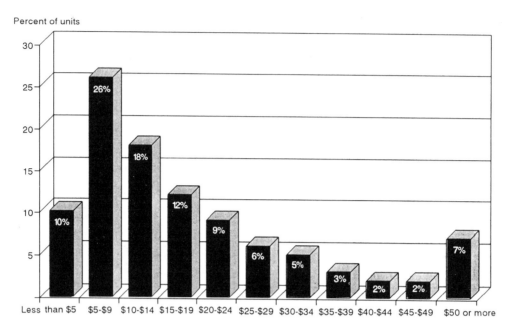

E2-7. Median Family Income, by Age, Race, and Hispanic Origin: 1990

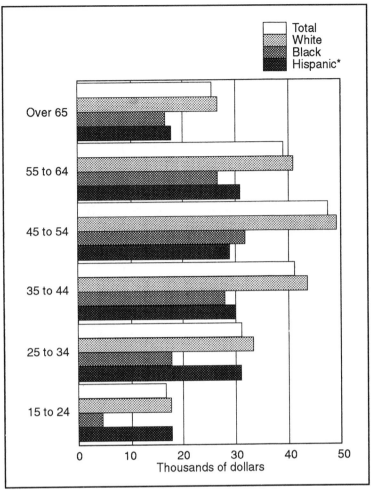

*May be of any race

E2-8. Median Income and Percent of Aged Units, by Age, Sex, and Marital Status

Sex and marital status	65-69	70-74	75-79	80-84	85 or older
	Median income				
Married couples............	$26,202	$23,954	$20,719	$17,710	$16,964
Nonmarried men...........	12,792	11,181	10,224	10,325	9,140
Nonmarried women........	10,111	9,281	8,573	8,379	7,416
	Percent of units				
Total number (in thousands).........	6,913	6,165	4,682	3,139	2,250
Total percent............	100	100	100	100	100
Married couples............	54	44	34	28	17
Nonmarried men...........	12	14	14	14	18
Nonmarried women........	33	42	51	58	65

E2-9. Median Income of Elderly Units, by Marital Status, Race, and Hispanic Origin: 1990

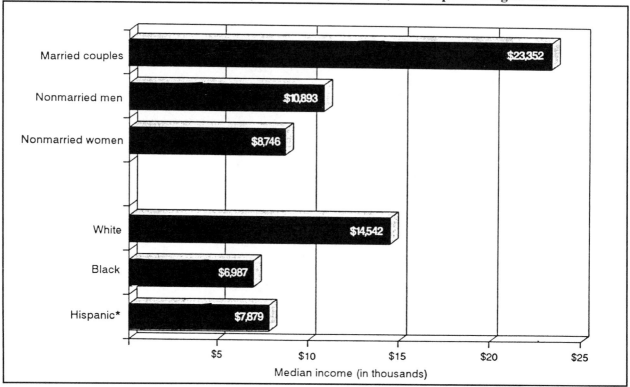

*Persons of Hispanic origin may be of any race.

E2-10. Income Level for the Elderly, by Residence: 1987

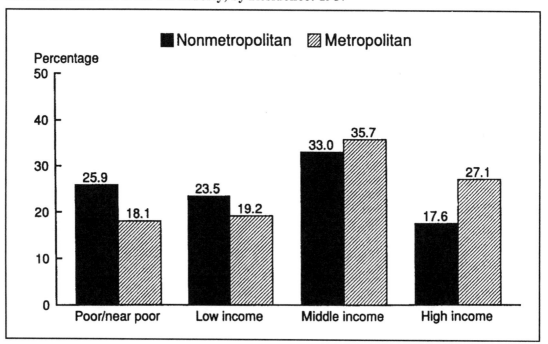

Source: Agency for Health Care Policy and Research. National Medical Expenditure Survey - Household Survey, 1987.

E2-11. Median Income of Households, by Selected Characteristics, Race, and Hispanic Origin of Householder: 1991, 1990, and 1989

[Households as of March of the following year. An asterisk (*) preceding percent change indicates statistically significant change at the 90-percent confidence level.]

Characteristic	1991			1990			1989			Percent change in real median income (1990-91)
	Number (thous.)	Median income Value (dollars)	Standard error (dollars)	Number (thous.)	Median income Value (dollars)	Standard error (dollars)	Number (thous.)	Median income Value (dollars)	Standard error (dollars)	
ALL RACES										
All households	95 669	30 126	144	94 312	29 943	153	93 347	28 906	159	* -3.5
Type of Residence										
Nonfarm	94 104	30 123	146	92 670	29 901	158	91 710	28 908	162	* -3.3
Farm	1 565	30 270	1 304	1 642	31 589	1 262	1 637	28 824	1 091	* -8.0
Inside metropolitan areas	74 535	31 975	164	73 135	31 823	154	72 331	31 124	160	* -3.6
One million or more	47 675	34 472	286	46 601	33 826	245	45 970	33 163	254	* -2.2
Inside central cities	18 851	26 891	308	18 388	26 732	298	18 326	26 049	284	* -3.5
Outside central cities	28 824	39 998	322	28 213	38 831	337	27 644	38 510	333	-1.2
Under 1 million	26 859	28 551	280	26 534	28 579	305	26 362	27 827	283	* -4.1
Inside central cities	11 461	24 959	389	11 509	24 900	395	11 413	25 000	382	* -3.8
Outside central cities	15 399	31 255	341	15 025	31 395	329	14 949	30 442	324	* -4.5
Outside metropolitan areas	21 134	24 691	329	21 177	23 709	314	21 016	22 417	298	-.1
Region										
Northeast	19 314	33 467	386	19 271	32 676	337	19 127	32 643	339	-1.7
Midwest	23 327	29 927	298	23 223	29 897	307	22 760	28 750	295	* -3.9
South	33 073	27 178	214	32 312	26 942	221	32 262	25 870	218	* -3.2
West	19 955	32 253	307	19 506	31 761	292	19 197	31 086	324	* -2.6
Type of Household										
Family households	67 173	36 404	177	66 322	35 707	167	66 090	34 633	191	* -2.2
Married-couple families	52 457	41 075	204	52 147	39 996	206	52 317	38 664	211	* -1.4
Male householder, no wife present	3 025	31 010	702	2 907	31 552	639	2 884	30 336	735	* -5.7
Female householder, no husband present	11 692	17 961	336	11 268	18 069	351	10 890	17 383	290	* -4.6
Nonfamily households	28 496	17 774	204	27 990	17 690	205	27 257	17 115	168	* -3.6
Male householder	12 428	23 022	390	12 150	22 489	305	11 606	22 423	305	-1.8
Living alone	9 613	20 259	273	9 450	19 964	298	9 049	19 617	331	* -2.6
Female householder	16 068	14 321	207	15 840	14 099	211	15 651	13 755	218	-2.5
Living alone	14 361	12 834	208	14 141	12 548	190	13 950	12 190	158	-1.9
Age of Householder										
Under 65 years	74 748	34 876	193	73 785	33 920	173	73 191	33 019	181	* -1.3
15 to 24 years	4 859	18 313	405	4 882	18 002	488	5 121	18 663	357	-2.4
25 to 34 years	20 007	30 842	239	20 323	30 359	234	20 472	29 823	271	* -2.5
35 to 44 years	21 774	39 349	364	21 304	38 561	349	20 554	37 635	327	* -2.1
45 to 54 years	15 547	43 751	539	14 751	41 922	412	14 514	41 523	411	.1
55 to 64 years	12 560	33 304	538	12 524	32 365	426	12 529	30 819	401	-1.3
65 years and over	20 921	16 975	175	20 527	16 855	183	20 156	15 771	175	* -3.4
65 to 74 years	12 043	20 063	269	12 001	20 292	271	11 733	18 959	267	* -5.1
75 years and over	8 878	13 933	208	8 526	13 150	238	8 423	12 101	177	1.7
Size of Household										
One person	23 974	15 441	176	23 590	15 344	182	22 999	14 829	174	* -3.4
Two persons	30 734	31 221	228	30 181	31 358	226	30 114	29 862	241	* -4.5
Three persons	16 398	38 244	374	16 082	36 765	345	16 128	36 277	327	-.2
Four persons	14 710	43 054	427	14 556	41 473	350	14 456	40 744	328	-.4
Five persons	6 389	40 792	524	6 206	39 275	566	6 213	39 281	613	-.3
Six persons	2 126	36 894	1 224	2 237	38 159	1 333	2 143	35 305	1 015	* -7.2
Seven persons or more	1 338	34 136	1 484	1 459	36 108	1 433	1 295	32 643	1 717	* -9.3
Number of Earners										
No earners	20 741	11 510	124	19 878	11 159	126	19 542	10 706	126	-1.0
One earner	31 818	24 834	194	31 413	24 575	197	30 958	23 809	192	* -3.0
Two earners or more	43 111	46 189	210	43 021	44 887	220	42 847	43 365	224	* -1.3
Two earners	33 300	43 034	243	33 021	41 656	218	32 682	40 211	210	-.9
Three earners	7 223	55 409	476	7 271	53 259	507	7 349	51 527	473	-.2
Four earners or more	2 588	69 167	1 164	2 729	67 000	1 035	2 815	65 202	891	-.9
Work Experience of Householder										
Total	95 669	30 126	144	94 312	29 943	153	93 347	28 906	159	* -3.5
Worked	68 876	37 333	163	68 658	36 252	154	68 148	35 500	155	* -1.2
Worked year-round, full-time	49 471	42 286	187	50 012	40 798	191	50 458	39 806	206	-.5
Did not work	26 793	14 180	145	25 654	13 819	159	25 199	13 092	155	-1.5
Tenure										
Owner occupied	61 310	37 257	191	60 395	36 298	185	59 846	35 481	185	* -1.5
Renter occupied	32 705	20 696	170	32 218	20 722	163	31 895	20 302	168	* -4.2
Occupier paid no cash rent	1 654	15 629	674	1 698	15 868	608	1 606	15 829	805	-5.5

E2-11. Median Income of Households, by Selected Characteristics, Race, and Hispanic Origin of Householder: 1991, 1990, and 1989 (continued)

[Households as of March of the following year. An asterisk (*) preceding percent change indicates statistically significant change at the 90-percent confidence level.]

	1991			1990			1989			Percent change in real median income (1990-91)
		Median income			Median income			Median income		
Characteristic	Number (thous.)	Value (dollars)	Standard error (dollars)	Number (thous.)	Value (dollars)	Standard error (dollars)	Number (thous.)	Value (dollars)	Standard error (dollars)	
WHITE										
All households	81 675	31 569	153	80 968	31 231	143	80 163	30 406	147	* -3.0
Type of Residence										
Nonfarm	80 157	31 594	155	79 373	31 216	145	78 556	30 442	149	* -2.9
Farm	1 518	30 585	1 265	1 595	31 819	1 337	1 608	29 039	1 104	* -7.8
Inside metropolitan areas	62 635	33 988	238	61 842	33 460	203	61 155	32 754	215	* -2.5
One million or more	39 173	36 732	251	38 563	35 837	244	37 902	35 417	255	* -1.6
Inside central cities	13 396	30 027	392	13 135	29 630	446	13 112	29 061	428	* -2.8
Outside central cities	25 777	40 652	312	25 429	39 670	367	24 789	39 257	354	* -1.7
Under 1 million	23 462	29 995	286	23 278	30 043	291	23 253	29 275	303	* -4.2
Inside central cities	9 292	26 885	409	9 300	26 845	428	9 334	26 587	380	* -3.9
Outside central cities	14 170	31 871	349	13 978	31 881	340	13 919	31 082	326	* -4.1
Outside metropolitan areas	19 040	25 804	290	19 127	24 887	329	19 009	23 611	342	-.5
Region										
Northeast	16 934	35 208	334	16 870	34 387	373	16 773	34 225	382	-1.7
Midwest	20 710	31 177	297	20 772	31 054	269	20 339	29 948	300	* -3.7
South	26 582	29 525	276	26 104	29 162	297	26 155	27 887	294	* -2.8
West	17 449	32 404	355	17 222	31 794	306	16 896	31 406	342	* -2.2
Type of Household										
Family households	57 224	38 229	206	56 803	37 219	177	56 590	36 325	183	* -1.4
Married-couple families	47 124	41 584	213	47 014	40 433	212	46 981	39 328	223	* -1.3
Male householder, no wife present	2 374	31 634	771	2 276	32 869	814	2 303	32 218	767	* -7.6
Female householder, no husband present	7 726	21 213	383	7 512	20 867	356	7 306	20 164	356	-2.4
Nonfamily households	24 451	18 461	218	24 166	18 449	220	23 573	17 715	227	* -4.0
Male householder	10 476	24 531	412	10 312	23 778	384	9 951	23 799	388	-1.0
Living alone	8 029	21 126	298	7 963	20 900	287	7 718	20 644	303	* -3.0
Female householder	13 975	14 790	214	13 853	14 629	218	13 622	14 205	225	* -3.0
Living alone	12 490	13 317	214	12 356	13 094	217	12 161	12 582	205	-2.4
Age of Householder										
Under 65 years	63 045	36 766	177	62 538	35 646	168	62 019	35 012	179	* -1.0
15 to 24 years	3 980	19 803	396	4 046	19 662	489	4 222	19 903	386	-3.3
25 to 34 years	16 677	32 315	266	17 069	31 859	247	17 137	31 395	238	* -2.7
35 to 44 years	18 331	41 202	309	18 013	40 423	311	17 395	39 502	383	* -2.2
45 to 54 years	13 297	46 215	466	12 534	44 098	524	12 404	43 667	495	.6
55 to 64 years	10 760	35 550	465	10 876	34 249	524	10 862	32 665	491	-.4
65 years and over	18 629	17 794	222	18 431	17 539	208	18 144	16 382	180	* -2.6
65 to 74 years	10 581	21 087	262	10 663	21 089	285	10 477	19 783	281	* -4.0
75 years and over	8 048	14 343	216	7 768	13 714	243	7 667	12 526	219	.4
Size of Household										
One person	20 518	15 985	183	20 319	15 981	190	19 879	15 384	179	* -4.0
Two persons	27 108	32 527	293	26 861	32 561	259	26 714	31 037	245	* -4.1
Three persons	13 807	40 330	387	13 596	38 930	422	13 585	38 298	388	-.6
Four persons	12 437	45 240	408	12 322	43 363	404	12 389	42 103	333	.1
Five persons	5 250	42 519	569	5 146	40 715	604	5 104	41 131	571	.2
Six persons	1 643	40 274	1 249	1 735	40 420	1 188	1 615	39 550	1 301	-4.4
Seven persons or more	912	38 033	1 586	990	40 822	1 789	877	38 108	2 188	* -10.6
Number of Earners										
No earners	17 500	12 771	159	16 876	12 395	137	16 626	11 900	130	-1.1
One earner	26 530	26 147	177	26 342	25 801	178	25 978	25 254	179	* -2.8
Two earners or more	37 645	47 100	219	37 751	45 705	225	37 560	44 257	235	* -1.1
Two earners	29 118	44 056	264	29 028	42 498	242	28 711	41 032	218	-.5
Three earners	6 259	56 228	483	6 387	54 264	536	6 368	52 321	506	-.6
Four earners or more	2 268	69 305	1 324	2 336	66 876	1 076	2 481	66 113	925	-.6
Work Experience of Householder										
Total	81 675	31 569	153	80 968	31 231	143	80 163	30 406	147	* -3.0
Worked	59 285	38 814	196	59 386	37 361	168	59 002	36 692	166	-.3
Worked year-round, full-time	42 965	43 572	244	43 616	41 853	201	44 023	40 902	184	-.1
Did not work	22 390	15 488	186	21 583	15 143	181	21 162	14 342	162	-1.9
Tenure										
Owner occupied	55 117	37 913	228	54 527	36 810	193	54 094	36 067	194	* -1.2
Renter occupied	25 167	21 918	187	24 976	21 962	180	24 685	21 634	188	* -4.2
Occupier paid no cash rent	1 391	16 350	662	1 466	16 868	624	1 384	16 897	800	* -7.0

E2-11. Median Income of Households, by Selected Characteristics, Race, and Hispanic Origin of Householder: 1991, 1990, and 1989 (continued)

[Households as of March of the following year. An asterisk (*) preceding percent change indicates statistically significant change at the 90-percent confidence level.

Characteristic	1991			1990			1989			Percent change in real median income (1990-91)
	Number	Median income		Number	Median income		Number	Median income		
		Value	Standard error		Value	Standard error		Value	Standard error	
	(thous.)	(dollars)	(dollars)	(thous.)	(dollars)	(dollars)	(thous.)	(dollars)	(dollars)	
BLACK										
All households	11 083	18 807	394	10 671	18 676	426	10 486	18 083	368	-3.4
Type of Residence										
Nonfarm	11 057	18 838	397	10 645	18 734	426	10 464	18 119	368	-3.5
Farm	25	(B)	(B)	27	(B)	(B)	21	(B)	(B)	(X)
Inside metropolitan areas	9 402	20 211	425	8 967	20 121	409	8 816	19 564	395	-3.6
One million or more	6 595	21 534	525	6 281	21 086	466	6 299	20 764	461	-2.0
Inside central cities	4 514	18 243	563	4 356	18 156	662	4 314	17 325	526	-3.6
Outside central cities	2 081	29 776	898	1 925	28 444	1 113	1 985	29 725	1 270	.5
Under 1 million	2 808	17 260	640	2 686	17 562	706	2 517	17 056	657	-5.7
Inside central cities	1 829	15 963	655	1 867	16 402	680	1 732	16 275	796	-6.6
Outside central cities	978	20 066	1 352	819	21 517	1 289	785	18 482	904	-10.5
Outside metropolitan areas	1 680	13 120	712	1 704	13 119	901	1 670	12 130	681	-4.0
Region										
Northeast	1 907	21 284	690	1 952	20 674	778	1 866	21 563	730	-1.2
Midwest	2 238	18 280	960	2 121	17 204	796	2 092	16 514	634	2.0
South	5 972	17 247	463	5 737	17 662	525	5 622	16 788	493	* -6.3
West	966	25 656	1 465	862	23 987	1 837	906	23 288	1 705	2.6
Type of Household										
Family households	7 716	22 203	470	7 471	21 899	380	7 470	20 911	430	-2.7
Married-couple families	3 631	33 369	758	3 569	33 893	669	3 750	30 833	649	* -5.5
Male householder, no wife present	504	26 428	1 758	472	24 048	1 749	446	20 044	1 102	5.5
Female householder, no husband present	3 582	12 196	427	3 430	12 537	458	3 275	12 170	375	* -6.7
Nonfamily households	3 367	12 202	477	3 200	11 789	462	3 015	11 193	519	-.7
Male householder	1 594	15 223	746	1 531	15 451	780	1 313	14 737	1 025	-5.5
Living alone	1 319	13 665	638	1 266	13 126	879	1 084	11 964	774	-.1
Female householder	1 773	9 520	491	1 670	8 661	578	1 702	8 944	598	5.5
Living alone	1 596	8 492	493	1 511	7 674	448	1 525	7 658	472	6.2
Age of Householder										
Under 65 years	9 135	21 606	393	8 883	21 011	352	8 790	20 389	353	-1.3
15 to 24 years	703	8 603	582	683	9 816	708	709	9 341	977	* -15.9
25 to 34 years	2 661	19 284	709	2 591	18 339	761	2 625	18 744	610	.9
35 to 44 years	2 636	26 233	762	2 578	26 011	834	2 456	26 134	837	-3.2
45 to 54 years	1 718	27 526	954	1 693	26 910	961	1 606	25 894	892	-1.8
55 to 64 years	1 418	20 103	1 115	1 337	19 226	1 308	1 395	16 207	1 006	.3
65 years and over	1 948	10 466	479	1 789	9 902	464	1 695	9 354	344	1.4
65 to 74 years	1 245	11 555	616	1 118	11 974	783	1 028	10 961	695	-7.4
75 years and over	702	9 151	488	671	7 831	521	668	7 840	432	12.1
Size of Household										
One person	2 915	10 650	499	2 778	10 156	468	2 610	9 451	477	.6
Two persons	2 887	19 230	674	2 685	20 122	632	2 721	18 721	536	* -8.3
Three persons	2 069	23 285	1 045	2 013	21 474	837	2 043	21 049	1 216	4.1
Four persons	1 661	26 187	1 246	1 674	25 683	1 469	1 550	26 246	1 082	-2.2
Five persons	878	24 371	1 803	805	24 342	2 188	858	24 963	2 277	-3.9
Six persons	368	25 251	3 097	371	26 742	2 701	412	20 288	1 771	-9.4
Seven persons or more	304	23 806	1 166	346	22 361	1 360	293	21 534	3 384	2.2
Number of Earners										
No earners	2 820	6 332	128	2 603	5 870	150	2 527	5 707	143	3.5
One earner	4 301	17 230	362	4 173	17 040	336	4 041	16 532	345	-3.0
Two earners or more	3 962	37 268	657	3 895	36 404	536	3 917	34 897	619	-1.8
Two earners	3 078	33 991	742	3 029	33 657	741	2 978	31 977	606	-3.1
Three earners	707	45 882	1 505	633	42 897	1 750	716	43 176	1 453	2.6
Four earners or more	176	59 256	3 930	234	60 323	3 629	223	54 164	3 146	-5.7
Work Experience of Householder										
Total	11 083	18 807	394	10 671	18 676	426	10 486	18 083	368	-3.4
Worked	7 328	26 424	415	7 202	25 765	475	7 060	25 117	444	-1.6
Worked year-round, full-time	4 928	31 866	508	4 840	31 015	432	4 874	29 993	508	-1.4
Did not work	3 755	7 494	202	3 469	7 249	161	3 425	7 059	150	-.8
Tenure										
Owner occupied	4 683	27 052	662	4 526	27 377	725	4 445	25 873	701	* -5.2
Renter occupied	6 183	14 169	449	5 945	13 929	436	5 862	14 011	421	-2.4
Occupier paid no cash rent	217	9 958	1 237	200	7 853	1 120	178	7 237	1 050	21.7

E2-11. Median Income of Households, by Selected Characteristics, Race, and Hispanic Origin of Householder: 1991, 1990, and 1989 (continued)

[Households as of March of the following year. An asterisk (*) preceding percent change indicates statistically significant change at the 90-percent confidence level.

Characteristic	1991			1990			1989			Percent change in real median income (1990-91)
		Median income			Median income			Median income		
	Number (thous.)	Value (dollars)	Standard error (dollars)	Number (thous.)	Value (dollars)	Standard error (dollars)	Number (thous.)	Value (dollars)	Standard error (dollars)	
HISPANIC ORIGIN[1]										
All households	6 379	22 691	471	6 220	22 330	458	5 933	21 921	425	-2.5
Type of Residence										
Nonfarm	6 355	22 719	475	6 180	22 326	459	5 897	21 932	426	-2.4
Farm	24	(B)	(B)	40	(B)	(B)	36	(B)	(B)	(X)
Inside metropolitan areas	5 928	23 052	539	5 776	22 737	500	5 479	22 355	493	-2.7
One million or more	4 554	24 322	625	4 426	23 436	560	4 145	23 624	643	-.4
Inside central cities	2 581	20 776	675	2 498	19 818	742	2 415	20 425	643	.6
Outside central cities	1 973	29 079	1 033	1 928	28 727	1 186	1 730	29 483	1 148	-2.9
Under 1 million	1 374	19 858	858	1 350	20 672	889	1 333	19 307	733	* -7.8
Inside central cities	828	19 076	1 296	815	20 113	1 208	784	18 431	993	-9.0
Outside central cities	546	20 651	1 072	535	21 444	1 466	550	20 695	1 539	-7.6
Outside metropolitan areas	451	19 354	2 094	444	18 392	1 453	454	17 383	1 680	1.0
Region										
Northeast	1 135	18 749	1 147	1 123	18 128	1 013	1 037	20 741	1 079	-.8
Midwest	456	24 581	2 179	408	24 346	2 053	398	25 739	1 447	-3.1
South	1 980	22 652	751	1 982	21 702	842	1 953	19 279	655	.2
West	2 807	24 008	796	2 706	24 148	777	2 544	24 032	879	-4.6
Type of Household										
Family households	5 177	24 551	519	4 981	24 552	557	4 840	24 080	620	* -4.0
Married-couple families	3 532	28 833	694	3 454	28 584	815	3 395	27 830	697	-3.2
Male householder, no wife present	383	23 298	1 750	342	25 456	1 859	329	26 257	1 687	* -12.2
Female householder, no husband present	1 261	13 323	835	1 186	12 603	764	1 116	12 888	827	1.4
Nonfamily households	1 202	15 733	769	1 238	14 274	788	1 093	13 923	999	5.8
Male householder	660	19 009	1 237	669	17 689	1 273	587	16 691	1 285	3.1
Living alone	444	15 455	1 043	456	13 716	1 153	415	13 582	986	8.1
Female householder	542	11 420	1 088	569	10 750	896	506	10 593	971	1.9
Living alone	443	9 160	664	469	8 933	765	442	8 918	879	-1.6
Age of Householder										
Under 65 years	5 724	23 939	515	5 566	23 788	517	5 262	23 118	585	* -3.4
15 to 24 years	556	16 554	1 368	594	14 732	1 127	542	15 440	762	7.8
25 to 34 years	1 821	22 664	780	1 808	21 695	755	1 721	22 016	601	.2
35 to 44 years	1 641	26 254	1 015	1 524	26 598	790	1 405	26 084	1 172	* -5.3
45 to 54 years	979	28 909	1 548	957	28 195	1 386	930	27 293	1 367	-1.6
55 to 64 years	728	24 952	1 884	682	24 757	1 608	664	25 475	1 763	-3.3
65 years and over	655	13 931	995	653	12 686	950	671	12 799	1 004	5.4
65 to 74 years	417	15 855	1 077	434	14 123	1 244	463	15 442	1 556	7.7
75 years and over	238	11 122	1 509	220	9 850	1 282	208	9 359	1 200	8.4
Size of Household										
One person	887	11 850	834	925	11 232	648	856	11 168	682	1.2
Two persons	1 364	22 587	949	1 354	20 712	828	1 292	20 967	848	4.6
Three persons	1 247	23 188	1 092	1 217	23 780	1 115	1 139	22 594	1 439	-6.4
Four persons	1 272	26 600	1 095	1 167	26 479	1 194	1 172	26 426	1 030	-3.6
Five persons	836	26 219	1 351	834	26 137	931	752	27 858	1 433	-3.7
Six persons	406	26 273	2 200	378	26 965	1 884	386	24 731	1 654	-6.5
Seven persons or more	367	27 212	1 686	345	31 185	1 821	336	26 898	2 180	* -16.3
Number of Earners										
No earners	1 038	7 471	276	1 022	7 048	238	925	6 724	222	1.7
One earner	2 219	17 250	415	2 111	17 176	478	2 051	17 307	483	-3.6
Two earners or more	3 122	34 500	757	3 086	33 393	660	2 957	33 298	710	-.9
Two earners	2 191	31 363	899	2 149	30 227	746	2 023	29 385	801	-.4
Three earners	616	38 399	1 554	647	38 247	1 566	591	39 939	1 519	-3.7
Four earners or more	315	49 479	2 817	290	50 909	2 852	343	47 534	2 492	-6.7
Work Experience of Householder										
Total	6 379	22 691	471	6 220	22 330	458	5 933	21 921	425	-2.5
Worked	4 800	27 337	563	4 659	26 864	463	4 479	26 523	539	-2.3
Worked year-round, full-time	3 238	31 785	644	3 138	31 490	570	3 104	30 500	690	* -3.1
Did not work	1 579	10 056	446	1 561	9 448	345	1 454	9 383	395	2.1
Tenure										
Owner occupied	2 547	33 556	946	2 423	32 321	786	2 443	31 574	903	-.4
Renter occupied	3 732	17 459	466	3 677	17 632	507	3 383	17 840	473	* -5.0
Occupier paid no cash rent	100	13 415	1 648	120	13 796	1 860	107	12 175	2 352	-6.7

[1]Persons of Hispanic origin may be of any race.

E2-12. Presence of Elderly—Households, by Total Money Income in 1991, Race, and Hispanic Origin of Householder

[Numbers in thousands. Households as of March 1992.

Total money income	Total	No persons 65 years and over	With persons 65 years and over					
			Total	All members elderly	Some, but not all elderly			
					Total	Elderly householder or spouse only	Elderly other relative only	Elderly nonrelative only
ALL RACES								
Total	95 669	72 838	22 831	15 827	7 004	5 416	1 305	114
Less than $5,000	4 576	3 365	1 211	1 069	141	122	18	1
$5,000 to $9,999	9 660	5 106	4 554	4 095	459	399	54	5
$10,000 to $14,999	8 992	5 237	3 755	3 037	718	620	62	19
$15,000 to $19,999	8 376	5 540	2 836	2 105	731	627	81	12
$20,000 to $24,999	8 255	5 902	2 353	1 675	679	577	80	4
$25,000 to $29,999	7 780	5 975	1 805	1 112	693	568	104	6
$30,000 to $34,999	6 773	5 544	1 229	662	567	448	91	7
$35,000 to $39,999	6 327	5 276	1 050	555	495	356	102	24
$40,000 to $44,999	5 620	4 876	743	317	426	327	85	6
$45,000 to $49,999	4 640	4 103	537	196	341	241	88	4
$50,000 to $54,999	4 173	3 739	435	181	254	172	65	4
$55,000 to $59,999	3 353	3 006	347	122	225	152	61	4
$60,000 to $64,999	2 944	2 618	327	134	192	115	73	1
$65,000 to $69,999	2 340	2 062	278	119	158	97	46	5
$70,000 to $74,999	1 899	1 724	175	47	128	91	32	1
$75,000 to $79,999	1 668	1 504	164	50	114	56	52	1
$80,000 to $84,999	1 341	1 209	132	42	90	74	13	2
$85,000 to $89,999	1 069	968	101	31	70	51	18	–
$90,000 to $94,999	875	748	127	41	86	52	31	–
$95,000 to $99,999	762	657	105	30	76	46	27	–
$100,000 and over	4 246	3 678	568	206	362	225	121	7
Median income ____ dollars	30 126	34 739	18 183	14 485	30 636	27 937	43 715	35 258
Standard error ____ dollars	145	202	209	161	469	521	1 348	3 205
Mean income ____ dollars	37 922	41 531	26 408	20 416	39 949	36 926	52 112	37 462
Standard error ____ dollars	156	182	271	252	617	671	1 621	3 808
Income per household member ____ dollars	14 455	14 562	13 941	14 464	13 382	13 690	13 007	10 749
Standard error ____ dollars	66	75	179	240	265	320	543	1 511
Gini ratio	.425	.401	.462	.442	.407	.410	.368	.385
Standard error	.0036	.0041	.0083	.0104	.0138	.0161	.0303	.1052
WHITE								
Total	81 675	61 503	20 172	14 361	5 811	4 559	1 019	94
Less than $5,000	3 014	2 115	899	814	85	70	13	1
$5,000 to $9,999	7 406	3 607	3 799	3 485	314	274	35	5
$10,000 to $14,999	7 445	4 120	3 325	2 795	530	459	46	14
$15,000 to $19,999	7 061	4 524	2 537	1 967	570	506	54	4
$20,000 to $24,999	7 070	4 892	2 178	1 589	589	499	70	4
$25,000 to $29,999	6 743	5 097	1 646	1 065	580	486	79	5
$30,000 to $34,999	5 866	4 738	1 128	638	489	397	69	7
$35,000 to $39,999	5 585	4 597	989	548	440	311	97	21
$40,000 to $44,999	4 932	4 247	684	310	374	288	74	4
$45,000 to $49,999	4 129	3 640	489	185	304	216	75	4
$50,000 to $54,999	3 758	3 374	384	171	214	146	51	4
$55,000 to $59,999	3 016	2 687	329	122	207	144	51	4
$60,000 to $64,999	2 657	2 380	277	128	149	100	46	1
$65,000 to $69,999	2 123	1 862	261	115	146	95	36	5
$70,000 to $74,999	1 730	1 568	162	46	116	87	27	1
$75,000 to $79,999	1 507	1 359	148	44	104	54	44	1
$80,000 to $84,999	1 262	1 135	127	42	84	70	13	2
$85,000 to $89,999	976	883	93	31	62	49	12	–
$90,000 to $94,999	780	668	111	37	74	49	22	–
$95,000 to $99,999	692	597	94	27	67	43	21	–
$100,000 and over	3 922	3 410	512	200	312	215	84	6
Median income ____ dollars	31 569	36 676	18 983	15 198	32 150	29 835	43 376	36 500
Standard error ____ dollars	153	180	219	198	515	555	1 425	2 845
Mean income ____ dollars	39 523	43 594	27 110	21 211	41 687	39 233	52 086	40 365
Standard error ____ dollars	172	201	294	270	697	762	1 869	4 283
Income per household member ____ dollars	15 322	15 442	14 760	14 886	14 605	15 075	13 749	11 886
Standard error ____ dollars	76	86	202	256	318	382	660	1 797
Gini ratio	.415	.387	.456	.435	.397	.402	.361	.372
Standard error	.0039	.0044	.0088	.0109	.0152	.0175	.0349	.1141

See footnote at end of table.

E2-12. Presence of Elderly—Households, by Total Money Income in 1991, Race, and Hispanic Origin of Householder (continued)

[Numbers in thousands. Households as of March 1992.

Total money income	Total	No persons 65 years and over	With persons 65 years and over					
					Some, but not all elderly			
			Total	All members elderly	Total	Elderly householder or spouse only	Elderly other relative only	Elderly nonrelative only
BLACK								
Total	11 083	8 917	2 166	1 254	912	721	148	15
Less than $5,000	1 394	1 110	284	232	52	49	3	-
$5,000 to $9,999	2 018	1 328	690	557	133	115	18	-
$10,000 to $14,999	1 291	943	347	190	157	139	9	3
$15,000 to $19,999	1 078	814	264	112	151	113	26	9
$20,000 to $24,999	940	807	133	58	75	69	3	-
$25,000 to $29,999	843	710	133	43	90	67	19	-
$30,000 to $34,999	690	612	78	19	59	41	13	-
$35,000 to $39,999	574	522	52	6	46	39	3	2
$40,000 to $44,999	536	496	40	7	33	27	6	-
$45,000 to $49,999	373	342	31	5	26	17	9	-
$50,000 to $54,999	271	246	25	8	17	10	7	-
$55,000 to $59,999	230	220	10	-	10	7	3	-
$60,000 to $64,999	170	145	25	2	23	10	13	-
$65,000 to $69,999	149	144	5	-	5	2	3	-
$70,000 to $74,999	112	106	6	-	6	3	2	-
$75,000 to $79,999	82	78	4	3	1	-	1	-
$80,000 to $84,999	56	52	4	-	4	3	-	-
$85,000 to $89,999	52	51	1	-	1	1	-	-
$90,000 to $94,999	53	47	5	2	3	1	2	-
$95,000 to $99,999	37	33	3	2	1	-	1	-
$100,000 and over	135	110	25	7	18	8	8	1
Median income _____ dollars	18 807	21 476	11 506	7 533	18 721	17 586	29 171	(B)
Standard error	395	396	480	296	767	890	2 521	(B)
Mean income _____ dollars	25 043	26 888	17 447	11 719	25 330	22 686	36 933	(B)
Standard error	327	372	617	566	1 131	1 137	3 491	(B)
Income per household member ____ dollars	8 924	9 079	8 055	9 328	7 411	7 006	9 025	(B)
Standard error	124	141	379	712	439	474	1 199	(B)
Gini ratio	.461	.447	.474	.440	.414	.400	.403	(B)
Standard error	.0107	.0116	.0289	.0417	.0411	.0465	.0924	(B)
HISPANIC ORIGIN[1]								
Total	6 379	5 519	860	359	501	310	163	9
Less than $5,000	435	369	66	49	18	10	7	-
$5,000 to $9,999	884	682	202	167	35	28	8	-
$10,000 to $14,999	771	657	114	47	67	48	14	2
$15,000 to $19,999	715	618	97	27	71	54	14	1
$20,000 to $24,999	662	588	74	20	53	40	11	-
$25,000 to $29,999	542	472	70	22	48	30	17	1
$30,000 to $34,999	465	417	47	8	39	28	9	2
$35,000 to $39,999	393	355	38	6	32	17	12	2
$40,000 to $44,999	313	286	26	4	24	11	11	-
$45,000 to $49,999	239	218	21	1	20	7	12	-
$50,000 to $54,999	197	182	15	1	13	4	7	1
$55,000 to $59,999	140	121	19	2	16	5	11	-
$60,000 to $64,999	137	129	8	1	7	6	-	-
$65,000 to $69,999	98	81	17	-	16	3	11	-
$70,000 to $74,999	69	64	5	-	5	2	2	-
$75,000 to $79,999	60	52	8	1	7	3	4	-
$80,000 to $84,999	42	40	2	-	2	1	1	-
$85,000 to $89,999	35	32	3	-	3	1	2	-
$90,000 to $94,999	24	21	3	-	3	1	1	-
$95,000 to $99,999	25	20	5	-	5	2	3	-
$100,000 and over	134	115	18	3	15	9	5	1
Median income _____ dollars	22 691	23 565	16 968	8 740	25 686	21 720	36 037	(B)
Standard error	472	519	1 035	494	1 853	1 555	4 384	(B)
Mean income _____ dollars	26 872	29 489	24 910	13 518	33 078	28 358	41 419	(B)
Standard error	462	496	1 253	1 148	1 798	1 964	3 705	(B)
Income per household member ____ dollars	8 357	8 304	8 786	9 520	8 592	8 755	8 503	(B)
Standard error	147	156	584	1 277	636	864	1 037	(B)
Gini ratio	.425	.417	.468	.442	.401	.391	.382	(B)
Standard error	.0143	.0153	.0420	.0749	.0525	.0695	.0685	(B)

[1]Persons of Hispanic origin may be of any race.

(B) Base less than 75,000

E2-13. Income from Earnings, by Race, Hispanic Origin, and Marital Status: Percent Distribution of Aged Units 65 or Older: 1990

Unit earnings (recipients only)	White			Black			Hispanic origin [1]		
	All units	Married couples	Nonmarried persons	All units	Married couples	Nonmarried persons	All units	Married couples	Nonmarried persons
Number (in thousands)........	4,455	2,925	1,530	429	213	217	168	113	55
Total percent	100.0	100.0	100.0	100.0	100.0	100.0	100.0	100.0	100.0
Less than $1,000	11.6	8.2	18.0	13.6	6.3	20.8	8.4	7.7	([2])
$1,000-$1,999	6.1	4.6	8.8	10.3	7.1	13.5	3.8	1.1	([2])
$2,000-$2,999	6.4	5.2	8.5	10.5	8.3	12.7	4.4	3.3	([2])
$3,000-$3,999	4.5	4.1	5.1	4.5	5.0	3.9	6.7	5.3	([2])
$4,000-$4,999	4.7	4.5	5.1	6.6	5.7	7.5	6.5	5.7	([2])
$5,000-$5,999	5.0	4.4	6.1	4.8	3.8	5.8	7.1	6.5	([2])
$6,000-$6,999	5.4	5.0	6.1	3.3	1.1	5.4	2.9	2.5	([2])
$7,000-$7,999	3.5	3.7	3.3	4.3	4.1	4.6	5.2	5.6	([2])
$8,000-$8,999	4.3	4.3	4.5	3.5	6.1	.9	7.2	4.2	([2])
$9,000-$9,999	3.2	3.6	2.3	2.0	3.9	.0	3.8	3.7	([2])
$10,000-$10,999	3.1	3.2	3.0	2.2	3.6	1.0	5.8	5.8	([2])
$11,000-$11,999	1.7	1.8	1.5	1.5	1.7	1.3	3.2	4.0	([2])
$12,000-$12,999	2.7	2.8	2.4	3.4	4.2	2.5	4.5	5.4	([2])
$13,000-$13,999	1.8	1.6	2.2	1.6	3.3	.0	3.1	4.3	([2])
$14,000-$14,999	1.3	1.2	1.4	1.5	3.0	.0	.6	.4	([2])
$15,000-$19,999	6.8	7.6	5.3	6.5	6.2	6.8	8.1	10.7	([2])
$20,000-$24,999	5.1	5.3	4.7	4.9	6.2	3.6	5.3	6.8	([2])
$25,000-$29,999	4.5	5.6	2.5	4.1	3.0	5.1	4.0	5.2	([2])
$30,000-$34,999	4.2	4.8	3.1	3.6	5.8	1.5	4.2	4.5	([2])
$35,000-$39,999	2.2	2.8	1.1	1.4	2.9	.0	1.8	2.7	([2])
$40,000-$44,999	2.4	2.3	2.6	1.9	3.9	.0	.0	.0	([2])
$45,000-$49,999	1.5	1.9	.8	1.8	1.8	1.8	.0	.0	([2])
$50,000-$54,999	1.8	2.4	.6	.4	.8	.0	1.0	1.5	([2])
$55,000-$59,999	.6	.8	.1	.4	.7	.0	.0	.0	([2])
$60,000-$64,999	.7	.8	.5	.0	.0	.0	.0	.0	([2])
$65,000-$69,999	.6	.8	.1	.0	.0	.0	.4	.7	([2])
$70,000-$74,999	.7	1.0	.2	.4	.0	.7	.0	.0	([2])
$75,000 or more	3.7	5.5	.1	1.1	1.7	.6	1.8	2.7	([2])
Median income	$8,491	$10,522	$5,529	$5,738	$9,119	$3,488	$8,169	$10,696	([2])

[1] Persons of Hispanic origin may be of any race.
[2] Fewer than 75,000 weighted cases.

E2-14. Income from Private Pensions or Annuities, by Age and Marital Status: Percent Distribution of Aged Units 55 or Older: 1990

Unit private pensions (recipients only)	All units			Married couples			Nonmarried persons		
	55-61	62-64	65 or older	55-61	62-64	65 or older	55-61	62-64	65 or older
Number (in thousands)..................	1,128	1,096	6,951	740	758	3,852	388	338	3,098
Total percent	100.0	100.0	100.0	100.0	100.0	100.0	100.0	100.0	100.0
$1-$499	4.8	3.2	5.4	4.1	3.4	3.4	6.1	2.8	7.9
$500-$999	5.2	5.5	7.5	4.6	4.2	5.3	6.4	8.4	10.2
$1,000-$1,499	7.0	3.9	8.7	6.7	3.0	6.2	7.6	5.9	11.9
$1,500-$1,999	3.6	4.0	6.4	3.0	2.4	5.2	4.9	7.5	7.9
$2,000-$2,499	4.8	5.5	7.0	3.0	3.1	6.1	8.4	10.9	8.2
$2,500-$2,999	3.7	2.2	4.4	2.1	2.5	3.5	6.8	1.6	5.4
$3,000-$3,499	4.0	2.6	4.3	3.0	2.3	4.1	5.8	3.4	4.4
$3,500-$3,999	3.9	5.9	4.8	4.5	6.8	4.3	2.8	4.1	5.3
$4,000-$4,499	3.3	3.5	3.9	3.2	3.1	3.3	3.5	4.6	4.6
$4,500-$4,999	2.4	4.4	4.4	2.4	5.0	4.7	2.4	3.0	3.9
$5,000-$5,999	6.1	7.3	6.8	4.6	5.6	7.3	9.0	11.1	6.2
$6,000-$6,999	5.2	5.2	6.8	6.0	5.0	7.8	3.7	5.6	5.5
$7,000-$7,999	4.6	5.5	4.8	4.2	6.1	5.4	5.5	4.1	3.9
$8,000-$8,999	2.3	3.2	4.2	3.5	3.6	4.9	.1	2.3	3.3
$9,000-$9,999	3.5	4.8	3.2	3.7	3.6	3.8	3.0	7.5	2.4
$10,000-$10,999	3.1	4.7	2.9	4.3	6.3	3.9	.8	1.3	1.7
$11,000-$11,999	2.3	2.2	1.6	2.3	2.6	2.0	2.3	1.3	1.0
$12,000-$12,999	5.4	3.3	2.0	6.2	3.7	2.7	3.9	2.6	1.2
$13,000-$13,999	2.5	1.0	1.4	2.6	1.1	1.8	2.4	.9	.8
$14,000-$14,999	2.9	2.1	1.3	3.6	3.0	1.4	1.7	.0	1.2
$15,000-$19,999	6.5	9.9	4.1	8.1	12.7	6.1	3.3	3.5	1.7
$20,000 or more	12.8	9.9	4.4	14.4	10.9	6.7	9.7	7.6	1.5
Median income	$5,959	$6,197	$4,161	$7,491	$7,458	$5,409	$3,990	$4,599	$2,833

E2-15. Income from Employer Pensions, by Sex, Marital Status, and Social Security Beneficiary Status: Percent Distribution of Persons Aged 65 or Older: 1990

Person pension income (recipients only) [1]	Beneficiaries [2]			Nonbeneficiaries		
	Total	Married	Nonmarried	Total	Married	Nonmarried
	Men					
Number (in thousands)	5,624	4,440	1,184	383	306	76
Total percent	100.0	100.0	100.0	100.0	100.0	100.0
$1-$499	2.0	2.0	1.7	.8	1.0	.0
$500-$999	4.4	4.2	5.4	1.4	1.7	.0
$1,000-$1,499	4.6	4.5	5.2	2.2	1.4	5.5
$1,500-$1,999	5.2	4.6	7.5	.8	1.0	.0
$2,000-$2,499	5.8	5.5	7.0	3.5	3.3	4.5
$2,500-$2,999	3.0	3.2	2.6	.4	.4	.0
$3,000-$3,999	8.4	8.0	10.1	2.3	2.3	2.0
$4,000-$4,999	7.0	6.8	7.8	3.3	3.5	2.5
$5,000-$5,999	6.5	6.4	6.8	.6	.8	.0
$6,000-$6,999	7.5	7.7	6.7	4.6	4.6	4.5
$7,000-$7,999	5.1	5.1	5.0	3.5	4.3	.0
$8,000-$8,999	4.9	5.1	4.1	2.7	2.2	5.0
$9,000-$9,999	4.8	4.4	6.5	1.9	1.0	5.7
$10,000-$10,999	4.2	4.1	4.5	1.0	.6	2.7
$11,000-$11,999	2.0	2.2	1.2	2.0	1.0	6.2
$12,000-$12,999	3.3	3.3	3.2	7.5	8.4	3.8
$13,000-$13,999	2.1	2.1	2.3	3.4	3.4	3.0
$14,000-$14,999	1.4	1.5	1.2	5.2	6.0	1.8
$15,000-$19,999	7.6	8.3	4.8	16.6	15.3	21.7
$20,000-$24,999	3.6	4.1	2.0	13.3	13.9	10.8
$25,000 or more	6.4	7.0	4.3	23.1	23.8	20.4
Median income	$6,142	$6,460	$5,280	$15,735	$15,736	$15,731
	Women					
Number (in thousands)	4,372	1,295	3,078	226	41	185
Total percent	100.0	100.0	100.0	100.0	100.0	100.0
$1-$499	6.9	7.5	6.6	.4	(3)	.0
$500-$999	9.5	12.0	8.5	2.9	(3)	2.6
$1,000-$1,499	10.8	10.1	11.1	4.3	(3)	4.1
$1,500-$1,999	7.1	7.2	7.0	3.6	(3)	4.4
$2,000-$2,499	7.3	6.1	7.9	.2	(3)	.0
$2,500-$2,999	5.8	6.0	5.7	1.6	(3)	1.5
$3,000-$3,999	8.7	8.8	8.7	3.8	(3)	2.8
$4,000-$4,999	7.7	6.8	8.0	5.2	(3)	5.8
$5,000-$5,999	5.9	6.4	5.7	6.3	(3)	7.0
$6,000-$6,999	5.7	6.6	5.4	11.7	(3)	10.2
$7,000-$7,999	4.1	3.7	4.3	9.9	(3)	10.9
$8,000-$8,999	3.7	2.8	4.0	3.4	(3)	4.2
$9,000-$9,999	3.1	4.1	2.7	2.3	(3)	2.0
$10,000-$10,999	2.7	3.5	2.4	3.5	(3)	3.1
$11,000-$11,999	2.0	2.2	1.9	1.9	(3)	2.3
$12,000-$12,999	1.6	1.8	1.5	3.6	(3)	4.4
$13,000-$13,999	1.1	1.2	1.0	4.5	(3)	4.4
$14,000-$14,999	1.8	.3	2.5	7.2	(3)	6.4
$15,000-$19,999	2.4	2.4	2.4	10.8	(3)	13.2
$20,000-$24,999	.9	.2	1.2	9.3	(3)	6.7
$25,000 or more	1.1	.6	1.3	3.6	(3)	4.0
Median income	$3,277	$3,126	$3,335	$8,102	(3)	$8,160

[1]Includes federal, state, local, and military pensions, and private pensions or annuities.

[2]Social Security beneficiaries may be receiving retired-worker benefits, dependents' or survivors' benefits, disability benefits, transitionally insured, or special age-72 benefits.

[3]Fewer than 75,000 weighted cases.

E2-16. Income from Government Employee Pension, by Sex and Marital Status: Percent Distribution of Persons Aged 65 or Older: 1990

Person government employee pensions (recipients only)[1]	Men			Women		
	Total	Married	Nonmarried	Total	Married	Nonmarried
Number (in thousands)..................	1,819	1,457	362	1,828	556	1,272
Total percent	100.0	100.0	100.0	100.0	100.0	100.0
$1-$499	.3	.2	.6	2.1	2.0	2.1
$500-$999	2.2	2.2	2.0	4.2	7.5	2.8
$1,000-$1,499	2.4	2.1	3.2	4.8	4.7	4.9
$1,500-$1,999	3.2	2.7	5.2	5.6	6.8	5.0
$2,000-$2,499	2.9	3.1	1.9	5.6	1.8	7.2
$2,500-$2,999	1.3	1.1	2.1	4.8	8.0	3.4
$3,000-$3,999	4.0	4.0	4.3	8.2	9.3	7.7
$4,000-$4,999	3.4	3.1	4.7	7.6	7.2	7.7
$5,000-$5,999	3.5	3.8	2.4	6.0	6.4	5.9
$6,000-$6,999	4.8	5.5	2.0	8.1	7.5	8.3
$7,000-$7,999	4.4	4.1	5.3	5.6	5.8	5.5
$8,000-$8,999	4.3	4.1	5.0	5.8	5.1	6.1
$9,000-$9,999	6.1	5.9	6.8	4.9	5.8	4.6
$10,000-$10,999	4.1	3.9	5.2	5.0	5.9	4.7
$11,000-$11,999	2.6	2.1	4.8	3.7	4.1	3.5
$12,000-$12,999	6.0	5.8	6.7	3.2	3.5	3.1
$13,000-$13,999	3.1	2.7	4.6	2.0	1.1	2.4
$14,000-$14,999	3.1	3.5	1.4	3.3	.8	4.4
$15,000-$19,999	14.0	14.5	11.7	4.9	4.0	5.2
$20,000-$24,999	8.6	9.3	6.1	2.3	1.9	2.4
$25,000 or more	15.8	16.3	14.1	2.3	.6	3.0
Median income	$11,684	$11,909	$10,968	$5,947	$5,036	$6,146

[1]Includes federal, state, local, and military pensions.

E2-17. Age of Householder—Households, by Median Money Income: 1967 to 1991

(Income in 1991 CPI-U-X1 adjusted dollars. Numbers in thousands as of March of the following year. Income years 1979 and earlier include householders 14 years old and over)

Year	15 to 24 years		25 to 34 years		35 to 44 years		45 to 54 years		55 to 64 years		65 years and over	
	Number of households	Median income	Number of households	Median income	Number of households	Median income	Number of households	Median income	Number of households	Median income	Number of households	Median income
1991.........	4,859	$18,313	20,007	$30,842	21,774	$39,349	15,547	$43,751	12,560	$33,304	20,921	$16,975
1990.........	4,882	18,760	20,323	31,637	21,304	40,184	14,751	43,686	12,524	33,727	20,527	17,564
1989.........	5,121	20,499	20,472	32,757	20,554	41,338	14,514	45,608	12,529	33,851	20,156	17,323
1988.........	5,415	19,618	20,924	32,706	19,952	42,085	14,018	43,995	12,805	33,276	19,716	17,181
1987[1]......	5,306	19,719	20,621	32,331	19,327	42,185	13,600	44,607	12,858	33,043	19,412	17,316
1986.........	5,197	19,026	20,502	32,183	18,703	40,744	13,211	44,315	12,868	33,275	18,998	17,205
1985.........	5,503	19,049	20,410	31,753	17,997	39,323	13,099	42,054	12,852	32,350	18,596	16,777
1984.........	5,438	18,389	20,013	31,114	17,481	39,043	12,628	41,314	13,073	31,584	18,155	16,778
1983[2]......	5,458	18,291	19,786	29,712	16,569	37,890	12,523	41,481	13,128	31,434	17,827	16,371
1982.........	5,695	19,683	19,104	30,319	16,020	37,569	12,354	39,870	13,074	31,450	17,671	15,730
1981.........	6,110	20,017	19,327	31,009	15,326	38,372	12,505	40,881	12,947	31,807	17,312	14,970
1980.........	6,443	21,036	19,153	32,001	14,462	39,101	12,694	41,573	12,704	32,349	16,912	14,532
1979[3]......	6,570	21,926	18,504	33,503	13,980	40,669	12,654	42,421	12,525	33,012	16,544	14,502
1978.........	6,342	22,224	16,996	33,297	13,328	40,210	12,585	42,739	12,284	32,341	15,795	14,288
1977.........	6,220	20,626	16,831	32,488	12,969	38,955	12,602	41,759	12,183	30,841	15,225	13,678
1976.........	5,991	20,320	16,167	32,090	12,482	38,340	12,905	40,502	11,780	30,753	14,816	13,670
1975.........	5,877	19,722	15,510	31,813	12,227	37,666	12,820	39,556	11,631	30,257	14,802	13,535
1974[4]......	5,866	21,288	14,949	32,730	11,886	39,094	12,901	40,514	11,299	30,100	14,263	13,888
1973.........	5,857	21,630	14,332	34,148	11,703	40,292	12,939	40,632	11,149	31,387	13,879	13,225
1972.........	5,476	21,660	13,562	33,366	11,721	38,921	12,805	40,262	11,212	30,780	13,473	12,789
1971.........	5,194	20,797	12,802	31,844	11,529	36,708	12,758	37,972	11,138	29,528	13,255	12,049
1970.........	4,707	21,993	11,847	31,956	11,739	36,708	12,509	37,638	10,952	29,370	12,622	11,536
1969.........	4,305	21,986	11,654	32,239	11,687	37,099	12,237	37,808	10,741	28,578	12,252	11,508
1968.........	4,068	21,778	11,282	31,041	11,739	35,499	12,149	35,304	10,552	27,562	12,014	11,488
1967.........	3,829	21,068	10,597	30,062	11,931	33,754	11,965	34,136	10,331	26,103	11,792	10,356

[1]Implementation of a new March CPS processing system.
[2]Implementation of Hispanic population weighting controls.
[3]Implementation of 1980 census population controls.
[4]Implementation of a new March CPS processing system.

E2-18. Median Value and Ratio of Owned House Value to Current Income for the Elderly, by Residence: 1989

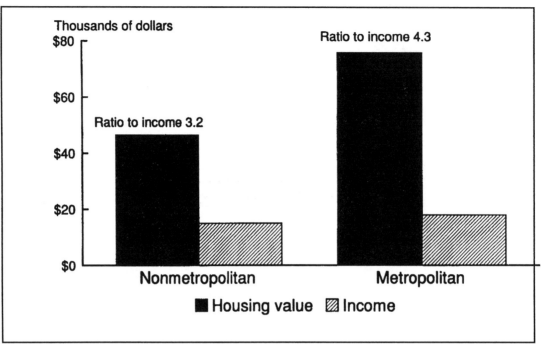

Source: Department of Housing and Urban Development, 1989 American Housing Survey.

E3. Living Costs

E3-1. CPI-U: All Items and Food and Beverages: 1981 to 1992

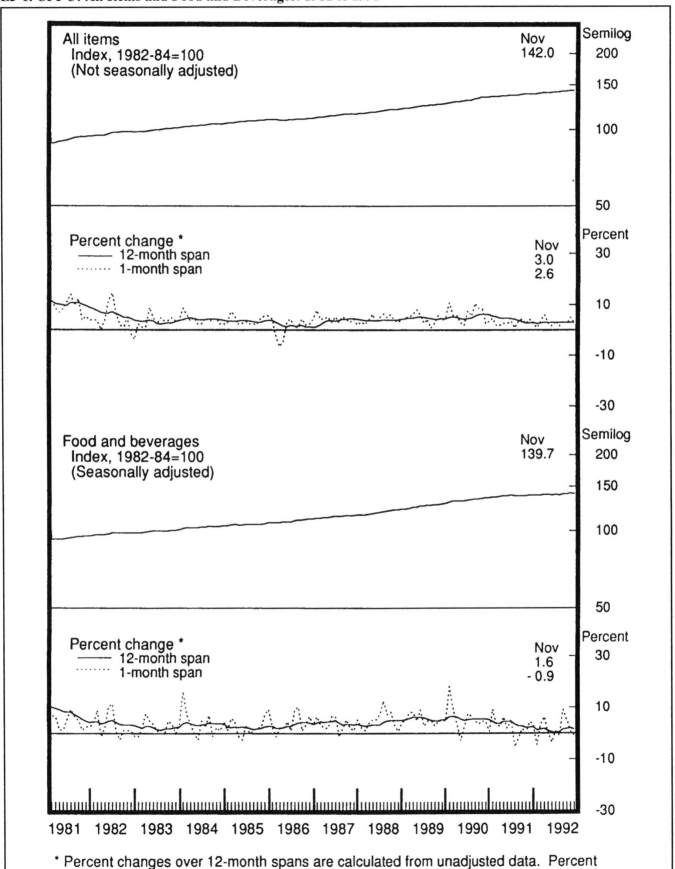

* Percent changes over 12-month spans are calculated from unadjusted data. Percent
changes over 1-month spans are annual rates calculated from seasonally adjusted data.

E3-2. CPI-U: Housing and Apparel and Upkeep: 1981 to 1992

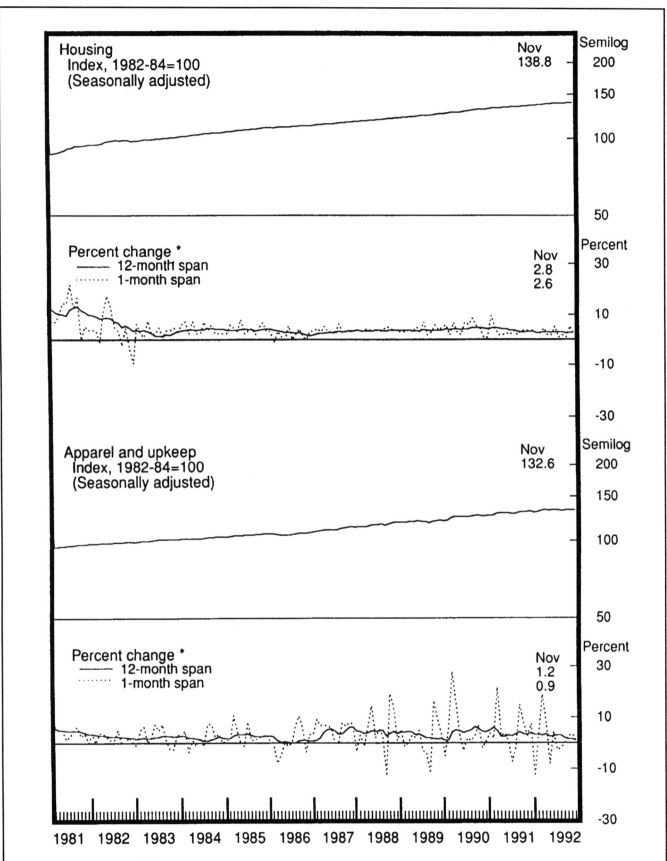

* Percent changes over 12-month spans are calculated from unadjusted data. Percent changes over 1-month spans are annual rates calculated from seasonally adjusted data.

E3-3. CPI-U: Transportation and Medical Care: 1981 to 1992

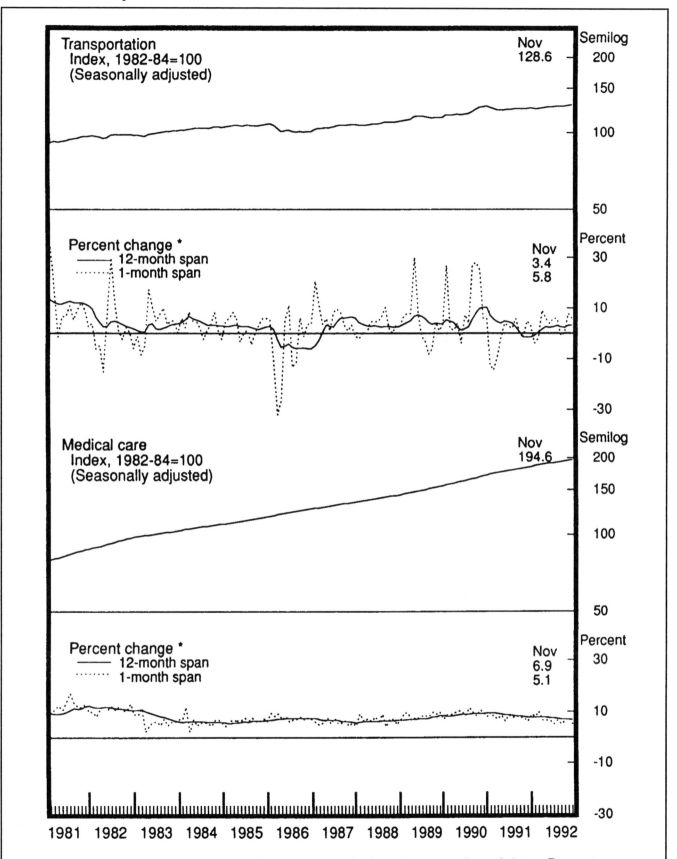

Transportation
Index, 1982-84=100
(Seasonally adjusted)

Nov
128.6

Semilog
200
150

100

50

Percent change *
— 12-month span
.... 1-month span

Nov
3.4
5.8

Percent
30

10

-10

-30

Medical care
Index, 1982-84=100
(Seasonally adjusted)

Nov
194.6

Semilog
200
150

100

50

Percent change *
— 12-month span
..... 1-month span

Nov
6.9
5.1

Percent
30

10

-10

-30

1981 1982 1983 1984 1985 1986 1987 1988 1989 1990 1991 1992

* Percent changes over 12-month spans are calculated from unadjusted data. Percent
changes over 1-month spans are annual rates calculated from seasonally adjusted data.

E3-4. CPI-U: Entertainment and Other Goods and Services: 1981 to 1992

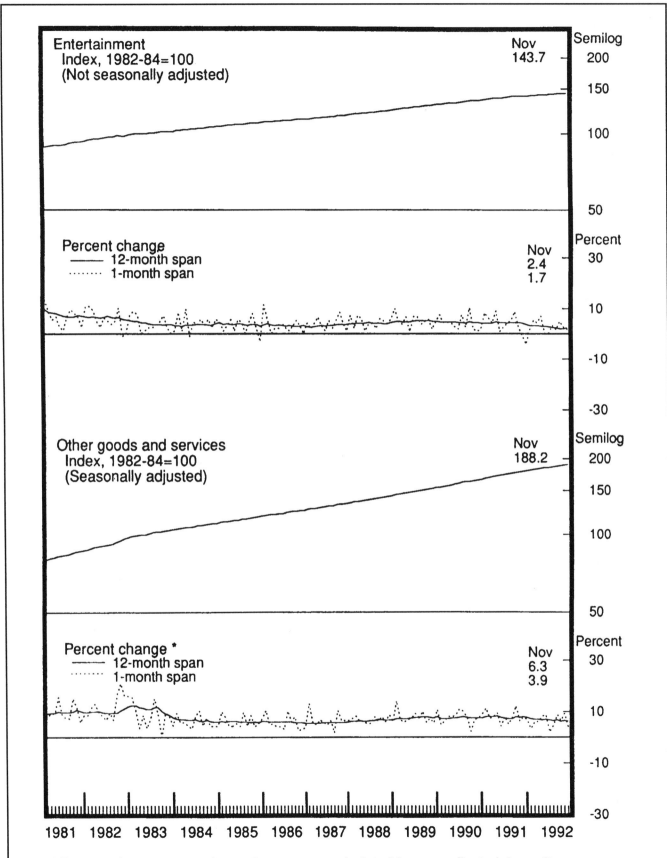

* Percent changes over 12-month spans are calculated from unadjusted data. Percent changes over 1-month spans are annual rates calculated from seasonally adjusted data.

E3-5. Selected Characteristics, Annual Expenditures, Sources of Income, and Shares of Expenditures and Income, for Older Consumer Units, by Income Class, Consumer Expenditure Survey: 1988 to 1989

Item	All consumer units age 65 and over[1]	Age 65 to 74 Less than $15,000	Age 65 to 74 $15,000 to $29,999	Age 65 to 74 $30,000 and over	Age 75 and over Less than $15,000	Age 75 and over $15,000 to $29,999	Age 75 and over $30,000 and over
Number of consumer units (in thousands)	17,621	4,961	3,288	2,052	5,322	1,336	661
Average number of persons	1.8	1.6	2.2	2.4	1.4	1.9	2.1
Age of reference person	73.8	69.4	69.2	68.4	80.8	79.3	79.1
Number of earners	.5	.4	.7	1.2	.1	.3	.5
Percent:							
Male	56	49	72	79	36	75	78
Homeowner	77	67	87	91	70	83	90
Black	10	14	9	3	12	2	2
College	25	15	29	57	15	29	52
Own at least one vehicle	78	76	96	99	58	89	92
Total expenditures	$18,372	$13,614	$20,862	$39,354	$10,424	$21,396	$37,656
Percent distribution:							
Food	15.3	16.4	16.8	14.1	17.7	13.7	11.3
Food at home	10.2	11.9	11.1	7.6	13.5	9.2	6.0
Food away from home	5.1	4.5	5.7	6.4	4.2	4.5	5.3
Housing	31.8	35.3	29.7	28.1	38.7	28.7	27.2
Apparel and services	4.5	4.7	5.3	5.3	3.3	3.5	4.2
Transportation	17.1	16.1	18.7	20.0	10.3	20.9	15.1
Health care	11.6	12.4	10.6	6.3	16.7	15.6	12.2
Entertainment	3.7	3.1	3.9	4.7	2.2	3.4	4.7
Other[2]	11.8	9.6	11.1	13.0	10.1	11.4	20.1
Personal insurance, pensions	4.3	2.4	4.0	8.5	1.0	2.8	5.2
Income before taxes[3]	$18,746	$8,654	$20,990	$52,875	$8,016	$21,049	$59,095
Percent distribution:							
Wages and salaries	19.7	6.4	21.8	37.2	1.9	8.1	10.1
Social security, retirement	58.3	85.9	66.3	33.3	88.5	72.4	39.8
Interest, dividends	15.2	4.2	8.2	16.6	6.2	16.5	44.5
Other income	6.8	3.5	3.7	12.9	3.5	2.9	5.6

[1]"Complete income reporters" only.
[2]Includes expenditures for alcoholic beverages, personal care, reading, education, tobacco, miscellaneous expenditures, and cash contributions.
[3]Income values are derived from "complete income reporters" only.

E3-6. Annual Expenditures, Expenditure Shares, and Characteristics of Single Consumer Units Classified by Sex and Selected Age Groups, Consumer Expenditure Survey: 1988 to 1989

	Single men All ages	Single men 25-34	Single men 65 and over	Single women All ages	Single women 25-34	Single women 65 and over
Income before taxes	$20,941	$22,931	$15,383	$13,803	$19,270	$9,989
Age of reference person	42	29	74	55	29	76
Percent homeowner	33	25	60	47	19	65
Number of earners	.8	1.0	.2	.5	.9	.1
Total expenditures	$18,668	$20,878	$13,977	$14,275	$17,416	$11,058
Percent distribution:						
Food	13	13	15	13	12	15
Food at home	5	5	8	8	5	11
Food away from home	8	9	7	5	7	4
Housing	31	32	34	37	34	41
Shelter	21	22	19	22	23	21
Utilities	6	5	8	8	6	11
Other housing[1]	5	5	6	7	5	9
Apparel and services	4	5	3	7	8	5
Transportation	20	22	20	14	18	9
Health care	4	2	12	7	4	13
Entertainment	5	5	3	4	6	3
Other[2]	22	21	14	17	18	14

[1]Includes household operations, housekeeping supplies, and household furnishings and equipment.
[2]Includes alcoholic beverages, personal care, reading, education, tobacco, miscellaneous, cash contributions, and personal insurance and pensions.

E3-7. Consumer Units with Reference Person Age 65 and Over, by Income before Taxes: Average Annual Expenditures and Characteristics, Consumer Expenditure Survey: 1988 to 1989

Item	Complete reporting of income							
	Total complete reporting	Less than $5,000	$5,000 to $9,999	$10,000 to $14,999	$15,000 to $19,999	$20,000 to $29,999	$30,000 to $39,999	$40,000 and over
Number of consumer units (in thousands)	17,621	1,692	5,209	3,383	2,187	2,438	1,143	1,571
Consumer unit characteristics:								
Income before taxes [1]	$18,746	$3,313	$7,370	$12,299	$17,300	$24,334	$34,515	$68,850
Income after taxes [1]	17,717	3,271	7,257	12,010	16,631	23,462	33,179	61,607
Average number of persons in consumer unit	1.8	1.3	1.4	1.7	2.0	2.2	2.3	2.3
Age of reference person	73.8	75.4	75.8	74.5	72.5	71.8	70.7	71.3
Average number in consumer unit:								
Earners	.5	.2	.2	.3	.5	.7	.9	1.2
Vehicles	1.4	.7	.8	1.4	1.8	2.0	2.3	2.5
Children under 18	.1	(²)	.1	(²)	.1	.1	.1	.1
Persons 65 and over	1.4	1.1	1.2	1.5	1.5	1.5	1.5	1.5
Percent distribution								
Sex of reference person:								
Male	56	28	35	61	69	77	73	83
Female	44	72	65	39	31	23	27	17
Housing tenure:								
Homeowner with mortgage	16	10	10	10	20	22	25	32
Homeowner without mortgage	61	45	59	63	64	67	63	61
Renter	24	44	31	27	16	12	12	7
Race of reference person:								
Black	10	27	13	7	7	7	3	3
White and other	90	73	87	93	93	93	97	97
Education of reference person:								
Elementary (1-8)	29	47	40	31	23	19	10	7
High school (9-12)	44	38	44	47	53	46	41	31
College	25	11	14	19	23	34	49	61
Never attended and other	1	4	2	2	1	(³)	(³)	(⁴)
At least one vehicle owned	78	53	60	83	91	96	98	97
Average annual expenditures	$18,372	$9,066	$10,258	$16,175	$18,656	$23,109	$29,953	$45,460
Food	2,805	1,506	1,824	2,672	3,132	3,489	4,790	5,504
Food at home	1,868	1,227	1,413	1,840	2,124	2,274	2,781	2,839
Cereals and bakery products	288	189	229	280	341	346	398	414
Cereals and cereal products	99	80	79	99	110	120	132	125
Bakery products	189	109	150	181	231	226	267	289
Meats, poultry, fish, and eggs	494	322	360	478	579	610	746	779
Beef	152	78	108	143	212	198	231	204
Pork	108	77	85	115	107	130	132	181
Other meats	66	47	50	70	75	84	90	86
Poultry	82	64	60	75	92	89	135	147
Fish and seafood	59	37	34	46	65	81	127	123
Eggs	27	19	23	28	28	28	31	38
Dairy products	227	161	183	232	253	267	310	315
Fresh milk and cream	115	94	96	121	123	132	145	136
Other dairy products	113	67	87	111	130	135	165	179
Fruits and vegetables	378	247	288	389	408	444	637	541
Fresh fruits	131	78	95	130	127	167	275	195
Fresh vegetables	114	77	88	118	132	127	185	155
Processed fruits	81	51	64	87	92	91	112	110
Processed vegetables	52	40	41	53	56	59	65	81

See footnotes at end of table.

E3-7. Consumer Units with Reference Person Age 65 and Over, by Income before Taxes: Average Annual Expenditures and Characteristics, Consumer Expenditure Survey: 1988 to 1989 (continued)

Item	Total complete reporting	Complete reporting of income						
		Less than $5,000	$5,000 to $9,999	$10,000 to $14,999	$15,000 to $19,999	$20,000 to $29,999	$30,000 to $39,999	$40,000 and over
Other food at home	$481	$308	$353	$461	$544	$607	$690	$791
Sugar and other sweets	66	49	48	59	69	86	117	105
Fats and oils	54	41	42	53	61	63	72	74
Miscellaneous foods	191	110	140	186	221	251	261	316
Nonalcoholic beverages	149	102	117	148	172	178	196	216
Food prepared by consumer unit on out-of-town trips	21	⁵ 6	5	14	21	29	45	79
Food away from home	937	280	411	832	1,009	1,215	2,009	2,665
Alcoholic beverages	139	40	46	134	166	173	268	471
Housing	5,846	3,612	3,990	5,468	5,603	6,689	8,239	12,733
Shelter	2,815	1,873	1,904	2,642	2,546	2,959	3,905	6,576
Owned dwellings	1,637	684	949	1,330	1,522	1,983	2,466	4,625
Mortgage interest	333	191	156	205	349	303	673	1,125
Property taxes	615	225	338	567	590	793	917	1,602
Maintenance, repairs, insurance, other expenses	688	267	456	558	583	886	876	1,898
Rented dwellings	859	1,125	853	1,087	733	608	759	739
Other lodging	319	64	102	225	292	368	681	1,212
Utilities, fuels, and public services	1,628	1,165	1,243	1,564	1,762	1,954	2,022	2,555
Natural gas	257	139	206	266	277	315	279	396
Electricity	650	471	485	637	713	773	816	1,023
Fuel oil and other fuels	133	134	105	127	149	151	141	183
Telephone	414	315	323	383	430	489	563	644
Water and other public services	173	107	124	151	194	226	224	308
Household operations	369	133	250	300	257	388	440	1,236
Personal services	71	⁵ 9	⁵ 97	⁵ 81	⁵ 24	⁵ 41	⁵ 98	⁵ 125
Other household expenses	297	124	154	218	233	347	342	1,111
Housekeeping supplies	361	182	241	451	362	453	599	526
Laundry and cleaning supplies	81	68	56	76	90	119	126	105
Other household products	151	64	69	268	134	174	232	225
Postage and stationery	129	50	116	107	138	160	240	197
Household furnishings and equipment	674	258	350	511	676	935	1,272	1,839
Household textiles	86	16	32	64	95	174	157	214
Furniture	150	82	63	132	133	184	221	472
Floor coverings	34	⁵ 5	⁵ 9	33	57	⁵ 49	⁵ 87	⁵ 66
Major appliances	121	83	65	100	140	174	175	241
Small appliances, miscellaneous housewares	45	15	21	47	38	54	102	112
Miscellaneous household equipment	238	58	159	135	213	300	530	734
Apparel and services	825	298	428	694	777	1,187	1,772	2,106
Men and boys	187	35	73	172	239	266	334	519
Men, 16 and over	163	⁵ 30	57	139	221	211	317	499
Boys, 2 to 15	24	⁵ 5	16	32	18	55	17	21
Women and girls	380	149	225	289	335	584	893	898
Women, 16 and over	359	144	216	274	313	549	839	845
Girls, 2 to 15	21	⁵ 4	10	15	22	35	54	53
Children under 2	18	⁵ 2	7	15	20	17	36	62
Footwear	117	⁵ 50	73	131	96	141	251	250
Other apparel products and services	123	62	50	88	86	179	257	376
Transportation	3,137	1,278	1,141	2,510	3,345	4,711	6,481	7,976
Vehicle purchases (net outlay)	1,369	⁵ 562	307	1,038	1,488	2,132	3,299	3,717
Cars and trucks, new	819	⁵ 244	⁵ 163	574	804	1,180	2,112	2,668
Cars and trucks, used	549	⁵ 318	144	464	684	952	1,179	1,049
Other vehicles	⁵ 1	(⁴)	(⁴)	(³)	(⁴)	(⁴)	⁵ 8	(⁴)
Gasoline and motor oil	586	321	299	527	673	841	953	1,171

See footnotes at end of table.

E3-7. Consumer Units with Reference Person Age 65 and Over, by Income before Taxes: Average Annual Expenditures and Characteristics, Consumer Expenditure Survey: 1988 to 1989 (continued)

Item	Complete reporting of income							
	Total complete reporting	Less than $5,000	$5,000 to $9,999	$10,000 to $14,999	$15,000 to $19,999	$20,000 to $29,999	$30,000 to $39,999	$40,000 and over
Other vehicle expenses	$949	$304	$449	$797	$1,034	$1,398	$1,762	$2,262
Vehicle finance charges	103	26	38	80	98	155	240	275
Maintenance and repairs	374	123	194	315	385	582	734	804
Vehicle insurance	380	130	186	329	452	532	588	917
Vehicle rental, licenses, other charges	92	26	31	73	99	129	201	266
Public transportation	232	91	85	149	150	339	466	826
Health care	2,124	1,175	1,453	2,396	2,506	2,566	2,395	3,471
Health insurance	923	505	723	1,042	1,021	1,199	1,004	1,155
Medical services	673	333	346	820	915	762	826	1,217
Drugs	412	287	324	445	439	509	434	575
Medical supplies	117	50	60	89	131	96	131	524
Entertainment	679	178	283	469	632	946	1,390	2,153
Fees and admissions	217	43	53	115	177	263	483	958
Television, radios, sound equipment	235	85	136	207	274	318	383	510
Pets, toys, and playground equipment	141	40	68	97	114	266	306	331
Other entertainment supplies, equipment, and services	86	11	26	49	67	99	218	354
Personal care products and services	256	139	128	240	323	353	500	491
Reading	136	57	76	112	153	183	227	311
Education	65	[5] 7	[5] 9	67	[5] 43	133	91	222
Tobacco products and smoking supplies	145	83	122	141	146	199	170	196
Miscellaneous	428	420	273	312	420	538	630	914
Cash contributions	1,002	154	338	612	744	1,092	1,361	4,917
Personal insurance and pensions	785	119	148	348	665	852	1,641	3,995
Life and other personal insurance	289	108	115	245	412	297	299	969
Pensions and Social Security	496	11	33	102	254	555	1,342	3,026
Sources of income and personal taxes: [1]								
Money income before taxes	18,746	3,313	7,370	12,299	17,300	24,334	34,515	68,850
Wages and salaries	3,698	99	170	735	2,115	5,204	9,029	21,642
Self-employment income	868	[5] -383	16	113	202	328	1,451	8,011
Social Security, private and government retirement	10,925	3,113	6,514	10,474	13,027	15,441	17,193	20,436
Interest, dividends, rental income, other property income	2,845	130	302	775	1,443	2,943	6,216	18,008
Unemployment and workers' compensation, veterans' benefits	148	[5] 20	103	80	113	137	451	426
Public assistance, supplemental security income, food stamps	178	298	228	63	302	129	[5] 63	[5] 114
Regular contributions for support	58	[5] 6	22	[5] 22	[5] 74	[5] 134	[5] 75	[5] 159
Other income	26	[5] 31	[5] 14	[5] 35	[5] 24	[5] 17	[5] 38	[5] 55
Personal taxes	1,029	42	113	289	668	872	1,337	7,243
Federal income taxes	796	27	81	219	467	690	1,011	5,700
State and local income taxes	169	2	7	26	131	134	192	1,282
Other taxes	64	13	24	43	70	48	134	261
Income after taxes	17,717	3,271	7,257	12,010	16,631	23,462	33,179	61,607

See footnotes at end of table.

E3-7. Consumer Units with Reference Person Age 65 and Over, by Income before Taxes: Average Annual Expenditures and Characteristics, Consumer Expenditure Survey: 1988 to 1989 (continued)

Item	Total complete reporting	Complete reporting of income						
		Less than $5,000	$5,000 to $9,999	$10,000 to $14,999	$15,000 to $19,999	$20,000 to $29,999	$30,000 to $39,999	$40,000 and over
Addenda:								
Net change in total assets	$681	$633	$153	-$1,069	-$787	$1,443	$777	$7,040
Net change in total liabilities	327	53	194	51	827	21	1,132	852
Other money receipts	684	5 569	143	156	758	304	424	4,418
Mortgage principal paid on owned property	-180	-62	-114	-111	-203	-229	-377	-424
Estimated market value of owned home	64,747	34,496	40,264	52,404	65,397	77,042	96,574	161,975
Estimated monthly rental value of owned home	382	197	270	326	426	451	548	784
Gifts of goods and services:								
Clothing, males 2 and over	63	5 9	34	54	86	110	65	149
Clothing, females 2 and over	69	5 11	51	43	67	107	100	211
Clothing, infants less than 2	16	5 2	7	15	18	16	30	55
Jewelry and watches	11	5 1	2	7	9	29	38	16
Small appliances and miscellaneous housewares	14	5 3	6	20	8	12	13	60
Household textiles	11	5 2	5 6	5 11	5 10	5 17	5 27	5 20
All other gifts	602	467	264	484	566	970	669	1,628

[1]Components of income and taxes are derived from "Complete income reporters."

[2]Value less than 0.05.

[3]Value less than 0.5.

[4]No data reported.

[5]Data are likely to have large sampling errors.

E3-8. Monthly Housing Costs as a Percent of Income, by Tenure and Age of Householder: 1987

(number of housing units in thousands)

Monthly housing costs as percent of income	Specified owner[1]				Specified renter[2]	
	With mortgage		Without mortgage			
	Householder 65+	Householder under 65 years	Householder 65+	Householder under 65 years	Householder 65+	Householder under 65 years
Total units	1,511	22,004	9,328	9,381	4,394	25,667
Less than 5 percent	16	198	380	1,211	16	176
5 to 9 percent	111	1,941	1,724	3,761	59	853
10 to 14 percent	202	3,840	1,933	1,979	174	2,418
15 to 19 percent	182	4,414	1,523	898	269	3,586
20 to 24 percent	213	4,001	1,058	469	391	3,685
25 to 29 percent	153	2,611	765	285	633	3,228
30 to 34 percent	149	1,746	520	154	541	2,404
35 to 39 percent	123	969	323	97	378	1,588
40 to 49 percent	130	902	423	163	581	2,134
50 to 59 percent	71	463	201	82	394	1,349
60 to 69 percent	52	258	99	57	293	899
70 percent or more	109	661	379	225	666	3,347
Median percent	26.0	20.8	17.1	9.6	36.5	28.3

[1]Limited to one-unit structures on less than 10 acres and no business on property.

[2]Excludes one-unit structures on 10 acres or more.

NOTE: Data exclude units with zero or negative income, no cash rent, or mortgage payment not reported.

Source: U.S. Bureau of the Census and U.S. Department of Housing and Urban Development, "American Housing Survey for the United States in 1987," *Current Housing Reports* H-150-87 (December 1989).

E3-9. Monthly Housing Costs as Percent of Income, by Age and Tenure of Householder: 1987

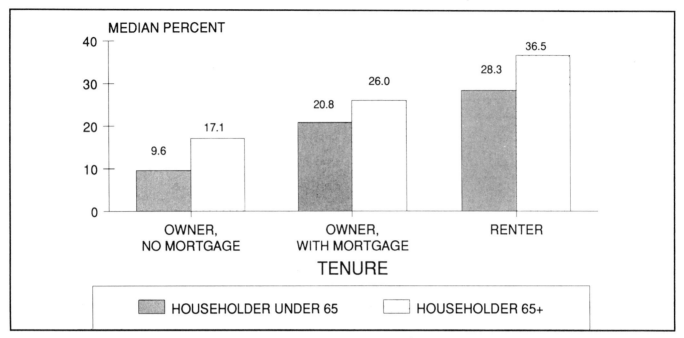

Source: U.S. Bureau of the Census and U.S. Department of Housing and Urban Development, "American Housing Survey of the United States in 1987," *Current Housing Reports* H-150-87 (December 1989).

E3-10. Personal Health-Care Expenditures, by Age: 1977 and 1987

Age and type of expenditure	Aggregate amount (billions)			Per capita amount		
	1987	1977	1977[1]	1987	1977	1977[1]
Total Expenditures						
All ages	$447.0	$150.3	$281.9	$1,776.0	$658.0	$1,234.1
Under 19 years	$51.9	$19.5	$36.6	$745.0	$269.0	$504.5
19 to 64 years	$233.1	$85.6	$160.5	$1,535.0	$651.0	$1,220.9
65 years and over	$162.0	$45.2	$84.8	$5,360.0	$1,856.0	$3,480.9
Private Expenditures						
All ages	$271.8	$92.6	$173.7	$1,079.0	$405.0	$759.6
Under 19 years	$38.1	$14.4	$27.0	$547.0	$198.0	$371.3
19 to 64 years	$173.0	$62.3	$116.8	$1,139.0	$474.0	$889.0
65 years and over	$60.6	$15.9	$29.8	$2,004.0	$653.0	$1,224.7
Public Expenditures						
All ages	$175.3	$57.8	$108.4	$696.0	$253.0	$474.5
Under 19	$13.8	$5.2	$9.8	$198.0	$711.0	$133.2
19 to 64 years	$60.0	$23.2	$43.5	$395.0	$177.0	$332.0
65 years and over	$101.5	$29.3	$55.0	$3,356.0	$1,204.0	$2,258.1

[1]1977 in 1987 constant dollars.
Source: Health Care Financing Administration, Office of the Actuary, data from the Office of National Cost Estimates.

E3-11. Total Out-of-Pocket Health Expenditures by the Elderly[a]

(in millions of nominal dollars)

	1961	1972	1984	1989	1991[b]
Total	$3,816	$8,293	$35,002	$57,047	$67,497
Direct Out-of-Pocket	3,087	5,951	24,630	39,728	47,626
Hospital	546	780	1,080	1,595	1,838
Physician	760	826	5,504	6,884	8,333
Nursing Home[c]	690	2,600	12,600	20,600	24,385
Other	1,091	1,745	5,436	10,649	13,070
Insurance	729	2,342	10,382	17,319	19,871
Private Insurance	729	1,382	7,180	10,860	13,336
Medicare Premium	NA	960	3,202	6,459[d]	6,535

[a]Data for health expenditures other than nursing home care for 1961, 1972, 1984, and 1989 are based on the Consumer Expenditure Survey (CEX). Nursing home care was added based on estimates from the Office of National Cost Estimates and the Brookings/ICF Long Term Care Financing Model.

[b]Data for 1991 were estimated by Lewin/ICF.

[c]The CEX is a survey of noninstitutionalized consumer units and does not capture nursing home expenditures. Nursing home care was added based on estimates from the Office of National Cost Estimates and the Brookings/ICF Long Term Care Financing Model. Adjustments were made to account for the change in the number of families when including nursing home residents.

[d]Medicare premiums in 1989 are unusually high because the $31.90 monthly Part B premiums contained an additional $4.00 per month for Part B services to cover the costs of benefits added by the 1988 Medicare Catastrophic Coverage Act (MCCA). MCCA was repealed, therefore the 1991 monthly premium of $29.90 was lower than in 1989.

NOTE: Expenditures are for consumer units headed by someone age 65 or older. A consumer unit comprises either: 1) all members of a particular household who are related by blood, marriage, adoption, or other legal arrangements; 2) a person living alone or sharing a household with others or living as a roomer in a private home or lodging house or in permanent living quarters in a hotel or motel, but who is financially independent; or 3) two or more persons living together who pool their income to make joint expenditure decisions.

E3-12. Per Family Out-of-Pocket Health Expenditures by the Elderly[a]

(in 1991 dollars)

	1961	1972	1984	1989	1991[b]
Total	$1,589	$1,854	$2,698	$3,249	$3,305
Direct Out-of-Pocket	1,285	1,331	1,898	2,262	2,332
Hospital	228	175	83	91	90
Physician	316	184	424	392	408
Nursing Home[c]	287	582	972	1,173	1,194
Other	454	390	419	606	640
Insurance	304	523	800	987	973
Private Insurance	304	309	553	619	653
Medicare Premium	NA	214	247	368[d]	320

[a]Data for health expenditures, other than nursing home care, for 1961, 1972, 1984, and 1989 are based on the Consumer Expenditure Survey (CEX). Nursing home care was added based on estimates from the Office of National Cost Estimates and the Brookings/ICF Long Term Care Financing Model.

[b]Data for 1991 were estimated by Lewin/ICF.

[c]The CEX is a survey of noninstitutionalized consumer units and does not capture nursing home expenditures. Nursing home care was added based on estimates from the Office of National Cost Estimates and the Brookings/ICF Long Term Care Financing Model. Adjustments were made to account for the change in the number of families when including nursing home residents.

[d]Medicare premiums in 1989 are unusually high because the $31.90 monthly Part B premiums contained an additional $4.00 per month for Part B services to cover the costs of benefits added by the 1988 Medicare Catastrophic Coverage Act (MCCA). MCCA was repealed, therefore the 1991 monthly premium of $29.90 was lower than in 1989.

NOTE: Expenditures are for consumer units headed by someone age 65 or older. A consumer unit comprises either: 1) all members of a particular household who are related by blood, marriage, adoption, or other legal arrangements; 2) a person living alone or sharing a household with others or living as a roomer in a private home or lodging house or in permanent living quarters in a hotel or motel, but who is financially independent; or 3) two or more persons living together who pool their income to make joint expenditure decisions.

E3-13. Percent Distribution of Per Family Out-of-Pocket Health Expenditures by Elderly Families[a]

	1961	1972	1984	1989	1991[b]
Total	100.0%	100.0%	100.0%	100.0%	100.0%
Direct Out-of-Pocket	80.9	71.8	70.3	69.7	70.6
Hospital	14.3	9.4	3.1	2.8	2.7
Physician	19.9	10.0	15.7	12.1	12.4
Nursing Home[c]	18.1	31.4	36.0	36.1	36.1
Other	28.6	21.0	15.5	18.7	19.4
Insurance	19.1	28.2	29.7	30.3	29.4
Private Insurance	19.1	16.6	20.5	19.0	19.7
Medicare Premium	NA	11.6	9.2	11.3[d]	9.7

[a]Data for health expenditures other than nursing home care for 1961, 1972, 1984, and 1989 are based on the Consumer Expenditure Survey (CEX). Nursing home care was added based on estimates from the Office of National Cost Estimates and the Brookings/ICF Long Term Care Financing Model.

[b]Data for 1991 were estimated by Lewin/ICF.

[c]The CEX is a survey of noninstitutionalized consumer units and does not capture nursing home expenditures. Nursing home care was added based on estimates from the Office of National Cost Estimates and the Brookings/ICF Long Term Care Financing Model. Adjustments were made to account for the change in the number of families when including nursing home residents.

[d]Medicare premiums in 1989 are unusually high because the $31.90 monthly Part B premiums contained an additional $4.00 per month for Part B services to cover the costs of benefits added by the 1988 Medicare Catastrophic Coverage Act (MCCA). MCCA was repealed, therefore the 1991 monthly premium of $29.90 was lower than in 1989.

NOTE: Expenditures are for consumer units headed by someone age 65 or older. A consumer unit comprises either: 1) all members of a particular household who are related by blood-marriage, adoption, or other legal arrangements; 2) a person living alone or sharing a household with others or living as a roomer in a private home or lodging house or in permanent living quarters in a hotel or motel, but who is financially independent; or 3) two or more persons living together who pool their income to make joint expenditure decisions.

E3-14. Elderly Family Out-of-Pocket Health Expenditures as a Percent of After-Tax Income[a]

	1961	1972	1984	1989	1991[b]
Total	10.6%	10.6%	16.2%	16.6%	17.1%
Direct Out-of-Pocket	8.6	7.6	11.4	11.5	12.1
Insurance	2.0	3.0	4.8	5.1	5.0
Private Insurance	2.0	1.8	3.3	3.2	3.3
Medicare Premium	NA	1.2	1.5	1.9[c]	1.7

[a]Data for health expenditures other than nursing home care for 1961, 1972, 1984, and 1989 are based on the Consumer Expenditure Survey (CEX). Nursing home care was added based on estimates from the Office of National Cost Estimates and the Brookings/ICF Long Term Care Financing Model.

[b]Data for 1991 were estimated by Lewin/ICF.

[c]Medicare premiums in 1989 are unusually high because the $31.90 monthly Part B premiums contained an additional $4.00 per month for Part B services to cover the costs of benefits added by the 1988 Medicare Catastrophic Coverage Act (MCCA). MCCA was repealed, therefore the 1991 monthly premium of $29.90 was lower than in 1989.

NOTE: Expenditures are for consumer units headed by someone age 65 or older. A consumer unit comprises either: 1) all members of a particular household who are related by blood, marriage, adoption, or other legal arrangements; 2) a person living alone or sharing a household with others or living as a roomer in a private home or lodging house or in permanent living quarters in a hotel or motel, but who is financially independent; or 3) two or more persons living together who pool their income to make joint expenditure decisions.

E3-15. Elderly Out-of-Pocket Health Costs Per Elderly Family

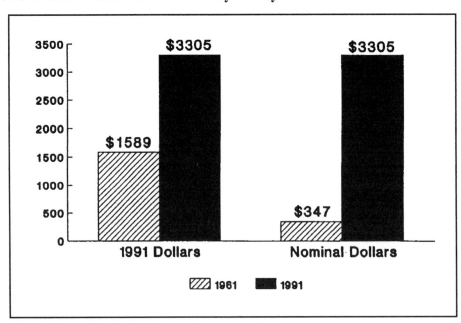

E3-16. Distribution of Out-of-Pocket Health Care Costs Per Elderly Family

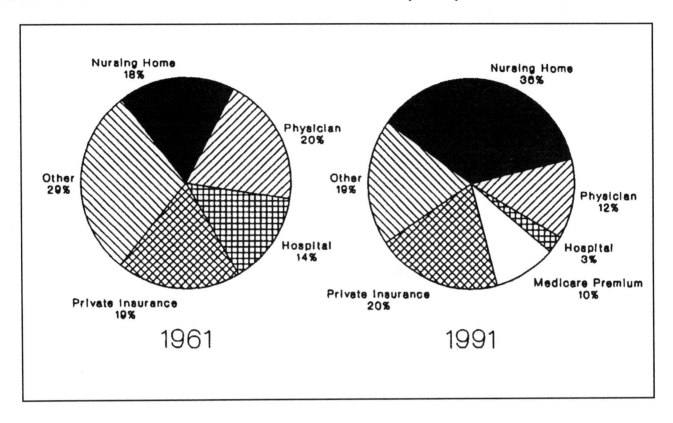

E3-17. Elderly Out-of-Pocket Health Care Expenses as a Portion of After-Tax Income

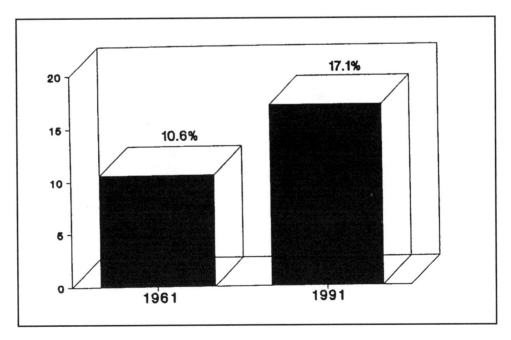

E4. Poverty

E4-1. Number of Poor and Poverty Rate: 1959 to 1991

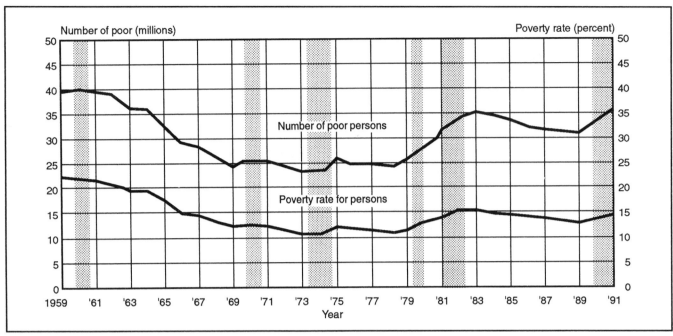

NOTE: The data points represent the midpoints of the respective years. The latest recessionary period began in July of 1990.

E4-2. Distribution of the Population Above and Below the Poverty Level, by Age: 1991

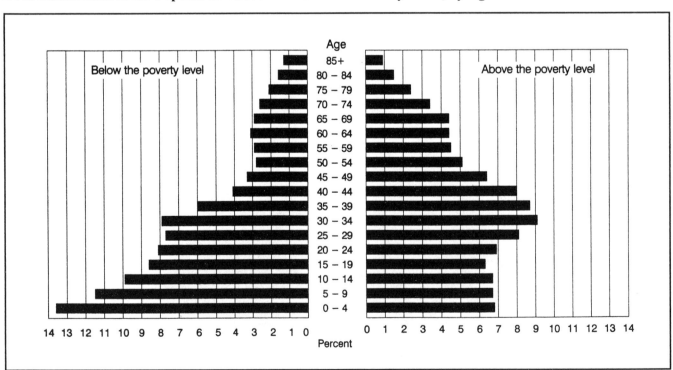

E4-3. Persons Below Poverty Level, by Race, Hispanic Origin, Age, and Region: 1990

[Persons as of March 1991.

AGE AND REGION	NUMBER BELOW POVERTY LEVEL (1,000)				PERCENT BELOW POVERTY LEVEL			
	All races [1]	White	Black	Hispanic [2]	All races [1]	White	Black	Hispanic [2]
Total	33,585	22,326	9,837	6,006	13.5	10.7	31.9	28.1
Under 16 years old.....	12,342	7,605	4,166	2,632	21.1	16.3	45.6	39.2
16 to 21 years old.....	3,351	2,162	1,020	669	16.2	13.0	32.9	29.7
22 to 44 years old.....	10,170	7,045	2,688	1,922	11.0	9.1	24.0	23.0
45 to 54 years old.....	2,002	1,358	569	311	7.8	6.2	21.1	17.9
55 to 59 years old.....	963	681	246	122	9.0	7.4	22.0	18.5
60 to 64 years old.....	1,098	768	288	105	10.3	8.2	27.9	18.1
65 years old and over...	3,658	2,707	860	245	12.2	10.1	33.8	22.5
Northeast...........	5,794	4,006	1,604	1,287	11.4	9.2	28.9	36.4
Midwest............	7,458	5,027	2,156	318	12.4	9.5	36.0	22.7
South..............	13,456	7,708	5,538	1,777	15.8	11.6	32.6	26.9
West..............	6,877	5,584	538	2,624	13.0	12.2	23.7	26.6

[1]Includes other races not shown separately.
[2]Hispanic persons may be of any race.
Source: U.S. Bureau of the Census, *Current Population Reports*, Series P-60, No. 175.

E4-4. Persons 65 Years Old and Over Below Poverty Level, by Selected Characteristics: 1970 to 1990

[Persons as of March of following year.

CHARACTERISTIC	NUMBER BELOW POVERTY LEVEL (1,000)					PERCENT BELOW POVERTY LEVEL				
	1970	1979 [1]	1985 [2]	1989 [3]	1990	1970	1979 [1]	1985 [2]	1989 [3]	1990
Persons, 65 yr. and over [4].....	4,793	3,682	3,456	3,363	3,658	24.6	15.2	12.6	11.4	12.2
White...................	4,011	2,911	2,698	2,539	2,707	22.6	13.3	11.0	9.6	10.1
Black...................	735	740	717	763	860	47.7	36.3	31.5	30.7	33.8
Hispanic [5]...............	(NA)	154	219	211	245	(NA)	26.8	23.9	20.6	22.5
In families...............	2,013	1,380	1,173	1,204	1,172	14.8	8.4	6.4	6.1	5.8
Unrelated individuals.........	2,779	2,299	2,281	2,160	2,479	47.2	29.4	25.6	22.0	24.7
Persons, 60 yr. and over......	5,977	4,753	4,677	4,389	4,756	21.3	13.9	12.3	10.9	11.7

[1]Population controls based on 1980 census.
[2]Beginning 1985, based on revised Hispanic population controls; data not directly comparable with prior years.
[3]Beginning 1989, based on revised processing procedures; data not directly comparable with prior years.
[4]Beginning 1979, includes members of unrelated subfamilies not shown separately. For earlier years, unrelated subfamily members are included in the "In families" category.
[5]Hispanic persons may be of any race.
NA Not available.
Source: U.S. Bureau of the Census, *Current Population Reports,* Series P-60, No. 175, and earlier issues.

E4-5. Number and Percent Poor in 1989 of Persons Aged 65 Years and Over, Ranked by State

State	Number
United States	3,780,585
1 Texas	296,690
2 New York	265,863
3 Florida	247,426
4 California	228,441
5 Pennsylvania	183,095
6 North Carolina	148,381
7 Illinois	144,439
8 Ohio	140,798
9 Georgia	126,206
10 Tennessee	122,767
11 Alabama	119,799
12 Michigan	114,086
13 Louisiana	106,026
14 Missouri	99,306
15 Kentucky	91,091
16 Mississippi	90,243
17 Virginia	88,570
18 New Jersey	84,200
19 South Carolina	78,092
20 Arkansas	75,625
21 Massachusetts	72,323
22 Oklahoma	71,042
23 Indiana	69,944
24 Minnesota	61,156
25 Wisconsin	54,806
26 Maryland	51,830
27 Arizona	49,917
28 Washington	49,509
29 Iowa	43,757
30 West Virginia	43,194
31 Kansas	38,303
32 Oregon	38,007
33 Colorado	34,258
34 Connecticut	30,010
35 New Mexico	25,839
36 Nebraska	25,032
37 Maine	21,479
38 Rhode Island	16,325
39 South Dakota	14,601
40 Idaho	13,223
41 Utah	12,682
42 District of Columbia	12,435
43 Montana	12,433
44 North Dakota	12,160
45 New Hampshire	11,900
46 Nevada	11,897
47 Hawaii	9,701
48 Delaware	7,697
49 Vermont	7,637
50 Wyoming	4,738
51 Alaska	1,606

State	Percent
United States	12.8
1 Mississippi	29.4
2 Louisiana	24.1
3 Alabama	24.0
4 Arkansas	22.9
5 Tennessee	20.9
6 Kentucky	20.6
7 South Carolina	20.5
8 Georgia	20.4
9 North Carolina	19.5
10 Texas	18.4
11 Oklahoma	17.9
12 District of Columbia	17.2
13 West Virginia	16.7
14 New Mexico	16.5
15 South Dakota	15.5
16 Missouri	14.8
17 North Dakota	14.6
18 Virginia	14.1
19 Maine	14.0
20 Montana	12.5
21 Vermont	12.4
22 Nebraska	12.2
23 Minnesota	12.1
24 Kansas	12.0
25 New York	11.9
26 Rhode Island	11.6
27 Idaho	11.5
28 Iowa	11.2
29 Colorado	11.0
30 Michigan	10.8
30 Florida	10.8
30 Arizona	10.8
30 Indiana	10.8
34 Illinois	10.7
34 Wyoming	10.7
34 Ohio	10.7
37 Pennsylvania	10.6
38 Maryland	10.5
39 New Hampshire	10.2
40 Oregon	10.1
40 Delaware	10.1
42 Nevada	9.6
43 Massachusetts	9.4
44 Washington	9.1
44 Wisconsin	9.1
46 Utah	8.8
47 New Jersey	8.5
48 Hawaii	8.0
49 California	7.6
49 Alaska	7.6
51 Connecticut	7.2

E4-6. Percent Poor in 1990 for Persons 65 Years and Over, by Race and Hispanic Origin: March 1991

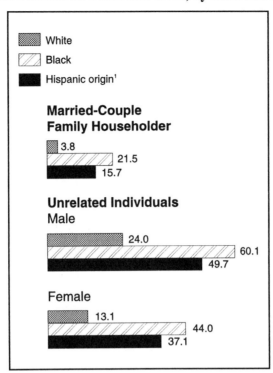

White

Black

Hispanic origin[1]

Married-Couple Family Householder

3.8

21.5

15.7

Unrelated Individuals
Male

24.0

60.1

49.7

Female

13.1

44.0

37.1

[1]Hispanic origin may be of any race.
Source: Mark Littman, U.S. Bureau of the Census, Poverty in the United States: 1990, *Current Population Reports,* Series P-60, No. 175. U.S. Government Printing Office, Washington, DC, 1991, table 5.

E4-7. Percent Poor Elderly in 1990, by Age, Sex, Race, and Hispanic Origin: March 1991

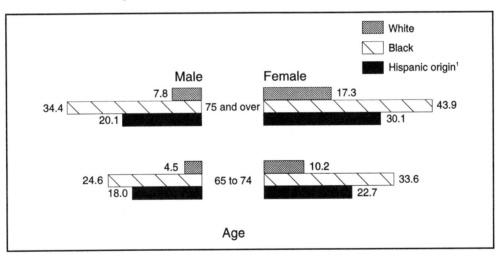

White

Black

Hispanic origin[1]

Male

Female

7.8   17.3
34.4   75 and over   43.9
20.1   30.1

4.5   10.2
24.6   65 to 74   33.6
18.0   22.7

Age

[1]Hispanic origin may be of any race.
Source: Mark Littman, U.S. Bureau of the Census, Poverty in the United States: 1990, *Current Population Reports,* Series P-60, No. 175. U.S. Government Printing Office, Washington, DC, 1991, table 5.

E4-8. Poverty Rates of Persons 85 Years and Over: 1981 to 1990

Year	White males	White females	Black females[1]
1990	4.3 to 15.3	17.4 to 28.4	15.2 to 55.6
1989	4.1 to 15.5	14.4 to 25.2	24.2 to 67.2
1988	5.3 to 19.1	11.9 to 22.9	16.3 to 61.5
1987	7.8 to 15.2	15.5 to 21.7	41.5 to 67.7
1986	9.2 to 16.8	14.6 to 20.6	29.8 to 57.8
1985	10.1 to 18.9	14.0 to 20.4	31.1 to 56.5
1984	8.0 to 16.0	14.3 to 20.9	32.8 to 60.4
1983	8.0 to 16.2	18.9 to 26.1	30.6 to 61.0
1982	9.3 to 17.9	18.0 to 25.4	30.1 to 59.9
1981	8.3 to 16.1	21.0 to 28.0	35.4 to 63.6

[1]There are not enough Black males 85 years and over in the survey to show statistically reliable data.

Source: U.S. Bureau of the Census, unpublished data from March 1982 to 1991, Current Population Survey, available from Mark Littman, Housing and Household Economic Statistics.

E4-9. Poverty Status of Persons, by Age, Race, and Hispanic Origin: 1959 to 1990

(Numbers in thousands. Persons as of March of the following year)

Year and race	All persons below poverty		Persons under 18 years below poverty		Persons 65 years and over below poverty	
	Number	Percent	Number	Percent	Number	Percent
All Races						
1990	33,585	13.5	13,431	20.6	3,658	12.2
1985	33,064	14.0	13,110	20.7	3,456	12.6
1980	29,272	13.0	11,543	18.3	3,871	15.7
1975	25,877	12.3	11,104	17.1	3,317	15.3
1970	25,420	12.6	10,440	15.1	4,793	24.6
1966	28,510	14.7	12,389	17.6	5,114	28.5
1959	39,490	22.4	17,552	27.3	5,481	35.2
White						
1990	22,326	10.7	8,232	15.9	2,707	10.1
1985	22,860	11.4	8,253	16.2	2,698	11.0
1980	19,699	10.2	7,181	13.9	3,042	13.6
1975	17,770	9.7	6,927	12.7	2,634	13.4
1970	17,484	9.9	(NA)	(NA)	4,011	22.6
1966	19,290	11.3	(NA)	(NA)	4,357	26.4
1959	28,484	18.1	(NA)	(NA)	4,744	33.1
Black						
1990	9,837	31.9	4,550	44.8	860	33.8
1985	8,926	31.3	4,157	43.6	717	31.5
1980	8,579	32.5	3,961	42.3	783	38.1
1975	7,545	31.3	3,925	41.7	652	36.3
1970	7,548	33.5	(NA)	(NA)	683	48.0
1966	8,867	41.8	(NA)	(NA)	722	55.1
1959	9,927	55.1	(NA)	(NA)	711	62.5
Hispanic Origin[1]						
1990	6,006	28.1	2,865	38.4	245	22.5
1985	5,236	29.0	2,606	40.3	219	23.9
1980	3,491	25.7	1,749	33.2	179	30.8
1975	2,991	26.9	(NA)	(NA)	137	32.6
1970	(NA)	(NA)	(NA)	(NA)	(NA)	(NA)
1966	(NA)	(NA)	(NA)	(NA)	(NA)	(NA)
1959	(NA)	(NA)	(NA)	(NA)	(NA)	(NA)

[1]Hispanic origin may be of any race.

NA Not available.

Source: Mark Littman, U.S. Bureau of the Census, "Poverty in the United States: 1990," *Current Population Reports,* Series P-60, No. 175. U.S. Government Printing Office, Washington, DC, 1991, tables 2 and 3.

E4-10. Poverty Rates for Persons Aged 65 to 74: 1990

(In percent)

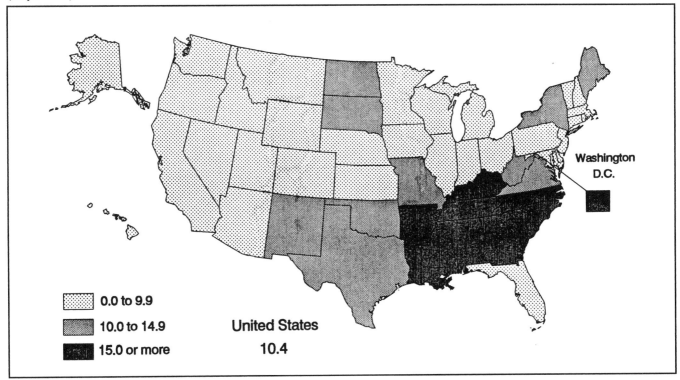

Source: U.S. Bureau of the Census, 1990 CPH-L-95.

E4-11. Poverty Rates for Persons Aged 75 and Over: 1990

(In percent)

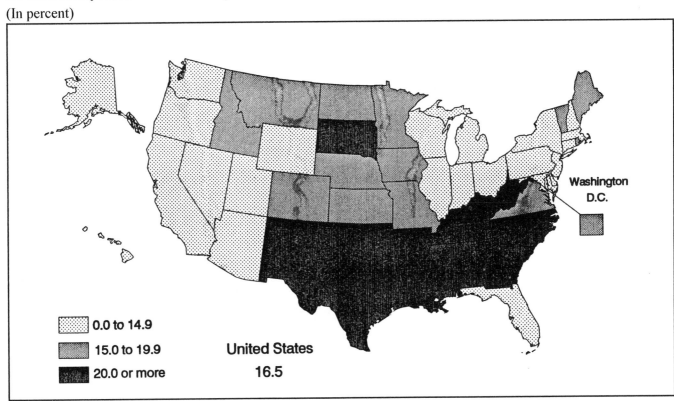

Source: U.S. Bureau of the Census, 1990 CPH-L-95.

E4-12. Poverty Rates for White Persons Aged 65 to 74: 1990

(In percent)

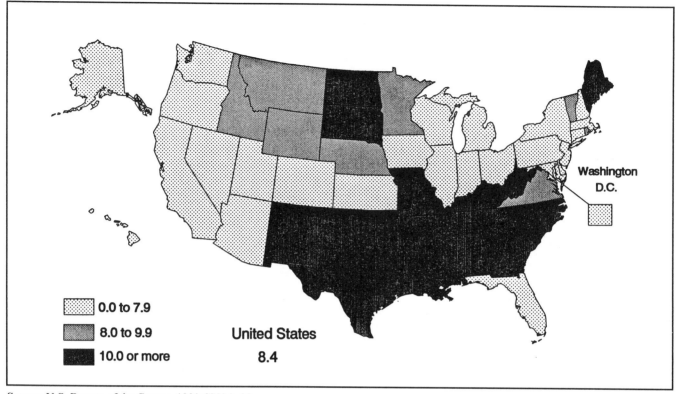

Source: U.S. Bureau of the Census, 1990 CPH-L-95.

E4-13. Poverty Rates for White Persons Aged 75 and Over: 1990

(In percent)

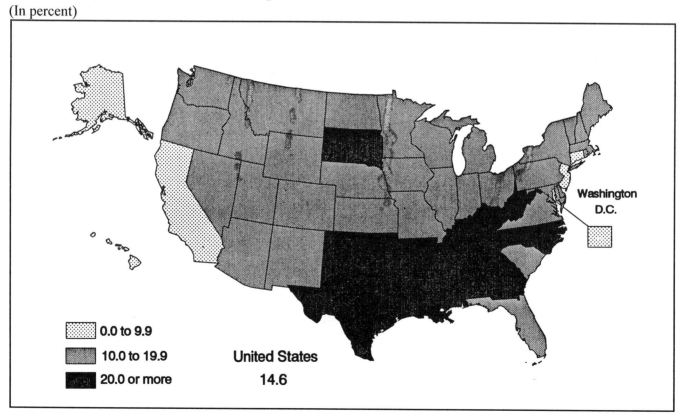

Source: U.S. Bureau of the Census, 1990 CPH-L-95.

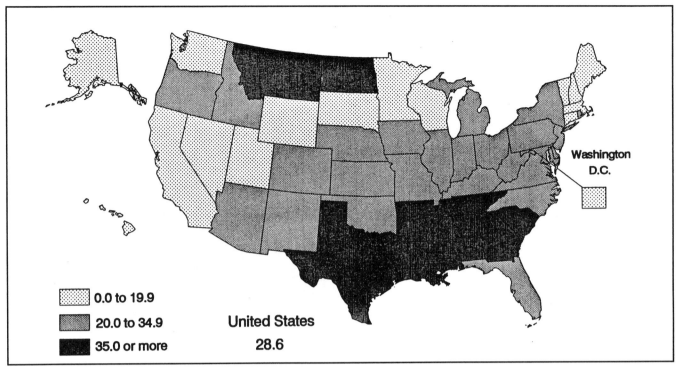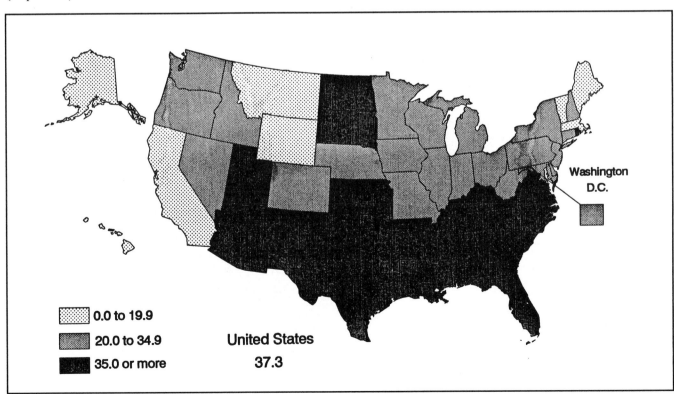

E4-14. Poverty Rates for Black Persons Aged 65 to 74: 1990

(In percent)

Washington D.C.

0.0 to 19.9
20.0 to 34.9
35.0 or more

United States
28.6

Source: U.S. Bureau of the Census, 1990 CPH-L-95.

E4-15. Poverty Rates for Black Persons Aged 75 and Over: 1990

(In percent)

Washington D.C.

0.0 to 19.9
20.0 to 34.9
35.0 or more

United States
37.3

Source: U.S. Bureau of the Census, 1990 CPH-L-95.

E4-16. Poverty Rates for Persons of Hispanic Origin Aged 65 to 74: 1990

(In percent; Persons of Hispanic origin may be of any race.)

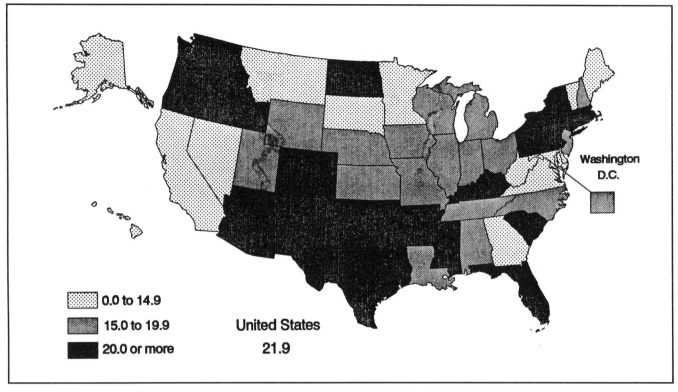

Source: U.S. Bureau of the Census, 1990 CPH-L-95.

E4-17. Poverty Rates for Persons of Hispanic Origin Aged 75 and Over: 1990

(In percent; Persons of Hispanic origin may be of any race.)

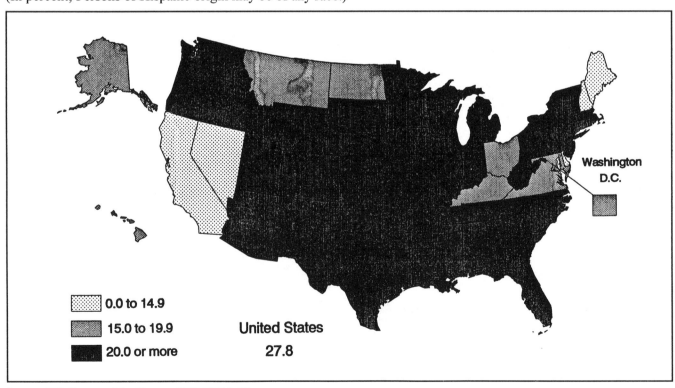

Source: U.S. Bureau of the Census, 1990 CPH-L-95.

E4-18. Families Below Poverty Level—Selected Characteristics, by Race and Hispanic Origin: 1990

[Families as of March 1991.

CHARACTERISTIC	NUMBER BELOW POVERTY LEVEL (1,000)				PERCENT BELOW POVERTY LEVEL			
	All races[1]	White	Black	Hispanic[2]	All races[1]	White	Black	Hispanic[2]
Total	**7,098**	**4,622**	**2,193**	**1,244**	**10.7**	**8.1**	**29.3**	**25.0**
Age of householder:								
15 to 24 years old	955	617	311	182	35.0	28.5	65.3	43.0
25 to 34 years old	2,377	1,568	734	441	16.3	12.9	37.8	29.5
35 to 44 years old	1,648	1,063	482	322	9.8	7.4	23.8	24.4
45 to 54 years old	806	508	263	161	6.9	5.1	21.0	20.0
55 to 64 years old	827	422	180	67	6.7	5.1	21.0	12.7
65 years old and over	686	443	224	69	6.3	4.5	24.2	17.0
Northeast	1,234	839	360	297	9.2	7.1	27.4	33.8
Midwest	1,583	1,050	479	73	9.8	7.3	33.3	22.5
South	2,942	1,661	1,231	385	12.6	8.9	29.5	23.8
West	1,339	1,072	123	488	9.9	9.1	22.4	22.6
Size of family:								
Two persons	2,234	1,587	566	235	8.1	6.5	22.7	19.1
Three persons	1,698	1,053	587	285	11.1	8.1	30.3	24.0
Four persons	1,507	954	488	295	10.7	8.0	30.5	25.8
Five persons	878	570	284	214	14.7	11.6	36.0	27.5
Six persons	415	275	108	117	20.2	17.1	33.0	34.2
Seven persons or more	368	183	160	98	28.6	21.3	50.0	32.9
Mean size	3.55	3.45	3.71	4.09	(X)	(X)	(X)	(X)
Mean number of children per family with children	2.24	2.17	2.34	2.53	(X)	(X)	(X)	(X)
Education of householder:[3]								
Elementary: Less than 8 years	910	595	268	344	26.3	22.8	38.7	31.8
8 years	479	365	107	104	17.0	14.6	39.5	34.5
High school: 1 to 3 years	1,460	889	540	270	20.7	15.9	41.5	35.9
4 years	2,188	1,411	703	190	9.3	6.9	26.2	15.0
College: 1 year or more	996	675	238	93	3.8	2.9	11.9	9.3
Work experience of householder in 1989:[4]								
Total[5]	7,098	4,622	2,193	1,244	10.7	8.1	29.3	25.0
Worked	3,533	2,481	931	626	7.0	5.6	18.1	16.7
50 to 52 weeks	1,442	1,029	360	291	3.8	2.9	9.6	10.7
49 weeks or less	2,091	1,452	571	335	19.5	16.1	40.8	32.5
Did not work	3,527	2,114	1,252	614	23.7	17.2	56.7	51.8

[1]Includes other races not shown separately.

[2]Hispanic persons may be of any race.

[3]Householder 25 years old and over.

[4]Restricted to families with civilian workers.

[5]Includes Armed Forces not shown separately.

X Not applicable.

Source: U.S. Bureau of the Census, *Current Population Reports,* Series P-60, No. 175.

E4-19. Percent of Elderly Persons Below the Poverty Level, by Race, Sex, and Residence: 1990

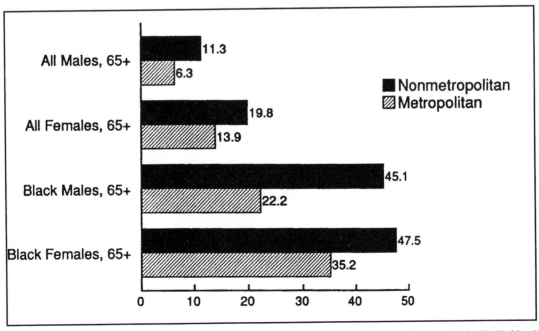

Source: U.S. Bureau of the Census, "Poverty in the United States: 1990," *Current Population Reports*, Series P-60, No. 175.

E4-20. Poverty Status of Persons, by Age, Race, and Hispanic Origin: 1959 to 1991

(Numbers in thousands. Persons as of March of the following year.

Year and characteristic	Under 18 years						18 to 64 years			65 years and over		
	All persons			Related children in families			Below poverty			Below poverty		
		Below poverty			Below poverty							
	Total	Number	Percent	Total	Number	Percent	Total	Number	Percent	Total	Number	Percent
ALL RACES												
1991	65 918	14 341	21.8	64 800	13 658	21.1	154 671	17 585	11.4	30 590	3 781	12.4
1990	65 049	13 431	20.6	63 908	12 715	19.9	153 502	16 496	10.7	30 093	3 658	12.2
1989	64 144	12 590	19.6	63 225	12 001	19.0	152 282	15 575	10.2	29 566	3 363	11.4
1988ʳ	63 747	12 455	19.5	62 906	11 935	19.0	150 761	15 809	10.5	29 022	3 481	12.0
1987ʳ	63 294	12 843	20.3	62 423	12 275	19.7	149 201	15 815	10.6	28 487	3 563	12.5
1986	62 948	12 876	20.5	62 009	12 257	19.8	147 631	16 017	10.8	27 975	3 477	12.4
1985	62 876	13 010	20.7	62 019	12 483	20.1	146 396	16 598	11.3	27 322	3 456	12.6
1984	62 447	13 420	21.5	61 681	12 929	21.0	144 551	16 952	11.7	26 818	3 330	12.4
1983	62 334	13 911	22.3	61 578	13 427	21.8	143 052	17 767	12.4	26 313	3 625	13.8
1982	62 345	13 647	21.9	61 565	13 139	21.3	141 328	17 000	12.0	25 738	3 751	14.6
1981	62 449	12 505	20.0	61 756	12 068	19.5	139 477	15 464	11.1	25 231	3 853	15.3
1980	62 914	11 543	18.3	62 168	11 114	17.9	137 428	13 858	10.1	24 686	3 871	15.7
1979	63 375	10 377	16.4	62 646	9 993	16.0	135 333	12 014	8.9	24 194	3 682	15.2
1978	62 311	9 931	15.9	61 987	9 722	15.7	130 169	11 332	8.7	23 175	3 233	14.0
1977	63 137	10 288	16.2	62 823	10 028	16.0	128 262	11 316	8.8	22 468	3 177	14.1
1976	64 028	10 273	16.0	63 729	10 081	15.8	126 175	11 389	9.0	22 100	3 313	15.0
1975	65 079	11 104	17.1	64 750	10 882	16.8	124 122	11 456	9.2	21 662	3 317	15.3
1974	66 134	10 156	15.4	65 802	9 967	15.1	122 101	10 132	8.3	21 127	3 085	14.6
1973	66 959	9 642	14.4	66 626	9 453	14.2	120 060	9 977	8.3	20 602	3 354	16.3
1972	67 930	10 284	15.1	67 592	10 082	14.9	117 957	10 438	8.8	20 117	3 738	18.6
1971	68 816	10 551	15.3	68 474	10 344	15.1	115 911	10 735	9.3	19 827	4 273	21.6
1970	69 159	10 440	15.1	68 815	10 235	14.9	113 554	10 187	9.0	19 470	4 793	24.6
1969	69 090	9 691	14.0	68 746	9 501	13.8	111 528	9 669	8.7	18 899	4 787	25.3
1968	70 385	10 954	15.6	70 035	10 739	15.3	108 684	9 803	9.0	18 559	4 632	25.0
1967	70 408	11 656	16.6	70 058	11 427	16.3	107 024	10 725	10.0	18 240	5 388	29.5
1966	70 218	12 389	17.6	69 869	12 146	17.4	105 241	11 007	10.5	17 929	5 114	28.5
1965	69 986	14 676	21.0	69 638	14 388	20.7	(NA)	(NA)	(NA)	(NA)	(NA)	(NA)
1964	69 711	16 051	23.0	69 364	15 736	22.7	(NA)	(NA)	(NA)	(NA)	(NA)	(NA)
1963	69 181	16 005	23.1	68 837	15 691	22.8	(NA)	(NA)	(NA)	(NA)	(NA)	(NA)
1962	67 722	16 963	25.0	67 385	16 630	24.7	(NA)	(NA)	(NA)	(NA)	(NA)	(NA)
1961	66 121	16 909	25.6	65 792	16 577	25.2	(NA)	(NA)	(NA)	(NA)	(NA)	(NA)
1960	65 601	17 634	26.9	65 275	17 288	26.5	(NA)	(NA)	(NA)	(NA)	(NA)	(NA)
1959	64 315	17 552	27.3	63 995	17 208	26.9	96 685	16 457	17.0	15 557	5 481	35.2
WHITE												
1991	52 523	8 848	16.8	51 627	8 316	16.1	130 300	12 098	9.3	27 297	2 802	10.3
1990	51 929	8 232	15.9	51 028	7 696	15.1	129 784	11 387	8.8	26 898	2 707	10.1
1989	51 400	7 599	14.8	50 704	7 164	14.1	128 974	10 647	8.3	26 479	2 539	9.6
1988ʳ	51 203	7 435	14.5	50 590	7 095	14.0	128 031	10 687	8.3	26 001	2 593	10.0
1987ʳ	51 012	7 788	15.3	50 360	7 398	14.7	126 991	10 703	8.4	25 602	2 704	10.6
1986	51 111	8 209	16.1	50 356	7 714	15.3	125 998	11 285	9.0	25 173	2 689	10.7
1985	51 031	8 253	16.2	50 358	7 838	15.6	125 258	11 909	9.5	24 629	2 698	11.0
1984	50 814	8 472	16.7	50 192	8 086	16.1	123 922	11 904	9.6	24 206	2 579	10.7
1983	50 726	8 862	17.5	50 183	8 534	17.0	123 014	12 347	10.0	23 754	2 776	11.7
1982	50 920	8 678	17.0	50 305	8 282	16.5	121 766	11 971	9.8	23 234	2 870	12.4
1981	51 140	7 785	15.2	50 553	7 429	14.7	120 574	10 790	8.9	22 791	2 978	13.1
1980	51 653	7 181	13.9	51 002	6 817	13.4	118 935	9 478	8.0	22 325	3 042	13.6
1979	52 262	6 193	11.8	51 687	5 909	11.4	117 583	8 110	6.9	21 898	2 911	13.3
1978	51 669	5 831	11.3	51 409	5 674	11.0	113 832	7 897	6.9	20 950	2 530	12.1
1977	52 563	6 097	11.6	52 299	5 943	11.4	112 374	7 893	7.0	20 316	2 426	11.9
1976	53 428	6 189	11.6	53 167	6 034	11.3	110 717	7 890	7.1	20 020	2 633	13.2
1975	54 405	6 927	12.7	54 126	6 748	12.5	109 105	8 210	7.5	19 654	2 634	13.4
1974	55 590	6 223	11.2	55 320	6 079	11.0	107 579	7 053	6.6	19 206	2 460	12.8
1973	(NA)	(NA)	(NA)	56 211	5 462	9.7	(NA)	(NA)	(NA)	(NA)	2 698	14.4
1972	(NA)	(NA)	(NA)	57 181	5 784	10.1	(NA)	(NA)	(NA)	(NA)	3 072	16.8
1971	(NA)	(NA)	(NA)	58 119	6 341	10.9	(NA)	(NA)	(NA)	(NA)	3 605	19.9
1970	(NA)	(NA)	(NA)	58 472	6 138	10.5	(NA)	(NA)	(NA)	(NA)	4 011	22.6
1969	(NA)	(NA)	(NA)	58 578	5 667	9.7	(NA)	(NA)	(NA)	(NA)	4 052	23.3
1968	(NA)	(NA)	(NA)	(NA)	6 373	10.7	(NA)	(NA)	(NA)	17 062	3 939	23.1
1967	(NA)	(NA)	(NA)	(NA)	6 729	11.3	(NA)	(NA)	(NA)	16 791	4 646	27.7
1966	(NA)	(NA)	(NA)	(NA)	7 204	12.1	(NA)	(NA)	(NA)	16 514	4 357	26.4
1965	(NA)	(NA)	(NA)	(NA)	8 595	14.4	(NA)	(NA)	(NA)	(NA)	(NA)	(NA)
1960	(NA)	(NA)	(NA)	(NA)	11 229	20.0	(NA)	(NA)	(NA)	(NA)	(NA)	(NA)
1959	(NA)	(NA)	(NA)	(NA)	11 386	20.6	(NA)	(NA)	(NA)	(NA)	4 744	33.1

See footnotes at end of table.

E4-20. Poverty Status of Persons, by Age, Race, and Hispanic Origin: 1959 to 1991 (continued)

(Numbers in thousands. Persons as of March of the following year.)

Year and characteristic	Under 18 years						18 to 64 years			65 years and over		
	All persons			Related children in families								
		Below poverty			Below poverty			Below poverty			Below poverty	
	Total	Number	Percent	Total	Number	Percent	Total	Number	Percent	Total	Number	Percent
BLACK												
1991	10 350	4 755	45.9	10 178	4 637	45.6	18 355	4 607	25.1	2 606	880	33.8
1990	10 162	4 550	44.8	9 980	4 412	44.2	18 097	4 427	24.5	2 547	860	33.8
1989	10 012	4 375	43.7	9 847	4 257	43.2	17 833	4 164	23.3	2 487	763	30.7
1988ʳ	9 865	4 296	43.5	9 681	4 148	42.8	17 548	4 275	24.4	2 436	785	32.2
1987ʳ	9 730	4 385	45.1	9 546	4 234	44.4	17 245	4 361	25.3	2 387	774	32.4
1986	9 629	4 148	43.1	9 467	4 037	42.7	16 911	4 113	24.3	2 331	722	31.0
1985	9 545	4 157	43.6	9 405	4 057	43.1	16 667	4 052	24.3	2 273	717	31.5
1984	9 480	4 413	46.6	9 356	4 320	46.2	16 369	4 368	26.7	2 238	710	31.7
1983	9 417	4 398	46.7	9 245	4 273	46.2	16 065	4 694	29.2	2 197	791	36.0
1982	9 400	4 472	47.6	9 269	4 388	47.3	15 692	4 415	28.1	2 124	811	38.2
1981	9 374	4 237	45.2	9 291	4 170	44.9	15 358	4 117	26.8	2 102	820	39.0
1980	9 368	3 961	42.3	9 287	3 906	42.1	14 987	3 835	25.6	2 054	783	38.1
1979	9 307	3 833	41.2	9 172	3 745	40.8	14 596	3 478	23.8	2 040	740	36.2
1978	9 229	3 830	41.5	9 168	3 781	41.2	13 774	3 133	22.7	1 954	662	33.9
1977	9 296	3 888	41.8	9 253	3 850	41.6	13 483	3 137	23.3	1 930	701	36.3
1976	9 322	3 787	40.6	9 291	3 758	40.4	13 224	3 163	23.9	1 852	644	34.8
1975	9 421	3 925	41.7	9 374	3 884	41.4	12 872	2 968	23.1	1 795	652	36.3
1974	9 439	3 755	39.8	9 384	3 713	39.6	12 539	2 836	22.6	1 721	591	34.3
1973	(NA)	(NA)	(NA)	9 405	3 822	40.6	(NA)	(NA)	(NA)	1 672	620	37.1
1972	(NA)	(NA)	(NA)	9 426	4 025	42.7	(NA)	(NA)	(NA)	1 603	640	39.9
1971	(NA)	(NA)	(NA)	9 414	3 836	40.4	(NA)	(NA)	(NA)	1 584	623	39.3
1970	(NA)	(NA)	(NA)	9 448	3 922	41.5	(NA)	(NA)	(NA)	1 422	683	48.0
1969	(NA)	(NA)	(NA)	9 290	3 677	39.6	(NA)	(NA)	(NA)	1 373	689	50.2
1968	(NA)	(NA)	(NA)	(NA)	4 188	43.1	(NA)	(NA)	(NA)	1 374	655	47.7
1967	(NA)	(NA)	(NA)	(NA)	4 558	47.4	(NA)	(NA)	(NA)	1 341	715	53.3
1966	(NA)	(NA)	(NA)	(NA)	4 774	50.6	(NA)	(NA)	(NA)	1 311	722	55.1
1959	(NA)	(NA)	(NA)	(NA)	5 022	65.6	(NA)	(NA)	(NA)		711	62.5
HISPANIC ORIGIN[1]												
1991	7 648	3 094	40.4	7 473	2 977	39.8	13 279	3 009	22.7	1 143	237	20.8
1990	7 457	2 865	38.4	7 300	2 750	37.7	12 857	2 896	22.5	1 091	245	22.5
1989	7 186	2 603	36.2	7 040	2 496	35.5	12 536	2 616	20.9	1 024	211	20.6
1988ʳ	7 003	2 631	37.6	6 908	2 576	37.3	12 056	2 501	20.7	1 005	225	22.4
1987ʳ	6 792	2 670	39.3	6 692	2 606	38.9	11 718	2 509	21.4	885	243	27.5
1986	6 646	2 507	37.7	6 511	2 413	37.1	11 206	2 406	21.5	906	204	22.5
1985	6 475	2 606	40.3	6 346	2 512	39.6	10 685	2 411	22.6	915	219	23.9
1984	6 068	2 376	39.2	5 982	2 317	38.7	10 029	2 254	22.5	819	176	21.5
1983	6 066	2 312	38.1	5 977	2 251	37.7	9 697	2 148	22.5	782	173	22.1
1982	5 527	2 181	39.5	5 436	2 117	38.9	8 262	1 963	23.8	596	159	26.6
1981	5 369	1 925	35.9	5 291	1 874	35.4	8 084	1 642	20.3	568	146	25.7
1980	5 276	1 749	33.2	5 211	1 718	33.0	7 740	1 563	20.2	582	179	30.8
1979	5 483	1 535	28.0	5 426	1 505	27.7	7 314	1 232	16.8	574	154	26.8
1978	5 012	1 384	27.6	4 972	1 354	27.2	6 527	1 098	16.8	539	125	23.2
1977	5 028	1 422	28.3	5 000	1 402	28.0	6 164	1 164	17.9	518	113	21.9
1976	4 771	1 443	30.2	4 736	1 424	30.1	6 034	1 212	20.1	464	128	27.7
1975	(NA)	(NA)	(NA)	4 896	1 619	33.1	(NA)	(NA)	(NA)	(NA)	137	32.6
1974	(NA)	(NA)	(NA)	4 939	1 414	28.6	(NA)	(NA)	(NA)	(NA)	117	28.9
1973	(NA)	(NA)	(NA)	4 910	1 364	27.8	(NA)	(NA)	(NA)	(NA)	95	24.9

ʳFigures based on new processing procedures. The 1987 and 1988 figures are also revised to reflect corrections to files after publication of the 1988 advance report, "Money Income and Poverty Status in the United States," 1988, p-60, No. 166.

[1]Persons of Hispanic origin may be of any race.

E4-21. Family Income Below the Poverty Line[1] and 125 Percent of the Poverty Line, by Age, Sex, Marital Status, Social Security Beneficiary Status, Living Arrangements, Race, and Hispanic Origin: Percent of Aged Units 55 or Older: 1990

Family poverty status	All units			Married couples			Nonmarried persons								
---	---	---	---	---	---	---	Total			Men			Women		
	55-61	62-64	65 or older	55-61	62-64	65 or older	55-61	62-64	65 or older	55-61	62-64	65 or older	55-61	62-64	65 or older
All units															
Number (in thousands)	10,067	4,120	23,148	6,026	2,351	9,343	4,041	1,768	13,805	1,552	580	3,225	2,489	1,188	10,580
Percent--															
Below poverty line	12	13	14	5	6	5	22	22	20	20	19	15	24	23	22
Below 125% of poverty line	15	19	22	7	9	9	27	31	31	26	25	23	28	33	33
Beneficiary units[2]															
Number (in thousands)	1,269	2,301	21,250	668	1,314	8,659	601	987	12,591	185	305	2,873	416	682	9,718
Percent--															
Below poverty line	21	13	14	10	6	5	34	23	20	33	18	13	34	25	22
Below 125% of poverty line	29	21	22	15	11	9	45	34	30	53	25	22	42	38	33
Nonbeneficiary units															
Number (in thousands)	8,798	1,818	1,898	5,358	1,038	684	3,440	781	1,214	1,367	274	352	2,073	506	862
Percent--															
Below poverty line	10	12	22	4	5	12	20	21	28	18	20	25	22	21	30
Below 125% of poverty line	13	15	28	6	7	16	24	27	35	23	26	31	25	27	37
Live with other family members															
Number (in thousands)	4,139	1,354	5,458	2,611	704	1,684	1,528	649	3,774	415	196	931	1,113	453	2,843
Percent--															
Below poverty line	9	10	8	5	7	7	15	14	9	9	12	8	18	14	9
Below 125% of poverty line	13	15	13	7	10	9	23	21	14	20	18	13	23	23	15
Live with no family members															
Number (in thousands)	5,928	2,766	17,690	3,415	1,647	7,659	2,513	1,119	10,031	1,137	384	2,294	1,376	735	7,737
Percent--															
Below poverty line	14	14	16	5	5	5	27	27	25	24	22	17	29	29	27
Below 125% of poverty line	17	20	25	7	9	9	30	36	37	29	29	27	32	40	40

Family poverty status	All units			Married couples			Nonmarried persons								
---	---	---	---	---	---	---	Total			Men			Women		
	55-61	62-64	65 or older	55-61	62-64	65 or older	55-61	62-64	65 or older	55-61	62-64	65 or older	55-61	62-64	65 or older
White															
Number (in thousands)	8,471	3,563	20,489	5,451	2,162	8,579	3,020	1,401	11,910	1,137	473	2,676	1,883	928	9,234
Percent--															
Below poverty line	9	11	12	4	5	4	19	19	18	17	15	11	20	21	20
Below 125% of poverty line	12	16	19	6	8	7	23	27	28	22	20	19	23	31	30
Black															
Number (in thousands)	1,277	445	2,147	401	143	569	877	303	1,577	374	92	462	502	211	1,115
Percent--															
Below poverty line	27	29	36	10	16	22	35	35	42	31	35	35	38	34	44
Below 125% of poverty line	35	39	48	15	23	31	44	47	55	41	51	48	46	46	57
Hispanic origin[3]															
Number (in thousands)	638	234	860	319	116	345	319	118	515	117	44	120	202	74	395
Percent--															
Below poverty line	22	22	25	10	11	14	33	32	32	26	(4)	31	37	(4)	33
Below 125% of poverty line	28	29	37	16	17	22	40	40	47	35	(4)	42	42	(4)	48

[1]The money income of families containing aged units is compared with the official poverty lines of families in 1990.

[2]Social Security beneficiaries may be receiving retired-worker benefits, dependents' or survivors' benefits, disability benefits, transitionally insured, or special age-72 benefits.

[3]Persons of Hispanic origin may be of any race.

[4]Fewer than 75,000 weighted cases.

E4-22. Percent of Elderly Persons in Poverty, by Definition of Income: 1979 to 1991

[Numbers in thousands. Persons as of March of the following year.

Characteristics	1979	1980	1981	1982	1983	1984	1985	1986	1987	1988	1989	1990	1991
PERSONS 65 YEARS AND OVER													
Total	24 194	24 686	25 231	25 738	26 313	26 818	27 322	27 975	28 487	29 022	29 566	30 093	30 590
Poverty Rate by Definition of Income													
Definition 1: Money income, before taxes, excluding capital gains	15.2	15.7	15.3	14.6	13.8	12.4	12.6	12.4	12.5	12.0	11.4	12.2	12.4
Definition 2: Definition 1 less government cash transfers	54.2	54.2	53.7	52.4	50.4	49.1	49.2	48.5	47.6	47.7	47.6	46.4	48.3
Definition 3: Definition 2 plus capital gains	53.9	53.8	53.2	52.0	49.3	48.0	47.9	47.1	47.3	47.6	47.6	46.3	48.1
Definition 4: Definition 3 plus health insurance supplements to wage or salary income	53.6	53.7	53.0	51.8	49.0	47.9	47.8	47.0	47.2	47.4	47.3	46.1	47.9
Definition 5: Definition 4 less Social Security payroll taxes	54.0	54.1	53.5	52.2	49.4	48.2	48.2	47.2	47.4	47.8	47.7	46.5	48.2
Definition 6: Definition 5 less Federal income taxes	54.0	54.2	53.6	52.4	49.6	48.5	48.4	47.4	47.5	48.0	47.9	46.6	48.4
Definition 7: Definition 6 plus earned income tax credits	54.0	54.2	53.6	52.4	49.5	48.4	48.4	47.4	47.5	47.9	47.8	46.6	48.3
Definition 8: Definition 7 less State income taxes	54.1	54.3	53.7	52.5	49.7	48.5	48.6	47.5	47.6	48.1	48.1	46.7	48.5
Definition 9: Definition 8 plus nonmeans-tested government cash transfers	17.3	17.6	16.8	16.0	15.4	14.2	14.5	14.0	14.3	13.9	13.6	13.7	14.2
Definition 10: Definition 9 plus fungible value of Medicare	15.4	15.0	13.9	13.5	13.0	12.2	12.5	11.6	12.0	11.8	11.4	12.0	12.2
Definition 11: Definition 10 plus subsidy value of regular-price school lunches	15.4	15.0	13.9	13.5	13.0	12.2	12.5	11.6	12.0	11.8	11.4	12.0	12.2
Definition 12: Definition 11 plus means-tested government cash transfers	13.6	13.3	12.5	12.1	11.3	10.4	10.9	10.1	10.7	10.3	9.7	10.7	10.5
Definition 13: Definition 12 plus fungible value of Medicaid	13.3	12.8	12.1	11.8	10.9	10.0	10.5	9.8	10.3	10.1	9.4	10.5	10.4
Definition 14: Definition 13 plus value of means-tested food and housing benefits	12.3	11.7	11.1	10.9	10.1	9.2	9.7	9.0	9.3	9.0	8.6	9.5	9.3
Definition 15: Definition 14 plus net imputed return on equity in own home	8.4	6.8	5.0	5.8	5.7	4.8	5.7	5.7	5.6	5.3	5.3	6.2	6.1
PERSONS 75 YEARS AND OVER													
Total	8 901	9 163	9 534	9 756	9 962	10 242	10 442	10 743	10 986	11 276	11 587	11 855	12 149
Poverty Rate by Definition of Income													
Definition 1: Money income, before taxes, excluding capital gains	19.4	20.1	19.3	18.1	17.0	15.8	16.0	15.8	16.6	15.2	15.4	16.0	15.0
Definition 2: Definition 1 less government cash transfers	62.6	62.6	61.4	60.7	58.6	56.6	56.9	57.6	57.1	56.4	57.8	56.5	57.3
Definition 3: Definition 2 plus capital gains	62.2	62.3	61.0	60.3	57.6	55.5	55.7	56.2	56.7	56.3	57.8	56.5	57.1
Definition 4: Definition 3 plus health insurance supplements to wage or salary income	62.0	62.2	60.9	60.2	57.5	55.4	55.6	56.0	56.7	56.3	57.6	56.4	56.9
Definition 5: Definition 4 less Social Security payroll taxes	62.2	62.4	61.2	60.5	57.8	55.6	55.9	56.2	56.9	56.6	57.9	56.5	57.2
Definition 6: Definition 5 less Federal income taxes	62.3	62.4	61.3	60.6	57.9	56.0	56.2	56.5	56.9	56.6	58.1	56.7	57.4
Definition 7: Definition 6 plus earned income tax credits	62.3	62.4	61.3	60.6	57.9	56.0	56.2	56.5	56.9	56.6	58.0	56.7	57.3
Definition 8: Definition 7 less State income taxes	62.4	62.5	61.4	60.7	58.0	56.0	56.3	56.6	57.1	56.7	58.3	56.8	57.5
Definition 9: Definition 8 plus nonmeans-tested government cash transfers	22.0	22.5	20.8	19.8	19.4	18.3	18.2	18.0	18.4	17.6	17.8	17.5	17.0
Definition 10: Definition 9 plus fungible value of Medicare	19.6	18.9	17.5	16.8	16.4	15.7	15.8	15.0	16.1	14.7	15.4	15.7	14.5
Definition 11: Definition 10 plus subsidy value of regular-price school lunches	19.6	18.9	17.5	16.8	16.4	15.7	15.8	15.0	16.1	14.7	15.4	15.7	14.5
Definition 12: Definition 11 plus means-tested government cash transfers	17.5	16.9	15.8	15.3	14.0	13.5	13.8	13.0	14.6	13.0	13.2	14.2	13.1
Definition 13: Definition 12 plus fungible value of Medicaid	17.1	16.4	15.2	14.9	13.6	13.0	13.5	12.6	14.3	12.8	12.7	14.0	12.9
Definition 14: Definition 13 plus value of means-tested food and housing benefits	15.9	15.1	14.0	13.6	12.6	12.1	12.4	11.8	13.2	11.4	11.7	12.9	11.7
Definition 15: Definition 14 plus net imputed return on equity in own home	10.6	8.4	5.8	7.1	6.7	6.1	6.9	7.4	7.7	6.6	7.2	8.2	7.3

F. Expenditures for the Elderly

OVERVIEW OF EXPENDITURES

In 1991, the federal government spent almost $390 billion, or 30% of the total federal budget, on expenses benefiting the elderly. Of this amount, over half (54%) is for Social Security and almost one-third (32%) for Medicare and Medicaid. The remainder goes for the support of older veterans, for retirement pay of military and civil service employees and their survivors, for supplemental social insurance (SSI), and for miscellaneous other programs.

SOCIAL SECURITY

Social Security and all but a portion of Medicare are financed through dedicated taxes collected expressly and exclusively for that purpose. The income of the 1990 OASDI Trust Fund was $272 billion; $223 billion were paid out in benefits, and the fund's assets were $214 billion. Thirty million of the 41 million Social Security beneficiaries in 1992 were 65 years or older; 2 million elderly received SSI payments. In 1990, the average monthly Social Security benefits to the elderly was $600 in metropolitan and $540 in nonmetropolitan areas; benefits to men are considerably higher than to women.

HEALTH CARE EXPENDITURES

The elderly population is a major user of health care services. Health care costs are highest during the last two years of a person's life. Medicare was created in 1965 to help pay the health costs of older Americans and the disabled; Medicaid is a federal and state program that helps low-income individuals of all ages get health care. Due to inflation and the high price of advanced medical technology and drugs, expenditures for health care for all age groups have been rising faster than any other category of the Consumer Price Index, requiring ever larger funding from public and private sources. One-third of federal spending for the elderly was spent on health programs in 1991. The increase is projected to be even more rapid unless new legislation is able to curtail it.

PUBLIC AND PRIVATE PENSIONS

Federal pension programs other than Social Security amount to about 10% of all federal outlays for the elderly distributed through Civil Service, Armed Forces, and other retirement programs. State and local governments operate over 2,000 separate retirement pension plans; average annual benefits under these plans are considerably lower than for federal retirees. Approximately one-half of all employees in the private sector are covered by pension plans.

VETERANS

Veterans represent an increasing proportion of the elderly male population; their numbers are expected to peak in the mid-1990s and to decline in the next century. The largest expenditure of the Veterans Administration is for health care of older veterans; other expenditures are for disability compensation, disability pension, and death compensation.

F1. Overview of Expenditures

F1-1. Federal Outlays Benefiting the Elderly: 1991

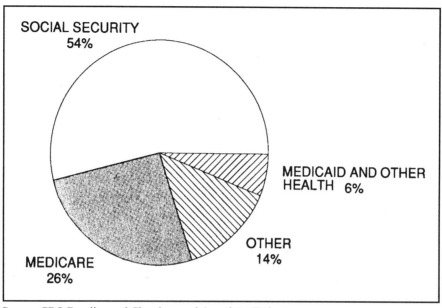

Source: CBO Baseline and Chambers and Associates Estimates.

F1-2. Federal Outlays Benefiting the Elderly: 1990 and 1991

(in millions of dollars)	Fiscal year	
Type of outlay	1990	1991
Medicare	93,510	101,949
Medicaid	14,862	16,975
Other federal health	5,927	6,698
Health subtotal	114,299	125,622
Social Security	194,073	207,329
Supplemental Security Income (SSI)	4,606	5,345
Veterans compensation-pensions	4,809	5,313
Other retired, disabled, and survivors benefits	29,389	30,506
Retirement/disability subtotal	232,877	248,493
Older American volunteer programs	119	121
Senior community service employment	346	359
Subsidized housing	5,778	6,078
Section 202 elderly housing loans	390	401
Farmers Home Administration housing	596	633
Food stamps	1,292	1,385
Older Americans Act	730	819
Social Services (Title XX)	581	588
Low-income home energy assistance	436	468
Other miscellaneous	1,055	2,375
Other subtotal	11,323	13,227
Total elderly outlays	358,499	387,342
Percentage of total federal outlays	30	30

Source: Calculated by Chambers and Associates for the American Association of Retired Persons.

F1-3. Federal Pension and Health Programs as a Percent of GNP and the Budget: 1965 to 2040

Year	Pension programs as a percent of GNP[1]	Health programs as a percent of GNP[1]	Total as a percent of GNP[1]	Total as a percent of budget[2]
1965	4.1	0.3	4.4	24.9
1970	4.7	1.4	6.1	30.0
1975	6.4	2.0	8.4	37.1
1980	6.5	2.3	8.8	38.2
1982	7.1	2.7	9.7	39.6
1984	7.0	2.8	9.8	39.7
1986	6.6	3.0	9.6	39.4
1988	6.4	3.2	9.6	39.4
1990	6.6[3]	3.1[3]	9.7	40.4
1995	6.2	3.7	9.9	41.3
2000	5.8	4.0	9.8	40.8
2005	5.6	4.4	10.0	41.7
2010	6.0	4.7	10.7	44.6
2015	6.0	5.0	11.0	45.8
2020	6.5	5.4	11.9	49.6
2025	7.0	5.9	12.9	53.9
2030	7.1	6.4	13.5	56.3
2035	7.1	7.0	14.1	58.8
2040	7.0	7.5	14.5	60.4

[1]Estimates for 1984-1988 are based on CBO baseline assumptions (August 1983); forecasts for 1990 and beyond are based on intermediate assumptions of the Social Security and Medicare actuaries.

[2]Forecasts for 1990 and beyond are based on the assumption that the budget accounts for 24 percent of GNP.

[3]The discontinuity in the estimates of pension and health benefits as a percent of GNP between 1986 and 1990 is due to the Social Security trustees assuming that OASDI will grow at a faster rate in the late 1980s than CBO assumes, and the Health Insurance trustees assuming that Medicare will grow at a slower rate than CBO assumes.

Source: John L. Palmer and Barbara B. Torrey, "Health Care Financing and Pension Programs." Paper prepared for the Urban Institute Conference on "Federal Budget Policy in the 1980s," September 29-30, 1983.

F1-4. Gross National Product (GNP), National Health Care (NHC) Expenditures, National Physician Expenditures¹, Medicare Expenditures¹, and Medicare Physician Expenditures: Selected Calendar Years 1970 to 1988

Calendar year	NHC expenditures²						Medicare expenditures²							
	Total			Total NHC physician³			Total Medicare			Medicare physician expenditures³				
	GNP in billions	Amount in billions	Relative index⁴	Amount in billions	Relative index⁴	Percent of NHC	Amount in billions	Relative index⁴	Percent of NHC	Amount in billions	Relative index⁴	Percent of NHC expenditures	Percent of Medicare expenditures	Percent of total physician expenditures
1970	$993	$74.4	100	$13.6	100	18.3	$7.5	100	10.1	$1.6	100	2.2	21.3	11.8
1975	1,549	132.9	179	23.3	171	17.5	16.3	217	12.3	3.4	212	2.6	20.9	14.6
1980	2,732	249.1	335	41.9	308	16.8	36.4	485	14.6	7.9	494	3.2	21.7	18.9
1981	3,053	285.2	383	54.8	404	19.2	44.7	596	15.7	9.7	606	3.4	21.7	17.7
1982	3,166	321.2	432	61.8	454	19.2	52.4	698	16.3	11.4	690	3.5	21.8	18.4
1983	3,406	355.1	478	68.4	503	19.3	58.8	784	16.6	13.4	837	3.8	22.8	19.6
1984	3,765	387.4	521	75.4	554	19.5	64.4	859	16.6	14.7	919	3.8	22.8	19.5
1985	3,998	420.1	565	74.0	544	17.6	70.1	935	16.7	16.6	1,038	4.0	23.7	22.4
1986	4,232	452.3	608	82.1	604	18.2	76.9	1,025	17.0	18.8	1,175	4.2	24.4	22.9
1987	4,516	492.5	662	93.0	684	18.9	82.9	1,105	16.8	21.6	1,350	4.4	26.1	23.2
1988	4,874	544.0	731	105.1	773	19.3	90.5	1,207	16.6	24.2	1,513	4.4	26.7	23.0
						Average annual rate of growth								
1970-84	10.0	12.5	—	13.0	—	—	16.6	—	—	17.2	—	—	—	—
1984-88	6.7	8.9	—	8.7	—	—	8.9	—	—	13.3	—	—	—	—
1970-88	9.2	11.7	—	12.0	—	—	14.8	—	—	16.3	—	—	—	—

¹Expenditures shown in this table, as reported by the Office of the Actuary (OACT), are substantially higher than the corresponding program payments reported in this article. The difference is due, for the most part, to OACT's process of projecting total payment based on a complete (100 percent) population of bill records. The program payments reported in this article reflect only those bill records received and processed by the Health Care Financing Administration as of a given processing cutoff date.

²Represents expenditures aggregated on an incurred basis (when the claim was paid).

³Excludes expenditures for supplier services, with the exception of independent laboratories.

⁴Relative Index for 1970 = 100.

Source: Health Care Financing Administration, Office of the Actuary.

F1-5. Estimates of Monthly Rent Subsidies, by Number of Bedrooms, Region, and Income Level: 1991

Region and income level of family	One bedroom	Two bedroom	Three or more bedroom
Northeast:			
Income under $6,000...	$232	$272	$305
Income $6,000 to $9,999	211	251	281
Income $10,000 and over..................................	88	105	116
Midwest:			
Income under $6,000...	140	180	204
Income $6,000 to $9,999	128	165	188
Income $10,000 and over..................................	54	69	78
South:			
Income under $6,000...	162	194	244
Income $6,000 to $9,999	149	178	225
Income $10,000 and over..................................	61	74	93
West:			
Income under $6,000...	194	243	321
Income $6,000 to $9,999	178	224	294
Income $10,000 and over..................................	74	93	122

NOTE: Data from the American Housing Survey were used to determine how much families living in nonsubsidized units with characteristics similar to the subsidized units pay for rent. The difference is the rent subsidy.

F1-6. Cost of Thrifty Food Plan: 1991

Sex and age	Annual amount
Child:	
1 and 2 years............................	$673
3 to 5 years...............................	724
6 to 8 years...............................	883
9 to 11 years.............................	1,051
Male:	
12 to 14 years...........................	1,090
15 to 19 years...........................	1,132
20 to 50 years...........................	1,214
51 years and over......................	1,105
Female:	
12 to 19 years...........................	1,102
20 to 50 years...........................	1,102
51 years and over......................	1,092
Family size adjustment:	
1 person	add 20 percent
2 persons	add 10 percent
3 persons	add 5 percent
4 persons	none
5 or 6 persons	subtract 5 percent
7 persons or more	subtract 10 percent

Source: U.S. Department of Agriculture.

F1-7. Private Pension Plans—Summary, by Type of Plan: 1975 to 1988

["Pension plan" is defined by the Employee Retirement Income Security Act (ERISA) as "any plan, fund, or program which was heretofore or is hereafter established or maintained by an employer or an employee organization, or by both, to the extent that such plan (a) provides retirement income to employees, or (b) results in a deferral of income by employees for periods extending to the termination of covered employment or beyond, regardless of the method of calculating the contributions made to the plan, the method of calculating the benefits under the plan, or the method of distributing benefits from the plan." A defined benefit plan provides a definite benefit formula for calculating benefit amounts - such as a flat amount per year of service or a percentage of salary or a percentage of salary times years of service. A defined contribution plan is a pension plan in which the contributions are made to an individual account for each employee. The retirement benefit is dependent upon the account balance at retirement. The balance depends upon amounts contributed, investment experience, and, in the case of profit sharing plans, amounts which may be allocated to the account due to forfeitures by terminating employees. Employee Stock Ownership Plans (ESOP) (see table 855) and 401(k) plans are included among defined contribution plans. Data are based on Form 5500 series reports filed with the Internal Revenue Service]

ITEM	Unit	TOTAL				DEFINED CONTRIBUTION PLAN				DEFINED BENEFIT PLAN			
		1975	1980	1985	1988	1975	1980	1985	1988	1975	1980	1985	1988
Number of plans [1]	1,000...	311.1	488.9	632.1	729.9	207.7	340.8	462.0	584.0	103.3	148.1	170.2	146.0
Total participants [2][3]	Million..	44.5	57.9	74.7	77.7	11.5	19.9	35.0	37.0	33.0	38.0	39.7	40.7
Active participants [2][4]	Million..	38.4	49.0	62.3	62.4	11.2	18.9	33.2	34.5	27.2	30.1	29.0	27.9
Contributions	Bil. dol. .	37.1	66.2	95.1	91.2	12.8	23.5	53.1	64.9	24.2	42.6	42.0	26.3
Benefits [5]	Bil. dol. .	19.1	35.3	101.9	118.6	6.2	13.1	47.4	58.2	12.9	22.1	54.5	60.4

[1] Excludes all plans covering only one participant. [2] Includes double counting of workers in more than one plan. [3] Total participants include active participants, vested separated workers, and retirees. [4] Any workers currently in employment covered by a plan and who are earning or retaining credited service under a plan. Includes any nonvested former employees who have not yet incurred breaks in service. [5] Benefits paid directly from trust and premium payments made from plan to insurance carriers. Excludes benefits paid directly by insurance carriers.

Source: U.S. Dept. of Labor, Pension and Welfare Benefits Administration, *Trends in Pensions*, 1989 and unpublished data.

F2. Social Security

F2-1. Social Security at a Glance: 1992

OASDI

Benefits and beneficiaries—May 1992

Number of beneficiaries..................................41.0 million
  Retired workers, spouses, and children.................29.0 million
    Retired workers....................................25.4 million
  Survivors of deceased workers.........................7.3 million
  Disabled workers, spouses, and children................4.7 million
    Disabled workers....................................3.3 million
  Age 65 or older..................................... 30.0 million

Average monthly benefit for—	Benefits	Awards
Retired workers	$631	$601
Disabled workers	$608	$599
Nondisabled widow(er)s	$586	$587
Children of deceased workers	$421	$414

Earnings amounts in 1992

Maximum taxable earnings
  Social Security...$55,500
  Medicare..$130,200

Earnings required for work credits (quarters of coverage)
  One work credit...$570
  Maximum of four work credits per year....................$2,280

Earnings test exempt amounts
  Under age 65.............................$7,440 ($620 monthly)
  Age 65-69..............................$10,200 ($850 monthly)

SSI

Number of persons receiving SSI and payment amounts

Category	Federally administered payments (May 1992)		Recipients of State-administered payments (January 1992)
	Number	Average payment	
All recipients	5.3 million	$357	308 thousand
Aged	1.5 million	$229	120 thousand
Blind	85 thousand	$374	4 thousand
Disabled	3.8 million	$406	183 thousand
Age 65 or older	2.1 million	. . .	. . .

Federal payment, 1992 (for persons in their own household, no other countable income)

Individual $422
Couple (both eligible).............................$633

F2-2. Social Security Trust Funds: 1980 to 1990

[In billions of dollars, except percent. See also *Historical Statistics, Colonial Times to 1970*, series H 238-242]

TYPE OF TRUST FUND	1980	1983	1984	1985	1986	1987	1988	1989	1990
Old-age and survivors insurance (OASI):									
Net contribution income [1]	103.5	138.3	167.0	180.2	194.2	206.0	233.2	252.6	272.4
Interest received [2]	1.8	6.7	2.6	1.9	3.1	4.7	7.6	12.0	16.4
Benefit payments [3]	105.1	149.2	157.8	167.2	176.8	[4]183.6	[4]195.5	208.0	223.0
Assets, end of year	22.8	[5]19.7	[6]27.1	[6]35.8	39.1	62.1	102.9	155.1	214.2
Disability insurance (DI):									
Net contribution income [1]	13.3	18.0	16.1	17.4	18.6	19.7	22.1	24.1	28.7
Interest received [2]	0.5	1.6	1.2	0.9	0.8	0.6	0.6	0.7	0.9
Benefit payments [3]	15.5	17.5	17.9	18.8	19.9	[4]20.5	[4]21.7	22.9	24.8
Assets, end of year	3.6	[5]5.2	[6]4.0	[6]6.3	7.8	6.7	6.9	7.9	11.1
Hospital insurance (HI): [1][7]									
Net contribution income [1][7]	23.9	38.2	42.5	47.7	54.7	58.8	62.6	68.5	71.1
Interest received [2]	1.1	2.6	3.0	3.4	3.6	4.5	5.8	7.3	8.5
Benefit payments	25.1	39.3	43.3	47.5	49.8	49.5	52.5	60.0	66.2
Assets, end of year	13.7	[6]12.9	[6]15.7	[6]20.5	40.0	53.7	69.6	85.6	98.9
Supplementary medical insurance (SMI):									
Net premium income	3.0	4.2	5.2	5.6	5.7	7.4	8.8	10.8	11.3
Transfers from general revenue	7.5	14.9	17.1	18.3	17.8	23.6	26.2	30.9	33.0
Interest received	0.4	0.7	1.0	1.2	1.1	0.9	0.9	1.1	1.6
Benefit payments	10.6	18.1	19.7	22.9	26.2	30.8	34.0	38.4	42.5
Assets, end of year	4.5	7.1	9.7	10.9	8.3	8.4	9.0	12.2	15.5

[1]Includes deposits by states and deductions for refund of estimated employee-tax overpayment. Beginning in 1983, includes government contributions on deemed wage credits for military service in 1957 and later. Beginning 1984 includes tax credits on wages paid in 1984 and net earnings from self-employment in 1984-89; and taxation of benefits (OASI and DI, only).

[2]Beginning in 1983, includes interest on deemed wage credits for military service performed after 1956. Data for 1983-1986 reflect interest on interfund borrowing.

[3]Includes payments for vocational rehabilitation services furnished to disabled persons receiving benefits because of their disabilities. Beginning in 1983, amounts relfect deductions for unnegotiated benefit checks.

[4]Data adjusted to reflect 12 months of benefit payments.

[5]Includes $18 billion borrowed from the DI and HI Trust Funds. Repayments on Jan. 31, 1985, reduced such amounts to $13.2 billion.

[6]Excludes $5 billion lent to the OASI Trust Fund. Repayment on Jan. 31, 1985, reduced the total to $2.5 billion. Includes premiums from aged ineligibles enrolled in HI.

[7]Excludes $12 billion lent to the OASI Trust Fund. Repayment on Jan. 31, 1985, reduced the total to $10.6 billion.

Source: U.S. Social Security Administration, Annual Report of Board of Trustees, OASI, DI, HI, and SMI Trust Funds. Also published in Social Security Bulletin, monthly.

F2-3. Social Security—Covered Employment, Earnings, and Contribution Rates: 1970 to 1990

[Includes Puerto Rico, Virgin Islands, American Samoa, and Guam. Represents all reported employment. Data are estimated. OASDHI= Old-age, survivors, disability, and health insurance; SMI= Supplementary medical insurance. See also *Historical Statistics, Colonial Times to 1970,* series H 172-185]

ITEM	Unit	1970	1980	1983	1984	1985	1986	1987	1988	1989	1990
Workers with insured status [1]	Million . . .	105.7	137.4	145.0	147.0	148.7	150.6	152.7	155.4	158.0	160.4
Male	Million . . .	61.9	75.4	78.4	78.8	79.7	80.7	81.5	82.6	83.7	84.7
Female	Million . . .	43.8	62.0	66.6	68.2	69.0	69.9	71.2	72.8	74.3	75.7
Under 25 years old	Million . . .	17.7	25.5	24.4	23.1	22.3	21.9	21.3	21.3	21.1	20.9
25 to 34 years old	Million . . .	22.3	34.9	38.0	39.7	39.9	40.0	40.6	41.0	41.3	41.4
35 to 44 years old	Million . . .	19.0	22.4	25.8	27.2	28.5	29.8	31.2	32.3	33.5	34.8
45 to 54 years old	Million . . .	19.0	18.6	18.6	18.8	18.8	19.3	19.8	20.5	21.4	22.1
55 to 59 years old	Million . . .	7.8	9.2	9.2	9.1	9.1	9.0	8.9	8.8	8.7	8.7
60 to 64 years old	Million . . .	6.3	7.9	8.4	8.6	8.7	8.8	8.7	8.7	8.7	8.6
65 to 69 years old	Million . . .	5.1	6.7	7.1	7.1	7.3	7.5	7.6	7.7	7.9	8.0
70 years old and over	Million . . .	8.5	12.1	13.4	13.4	13.9	14.3	14.7	15.0	15.4	15.8
Workers reported with—											
Taxable earnings [2]	Million . . .	93	112	112	116	120	123	125	130	133	134
Maximum earnings [2]	Million . . .	24	10	7	7	7	7	8	8	8	8
Earnings in covered employment	Bil. dol . .	532	1,326	1,608	1,772	1,912	2,035	2,198	2,411	2,593	2,722
Reported taxable [2]	Bil. dol . .	416	1,176	1,454	1,609	1,724	1,844	1,960	2,101	2,243	2,370
Percent of total	Percent . .	78.2	88.7	90.4	90.8	90.2	90.6	89.2	87.1	86.5	87.1
Average per worker:											
Total earnings [2]	Dollars . . .	5,711	11,817	14,345	15,260	15,955	16,587	17,584	18,610	19,494	20,373
Taxable earnings [2]	Dollars . . .	4,464	10,500	12,982	13,871	14,367	14,992	15,680	16,215	16,863	17,739
Annual maximum taxable earnings	Dollars . . .	7,800	25,900	35,700	37,800	39,600	42,000	43,800	45,000	48,000	51,300
Maximum tax [3]	Dollars . . .	374	1,588	2,392	[5]2,533	2,792	3,003	3,132	3,380	3,605	3,924
Contribution rates for OASDHI: [4]											
Each employer and employee	Percent . .	4.80	6.13	6.70	[5]7.00	7.05	7.15	7.15	7.51	7.51	7.65
Self-employed	Percent . .	6.90	8.10	9.35	[6]14.00	[6]14.10	[6]14.30	[6]14.30	[6]15.02	[6]15.02	[6]15.30
SMI, monthly premium [7]	Dollars . . .	5.30	9.60	12.20	14.60	15.50	15.50	17.90	24.80	31.90	28.60

[1]Fully insured for retirement and/or survivor benefits as of beginning of year.

[2]Includes self-employment.

[3]Employee's maximum tax; see footnote5.

[4]As of January 1, 1991 each employee and employer pays 7.65 percent and the self-employed pay 15.3 percent.

[5]Employee pays 6.7 percent. Employee's additional .3 percent is supplied from general revenues.

[6]Self-employed pays 11.3 percent in 1984, 11.8 percent in 1985, 12.3 percent in 1986 and 1987, and 13.02 percent in 1988 and 1989. The additional amount is supplied from general revenues. Beginning 1990, self-employed pays 15.3 percent, and half of the tax is deductible for income tax purposes and for computing and self-employment income subject to social security tax. 1970-82 as of July 1; beginning 1983, as of January 1. As of January 1, 1991 the monthly premium is $29.90.

Source: U.S. Social Security Administration, Annual Statisitical Supplement to the Social Security Bulletin, and unpublished data.

F2-4. OASDI Benefits: Number and Average Monthly Benefit in Current-Payment Status for Adult Beneficiaries, by Type of Benefit, Sex, and Age: March 1992

[Numbers in thousands]

Type of benefit and sex	Number of beneficiaries				Average monthly benefit			
	Total	Under 62	62–64	65 or older	Total	Under 62	62–64	65 or older
Total [1]	38,030	4,092	4,015	29,923	$587.61	$522.58	$527.92	$604.52
Retired workers	25,342	...	2,546	22,797	630.09	...	544.67	639.62
Disabled workers	3,253	2,722	531	...	608.59	602.62	639.15	...
Wives and husbands of retired workers	3,093	74	434	2,585	325.21	209.72	304.74	331.95
Wives and husbands of disabled workers	267	204	35	28	151.98	133.26	214.08	209.45
Nondisabled widows and widowers	5,030	163	414	4,453	584.91	540.06	559.57	588.91
Disabled widows and widowers	118	88	30	...	407.52	409.76	400.92	...
Mothers and fathers	296	287	8	1	416.30	414.81	473.06	416.07
Disabled adult children	619	554	17	48	379.67	382.88	370.17	346.17
Men [1]	15,794	2,101	1,746	11,947	696.14	616.83	667.58	714.27
Retired workers	13,256	...	1,381	11,875	710.26	...	654.69	716.72
Disabled workers	2,100	1,754	345	...	676.90	665.59	734.32	...
Husbands of retired workers	30	(2)	1	29	202.71	127.38	163.32	204.28
Husbands of disabled workers	7	6	(2)	1	101.95	95.41	125.00	129.13
Nondisabled widowers	35	6	9	20	427.98	369.66	465.40	429.68
Disabled widowers	2	2	(2)	...	262.42	266.28	248.02	...
Fathers	16	16	(2)	(2)	276.74	276.44	325.74	259.48
Disabled adult children	346	317	9	21	378.19	380.59	367.03	345.82
Women [1]	22,236	1,991	2,269	17,976	510.53	423.12	420.47	531.57
Retired workers	12,086	...	1,165	10,922	542.16	...	414.22	555.80
Disabled workers	1,154	968	186	...	484.26	488.51	462.11	...
Wives of retired workers	3,063	74	433	2,556	326.42	209.83	305.07	333.41
Wives of disabled workers	260	198	35	27	153.34	134.33	214.92	212.64
Nondisabled widowers	4,995	157	405	4,433	586.02	546.91	561.63	589.63
Disabled widowers	116	87	30	...	410.00	412.35	403.09	...
Mothers	279	271	7	1	424.53	423.16	475.19	419.40
Disabled adult children	273	237	9	28	382.15	385.95	373.39	352.28

F2-5. Amount of OASDI Benefits in Current-Payment Status, by Type of Benefit, Sex of Beneficiaries Aged 65 or Older, and State, December 1990

[In thousands]

State and county	Total	Retirement benefits			Survivor benefits		Disability benefits			Aged 65 or older	
		Retired workers	Wives and husbands	Children	Widows and widowers [2]	Children	Disabled workers	Wives and husbands	Children	Men	Women
United States, total	$21,684,924	$14,966,659	$964,815	$109,463	$2,953,871	$720,172	$1,768,208	$39,843	$161,893	$8,012,120	$8,984,869
Alabama...............................	344,812	212,735	15,755	2,474	54,151	15,909	38,696	1,032	4,060	115,132	134,505
Alaska..................................	17,750	11,511	583	147	1,851	1,599	1,833	31	195	6,434	5,602
Arizona................................	328,404	235,094	15,354	1,507	37,175	9,879	26,541	585	2,269	128,847	128,844
Arkansas..............................	225,109	143,762	10,170	1,296	31,921	8,520	26,083	653	2,704	79,666	86,424
California.............................	2,048,747	1,449,275	96,453	10,403	248,046	63,960	164,762	2,911	12,937	790,880	845,719
Colorado..............................	225,655	152,058	11,939	874	30,138	7,940	20,479	414	1,813	84,603	89,015
Connecticut..........................	323,530	246,471	10,857	1,349	37,370	7,742	18,150	249	1,342	126,259	145,374
Delaware..............................	60,100	42,611	2,463	274	7,784	1,834	4,670	87	377	22,406	24,464
District of Columbia...............	36,897	25,926	1,168	167	4,859	1,642	2,959	20	156	12,153	17,892
Florida.................................	1,475,328	1,092,881	64,308	5,713	172,933	33,679	95,678	2,097	8,039	596,742	608,689
Georgia................................	440,248	282,483	16,496	2,331	60,482	21,472	50,899	1,046	5,039	143,976	175,627
Hawaii..................................	79,859	60,721	3,195	892	7,604	2,512	4,491	84	360	34,410	29,340
Idaho...................................	83,484	58,548	4,421	427	10,356	2,910	6,062	160	600	33,474	32,312
Illinois.................................	1,024,886	720,644	41,809	4,747	143,135	33,167	73,377	1,330	6,677	379,494	443,628
Indiana................................	522,564	358,877	22,112	2,591	72,878	17,749	43,069	947	4,341	187,199	217,172
Iowa....................................	288,985	201,406	16,408	1,232	42,593	7,546	17,872	349	1,579	111,152	125,122
Kansas.................................	229,097	162,552	11,851	949	32,050	6,741	13,484	249	1,221	88,547	100,147
Kentucky.............................	314,429	187,458	15,384	1,794	50,998	12,742	40,352	1,377	4,324	104,465	119,862
Louisiana.............................	315,665	179,630	18,047	2,224	56,110	16,952	36,836	1,377	4,489	107,424	115,434
Maine...................................	109,395	75,924	4,821	497	14,665	3,205	9,265	206	812	40,258	45,307
Maryland..............................	338,874	237,456	13,776	1,482	47,570	12,159	24,184	402	1,845	122,725	146,065
Massachusetts.......................	546,471	398,913	19,781	2,142	69,551	13,185	39,350	665	2,884	200,160	250,219
Michigan..............................	868,130	586,000	39,288	4,829	122,897	30,177	75,776	1,665	7,498	314,580	347,436
Minnesota............................	361,158	256,112	18,764	1,709	49,873	9,957	22,471	365	1,907	139,309	154,062
Mississippi...........................	204,653	123,993	7,895	1,585	29,431	10,741	27,158	750	3,100	65,652	77,457
Missouri...............................	489,698	335,505	21,448	2,277	68,336	15,884	41,471	878	3,899	175,768	206,460
Montana...............................	72,905	48,814	3,881	345	9,813	2,559	6,665	168	660	28,253	27,898
Nebraska..............................	145,647	102,737	7,947	569	20,914	4,078	8,449	160	793	56,450	63,890
Nevada................................	94,662	69,346	3,325	417	9,660	3,038	8,136	137	603	38,254	34,482
New Hampshire.....................	91,208	67,779	3,236	360	10,377	2,620	6,182	111	543	34,249	38,892
New Jersey...........................	749,141	554,856	24,016	2,943	93,222	20,211	49,248	832	3,813	283,639	332,453
New Mexico..........................	108,440	70,823	5,991	720	14,339	4,986	10,177	321	1,083	40,837	39,827
New York.............................	1,674,442	1,212,533	56,641	8,218	208,240	48,275	127,812	2,509	10,214	604,107	741,319
North Carolina......................	544,748	371,651	19,096	2,526	68,593	20,663	56,443	1,004	4,772	185,511	220,961
North Dakota........................	57,171	37,974	4,032	308	9,246	1,737	3,493	73	308	23,416	23,200
Ohio....................................	1,007,531	663,216	52,591	5,139	160,521	32,047	84,114	2,037	7,866	367,617	414,684
Oklahoma.............................	275,405	185,448	13,704	1,287	40,993	10,241	21,257	498	1,977	100,279	114,423
Oregon.................................	278,008	202,205	12,952	1,189	33,108	7,622	18,991	411	1,530	109,724	113,341
Pennsylvania.........................	1,282,597	901,911	57,625	5,225	192,984	32,868	83,750	1,926	6,308	479,589	555,555
Rhode Island........................	101,706	76,613	2,756	369	11,566	2,302	7,466	126	508	37,422	45,830
South Carolina......................	271,849	180,015	9,460	1,479	33,667	12,573	31,167	604	2,884	90,799	106,229
South Dakota........................	63,804	43,433	3,858	309	9,602	1,900	4,216	95	391	25,224	26,595
Tennessee.............................	412,241	266,661	18,106	2,251	59,995	16,192	43,840	1,030	4,166	141,630	165,594
Texas...................................	1,134,174	739,383	62,704	6,903	177,915	51,740	84,644	2,315	8,570	418,066	451,023
Utah....................................	104,320	73,116	5,500	647	12,294	4,700	7,123	150	790	40,919	40,796
Vermont...............................	47,204	33,163	2,014	216	6,289	1,466	3,666	73	317	17,448	19,893
Virginia...............................	430,114	287,902	18,269	2,030	60,883	15,880	40,473	1,035	3,642	149,470	178,467
Washington...........................	408,534	292,423	19,615	1,744	48,734	11,724	31,070	601	2,623	160,046	165,121
West Virginia........................	192,238	112,074	10,386	1,262	34,706	7,232	22,999	1,017	2,562	65,199	72,928
Wisconsin.............................	473,950	336,463	21,128	2,292	62,795	12,967	34,386	677	3,242	180,224	196,602
Wyoming..............................	34,151	23,593	1,569	143	4,414	1,420	2,696	56	260	13,054	13,073
Outlying Areas:											
American Samoa.....................	916	337	39	49	125	164	166	7	29	221	152
Guam...................................	1,721	942	115	52	221	246	119	6	20	655	396
Northern Mariana Islands	80	34	3	4	8	18	11	0	2	21	5
Puerto Rico...........................	182,676	91,298	10,171	2,688	23,067	10,958	37,196	1,589	5,709	58,544	49,000
Virgin Islands........................	4,335	2,823	170	61	449	362	409	11	50	1,561	1,440
Abroad.................................	131,033	77,729	8,972	1,468	29,712	6,574	5,625	258	695	47,646	57,890
Unknown..............................	3,729	818	397	297	663	745	252	78	479	331	725

[1]Includes special age-72 beneficiaries.

[2]Includes nondisabled widows and widowers, disabled widows and widowers, widowed mothers and fathers, and parents.

F2-6. OASDI Benefits in Current-Payment Status: Number and Percent of OASDI Beneficiaries Also Receiving Federally Administered SSI Payments, by Reason for SSI Eligibility and Type of OASDI Benefit: March 1992

Type of benefit	All OASDI beneficiaries [1]	OASDI beneficiaries with SSI					
		Number			Percent of all OASDI benefits		
		Total	Aged	Blind and disabled	Total	Aged	Blind and disabled
Total	40,810,155	2,278,115	980,187	1,297,928	5.6	2.4	3.2
Retirement	28,867,214	1,130,509	717,223	413,286	3.9	2.5	1.4
Workers age 65 or older	22,796,766	882,070	644,065	238,005	3.9	2.8	1.0
Men	11,875,238	323,162	231,109	92,053	2.7	1.9	.8
Women	10,921,528	558,908	412,956	145,952	5.1	3.8	1.3
Wives and husbands age 65 or older	2,585,269	119,179	73,087	46,092	4.6	2.8	1.8
Disabled adult children age 65 or older	1,566	777	71	706	49.6	4.5	45.1
Disabled adult children age 18–64	175,615	90,653	...	90,653	51.6	...	51.6
Workers age 62–64	2,545,545	21,925	...	21,925	.9	...	.9
Men	1,380,965	12,117	...	12,117	.9	...	.9
Women	1,164,580	9,808	...	9,808	.8	...	.8
Wives and husbands age 62–64	421,423	10,780	...	10,780	2.6	...	2.6
Children under age 18 and students age 18–19	254,225	2,867	...	2,867	1.1	...	1.1
Wives and husbands with children	86,805	2,258	...	2,258	2.6	...	2.6
Disability	4,669,107	581,911	1,634	580,277	12.5	(2)	12.4
Workers under age 65	3,253,443	526,274	...	526,274	16.2	...	16.2
Men	2,099,757	270,764	...	270,764	12.9	...	12.9
Women	1,153,686	255,510	...	255,510	22.1	...	22.1
Wives and husbands age 65 or older	28,255	3,652	1,634	2,018	12.9	5.8	7.1
Disabled adult children	39,188	27,410	...	27,410	69.9	...	69.9
Wives and husbands age 62–64	33,487	1,455	...	1,455	4.3	...	4.3
Children under age 18 and students age 18–19	1,045,838	17,975	...	17,975	1.7	...	1.7
Wives and husbands with children	268,896	5,145	...	5,145	1.9	...	1.9
Survivors	7,273,834	565,695	261,330	304,365	7.8	3.6	4.2
Widows and widowers age 65 or older	4,453,463	365,622	258,100	107,522	8.2	5.8	2.4
Disabled widows and widowers	118,366	26,725	...	26,725	22.6	...	22.6
Disabled adult children age 65 or older	46,571	15,880	2,689	13,191	34.1	5.8	28.3
Disabled adult children age 18–64	356,510	124,476	...	124,476	34.9	...	34.9
Parents age 65 or older	5,232	618	541	77	11.8	10.3	1.5
Parents age 62–64	93	5	...	5	5.4	...	5.4
Nondisabled widows and widowers age 60–64	576,757	16,561	...	16,561	2.9	...	2.9
Children under age 18 and students age 18–19	1,420,970	10,525	...	10,525	.7	...	.7
Widowed mothers and fathers	295,872	5,283	...	5,283	1.8	...	1.8

[1]Excludes 4,727 special age-72 beneficiaries.
[2]Less than 0.05 percent.

F2-7. OASDI Benefits: Number of Monthly Benefits Awarded to Retired Workers and Their Spouses and Children and to Survivors: 1940 to 1992

Period	Total	Retired workers and their spouses and children			Survivors of deceased workers		
		Retired workers	Wives and husbands	Children	Widows, widowers, and parents [3]	Widowed mothers and fathers	Children
1940	254,984	132,335	34,555	8,249	5,452	23,260	51,133
1950	962,628	567,131	162,768	25,495	68,987	41,101	97,146
1960	1,969,842	981,717	339,987	69,979	244,122	92,607	241,430
1970	2,959,199	1,338,107	339,447	182,595	365,068	112,377	591,724
1980	3,330,624	1,620,100	360,363	287,694	452,883	107,810	500,099
1985	3,082,487	1,690,490	356,558	128,076	502,054	72,241	332,531
1986	3,095,987	1,734,248	358,115	122,652	491,396	69,340	319,808
1987	2,983,947	1,681,716	333,333	117,984	475,321	64,777	310,573
1988	2,932,663	1,654,068	316,929	116,659	457,837	62,676	324,346
1989	2,890,267	1,656,744	310,498	106,491	449,420	59,525	307,484
1990	2,895,694	1,664,754	308,980	108,105	452,095	58,060	303,616
1991	2,938,050	1,695,346	307,000	107,261	469,034	57,896	301,459
1991							
August	229,371	132,929	24,820	7,859	36,823	4,753	22,184
September	241,616	136,744	26,057	9,027	39,185	5,271	25,328
October	214,311	123,179	22,170	7,883	32,982	4,446	23,649
November	259,237	138,649	25,986	9,587	47,018	6,257	31,737
December	163,419	97,181	18,052	6,070	22,282	2,596	17,237
1992							
January	327,545	203,608	30,805	10,488	50,088	4,911	27,641
February	264,775	153,679	26,795	9,321	43,548	4,727	26,702
March	277,839	157,501	28,412	10,764	46,117	5,387	29,654
April	250,371	143,752	26,466	9,919	39,222	4,706	26,297
May	248,998	141,176	26,508	9,854	40,845	4,787	25,820
June	237,383	135,729	25,214	8,896	39,017	4,840	23,674
July	245,719	143,393	25,621	8,734	40,022	4,857	23,085
August	236,824	137,222	25,005	8,189	38,097	4,825	23,481

[1]For a historical description of requirements for entitlement to benefits see Section 2, "History of Program Provisions—Type of Monthly Benefits," in the current Annual Statistical Supplement to the Social Security Bulletin.
[2]Includes persons with special age-72 benefits.
[3]Includes nondisabled widows and widowers, aged 60 or older, disabled widows and widowers aged 50 or older, and surviving parents.

F2-8. Proportion of Elderly Social Security Beneficiaries, by Sex and Residence: December 1990

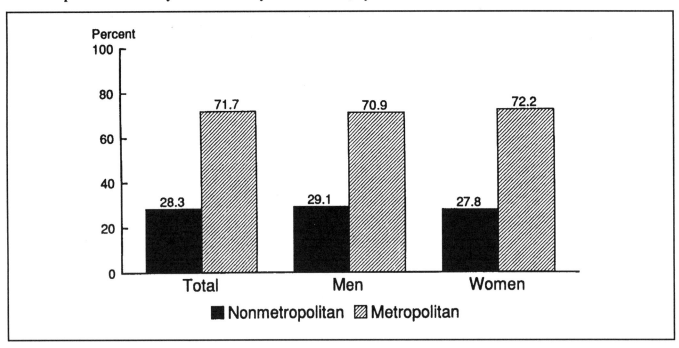

Source: Social Security Administration, Office of Research and Statistics 100 percent data from administrative records, December, 1990.

F2-9. Average Social Security Benefit for Elderly Beneficiaries, by Sex and Residence: December 1990

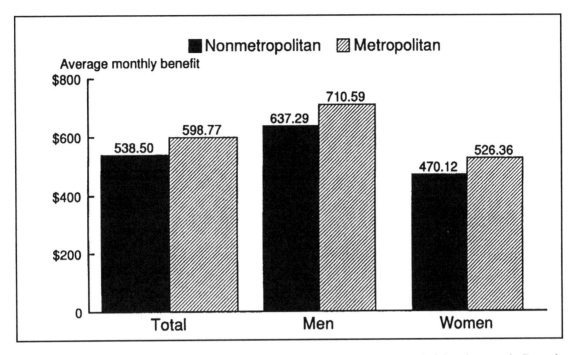

Source: Social Security Administration, Office of Research and Statistics 100 percent data from administrative records, December, 1990.

F2-10. SSI: Number of Persons Awarded Federally Administered Payments, by Category, 1974 to 1992

Period	Total	Aged	Blind	Disabled
1974 [1]	890.768	498.555	5.206	387.007
1980	496.137	169.862	7.576	318.699
1985 [2]	463.989	130.814	6.376	326.799
1986	572.122	148.618	6.591	416.913
1987	554.490	154.144	6.262	394.084
1988	548.598	154.809	5.850	387.939
1989	598.238	175.026	5.897	417.315
1990	685.398	179.447	6.077	499.874
1991	776.931	174.656	6.092	596.183
1991				
June	74.656	15.845	588	58.223
July	59.759	15.080	457	44.222
August	65.158	15.125	488	49.545
September	80.014	18.083	659	61.272
October	62.418	14.281	439	47.698
November	62.725	13.407	486	48.832
December	78.913	16.431	523	61.959
1992				
January	55.026	11.525	414	43.087
February	85.185	16.960	582	67.643
March	78.871	14.417	579	63.875
April	81.394	13.726	587	67.081
May	91.187	16.462	655	81.080
June	76.500	13.888	484	62.128

[1]Reflects data for May-December.
[2]Data not available for October.

F2-11. SSI: Number and Percent Distribution of Children and Adults Receiving Federally Administered Payments, by Age and Category: June 1992

Age	Total	Aged	Blind	Disabled
		Children		
Total number	530.198	...	9.138	521.060
Total percent	100.0	...	100.0	100.0
Under 5	16.7	...	15.8	16.7
5–9	27.1	...	26.1	27.1
10–14	30.2	...	26.9	30.3
15–17	15.8	...	15.6	15.8
18–21 [1]	10.1	...	15.6	10.0
		Adults		
Total number	4.829.684	1.470.293	76.525	3.282.866
Total percent	100.0	100.0	100.0	100.0
18–21 [1]	2.3	...	3.5	3.3
22–29	8.9	...	13.7	12.7
30–39	13.2	...	16.6	19.0
40–49	11.6	...	13.6	16.8
50–59	12.9	...	14.5	18.7
60–64	7.7	...	9.2	11.1
65–69	11.8	20.5	8.6	8.0
70–74	10.4	22.8	6.5	5.0
75–79	8.4	19.4	5.3	3.6
80 or older	12.7	37.2	8.5	1.8

[1]Persons age 18-21 can be classified as either children or adults depending on their student status.

F3. Health Care Expenditures

F3-1. Federal Health Outlays, by Several Measures: 1960 to 1995

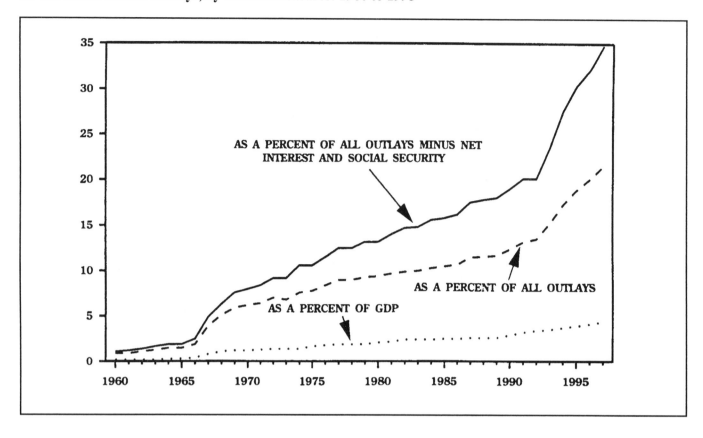

F3-2. Real Per Capita National Health Expenditures: 1929 to 1989

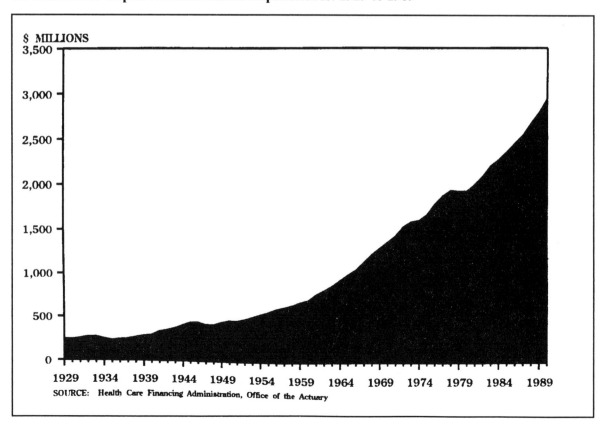

SOURCE: Health Care Financing Administration, Office of the Actuary

F3-3. Federal Health Spending: 1965 to 1995

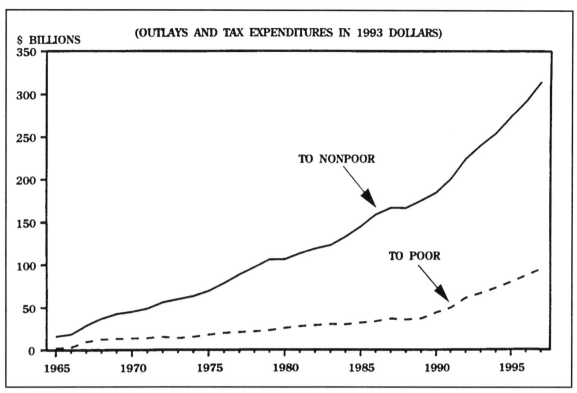

NOTE: Federal spending for Medicare, Medicaid, hospital and medical care for veterans, and other payments to individuals for health purposes; and tax expenditures for employment provided health plans and for deductions of health expenses. Spending share to poor reflects percent of recipients with money incomes below poverty thresholds.
Source: Census Bureau publication on receipt of noncash benefits.

F3-4. Health Care and General Inflation Rates in the 1980s

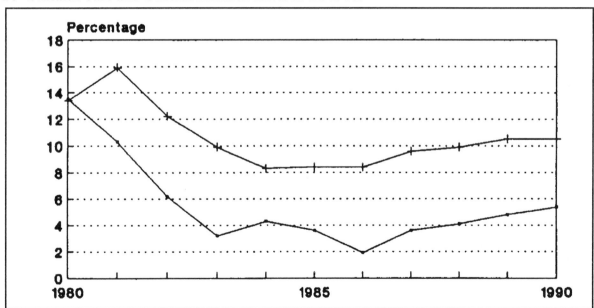

F3-5. Relative Growth in Total National Health Care Expenditures, Physician Expenditures, Total Medicare Expenditures, and Medicare Physician Expenditures: Selected Calendar Years 1970 to 1988

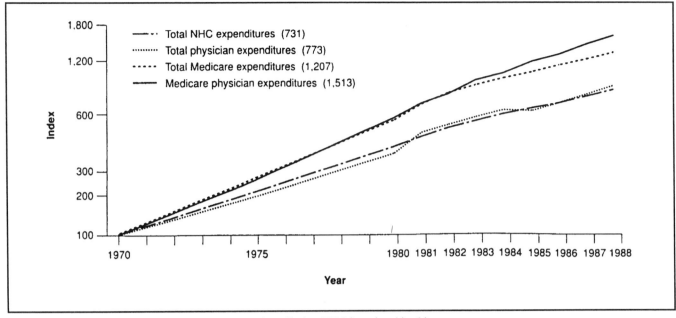

NOTE: The numbers in parentheses represent 1988 value of index. NHC is national health care.
Source: Health Care Financing Administration, Bureau of Data Management and Strategy: data from the Medicare Decision Support System: data development by the Office of Research and Demonstrations.

F3-6. Per Capita Personal Health Care Expenditures for Persons 65 Years and More, by Age, Type of Service, and Source of Payment: 1987

Age	Total	Source of funds			
		Private	Medicare	Medicaid	Other
65 years or more	$5,360	$2,004	$2,391	$ 645	$321
65–69 years	3,728	1,430	1,849	245	204
70–74 years	4,424	1,564	2,234	357	268
75–79 years	5,455	1,843	2,685	569	358
80–84 years	6,717	2,333	3,023	908	453
85 years and more	9,178	3,631	3,215	1,742	591
Hospital care					
65 years or more	2,248	333	1,566	110	239
65–69 years	1,682	312	1,144	67	158
70–74 years	2,062	327	1,431	93	212
75–79 years	2,536	341	1,786	127	283
80–84 years	2,935	355	2,070	161	348
85 years and more	3,231	376	2,246	198	411
Physicians' services					
65 years or more	1,107	393	671	17	26
65–69 years	974	380	558	14	22
70–74 years	1,086	389	655	17	25
75–79 years	1,191	398	745	19	29
80–84 years	1,246	407	789	20	31
85 years and more	1,262	420	792	20	31
Nursing home care					
65 years or more	1,085	634	19	395	38
65–69 years	165	94	5	60	6
70–74 years	360	205	11	131	13
75–79 years	802	461	22	292	28
80–84 years	1,603	927	37	584	56
85 years and more	3,738	2,191	56	1,361	131
Other personal health care					
65 years or more	920	644	135	123	18
65–69 years	907	644	142	103	18
70–74 years	916	644	137	117	18
75–79 years	825	644	133	130	18
80–84 years	934	644	128	144	18
85 years and more	947	645	121	164	18

NOTE: Hospital care and physicians' services include both inpatient and outpatient care.
Source: Health Care Financing Administration, HCFA Review. Summer 1989.

F3-7. Mean Medicare Outlays Per Enrollee, by State and Risk Class: 1991

(Figures in dollars)

State	Risk class	
	Age 65 and over	Blind and disabled
Alabama	3,429	3,533
Alaska	3,271	4,095
Arizona	3,155	3,586
Arkansas	3,069	2,863
California	3,293	4,545
Colorado	2,649	3,255
Connecticut	3,317	4,275
Delaware	3,308	3,678
District of Columbia	4,429	7,447
Florida	3,337	3,959
Georgia	3,258	3,701
Hawaii	2,019	3,919
Idaho	2,460	2,294
Illinois	3,343	4,264
Indiana	3,039	3,499
Iowa	2,652	3,286
Kansas	3,021	3,476
Kentucky	3,232	2,940
Louisiana	4,036	4,223
Maine	2,679	2,752
Maryland	3,924	5,277
Massachusetts	3,699	4,148
Michigan	3,663	3,812
Minnesota	2,379	3,055
Mississippi	2,979	3,048
Missouri	3,236	3,644
Montana	2,763	2,754
Nebraska	2,489	3,297
Nevada	3,017	3,315
New Hampshire	2,686	3,250
New Jersey	3,243	4,277
New Mexico	2,675	3,132
New York	3,876	4,481
North Carolina	2,654	3,310
North Dakota	2,841	2,718
Ohio	3,628	3,811
Oklahoma	3,093	3,412
Oregon	2,238	2,942
Pennsylvania	3,749	4,421
Rhode Island	3,121	3,415
South Carolina	2,491	3,052
South Dakota	2,498	2,901
Tennessee	3,252	3,415
Texas	3,280	4,286
Utah	2,499	2,910
Vermont	2,511	2,746
Virginia	2,956	3,724
Washington	2,738	3,329
West Virginia	2,985	2,539
Wisconsin	2,733	3,112
Wyoming	2,761	3,663

Source: Health Care Financing Administration.

F3-8. Medicare Supplementary Medical Insurance Expenditures[1], Relative Index, and Percent Distribution, by Type of Provider: Selected Calendar Years 1970 to 1988

Type of provider	1970	1975	1983	1984	1985	1986	1987	1988	Average annual rate of growth	
									1970-88	1984-88
				Dollars in millions						
Total	$1,975	$4,273	$18,106	$19,661	$22,947	$26,239	$30,820	$33,969	17.1	16.6
Physicians and suppliers	1,801	3,454	14,287	15,715	17,869	19,937	23,503	25,353	15.8	12.7
Outpatient facilities[2]	117	652	3,387	3,450	4,304	5,144	5,903	6,549	25.1	17.4
All other[3]	57	167	442	496	774	1,158	1,414	2,067	22.1	42.9
				Relative index[4]						
Total	100	216	917	995	1,162	1,329	1,561	1,720	—	—
Physicians and suppliers	100	192	793	873	984	1,106	1,305	1,408	—	—
Outpatient facilities[2]	100	557	2,895	2,949	3,679	4,397	5,045	5,597	—	—
All other[3]	100	464	1,228	1,377	2,150	3,217	3,928	5,742	—	—
				Percent distribution						
Total	100.0	100.0	100.0	100.0	100.0	100.0	100.0	100.0	—	—
Physicians and suppliers	91.2	80.8	78.9	79.9	77.9	76.0	76.3	74.6	—	—
Outpatient facilities[2]	5.9	15.3	18.7	17.5	18.8	19.6	19.2	19.3	—	—
All other[3]	2.9	3.9	2.4	2.5	3.4	4.4	4.6	6.1	—	—

[1]Expenditures shown in this table reported by the Office of the Actuary (OACT).

[2]Includes outpatient hospital facilities, end stage renal disease freestanding facilities, rural health clinics, and outpatient rehabilitation facilities.

[3]Includes health maintenance organizations, competitive medical plans, and other prepaid health plans, and home health agency (HHA) services covered under supplementary medical insurance. As a result of the Omnibus Reconciliation Act 1980 legislation, most HHA services were covered under the hospital insurance program.

[4]Relative index for 1970 = 100.

Source: Health Care Financing Administration, Office of the Actuary.

F3-9. Medicare Enrollment, Persons Served, and Payments for Medicare Enrollees 65 Years of Age and Over, by Selected Characteristics: 1967, 1977, and 1986

Characteristic	Enrollment in millions [1]			Persons served per 1,000 enrollees [2]			Payments per person served [3]			Payments per enrollee [3]		
	1967	1977	1986	1967	1977	1986	1967	1977	1986	1967	1977	1986
Total	19.5	23.8	28.8	367	570	732	$592	$1,332	$2,870	$217	$ 759	$2,100
Age												
65–66 years	2.8	3.3	3.9	300	533	652	496	1,075	2,118	149	573	1,381
67–68 years	2.6	3.2	3.5	326	511	656	521	1,173	2,441	170	599	1,601
69–70 years	2.4	2.9	3.3	339	531	689	530	1,211	2,579	180	643	1,777
71–72 years	2.3	2.6	3.1	351	555	719	560	1,228	2,777	197	681	1,997
73–74 years	2.1	2.3	2.8	369	576	735	574	1,319	2,910	212	759	2,140
75–79 years	3.9	4.5	5.6	398	597	768	624	1,430	3,100	248	853	2,380
80–84 years	2.2	3.0	3.6	430	623	808	693	1,549	3,310	298	965	2,674
85 years and over	1.3	2.1	2.9	465	652	827	740	1,636	3,477	345	1,068	2,875
Sex												
Male	8.3	9.6	11.5	357	546	691	647	1,505	3,272	231	821	2,261
Female	11.3	14.2	17.3	373	586	759	554	1,223	2,626	207	717	1,992
Race [4]												
White	17.4	21.1	25.2	375	576	738	593	1,328	2,842	222	765	2,097
All other	1.5	2.1	2.7	260	514	683	557	1,404	3,185	145	722	2,174
Geographic region [5]												
Northeast	5.1	5.7	6.5	385	613	775	604	1,426	2,933	233	874	2,274
Midwest	5.6	6.3	7.3	352	541	729	599	1,401	2,894	211	757	2,110
South	5.6	7.5	9.4	351	556	736	528	1,198	2,744	186	666	2,018
West	2.9	3.8	5.0	455	632	727	620	1,341	3,051	282	848	2,218

[1]Includes fee-for-service and health maintanance organization (HMO) enrollees; as of July 1 each year.
[2]Excludes HMO enrollees.
[3]Excludes amounts for HMO services.
[4]Excludes persons of unknown race.
[5]Includes the resident population of the United States but not residence unknown.

NOTE: Data include the United States, residence unknown, Puerto Rico, Virgin Islands, Guam, other outlying areas, and foreign countries. Some numbers in this table have been revised and differ from those shown in previous editions of Health, United States.

Source: National Center for Health Statistics: Health, United States, 1989; based on unpublished data from the Bureau of Data Management and Strategy, Health Care Financing Administration.

F3-10. Where the Medicaid Dollar for the Elderly Goes: 1989

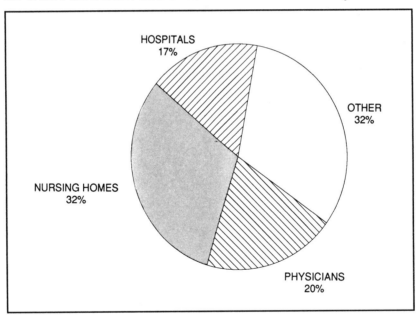

Source: Thomas W. Reilly, Steven B. Clauser, and David K. Baugh, "Trends in Medicaid Payments and Utilization, 1975-1989," *Health Care Financing Review* (1990 Annual Supplement).

F3-11. Where the Private Health Care Dollar for the Elderly Goes: 1987

NOTE: Total exceeds 100 percent due to rounding.
Source: Daniel R. Waldo, Sally T. Sonnefeld, David R. McKusick, and Ross H. Arnett, III, "Health Expenditures by Age Group, 1977 and 1987," *Health Care Financing Review,* Vol. 10, No. 4 (Summer 1989).

F3-12. Projected Nursing Home Expenditures for People Age 65+, by Source of Payment in 1990, 2005, and 2020

(in billions of 1989 dollars)			
Source of payment	1990	2005	2020
Nursing Home Care			
Medicare	$ 1.1	$ 1.8	$ 3.2
Medicaid..	$15.7	$27.0	$45.0
Out-of-Pocket..................................	$20.8	$35.2	$64.4
Total	$37.6	$64.0	$112.6

F3-13. Sources of Payment of Health Care Expenditures for the Elderly, by Functional Status of User: 1987

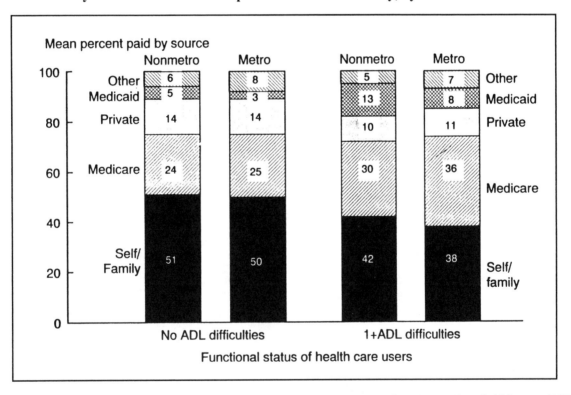

Source: Agency for Health Care Policy and Research, National Medical Expenditure Survey-Household Survey, 1987.

F3-14. Total Health Care Expenditures for the Elderly, by Functional Status of User and Residence: 1987

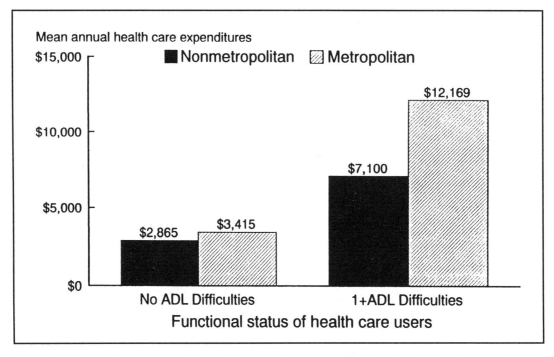

Source: Agency for Health Care Policy and Research, National Medical Expenditure Survey-Household Survey, 1987.

F4. Public and Private Pensions

F4-1. Assets of Private and Public Pension Funds, by Type of Fund: 1989 to 1991

TYPE OF PENSION FUND	1980	1983	1984	1985	1986	1987	1988	1989	1990	1991
Total, all types	916	1,350	1,498	1,795	2,063	2,182	2,451	2,848	2,963	3,473
Private funds.	642	926	1,011	1,241	1,424	1,476	1,637	1,884	1,961	2,320
Insured	172	286	332	400	477	549	628	714	798	893
Noninsured [1]	470	640	680	841	947	928	1,009	1,171	1,163	1,427
Corporate equities [2]	231	309	295	393	454	453	506	625	585	781
U.S. Government securities	51	98	115	136	147	142	146	163	171	194
Corporate bonds [3]	78	66	78	92	96	92	94	103	107	120
Time deposits	25	49	63	74	88	82	92	97	97	107
Public funds	275	423	487	554	639	706	814	964	1,002	1,153
State and local government .	198	311	357	405	469	517	606	735	752	877
Corporate bonds [3]	95	107	118	129	140	125	146	182	188	199
Corporate equities [2]	44	90	97	120	150	170	220	300	296	373
U.S. Government securities	40	88	111	124	144	169	185	198	220	250
Other.	19	27	31	32	35	54	56	54	47	55
U.S. Government	76	112	130	149	170	188	208	229	251	276
Civil service [4]	74	111	127	145	163	182	200	220	241	266
Railroad retirement	3	1	3	4	6	7	8	9	9	11

[1]Covers all pension funds of corporations, nonprofit organizations, unions, and multi-employer groups. Also includes deferred profit-sharing plans and Federal Employees Retirement System (FERS) Thrift Savings Fund. Excludes health, welfare and bonus plans. Includes other types of assets not shown separately.

[2]Includes mutual fund shares.

[3]Includes foreign bonds.

[4]Includes U.S. Foreign Service Retirement and Disability Trust Fund and the Federal Employees Retirement System.

Source: Board of Governors of the Federal Reserve System, Annual Statistical Digest, and unpublished data.

F4-2. Accrual Costs and Funding for Major Federal Retirement Systems: 1991 Estimates

	Number of Active Personnel (thousands)	Actuaries Estimated Accrual Cost	Current Payments	
			Agency Payroll Charges	Employee Contributions Percent of Basic Pay
Plans on Full or Partial Accrual				
Military Retirement: [1]				
FINAL PAY	575	49.6	49.6	—
HI–3	523	43.6	43.6	—
REDUX	967	36.8	36.8	—
Civil Service Retirement: [2]				
CSRS	1,691	28.3	7.0	7.0
FERS	1,194	13.7	12.9	0.8
Foreign Service Retirement:				
FSRS	7	36.2	7.0	7.0
FSPS	5	23.2	21.7	1.4
Pay-As-You-Go Plans				
Coast Guard	37	29.2	—	—
Public Health Service	6	37.1	—	—

[1] FINAL PAY is the plan for military personnel entering the armed forces prior to September 1980. REDUX applies to all entrants since August 1986. HI-3 is the plan for entrants in the intervening time period. Military pay is only about 70 percent of total salary, and the percentages would be lower if computed on the basis of total compensation.

[2] Costs given for the typical employee. Costs for certain employees (law enforcement officers, firefighters, congressional staff and members, etc.) are higher than shown. For FERS, costs do not include government contributions for social security or matching Thrift Savings Plan contributions.

F4-3. Private and State and Local Government Pension Assets: 1950 to 1989

[Billions of Dollars]

Year	Total pension plans	Private pension plans			State and local pension plans
		Total	Insured	Non-insured	
1950	16.8	11.9	4.8	7.1	4.9
1951	19.4	13.8	5.6	8.2	5.6
1952	22.9	16.3	6.5	9.8	6.6
1953	27.3	19.3	7.6	11.7	8.0
1954	32.1	22.6	8.8	13.8	9.5
1955	39.2	28.4	10.1	18.3	10.8
1956	44.4	32.3	11.2	21.1	12.1
1957	49.8	36.0	12.6	23.4	13.8
1958	58.8	43.2	14.0	29.2	15.6
1959	67.2	49.6	15.5	34.1	17.6
1960	74.6	54.9	16.8	38.1	19.7
1961	86.7	64.4	18.3	46.1	22.3
1962	91.7	67.2	19.7	47.5	24.5
1963	104.0	76.6	21.2	55.4	27.4
1964	118.5	87.9	23.0	64.9	30.6
1965	134.0	99.9	25.5	74.4	34.1
1966	142.0	103.9	27.3	76.6	38.1
1967	162.9	120.3	29.9	90.4	42.6
1968	183.2	135.2	32.5	102.7	48.0
1969	192.0	138.8	35.0	103.8	53.2
1970	209.8	149.5	37.5	112.0	60.3
1971	243.8	174.8	42.4	132.4	69.0
1972	294.4	213.8	48.5	165.3	80.6
1973	297.6	212.9	51.2	161.7	84.7
1974	300.1	212.1	53.4	158.7	88.0
1975	394.4	289.6	64.6	225.0	104.8
1976	451.9	331.5	79.6	251.9	120.4
1977	495.9	363.4	91.7	271.7	132.5
1978	588.0	434.1	107.9	326.2	153.9
1979	683.1	513.4	127.3	386.1	169.7
1980	819.9	621.8	152.2	469.6	198.1
1981	883.4	659.2	172.5	486.7	224.2
1982	1,044.1	781.6	205.8	575.8	262.5
1983	1,234.4	923.2	240.7	682.5	311.2
1984	1,350.7	994.1	280.2	713.9	356.6
1985	1,591.0	1,186.3	337.9	848.4	404.7
1986	1,783.1	1,313.7	397.8	915.9	469.4
1987	1,909.8	1,392.8	435.3	957.5	517.0
1988	2,128.2	1,522.1	481.5	1,040.6	606.1
1989	2,416.7	1,689.3	525.8	1,163.5	727.4

Source: Federal Reserve Board Flow of Funds Accounts, Financial Assets and Liabilities, year-end 1966-89 and earlier reports; American Council of Life Insurance, Life Insurance Fact Book, 1990 and previous issues.

F4-4. Benefits and Beneficiaries Under Public Employee Retirement Systems, by Reason for Benefit Receipt: Fiscal Year 1988

Systems	Total	Age and service	Disability	Survivor [1] Monthly	Survivor [1] Lump sum
	Benefits (in millions)				
Total [2]	$77,242.0	$62,703.6	$8,379.2	$6,072.2	$87.0
Federal employees [2]	47,518.0	36,397.6	6,209.2	4,824.2	87.0
Civil Service	27,638.0	18,814.5	4,733.1	4,007.5	82.9
Armed Forces [3]	18,990.7	16,856.0	1,395.6	739.1	...
Other Federal programs [2]	889.3	727.1	80.5	77.6	4.1
Contributory systems	362.8	311.5	20.7	28.0	2.6
Federal judiciary survivors [4]	3.7	...	...	3.7	...
Foreign Service	267.8	235.7	13.4	16.1	2.6
Tennessee Valley Authority	91.3	75.8	7.3	8.2	...
Noncontributory systems [2]	526.5	415.6	59.8	49.6	1.5
Coast Guard [3,5]	354.4	263.9	52.0	38.5	...
Federal judiciary [3,6]	23.0	23.0	...	...	...
Federal Reserve [7,8]	64.9	54.8	2.5	6.1	1.5
NOAA [3,9]	5.0	3.9	.6	.5	...
Public Health Service [3,10]	78.0	69.0	4.7	4.3	...
State and local employees [11]	29,724.0	26,306.0	2,170.0	1,248.0	...
	Beneficiaries at end of year (in thousands)				
Total [2]	7,422.1	5,764.6	698.2	959.3	...
Federal employees [2]	3,714.1	2,571.6	454.2	688.3	...
Civil Service	2,089.4	1,237.1	311.3	541.0	...
Armed Forces [3]	1,566.9	1,290.0	137.1	139.8	...
Other Federal programs [2]	57.8	44.5	5.8	7.5	...
Contributory systems	19.5	15.0	1.4	3.1	...
Federal judiciary survivors [4]	.2	...	...	.2	...
Foreign Service	10.2	8.3	.4	1.5	...
Tennessee Valley Authority	9.1	6.7	1.0	1.4	...
Noncontributory systems [2]	38.3	29.5	4.4	4.4	...
Coast Guard [3,5]	25.2	18.7	3.7	2.8	...
Federal judiciary [3,6]	.3	.3	...	...	...
Federal Reserve [7,8]	10.0	8.3	.5	1.2	...
NOAA [3,9]	.2	.1	...	.1	...
Public Health Service [3,10]	2.6	2.1	.2	.3	...
State and local employees [11]	3,708.0	3,193.0	244.0	271.0	...

[1]Unless otherwise specified, number of survivor beneficiaries represents number of individuals.

[2]Totals include benefits and beneficiaries of the Federal Tax Court retirement system, not shown separately.

[3]Survivor beneficiaries represent families.

[4]Excludes annuities to widows of Supreme Court justices; see footnote 6.

[5]Includes Lighthouse Service widows.

[6]Includes Supreme Court justices, their widows, and other federal judges retired on salary.

[7]Lump-sum benefits relate to the Federal Reserve Board plan only.

[8]Survivor beneficiaries represent widows only.

[9]National Oceanic and Atmospheric Administration commissioned officers.

[10]Commissioned officers.

[11]Survivor beneficiary number represents payees, not necessarily individuals. Lump-sum data not available for 1987.

F4-5. Percent Distribution of Benefits and Beneficiaries Under Public Employee Retirement Systems, by Reason for Benefit Receipt and Level of Administering Government: 1978 and 1986 to 1988

All levels of government, by reason for receipt	1978	1986	1987	1988	All reasons for receipt, by level of government	1978	1986	1987	1988
Benefits	100	100	100	100	Benefits	100	100	100	100
Age and service..............	79	80	81	81	Federal.....................	67	63	62	62
Disability	13	12	11	11	Civil Service..............	35	35	35	36
Survivor, monthly benefits......	7	7	8	8	Armed Forces............	31	27	25	25
Survivor, lump-sum benefits....	1	1	0	0	Other	1	1	1	1
					State and local..............	33	37	38	38
Beneficiaries	100	100	100	100	Beneficiaries	100	100	100	100
Age and service..............	73	77	79	78	Federal.....................	55	50	50	50
Disability	13	11	9	9	Civil Service..............	30	28	28	28
Survivor, monthly benefits......	14	13	12	13	Armed Forces............	24	21	21	21
					Other	1	1	1	1
					State and local..............	45	50	50	50

F4-6. Average Annual Benefit Amounts, by Reason for Benefit Receipt and Level of Government: 1978 and 1986 to 1988, in Current and Constant (1988) Dollars

Reason for receipt	1978	1986	1987	1988	Percentage Increase, 1978-88	1978	1986	1987	1988	Percentage Increase, 1978-88
		Current dollars					Constant (1988) dollars			
All public employee retirement systems	$5,903	$9,354	$9,743	$10,395	76	$10,240	$10,164	$10,118	$10,395	2
Age and service.....................	6,450	9,693	10,086	10,877	69	11,188	10,533	10,474	10,877	-3
Disability	6,154	11,359	11,859	12,001	95	10,675	12,343	12,315	12,001	12
Survivor, monthly benefits............	2,865	5,679	5,982	6,330	121	4,970	6,171	6,212	6,330	27
Federal employee retirement systems......................	7,237	11,769	12,127	12,771	76	12,554	12,788	12,593	12,771	2
Age and service.....................	8,343	13,073	13,461	14,154	70	14,472	14,205	13,979	14,154	-2
Disability	8,141	12,591	12,978	13,671	68	14,122	13,682	13,477	13,671	-3
Survivor, monthly benefits............	3,390	6,179	6,514	7,009	107	5,880	6,714	6,765	7,009	19
State and local employee retirement systems............................	4,258	6,908	7,406	8,016	88	7,386	7,506	7,691	8,016	9
Age and service.....................	4,541	6,995	7,506	8,239	81	7,877	7,601	7,795	8,239	5
Disability	4,748	8,646	9,219	8,893	87	8,236	9,395	9,574	8,893	8
Survivor, monthly benefits............	1,924	4,228	4,468	4,605	139	3,337	4,594	4,640	4,605	38

F4-7. Benefits and Beneficiaries Under Public Employee Retirement Systems, by Reason for Benefit Receipt: 1954 to 1988

Year	Benefits (in millions)					Beneficiaries (in thousands)			
				Survivor					
	Total	Age and service	Disability	Monthly	Lump sum	Total	Age and service	Disability	Monthly survivor
1954	$1,300	$831	$301	$69	$50	850	559	180	110
1955	1,463	993	335	81	50	917	606	189	122
1956	1,665	1,153	360	96	56	1,004	672	197	136
1957	1,881	1,331	377	112	62	1,108	756	201	150
1958	2,156	1,534	419	135	68	1,222	835	217	170
1959	2,424	1,736	459	162	67	1,341	907	232	203
1960	2,674	1,921	492	185	76	1,448	977	247	224
1961	3,008	2,181	530	208	88	1,578	1,072	263	243
1962	3,303	2,401	571	229	97	1,688	1,150	280	259
1963	3,754	2,763	625	266	101	1,838	1,263	294	280
1964	4,253	3,151	693	296	113	1,984	1,372	310	301
1965	4,720	3,520	751	324	125	2,117	1,472	326	319
1966	5,479	4,104	857	382	135	2,293	1,607	346	340
1967	6,172	4,636	942	448	145	2,474	1,744	364	366
1968	6,926	5,250	1,022	492	162	2,666	1,890	378	388
1969	7,920	6,052	1,135	554	179	2,854	2,049	398	406
1970	9,355	7,210	1,312	645	189	3,050	2,204	419	427
1971	10,947	8,553	1,491	734	200	3,265	2,375	439	451
1972	12,783	10,039	1,687	837	220	3,474	2,543	456	476
1973	14,975	11,867	1,907	965	236	3,796	2,785	487	525
1974	18,052	14,382	2,241	1,171	258	4,136	3,035	518	583
1975	21,617	17,200	2,707	1,439	271	4,428	3,243	549	636
1976	24,526	19,506	3,096	1,641	282	4,739	3,747	577	688
1977	27,429	21,795	3,500	1,842	292	5,006	3,660	611	735
1978	30,873	24,452	3,985	2,111	324	5,175	3,791	648	737
1979	35,068	27,730	4,560	2,445	333	5,409	3,982	679	749
1980	41,060	32,416	5,371	2,896	377	5,659	4,200	708	751
1981	46,821	36,806	6,219	3,382	414	5,969	4,427	751	791
1982	59,906	40,234	6,896	3,735	438	6,202	4,611	778	813
1983	55,371	43,666	7,165	4,049	491	6,447	4,825	781	841
1984	59,024	46,735	7,360	4,495	434	6,639	5,056	745	838
1985	63,499	50,562	7,623	4,856	544	6,890	5,271	745	874
1986	67,438	53,866	7,747	4,986	840	7,120	5,557	682	878
1987	71,412	58,178	7,812	5,366	56	7,323	5,768	658	897
1988	77,242	62,704	8,379	6,072	87	7,422	5,765	698	959

F4-8. Average Annual Retirement Pension from Private Pension Plans in Selected Countries: 1970 to 1989

Year	Australia	Canada	France	Germany	Japan	Netherlands	Switzerland	United Kingdom	United States
1970	—	—	—	—	—	387	896	—	1,767
1975	—	—	—	—	—	935	1,995	—	2,421
1980	—	—	2,308	—	520	1,834	3,954	—	3,470
1981	—	3,764	2,075	—	614	1,586	3,512	—	3,810
1982	—	3,989	1,908	1,484	658	1,616	3,612	—	4,080
1983	—	4,356	1,775	—	740	1,629	3,624	1,735	4,310
1984	—	4,511	1,722	—	834	1,537	3,434	—	4,530
1985	—	4,510	1,684	—	931	1,725	—	—	4,700
1986	—	4,597	2,381	—	1,490	2,512	—	—	4,950
1987	—	5,100	2,986	—	1,867	3,178	6,326	—	—
1988	—	5,859	3,203	2,940	2,292	3,505	—	—	—
1989	—	—	3,226	—	2,304	3,450	—	—	6,359

(U.S. Dollars)

NOTE: Statistics for Canada include both private pension plans and plans for government employees.
—Data not available.

F5. Veterans

F5-1. Number of Veterans Over 65 Years: 1965 to 2000

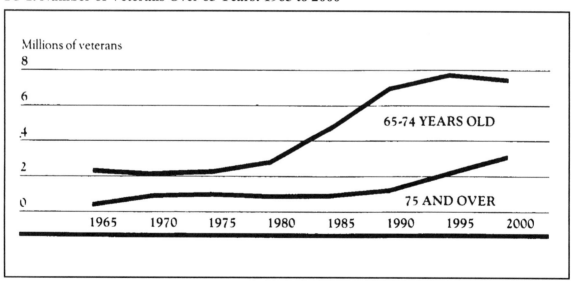

Source "A Report on the Aging Veteran," U.S. Senate Committee on Veterans' Affairs. 1978. p. v.

F5-2. Percent of Elderly Males Who Are Veterans, by Age: 1987

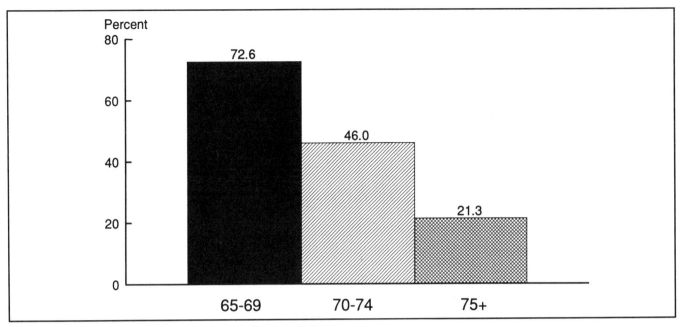

Source: Department of Veterans Affairs, *Survey of Veterans*, 1987.

F5-3. Veterans Over 65 Years as Percent of All U.S. Males Over 65 Years: 1970 to 2000

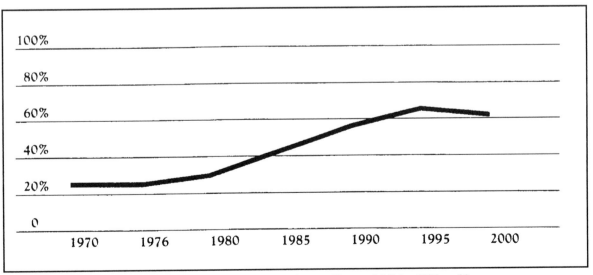

Source: "A Report on the Aging Veteran," U.S. Senate Committee on Veterans' Affairs, 1978, p. 23.

F5-4. Estimates and Projections of the Elderly Veteran Population, by Age: 1980 to 2040

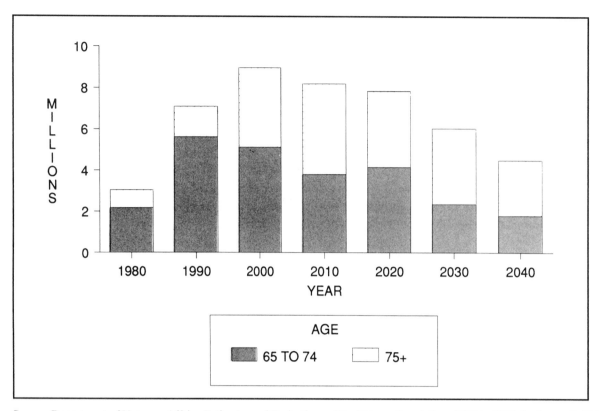

Source: Department of Veterans Affairs. Estimates and Projections of the Veteran Population: 1980 to 2040, by Lynne R. Heltman and Thomas P. Bonczar. (March 1990).

F5-5. Department of Veterans Affairs Medical Budget Obligations: 1993

(dollars in thousands)

	1992 Actual	1993 Budget Estimate	1993 Current Estimate	1994 Estimate	Increase/ Decrease
Medical bed sections	$3,293,964	$3,511,631	$3,668,145	$3,824,487	$156,342
Surgical bed sections	2,117,256	2,240,689	2,257,864	2,354,098	96,234
Psychiatric bed sections	1,525,930	1,717,954	1,655,859	1,726,434	70,575
Intermediate bed sections	706,024	850,705	778,264	811,435	33,171
VA hospital	7,643,174	8,320,979	8,360,132	8,716,454	356,322
VA nursing homes	881,579	1,016,864	1,014,990	1,108,734	93,744
VA domiciliary	200,010	218,569	227,774	236,434	8,660
Outpatient care	3,707,113	3,778,816	3,962,241	4,192,803	230,562
Misc benefits and svcs	610,954	608,804	635,392	663,612	28,220
VA facilities	13,042,830	13,944,032	14,200,529	14,918,037	717,508
Contract hospitals	130,454	147,647	135,728	143,112	7,384
Community nursing homes	283,771	351,341	349,665	378,442	28,777
State home domiciliaries	17,358	20,521	17,695	20,093	2,398
State home nursing homes	100,314	132,321	117,654	148,117	30,463
State home hospitals	4,445	5,181	4,724	5,264	540
CHAMPVA	102,888	95,877	100,043	103,450	3,407
(Inpatient)	(40,775)	(41,599)	(39,760)	(41,144)	(1,384)
(Outpatient)	(62,113)	(54,278)	(60,283)	(62,306)	(2,023)
Non-VA facilities	639,230	752,888	725,509	798,478	72,969
Total obligations	$13,682,060	$14,696,920	$14,926,038	$15,716,515	$790,477
Less reimbursements	(70,121)	(65,000)	(70,258)	(74,063)	(3,805)
Lapse	3,373				
Unobligated balance available	10,373		(10,373)		10,373
Total budget authority	$13,625,685	$14,631,920	$14,845,407	$15,642,452	$797,045

F5-6. Department of Veterans Affairs Budget Obligations for Patient Care: 1993

	1992 Actual	1993 Budget Estimate	1993 Current Estimate	1994 Estimate	Increase/ Decrease
Average obligation/Patient day					
Medical bed sections	$612.24	$668.82	$682.03	$711.00	$28.97
Surgical bed sections	959.03	1,008.85	1,063.79	1,131.70	67.91
Psychiatric bed sections	294.39	355.01	307.55	312.83	5.28
Intermediate bed sections	245.36	270.76	284.64	297.92	13.28
VA hospital	488.42	538.48	535.25	555.13	19.88
VA nursing	183.73	195.04	201.43	207.60	6.17
VA domiciliary	84.86	86.29	92.89	96.42	3.53
Contract hospitals	950.04	965.05	989.80	1,043.25	53.45
Community nursing homes	88.25	101.68	98.12	106.36	8.24
State home domiciliaries 1/	10.83	11.79	11.79	12.55	0.76
State home nursing homes 1/	25.35	27.61	27.61	30.40	2.79
State home hospitals 1/	25.35	27.61	27.61	31.03	3.42
Average obligation/Patient treated					
Medical bed sections	$6,881	$7,316	$7,724	$8,029	$305
Surgical bed sections	8,245	8,787	8,947	9,393	446
Psychiatric bed sections	8,009	9,337	8,457	8,622	165
Intermediate bed sections	17,233	17,361	20,481	21,662	1,181
VA hospital	7,904	8,596	8,699	9,036	337
VA nursing	28,995	31,170	31,725	32,697	972
VA domiciliary	10,318	10,596	11,286	11,667	381
Contract hospitals	6,431	7,463	6,798	7,165	367
Community nursing homes	10,082	11,129	10,739	11,641	902
State home domiciliaries 1/	2,488	2,302	2,417	2,717	300
State home nursing homes 1/	5,938	6,530	6,406	7,199	793
State home hospitals 1/	1,860	1,876	2,016	2,265	249

1/ All State home per diems in accordance with PL 101-322

F5-7. Percent of Elderly Veterans Receiving Selected Benefits, by Residence: 1987

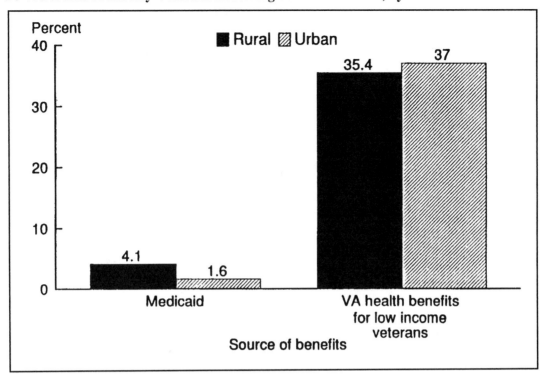

Source: Dept. of Veterans Affairs, *Survey of Veterans*, 1987.

F5-8. Source of Assistance for Elderly Veterans Receiving ADL*/IADL** Aid, by Residence: 1987

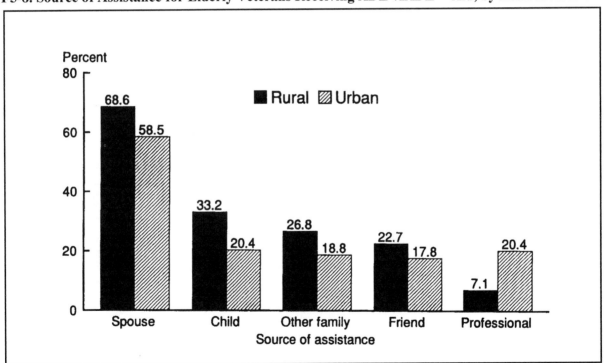

*Includes eating, dressing, toileting, bathing, transferring.
**Includes meal preparation, getting around community, shopping, managing money, using telephone, light housework.
Source: Dept. of Veterans Affairs, *Survey of Veterans*, 1987

F5-9. Expenditures/Outlays[1] for Disability Compensation: 1967 to 1991

(In thousands of dollars)

Fiscal Year	Total	Vietnam Era	Korean Conflict	World War II (2)	World War I (2)	All Other
1967	1,917,840		251,006	1,331,920	163,464	171,451
1968	1,953,879	38,974	257,515	1,334,886	152,850	169,655
1969	2,146,083	118,021	281,248	1,419,159	154,561	173,094
1970	2,392,737	227,233	308,306	1,511,210	154,955	191,034
1971	2,729,254	355,347	344,843	1,657,282	157,055	214,727
1972	2,801,572	434,438	351,577	1,654,273	142,697	218,586
1973	3,113,133	535,324	388,596	1,806,160	140,503	242,550
1974	3,285,411	591,581	404,745	1,844,036	130,349	314,701
1975	3,797,330	739,926	463,762	2,094,047	133,262	366,333
1976	4,238,116	881,685	514,895	2,296,677	132,886	411,974
TQ76	1,079,074	232,983	130,242	577,984	31,256	106,610
1977	4,701,901	1,046,174	566,829	2,488,563	124,329	476,007
1978	5,077,340	1,171,343	606,227	2,637,895	117,134	544,741
1979	5,554,098	1,320,729	660,947	2,830,670	109,545	632,208
1980	6,103,643	1,495,831	717,772	3,047,037	103,788	739,215
1981	6,939,022	1,748,185	804,521	3,392,715	100,985	892,615
1982	7,593,642	1,961,241	873,933	3,638,997	93,093	1,026,378
1983	8,006,995	2,120,410	913,501	3,761,227	82,418	1,129,439
1984	8,041,179	2,178,438	910,471	3,702,793	68,001	1,181,475
1985	8,270,080	2,292,011	928,320	3,727,176	57,362	1,265,211
1986	8,379,118	2,380,493	936,330	3,688,868	47,105	1,326,323
1987	8,424,213	2,473,735	940,540	3,611,755	37,954	1,360,230
1988	8,721,951	2,632,871	961,511	3,659,437	30,230	1,437,902
1989	8,936,619	2,790,531	985,560	3,596,365	23,879	1,540,285
1990	8,337,396	2,988,079	1,016,016	2,667,916	18,502	1,646,883
1991	9,612,170	3,202,536	1,031,311	3,590,606	14,076	1,773,641

(1) Beginning with FY 1988 data are for outlays.
(2) Excludes expenditures for World War I Emergency Officers and World War II Retired Reserve Officers.

F5-10. Expenditures/Outlays[1] for Disability Pension: 1967 to 1991

(In thousands of dollars)

Fiscal Year	Total	Vietnam Era	Korean Conflict	World War II	World War I	All Other
1967	1,263,193		22,139	312,462	914,304	14,288
1968	1,272,446	287	25,735	358,458	876,131	11,835
1969	1,317,919	1,062	30,359	418,715	858,141	9,643
1970	1,357,113	2,100	36,143	483,978	827,316	7,576
1971	1,386,343	3,416	42,671	555,299	778,880	6,078
1972	1,476,626	5,507	53,543	665,388	746,828	5,359
1973	1,476,651	7,644	62,936	732,359	669,524	4,188
1974	1,475,548	9,708	71,412	791,952	599,331	3,145
1975	1,572,884	13,447	88,731	912,194	555,819	2,694
1976	1,654,315	17,239	108,244	1,025,064	501,639	2,128
TQ76	414,906	5,057	29,593	264,199	115,611	447
1977	1,838,462	24,186	134,936	1,163,146	514,451	1,742
1978	1,926,998	29,750	154,119	1,244,048	497,629	1,452
1979	2,150,311	37,486	192,521	1,440,778	478,194	1,332
1980	2,227,079	51,085	230,476	1,511,355	433,300	863
1981	2,380,186	66,175	274,660	1,634,358	404,267	726
1982	2,458,382	82,502	313,087	1,694,386	367,859	548
1983	2,492,541	97,500	343,726	1,727,177	323,704	434
1984	2,491,975	110,050	370,157	1,730,943	280,449	376
1985	2,472,178	118,116	387,489	1,720,970	245,240	362
1986	2,471,454	128,890	409,257	1,720,403	212,579	325
1987	2,440,289	140,553	430,346	1,687,950	181,086	353
1988 (1)	2,502,525	160,739	466,447	1,720,864	153,938	537
1989	2,516,253	179,974	499,688	1,707,365	128,726	500
1990	2,666,954	208,939	541,097	1,809,741	106,436	741
1991	2,660,716	241,808	576,090	1,760,110	81,622	1,086

(1) Beginning with FY 1988 data are for outlays.

F5-11. Expenditures/Outlays for Dependency and Indemnity Compensation or Death Compensation: 1967 to 1991

(In thousands of dollars)

Fiscal Year	Total	Vietnam Era	Korean Conflict	World War II	World War I	All Other
1967	497,218		57,278	273,701	64,423	101,817
1968	516,693	19,458	58,117	276,410	64,049	98,660
1969	535,754	49,745	59,083	275,265	63,885	87,776
1970	594,618	71,499	63,303	289,972	72,568	97,275
1971	645,319	89,943	66,856	305,231	78,296	104,993
1972	699,677	104,188	72,011	326,593	83,741	113,145
1973	737,346	116,786	75,408	340,017	86,485	118,650
1974	760,060	127,252	78,005	346,176	87,336	121,291
1975	860,167	153,129	88,392	383,777	97,462	137,407
1976	955,956	179,556	98,544	420,409	106,371	151,077
TQ76	242,563	46,393	25,155	106,573	26,405	38,037
1977	1,046,240	205,585	108,254	454,739	111,894	165,768
1978	1,120,057	225,434	116,698	482,326	115,307	180,291
1979	1,215,677	247,151	127,137	521,698	121,220	198,470
1980	1,344,644	276,498	141,292	574,742	129,329	222,782
1981	1,534,942	322,344	162,774	651,066	141,160	257,598
1982	1,701,595	362,832	182,156	718,493	148,690	289,422
1983	1,825,997	395,607	197,114	769,299	150,725	313,251
1984	1,868,747	410,826	203,857	785,428	143,805	324,831
1985	1,957,986	437,990	216,188	821,884	139,866	342,057
1986	2,020,680	462,646	227,167	846,108	132,654	352,105
1987	2,062,303	485,876	235,332	859,619	123,436	358,041
1988 (1)	2,161,808	519,946	249,693	905,664	116,401	370,103
1989	2,247,408	555,947	265,100	933,750	108,738	383,873
1990	2,351,699	597,521	281,283	973,753	101,827	397,315
1991	2,482,294	654,453	297,897	1,022,795	95,011	412,138

(1) Beginning with FY 1988 data are for outlays.

F5-12. Expenditures/Outlays for Death Pension: 1967 to 1991

(In thousands of dollars)

Fiscal Year	Total	Vietnam Era	Korean Conflict	World War II	World War I	All Other
1967	712,330		33,979	290,847	343,978	43,527
1968	779,419	309	41,464	325,084	368,455	44,107
1969	849,216	944	48,921	356,334	400,314	42,703
1970	907,434	2,182	56,877	385,277	423,188	39,910
1971	963,656	4,480	64,947	409,686	447,477	37,066
1972	1,065,583	7,262	76,524	455,841	491,450	34,506
1973	1,097,844	10,096	85,462	478,348	491,533	32,406
1974	1,092,989	12,979	92,518	488,776	469,097	29,619
1975	1,153,096	17,302	105,329	530,500	472,564	27,402
1976	1,226,101	23,446	120,192	581,380	475,536	25,547
TQ76	303,917	6,745	31,113	144,759	115,272	6,029
1977	1,288,117	31,586	135,447	627,882	470,295	22,907
1978	1,331,359	38,737	145,970	656,487	469,105	21,059
1979	1,402,098	41,311	140,180	683,067	517,997	19,543
1980	1,369,088	38,845	127,550	672,289	511,505	18,899
1981	1,370,878	36,906	118,500	685,393	512,536	17,543
1982	1,379,048	36,228	114,075	693,235	519,138	16,373
1983	1,372,408	35,759	111,805	698,863	511,118	14,862
1984	1,346,020	33,482	108,875	693;574	496,509	13,580
1985	1,336,876	32,918	110,418	686,546	494,787	12,207
1986	1,347,904	31,788	117,832	691,744	495,118	11,422
1987	1,314,493	30,641	120,698	664,965	487,709	10,479
1988 (1)	1,323,936	30,886	130,672	675,067	477,234	10,076
1989	1,308,762	31,650	139,523	664,170	463,719	9,699
1990	1,318,362	34,319	151,578	669,967	453,017	9,481
1991	1,324,600	37,847	161,867	674,260	441,194	9,432

(1) Beginning with FY 1988 data are for outlays.

F5-13. Monthly Disability Compensation Age of Veteran, by Combined Degree of Impairment: September 1992

AGE	NUMBER	MO. VALUE	0%	10%	20%	30%	40%	50%	60%	70%	80%	90%	100%
15	2	$323		1		1							
16	2	$914			1	1							
17	5	$4,714							1	1	1	1	1
18	1	$83		1									
19	72	$15,412		45	16	6	1		1				3
20	466	$100,160		274	96	44	16	15	2	1	1		17
21	1,404	$308,264		843	283	113	61	30	17	4	3	1	49
22	2,765	$620,905		1670	539	235	102	62	33	18	8	4	94
23	4,409	$923,145	1	2693	854	378	165	83	55	26	18	3	133
24	5,753	$1,302,864	3	3392	1137	532	250	106	76	37	21	6	193
25	6,947	$1,572,861	2	3993	1442	665	303	135	88	51	23	19	226
26	7,839	$1,938,147	7	4350	1590	785	388	187	141	60	38	24	269
27	8,896	$2,291,665	7	4836	1775	918	441	226	181	94	58	21	339
28	10,153	$2,708,470	14	5399	1984	1162	516	279	196	102	69	28	404
29	10,944	$3,102,523	10	5620	2210	1200	615	327	258	112	56	32	504
30	11,806	$3,638,988	10	5892	2258	1377	684	375	277	172	89	33	639
31	13,141	$4,086,190	13	6361	2540	1527	828	475	342	197	90	36	732
32	13,955	$4,535,298	23	6694	2626	1652	900	482	341	238	106	58	835
33	15,549	$5,329,598	11	7437	2840	1794	963	606	396	274	109	48	1071
34	16,764	$5,624,615	15	8085	3009	1943	984	695	414	302	122	69	1126
35	18,569	$6,467,410	20	9028	3235	2118	1122	668	494	342	120	49	1373
36	20,127	$7,018,000	25	9684	3553	2309	1174	810	522	388	150	61	1451
37	21,242	$7,513,517	14	10165	3690	2470	1265	821	552	436	152	78	1599
38	22,479	$8,126,190	19	10701	3847	2600	1330	874	595	455	166	55	1837
39	24,161	$8,897,168	19	11280	4135	2856	1440	983	667	534	204	97	1946
40	27,923	$10,363,222	20	13005	4660	3323	1691	1222	799	604	236	111	2252
41	32,786	$12,643,624	18	14686	5443	4130	1979	1568	1040	751	321	174	2676
42	44,630	$18,284,126	31	19027	7015	5539	3107	2355	1619	1274	627	326	3710
43	61,645	$25,935,107	36	25274	9486	7962	4595	3252	2525	2000	1097	545	4873
44	72,837	$30,539,205	70	29520	11287	9237	5622	4061	3089	2382	1402	750	5417
45	76,014	$31,335,948	70	30645	12057	9951	6027	4145	3258	2417	1400	723	5321
46	60,823	$24,274,668	124	25214	9794	7940	4683	2948	2553	1823	1043	525	4176
47	42,750	$16,792,592	110	17703	7111	5606	3370	2004	1777	1171	631	323	2944
48	37,736	$14,690,648	175	15569	6473	5049	2966	1688	1494	942	520	260	2600
49	36,546	$14,017,285	193	15067	6332	4878	2961	1567	1507	887	475	238	2441
50	33,946	$12,844,376	186	13986	5958	4523	2853	1394	1450	749	450	200	2197

F5-13. Monthly Disability Compensation Age of Veteran, by Combined Degree of Impairment: September 1992 (continued)

AGE	NUMBER	MO. VALUE	0%	10%	20%	30%	40%	50%	60%	70%	80%	90%	100%
51	29,283	$10,993,079	185	11914	5319	4037	2411	1203	1188	627	355	162	1882
52	27,276	$10,243,758	201	11136	4940	3718	2185	1059	1171	602	354	157	1753
53	26,015	$9,521,762	237	10484	4859	3623	2170	949	1128	578	292	164	1531
54	26,791	$9,976,647	279	10540	5012	3755	2267	1011	1210	598	326	160	1633
55	27,668	$10,352,424	325	10921	5045	3934	2396	1038	1179	618	333	136	1743
56	29,260	$10,898,227	363	11634	5260	4078	2507	1082	1416	656	362	141	1761
57	30,067	$11,383,131	449	11845	5298	4230	2541	1154	1479	691	387	162	1831
58	32,025	$12,353,806	497	12377	5450	4552	2772	1330	1610	795	435	189	2018
59	35,832	$14,127,970	776	13626	6024	5058	3028	1488	1799	915	543	262	2313
60	42,936	$17,406,641	898	15871	7016	5964	3757	1957	2337	1226	773	338	2799
61	44,342	$18,038,198	858	15968	7213	6352	4019	2067	2505	1362	853	358	2787
62	46,079	$18,889,428	991	16324	7537	6502	4180	2270	2662	1450	872	381	2910
63	42,522	$17,538,847	946	15028	6867	6068	3937	2063	2400	1324	790	363	2736
64	39,818	$16,453,144	949	14304	6238	5651	3552	1863	2291	1233	795	272	2670
65	36,150	$14,695,117	1040	13664	5040	5402	2832	1633	2155	1079	658	201	2446
66	49,595	$19,171,079	1035	19515	7133	7198	3919	2473	2708	1416	916	375	2907
67	75,286	$28,783,422	1155	28394	10823	11326	6608	4225	4258	2467	1536	622	3872
68	82,872	$32,090,460	1183	30680	11963	12601	7467	4727	4778	2714	1739	699	4321
69	79,657	$30,724,801	1133	29806	11515	12236	7064	4512	4459	2537	1517	643	4235
70	82,759	$32,181,023	1137	30974	11962	12564	7285	4684	4752	2673	1710	628	4390
71	82,493	$32,054,655	1066	30801	12242	12285	7314	4715	4774	2556	1683	635	4422
72	74,040	$28,981,441	907	27361	11079	11079	6845	4084	4332	2454	1433	581	3885
73	68,373	$26,460,524	762	25468	10168	10276	6289	3895	4010	2245	1364	477	3419
74	61,157	$23,766,659	706	22840	9350	8938	5578	3429	3596	1986	1180	453	3101
75	47,759	$18,142,141	561	18088	7450	7001	4232	2571	2776	1524	893	346	2317
76	39,426	$14,998,770	434	14948	6149	5732	3572	2118	2406	1201	746	273	1847
77	32,563	$12,250,560	331	12563	5083	4599	2962	1730	1967	988	666	213	1461
78	26,732	$10,182,986	243	10101	4287	3791	2406	1467	1656	866	488	174	1253
79	21,176	$8,012,810	210	8117	3398	2935	1959	1102	1303	639	393	131	989
80	17,508	$6,551,613	169	6667	2854	2470	1618	939	1055	537	289	99	811
81	13,625	$5,090,029	112	5118	2312	1964	1249	694	819	425	240	92	600
82	11,188	$4,161,847	111	4250	1845	1574	1006	613	689	344	189	76	491
83	8,664	$3,210,139	73	3274	1523	1159	812	451	572	247	163	54	336
84	6,932	$2,534,936	57	2612	1235	945	660	373	426	207	120	35	262
85	5,578	$2,128,137	50	2064	980	728	550	281	364	187	97	31	246
86	3,926	$1,476,765	34	1444	706	538	372	206	259	122	51	19	175

F5-13. Monthly Disability Compensation Age of Veteran, by Combined Degree of Impairment: September 1992 (continued)

AGE	NUMBER	MO. VALUE	0%	10%	20%	30%	40%	50%	60%	70%	80%	90%	100%
87	2,426	$929,173	25	875	407	349	228	129	173	70	50	14	106
88	1,087	$441,780	18	340	190	155	128	65	73	34	24	7	53
89	753	$330,035	7	233	135	119	66	40	57	28	17	6	45
90	605	$252,695	8	195	105	85	70	40	29	18	15	5	35
91	451	$198,418	9	134	66	71	47	35	34	14	9	6	26
92	520	$230,637	10	145	102	67	58	30	41	19	7	3	38
93	448	$212,657	7	105	96	64	44	33	38	14	11	3	33
94	446	$203,511	5	118	104	61	35	24	29	23	13	2	32
95	308	$140,648	3	61	83	52	30	14	21	13	9		22
96	390	$163,258	6	86	105	62	43	22	15	13	10	1	27
97	347	$142,638	4	83	90	47	30	34	21	10	8	3	17
98	196	$86,156	3	56	41	25	16	12	19	8	4	1	11
99	129	$53,940	1	36	29	24	9	8	10	4	3	1	7
100	72	$38,299	1	17	14	9	9	3	6		4	1	8
101	51	$16,126	2	13	10	15	4	2	2	1			2
102	32	$20,374		5	6	6	3		5	2	2		3
103	25	$9,473		7	9	3	1	1	1		1		2
104	7	$8,131			1			1			1		3
105	6	$4,445	1	1	1	1		1	1				1
106	5	$2,470		1	1		1			1		1	
107	9	$5,971		3	1	1	1				1		1
108	5	$2,805	1	3					2	2	1		
109	6	$5,254				1	1	1	1	1		1	1
110	4	$3,542		1			2						1
111	5	$3,020		4	1	1	1	1	1	1			
112	7	$2,097				1			1				
113	3	$1,101		1		2	1						
114	5	$1,549											
BLANK	133	$26,800		82	19	16	2	1	2	2			4

F5-14. VA Nursing Home Census*: FY 1988 to 2010

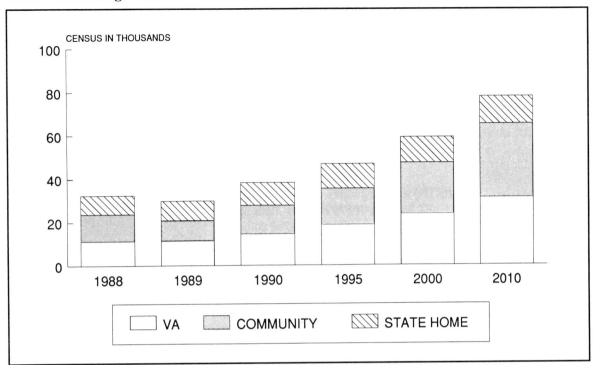

*Average Daily Census.
Source: Department of Veterans Affairs.

Guide to Relevant Information Resources

Many federal agencies and private organizations provide statistical information on a great variety of topics. The Bureau of the Census, the Bureau of Labor Statistics, the National Center for Health Statistics, and the National Center for Education Statistics are the major government sources for the collection and analysis of statistical data. Most private organizations base their analyses on data collected by government agencies. This handbook was created to simplify the task of researchers who want to locate data on aging Americans. For users who need more specific or detailed information, contacts for statistical agencies and other organizations concerned with the aging population are provided below. The Census Bureau "Telephone Contacts for Data Users," which is reproduced here, lists all offices that produce statistics on specific topics.

American Association of Retired Persons
601 E Street, NW
Washington, DC 20049
Information Center: (202) 434-6240

Federal Council on Aging
330 Independence Avenue, SW
Washington, DC 20201
(202) 479-1200

Population Reference Bureau
1875 Connecticut Avenue, NW
Suite 520
Washington, DC 20009
(202) 483-1100

U.S. Department of Commerce
Bureau of the Census
Washington, DC 20233
Aging Population: Arnold Goldstein, Cynthia Taeuber
(301) 763-7883

U.S. Department of Education
National Center for Education Statistics
Washington, DC 20208-5652
(202) 219-1659

U.S. Department of Health and Human Services
Administration on Aging
Washington, DC 20201
(202) 619-0724

U.S. Department of Health and Human Services
National Center for Health Statistics
6525 Belcrest Road
Hyattsville, MD
(301) 436-8500
Health Data on Older Americans: (301) 436-7104

U.S. Department of Health and Human Services
National Institute on Aging
Gateway Bldg 2C-234
7201 Wisconsin Ave
Bethesda, MD 20892
(301) 496-3136

U.S. Department of Health and Human Services
Social Security Administration
Office of Research and Statistics
4301 Connecticut Avenue, Suite 209
Washington, DC 20008
Income of Older Americans: Susan Grad (202) 282-7094

U.S. Department of Justice
Bureau of Justice Statistics
Drugs and Crime Data Center
1600 Research Boulevard
Rockville, MD 20850
(800) 666-3332

U.S. Department of Labor
Bureau of Labor Statistics
441 G Street, NW
Washington, DC 20212
(202) 523-1208
Older Workers: Philip Rones (202) 523-1944

United States Senate
Special Committee on Aging
Washington, DC 20510
(202) 224-5364

U.S. BUREAU OF THE CENSUS

telephone contacts for data users

April 1993

Use area code 301 unless otherwise noted.

General Information Contacts

Frequently called numbers

Census Customer Services
(Data product & ordering information for computer tapes,
CD-ROM's, microfiche, & some publications) 763-4100
  FAX 763-4794
  TDD 763-2811
Agriculture Information 1-800-523-3215
Business Information 763-1792
Census Job Information (Recording) 763-6064
Census Personnel Locator 763-7662
Congressional Affairs 763-2446
Foreign Trade Information .... 763-5140 / 7754
General Information 763-4100
Library 763-5042
Population Information .... 763-5002 / 5020 (TTY)
Public Information Office (Press) 763-4040

Census regional offices
(Information services, data product information)

Atlanta, GA 404-730-3833
Boston, MA 617-565-7078
Charlotte, NC 704-344-6144
Chicago, IL 312-353-0980
Dallas, TX 214-767-7105
Denver, CO 303-969-7750
Detroit, MI 313-354-4654
Kansas City, KS 913-236-3711
Los Angeles, CA 818-904-6339
New York, NY 212-264-4730
Philadelphia, PA 215-597-8313
Seattle, WA 206-728-5314

Regional Office Liaison — FLD 763-4683

U.S. Department of Commerce
Economics and Statistics Administration
BUREAU OF THE CENSUS

Data products — reference

Bulletin Board — Nancy Smith (DUSD) 763-1580
CENDATA (Online Service) — DUSD 763-2074
Census & You (Newsletter) —
  Neil Tillman (DUSD) 763-1584
Census Catalog — John McCall (DUSD) 763-1584
County & City, State & Metropolitan Area
  Data Books — Wanda Cevis (DUSD) 763-1034
Factfinders (General information booklets) —
  Frederick Bohme (DUSD) 763-7936
Guides — Gary Young (DUSD) 763-1584
Historical Statistics — DUSD 763-1034
Monthly Product Announcement —
  Mary Kilbride (DUSD) 763-1584
Statistical Abstract — Glenn King (DUSD) 763-5299
Statistical Briefs —
  Robert Bernstein (DUSD) 763-1584

Other key contacts

Access to Census Records (Age Search) —
  DPD 812-285-5314
Census History —
  Frederick Bohme (DUSD) 763-7936
Confidentiality & Privacy —
  Jerry Gates (PPDO) 763-5063
Economic Studies — Arnold Reznek (CES) ... 763-2705
Education Support — George Daily /
  Dorothy Jackson (DUSD) 763-1510
Exhibits & Conventions —
  Joanne Dickinson (DUSD) 763-2370
International Visitors Program —
  Nina Pane Pinto / Gene Vandrovec (ISPC) ... 763-2839
Legislation — Thomas Jones (PPDO) 763-4001
Litigation — Valerie Gregg (PPDO) 763-7787
Marketing — DUSD 763-1510
Microdata Files —
  Carmen Campbell (DUSD) 763-2005
Statistical Research:
  Demographic — Lawrence Ernst (SRD) 763-7880
  Economic — C. Easley Hoy (SRD) 763-5702
1990 Census Tabulations & Publications —
  U.S.: Gloria Porter (DMD) 763-3938
  Puerto Rico & Outlying Areas —
    Lourdes Flaim (DMD) 763-2903

2   Census Bureau Telephone Contacts

Business Economics

Agriculture

Crop Statistics — Donald Jahnke (AGR) 763-8567
Data Requirements & Outreach —
     Douglas Miller (AGR) 763-8561
Farm Economics — James Liefer (AGR) 763-8514
General Information —
     Tom Manning (AGR) 1-800-523-3215
Irrigation & Horticulture Statistics —
     John Blackledge (AGR) 763-8559
Livestock Statistics — Linda Hutton (AGR) 763-8569
Puerto Rico, Virgin Islands, Guam, Northern
     Marianas, & American Samoa —
     Kent Hoover (AGR) 763-8564
Special Surveys & Custom Tabulations —
     John Blackledge (AGR) 763-8559

U.S. Bureau of the Census Telephone Contacts for Data Users

Editor: Mary G. Thomas   April 1993

To contact any of the specialists by mail, use their name, the division, and the address — Bureau of the Census, Washington, DC 20233. To receive copies of *U.S. Bureau of the Census Telephone Contacts for Data Users,* contact Customer Services (301-763-4100). Send comments on this publication to Mary G. Thomas, DUSD, Bureau of the Census, Washington, DC 20233 (301-763-1584).

Key to Office Abbreviations

AGR	Agriculture
BUS	Business
CES	Center for Economic Studies
CIR	Center for International Research
CSD	Construction Statistics Division
CSMR	Center for Survey Methods Research
DMD	Decennial Management Division
DPD	Data Preparation Division
DSD	Demographic Surveys Division
DSMD	Demographic Statistical Methods Division
DSSD	Decennial Statistical Studies Division
DUSD	Data User Services Division
ECSD	Economic Census & Surveys Division
EPD	Economic Programming Division
ESMD	Economic Statistical Methods Division
FLD	Field Division
FTD	Foreign Trade Division
GEO	Geography
GOVS	Governments
HHES	Housing & Household Economic Statistics
IND	Industry
ISPC	International Statistical Program Center
PIO	Public Information Office
POP	Population
PPDO	Program & Policy Development Office
SRD	Statistical Research Division
2KS	Year 2000 Research & Development Staff

Communications & utilities

Census — Dennis Shoemaker (BUS) 763-2662
Current Programs —
     Tom Zabelsky (BUS) 763-5528

Construction

Building Permits — Linda Hoyle (CSD) 763-7244
Census — Bill Visnansky (CSD) 763-7546
Construction in MSA's —
     Joseph Gilvary (CSD) 763-7842
Housing Starts & Completions —
     David Fondelier (CSD) 763-5731
Residential Characteristics, Price Index, Sales —
     Steve Berman (CSD) 763-7842
Residential Improvements & Repairs —
     George Roff (CSD) 763-5705
Value of New Construction —
     Allan Meyer (CSD) 763-5717

Finance, insurance, & real estate

Census — Sidney Marcus (BUS) 763-1386

Foreign trade

Data Services —
     Haydn Mearkle (FTD) .... 763-5140 / 7754
Shipper's Declaration —
     Hal Blyweiss (FTD) 763-5310

Manufacturing

Concentration, Exports From Manufacturing
     Establishments, & Production Index —
     Bruce Goldhirsch (IND) 763-1503
Durables:
     Census & Annual Survey —
       Kenneth Hansen (IND) 763-7304
     Current Industrial Reports — Ken McBeth /
       Milbren Thomas (IND) 763-2518
Fuels & Electric Energy Consumed —
     John McNamee (IND) 763-5938
Industries — John P. Govoni (IND) 763-7666
Monthly Shipments, Inventories, Orders —
     Steve Andrews (IND) 763-2502
Nondurables:
     Census & Annual Survey —
       Michael Zampogna (IND) 763-2510
     Current Industrial Reports —
       Judy Dodds (IND) 763-5911
Research & Development, Capacity,
     Pollution Abatement —
     Elinor Champion (IND) 763-5616

Retail trade

Advance Monthly —
     Ronald Piencykoski (BUS) 763-5294
Census — Anne Russell (BUS) 763-7038
Monthly Report — Irving True (BUS) 763-7128

Services

Census — Jack Moody (BUS) 763-7039
Current Reports — Thomas Zabelsky (BUS) ... 763-5528

Use area code 301 unless otherwise noted.

Census Bureau Telephone Contacts   3

Transportation

Census — Dennis Shoemaker (BUS) 763-2662
Commodity Flow Survey —
    John Fowler (BUS) 763-6087
Truck Inventory and Use —
    Bill Bostic (BUS) 763-2735
Warehousing & Trucking —
    Tom Zabelsky (BUS) 763-5528

Wholesale trade

Census — John Trimble (BUS) 763-5281
Current Sales & Inventories —
    Nancy Piesto (BUS) 763-3916

Special topics

Business Owners — Eddie Salyers (ECSD) ... 763-5470
Census Products — Paul Zeisset (ECSD) 763-1792

County Business Patterns —
    Zigmund Decker (ECSD) 763-5430
Enterprise Statistics —
    Eddie Salyers (ECSD) 763-5470
Industry & Commodity Classification —
    James Kristoff (ECSD) 763-1935
Investment in Plant & Equipment —
    John Gates (IND) 763-5596
Mineral Industries —
    John McNamee (IND) 763-5938
Minority- & Women-Owned Businesses —
    Eddie Salyers (ECSD) 763-5470
Quarterly Financial Report —
    Paul Zarrett (ECSD) 763-2718
Puerto Rico & Outlying Areas —
    Kent Hoover (AGR) .... 763-8559 / 8564

Demographics & Population

Aging Population, U.S. —
    Arnold Goldstein (POP) 763-7883
Ancestry — Susan Lapham (POP) 763-7955
Apportionment — Robert Speaker (POP) 763-7962
Child Care — Martin O'Connell /
    Amara Bachu (POP) .... 763-5303 / 4547
Children — Donald Hernandez (POP) 763-7987
Citizenship — Susan Lapham (POP) 763-7955
Commuting, Means of Transportation, &
    Place of Work — Phil Salopek /
    Celia Boertlein (POP) 763-3850
Crime — Gail Hoff (DSD) 763-1735
Current Population Survey:
  General Information — DUSD 763-4100
  Questionnaire Content —
    Ron Tucker (DSD) 763-2773
  Sampling Methods —
    Preston Waite (DSMD) 763-2672
Disability — Jack McNeil /
    Bob Bennefield (HHES) .... 763-8300 / 8578
Education — POP 763-1154
Equal Employment Opportunity Data —
    Tom Scopp (HHES) 763-8199
Fertility & Births — Martin O'Connell /
    Amara Bachu (POP) .... 763-5303 /4547
Foreign Born — Susan Lapham (POP) 763-7955
Group Quarters Population —
    Denise Smith (POP) 763-2784
Health Surveys — Robert Mangold (DSD) 763-5684
Hispanic & Ethnic Statistics — POP 763-7955
Homeless — Annetta Clark (POP) 763-2784
Household Estimates — POP 763-5002
Households & Families —
    Steve Rawlings (POP) 763-7987
Immigration (Legal / Undocumented) & Emigration —
    Edward Fernandez (POP) 763-5590

Journey to Work — Phil Salopek /
    Gloria Swieczkowski (POP) 763-3850
Language — POP 763-1154
Longitudinal Surveys —
    Sarah Higgins (DSD) 763-2767
Marital Status & Living Arrangements —
    Arlene Saluter (POP) 763-7987
Metropolitan Areas (MA's):
  Population — POP 763-5002
  Standards — James Fitzsimmons (POP) 763-5158
Migration — Kristen Hansen /
    Diana DeAre (POP) 763-3850
National Estimates & Projections — POP 763-5002
Outlying Areas — Michael Levin (POP) 763-5134
Place of Birth — Kristin Hansen (POP) 763-3850
Population Information — POP ... 763-5002 / 5020 (TTY)
Prisoner Surveys — Gail Hoff (DSD) 763-1735
Puerto Rico — Lourdes Flaim (DMD) 763-2903
Race Statistics — POP .... 763-2607 / 7572
Reapportionment & Redistricting —
    Marshall Turner, Jr. (DUSD) 763-3856
Sampling Methods, Decennial Census —
    Henry Woltman (DSSD) 763-5987
School District Data — Jane Ingold (POP) 763-5476
Special Population Censuses —
    Elaine Csellar (ISPC) 763-5604
Special Surveys — Sarah Higgins (DSD) 763-2767
Special Tabulations — Rose Cowan (POP) 763-5476
State & County Estimates — POP 763-5002
State Projections — POP 763-5002
Travel Surveys — John Cannon (DSD) 763-5468
Undercount, Demographic Analysis —
    Gregg Robinson (POP) 763-5590
Veterans Status — Thomas Palumbo /
    Selwyn Jones (HHES) 763-8574
Women — Denise Smith (POP) 763-2784

Use area code 301 unless otherwise noted.

4 Census Bureau Telephone Contacts

Geographic Concepts

Annexations, Boundary Changes —
Nancy Goodman (GEO) 763-3827
Area Measurement — Jim Davis (GEO) 763-3827
Census Geographic Concepts — GEO 763-3827
State Boundary Certification —
Louise Stewart (GEO) 763-3827
Census Tracts — Cathy Miller (GEO) 763-3827
Centers of Population — Jim Davis (GEO) 763-3827
Congressional Districts:
Address Allocations — GEO 763-5692
Boundaries, Component Areas —
Cathy McCully (GEO) 763-3827
Fee-Paid Block Splits — Joel Miller (GEO) 763-3827
FIPS Codes — Virgeline Davis (GEO) 763-3827
Maps:
Computer Mapping —
Fred Broome (GEO) 763-3973
School Districts — Dave Aultman (GEO) 763-3827
1980 Census Map Orders —
Ann Devore (DPD) 812-288-3192
1990 Census Maps — DUSD 763-4100

Metropolitan Areas —
James Fitzsimmons (POP) 763-5158
Outlying Areas — Virgeline Davis (GEO) 763-3827
TIGER System:
Applications & Product Information —
Larry Carbaugh (DUSD) 763-1384
Future Plans — GEO 763-4664
Product Sales — DUSD 763-4100
Urban / Rural Residence —
Robert Speaker (POP) 763-7962
Urbanized Areas & Urban / Rural Concepts —
Nancy Torrieri (GEO) 763-3827
User-Defined Areas Program (Neighborhood
Statistics) — Adrienne Quasney (DMD) 763-4282
Voting Districts — Cathy McCully (GEO) 763-3827
ZIP Codes:
Demographic Data — DUSD 763-4100
Economic Data — Anne Russell (BUS) 763-7038
Geographic Relationships —
Rose Quarato (GEO) 763-4667

Governments

Criminal Justice — Alan Stevens (GOVS) 763-7789
Employment — Larry McDonald (GOVS) 763-5086
Federal Expenditure Data —
Robert McArthur (GOVS) 763-5276
Finance — Gerard Keffer (GOVS) 763-5356

Governmental Organization —
Alan Stevens (GOVS) 763-7789
Survey Operations —
Genevieve Speight (GOVS) 763-7783
Taxation — Gerard Keffer (GOVS) 763-5356

Housing

American Housing Survey —
Edward Montfort (HHES) 763-8551
Census — Bill Downs (HHES) 763-8553
Components of Inventory Change Survey —
Barbara Williams (HHES) 763-8551

Market Absorption / Residential Finance —
Anne Smoler / Peter Fronczek (HHES) 763-8165
New York City Housing & Vacancy Survey —
Margaret Harper (HHES) 763-8171
Vacancy Data —
Wallace Fraser / Robert Callis (HHES) 763-8165

Income, Poverty, & Wealth

Consumer Expenditure Survey —
Ron Dopkowski (DSD) 763-2063
Household Wealth — T. J. Eller (HHES) 763-8578
Income Statistics — HHES 763-8576
Poverty Statistics — HHES 763-8578

Survey of Income & Program Participation
(SIPP) — Enrique Lamas (HHES) 763-8018
General Information — Don Fischer (DSD) 763-2764
Microdata Files—
Carmen Campbell (DUSD) 763-2005
Statistical Methods — Raj Singh (DSMD) ... 763-7944

International Statistics

Africa, Asia, Latin America, North America,
& Oceania — Frank Hobbs (CIR) 763-4221
Aging Population — Kevin Kinsella (CIR) 763-4884
China, People's Republic —
Loraine West (CIR) 763-4012
Europe — Godfrey Baldwin (CIR) 763-4020

Former Soviet Union — Marc Rubin (CIR) 763-4020
Health — Karen Stanecki (CIR) 763-4086
International Data Base —
Peter Johnson (CIR) 763-4811
Women in Development —
Patricia Rowe (CIR) 763-4221

Use area code 301 unless otherwise noted.

Census Bureau Telephone Contacts   5

Labor Force

Commuting, Means of Transportation, & Place
of Work — Phil Salopek /
Celia Boertlein (POP) 763-3850
Employment & Unemployment — Thomas Palumbo /
Selwyn Jones (HHES) 763-8574

Journey to Work — Phil Salopek /
Gloria Swieczkowski (POP) 763-3850
Occupation & Industry Statistics —
HHES 763-8574

State & Local Data Centers

Business / Industry Data Centers —
John Rowe (DUSD) 763-1580
Clearinghouse for Census Data Services —
Larry Carbaugh (DUSD) 763-1384

National Census Information Centers —
Barbara Harris (DUSD) 763-1580
State Data Center Program —
Sam Johnson (DUSD) 763-1580

State data centers (SDC's) and business / industry data centers (BIDC's)

(All States have SDC's. Data centers are usually State government agencies, universities, and libraries that head up a network of affiliate centers. Below we list the SDC and BIDC lead agency contacts. Asterisks identify States that also have BIDC's. In some States, one agency serves as the lead for both the SDC and the BIDC; we list the BIDC separately where there is a separate agency serving as the lead.)

Alabama — Annette Watters,
University of Alabama 205-348-6191
Alaska — Kathryn Lizik,
Department of Labor 907-465-6026
* **Arizona** — Betty Jeffries,
Department of Security 602-542-5984
Arkansas — Sarah Breshears, University
of Arkansas at Little Rock 501-569-8530
California — Linda Gage,
Department of Finance 916-322-4651
Colorado — Reid Reynolds,
Department of Local Affairs 303-866-2156
* **Connecticut** — Bill Kraynak,
Office of Policy & Management 203-566-8285
* **Delaware** — Judy McKinney-Cherry,
Development Office 302-739-4271
District of Columbia — Gan Ahuja,
Mayor's Office of Planning 202-727-6533
* **Florida** — Steve Kimble,
State Data Center 904-487-2814
BIDC — Amy Schmeling,
Department of Commerce 904-487-2971
Georgia — Marty Sik,
Office of Planning & Budget 404-656-0911
Guam — Peter Barcinas,
Department of Commerce 671-646-5841
Hawaii — Jan Nakamoto,
Department of Business &
Economic Development & Tourism 808-586-2493
Idaho — Alan Porter,
Department of Commerce 208-334-2470
Illinois — Suzanne Ebetsch,
Bureau of the Budget 217-782-1381
* **Indiana** — Roberta Eads,
State Library 317-232-3733
BIDC — Carol Rogers,
Business Research Center 317-274-2205
Iowa — Beth Henning, State Library 515-281-4350

Kansas — Marc Galbraith,
State Library 913-296-3296
* **Kentucky** — Ron Crouch, Center
for Urban & Economic Research 502-588-7990
Louisiana — Karen Paterson, Office of
Planning & Budget 504-342-7410
Maine — Jean Martin,
Department of Labor 207-289-2271
* **Maryland** — Robert Dadd / Jayne Traynham,
Department of State Planning 410-225-4450
* **Massachusetts** — Stephen Coelen,
University of Massachusetts 413-545-3460
Michigan — Eric Swanson, Department
of Management & Budget 517-373-7910
* **Minnesota** — David Birkholz,
State Demographer's Office 612-297-2557
BIDC — David Rademacher,
State Demographer's Office 612-297-3255
* **Mississippi** — Rachael McNeely,
University of Mississippi 601-232-7288
BIDC — Bill Rigby, Division of
Research & Information System 601-359-2674
* **Missouri** — Kate Graf, State Library 314-751-1823
BIDC — Max E. Summers, Small
Business Development Centers 314-882-0344
* **Montana** — Patricia Roberts,
Department of Commerce 406-444-2896
Nebraska — Jerome Deichert /
Tim Himberger, University of
Nebraska-Omaha 402-595-2311
Nevada — Betty McNeal,
State Library 702-687-8326
New Hampshire — Thomas J. Duffy,
Office of State Planning 603-271-2155
* **New Jersey** — Connie O. Hughes,
Department of Labor 609-984-2593
* **New Mexico** — Kevin Kargacin,
University of New Mexico 505-277-6626
BIDC — Bobby Leitch, University
of New Mexico 505-277-2216

Use area code 301 unless otherwise noted.

6   Census Bureau Telephone Contacts

* **New York** — Robert Scardamalia,
  Department of Economic Development .. 518-474-1141
* **North Carolina** — Francine Stephenson,
  Office of State Planning 919-733-4131
  North Dakota — Dr. Richard Rathge,
  North Dakota State University 701-237-8621
* **Ohio** — Barry Bennett,
  Department of Development 614-466-2115
* **Oklahoma** — Jeff Wallace,
  Department of Commerce 405-841-5184
  Oregon — Maria Wilson-Figueroa,
  Portland State University 503-725-5159
* **Pennsylvania** — Michael Behney,
  Pennsylvania State University
  at Harrisburg 717-948-6336
  Puerto Rico — Jose Jiminez,
  Planning Board 809-728-4430
  Rhode Island — Paul Egan,
  Department of Administration 401-277-6493
  South Carolina — Mike MacFarlane,
  Budget & Control Board 803-734-3780
  South Dakota — DeVee Dykstra,
  University of South Dakota 605-677-5287
  Tennessee — Charles Brown,
  State Planning Office 615-741-1676

  Texas — Susan Tully,
  Department of Commerce 512-320-9667
* **Utah** — Julie Johnson,
  Office of Planning & Budget 801-538-1036
  Vermont — Sybil McShane,
  Department of Libraries 802-828-3261
  Virgin Islands — Frank Mills,
  University of the Virgin Islands 809-776-9200
  Virginia — Dan Jones,
  Virginia Employment Commission 804-786-8308
* **Washington** — George Hough,
  Office of Financial Management 206-586-2504
* **West Virginia** — Mary C. Harless,
  Office of Community &
  Industrial Development 304-558-4010
  BIDC — Randy Childs,
  Center for Economic Research 304-293-7832
* **Wisconsin** — Robert Naylor,
  Department of Administration 608-265-1927
  BIDC — Michael Knight,
  University of Wisconsin-Madison 608-265-3044
  Wyoming — Steve Furtney,
  Department of Administration &
  Fiscal Control 307-777-7504

National census information centers

(National Census Information Centers, in partnership with the Census Bureau, coordinate information networks that disseminate census data on the Black, Hispanic, Asian, and Pacific Islander, and American Indian/Alaska Native populations.)

Asian / Pacific Islander Data Consortium,
San Francisco — Clarissa Tom 415-541-0866
IndianNet Information Center,
Washington, DC — Ellen Hornbeck 202-544-7743
National Council of La Raza,
Washington, DC — Sonia Perez 202-289-1380

National Urban League, Washington, DC —
Billy Tidwell 202-898-1604
Southwest Voter Research Institute,
San Antonio, Texas —
Robert Brischetto 210-222-8014

U.S. Bureau of the Census Management

Director —
Harry A. Scarr (Acting) 763-5190

Associate Directors

Administration .... Vacant

Decennial Census —
Charles D. Jones 763-5180

Demographic Programs —
William P. Butz 763-5167

Economic Programs —
Charles A. Waite 763-5274

Field Operations —
Bryant Benton 763-7980

Information Technology .... Vacant

Statistical Design, Methodology, & Standards —
Robert D. Tortora 763-2562

Assistant Directors

Administration —
Clifford J. Parker 763-2350

Automated Data Processing —
Arnold A. Jackson 763-2360

Communications —
Clifford J. Parker (Acting) 763-2350

Decennial Censuses —
Peter A. Bounpane 763-5613

Economic Censuses —
Roger H. Bugenhagen 763-2076

Use area code 301 unless otherwise noted.

Glossary

(Based on definitions found in listed sources. Terms defined in head or footnotes are not repeated here.)

ADL. Personal activities of daily living, such as eating, toileting, dressing, walking, and getting in and out of bed.

Aged Unit. A housing unit owned, rented, or maintained by an elderly person.

Assets. Interest-earning assets (bank accounts, bonds, U.S. government securities), stocks and mutual fund shares, real estate, mortgages, own business or profession, motor vehicles.

CHAMPUS. Civilian Health and Medical Program of the Uniformed Services. All active and retired military personnel and their dependents are eligible for medical treatment at any Department of Defense medical facility. CHAMPUS provides reimbursement for covered medical care rendered in civilian facilities to dependents of active, retired, or deceased military personnel.

Civilian labor force. The civilian labor force comprises all civilians 15 years old or over classified as employed or unemployed.

Civilian noninstitutional population. The U.S. population excluding military personnel and their families living on post, and inmates of institutions.

CPI. Consumer Price Index. Measures the average change in the cost of a fixed market basket of goods and services purchased by consumers.

CPI-U. CPI for all urban consumers.

CPS. Current Population Survey. Continuing monthly series of surveys of a sample of the civilian noninstitutional population conducted by the Bureau of the Census.

Death rate. Number of deaths per 100,000 population. Actual number is crude death rate. Number calculated to show what the number of deaths would be if there were no changes in the age composition of the population from year to year is the age adjusted death rate.

Educational attainment. The highest grade of regular school attended and completed.

Elderly. Persons over 65 years of age.

Employed. Employed persons comprise all civilians who during a survey week did any work as paid employees or in their own business, profession, or farm, or who were only temporarily absent from their jobs or businesses.

Enrollment. The total number of students registered in a given school unit at a given time, generally in the fall of a year.

Family. A group of two or more persons related by birth, marriage, or adoption who reside together.

Farm/nonfarm residence. A farm is any place in rural territory from which $1,000 or more of agricultural products were sold in the reporting year. All other households are classified as nonfarm, whether living in urban or rural areas but not on farms.

Food Stamp Program. Provides eligible households with coupons that can be used to purchase food to permit low-income households to obtain a more nutritious diet.

Gini Ratio. Index of income concentration; a statistical measure of income equality, ranging from 0 to 1.

GNP. Gross National Product. The total national output of goods and services valued at market prices.

Government transfer payments. Include Social Security, railroad retirement, public assistance, welfare payments, Supplemental Security Income, retirement and annuities, veteran's payments, and unemployment and worker's compensation.

Group quarters. Noninstitutional living arrangements for groups living in unconventional housing units containing nine or more persons who are unrelated to the person in charge. Military quarters, college dormitories, rooming houses, and halfway houses are defined as group quarters.

Head of household. *See* Householder.

Hispanic origin. Persons indicating that their origin is Mexican, Puerto Rican, Cuban, Central American, Spanish South American, or other Spanish origin, according to self-identification in response to census origin or descent question.

Household. Consists of all persons—related family members and unrelated persons—who occupy a housing unit. The count of households excludes group quarters.

Householder. The person in whose name a housing unit is owned, rented, or maintained.

IADL. Instrumental activities of daily living requiring tools or appliances, such as preparing meals, shopping, using the telephone, cleaning house.

Institutions. Institutions include correctional institutions, mental and chronic disease hospitals, homes for the aged, and special schools.

Labor force/not in the labor force. Persons are classified as in the labor force if they were employed as civilians, unemployed, or in the Armed Forces during the survey week. The "civilian labor force" comprises all civilians classified as employed or unemployed. All civilians 15 years old and over who are not classified as employed or unemployed are defined as "not in the labor force."

Married couple. A married couple is a husband and wife enumerated as members of the same household.

Medicaid. The Medicaid program is administered by state agencies through grants from the Health Care Financing Administration of the Department of Health and Human Services to furnish medical assistance to needy families with dependent children, and aged, blind, or disabled individuals whose incomes and resources are insufficient to meet the costs of necessary medical services.

Medicare. The Medicare program provides adequate medical care for the aged and disabled.

Migration. Geographic mobility involving a change of usual residence between clearly defined geographic units, that is, between counties, states, or regions.

Money earnings. The sum of money wages or salary and net income from farm and nonfarm self-employment.

Money income. Money income excluding capital gains before taxes.

MSA. Metropolitan Statistical Area. A large population nucleus and nearby communities that have a high degree of economic and social integration with that nucleus. An MSA must include a city of at least 50,000 population.

Net worth. Value of assets less any debts. *See also* Assets.

Noncash benefits. Benefits received in a form other than money that serve to enhance or improve the economic well-being of the recipient, such as food stamps, school lunches, subsidized housing, Medicare, Medicaid, and military health care.

OASDI. Old-Age, Survivors, and Disability Insurance under Social Security.

Occupation. Persons are classified according to the civilian job held longest during the year. Occupational groupings are based on the 1980 Standard Occupational Classification System (SOC) of the Bureau of the Census.

Poverty. Persons and families are classified as being above or below poverty level according to the Federal Interagency Committee Poverty Index. The index is based solely on money income and is updated every year to reflect changes in the Consumer Price Index.

Public assistance/welfare payments. Include Aid to Families with Dependent Children, Supplemental Security Income (SSI), and general cash assistance.

Resident population. Includes civilian population and armed forces personnel residing within the United States. Excludes armed forces personnel residing overseas.

Rural population. *See* Urban population.

SES. Socioeconomic Status Index. A composite of father's education, mother's education, family income, father's occupation, and household items.

SIPP. Survey of Income and Program Participation. Conducted by the Bureau of the Census.

SMSA Standard Metropolitan Statistical Area. *See* MSA.

SOC. Standard Occupational Classification System. *See also* Occupation.

Social Security. Includes Social Security pensions and survivors benefits, and permanent disability insurance payments made by the Social Security Administration.

SSI. Supplemental Security Income. Includes payments made by federal, state, and local welfare agencies to low-income persons who are 65 years old or over, blind, and/or disabled.

Subfamily. A married couple with or without children, or one parent with one or more children living in a household, but not including among its members the person or couple maintaining the household. Because a subfamily does not include the householder, it is excluded from the count of families. *See also* Family, Household, Householder.

Supplemental Security Income. *See* SSI.

Unemployed. Civilian persons who, during a survey week, had no employment but were available for work and had engaged in job-seeking activity within the past four weeks, were waiting to be called back to a job, or were waiting to report for a new job.

Urban Population. Persons living in an urbanized area comprising one or more places and the adjacent densely settled territory that together have a minimum population of 50,000 persons.

List of Sources

A. DEMOGRAPHICS

A1. Age and Sex Distribution

A1-1 Taeuber, Cynthia M. *Sixty-Five Plus in America.* U.S. Department of Commerce, Bureau of the Census, unpublished series of tables and charts, 1992, n.p.

A1-2 Taeuber. *Sixty-Five Plus in America,* unpublished series, n.p.

A1-3 Taeuber. *Sixty-Five Plus in America,* unpublished series, n.p.

A1-4 Taeuber. *Sixty-Five Plus in America,* unpublished series, n.p.

A1-5 Taeuber. *Sixty-Five Plus in America,* unpublished series, n.p.

A1-6 Taeuber. *Sixty-Five Plus in America,* unpublished series, n.p.

A1-7 *Statistical Abstract of the United States, 1992.* U.S. Department of Commerce, Bureau of the Census, Economics and Statistics Administration, 1992, p. 19.

A1-8 "Elderly Population Growth in the 1980's." *Census and You,* Vol. 27, No. 4 (April 1992), p. 5.

A1-9 Taeuber, Cynthia M. *Sixty-Five Plus in America.* U.S. Department of Commerce, Bureau of the Census, Current Population Reports, P23-178, August 1992, p. 2-2 (revised).

A1-10 Taeuber. *Sixty-Five Plus in America,* August 1992, p. 2-10 (revised).

A1-11 Taeuber. *Sixty-Five Plus in America,* August 1992, p. 1-2.

A1-12 Taeuber. *Sixty-Five Plus in America,* August 1992, p. 1-2 (revised).

A1-13 Taeuber. *Sixty-Five Plus in America,* August 1992, p. 2-8 (revised).

A1-14 Taeuber. *Sixty-Five Plus in America,* August 1992, p. 2-9 (revised).

A1-15 Taeuber. *Sixty-Five Plus in America,* August 1992, p. 2-9 (revised).

A2. Life Expectancy

A2-1 *Statistical Abstract of the United States, 1992.* U.S. Department of Commerce, Bureau of the Census, Economics and Statistics Administration, 1992, p. 77.

A2-2 *Statistical Abstract of the United States, 1992,* p. 76.

A2-3 "Advance Report of Final Mortality Statistics, 1990." *Monthly Vital Statistics Report,* Vol. 41, No. 7, Supplement (7 January 1993), p. 5.

A2-4 Taeuber, Cynthia M. *Sixty-Five Plus in America.* U.S. Department of Commerce, Bureau of the Census, Current Population Reports, P23-178, August 1992, p. 3-1.

A2-5 Based on J.F. Van Nostrand, S.E. Furner, and R. Suzman. *Health Data on Older Americans, United States, 1992.* U.S. Department of Health and Human Services, Public Health Service, Centers for Disease Control: National Center for Health Statistics, Vital and Health Statistics, Series 3 (Computer Disk), 1992, Chapter 4, Table D.

A2-6 "U.S. Longevity at a Standstill." *Metropolitan Life Insurance Statistical Bulletin,* Vol. 73, No. 3 (July 1992), p. 7.

A2-7 U.S. Senate Special Committee on Aging, American Association of Retired Persons, Federal Council on Aging, and U.S. Administration on Aging. *Aging America: Trends and*

Projections. 1991 Edition. U.S. Department of Health and Human Services, (FCoA) 91-28001, 1991, p. 24.

A2-8 Based on J.F. Van Nostrand, S.E. Furner, and R. Suzman. *Health Data on Older Americans, United States, 1992.* U.S. Department of Health and Human Services, Public Health Service, Centers for Disease Control: National Center for Health Statistics, Vital and Health Statistics, Series 3 (Computer Disk), 1992, Chapter 9, Table 13.

A2-9 U.S. Senate Special Committee on Aging, American Association of Retired Persons, Federal Council on Aging, and U.S. Administration on Aging. *Aging America: Trends and Projections. 1991 Edition.* U.S. Department of Health and Human Services, (FCoA) 91-28001, 1991, p. 23.

A3. Race and Ethnicity

A3-1 Taeuber, Cynthia M. *Sixty-Five Plus in America.* U.S. Department of Commerce, Bureau of the Census, unpublished series of tables and charts, 1992, n.p.

A3-2 Taeuber. *Sixty-Five Plus in America,* unpublished series, n.p.

A3-3 Taeuber. *Sixty-Five Plus in America,* unpublished series, n.p.

A3-4 U.S. Senate Special Committee on Aging. *Common Beliefs About the Rural Elderly: Myth or Fact?* U.S. Government Printing Office, Serial No. 102-N, July 1992, p. 26.

A3-5 Taeuber, Cynthia M. *Sixty-Five Plus in America* U.S. Department of Commerce, Bureau of the Census, unpublished series of table and charts, 1992, n.p.

A3-6 Taeuber. *Sixty-Five Plus in America,* unpublished series, n.p.

A3-7 Taeuber. *Sixty-Five Plus in America,* unpublished series, n.p.

A3-8 Taeuber. *Sixty-Five Plus in America,* unpublished series, n.p.

A3-9 U.S. Senate Special Committee on Aging, American Association of Retired Persons, Federal Council on Aging, and U.S. Administration on Aging. *Aging America: Trends and*

Projections. 1991 Edition. U.S. Department of Health and Human Services, (FCoA) 91-28001, 1991, p. 16.

A3-10 Taeuber, Cynthia M. *Sixty-Five Plus in America.* U.S. Department of Commerce, Bureau of the Census, Current Population Reports, P23-178, August 1992, p. 2-16 (revised).

A3-11 Taeuber. *Sixty-Five Plus in America,* August 1992, p. 2-15 (revised).

A3-12 Taeuber. *Sixty-Five Plus in America,* August 1992, p. 2-13 (revised).

A3-13 Taeuber. *Sixty-Five Plus in America,* August 1992, p. 2-14 (revised).

A3-14 Taeuber. *Sixty-Five Plus in America,* August 1992, p. 2-14 (revised).

A3-15 Taeuber. *Sixty-Five Plus in America,* August 1992, p. 2-15.

A4. Geographic Distribution and Mobility

A4-1 Taeuber, Cynthia M. *Sixty-Five Plus in America.* U.S. Department of Commerce, Bureau of the Census, Current Population Reports, P23-178, August 1992, p. 5-14.

A4-2 Taeuber. *Sixty-Five Plus in America,* August 1992, p. 5-2.

A4-3 Taeuber. *Sixty-Five Plus in America,* August 1992, p. 5-7.

A4-4 Taeuber. *Sixty-Five Plus in America,* August 1992, p. 5-13.

A4-5 U.S. Senate Special Committee on Aging. *Common Beliefs About the Rural Elderly: Myth or Fact?* U.S. Government Printing Office, Serial No. 102-N, July 1992, p. 21.

A4-6 U.S. Senate Special Committee on Aging. *Common Beliefs About the Rural Elderly,* p. 22.

A4-7 *Geographic Mobility: March 1990 to March 1991.* U.S. Bureau of the Census, Current Population Reports, P20-463, 1992, p. xvi.

A4-8 *Geographic Mobility: March 1990 to March 1991,* p. xiv-xv.

A4-9 *Geographic Mobility: March 1990 to March 1991,* p. 3-6.

A5. Aging Around the World

A5-1   Taeuber, Cynthia M. *Sixty-Five Plus in America* U.S. Department of Commerce, Bureau of the Census, Current Population Reports, P23-178, August 1992, p. 2-20.

A5-2   Torrey, Barbara Boyle, Kevin Kinsella, and Cynthia M. Taeuber. *An Aging World.* U.S. Department of Commerce, Bureau of the Census, International Population Reports, P95-78, 1987, p. 4.

A5-3   U.S. Senate Special Committee on Aging, American Association of Retired Persons, Federal Council on Aging, and U.S. Administration on Aging. *Aging America: Trends and Projections. 1991 Edition.* U.S. Department of Health and Human Services, (FCoA) 91-28001, 1991, p. 249.

A5-4   Torrey, Barbara Boyle, Kevin Kinsella, and Cynthia M. Taeuber. *An Aging World.* U.S. Department of Commerce, Bureau of the Census, International Population Reports, P95-78, 1987, p. 7.

A5-5   Torrey, Kinsella, and Taeuber. *An Aging World,* p. 7.

A5-6   Taeuber, Cynthia M. *Sixty-Five Plus in America.* U.S. Department of Commerce, Bureau of the Census, Current Population Reports, P23-178, August 1992, p. 2-21.

A5-7   Taeuber. *Sixty-Five Plus in America,* August 1992, p. 2-21.

A5-8   Taeuber. *Sixty-Five Plus in America,* August 1992, p. 2-22.

A5-9   Taeuber. *Sixty-Five Plus in America,* August 1992, p. 2-22.

A5-10   Taeuber. *Sixty-Five Plus in America,* August 1992, p. 2-22.

A5-11   Torrey, Barbara Boyle, Kevin Kinsella, and Cynthia M. Taeuber. *An Aging World.* U.S. Department of Commerce, Bureau of the Census, International Population Reports, P95-78, 1987, p. 8.

B. SOCIAL CHARACTERISTICS

B1. Living Arrangements and Marital Status

B1-1   Saluter, Arlene F. *Marital Status and Living Arrangements: March 1991.* U.S. Bureau of the Census, Current Population Reports, P20-461, 1992, p. 11.

B1-2   Saluter, Arlene F. *Marital Status and Living Arrangements: March 1992.* U.S. Bureau of the Census, Current Population Reports, P20-468, December 1992, p. xv.

B1-3   Saluter, Arlene F. *Marital Status and Living Arrangements: March 1991.* U.S. Bureau of the Census, Current Population Reports, P20-461, 1992, p. 12.

B1-4   Saluter, Arlene F. *Marital Status and Living Arrangements: March 1990.* U.S. Bureau of the Census, Current Population Reports, P20-450, May 1991, p. 12.

B1-5   U.S. Senate Special Committee on Aging. *Common Beliefs About the Rural Elderly: Myth or Fact?* U.S. Government Printing Office, Serial No. 102-N, July 1992, p. 41.

B1-6   Van Nostrand, J.F., S.E. Furner, and R. Suzman. *Health Data on Older Americans, United States, 1992.* U.S. Department of Health and Human Services, Public Health Service, Centers for Disease Control: National Center for Health Statistics, Vital and Health Statistics, Series 3(27), DHHS Publication No. (PHS)93-1411, January 1993, p. 249.

B1-7   Taeuber, Cynthia M. *Sixty-Five Plus in America.* U.S. Department of Commerce, Bureau of the Census, Current Population Reports, P23-178, August 1992, p. 6-9.

B1-8   Saluter, Arlene F. *Marital Status and Living Arrangements: March 1990.* U.S. Bureau of the Census, Current Population Reports, P20-450, p. 13.

B1-9   *The Black Population in the United States: March 1991.* U.S. Bureau of the Census, Current Population Reports, P20-464, 1992, p. 35.

B1-10 U.S. Senate Special Committee on Aging, American Association of Retired Persons, Federal Council on Aging, and U.S. Administration on Aging. *Aging America: Trends and Projections. 1991 Edition.* U.S. Department of Health and Human Services, (FCoA) 91-28001, 1991, p. 184.

B1-11 Taeuber, Cynthia M. *Sixty-Five Plus in America.* U.S. Department of Commerce, Bureau of the Census, Current Population Reports, P23-178, August 1992, p. 6-2.

B1-12 U.S. Senate Special Committee on Aging, American Association of Retired Persons, Federal Council on Aging, and U.S. Administration on Aging. *Aging America: Trends and Projections. 1991 Edition.* U.S. Department of Health and Human Services, (FCoA) 91-28001, 1991, p. 185.

B1-13 Saluter, Arlene F. *Marital Status and Living Arrangements: March 1992.* U.S. Bureau of the Census, Current Population Reports, P20-468, December 1992, p. viii.

B1-14 Saluter. *Marital Status and Living Arrangements: March 1992*, p. ix.

B2. Households, Housing, and Informal Supports

B2-1 Saluter, Arlene F. *Marital Status and Living Arrangements: March 1990.* U.S. Bureau of the Census, Current Population Reports, P20-450, p. 15.

B2-2 Taeuber, Cynthia M. *Sixty-Five Plus in America.* U.S. Department of Commerce, Bureau of the Census, Current Population Reports, P23-178, August 1992, p. 6–10.

B2-3 Saluter, Arlene F. *Marital Status and Living Arrangements: March 1991.* U.S. Bureau of the Census, Current Population Reports, P20-461, 1992, p. 11.

B2-4 Taeuber, Cynthia M. *Sixty-Five Plus in America—Revisions.* U.S. Department of Commerce, Bureau of the Census, Current Population Reports, P23-178; unpublished revisions based on projections from P25-1092, December 1992, p. 2-20.

B2-5 Federal Council on the Aging. *Annual Report to the President, 1985.* Department of Health and Human Services Publication No. 86-20824, 1986, p. 12.

B2-6 U.S. Senate Special Committee on Aging. *Common Beliefs About the Rural Elderly: Myth or Fact?* U.S. Government Printing Office, Serial No. 102-N, July 1992, p. 37.

B2-7 U.S. Senate Special Committee on Aging. *Common Beliefs About the Rural Elderly*, p. 40.

B2-8 U.S. Senate Special Committee on Aging, American Association of Retired Persons, Federal Council on Aging, and U.S. Administration on Aging. *Aging America: Trends and Projections. 1991 Edition.* U.S. Department of Health and Human Services, (FCoA) 91-28001, 1991, p. 199.

B3. Education

B3-1 *Statistical Abstract of the United States, 1992.* U.S. Department of Commerce, Bureau of the Census, Economics and Statistics Administration, 1992, p. 144.

B3-2 U.S. Senate Special Committee on Aging, American Association of Retired Persons, Federal Council on Aging, and U.S. Administration on Aging. *Aging America: Trends and Projections. 1991 Edition.* U.S. Department of Health and Human Services, (FCoA) 91-28001, 1991, p. 189.

B3-3 U.S. Senate Special Committee on Aging, et al. *Aging America: Trends and Projections. 1991 Edition*, p. 190.

B3-4 U.S. Senate Special Committee on Aging, et al. *Aging America: Trends and Projections. 1991 Edition*, p. 193.

B3-5 U.S. Senate Special Committee on Aging. *Common Beliefs About the Rural Elderly: Myth or Fact?* U.S. Government Printing Office, Serial No. 102-N, July 1992, p. 35.

B3-6   U.S. Senate Special Committee on Aging, American Association of Retired Persons, Federal Council on Aging, and U.S. Administration on Aging. *Aging America: Trends and Projections. 1991 Edition.* U.S. Department of Health and Human Services, (FCoA) 91-28001, 1991, p. 192.

B3-7   Taeuber, Cynthia M. *Sixty-Five Plus in America* U.S. Department of Commerce, Bureau of the Census, Current Population Reports, P23-178, August 1992, pp. 6-15 and 6-16.

B3-8   *Statistical Abstract of the United States, 1992.* U.S. Department of Commerce, Bureau of the Census, Economics and Statistics Administration, 1992, p. 145.

B3-9   *Demographic and Socioeconomic Aspects of Aging in the US: 1920–2040.* U.S. Department of Commerce, Bureau of the Census, August 1984, p. 99.

B3-10   *Enrollment in Higher Education, Fall 1989.* U.S. Department of Education, National Center for Education Statistics, E.D.TABS, DR-IPEDS-89/90, NCES 91-217, July 1991, p. 23.

B3-11   *Enrollment in Higher Education, Fall 1989,* p. 24.

B3-12   *Money Income of Households, Families, and Persons in the United States: 1991.* Current Population Reports, Consumer Income, P60-180: U.S. Department of Commerce, Bureau of the Census, Economics and Statistics Administration, 1992, pp. 144–47.

B3-13   *Poverty in the United States: 1991.* Current Population Reports, Consumer Income, P60-181: U.S. Department of Commerce, Bureau of the Census, Economics and Statistics Administration, August 1992, pp. 70–73.

B4. Social Attitudes and Activities

B4-1   *The Nation's Great Overlooked Resource: The Contributions of Americans 55+.* New York: The Commonwealth Fund. Based on a national survey conducted for the Commonwealth Fund by Louis Harris and Associates, June 1992, inside front cover.

B4-2   *Chartbook on Aging in America.* 1981 White House Conference on Aging, 1981, p. 139.

B4-3   *Chartbook on Aging in America,* p. 141.

B4-4   U.S. Senate Special Committee on Aging. *Common Beliefs About the Rural Elderly: Myth or Fact?* U.S. Government Printing Office, Serial No. 102-N, July 1992, p. 42.

B4-5   U.S. Senate Special Committee on Aging. *Common Beliefs About the Rural Elderly,* p. 43.

B4-6   U.S. Senate Special Committee on Aging. *Common Beliefs About the Rural Elderly,* p. 44.

B4-7   U.S. Senate Special Committee on Aging. *Common Beliefs About the Rural Elderly,* p. 45.

B4-8   *Statistical Abstract of the United States, 1992.* U.S. Department of Commerce, Bureau of the Census, Economics and Statistics Administration, 1992, p. 374.

B4-9   U.S. Senate Special Committee on Aging, American Association of Retired Persons, Federal Council on Aging, and U.S. Administration on Aging. *Aging America: Trends and Projections. 1991 Edition.* U.S. Department of Health and Human Services, (FCoA) 91-28001, 1991, p. 204.

B4-10   U.S. Senate Special Committee on Aging, et al. *Aging America: Trends and Projections. 1991 Edition,* p. 205.

B4-11   Hayghe. "Volunteers in the U.S.: Who donates the time?" *Monthly Labor Review,* Vol. 114, No. 2 (February 1991), p. 8.

B4-12   *The Nation's Great Overlooked Resource: The Contributions of Americans 55+.* New York: The Commonwealth Fund. Based on a national survey conducted for the Commonwealth Fund by Louis Harris and Associates, June 1992, p. 11.

B4-13   *The Nation's Great Overlooked Resource,* p. 25.

B4-14   *The Nation's Great Overlooked Resource,* p. 8.

B4-15   *Statistical Abstract of the United States, 1992.* U.S. Department of Commerce, Bureau of the Census, Economics and Statistics Administration, 1992, p. 269.

B4-16 *Voting and Voting Registration in the Election of November 1990.* U.S. Bureau of the Census, Current Population Reports, P20-453, March 1991, p.1.

B4-17 *Voting and Voting Registration,* p. 6.

B4-18 Jennings, Jerry T. *Voting and Registration in the Election of November 1992.* U.S. Bureau of the Census, Current Population Reports, P20-466, April 1993, p. v.

B4-19 *Voting and Voting Registration in the Election of November 1990.* U.S. Bureau of the Census, and Current Population Reports, P20-453, March 1991, p. 2.

B4-20. Jennings, Jerry T. *Voting and Registration in the Election of November 1992.* U.S. Bureau of the Census, Current Population Reports, P20-466, April 1993, p. vi.

B4-21 Hu, Patricia S., and Jennifer Young. *Summary of Travel Trends: 1990 Nationwide Personal Transportation Survey.* U.S. Department of Transportation, Federal Highway Administration, Office of Highway Information Management, FHWA-PL-92-027, March 1992, p. 36.

B4-22 Hu and Young. *Summary of Travel Trends: 1990 Nationwide Personal Transportation Survey,* p. 39.

B4-23 Hu and Young. *Summary of Travel Trends: 1990 Nationwide Personal Transportation Survey,* p. 42.

B5. Victimization and Abuse of the Elderly

B5-1 Bachman, Ronet. *Elderly Victims.* U.S. Department of Justice, Bureau of Justice Statistics, NCJ-138330, October 1992, p. 2.

B5-2 Bachman. *Elderly Victims,* p. 2.

B5-3 Bachman. *Elderly Victims,* p. 2.

B5-4 Bachman. *Elderly Victims,* p. 3.

B5-5 Bachman. *Elderly Victims,* p. 3.

B5-6 Bachman. *Elderly Victims,* p. 5.

B5-7 Bachman. *Elderly Victims,* p. 5.

B5-8 Bachman. *Elderly Victims,* p. 6.

B5-9 Bachman. *Elderly Victims,* p. 6.

B5-10 Bachman. *Elderly Victims,* p. 7.

B5-11 Bachman. *Elderly Victims,* p. 7.

B5-12 Bachman. *Elderly Victims,* p. 4.

B5-13 *Criminal Victimization in the United States, 1991.* U.S. Department of Justice, Bureau of Justice Statistics, NCJ-139563, National Crime Victimization Survey Report, December 1992, p. 106.

B5-14 *Criminal Victimization in the United States, 1991,* p. 106.

B5-15 Bachman, Ronet. *Elderly Victims.* U.S. Department of Justice, Bureau of Justice Statistics, NCJ-138330, October 1992, p. 8.

B5-16 Bachman. *Elderly Victims,* p. 8.

B5-17 Tataro, Toshio. *Summaries of the Statistical Data on Elder Abuse in Domestic Settings for FY 90 and FY 91.* Washington: National Aging Resource Center on Elder Abuse (NARCEA), February 1993, p. 20.

B5-18 *Elder Abuse: Effectiveness of Reporting Laws and Other Factors.* U. S. General Accounting Office, GAO/HRD-91-74, Report to the Chairman, Subcommittee on Human Services, Select Committee on Aging, House of Representatives, April 1991, p. 6.

B5-19 *Elder Abuse: Effectiveness of Reporting Laws and Other Factors,* p. 8.

B5-20 Tataro, Toshio. *Summaries of the Statistical Data on Elder Abuse in Domestic Settings for FY 90 and FY 91.* Washington: National Aging Resource Center on Elder Abuse (NARCEA), February 1993, p. 24.

B5-21 Tataro. *Summaries of the Statistical Data on Elder Abuse in Domestic Settings for FY 90 and FY 91,* p. 25.

B5-22 Tataro. *Summaries of the Statistical Data on Elder Abuse in Domestic Settings for FY 90 and FY 91,* p. 22.

B5-23 *Elder Abuse: Effectiveness of Reporting Laws and Other Factors.* U. S. General Accounting Office, GAO/HRD-91-74, Report to the Chairman, Subcommittee on Human Services, Select Committee on Aging, House of Representatives, April 1991, p. 10.

B6. Other Social Problems

B6-1 *Alcohol and Health.* Eighth Special Report to the U.S. Congress from the Secretary of Health and Human Services, U.S. Department of Health and Human Services, National Institute on Alcohol Abuse and Alcoholism, September 1993, p. 1–29.

B6-2 U.S. Senate Special Committee on Aging. *Common Beliefs About the Rural Elderly: Myth or Fact?* U.S. Government Printing Office, Serial No. 102-N, July 1992, p. 66.

B6-3 *Fatal Accident Reporting System, 1990: A Review of Information on Fatal Traffic Crashes in the United States.* U.S. Department of Transportation, National Highway Traffic Safety Administration, DOT HS 807 794, December 1991, p. 32.

B6-4 U.S. Senate Special Committee on Aging. *Common Beliefs About the Rural Elderly: Myth or Fact?* U.S. Government Printing Office, Serial No. 102-N, July 1992, p. 65.

B6-5 Taeuber, Cynthia M. *Sixty-Five Plus in America.* U.S. Department of Commerce, Bureau of the Census, Current Population Reports, P23-178, August 1992, p. 3-9.

B6-6 Cerrelli, Ezio. *Older Drivers, the Age Factor in Traffic Safety.* U.S. Department of Transportation, National Highway Traffic Safety Administration, DOT HS 807 402, February 1989, p. 6.

B6-7 *Transportation in an Aging Society: Improving Mobility and Safety for Older Persons, Volume 1.* Washington: Transportation Research Board, National Research Council, Special Report 218, 1988, p. 55.

B6-8 Cerrelli, Ezio. *Older Drivers, the Age Factor in Traffic Safety.* U.S. Department of Transportation, National Highway Traffic Safety Administration, DOT HS 807 402, February 1989, p. 11.

B6-9 Cerrelli. *Older Drivers, the Age Factor in Traffic Safety*, p. 15.

B6-10 *Fatal Accident Reporting System, 1990: A Review of Information on Fatal Traffic Crashes in the United States.* U.S. Department of Transportation, National Highway Traffic Safety Administration, DOT HS 807 794, December 1991, p. 6.

B6-11 *Statistical Abstract of the United States, 1992.* U.S. Department of Commerce, Bureau of the Census, Economics and Statistics Administration, 1992, p. 197.

C. HEALTH STATUS

C1. Health Assessment

C1-1 Adams, Patricia F., and Veronica Benson. *Current Estimates from the National Health Interview Survey, 1990.* U.S. Department of Health and Human Services, National Center for Health Statistics, Vital and Health Statistics, Series 10, No. 181, December 1991, pp. 112–13.

C1-2 *Health United States, 1991.* Hyattsville, MD: U.S. Department of Health and Human Services, Public Health Service, (PHS)92-1232, 1992, p. 202.

C1-3 Van Nostrand, J.F., S.E. Furner, and R. Suzman. *Health Data on Older Americans, United States, 1992.* U.S. Department of Health and Human Services, Public Health Service, Centers for Disease Control: National Center for Health Statistics, Vital and Health Statistics, Series 3(27), DHHS Publication No. (PHS)93-1411, January 1993, p. 14.

C1-4 Van Nostrand, Furner, and Suzman. *Health Data on Older Americans, United States, 1992*, p. 15.

C1-5 U.S. Senate Special Committee on Aging. *Common Beliefs About the Rural Elderly: Myth or Fact?* U.S. Government Printing Office, Serial No. 102-N, July 1992, p. 58.

C2. Diseases and Disabilities

C2-1 Adams, Patricia F., and Veronica Benson. *Current Estimates from the National Health Interview Survey, 1990.* U.S. Department of Health and Human Services, National Center for Health Statistics, Vital and Health Statistics, Series 10, No. 181, December 1991, p. 19.

C2-2 Adams and Benson. *Current Estimates from the National Health Interview Survey, 1990*, p. 13.

C2-3   Van Nostrand, J.F., S.E. Furner, and R. Suzman. *Health Data on Older Americans, United States, 1992.* U.S. Department of Health and Human Services, Public Health Service, Centers for Disease Control: National Center for Health Statistics, Vital and Health Statistics, Series 3(27), DHHS Publication No. (PHS)93-1411, January 1993, p. 21.

C2-4   Adams, Patricia F., and Veronica Benson. *Current Estimates from the National Health Interview Survey, 1990.* U.S. Department of Health and Human Services, National Center for Health Statistics, Vital and Health Statistics, Series 10, No. 181, December 1991, pp. 82–83.

C2-5   Adams and Benson. *Current Estimates from the National Health Interview Survey, 1990,* pp. 84–85.

C2-6   Van Nostrand, J.F., S.E. Furner, and R. Suzman. *Health Data on Older Americans, United States, 1992.* U.S. Department of Health and Human Services, Public Health Service, Centers for Disease Control: National Center for Health Statistics, Vital and Health Statistics, Series 3(27), DHHS Publication No. (PHS)93-1411, January 1993, p. 283.

C2-7   Based on J.F. Van Nostrand, S.E. Furner, and R. Suzman. *Health Data on Older Americans, United States, 1992.* U.S. Department of Health and Human Services, Public Health Service, Centers for Disease Control: National Center for Health   Statistics, Vital and Health Statistics, Series 3 (Computer Disk), 1992, Chapter 9, Table 4.

C2-8   *Prevalence of Chronic Diseases: A Summary of Data from the Survey of American Indians and Alaska Natives, Data Summary 3.* U.S. Department of Health and Human Services, Public Health Service, Agency for Health Care Policy and   Research, 1991, p. 6.

C2-9   Adams, Patricia F., and Veronica Benson. *Current Estimates from the National Health Interview Survey, 1990.* U.S. Department of Health and Human Services, National Center for Health Statistics, Vital and Health Statistics, Series 10, No. 181, December 1991, p. 37.

C2-10 Adams and Benson. *Current Estimates from the National Health Interview Survey, 1990,* p. 31.

C2-11 Adams and Benson. *Current Estimates from the National Health Interview Survey, 1990,* pp. 110–11.

C2-12 Van Nostrand, J.F., S.E. Furner, and R. Suzman. *Health Data on Older Americans, United States, 1992.* U.S. Department of Health and Human Services, Public Health Service, Centers for Disease Control: National Center for Health Statistics, Vital and Health Statistics, Series 3(27), DHHS Publication No. (PHS)93-1411, January 1993, p. 26.

C2-13 U.S. Senate Special Committee on Aging. *Common Beliefs About the Rural Elderly: Myth or Fact?* U.S. Government Printing Office, Serial No. 102-N, July 1992, p. 73.

C2-14 Van Nostrand, J.F., S.E. Furner, and R. Suzman. *Health Data on Older Americans, United States, 1992.* U.S. Department of Health and Human Services, Public Health Service, Centers for Disease Control: National Center for Health Statistics, Vital and Health Statistics, Series 3(27), DHHS Publication No. (PHS)93-1411, January 1993, p. 31.

C3. Death Rates and Causes of Death

C3-1   Van Nostrand, J.F., S.E. Furner, and R. Suzman. *Health Data on Older Americans, United States, 1992.* U.S. Department of Health and Human Services, Public Health Service, Centers for Disease Control: National Center for Health Statistics, Vital and Health Statistics, Series 3(27), DHHS Publication No. (PHS)93-1411, January 1993, p. 78.

C3-2   "Advance Report of Final Mortality Statistics, 1990." *Monthly Vital Statistics Report,* Vol. 41, No. 7, Supplement (7 January 1993), p. 3.

C3-3   "Advance Report of Final Mortality Statistics, 1990," p. 15.

C3-4   "Advance Report of Final Mortality Statistics, 1990," p. 3.

C3-5   *Statistical Abstract of the United States, 1992.* U.S. Department of Commerce, Bureau of the Census, Economics and Statistics Administration, 1992, p. 83.

C3-6   "Advance Report of Final Mortality Statistics, 1990." *Monthly Vital Statistics Report,* Vol. 41, No. 7, Supplement (7 January 1993), p. 21.

C3-7   *Health United States, 1991.* Hyattsville, MD: U.S. Department of Health and Human Services, Public Health Service, (PHS)92-1232, 1992, p.184.

C3-8   Van Nostrand, J.F., S.E. Furner, and R. Suzman. *Health Data on Older Americans, United States, 1992.* U.S. Department of Health and Human Services, Public Health Service, Centers for Disease Control: National Center for Health Statistics, Vital and Health Statistics, Series 3(27), DHHS Publication No. (PHS)93-1411, January 1993, p. 254.

C3-9   Taeuber, Cynthia M. *Sixty-Five Plus in America.* U.S. Department of Commerce, Bureau of the Census, Current Population Reports, P23-178, August 1992, p. 3-8.

C3-10   Taeuber. *Sixty-Five Plus in America,* August 1992, p. 3-8.

C3-11   Taeuber. *Sixty-Five Plus in America,* August 1992, p. 3-9.

C3-12   *Health United States, 1991.* Hyattsville, MD: U.S. Department of Health and Human Services, Public Health Service, (PHS)92-1232, 1992, pp.163–64.

C3-13   *Health United States, 1991,* pp. 167–68.

C3-14   *Health United States, 1991,* pp. 165–66.

C3-15   Van Nostrand, J.F., S.E. Furner, and R. Suzman. *Health Data on Older Americans, United States, 1992.* U.S. Department of Health and Human Services, Public Health Service, Centers for Disease Control: National Center for Health Statistics, Vital and Health Statistics, Series 3(27), DHHS Publication No. (PHS)93-1411, January 1993, p. 80.

C3-16   Van Nostrand, Furner, and Suzman. *Health Data on Older Americans, United States, 1992,* p. 81.

C3-17   Van Nostrand, Furner, and Suzman. *Health Data on Older Americans, United States, 1992,* p. 82.

C3-18   Van Nostrand, Furner, and Suzman. *Health Data on Older Americans, United States, 1992,* p. 84.

C4. Health Care Access and Utilization

C4-1   Densen, Paul M. *Tracing the Elderly Through the Health Care System: An Update.* U.S. Department of Health and Human Services, Public Health Service, Agency for Health Care Policy and Research, AHCPR 91-11, January 1991, p. 6.

C4-2   Densen. *Tracing the Elderly Through the Health Care System,* p. 7.

C4-3   U.S. Senate Special Committee on Aging. *Common Beliefs About the Rural Elderly: Myth or Fact?* U.S. Government Printing Office, Serial No. 102-N, July 1992, p. 49.

C4-4   U.S. Senate Special Committee on Aging. *Common Beliefs About the Rural Elderly,* p. 50.

C4-5   U.S. Senate Special Committee on Aging. *Common Beliefs About the Rural Elderly,* p. 64.

C4-6   Van Nostrand, J.F., S.E. Furner, and R. Suzman. *Health Data on Older Americans, United States, 1992.* U.S. Department of Health and Human Services, Public Health Service, Centers for Disease Control: National Center for Health Statistics, Vitaland Health Statistics, Series 3(27), DHHS Publication No. (PHS)93-1411, January 1993, p. 121.

C4-7   Van Nostrand, Furner, and Suzman. *Health Data on Older Americans, United States, 1992,* p. 122.

C4-8   *Health United States, 1991.* Hyattsville, MD: U.S. Department of Health and Human Services, Public Health Service, (PHS)92-1232, 1992, p. 222.

C4-9   Van Nostrand, J.F., S.E. Furner, and R. Suzman. *Health Data on Older Americans, United States, 1992.* U.S. Department of Health and Human Services, Public Health Service, Centers for Disease Control: National Center for Health Statistics, Vital and Health Statistics, Series 3(27), DHHS Publication No. (PHS)93-1411, January 1993, p. 206.

C4-10 Van Nostrand, Furner, and Suzman. *Health Data on Older Americans, United States, 1992*, p. 270.

C5. Hospitals and Nursing Homes

C5-1 Van Nostrand, J.F., S.E. Furner, and R. Suzman. *Health Data on Older Americans, United States, 1992*. U.S. Department of Health and Human Services, Public Health Service, Centers for Disease Control: National Center for Health Statistics, Vital and Health Statistics, Series 3(27), DHHS Publication No. (PHS)93-1411, January 1993, p. 238.

C5-2 Densen, Paul M. *Tracing the Elderly Through the Health Care System: An Update.* U.S. Department of Health and Human Services, Public Health Service, Agency for Health Care Policy and Research, AHCPR 91-11, January 1991, p. 9.

C5-3 Densen. *Tracing the Elderly Through the Health Care System*, p. 9.

C5-4 *Health United States, 1991*. Hyattsville, MD: U.S. Department of Health and Human Services, Public Health Service, (PHS)92-1232, 1992, pp. 229–30.

C5-5 *Source Book of Health Insurance Data, 1991*. Washington: Health Insurance Association of America, 1991, pp. 83–84.

C5-6 *Source Book of Health Insurance Data, 1991*, p. 85.

C5-7 *Source Book of Health Insurance Data, 1991*, p. 86.

C5-8 Van Nostrand, J.F., S.E. Furner, and R. Suzman. *Health Data on Older Americans, United States, 1992*. U.S. Department of Health and Human Services, Public Health Service, Centers for Disease Control: National Center for Health Statistics, Vital and Health Statistics, Series 3(27), DHHS Publication No. (PHS)93-1411, January 1993, p. 144.

C5-9 *Health United States, 1991*. Hyattsville, MD: U.S. Department of Health and Human Services, Public Health Service, (PHS)92-1232, 1992, p. 236.

C5-10 Taeuber, Cynthia M. *Sixty-Five Plus in America*. U.S. Department of Commerce, Bureau of the Census, unpublished series of tables and charts, 1992, n.p.

C5-11 Taeuber. *Sixty-Five Plus in America,* unpublished series, n.p.

C5-12 U.S. Senate Special Committee on Aging, American Association of Retired Persons, Federal Council on Aging, and U.S. Administration on Aging. *Aging America: Trends and Projections. 1991 Edition.* U.S. Department of Health and Human Services, (FCoA) 91-28001, 1991, p. 164.

C5-13 U.S. Senate Special Committee on Aging, et al. *Aging America: Trends and Projections. 1991 Edition*, p. 163.

C5-14 U.S. Senate Special Committee on Aging, et al. *Aging America: Trends and Projections. 1991 Edition*, p. 165.

C5-15 *Health United States, 1991*. Hyattsville, MD: U.S. Department of Health and Human Services, Public Health Service, (PHS)92-1232, 1992, p. 239.

C5-16 *Health United States, 1991*, p. 240.

C5-17 *Health United States, 1991*, p. 241.

C6. Health Insurance Coverage

C6-1 "A Look at Health Insurance Coverage." *Census and You*, Vol. 27, No. 9 (September 1992), p. 8.

C6-2 *Money Income of Households, Families, and Persons in the United States: 1991*. Current Population Reports, Consumer Income, P60-180: U.S. Department of Commerce, Bureau of the Census, Economics and Statistics Administration, 1992, p. xxiii.

C6-3 Taeuber, Cynthia M. *Sixty-Five Plus in America*. U.S. Department of Commerce, Bureau of the Census, Current Population Reports, P23-178, August 1992, p. 3-17.

C6-4 *The Health Cost Squeeze on Older Americans.* Washington: Families USA Foundation, February 1992, p. 7.

C6-5 *Source Book of Health Insurance Data, 1991*. Washington: Health Insurance Association of America, 1991, pp. 25-26.

C6-6   *Source Book of Health Insurance Data, 1991*, p. 27.

C6-7   Van Nostrand, J.F., S.E. Furner, and R. Suzman. *Health Data on Older Americans, United States, 1992.* U.S. Department of Health and Human Services, Public Health Service, Centers for Disease Control: National Center for Health Statistics, Vital and Health Statistics, Series 3(27), DHHS Publication No. (PHS)93-1411, January 1993, p. 217.

C6-8   Van Nostrand, Furner, and Suzman. *Health Data on Older Americans, United States, 1992*, p. 217.

C6-9   Van Nostrand, Furner, and Suzman. *Health Data on Older Americans, United States, 1992*, p. 218.

C6-10 U.S. Senate Special Committee on Aging. *Common Beliefs About the Rural Elderly: Myth or Fact?* U.S. Government Printing Office, Serial No. 102-N, July   1992, p. 75.

C6-11 *Poverty in the United States: 1991.* Current Population Reports, Consumer Income, P60-181: U.S. Department of Commerce, Bureau of the Census, Economics and Statistics Administration, August 1992, p. xviii.

D. EMPLOYMENT

D1. Labor Force Participation

D1-1   U.S. Senate Special Committee on Aging, American Association of Retired Persons, Federal Council on Aging, and U.S. Administration on Aging. *Aging America: Trends and Projections. 1991 Edition.* U.S. Department of Health and Human Services, (FCoA) 91-28001, 1991, p. 91.

D1-2   U.S. Senate Special Committee on Aging, et al. *Aging America: Trends and Projections. 1991 Edition*, p. 91.

D1-3   Taeuber, Cynthia M. *Sixty-Five Plus in America.* U.S. Department of Commerce, Bureau of the Census, Current Population Reports, P23-178, August 1992, p. 4-1.

D1-4   Gendell, Murray, and Jacob S. Siegel. "Trends in Retirement Age by Sex, 1950–2005." *Monthly Labor Review,* Vol. 115, No. 7 (July 1992), p. 24.

D1-5   *Statistical Abstract of the United States, 1992.* U.S. Department of Commerce, Bureau of the Census, Economics and Statistics Administration, 1992, p. 381.

D1-6   *Statistical Abstract of the United States, 1992*, p. 389.

D1-7   *Statistical Abstract of the United States, 1992*, p. 389.

D1-8   Taeuber, Cynthia M. *Sixty-Five Plus in America.* U.S. Department of Commerce, Bureau of the Census, Current Population Reports, P23-178, August 1992, p. 4-2.

D1-9   U.S. Senate Special Committee on Aging, American Association of Retired Persons, Federal Council on Aging, and U.S. Administration on Aging. *Aging America: Trends and Projections. 1991 Edition.* U.S. Department of Health and Human Services, (FCoA) 91-28001, 1991, p. 100.

D1-10 U.S. Senate Special Committee on Aging, et al. *Aging America: Trends and Projections. 1991 Edition*, p. 98.

D1-11 U.S. Senate Special Committee on Aging, et al. *Aging America: Trends and Projections. 1991 Edition*, p. 99.

D1-12 U.S. Senate Special Committee on Aging, et al. *Aging America: Trends and Projections. 1991 Edition*, p. 97.

D1-13 *Employment and Earnings.* U.S. Department of Labor, Bureau of Labor Statistics, Vol. 40, No. 1 (January 1993), pp. 16–18.

D1-14 *Employment and Earnings,* p. 37.

D1-15 *Employment and Earnings,* p. 34.

D1-16 *Employment and Earnings,* p. 41.

D1-17 U.S. Senate Special Committee on Aging, American Association of Retired Persons, Federal Council on Aging, and U.S. Administration on Aging. *Aging America: Trends and Projections. 1991 Edition.* U.S. Department of Health and Human Services, (FCoA) 91-28001, 1991, p. 261.

D1-18 U.S. Senate Special Committee on Aging, et al. *Aging America: Trends and Projections. 1991 Edition*, p. 261.

D1-19 *Poverty in the United States: 1991.* Current Population Reports, Consumer Income, P60-181: U.S. Department of Commerce, Bureau of the Census, Economics and Statistics Administration, August 1992, pp. 84–87.

D2. Unemployment

D2-1 *Statistical Abstract of the United States, 1992.* U.S. Department of Commerce, Bureau of the Census, Economics and Statistics Administration, 1992, p. 399.

D2-2 *Employment and Earnings.* U.S. Department of Labor, Bureau of Labor Statistics, Vol. 40, No. 1 (January 1993), p. 31.

D2-3 *Employment and Earnings,* p. 64.

D2-4 *Employment and Earnings,* p. 63.

D2-5 *Employment and Earnings,* p. 65.

D2-6 *Employment and Earnings,* p. 33.

D2-7 *Poverty in the United States: 1991.* Current Population Reports, Consumer Income, P60-181: U.S. Department of Commerce, Bureau of the Census, Economics and Statistics Administration, August 1992, pp. 88–90.

D3. Retirement Trends and Pensions

D3-1 *Statistical Abstract of the United States, 1992.* U.S. Department of Commerce, Bureau of the Census, Economics and Statistics Administration, 1992, p. 363.

D3-2 Turner, John A., and Daniel J. Beller. *Trends in Pensions 1992.* U.S. Department of Labor, Pension and Welfare Benefits Administration, 1992, p. 21.

D3-3 Turner and Beller. *Trends in Pensions 1992,* p. 106.

D3-4 *Survey of Retiree Medical Benefits 1990.* Lincolnshire, IL: Hewitt Associates, 1990, inside cover.

D3-5 Iams, Howard M., and John L. McCoy. "Predictors of Mortality Among Newly Retired Workers." *Social Security Bulletin*, Vol. 54, No. 3 (March 1991), p. 6.

E. ECONOMIC CONDITIONS

E1. Sources of Income

E1-1 *Income of the Aged Chartbook, 1990.* U.S. Department of Health and Human Services, Social Security Administration, SSA Publication No. 13-11727, September 1992, p. 8.

E1-2 Grad, Susan. *Income of the Population 55 or Older, 1990.* U.S. Department of Health and Human Services, Social Security Administration, SSA Publication No. 13-11871, April 1992, pp. 1–5.

E1-3 Grad. *Income of the Population 55 or Older, 1990,* pp. 6–7.

E1-4 Grad. *Income of the Population 55 or Older, 1990,* pp. 8–10.

E1-5 Grad. *Income of the Population 55 or Older, 1990,* pp. 11–12.

E1-6 Radner, Daniel B. "Changes in the Incomes of Age Groups, 1984–89." *Social Security Bulletin,* Vol. 54, No. 12 (December 1991), p. 14.

E1-7 Grad, Susan. *Income of the Population 55 or Older, 1990.* U.S. Department of Health and Human Services, Social Security Administration, SSA Publication No. 13-11871, April 1992, pp. 87–90.

E1-8 *Income of the Aged Chartbook, 1990.* U.S. Department of Health and Human Services, Social Security Administration, SSA Publication No. 13-11727, September 1992, p. 14.

E1-9 Based on *Money Income of Households, Families, and Persons in the United States: 1991.* Current Population Reports, Consumer Income, P60-180: U.S. Department of Commerce, Bureau of the Census, Economics and Statistics Administration, 1992, pp. 178–79.

E1-10 U.S. Senate Special Committee on Aging, American Association of Retired Persons, Federal Council on Aging, and U.S. Administration on Aging. *Aging America: Trends and Projections. 1991 Edition.* U.S. Department of Health and Human Services, (FCoA) 91-28001, 1991, p. 264.

E1-11 U.S. Senate Special Committee on Aging, et al. *Aging America: Trends and Projections. 1991 Edition*, p. 263.

E2. Income and Assets

E2-1   *Statistical Abstract of the United States, 1992.* U.S. Department of Commerce, Bureau of the Census, Economics and Statistics Administration, 1992, p. 447.

E2-2   Radner, Daniel B. "The Economic Status of the Aged." *Social Security Bulletin*, Vol. 55, No. 3 (September 1992), p. 8.

E2-3   *Statistical Abstract of the United States, 1992.* U.S. Department of Commerce, Bureau of the Census, Economics and Statistics Administration, 1992, p. 462.

E2-4   Radner, Daniel B. "The Economic Status of the Aged." *Social Security Bulletin*, Vol. 55, No. 3 (September 1992), p. 13.

E2-5   *Income, Poverty and Wealth in the United States: A Chartbook.* U.S. Bureau of the Census, Current Population Reports, P60-179, 1992, p. 28.

E2-6   *Income of the Aged Chartbook, 1990.* U.S. Department of Health and Human Services, Social Security Administration, SSA Publication No. 13-11727, September 1992, p. 1.

E2-7   *Income, Poverty and Wealth in the United States: A Chartbook.* U.S. Bureau of the Census, Current Population Reports, P60-179, 1992, p. 5.

E2-8   *Income of the Aged Chartbook, 1990.* U.S. Department of Health and Human Services, Social Security Administration, SSA Publication No. 13-11727, September 1992, p. 4.

E2-9   *Income of the Aged Chartbook, 1990,* p. 2.

E2-10 U.S. Senate Special Committee on Aging. *Common Beliefs About the Rural Elderly: Myth or Fact?* U.S. Government Printing Office, Serial No. 102-N, July 1992, p. 29.

E2-11 *Money Income of Households, Families, and Persons in the United States: 1991.* Current Population Reports, Consumer Income, P60-180: U.S. Department of Commerce, Bureau of the Census, Economics and Statistics Administration, 1992, pp. 1–4.

E2-12 *Money Income of Households, Families, and Persons in the United States: 1991,* pp. 38–39.

E2-13 Grad, Susan. *Income of the Population 55 or Older, 1990.* U.S. Department of Health and Human Services, Social Security Administration, SSA Publication No. 13-11871, April 1992, p. 68.

E2-14 Grad. *Income of the Population 55 or Older, 1990,* p. 71.

E2-15 Grad. *Income of the Population 55 or Older, 1990,* pp. 78–79.

E2-16 Grad. *Income of the Population 55 or Older, 1990,* pp. 77.

E2-17 *Money Income of Households, Families, and Persons in the United States: 1991.*   Current Population Reports, Consumer Income, P60-180: U.S. Department of Commerce, Bureau of the Census, Economics and Statistics Administration, 1992, p. B-7.

E2-18 U.S. Senate Special Committee on Aging. *Common Beliefs About the Rural Elderly: Myth or Fact?* U.S. Government Printing Office, Serial No. 102-N, July 1992, p. 39.

E3. Living Costs

E3-1   *CPI Detailed Report.* U.S. Department of Labor, Bureau of Labor Statistics, Vol. 40, No. 1 (December 1992), p. 3.

E3-2   *CPI Detailed Report,* p. 4.

E3-3   *CPI Detailed Report,* p. 5.

E3-4   *CPI Detailed Report,* p. 6.

E3-5   *Consumer Expenditure Survey, 1988–89.* U.S. Department of Labor, Bureau of Labor Statistics, Bulletin 2383, Lab-441, August 1991, p. 5.

E3-6   *Consumer Expenditure Survey, 1988–89,* p. 9.

E3-7   *Consumer Expenditure Survey, 1988–89,* pp. 119–22.

E3-8   U.S. Senate Special Committee on Aging, American Association of Retired Persons, Federal Council on Aging, and U.S. Administration on Aging. *Aging America: Trends and Projections. 1991 Edition.* U.S. Department of Health and Human Services, (FCoA) 91-28001, 1991, p. 195.

E3-9   U.S. Senate Special Committee on Aging, et al. *Aging America: Trends and Projections. 1991 Edition,* p. 196.

E3-10   Taeuber, Cynthia M. *Sixty-Five Plus in America*. U.S. Department of Commerce, Bureau of the Census, Current Population Reports, P23-178, August 1992, p. 3-19.

E3-11   *The Health Cost Squeeze on Older Americans.* Washington: Families USA Foundation, February 1992, Appendix.

E3-12   *The Health Cost Squeeze on Older Americans,* p. 4.

E3-13   *The Health Cost Squeeze on Older Americans,* Appendix.

E3-14   *The Health Cost Squeeze on Older Americans,* p. 10.

E3-15   *The Health Cost Squeeze on Older Americans,* p. 1.

E3-16   *The Health Cost Squeeze on Older Americans,* p. 9.

E3-17   *The Health Cost Squeeze on Older Americans,* p. 11.

E4. Poverty

E4-1   *Poverty in the United States: 1991.* Current Population Reports, Consumer Income, P60-181: U.S. Department of Commerce, Bureau of the Census, Economics and Statistics Administration, August 1992, p. ix.

E4-2   *Poverty in the United States: 1991,* p. ix.

E4-3   *Statistical Abstract of the United States, 1992.* U.S. Department of Commerce, Bureau of the Census, Economics and Statistics Administration, 1992, p. 457.

E4-4   *Statistical Abstract of the United States, 1992,* p. 457.

E4-5   Taeuber, Cynthia M. *Sixty-Five Plus in America.* U.S. Department of Commerce, Bureau of the Census, unpublished series of table and charts, 1992, n.p.

E4-6   Taeuber, Cynthia M. *Sixty-Five Plus in America.* U.S. Department of Commerce, Bureau of the Census, Current Population Reports, P23-178, August 1992, p. 4-17.

E4-7   Taeuber. *Sixty-Five Plus in America,* August 1992, p. 4-14.

E4-8   Taeuber. *Sixty-Five Plus in America,* August 1992, p. 4-14.

E4-9   Taeuber. *Sixty-Five Plus in America,* August 1992, p. 4-13.

E4-10   *Poverty Rates for States by Age, Race and Hispanic Origin: 1990.* U.S. Department of Commerce, Bureau of the Census, unpublished tables, 1991, n.p.

E4-11   *Poverty Rates for States by Age, Race and Hispanic Origin: 1990,* n.p.

E4-12   *Poverty Rates for States by Age, Race and Hispanic Origin: 1990,* n.p.

E4-13   *Poverty Rates for States by Age, Race and Hispanic Origin: 1990,* n.p.

E4-14   *Poverty Rates for States by Age, Race and Hispanic Origin: 1990,* n.p.

E4-15   *Poverty Rates for States by Age, Race and Hispanic Origin: 1990,* n.p.

E4-16   *Poverty Rates for States by Age, Race and Hispanic Origin: 1990,* n.p.

E4-17   *Poverty Rates for States by Age, Race and Hispanic Origin: 1990,* n.p.

E4-18   *Statistical Abstract of the United States, 1992.* U.S. Department of Commerce, Bureau of the Census, Economics and Statistics Administration, 1992, p. 459.

E4-19   U.S. Senate Special Committee on Aging. *Common Beliefs About the Rural Elderly: Myth or Fact?* U.S. Government Printing Office, Serial No. 102-N, July 1992, p. 28.

E4-20   *Poverty in the United States: 1991.* Current Population Reports, Consumer Income, P60-181: U.S. Department of Commerce, Bureau of the Census, Economics and Statistics Administration, August 1992, pp. 4–5.

E4-21   Grad, Susan. *Income of the Population 55 or Older, 1990.* U.S. Department of Health and Human Services, Social Security Administration, SSA Publication No. 13-11871, April 1992, pp. 107–08.

E4-22   *Measuring the Effect of Benefits and Taxes on Income and Poverty: 1979 to 1991.* Current Population Reports, Consumer Income, P60-182-RD: U.S. Department of Commerce, Bureau of the Census, Economics and Statistics Administration, August 1992, p. 100.

F. EXPENDITURES FOR THE ELDERLY

F1. Overview of Expenditures

F1-1   U.S. Senate Special Committee on Aging, American Association of Retired Persons, Federal Council on Aging, and U.S. Administration on Aging. *Aging America: Trends and Projections. 1991 Edition.* U.S. Department of Health and Human Services, (FCoA) 91-28001, 1991, p. 238.

F1-2   U.S. Senate Special Committee on Aging, et al. *Aging America: Trends and Projections. 1991 Edition,* p. 239.

F1-3   U.S. Senate Special Committee on Aging, et al. *Aging America: Trends and Projections. 1991 Edition,* p. 242.

F1-4   Helbing, Charles, Viola B. Latta, and Roger E. Keene. "Medicare Expenditures for Physician and Supplier Services, 1970–88." *Health Care Financing Review,* Vol. 12, No. 3 (March 1991), p. 111.

F1-5   *Measuring the Effect of Benefits and Taxes on Income and Poverty: 1979 to 1991.* Current Population Reports, Consumer Income, P60-182-RD: U.S. Department of Commerce, Bureau of the Census, Economics and Statistics Administration, August 1992, p. B-2.

F1-6   *Measuring the Effect of Benefits and Taxes on Income and Poverty: 1979 to 1991,* p. B-2.

F1-7   *Statistical Abstract of the United States, 1992.* U.S. Department of Commerce, Bureau of the Census, Economics and Statistics Administration, 1992, p. 363.

F2. Social Security

F2-1   "Current Operating Statistics." *Social Security Bulletin,* Vol. 55, No. 3 (September 1992), p. 1.

F2-2   *Statistical Abstract of the United States, 1992.* U.S. Department of Commerce, Bureau of the Census, Economics and Statistics Administration, 1992, p. 360.

F2-3   *Statistical Abstract of the United States, 1992,* p. 360.

F2-4   "OASDI Benefits." *Social Security Bulletin,* Vol. 55, No. 2 (June 1992), p. 90.

F2-5   *OASDI Beneficiaries by State and County.* U.S. Department of Health and Human Services, Social Security Administration, December 1990, p. 2.

F2-6   "OASDI Benefits." *Social Security Bulletin,* Vol. 55, No. 2 (June 1992), p. 101.

F2-7   "Current Operating Statistics." *Social Security Bulletin,* Vol. 55, No. 3 (September 1992), p. 93.

F2-8   U.S. Senate Special Committee on Aging. *Common Beliefs About the Rural Elderly: Myth or Fact?* U.S. Government Printing Office, Serial No. 102-N, July 1992, p. 33.

F2-9   U.S. Senate Special Committee on Aging. *Common Beliefs About the Rural Elderly,* p. 31.

F2-10   "Current Operating Statistics." *Social Security Bulletin,* Vol. 55, No. 3 (September 1992), p. 102.

F2-11   "Current Operating Statistics," p. 102.

F3. Health Care Expenditures

F3-1   Office of the President. *Budget of the United States Government, Fiscal Year 1993.* U.S. Government Printing Office, 1992, p. 1-18.

F3-2   Office of the President. *Budget of the United States Government, Fiscal Year 1993,* p. 1-18.

F3-3   Office of the President. *Budget of the United States Government, Fiscal Year 1993,* p. 1-20.

F3-4   *The Health Cost Squeeze on Older Americans.* Washington: Families USA Foundation, February 1992, p. 3.

F3-5   Helbing, Charles, Viola B. Latta, and Roger E. Keene. "Medicare Expenditures for Physician and Supplier Services, 1970–88." *Health Care Financing Review,* Vol. 12, No. 3 (March 1991), p. 112.

F3-6   *Source Book of Health Insurance Data, 1991.* Washington: Health Insurance Association of America, 1991, p. 46.

F3-7   *Measuring the Effect of Benefits and Taxes on Income and Poverty: 1979 to 1991.* Current Population Reports, Consumer Income, P60-182-RD: U.S. Department of Commerce, Bureau of the Census, Economics and Statistics Administration, August 1992, p. B-3.

F3-8   Helbing, Charles, Viola B. Latta, and Roger E. Keene. "Medicare Expenditures for Physician and Supplier Services, 1970–88." *Health Care Financing Review*, Vol. 12, No. 3 (March 1991), p. 113.

F3-9   Van Nostrand, J.F., S.E. Furner, and R. Suzman. *Health Data on Older Americans, United States, 1992.* U.S. Department of Health and Human Services, Public Health Service, Centers for Disease Control: National Center for Health Statistics, Vital and Health Statistics, Series 3(27), DHHS Publication No. (PHS)93-1411, January 1993, p. 216.

F3-10   U.S. Senate Special Committee on Aging. *Common Beliefs About the Rural Elderly: Myth or Fact?* U.S. Government Printing Office, Serial No. 102-N, July 1992, p. 139.

F3-11   U.S. Senate Special Committee on Aging. *Common Beliefs About the Rural Elderly,* p. 140.

F3-12   U.S. Senate Special Committee on Aging, American Association of Retired Persons, Federal Council on Aging, and U.S. Administration on Aging. *Aging America: Trends and Projections. 1991 Edition.* U.S. Department of Health and Human Services, (FCoA) 91-28001, 1991, p. 172.

F3-13   U.S. Senate Special Committee on Aging. *Common Beliefs About the Rural Elderly: Myth or Fact?* U.S. Government Printing Office, Serial No. 102-N, July 1992, p. 77.

F3-14   U.S. Senate Special Committee on Aging. *Common Beliefs About the Rural Elderly,* p. 76.

F4. Public and Private Pensions

F4-1   *Statistical Abstract of the United States, 1992.* U.S. Department of Commerce, Bureau of the Census, Economics and Statistics Administration, 1992, p. 363.

F4-2   Office of the President. *Budget of the United States Government, Fiscal Year 1993.* U.S. Government Printing Office, 1992, p. 1-283.

F4-3   Turner, John A., and Daniel J. Beller. *Trends in Pensions 1992.* U.S. Department of Labor, Pension and Welfare Benefits Administration, 1992, p. 426.

F4-4   Bixby, Ann Kallman. "Benefits and Beneficiaries Under Public Employee Retirement Systems, Fiscal Year 1988." *Social Security Bulletin*, Vol. 54, No. 6 (June 1991), p. 29.

F4-5   Bixby. "Benefits and Beneficiaries Under Public Employee Retirement Systems, Fiscal Year 1988," p. 30.

F4-6   Bixby. "Benefits and Beneficiaries Under Public Employee Retirement Systems, Fiscal Year 1988," p. 31.

F4-7   Bixby. "Benefits and Beneficiaries Under Public Employee Retirement Systems, Fiscal Year 1988," p. 32.

F4-8   Turner, John A., and Daniel J. Beller. *Trends in Pensions 1992.* U.S. Department of Labor, Pension and Welfare Benefits Administration, 1992, p. 23.

F5. Veterans

F5-1   Horgan, Constance, Amy Taylor, and Gail Wilensky. "Aging Veterans: Will They Overwhelm the VA Medical System?" *Health Affairs* (September 1983), p. 79.

F5-2   U.S. Senate Special Committee on Aging. *Common Beliefs About the RuralElderly: Myth or Fact?* U.S. Government Printing Office, Serial No. 102-N, July 1992, p. 24.

F5-3   Horgan, Taylor, and Wilensky. "Aging Veterans," p. 78.

F5-4   U.S. Senate Special Committee on Aging, American Association of RetiredPersons, Federal Council on Aging, and U.S. Administration on Aging. *Aging America: Trends and Projections. 1991 Edition.* U.S. Department of Health and Human Services, (FCoA) 91-28001, 1991, p. 26.

F5-5   *Unpublished Reports.* U.S. Department of Veteran Affairs, 1993, p. 2-39.

F5-6   *Unpublished Reports,* p. 2-40.

F5-7   U.S. Senate Special Committee on Aging. *Common Beliefs About the Rural Elderly: Myth or Fact?* U.S. Government Printing Office, Serial No. 102-N, July 1992, p. 78.

F5-8   U.S. Senate Special Committee on Aging.
       Common Beliefs About the Rural Elderly, p. 46.

F5-9   *Unpublished Reports.* U.S. Department of
       Veteran Affairs, 1993, p. 5.

F5-10 *Unpublished Reports,* p. 6.

F5-11 *Unpublished Reports,* p. 7.

F5-12 *Unpublished Reports,* p. 8.

F5-13 *Unpublished Reports,* n.p.

F5-14 U.S. Senate Special Committee on Aging,
       American Association of Retired Persons,
       Federal Council on Aging, and U.S. Administra-
       tion on Aging. *Aging America: Trends and
       Projections. 1991 Edition.* U.S. Department of
       Health and Human Services, (FCoA) 91-28001,
       1991, p. 171.

Index

by Linda Webster

Abuse of elderly, 48, 98-102
Activities. See Social activities
Activities of daily living (ADLs), difficulty in, 114-15, 130-31, 281-82, 293
Acute conditions. *See* Diseases and disabilities
ADLs. *See* Activities of daily living (ADLs)
Administration on Aging, 303
African Americans. *See* Blacks
Age and age distribution
    alcohol use/abuse and, 103, 104
    blood alcohol content in fatal crashes, 104
    in colonial America, xxi
    by country, 1-2, 42-46
    crash involvements by, 106
    of crime victims, 93, 95-98
    death rates by, 11, 132-33, 135-44
    diseases and disabilities by, 116-31
    driver fatalities and serious injuries by, 107
    educational attainment and, 64-79
    of elder abuse victims, 101
    health assessment and, 110-13
    health care expenditures by, 240
    health insurance by, 165, 166, 168, 171
    hospital stay by, 153-56
    households and, 60-62
    housing costs by, 239-40
    income by, 215-19, 221-24, 229
    income sources by, 203-11, 213-14
    international statistics, 1-2, 41-46
    labor force participation by, 173-83
    life expectancy and, 12, 15-17
    living arrangements and, 48, 52, 54
    living costs by, 235
    marital status and, 55-60
    mobility and, 34-40
    from 1900, 8-9
    in 1990, xxi, 3-10
    nonmotorist fatality rate by, 108
    nursing home stay by, 157, 161
    population aged 65 and over, 1, 3-4, 41-46
    population aged 80/85 and over, 5-6, 8, 9, 42, 43, 45, 46
    poverty by, 245, 246-47, 249-58
    of prison inmates, 108
    projections to 21st century, 8-11, 41, 44-46
    psychiatric hospital stay by, 163-64
    by race and ethnicity, 1, 18-28
    by regions, 19, 29
    retirement trends and pensions by, 198-201

    self-reported driving difficulties and, 106
    by sex, 1, 7, 9-11, 18
    by state, 3-6
    support ratios of elderly persons, 62
    travel and, 91-92
    volunteerism and, 83-86
    voting and, 88-90
Agriculture, 175, 176, 181-82
Alcohol use/abuse, 48, 103-104
Aleuts, 18-20, 24, 29, 32
American Assocation of Retired Persons, 303
American Indians, 18-20, 24, 29, 32
Apparel and upkeep costs, 232, 235, 237
Arthritis, 123. *See also* Diseases and disabilities
Asian Americans, 18-20, 23, 29
Assault. *See* Crime
Attitudes, social, 80
Automobile driving. *See* Driving

Blacks
    alcohol use/abuse and, 103
    cigarette smoking and, 105
    as crime victims, 94
    death rates of, 11, 132-33, 137-44
    diseases and disabilities of, 123, 124, 128
    educational attainment and, 47, 64, 67-69, 76-79
    grandparents in households with grandchildren, 61
    health assessment and, 110, 112, 113, 115
    health care for, 147, 149, 151
    health insurance for, 165, 168, 171
    hospital stay of, 151, 155
    households of, 61, 62
    income of, 202, 207-209, 212, 215, 219-27
    labor force participation by, 173-75, 180, 183, 187
    life expectancy of, 1, 11, 14-16
    literacy of, 69
    living arrangements of, 49
    living costs of, 236
    marital status of, 55-56, 58, 59
    in metropolitan/nonmetropolitan areas, 20, 32
    mobility and, 35-36, 39
    nursing home stay by, 157, 158, 161
    population aged 65 and over, 18-21, 25-27
    population aged 85 and over, 21, 27
    poverty of, 245, 247, 249-50, 253, 255-58
    as prison inmates, 108
    projections into 21st century, 25-27
    by regions, 19, 29

Blacks (*continued*)
  retirement trends and pensions for, 198, 201
  by state, 21
  support ratios of elderly persons, 62
  unemployment of, 189-91, 193-94
  volunteerism and, 83, 86
  voting and, 88-90
Bureau of the Census, xxi, 304–09
Bureau of the Census Management, 309
Burglary. *See* Crime

Caregivers, 62
Census Bureau, xxi, 304-09
Cerebrovascular diseases, death rates for, 136, 138, 142-44
Children
  grandchildren in households with grandparents, 61
  in metropolitan/nonmetropolitan areas, 33
  OASDI benefits for, 271-72
  volunteerism for, 86
Chronic conditions. *See* Diseases and disabilities
Church membership and attendance, 47, 81
Cigarette smoking, 105
Colonial America, xxi
Commerce Department, 303
Costs. *See* Living costs
Crime, 47-48, 92-98

Daily living activities, difficulty in, 114–15, 130-31, 281-82, 293
Death rates
  by age, 11, 132-33, 135-44
  from 1940 to 1990, 132
  percent change in, 143-44
  by race and ethnicity, 11, 132-33, 137-44
  by sex, 11, 132-33, 137-44
  for specific diseases, 109, 135-44
Deaths, causes of, 134-44
Dental care, 147
Dentists, number of, 146
Developing countries, 41-46
Diabetes, 118, 124. *See also* Diseases and disabilities
Disabilities. *See* Diseases and disabilities
Diseases and disabilities
  acute conditions, by age and type of condition, 109, 116-17, 126-29
  age distribution of, 116-31
  as causes of death, 134-35
  chronic conditions, by age, and type of condition, 118-25, 128, 129
  days per person and days of activity restriction due to, 128-29
  death rates for, 135-44
  difficulty in activities of daily living, 130-31
  hospital stay by, 151, 153-54
  by income, 129
  by metropolitan/nonmetropolitan areas, 129
  by race and ethnicity, 123, 124, 128, 131
  by regions, 129
  by sex, 118, 121-25, 128, 130, 131
Divorce. *See* Marital status
Drinking alcohol. *See* Alcohol use/abuse
Driving
  blood alcohol content in fatal crashes, 104
  fatalities and serious injuries in, 104, 106, 107
  miles driven, 91
  self-reported driving difficulties by age, 106

Earnings. *See* Income
Economic conditions. *See* Income; Living costs; Poverty
Education Department, 303
Educational attainment
  by age, 64-79
  college education, 65, 67-79
  earnings and, 72-75
  by employment status, 64, 72-75
  graduate degrees, 67, 71-79
  health care by, 150-51
  health insurance by, 165
  high school education, 65, 67-69, 72-79
  households and, 76-79
  living costs by, 236
  by marital status, 64
  median years of school, 47, 65-67
  by metropolitan/nonmetropolitan areas, 67
  mobility and, 35-36
  poverty and, 76-79, 255
  of prison inmates, 108
  by race and ethnicity, 47, 64, 67-69, 76-79
  by regions, 64, 66
  by sex, 64, 67, 69-75
  survival status of new retired-worker beneficiaries, 200
  undergraduate enrollment, 70-71
  volunteerism and, 83, 86
Elder abuse, 48, 98-102
Employment
  by age, 173-83
  duration of unemployment, 189, 190
  educational attainment and, 64, 72-75
  full- or part-time status, 183
  health care coverage offered by employers, 199
  health insurance and firm size, 169
  by industry and occupation, 176-77
  international statistics, 184
  jobsearch methods used by unemployed, 194
  labor force participation, 172, 173-88
  by marital status, 175, 183
  mobility and, 35-36
  from 1950 to 1990, 173, 174, 176-77
  pension plan by size of firm, 199
  poverty and work experience, 255
  of prison inmates before arrest, 108
  projections into 21st century, 174, 176, 177
  by race and ethnicity, 173-75, 179-80, 183, 186-88
  reasons for unemployment, 191-93, 195-97
  by sex, 173-75, 177-88
  survival status of new retired-worker beneficiaries, 201
  unemployment, 172, 175, 178-80, 189-97
  volunteerism and, 86
  weekly hours of, 175
Employment Retirement Income Security Act (ERISA), 202
Entertainment costs, 234, 235, 238
ERISA. *See* Employment Retirement Income Security Act (ERISA)
Eskimos, 18-20, 24, 29, 32
Ethnicity. *See* Race and ethnicity
Expenditures for the elderly
  federal outlays, 260, 261-63
  health care, 260, 263, 274-82
  Medicare, 109, 170-71, 241-45, 260, 261, 263, 276-79
  overview of, 260, 261-65
  public and private pensions, 260, 282-88
  rent subsidies, 264
  Social Security, 202, 203-14, 228, 260, 261, 266-73

thrifty food plan, 264
veterans, 260, 288-301

Federal agencies, 303-09
Federal Council on Aging, 303
Federal expenditures for the elderly. *See* Expenditures for the elderly
Food
 national expenditures on, 264
 personal costs for, 231, 235, 236-37
Friends, 82, 83

Geographic distribution. *See also* Metropolitan/nonmetropolitan
 areas
  by age, 19, 29-33
  living arrangements and, 51, 53
  marital status and, 55
  metropolitan/nonmetropolitan areas, 20, 32-33
  percent change from 1980 to 1990, 30
  population aged 65 and over, 19, 29, 30, 32, 33
  population aged 85 and over, 31, 32, 33
  by regions, 19, 29-31
  by state, 30-31
Geographic mobility, 1, 34-40
Grandchildren
 in households with grandparents, 61
 volunteerism for, 86

Health and Human Services Department, 303
Health assessment, 109, 110-15, 147, 150-51, 201
Health care
 access and utilization, 109, 145-51
 of crime victims, 96
 dental care and toothlessness, 147
 employers offering health care coverage, 199
 hospitals, 109, 151-56
 mental health organizations, 109, 162-64
 movement through health care system, 145
 national expenditures for, 263, 274-82
 number of dentists, 146
 number of physicians, 146
 nursing homes, 109, 152, 157-61
 personal expenditures for, 233, 235, 238, 240-45
 physician visits, 147-49
 psychiatric organizations, 109, 162-64
 by race and ethnicity, 147, 149, 151
 by sex distribution, 147-51
 vitamin or mineral supplements, 150-51
Health insurance, 109, 165-71, 199, 200, 241–45
Heart diseases, death rates for, 109, 136, 137, 139, 143
Hispanics
 alcohol use/abuse and, 103
 educational attainment and, 47, 64, 67-69, 76-79
 grandparents in households with grandchildren, 61
 health insurance for, 165, 168, 171
 households of, 61, 62
 income by, 202, 207-09, 212
 income of, 215, 219-27
 labor force participation by, 174, 175, 188
 living arrangements of, 49
 marital status of, 55-56, 58, 59
 in metropolitan/nonmetropolitan areas, 20, 32
 mobility and, 35-36, 40
 population aged 65 and over, 18-20, 22, 25-27
 population aged 85 and over, 18, 22, 28
 poverty of, 245, 247, 249-50, 254-58

projections into 21st century, 25-28
by region, 19, 29
retirement trends and pensions for, 198
by sex, 18-20
by state, 22
support ratios of elderly persons, 62
unemployment of, 189, 191
volunteerism and, 83, 86
voting and, 88-90
Homes. *See* Housing
Homicide, 98. *See also* Crime
Hospitals
 duration of stay in, 109, 151-56
 expenditures for, 241-43, 245, 280-81
Household crimes. *See* Crime
Households. *See* Living arrangements
Housing. *See also* Living arrangements
 cost of, 232, 235, 237, 239-40
 of crime victims, 94
 home ownership, 47, 63-64, 230
 in metropolitan/nonmetropolitan areas, 63
 mobility and, 35-36
 by poverty status, 64
 value of, compared to income, 230
Humphrey, David, xxi
Hypertension, 118, 124. *See also* Diseases and disabilities

IADLs. *See* Instrumental activities of daily living (IADLs)
Illnesses. *See* Diseases and disabilities
Income. *See also* Poverty
 by age, 215-19, 221-24, 229
 of crime victims, 95
 diseases and disabilities and, 129
 from earnings, 227
 educational attainment and, 72-75
 health assessment and, 111, 113
 health care by, 150-51
 health insurance by, 165, 171
 hospital stay by, 155
 housing costs by, 239-40
 international statistics on, 214
 labor force participation by, 185-88
 by living arrangements, 215, 221-24
 living costs by, 235, 238
 by marital status, 203-208, 210-11, 219-24, 227-29
 mean/median income, 202, 215, 218-24, 229
 by metropolitan/nonmetropolitan areas, 220, 230
 net worth, 216-17
 from pensions or annuities, 227-29
 poverty by definition of income, 259
 by race and ethnicity, 202, 207-09, 212, 215-16, 219-27
 by regions, 215, 221-24
 by sex, 203-07, 210-11, 219, 229
 sources of, 202, 203-14, 238
 survival status of new retired-worker beneficiaries, 200
 unemployment by, 195-97
 value of owned house compared to, 230
Information resources, 303
Instrumental activities of daily living (IADLs), difficulty in, 130,
 293
Insurance. *See* Health insurance
International statistics
 demographic data, 1-2, 41-46
 income sources, 214

International statistics (*continued*)
    labor force participation, 184
    retirement trends and pensions, 198
    telephone contacts for, 307
Ischemic heart disease, 118, 124. *See also* Diseases and disabilities

Japan, 42-46
Jefferson, Thomas, xxi
Joint pain, 123. *See also* Diseases and disabilities
Justice Department, 303

Labor Department, 303
Labor force. *See* Employment
Leisure-time activities. *See* Social activities
Life expectancy, 1, 12-17
Literacy, 69. *See also* Educational attainment
Living arrangements, 47, 48-54, 60-64. *See also* Housing
    educational attainment and, 76-79
    income and, 215, 221-24
    labor force participation by, 185-88
    unemployment and, 195-97
Living costs
    all items, 202, 231-39
    apparal and upkeep, 232, 235, 237
    entertainment, 234, 235, 238
    food and beverages, 231, 235, 236-37
    housing, 232, 235, 237, 239-40
    medical care, 233, 235, 238, 240-45
    transportation, 233, 235, 237-38

Malignant neoplasms, death rates for, 136, 138, 140-41, 144
Marital status, 47, 55-60
    of crime victims, 94
    educational attainment and, 64
    employment by, 175, 183
    health insurance by, 165
    income by, 219-24, 227-29
    income sources by, 203-08, 210-11
    never married, 59, 60
    nursing home stay by, 161
    poverty by, 258
    of prison inmates, 108
    survival status of new retired-worker beneficiaries, 201
    unemployment by, 190
    volunteerism and, 86
Medicaid, 109, 170-71, 261, 276, 280
Medical care. *See* Health care
Medicare, 109, 170-71, 241-45, 260, 261, 263, 276-79
Mental health organizations, 109, 162-64
Mental illness, 109, 164
Metropolitan/nonmetropolitan areas
    age distribution in, 20, 32-33
    dentists in, 146
    diseases and disabilities by, 129, 130
    educational attainment and, 67
    health care expenditures by, 281-82
    health insurance by, 170
    health status and, 111, 112, 115
    housing in, 63
    income by, 220, 230
    physicians in, 146
    poverty in, 255
    race and ethnicity in, 20, 32
    Social Security benefits by, 272-73
    survival status of new retired-worker beneficiaries, 200
    veterans in, 293

Mineral or vitamin supplements, 150-51
Mobility, 1, 34-40

National Center for Health Statistics, 303
National Institute on Aging, 303
Native Americans. *See* American Indians
Nonmetropolitan areas. *See* Metropolitan/nonmetropolitan areas
Nursing homes
    duration of stay in, 109, 152, 157-61
    expenditures for, 241-43, 245, 280-81
    veterans in, 301

OASDI, 260, 269-72

Pacific Islanders, 18-20, 23, 29
Pensions, 172, 198-201, 203-14, 227-29, 260, 262, 265, 282-88
Physicians
    characteristics of physician visits, 149
    expenditures for, 241-43, 245, 280
    national expenditures to, 263, 276
    number of, 146
    number of physician visits, 147
    patient reason for physician visits, 148
    specialities of, 149
Police reporting of crimes, 97
Population Reference Bureau, 303
Poverty
    by age, 245, 246-47, 249-58
    by definition of income, 259
    educational attainment and, 76-79, 255
    family size and, 255
    health insurance and, 171
    housing tenure and, 64
    labor force participation and, 185-88
    by marital status, 258
    in metropolitan/nonmetropolitan areas, 255
    from 1959 to 1991, 246
    of population aged 85 and over, 250
    by race and ethnicity, 245, 247, 249-50, 253–58
    by regions, 255
    by sex, 202, 249
    by state, 248, 251-54
    unemployment and, 195-97
    work experience and, 255
Prison inmates, 108
Psychiatric organizations, 109, 162-64
Public assistance, 203-14

Race and ethnicity
    alcohol use/abuse and, 103
    cigarette smoking and, 105
    of crime victims, 94
    death rates by, 11, 132-33, 137-44
    diseases and disabilities by, 123, 124, 128, 131
    educational attainment and, 47, 64, 67-69, 76-79
    grandparents in households with grandchildren, 61
    health assessment and, 110, 112, 113, 115
    health care by, 147, 149, 151
    health insurance by, 165, 168, 171
    hospital stay by, 151, 155
    households and, 61, 62
    income by, 202, 215-16, 219-27
    income sources by, 202, 207-09, 212
    labor force participation by, 173-75, 179-80, 183, 186-88
    life expectancy and, 1, 12, 14-16

literacy and, 69
living arrangements and, 49
living costs by, 236
marital status and, 55-56, 58-59
by metropolitan/nonmetropolitan areas, 20, 32
mobility and, 35-40
nursing home stay by, 157, 158, 161
population aged 65 and over, 1, 18-27
population aged 85 and over, 21-24, 27-28
poverty by, 245, 247, 249-50, 253-58
of prison inmates, 108
projections into 21st century, 1, 25-28
psychiatric hospital stay by, 163
by regions, 19, 29
retirement trends and pensions by, 198, 201
by state, 21-24
support ratios of elderly persons, 62
unemployment by, 189-91, 193-94
volunteerism and, 83, 86
voting and, 88-90
Relatives, of help to elderly, 82
Religious attendance, 47, 81
Rent subsidies, 264
Retirement trends and pensions, 172, 198-201, 203-14, 227-29, 260, 262, 265, 282-88
Rural areas. *See* Metropolitan/nonmetropolitan areas

Senate Special Committee on Aging, 303
Sex distribution
by age, 1, 7, 9-11, 18
alcohol use/abuse and, 103-04
cigarette smoking and, 105
of crime victims, 94
death rates by, 11, 132-33, 137-44
diseases and disabilities by, 118, 121-25, 128, 130, 131
educational attainment and, 64, 67, 69-75
of elder abuse victims, 100
health assessment and, 110, 112-15
health care by, 147-51
health insurance by, 169, 170
hospital stay by, 151, 153-56
households and, 60
income by, 219, 229
income sources by, 203-07, 210-11
international statistics, 41, 45
labor force participation by, 173-75, 177-88
life expectancy and, 13, 14-17
living arrangements and, 47, 49-52, 54
living costs by, 236
marital status and, 47, 55-57, 59, 60
miles driven and, 91
mobility and, 35-40
nursing home stay by, 157-58, 161
OASDI benefits by, 269-70
poverty by, 202, 249
of prison inmates, 108
psychiatric hospital stay by, 163
retirement trends and pensions by, 198-201
Social Security benefits by, 269-70, 272-73
unemployment by, 189-97
volunteerism and, 83, 84, 86
voting and, 88-90
Single persons, 59-60. *See also* Marital status

Smoking, 105
Social activities
friendships, 82, 83
by metropolitan/nonmetropolitan areas, 81-83
miles driven and travel, 91-92
relatives that elderly can call on for help, 82
religious attendance and, 47, 81
specific leisure-time activities, 47, 80
volunteerism, 83-87
voting, 47, 88-90
Social attitudes, 80
Social Security, 202, 203-14, 228, 260, 261, 266-73
Social Security Administration, 303
Stamp, Sir Josiah, xxi
State prison inmates, 108

Taxes, 238
Theft. *See* Crime
Toothlessness, 147
Transportation costs, 233, 235, 237-38
Travel, 91-92

Unemployment, 172, 175, 178-80, 189-97. *See also* Employment
U.S. Bureau of the Census, xxi, 304-09
U.S. Bureau of the Census Management, 309
U.S. Department of Commerce, 303
U.S. Department of Education, 303
U.S. Department of Health and Human Services, 303
U.S. Department of Justice, 303
U.S. Department of Labor, 303
U.S. Senate, Special Committee on Aging, 303
Unmarried, 59-60. *See also* Marital status
Urban areas. *See* Metropolitan/nonmetropolitan areas

Veterans. *See also* Expenditures for the elderly
assistance in daily living activities for, 293
disability compensation for, 294-95, 298-300
expenditures for death compensation, 296-97
health care expenditures for, 291-93
number of, 288-90
in nursing homes, 301
projections into 21st century, 288-90
Victimization, 47-48, 92-98
Vitamin or mineral supplements, 150-51
Volunteerism, 83-87
Voting, 47, 88-90

Widows, 58, 60. *See also* Marital status

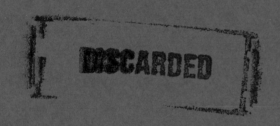